Frommer's®

New York City 2012

by Brian Silverman, Richard Goodman & Kelsy Chauvin

WILEY

Wiley Publishing, Inc.

Published by:
Wiley Publishing, Inc.
111 River St.
Hoboken, NJ 07030-5774

ISBN 978-1-118-02740-0 (paper); ISBN 978-1-118-07685-9 (paper); ISBN 978-1-118-09586-7 (ebk); ISBN 978-1-118-09587-4 (ebk); ISBN 978-1-118-09588-1 (ebk)

Editor: William Travis, with Kathleen Warnock
Production Editor: Katie Robinson
Cartographer: Roberta Stockwell
Cover photo editor: Richard Fox; photo editors: Alden Gewirtz, Cherie Cincilla
Design and Layout by Vertigo Design
Graphics and Prepress by Wiley Indianapolis Composition Services

Front cover photo: Detail of Chrysler Building with New York skyline at dusk ©Pete Seaward / Getty Images
Back cover photos, left to right: Brooklyn Bridge New York City DUMBO warehouse ©Randy Duchaine / Alamy Images; Imagine Memorial to John Lennon Strawberry Fields Central Park ©Picture Partners / Alamy Images; line of yellow taxis ©Quavondo / iStock Photo

Manufactured in China

5 4 3 2 1

CONTENTS

4 WHERE TO STAY 83

5 WHERE TO DINE 137

6 EXPLORING NEW YORK CITY 216

7 SHOPPING 338

8 NEW YORK CITY AFTER DARK 386

9 PLANNING YOUR TRIP TO NEW YORK CITY 445

LIST OF MAPS

ABOUT THE AUTHORS

Brian Silverman (Senior Writer, Best of New York City, Where to Stay, Where to Dine chapters) is a freelance writer whose work has been published in *Saveur, The New Yorker, Caribbean Travel & Life, Islands,* and *Four Seasons.* Among the many topics he writes about are food, travel, sports, and music. He is the author of numerous books including *Going, Going, Gone: History, Lore, and Mystique of the Home Run,* and the *Twentieth Century Treasury of Sports.* He is also the author of the blog *Fried Neck Bones . . . and Some Home Fries* at www.friedneckbones.wordpress.com. For Frommer's, he has written Complete, Portable, and Budget Guides to New York City, as well as *New York City for Dummies.* He lives in Manhattan with his wife and children.

Richard Goodman (Best of New York City, New York City in Depth, Planning Your Trip, Neighborhoods and Suggested Itineraries, and Exploring New York) has lived in New York City for 35 years. He is the author of *A New York Memoir,* which chronicles those years. His book, *The Bicycle Diaries: One New Yorker's Journey Through September 11th,* was published in 2011 in a fine press edition. He is also the author of *French Dirt: The Story of a Garden in the South of France* and *The Soul of Creative Writing.* He teaches creative nonfiction at Spalding University's MFA in Writing Program.

Kelsy Chauvin (Best of New York, Shopping, After Dark chapters) is a writer, photographer, and filmmaker. Her very first trip abroad was to Uzbekistan at age 15, a journey that sparked a lifelong thirst for travel. Her writing and photography have been published in magazines, online, and in various Frommer's publications. She has called Brooklyn home for 10 years. "Anywhere is walking distance, if you've got the time." Steven Wright

ACKNOWLEDGMENTS

To my wife, Heather, and my sons, Louis and Russell.

—Brian Silverman

I would like to thank Caroline Kinneberg for her meticulous research efforts. And a very special thank-you to my daughter.

—Richard Goodman

Thanks especially to Lauren LoGiudice, a profoundly diligent research partner and utter professional. I'd like to thank Rebecca Shalomoff and Ralee Bankston.

—Kelsy Chauvin

HOW TO CONTACT US

In researching this book, we discovered many wonderful places—hotels, restaurants, shops, and more. We're sure you'll find others. Please tell us about them, so we can share the information with your fellow travelers in upcoming editions. If you were disappointed with a recommendation, we'd love to know that, too. Please write to:

Frommer's New York City 2012
Wiley Publishing, Inc. • 111 River St. • Hoboken, NJ 07030-5774
frommersfeedback@wiley.com

ADVISORY & DISCLAIMER

Travel information can change quickly and unexpectedly, and we strongly advise you to confirm important details locally before traveling, including information on visas, health and safety, traffic and transport, accommodation, shopping and eating out. We also encourage you to stay alert while traveling and to remain aware of your surroundings. Avoid civil disturbances, and keep a close eye on cameras, purses, wallets and other valuables.

While we have endeavored to ensure that the information contained within this guide is accurate and up-to-date at the time of publication, we make no representations or warranties with respect to the accuracy or completeness of the contents of this work and specifically disclaim all warranties, including without limitation warranties of fitness for a particular purpose. We accept no responsibility or liability for any inaccuracy or errors or omissions, or for any inconvenience, loss, damage, costs or expenses of any nature whatsoever incurred or suffered by anyone as a result of any advice or information contained in this guide.

The inclusion of a company, organization or Website in this guide as a service provider and/or potential source of further information does not mean that we endorse them or the information they provide. Be aware that information provided through some Websites may be unreliable and can change without notice. Neither the publisher or author shall be liable for any damages arising herefrom.

FROMMER'S STAR RATINGS, ICONS & ABBREVIATIONS

Every hotel, restaurant, and attraction listing in this guide has been ranked for quality, value, service, amenities, and special features using a **star-rating system.** In country, state, and regional guides, we also rate towns and regions to help you narrow down your choices and budget your time accordingly. Hotels and restaurants are rated on a scale of zero (recommended) to three stars (exceptional). Attractions, shopping, nightlife, towns, and regions are rated according to the following scale: zero stars (recommended), one star (highly recommended), two stars (very highly recommended), and three stars (must-see).

In addition to the star-rating system, we also use **seven feature icons** that point you to the great deals, in-the-know advice, and unique experiences that separate travelers from tourists. Throughout the book, look for:

Special finds—those places only insiders know about

Fun facts—details that make travelers more informed and their trips more fun

Kids—Best bets for kids and advice for the whole family

Special moments—those experiences that memories are made of

Overrated—Places or experiences not worth your time or money

Insider tips—great ways to save time and money

Great values—where to get the best deals

The following **abbreviations** are used for credit cards:

AE	American Express	**DISC**	Discover	**V**	Visa
DC	Diners Club	**MC**	MasterCard		

TRAVEL RESOURCES AT FROMMERS.COM

Frommer's travel resources don't end with this guide. Frommer's website, **www.frommers. com**, has travel information on more than 4,000 destinations. We update features regularly, giving you access to the most current trip-planning information and the best airfare, lodging, and car-rental bargains. You can also listen to podcasts, connect with other Frommers.com members through our active-reader forums, share your travel photos, read blogs from guidebook editors and fellow travelers, and much more.

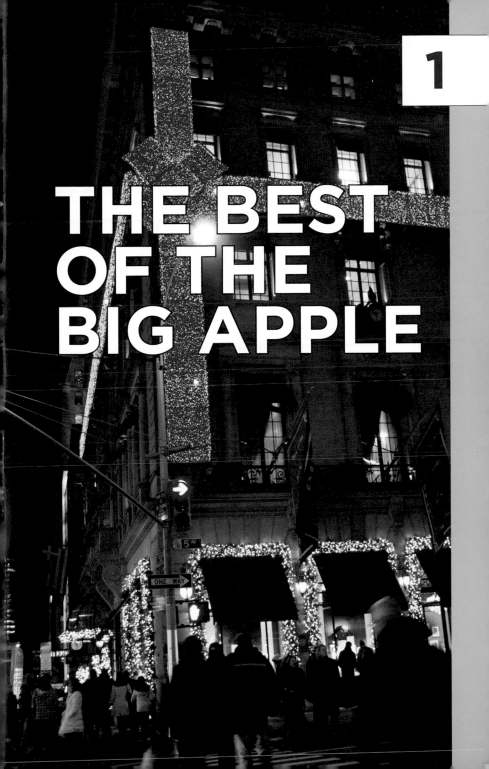

THE BEST OF THE BIG APPLE

conic, hip, trendsetting, and ever-changing, New York City lives up to its superlatives. Underneath the Big Apple's jagged sky-scraper skyline, museums dazzle with the latest collections, celebrity chefs unveil their newest creations, and Broadway continues to stage elaborate, glittering shows. Downtown, fashionistas linger on the cobblestone streets of the Meatpacking District, while artists paint urban portraits in Union Square. Beyond the bustle, though, is a diverse population, taking the city in stride and friendlier than you were led to believe.

THINGS TO DO   When you're planning your activities, think on your feet. Do what New Yorkers do: walk. Wander the angled tree-lined streets of **Greenwich Village** or the avenues of million-dollar townhouses on the Upper East Side. Art lovers should not miss the Warhols and Pollocks at **MoMA,** or the comprehen-

Crowds throng the Theater District for an 8 o'clock curtain.

sive and essential **Metropolitan Museum of Art.** Outdoors, min-gle with joggers and skaters in **Central Park** or smell the bloom-ing flowers at the **Brooklyn Botanic Garden.** Head to **Bat-tery Park** for sunset views over the Hudson River, or watch the world below from the top of the **Empire State Building.**

SHOPPING   And make sure your walking includes window-shopping. Couture designer shops line **Madison Avenue,** while the major department stores like **Saks Fifth Avenue** and **Bloomingda-le's** anchor Fifth Avenue in Mid-town. Cutting-edge designers show their wares in the **Meat-packing District,** while high-fashion boutiques and cool housewares peak out behind the cast-iron facades of **SoHo.** Rum-mage through vintage clothing boutiques on the **Lower East Side** or sift through knockoff sun-glasses, purses, and watches on crammed Canal Street in **Chinatown.** Head to **Greenwich Village** to browse music stores and boutique food shops.

PREVIOUS PAGE: Like a shiny gift about to be unwrapped, New York City at Christmas is waiting to be explored and enjoyed.

EATING & DRINKING To fuel your rambles, you can find your culinary bliss from high end to low budget, in every ethnic cuisine. With small apartment kitchens and a culinary smorgasbord around every corner, it's no wonder New Yorkers eat out so much. Start in **Chinatown** for Cantonese noodles or indulge in a juicy steak at a **Midtown** steak house. Mix with celebrities at a fusion spot in **Chelsea** or tuck into a steaming bowl of mussels at a cozy **Greenwich Village** bistro. If you're on the go, grab a slice of pizza or a bagel with a schmear of cream cheese. For cheap, good, ethnic eats, hop the subway to **Queens**, **Brooklyn** or **The Bronx**.

NIGHTLIFE & ENTERTAINMENT Make sure you save some energy for your nighttime activities. **Times Square**'s bright lights shine on elaborate stage productions in **Broadway**'s theaters. Dress up for a classical concert at **Carnegie Hall** or **Lincoln Center**. Lovers of soul head to Harlem's **Apollo Theatre**. The legendary **Blue Note** and **Village Vanguard** pack in jazz fans, while cutting-edge bars and clubs in the **Meatpacking District** lure the beautiful people.

Take a break from the hustle and bustle in Central Park.

most unforgettable NEW YORK CITY EXPERIENCES

o **Sailing to the Statue of Liberty,** on Liberty Island in New York Harbor: If you have time to do only one thing on your visit to New York, sail to the Lady in the Harbor. No other monument embodies the nation's—and the world's—notion of political freedom and economic potential more than Lady Liberty. It is also the ultimate symbol of New York, the personification of the city's vast diversity and tolerance. And, after nearly a decade of being off limits, you can once more ascend to the Lady's crown, re-opened in 2009 for the first time since September 11, 2001. See p. 243.

o **Visiting the Empire State Building Observatory at Dusk:** The Empire State Building, once again the tallest building in New York, is one of the city's definitive icons. Arrive at dusk and watch the lights of the city come on. It's pure magic. See p. 232.

- **Walking the Brooklyn Bridge:** Manhattan has five major bridges connecting the island to other shores, and the most historic and fascinating is the Brooklyn Bridge. For a close-up look at what was a marvel of civic engineering when it was built in 1883, and a true New York experience, walk across from Manhattan to Brooklyn (or vice versa!). See p. 228.

- **Jogging Around the Central Park Reservoir:** Okay, you don't even have to jog it. You can walk the jogging path around the Jacqueline Kennedy Onassis Reservoir and take in the beauty of Central Park, as well as the views of Central Park West, Fifth Avenue, and especially the skyline of midtown Manhattan. See p. 282.

Crossing the Brooklyn Bridge.

- **Sunday Morning in New York:** This might not sound so unforgettable, but to experience the city minus the noise and activity is something special. I've noticed quite a few tourists, usually jet-lagged Europeans, wandering the parks and streets early Sunday mornings.

- **Walking 125th Street:** Take a walk across this famous Harlem boulevard, and your senses will be overwhelmed with the music, the variety of stores, the restaurants, the stalls selling everything from homemade CDs to bean pies, and the street prophets and musicians. The energy is relentless.

- **Traveling Underground:** Don't be afraid of the subways. Go underground, MetroCard in hand, and use the fastest means of transport in the city. On the way, you might see music, art, even history in many of the city's refurbished stations.

- **TriBeCa in the Early Morning:** This marvelous part of New York, full of large, brick, rust-colored warehouses and cobblestone streets, looks like Monet painted it in the morning with a strong sun playing off its rich surfaces. This is the heart of the heart of New York, to my mind.

NEW YORK'S best EVENTS & SEASONS

- **Best Parade: West Indian–American Day Carnival and Parade.** Held on Eastern Parkway in Brooklyn, this is the biggest parade in New York. The music (calypso, soca, reggae, and Latin), the costumes, and the Caribbean food make this unforgettable. If you're lucky enough to be in town on Labor Day, don't miss it. See p. 46.

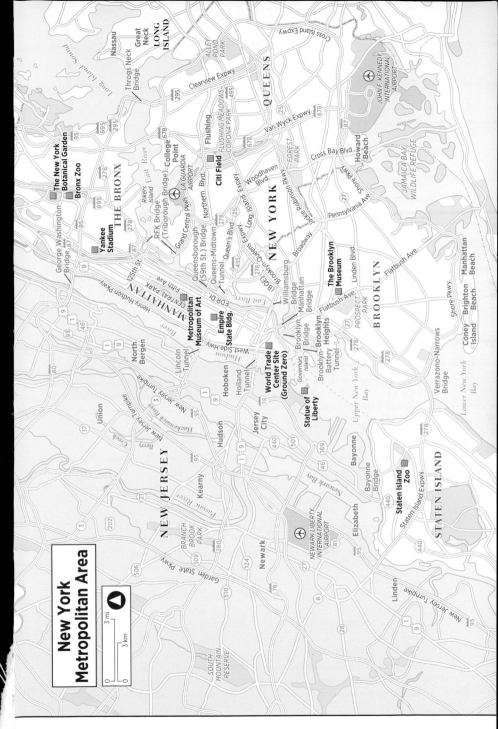

New York
Metropolitan Area

5

o **Best Season in New York: Christmas.** Come see the Christmas trees on Park Avenue, the big crystal snowflake hanging above the intersection of 57th Street and Fifth Avenue, the trees at Rockefeller Center and Lincoln Center, the menorah at Grand Army Plaza at Fifth and 59th Street, and the decorations in department store windows, restaurants, and hotels. And even though the crowds, especially around Midtown and Rockefeller Center, might bring out the Scrooge in you, the atmosphere is almost always festive and like no other time of year.

o **Best Time of Year to Come to New York: Summer.** Most people prefer the temperate days of fall to visit New York, and that's when the city is most crowded. But my personal favorite season is summer, when the streets are less crowded, restaurants and shows are easier to get into, and free outdoor cultural events abound.

Follow the star . . . to Fifth Avenue and 57th St. during the holiday season.

o **Best Day to Come to New York: New Year's Day.** The holidays are over; you've had enough festivity—see above—and you've wisely skipped the insanity of New Year's Eve and arisen fresh and (relatively) sober. Get out on the town early; you'll have the city practically to yourself.

NEW YORK'S best MUSEUMS

o **Best Overall Museum: American Museum of Natural History.** You can spend your entire visit to New York at this 4-square-block museum; there is that much to see. From the famed dinosaur halls to the Hall of Ocean Life, the Museum of Natural History houses the world's greatest natural science collection. See p. 220.

o **Best Art Museum: Metropolitan Museum of Art.** Not just the best art museum in New York, but the best in North America. The number of masterworks is mind-boggling. See p. 234.

o **Best-Looking Museum: Museum of Modern Art.** Though the exterior of the Guggenheim is certainly memorable, and the New Museum of Contemporary Art is oddly attractive, MoMA's $450-million renovation makes it the coolest-looking museum, inside and out, in town. See p. 237.

The dinosaurs are a big favorite at the American Museum of Natural History.

o **Best Art Museum that People Outside New York Love to Tell You They Love the Most:** The Frick. I (Richard) have met more Europeans in my travels who tell me their favorite museum in New York is the Frick. It's stately, restrained, gorgeous, elegant, and very tasteful—how some Europeans see themselves. And I adore it, too. See p. 251.

o **Best New York Museum about New York: Museum of the City of New York.** Start here and get a feel of what the city is like—from past to present. There are always fascinating exhibits. See p. 259.

o **Best Home Posing as a Museum: The Louis Armstrong House Museum.** This unassuming house in Queens was Satchmo's home for almost 30 years, and it's been preserved almost exactly as it was when he died in 1971. See p. 329.

best NEW YORK CITY BUILDINGS

o **Best Historic Building: Grand Central Terminal.** Despite all the steel-and-glass skyscrapers, many historic marvels are still standing, and the best is this Beaux Arts gem. This railroad station, built in 1913, was restored in the 1990s to recapture its brilliance. See p. 233.

o **Best Skyscraper: The Chrysler Building.** There is no observation deck, but this Art Deco masterpiece is best viewed from outside or from other observation decks, such as the Empire State Building's. See p. 271.

o **Most Impressive Place of Worship: Cathedral of St. John the Divine.** Construction began on the world's largest Gothic cathedral in 1892—and it's still going on. But this is one structure that benefits from being a work in progress. See p. 278.

best NEW YORK CITY PARKS

o **Central Park:** Period. One of the world's great urban refuges—a center of calm and tranquility among the noisy bustle that is Manhattan. See p. 282.

o **Riverside Park:** This 4-mile-long park along the Hudson River is a welcome alternative to the sometimes-overcrowded Central Park. See p. 294.

FROM TOP: The 70th St. Garden provides an elegant exterior view of the Frick Museum; the Chrysler Building is an Art Deco wonder in Midtown.

o **High Line:** Located in the Meatpacking District of Manhattan, this marvelous new park was once an elevated structure for freight trains. It's become immensely popular and shows how New York City is constantly reinventing itself. See p. 294.

best PLACES IN NEW YORK CITY TO TAKE THE KIDS

o **Central Park:** With its carousel, a zoo, two ice-skating rinks and pools (depending on the season), playgrounds, and ball fields, Central Park is a children's wonderland. See p. 282.

o **Bronx Zoo:** This is one of the great zoos in the world—and you don't have to be a kid to love it. See p. 312.

The High Line Park is an oasis above the Meatpacking District.

o **New York Hall of Science:** This Queens museum, in Flushing Meadows–Corona Park, has hands-on exhibits that thrill, from preschoolers on up. The surrounding park offers a carousel, zoo, and boat and bike rentals. See p. 310.

o **Coney Island:** It's not a theme park (yet!), just an old-fashioned amusement park on the beach. Nearby is the New York Aquarium, Keyspan Park (home of the minor league baseball team Brooklyn Cyclones), and Nathan's Famous hot dogs. What more could a kid, want? See p. 322.

Girl and gorilla at the Bronx Zoo.

Even in winter, Central Park's a great place for kids to slide around.

best NEIGHBORHOODS TO STROLL IN NEW YORK CITY

- **The Upper West Side:** With museums, parks, some old buildings and brownstones, inexpensive restaurants, and a residential feel, this is my favorite neighborhood to stroll.
- **Greenwich Village:** With its historic streets, hidden cafes, cozy restaurants, and eccentric characters, Greenwich Village is a constant, but pleasant, barrage on the senses.
- **Chinatown:** With the relentless activity and crowded sidewalks, Chinatown might not seem like ideal strolling territory, but it's so colorful, it's worth braving the mobs.
- **Brooklyn Heights:** A designated historic district, on your stroll you will be awed by the pristine condition of 19th-century row houses and mansions. But best of all is the view of Manhattan and New York Harbor, including the Statue of Liberty, from Brooklyn Heights's famous promenade.

best STREETS TO WALK UP OR DOWN

- **West 4th Street (Positively):** This street runs east/west (more or less) through the heart of Greenwich Village. It skirts the southern end of Washington Square Park and then plunges into the heart of the West Village. To my mind, this street, on the stretch between Seventh Avenue and West 12th

Street (yes, W. 4th St. runs into W. 12th St.) is the most beautiful in New York. If you're lucky enough to walk it on a snowy evening with the lamplights illuminating the falling flakes or at dusk on a warm summer evening with leafy shadows everywhere, you'll be transported.

o **Prince Street:** This SoHo street has a brief run of just 10 blocks, from Bowery to MacDougal, but it's an exquisite walk. It's chock-full of atmosphere and history. The walk will take you by the Old St. Patrick's Cathedral—the city's first cathedral—and its gorgeous old brick wall. Just a few steps west is McNally Jackson, a marvelous independent bookstore where you can pause and browse.

o **Irving Place:** This is another small gem, running a mere 6 blocks between 14th Street and Gramercy Park, not terribly far from Union Square. It takes you by Pete's Tavern, a grand old dive that's been around for 150 years. When you reach the street's apex, you can finish off this lovely little walk with a stroll around Gramercy Park, a tiny green gem that, alas, is surrounded by a wrought-iron fence and can only be entered by those who live in the neighborhood.

o **Fifth Avenue, Park Slope, Brooklyn:** The train ride from Manhattan is a small price to pay to enjoy the still-undiscovered-by-tourists vibe on this Brooklyn thoroughfare. The Park Slope neighborhood in general is full of hidden gems, but it's easy to spend a whole day checking out the cool shops, clubs, brownstones, and restaurants lining Fifth Avenue between Bergen and 9th streets. Streets like this are the reason people move to Brooklyn.

The winding streets of Greenwich Village are a great place for a stroll.

Interesting details make a walk in Chinatown fun and pretty.

best **THINGS TO DO FOR FREE IN NEW YORK**

- **Ride the Staten Island Ferry:** The Staten Island Ferry is used daily by thousands of commuters. Ride it for a great view of the Statue of Liberty, Ellis Island, New York Harbor, and the lower Manhattan skyline. You can't beat the price: free. See p. 242.

- **Attend a Gospel Service:** All around New York, you'll find Sunday gospel services, but for some special soul stirring, head to Harlem and the **Abyssinian Baptist Church** or Brooklyn and the **Brooklyn Tabernacle.** Services are free, but when the basket is passed, don't be stingy. See p. 278 and 322.

- **Visit Free Museums:** Believe it or not, there are museums in New York that don't charge admission. Two of my favorites are the **National Museum of the American Indian** and the **Federal Hall National Memorial.** See p. 260 and 276.

- **Take in a Game at the West 4th Street Basketball Courts:** On West 4th Street and Sixth Avenue, you'll find the legendary public hoops courts. I don't know what's more entertaining: the moves on the court or the inventive trash talk accompanying the games.

- **Walk. Anywhere:** New York City is the most walkable city in the world that I know of. Since most of it is planned on the grid system, it's hard to get lost (except in the West Village, where getting lost is part of the fun). Avenues go north and south, streets go east and west. (The Bronx is up and the Battery's down!) You will never find a better way to get to know New York. I would recommend starting at the foot of the city, where it all began over 400 years ago, then strolling up Broadway, the only street in Manhattan that goes from one end of the island to the other. You can actually walk the entire length of Manhattan, a walk that, done briskly, would probably take you about 6 hours. That's a 13½-mile hike, by the way!

Take a free ride on the Staten Island Ferry.

best OFFBEAT NEW YORK EXPERIENCES

○ **Visit the Little Italy of the Bronx:** With the demise of Little Italy in Manhattan, the area around Arthur Avenue, known as the Little Italy of the Bronx, is the place for old-fashioned Italian charm, food, and ambience.

○ **Museum of Sex:** How many cities can claim their own Museum of Sex? Not too many! We got your Museum of Sex right here . . . but you must be 18 or older to enter. See p. 259.

The Roosevelt Island Tram gives you a birds-eye view over the East Side.

○ **Roosevelt Island Tram:** Impress your family and friends with a spectacular view of the skyline from the Roosevelt Island Tram. During the 4-minute ride, you will be treated to a gorgeous vista down the East River, with views of the United Nations and the Queensboro, Williamsburg, Manhattan, and Brooklyn bridges. See p. 242.

○ **Bike Along the Hudson River:** If walking is not enough exercise for you, a good alternative is to rent a bike and ride the length of Manhattan via the work-in-progress **Hudson River Park.** As of this writing, you can bike from Battery Park to Fort Tryon Park, near the George Washington Bridge. There are detours along the way, which occasionally take you off the paths. For bike-rental info, see p. 293.

○ **Take a Food Tour:** Mmmmm! You'll find lots of groups that offer tours centered around food, and it's a fantastic way to learn about a specific neighborhood. What could be better than seeing Brooklyn by way of its pizzerias, or exploring Harlem by sampling African, Caribbean, Latin American, and soul foods along the way?

○ **Ride the International Express:** The no. 7 train is sometimes known as the "International Express." Take it through the borough of Queens (where it runs aboveground for most of its length), and you will pass one ethnic neighborhood after another, from Indian to Thai, from Peruvian to Colombian, from Chinese to Korean.

○ **Bastille Day in the City:** That's July 14, for you non-Francophiles. A consortium of French organizations puts on a big fête on East 60th Street between Fifth and Lexington avenues on the Sunday just before or after July 14. The fun starts at noon and continues until 6pm. Sample the cuisine of France and other French-speaking countries, browse the French-themed market stalls, and dance in the street in a French-style *"bal-musette."* There are even can-can dancers! Check out the details at http://bastilledaynyc.com.

best DAYS IN NEW YORK'S OTHER BOROUGHS

Visit the new Luna Park at Brooklyn's Coney Island.

o **In the Bronx:** Spend the morning at the **Bronx Zoo** (p. 312) or the **New York Botanical Garden** (p. 315), and then head to **Arthur Avenue,** the Little Italy of the Bronx (see "Best Offbeat New York Experiences," above), for an authentic Italian feast.

o **In Brooklyn:** You can take a look at what's on at the always-exciting **Brooklyn Museum of Art** (p. 321), then get some fresh air with a stroll in nearby, lovely **Prospect Park** (p. 326). Cap it off with a sandwich and a slice of cheesecake at **Junior's** (p. 207), on Flatbush Avenue. Or, head for **Coney Island** (p. 322), whose face will change forever within the life of this book. Go in the summer, hit the beach, the amusement park, the aquarium, Nathan's Famous hot dogs, and/or maybe a Cyclones baseball game. It's a schlep, but one you will never forget.

o **In Queens:** Take the 7 train, the **International Express** (see "Best Offbeat New York Experiences," above), to the **Queens Museum of Art** (p. 332), on the grounds of the 1964 World's Fair, or the **Louis Armstrong House Museum** (p. 329). If it's the right time of year, take in a **Mets game** (p. 334)

Jazz great Louis Armstrong's home in Queens is now a museum.

Barneys' decorated windows are a much-loved New York holiday tradition.

or wander the grounds of the U.S. Open. On your way back, stop for a meal at any of the ethnic restaurants you will find within close proximity of the no. 7 train.

best SHOPPING IN NEW YORK CITY

- **Best Store: Saks Fifth Avenue.** For versatility, Saks has it all—without being overwhelming like other big stores. And don't miss those legendary holiday window displays. See p. 354.

- **Best Clothes Store: Barneys.** This store is the pinnacle of big-ticket fashion, with twice-yearly warehouse sales. See p. 352.

- **Best Bargain Store: Century 21.** Come early on weekdays to avoid the crowds at this wild designer-markdown emporium. See p. 353.

- **Best Vintage Store: Beacon's Closet.** Its two Brooklyn shops stock some of the best, most affordable clothing in town. See p. 361.

- **Best Shopping Zone: SoHo, NoHo, and Nolita.** Three neighborhoods together create the best single area for roaming and shopping among the newest, trendiest boutiques. See chapter 7.

- **Best Bookstore: Bluestockings.** This "radical bookstore, fair-trade cafe, and activist center" on the Lower East Side packs a full arsenal of literature and events into its Allen Street storefront. See p. 358.

- **Best Old-World Italian Food Store: DiPalo's Dairy.** This 1910-originated store is one of the last vestiges New York's Little Italy—just ask lifelong owner Louie DiPalo. See p. 369.

- Best Music Store: Other Music. It's tough to find a good album these days, much less a good record store. Thank heaven for Other Music. See p. 381.

- Best Old-World Jewish Food Store: Russ & Daughters. This smoked-fish purveyor has been a mainstay on the Lower East Side since 1914 (or 1908, if you count its push-cart days). Like DiPalo's above, the Russ family has been in charge since the beginning. See p. 372.

best CULTURE & NIGHTLIFE IN NEW YORK

- Best Performance Space: Carnegie Hall. One of the world's great concert halls, with an array of world-class talent on display almost every night. See p. 404.

- Best Free Cultural Event: Shakespeare in the Park. Imagine Shakespeare performed by stars, under the stars, in Central Park. No wonder it's considered a New York institution. See p. 408.

- Best Children's Theater: Paper Bag Players. For children 4 to 9, the imaginative players put on colorful performances on homemade sets. See p. 392.

- Best Jazz Club: The Village Vanguard. You can't do better than this subterranean musical landmark for real-deal jazz. See p. 418.

- Best Rock Club: Southpaw. Outdoing any Manhattan club for its layout, acoustics, and breadth of programming, this Park Slope, Brooklyn, mainstay is not to be missed. See p. 415.

- Best Comedy Club: Gotham Comedy Club. Comfortable and sophisticated, this is where the best comedians come to hone their acts. See p. 423.

The stars come out in summer at Shakespeare in the Park.

Jazz aficionados flock to the classic Village Vanguard.

o **Best Cocktail: Flatiron Lounge.** Manhattan's best Manhattan is served up in this classic Deco lounge. See p. 432.

o **Best Pub: Ear Inn.** An old hanger-on in chic SoHo, this rumored-to-be-haunted joint continues to survive among the lush lounges that surround it. See p. 427.

o **Best Dive Bar: Rudy's Bar & Grill.** Midtown's dirt-cheap watering hole also serves free hot dogs! See p. 433.

o **Best Beer Bar: Spuyten Duyvil.** This Williamsburg, Brooklyn, bar is nirvana for beer fanatics. Kick back with a draught and enjoy the killer jukebox. See p. 438.

o **Best Club: Santos Party House.** Come dance at this low-cover-charge Chinatown club, with cutting-edge DJs, all kinds of bands, and always a good crowd. See p. 440.

o **Best Scenester Bar: Ace Hotel Lobby Bar.** This huge lobby bar is second to none when it comes to funky-modern decor and ace cocktails. See p. 434.

NEW YORK CITY IN DEPTH

National Park Service
U.S. Department of the Interior

Welcome

Ellis
Island

**Statue of Liberty
National Monument**

Welcome to the Big Apple . . . wait a minute. So why *is* New York City called "the Big Apple"? Some say it's a horse racing reference: The prize for the winning horse was an apple, and in the 1920s, with so many racetracks in New York, it was referred to as "the Big Apple"—the city that jockeys and trainers aspired to conquer. It was also Gotham, the Empire City, the City that Never Sleeps, the Melting Pot, the Capital of the World, a city "so nice, they named it twice." After all, when a place is world class in finance, culture, and media, it's difficult to sum up your grandeur in one moniker.

How do eight million people function, live, work, and even thrive on top of each other? It's mind boggling. For those of us who do live here, it's best not to ponder the enormity of it all. We're in too much of a hurry.

But forget the monuments, the glass towers, the arenas, and theaters; it is the people who made the city—for better, for worse! It's the place to prove yourself; to "make a brand new start of it"; and where "if [you] can make it there, [you can] make it anywhere." And it's the people, and their unique contributions who keep the city thriving. Whether they are from Ireland, Italy, West Africa, France, Israel, Pakistan, Mexico, Haiti, or Manhattan (Kansas), it's that mix of people and cultures that has always been the city's most solid foundation and source of energy.

The variety and diversity seem to form a collective unifying and feisty spirit that is essential to the city's character.

NEW YORK CITY TODAY

New Yorkers have heard the proud refrain from local politicos many times: New York is better than ever. Our city is cleaner (and greener) than it ever was. The number of hotels, restaurants, and clubs keeps growing—6,600 hotel rooms were added in 2010, for example—and they get better every year. In fact, the *New York Times* reported that a record 48.7 million visitors came to New York City in 2010—more than any year ever—an increase of 7% from 2009. The figure is getting nearer and nearer to Mayor Bloomberg's goal of 50 million visitors a year—a figure he wants to reach by 2011.

"Just think about that," the mayor said at a news conference heralding those stats, "the economy turns down in America and around the world, and we have a record year in tourism."

Those tourists will feel safer, too, in a city that is consistently ranked among the most safest, if not *the* safest, big city in America. The FBI reported that violent crime decreased 4.2 percent and property crime declined 5.3 percent in 2010 in the Big Apple.

FACING PAGE: **Generations of immigrants passed through Ellis Island, and helped create modern New York City.**

New York City is headed toward 50 million visitors a year . . . and they all seem to congregate in Times Square!

More welcome news: Despite the hard times, New York City, according to the latest figures, has continued to rebound faster from the recession than the rest of the nation. Unemployment is decreasing, and while we may not find ourselves loosening that collective belt a notch, we are optimists—and always have been.

Why, then, are some of us worried about our city? Even with this welcome number of tourists, those of us who have been here a long time and have seen the changes from a city in need to what it is today, fret that this renaissance is one without character. We worry that with a chain coffee shop on every corner and new glass-and-steel condos sprouting like mushrooms at the expense of an old favorite bookstore or our local Cuban/Chinese joint, that we are slowly losing our identity—the fear being that we will become like Everycity, U.S.A.

But change is inevitable. "Of the city's five boroughs, Manhattan, in particular, refuses to remain as it was. It is dynamic, not static. What seems permanent when you are 20 is too often a ghost when you are 30," Pete Hamill writes in his book *Downtown: My Manhattan.*

And the longer you live in this town, the more ghosts you will encounter. But New Yorkers adapt . . . sometimes painfully. Hamill explains, "The New York version of nostalgia is not simply about lost buildings or their presence in the youth of the individuals who lived with them. It involves an almost fatalistic acceptance of the permanent presence of loss. Nothing will ever stay the same . . . Irreversible change happens so often in New York that the experience affects character itself. New York toughens its people against sentimentality by allowing the truer emotion of nostalgia. Sentimentality is always about a lie. Nostalgia is about real things gone."

So though we might mourn loss, we also anticipate and expect change—it's part of our way of life. We know that a restaurant, show, club, or store might be the hottest thing now, but a couple months later, the next one has opened or been discovered and that once-hot spot quickly becomes passé.

But some icons and institutions are so entrenched in our daily lives that we could never accept their loss. What would we do without that reassuring sight of the Lady in the Harbor, or the gleaming spire of the Empire State Building? Or the perfect pizza? Or a Sunday in Central Park? Or the rumbling of the trains beneath the earth? Or the sounds of jazz from a Village club? So while New York is ever changing, as long as its core remains the same we might complain a bit, but we aren't going anywhere.

In fact, New York City is predicted to add one million *more* residents by 2030 and must figure out where to put them, how to move them around, and what they'll be doing. The city has embarked on an ambitious, long-term plan (called **PlaNYC 2030**) to improve the rapidly aging infrastructure, find ways to fuel its energy needs more sustainably, and expand the mass transit system to accommodate millions more people, as well as figure out ways to build housing that will keep lower- and middle-income people within its borders.

There's been a movement toward congestion pricing (charging vehicles a high premium to drive in Manhattan during the day), which was narrowly defeated in 2008; but because productivity goes down when traffic jams go up, expect to see a new take on solving the traffic crisis in the next several years. The city has created over 200 miles of new bike paths, for example. The crossroads of the world, Times Square, became a pedestrian mall mid-2009 in a 6-month experiment that drew all eyes to the lounge chairs sprouting up in an area that was once wall-to-wall taxis and buses. As of February 2010, Mayor Bloomberg declared the experiment a success and said it would continue, and even added another auto-free zone around Herald Square. And that's just the tip of the iceberg.

While Mayor Bloomberg may be right to crow about the increase in tourists to New York, he didn't get to be a billionaire by giving money away. So while he does everything he can to draw visitors to our fair city, he can be draconian when he has to in terms of cutting jobs (8,200 in the next fiscal year) and increasing taxes. In 2009, the mayor, with the city council's blessing, increased the city's already-steep sales tax to 8.875%. As of August 1, 2010, the sweet deal of paying no state sales tax on clothing items under $110 was no more. The mayor responded by declaring that clothing and footwear under $110 are exempt from New York City's 4.5% sales tax. In 2011, he declared that clothing and footwear under $55 will be exempt from the entire sales tax. The story of the state legislature's dysfunctional behavior in past years has been a source of astonishment, laughter, and anger. The new governor, Andrew Cuomo, has vowed to tame that unmanageable body, but Albany is littered with the bones of governors who have made that pledge. We will see.

But wait, there's more! For those of you who haven't paid a visit to New York since the days of subway tokens, or even in the last few years, the subway and bus fare went up to $2.25 per ride in June 2009, and $2.50 in 2011. Another fare hike is proposed for 2013.

It's all a big challenge, but as a city that has come up with ingenious solutions since its birth, you can bet New York will come up with some unique (and showy) ways to figure out what's going to happen in the next half-millennium or so.

LOOKING BACK AT NEW YORK CITY
Colonial Days (1524–1776)

The area that became New York City was the home to many Native Americans before Giovanni da Verrazano arrived in 1524. And it wasn't until 1609, when Henry Hudson, while searching for the Northwest Passage, claimed it for the Dutch East India Company, that New York was recognized as a potential, profitable settlement in the New World. (And it's 1609 that the city uses as its founding date.)

Hudson (the river that separates Manhattan from the mainland is named after him) said of New York, "It is as beautiful a land as one can hope to tread upon." The treading didn't really start until years later, but by 1625, Dutch

The first Congress was held at Federal Hall.

settlers established a fur trade with the locals and called their colony New Amsterdam. A year later, Peter Minuit of the Dutch West India Company made that famous deal for the island. He bought New Amsterdam from the Lenape Tribe for what has widely been reported as $24.

New Amsterdam became a British colony in the 1670s, and during the Revolutionary War it was occupied by British troops. England controlled New York

DATELINE

1524 Giovanni da Verrazano sails into New York Harbor.

1609 Henry Hudson sails up the Hudson River.

1621 The Dutch West India Company begins trading from New York City.

1626 The Dutch pay 60 guilders ($24) to the Lenape Tribe for the island of New Amsterdam.

1664 The Dutch surrender New Amsterdam to the British and the island is renamed after the

brother of King Charles II, the Duke of York.

1765 The Sons of Liberty burn the British governor in effigy.

1776 Independence from England is declared.

1789 The first Congress is held at Federal Hall on Wall Street, and George Washington is inaugurated.

1792 The first stock exchange is established on Wall Street.

until 1783, when it withdrew from the city 2 years *after* the end of the American Revolution.

Two years after that, New York was named the first capital of the United States. The first Congress was held at Federal Hall on Wall Street in 1789, and George Washington was inaugurated president. But New York's tenure as the capital didn't last long. A year later, the government headed south to Philadelphia, eventually finding its permanent home in the newly created District of Columbia.

A Melting Pot City

By 1825, New York City's population swelled to 250,000, rising to a half-million by midcentury. The city was a hotbed of Union recruitment during the Civil War; in the

Visitors walk the halls their ancestors might have arrived in.

1863 draft riots, Irish immigrants violently protested the draft and lynched 11 African-Americans.

With industry booming, the late 19th century was termed the "Gilded Age." New York City was an example of this label in action; millionaires built mansions on Fifth Avenue, while rows of tenements teeming with families (made up of the cheap, mostly immigrant laborers who were employed by the industrial barons) filled the city's districts. In 1880, the city's population boomed to 1.1 million.

1820 New York City is the nation's largest city, with a population of 124,000.

1859 Central Park opens.

1863 The draft riots rage throughout New York; 125 people die, including 11 African-Americans who are lynched by mobs of Irish immigrants.

1883 The Brooklyn Bridge opens.

1886 The Statue of Liberty is completed.

1892 Ellis Island opens, processing over a million immigrants yearly.

1904 The first subway departs from City Hall.

1920 Babe Ruth joins the New York Yankees.

1923 Old Yankee Stadium opens.

1929 The stock market crashes.

1931 The Empire State Building opens and is the tallest building in the world.

1939 The New York World's Fair opens in Flushing Meadows, Queens.

continues

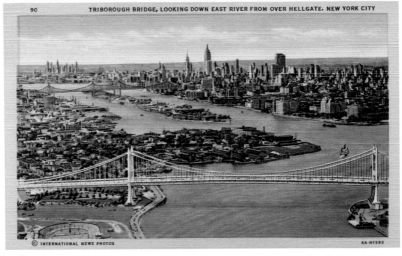

© INTERNATIONAL NEWS PHOTOS   6A-H1593

Robert Moses spearheaded projects like the Triborough Bridge, now called the Robert F. Kennedy Bridge.

More European immigrants poured into the city between 1900 and 1930, arriving at Ellis Island and then fanning out into such neighborhoods as the Lower East Side, Greenwich Village, Little Italy, and Harlem. With the city population in 1930 at seven million and a depression raging, New York turned to a feisty mayor named Fiorello La Guardia for help. With the assistance of civic planner Robert Moses, who masterminded a huge public works program, the city was remade. Moses did some things well, but his highway, bridge, tunnel,

DATELINE continued

1947   The Brooklyn Dodgers sign Jackie Robinson, the first African-American to play in the Major Leagues.

1957   Elvis Presley performs live in New York on the *Ed Sullivan Show*.

1969   The gay rights movement begins with the Stonewall Rebellion in Greenwich Village.

1990   David Dinkins becomes the first African-American mayor of New York City.

2000   The New York Yankees beat the New York Mets in the first Subway Series in 44 years. New York's population exceeds eight million.

2001   Terrorists use hijacked planes to crash into the Twin Towers of the World Trade Center, bringing the towers down and killing more than 3,000 people.

2003   Smoking is banned in all restaurants and bars.

and housing projects ran through (and sometimes destroyed) many vibrant neighborhoods.

Post–World War II Through Today

While most of the country prospered after World War II, New York, with those Moses-built highways and a newly forming car culture, endured an exodus to the suburbs. By 1958, the Dodgers had left Brooklyn and the Giants had left the Polo Grounds in upper Manhattan. This economic slide climaxed in the late 1970s with the city's declaration of bankruptcy.

As Wall Street rallied during the Reagan years of the 1980s, New York's fortunes also improved. It was a heady time to be living here. Ed Koch was the one and only mayor for the entire decade. It takes a tough man to govern New York; you have to have skin of titanium, and Ed—as everyone called him—proved this, alienating as many people as he endeared. There was no middle ground with Mr. "How'm I doin'?"

A book that captures well the excesses of the period, as typified by the frenetic downtown club scene, is Jay McInerney's *Bright Lights, Big City* (1984), with its urban equivalent of eat, drink, and be merry, for tomorrow we die (read "snort" for "drink" here). The movie Wall Street came out in 1987 with its now notorious, and sadly prescient, line, "Greed is good." Studio 54 was flourishing right up to 1986, when its infamous doors finally closed.

Not all was about surfeit, though. In the early 1980s, a college student named Barack Obama lived in an apartment on East 94th Street in Manhattan. He wrote about it in his memoir, *Dreams from My Father:* "It was an uninviting block, treeless and barren, lined with soot-colored walk-ups that cast heavy shadows for the rest of the day. The apartment was small, with slanting floors and irregular heat and a buzzer downstairs that didn't work."

The future president graduated from Columbia University in 1983.

2006 Construction begins on the controversial Freedom Tower (its name later changed to One World Trade), to be built at the site of the World Trade Center.

2008 QB Eli Manning leads the Giants to a win in Super Bowl XXV (they may play in New Jersey, but they still call themselves the New York Giants).

2009 Captain Chesley "Sully" Sullenberger successfully lands US Airways flight 1549 in the Hudson River, and all 155 people on board are saved in the so-called "Miracle on the Hudson."

Both the Yankees and the Mets move into new stadiums, just in time for the financial meltdown that left fans complaining about the sky-high ticket prices. To make up for this affront, the Yankees win the World Series—their 27th.

2010 The New Meadowlands Stadium opens in East Rutherford, New Jersey, new home to both the New York Giants and the New York Jets.

2011 The National 9/11 Memorial opens on September 11th, the 10th anniversary of the terrorist attacks.

Times Square used to be a bit more gritty . . .   . . . but now visitors can sit in the middle of it.

In the 1990s, with Rudolph Giuliani—whom they haven't named anything after yet—as the mayor, followed by the current mayor, Michael Bloomberg, the city rode a wave of prosperity that left it safer, cleaner, and more populated. The flip side of this boom was that Manhattan became more homogenized. Witness the Disneyfication of Times Square—the ultimate symbol of New York's homogenization—and the growing gap between the rich and poor.

Everything changed on September 11, 2001, when terrorists flew planes into the Twin Towers of the World Trade Center. But New York's grit and verve showed itself once more, as the city immediately began to rebound emotionally from that tragedy. The financial aftermaths of the attacks were also short-lived, and the city has experienced an unprecedented building boom in the first decade of the 21st century, which led to a drastic "readjustment" of the city's real estate market, along with everything else budgetary and financial with economic collapse/crisis/recession—or whatever you want to call it—at the end of 2008.

Federal stimulus money is making its way into New York City, but thousands of jobs have been lost in the financial sector, a loss felt in all of the support industries around it, from restaurants to computer sales. In spring 2010, the unemployment rate in the city stood at about 10%.

Tourism has always been essential for New York City's economic health, and the city government is trying to find a balance between necessary budget cuts and the support needed for big attractions to keep the visitors coming.

If you come here in 2010 or 2011, you are likely to find a city of both bargains and price hikes: Hotel rooms are more available and at better prices than ever before; restaurants are offering deals left and right; and some attractions are raising their admission prices and some curtailing their hours.

It's a challenging time here, as it is everywhere else, but New Yorkers are known for coming up with unique solutions in their unique environment.

NEW YORK CITY'S ARCHITECTURE

New York City contains a wealth of architectural styles, from modest row houses to ornate churches to soaring skyscrapers. Constructed over 300 years, these buildings represent the changing tastes of the city's residents from Colonial times to the present. A brief look at the city's most popular styles provides a unique perspective on the city's past, present, and future.

Georgian (1700–76)

This style reflects Renaissance ideas made popular in England, and later in the United States, through the publication of books on 16th-century Italian architects. In the United States, the style was seen as an appropriate expression of the relative prosperity and security of the colonies. It was a sharp contrast to the unadorned Colonial style that preceded it.

St. Paul's Chapel, on Broadway between Vesey and Fulton streets (1764–66, Thomas McBean), the only pre-Revolutionary building remaining in continuous use in Manhattan, is an almost perfect example of the Georgian style, with a pediment, colossal columns, Palladian window, quoins, and balustrade above the roof line. The **Morris-Jumel Mansion** in Harlem (p. 274), built in 1765 and billing itself as "Manhattan's oldest house," also survives from the late Colonial era. Although it's a 20th-century reconstruction of a formal English house built here in 1719, **Fraunces Tavern,** 54 Pearl St., is another fine example of the style.

The Morris-Jumel Mansion is a historic home from the Colonial era.

Federal (1780–1820)

Federal was the first truly American architectural style. Federal was popular with successful merchants throughout the cities and towns of the eastern seaboard. Its connection to the prosperous empires of Rome and Greece was seen as an appropriate reference for the young United States.

In New York, the Federal style was popular for row houses built after the 1811 creation of the city's grid pattern of avenues and streets.

In the **West Village,** near and along Bedford Street between Christopher and Morton streets, are more original Federal-style houses than anywhere else in Manhattan. House nos. 4 through 10 (1825–34) on Grove Street, just off Bedford, present one of the most authentic groups of late Federal–style houses in America. Another house from the period that you can see and visit is the **Dyckman Farmhouse Museum** (ca. 1784) in Inwood, at the northern tip of Manhattan.

Greek Revival (1820–60)

The Greek Revolution in the 1820s, in which Greece won its independence from the Turks, recalled to American intellectuals the democracy of ancient Greece and its elegant architecture, created around 400 B.C. At the same time, the War of 1812 diminished American affection for the British influence, including the still-dominant Federal style. The style was so popular it came to be known as the National Style, and was used for numerous state capitols, as well as the U.S. Capitol in Washington, D.C.

Perhaps the city's finest Greek Revival building is **Federal Hall National Memorial** (1834–42), at 26 Wall St., where George Washington took his presidential oath in 1789. It has a Greek temple front, with Doric columns and a simple pediment, resting on a high base, called a *plinth,* with a steep flight of steps.

Gothic Revival (1830–60)

The term *Gothic Revival* refers to a literary and aesthetic movement of the 1830s and 1840s that occurred in England and later in the United States. The revival style was used for everything from timber cottages to stone castles and churches. Some structures had only one or two Gothic features, most commonly a steeply pitched roof or pointed arches, whereas other buildings, usually churches, were accurate copies of English Gothic structures.

Trinity Church, at Broadway and Wall Street (Richard Upjohn, 1846), is one of the most celebrated, authentic Gothic Revival structures in the United States. Here you see all the features of a Gothic church: a steeple, battlements, pointed arches, Gothic tracery, stained-glass windows, flying buttresses (an external bracing system for supporting a roof or vault), and medieval sculptures. This was the tallest building in the area until the late 1860s.

Italianate (1840–80)

The architecture of Italy served as the inspiration for this building style. Its adaptability made it immensely popular in the 1850s. In New York, the style was used for urban row houses and commercial buildings. The development of cast iron at this time permitted the mass production of decorative features that few could have afforded in carved stone. This led to the creation of cast-iron districts in nearly every American city, including New York.

New York's **SoHo–Cast Iron Historic District** has 26 blocks jammed with cast-iron facades, many in the Italianate manner. The single richest section is **Greene Street** between Houston and Canal streets. Stroll along here and take in building after building of sculptural facades.

Early Skyscraper (1880–1920)

The invention of the skyscraper can be traced directly to the use of cast iron in the 1840s, such as those seen in New York's SoHo. Experimentation with cast and wrought iron eventually allowed buildings to rise higher. (Previously, buildings were restricted by the height supportable by their load-bearing walls.) Important technical innovations—involving safety elevators, electricity, fireproofing, foundations, plumbing, and telecommunications—combined with advances in skeletal construction to create a new building type, the skyscraper. These buildings were spacious, cost effective, efficient, and quickly erected—in short, the perfect architectural solution for America's growing downtowns.

Solving the technical problems of the skyscraper, however, did not resolve how the building should look.

New York's early skyscrapers relied heavily on historical decoration. A good early example in the Beaux Arts mode is the **American Surety Company,** at 100 Broadway (Bruce Price, 1895). The triangular **Flatiron Building,** at Fifth Avenue and 23rd Street (Daniel H. Burnham & Co., 1902), has strong tripartite divisions and Renaissance Revival detail. And, finally, the **Woolworth Building** (Cass Gilbert, 1913), on Broadway at Park Place, dubbed the "Cathedral of Commerce," is a neo-Gothic skyscraper with flying buttresses, spires, sculptured gargoyles, and pointed arches.

Beaux Arts (1890–1920)

This style takes its name from the Ecole des Beaux-Arts in Paris, where a number of prominent American architects (including **Richard Morris Hunt** [1827–95], **John Mervin Carrère** [1858–1911], and **Thomas Hastings** [1860–1929], to name only a few) received their training, beginning around the mid–19th century. These architects adopted the academic design principles of the Ecole, which emphasized the

The Flatiron Building.

Mercury presides over Grand Central Terminal.

study of Greek and Roman structures, composition, and symmetry, and the creation of elaborate presentation drawings. Because of the idealized origins and grandiose use of classical forms, the Beaux Arts in America was seen as the ideal style for expressing civic pride.

New York has several exuberant Beaux Arts buildings, exhibiting the style's key features. The **New York Public Library,** at Fifth Avenue and 42nd Street (Carrère & Hastings, 1911), is perhaps the best example. Others of note are **Grand Central Terminal,** at 42nd Street and Park Avenue (Reed & Stem and Warren & Whetmore, 1903–13), and the **U.S. Customs House** (Cass Gilbert, 1907), on Bowling Green between State and Whitehall streets.

International Style (1920–45)

In 1932, the Museum of Modern Art hosted its first architecture exhibit, titled simply "Modern Architecture." Displays included images of International Style buildings from around the world, many designed by architects from Germany's Bauhaus, a progressive design school. The structures shared a stark simplicity and functionalism, a definite break from historically based, decorative styles.

The International Style was popularized in the U.S. through the teachings and designs of **Ludwig Mies van der Rohe** (1886–1969), a German émigré based in Chicago. Interpretations of the "Miesian" International Style were built in most U.S. cities, including New York, as late as 1980.

Two famous examples of this style are the **Seagram Building,** at 375 Park Ave. (Ludwig Mies van der Rohe, 1958), and **Lever House,** 390 Park Ave., between 53rd and 54th streets (Skidmore, Owings & Merrill, 1952). The latter is credited for popularizing the use of plazas and glass curtain walls.

Another well-known example is the Secretariat building in the **United Nations** complex, at First Avenue and 46th Street (1947–53), designed by an international committee of architects.

Art Deco (1925–40)

Art Deco is a decorative style that took its name from a Paris exposition in 1925. The jazzy style embodied the idea of modernity. One of the first widely accepted styles not based on historic precedents, it influenced all areas of design, from jewelry and household goods to cars, trains, and ocean liners.

Art Deco buildings are characterized by a linear, hard edge, or angular composition, often with a vertical emphasis and highlighted with stylized decoration. The New York zoning law of 1916, which required setbacks in buildings above a certain height to ensure that light and air could reach the street, gave the style its distinctive profile.

Despite the effects of the Depression, several major Art Deco structures were built in New York in the 1930s, often providing crucial jobs. **Rockefeller Center** (Raymond Hood, 1932–40), a complex that sprawls from 48th to 50th streets, between Fifth and Sixth avenues, includes 30 Rockefeller Plaza, a tour de force of Art Deco style, with a soaring, vertical shaft and aluminum details. The **Chrysler Building,** Lexington Avenue at 42nd Street (William Van Alen, 1930), is a towering tribute to the automobile. The Chrysler's needlelike spire with zigzag patterns in glass and metal is a distinctive feature on the city's skyline. The famous **Empire State Building,** Fifth Avenue at 34th Street (Shreve, Lamb & Harmon, 1931), contains a black-and-silver-toned lobby among its many Art Deco features.

Postmodern (1975–90)

After years of steel-and-glass office towers in the International Style, postmodernism burst on the scene in the 1970s with the reintroduction of historical precedents in architecture. With many feeling that the office towers of the previous style were too cold, postmodernists began to incorporate classical details and recognizable forms into their designs—often applied in outrageous proportions.

The **Sony Building,** at 550 Madison Ave. (Philip Johnson/

The Empire State Building is a beautiful example of Art Deco architecture.

The Heart Building's intricate façade is the design of Sir Norman Foster.

John Burgee, 1984), brings the distinctive shape of a Chippendale cabinet to the New York skyline. The **Morgan Bank Headquarters,** 60 Wall St. (Kevin Roche, John Dinkeloo & Assocs., 1988), resembles a classical column, with modern interpretations of a base, shaft, and capital. The base of the column mirrors the style of the facade of the 19th-century building across the street.

21st-Century Architecture

The new building boom at the beginning of the 21st century has brought edifices designed by such modern architectural giants as Frank Gehry, who designed the **IAC Building** on West 18th Street with the look of billowing curtains; by Sir Norman Foster, who designed the geometrically patterned **Hearst Tower** at 300 W. 57th St.; and by Renzo Piano, who designed the 52-story headquarters of the *New York Times* at 620 Eighth Ave. at 42nd Street, which opened in 2007 (and was climbed by not one, but two, "human spiders" on the same day in June 2008!). Piano also took charge of the vast makeover and addition to the Morgan Library, completed in 2006.

Finally, construction at the World Trade Center site makes real progress with the focal point, the 1,776 feet-high One World Trade Center—also known as Freedom Tower—to be completed by 2013.

NEW YORK CITY IN POP CULTURE
Books

Where to begin? New York City has been the influence, inspiration, and site of libraries' worth of fiction, poetry, memoir, history, and drama. For the definitive history of the birth of New York City to the end of the 19th century, there is no better read than the Pulitzer Prize–winning *Gotham: A History of New York City to 1898,* by Edwin R. Burrows and Mike Wallace (Oxford University Press). Another recommended historical look at the growth of New York City, this one told in a breezy narrative tone, is *The Epic of New York City: A Narrative History,* by Edward Robb Ellis (Kodansha).

Luc Sante's *Low Life: Lures and Snares of Old New York* (Vintage Departures) details the bad old days of brothels, drug dens, and gambling saloons in New York in the early 20th century—it's a lively, fascinating read.

One of master biographer Robert Caro's early works, *The Power Broker: Robert Moses and the Fall of New York* (Random House), focuses on how the vision of master dealmaker Robert Moses transformed New York to what it became in the second half of the 20th century.

Downtown, by Pete Hamill (Little Brown & Co.), is as concise a history of the area to the south of Times Square as you will find—and told in Hamill's typically breezy and gritty style, while Hamill's 2003 novel, *Forever,* chronicles the 3 centuries of a man who has been given the gift of eternal life as long as he never leaves the island of Manhattan. In *The Great Bridge: The Epic Story of the Building of the Brooklyn Bridge* (Simon & Schuster), author David McCullough devotes his estimable talents to the tale of the Brooklyn–Manhattan span.

Speaking of water, you might try Philip Lopate's *Waterfront: A Walk Around Manhattan,* which is a personal look—mixed with historical, architectural, and cultural references—at New York City's waterfront.

The companion to the PBS series (see "Films," below) *New York,* by Ric Burns, Lisa Ades, and James Sanders (Knopf), uses lavish photographs and illustrations to show the growth of New York City.

My all-time favorite book about New York is a children's classic called *This Is New York* (Universe Publishing), written and illustrated by M. Sasek in 1960. The book was recently reissued and, with an update added, is as fresh as it was all those years ago.

E.B. White—who else?—captured the soul of the city in his splendid essay, *Here Is New York,* originally published in *Holiday.* Thankfully, it has been reissued by Little Bookroom books. If you read any single book or essay about New York—and this isn't that long—read White's poem to New York.

New York has been fertile fodder for novelists, short-story writers, and playwrights, and the city is often a character in itself. The novels, stories, and plays with New York as the backdrop are too numerous to begin to chronicle. Here are some of my personal favorites.

You might say it all begins with "Bartleby, the Scrivener," by Herman Melville, which is subtitled, "A Story of Wall Street." Published in 1853, it contains Bartleby's wonderful refrain when he is asked to do some work, "I would prefer not to." Haven't we all felt like saying that at one time or another? Edgar Allen Poe was living and working in New York City (you can still visit his cottage in the Bronx) when he lost his young wife, the model for "lost Lenore" in "The Raven."

The 1934 novel *Call It Sleep,* by Henry Roth, tells the story of a poor Jewish boy and his coming to terms with his old-world parents and the modern world of New York around him.

Much the same emotional and physical geography is covered in Elmer Rice's forceful 1929 Pulitzer Prize–winning play, *Street Scene.* It captures what that early, turn-of-the-20th-century immigrant life in a tenement building was like, where so much of it was played out on the front stoops.

For a taste of tenement life in the Bronx, read Vivian Gornick's searing memoir, *Fierce Attachments.*

Although Arthur Miller's *Death of a Salesman* is set in New York, the play he wrote that has an especially strong sense of the city is *A View from the Bridge,* which is set in the Red Hook section of Brooklyn.

New York native Mickey Spillane's 1947 potboiler *I, the Jury,* introduces tough-guy detective Mike Hammer as he investigates the dark side of the upper class of New York.

Last Exit to Brooklyn, by Hubert Selby, Jr., takes place in and around what is now the Red Hook/Brooklyn Navy Yard section of Brooklyn, and the 1964 novel is bleak in its portrait of the city, to say the least.

All of the novels in Chester Himes' Coffin Ed Johnson and Gravedigger Jones detective series are vivid looks at Harlem in the 1940s and 1950s, written, amazingly, when Himes was living in Paris. *A Rage in Harlem* is one of the best.

We can't have a list without Holden Caulfield's sad and funny New York as described in the late J.D. Salinger's classic *The Catcher in the Rye* (1951). New York is the backdrop for many of Salinger's works, including "The Laughing Man" from *Nine Stories* and *Franny and Zooey.*

Time and Again, a time-travel fantasy written in 1970 by Jack Finney, takes the main character from New York to the city in 1882, where Finney gets the period detail perfectly.

Famous as the author of *The Godfather,* Mario Puzo gives a more literary, semiautobiographical effort in *The Fortunate Pilgrim,* about an Italian-American family growing up in Hell's Kitchen. The book is a masterpiece and was sadly dismissed when it was published in 1965.

Lawrence Block, in his Matt Scudder mystery series, uses New York as a major character. *When the Sacred Ginmill Closes* is my favorite in the series.

The Mambo Kings Play Songs of Love, by Oscar Hijuelos, is about two Cuban musicians who emigrate to New York, specifically upper Manhattan, in the early 1950s, and deservedly won the Pulitzer Prize for fiction in 1990.

I just can't leave out Irwin Shaw's magnificent, chilling short story, "The Girls in Their Summer Dresses," which takes place on a walk to Washington Square Park.

Paul Auster produced a series of novels in the 1980s that have since been collected under the rubric *The New York Trilogy.* They include *City of Glass, Ghosts,* and *The Locked Room.*

Speaking of phantoms, don't forget *Exit Ghost,* by Philip Roth. An aging writer emerges from his Berkshires retreat and comes to New York to see if he can recapture some of his literary youth.

In recent years, some excellent younger authors have been publishing very fine novels that take place in New York. You might even say there seems to be a literary renaissance here. Some of these acclaimed books include *Motherless Brooklyn,* by Jonathan Lethem; *Netherland,* by Joseph O'Neill; *Let the Great World Spin,* by Colum McCann; and *Extremely Loud and Incredibly Close,* by Jonathan Safran Foer; and *A New York Memoir,* by award-winning travel writer (and Frommer's author) Richard Goodman.

New York has inspired the bards, as well. Walt Whitman (who worked as a writer and editor for various New York newspapers), in *Leaves of Grass,* wrote, "Walt Whitman, a cosmos, of Manhattan the son . . . ." Nearly a hundred years later, his spiritual descendant, Hart Crane, wrote the stirring "To Brooklyn Bridge," as part of his book, *The Bridge.*

Even the great Spanish poet Federico García Lorca got into the act, with his *Poeta en Nueva York,* published the same year as Crane's book, 1930.

Finally, we can't forget the feisty 6-year-old girl who lives in the Plaza Hotel—Eloise. In the classic children's book with the same name by Kay Thompson, we follow the adventures of this irrepressible girl who declares, "Getting bored is not allowed." For many children at least, Eloise *is* New York City.

Films

There are not many places as cinematic as New York City. Filmmakers, like novelists, view the city as a character. The list of movies in which New York plays a crucial role are too many to mention, but here are some of the top New York City movies that are worth renting before you visit.

The Empire State Building has never been the same since King Kong climbed it in the 1933 movie of the same name. Who will ever forget Kong futilely swatting at those planes at the top of the building?

There were shantytowns all over America during the Great Depression, and New York had one, too. This is where Carole Lombard finds "lost man" William Powell at the start of the 1936 screwball comedy *My Man Godfrey.* Powell has never been more dry, nor Lombard more bubbly.

The Great Depression produced films that belied the times and gave great doses of escapism to a beleaguered public. One of the most famous was *42nd Street,* choreographed by Busby Berkeley and starring the marvelous hoofer, Ruby Keeler. It's got the famous line, "You're going out there a youngster, but you've got to come back a star!" Young men and women are still streaming into the city with that dream in their hearts 75 years later—and probably always will.

Possibly the best New York City promotional film is the musical *On the Town* (1948), with Gene Kelly and Frank Sinatra, about three sailors with 24 hours' leave spent exploring Gotham. Shot on location, all the landmarks were captured in beautiful Technicolor.

Maybe the cattiest film ever made is set in New York, *All About Eve* (1950), starring Bette Davis as aging actress Margo Channing. She utters the delicious line, "Fasten your seatbelts, it's going to be a bumpy night!"

In 1954, Alfred Hitchcock presented his classic voyeuristic thriller, *Rear Window,* starring Jimmy Stewart and a ravishing Grace Kelly, set in an apartment in Greenwich Village. One year later, the musical *Guys and Dolls,* based on the Times Square stories of Damon Runyon, made its debut with a singing (!) Marlon Brando.

Leonard Bernstein wrote the music for *On the Town,* and he also wrote the music for the landmark musical, *West Side Story* (1961) with lyrics by a young—27 at the time!—Stephen Sondheim.

The same year (1961) was also when Audrey Hepburn had her *Breakfast at Tiffany's* in her classic role as the winningly eccentric Holly Golightly.

Director Paul Mazursky is Brooklyn born, and New York occupies a special place in his cinematic heart. *Next Stop, Greenwich Village* is his sweet 1976 film about a young artist's first taste of this famed part of New York. His *Moscow on the Hudson* has Robin Williams as a Russian circus performer defecting in Bloomingdale's. Where else?

Woody Allen is a New York filmmaker and shoots almost all his films—at least until recently—in the city. One of his best—and a good, but maybe a bit dated, look at neurotic New York—is *Annie Hall* (1977). Don't neglect his ultimate love letter to the city, *Manhattan* (1979).

Following in Woody Allen's footsteps are director Rob Reiner and writer Nora Ephron, who made *When Harry Met Sally* (1989). It's sort of a poor man's *Annie Hall* but a gorgeous cinematic tribute to New York. The famous "I'll have what she's having" scene was filmed in Katz's Delicatessen (p. 149).

Though no physical combat took place in New York during World War II, there was plenty of espionage. A classic 1945 black-and-white thriller is *The*

The Jets and Sharks danced and battled in *West Side Story.*

House on 92nd Street that tells the story of a Nazi spy ring—right on the exclusive Upper East Side.

"I love this dirty town," says Burt Lancaster in the gritty, crackling **Sweet Smell of Success** (1957). In the beautifully photographed black-and-white movie, Lancaster plays malicious gossip columnist J. J. Hunsecker, and Tony Curtis is perfectly despicable as the groveling publicist Sidney Falco.

There are a number of Christmas-themed films that are set in New York, and the granddaddy of them all is **Miracle on 34th Street,** released in 1947. The great department store Gimbel's was still around, and its fierce rivalry with Macy's is the backdrop for this sentimental favorite about Santa Claus on trial.

The Empire State Building has another supporting role in **Elf,** a 2003 comedy starring Will Ferrell. Dressed in an absurd green costume, Ferrell plays a human who was raised by elves in the North Pole and who comes to New York City at Christmas to find his long lost father (whose office is in the Empire State Building), who is none other than Sonny Corleone—James Caan.

But wait a minute. How is *that* possible, since the Empire State Building was destroyed by aliens in **Independence Day** (1996)?

In fact, New York has probably been the most-destroyed city, cinematically speaking, in history. It was creamed *four times* in 1 year—in **Deep Impact, Armageddon, The Siege,** and **Godzilla,** all released in 1998. (And don't forget about the damage wrought by the Stay-Puft marshmallow man in **Ghostbusters** [1984]!)

It seems like since the beginning of New York time, the city was the place people came to become famous. Joe Buck (Jon Voight) came to New York from Texas to be a big shot in the 1969 Academy Award–winner **Midnight Cowboy,** but it took a third-rate conman, Ratso Rizzo (Dustin Hoffman), to transform Voight into a pathetic male hustler. The movie is a bleak but realistic look at the timeless New York story.

One character in a New York-based film whose last wish is to be famous is Robert Redford's in Sydney Pollack's 1975 suspenseful, convoluted thriller, **Three Days of the Condor.** Redford plays a CIA analyst who "just reads books" but who is nevertheless being hunted by a rogue cell of "Company" agents. He takes refuge in Faye Dunaway's Brooklyn Heights apartment. They both never looked better.

Before there was the hit musical, there was the movie **The Producers** (1968) starring Zero Mostel and, in his first lead role, Gene Wilder, as the timid but eventually larcenous accountant Leo Bloom. There is no funnier film set in New York—or, in my humble opinion, anywhere.

Another filmmaker identified with New York is Martin Scorsese. He has made many films where New York plays a central role, from **Mean Streets** (1973) to **Gangs of New York** (2002), which was actually filmed in Italy. But the one film in which New York is a character, and not a very flattering one, is **Taxi Driver.** The Academy Award–nominated 1976 movie about an alienated and psychotic taxi driver is tough and bloody, but to see images of seedy Times Square as it was before its recent reincarnation, there is no better film.

Though long, Sergio Leone's **Once Upon A Time in America** (1984), about Jewish gangsters in the first part of the 20th century, evokes the period masterfully and features stunning New York City locations.

Al Pacino could have his very own New York–based film festival. The movies he's starred in that are set in New York include **The Panic in Needle Park** (1971); **Serpico** (1973); **Dog Day Afternoon** (1975)—remember "Attica! Attica!"?; **Sea of Love** (1989); **Scent of a Woman** (1992), for which he won an Academy Award; and **Donnie Brasco** (1997).

The fourth-largest city in America, Brooklyn, has also been a colorful location. John Travolta's strut under the elevated train in Bensonhurst to the tune of the Bee Gees' "Stayin' Alive" in **Saturday Night Fever** (1977) and Gene Hackman's frenetic and dizzying car chase under the same tracks in **The French Connection** (1971) are two of the best Brooklyn-centric movies.

The best history of New York on video is the Ric Burns documentary **New York: A Documentary Film** (1999), which aired on PBS. The seven-disc, 14-hour DVD (also available on VHS) is a must-see for anyone interested in the evolution of this great city.

The list goes on and on. I can hear the film fans crying out now— why didn't you mention *The Pawnbroker, The Odd Couple, Funny Girl,*

Annie Hall was one of Woody Allen's many love notes to New York City.

Your friendly neighborhood *Spider-Man* keeps NYC safe.

Rosemary's Baby, The Way We Were, Network, Kramer vs. Kramer, Wall Street, Do the Right Thing, Men in Black, Spider-Man—and what about *The Lost Weekend*, for gosh sakes?

I just did!

Television

The medium of television was born in New York City in the late 1940s and 1950s. Many early pioneering television programs were filmed in New York, often in front of live audiences. Breaking new ground, programs such as the *Philco Television Playhouse* and *Playhouse 90* featured original dramas by heavyweight writers, including Paddy Chayefsky, Gore Vidal, and Rod Serling; directors such as Sidney Lumet and Arthur Penn; and actors including Robert Redford, Jack Klugman, and Rod Steiger.

One of the first television shows to be filmed on location in New York, *Naked City* was a tough black-and-white series that ran from 1958 to 1963. I can still hear its trademark closing lines: "There are eight million stories in the Naked City. This has been one of them."

Comedy was a big part of the early days of television, and the talent level was impressive. Best among the programs was *Your Show of Shows* (1950–54), which showcased the talents of Sid Caesar, Carl Reiner, and Mel Brooks, among others, who would improvise and devise sketches in a 90-minute show each week; the show was an inspiration for another New York–based comedy sketch series, *Saturday Night Live.*

The sitcom was also hatched during this period in New York. The best, by far, was the story of the timeless travails of a city bus driver named Ralph Kramden; his wife, Alice; and their friends Ed and Trixie Norton—all who lived in Brooklyn. The ensemble team of Jackie Gleason, Art Carney, Audrey Meadows,

NEW YORK CITY playlist

The energy of New York City's streets provides inspiration to songwriters and musicians. New York is probably the most vibrant city for music in the world. From songsmiths crowding such storied places as Tin Pan Alley and the Brill Building, to the folkies wandering Bleecker Street, the styles of music and songs about New York are countless. Everyone has a song that means "New York" to them, so here are *my* top 10 . . . no, New York's too big for a top 10, here's an even dozen songs!

1. **"Autumn in New York":** This 1934 jazz standard has been performed by greats including Ella Fitzgerald, Frank Sinatra, Charlie Parker, and Louis Armstrong. My favorite rendition is the one performed by the Modern Jazz Quartet.

2. **"Downtown":** This 1965 megahit, performed by Petula Clark, is an early anthem to the thrill of nightlife "downtown." It's as timely today as it was 45 years ago.

3. **"I Guess the Lord Must Be in New York City":** Harry Nilsson wrote this song in 1968 for the movie *Midnight Cowboy,* but the director of that movie, John Schlesinger, used Nilsson's other song "Everybody's Talkin" instead. He really couldn't go wrong with either.

4. **"On Broadway":** This 1963 hit for the Drifters, another theme about making it in New York, has been covered by many, including guitarist George Benson, who had a huge hit with it and did not "catch the Greyhound bus for home."

5. **"Spanish Harlem":** This hit for Ben E. King in 1961, from songwriters Jerry Leiber and Phil Spector, had a distinctive Latin beat, evoking the influx of Puerto Ricans to the city at the time. The red rose in Spanish Harlem became a "black" rose when Aretha Franklin covered the song in 1971.

6. **"Summer in the City":** This 1966 hit by the Lovin' Spoonful captures the raw grit of a stifling New York summer. It really is "a pity the days can't be like the nights in the summer in the city."

7. **"Take the A Train":** The signature tune by Duke Ellington and lyrics by Billy Strayhorn refer to the A train that runs from Brooklyn, through Manhattan, and up to Harlem. And the A train is *still* the "quickest way to get to Harlem."

8. **"The Message":** "It's like a jungle sometimes . . ." This 1982 hip-hop classic by Grandmaster Flash and the Furious Five masterfully re-creates the urban rage of the time.

9. Theme from **"New York, New York":** Start spreadin' the news: This Kander and Ebb classic was the theme song for the Martin Scorsese movie of the same name. Liza Minnelli sang it in the film, but it's the Frank Sinatra version that has become synonymous with the city and all its challenges.

10. **"New York, New York":** From the great Broadway musical and, later, movie, *On the Town.* With those wonderful lines, "The Bronx is up, and the Battery's down. The people ride in a hole in the ground."

11. **"Walk on the Wild Side":** Lou Reed's 1972 classic was produced by David Bowie and was a big hit despite its obviously dark and downright perverse undertones. With "A hustle here and a hustle there/New York City is the place where they said . . ."

12. **"Empire State of Mind":** Jay-Z and Alicia Keys created a new NYC anthem in 2009 with a song that topped the charts and tips its lyrical hat to "New York, New York" with Jay-Z declaring: "I'm the new Sinatra/And since I made it here/I can make it anywhere."

and Joyce Randolph, and a very limited set, formed what is now history in *The Honeymooners* (1955–56).

In the 1960s, most television production moved to the West Coast, but a few mainstays remained, such as the *Ed Sullivan Show* and the *Tonight Show with Johnny Carson,* which migrated west in 1972.

While most sitcoms and dramas were produced in Los Angeles, there were a couple of notable exceptions that used New York as their home base, including classic shows *The Odd Couple* (1970–75) and *The Cosby Show* (1984–92).

In the 1990s and up to the present, New York has seen a resurgence of film and television production, including *Law and Order* (the original, sadly, cancelled in 2010), and its spinoffs, *The Late Show with David Letterman, Late Night with Jimmy Fallon,* the HBO series (and films) *Sex and the City, 30 Rock, The Daily Show, The Colbert Report,* and the award-winning *Mad Men.* The 'tween hit

live *NOT* FROM NEW YORK (BUT ABOUT NEW YORK)

Some of the best television shows about New York were never filmed in New York, with the exception of some stock footage. Here is my list of the best New York television not filmed in New York.

○ *Seinfeld* (1990–98): You couldn't get it any more accurate than this show. It was as if they bottled the New York attitude in so many ways and made sure it was let loose on the set. The show has even spawned location tours in the city led by the real-life Kramer. Not that there's anything wrong with that. He's real, and he's spectacular.

○ *All in the Family* (1971–79): Archie Bunker, brilliantly played by Carroll O'Connor, was the quintessential white, blue-collar New York bigot, who lived with his "dingbat" wife, Edith, and daughter and son-in-law ("Meathead") in a small house in Astoria.

○ *Taxi* (1978–83): The cross section of taxi drivers, at the time, showed the diversity of the city. Now, however, though still entertaining, it is very dated: You won't see a Checker cab on the street anymore, and you are most likely to be driven by drivers from countries ranging from the West

Indies to West Africa to Pakistan. But the haunting theme and opening shots of a taxi driving over the Queensboro Bridge remain classics.

○ *Welcome Back Kotter* (1975–79): Oh, to return to the innocent days of Brooklyn public schools when your only worries were "delinquent" Sweathogs such as Vinnie Barbarino, Arnold Horshack, a Puerto Rican Jew named Juan Epstein, and Freddie "Boom Boom" Washington—big afros and all—taught by a wisecracking teacher named Kotter. John Travolta, of course, is famous for playing another Brooklynite: *Saturday Night Fever*'s Tony Manero.

○ *Friends* (1994–2004): In their favorite hangout, "Central Perk," Ross, Rachel, Joey, Chandler, Phoebe, and Monica were NYC yuppies . . . on a soundstage in Hollywood. Could those apartments *be* any more huge? Though a real NY apartment just might have a view of an Ugly Naked Guy.

Gossip Girl both takes place and is produced in New York City. *The Good Wife* is set in Chicago but filmed in New York. Other popular shows made in NYC include *Damages, Rescue Me, Sesame Street* (shot in Queens), and *White Collar.*

WHEN TO GO

Summer or winter, rain or shine, there's always great stuff going on in New York City, so when you're planning a trip to New York City, there's no real "best" or "worst" time to go.

Culture hounds might come in fall, winter, and early spring, when the theater and performing-arts seasons reach their heights. During summer, many of the top cultural institutions, especially Lincoln Center, offer free, alfresco entertainment. Those who want to see the biggest hits on Broadway usually have the best luck getting tickets in the slower months of January and February.

Gourmands might find it easiest to land the best tables during July and August, when New Yorkers escape the city on weekends. If you prefer to walk every city block to take in the sights, spring and fall usually offer the mildest and most pleasant weather.

New York is a nonstop holiday party from early December through the start of the New Year. Celebrations of the season abound in festive holiday windows and events such as the lighting of the Rockefeller Center tree and the *Radio City Christmas Spectacular*—not to mention those terrific seasonal sales that make New York a holiday shopping bonanza.

However, keep in mind that hotel prices go sky high (more on that below), and the crowds are almost intolerable. If you'd rather have more of the city to yourself—better chances at restaurant reservations and shows, and easier access to museums and other attractions—choose another time of year to visit.

Money Matters

Hotel prices are always fairly high in New York, though the current economic troubles have softened the market considerably; still, you might want to follow these rough seasonal guidelines.

Bargain hunters might want to visit in winter, between the first of the year and early April. Sure, you might have to bear some cold weather, but that's when hotels are suffering from the post-holiday blues, and rooms often go for a relative song—a song in this case may mean a room with a private bathroom for as little as $150, or even less. AAA cardholders can do even better in many cases (around 10% savings at certain hotels). However, be aware that the occasional convention or event, such as February's annual Fashion Week, can sometimes throw a wrench in your winter savings plans.

Spring and fall are traditionally the busiest and most expensive seasons after holiday time. Don't expect hotels to be handing you deals, but you may be able to negotiate a decent rate.

The city is drawing more families these days, and they usually visit in the summer. Still, the prospect of heat and humidity keeps some people away, making July and the first half of August a cheaper time to visit than later in the year; good hotel deals are often available.

During the Christmas season, expect to pay top dollar for everything. The first 2 weeks of December—the shopping weeks—are the worst when it comes to scoring an affordable hotel room; that's when shoppers from around the world converge on the town to catch the holiday spirit and spend, spend, spend. But Thanksgiving can be a great time to come, believe it or not: Business travelers have gone home, and the holiday shoppers haven't yet arrived. It's a little-known secret that most hotels away from the Thanksgiving Day Parade route have empty rooms, and they're usually willing to make great deals to fill them.

Weather

Many consider that long week or 10 days that arrive each summer between mid-July and mid-August, when temperatures can go up to as high as 100°F (38°C) with 90% humidity, as New York's worst weather. Don't get put off by this—summer has its compensations, such as wonderful free open-air concerts and other events, as mentioned—but bear it in mind. If you are at all temperature sensitive, your odds of getting comfortable weather are better in June or September.

Another period when you might not like to stroll around the city is during January or February, when temperatures are commonly in the 20s (below 0°C) and those concrete canyons turn into wind tunnels. The city looks gorgeous for about a day after a snowfall, but the streets soon become a slushy mess. Again, you never know—temperatures have regularly been in the 30s and mild 40s (single digits Celsius) during the past few global-warmed winters. If you hit the weather jackpot, you could have a bargain bonanza (see "Money Matters," above).

Fall and spring are the best times in New York. From April to June and September to November, temperatures are mild and pleasant, and the light is beautiful. With the leaves changing in Central Park and just the hint of crispness in the air, October is a fabulous time to be here—but expect to pay for the privilege.

If you want to know what to pack just before you go, check the Weather Channel's online 10-day forecast at **www.weather.com**; I like to balance it against CNN's online 8-day forecast at **www.cnn.com/weather**. You can also get the local weather by calling ℭ **212/976-1212** or the **National Weather Service** at ℭ **631/924-0517.**

New York's Average Temperature & Rainfall

	JAN	FEB	MAR	APR	MAY	JUNE	JULY	AUG	SEPT	OCT	NOV	DEC
DAILY TEMP. (°F)	32	34	42	53	63	72	77	76	68	58	48	37
DAILY TEMP. (°C)	0	1	6	12	17	22	25	24	20	14	9	3
DAYS OF PRECIPITATION	11	10	11	11	11	10	11	10	8	8	9	10

Holidays

Banks, government offices, post offices, and many stores, restaurants, and museums are closed on the following legal national holidays: January 1 (New Year's Day), the third Monday in January (Martin Luther King, Jr., Day), the third Monday in February (Presidents' Day), the last Monday in May (Memorial Day), July 4 (Independence Day), the first Monday in September (Labor Day), the second Monday in October (Columbus Day), November 11 (Veterans Day/Armistice Day), the fourth Thursday in November (Thanksgiving Day), and December 25

(Christmas). The Tuesday after the first Monday in November is Election Day, a federal government holiday in presidential-election years (held every 4 years, and next in 2012).

New York City Calendar of Events

The following information is always subject to change. Confirm before you make plans around a specific event. Call the venue or the New York City Convention & Visitors Bureau at ℂ **212/484-1222,** go to **www.nycgo.com,** or buy a copy of *Time Out New York* at any newsstand for the latest details.

For an exhaustive list of events beyond those listed here, check **http://events.frommers.com,** where you'll find a searchable, up-to-the-minute roster of what's on in cities all over the world.

JANUARY

New York Boat Show. Slip on your Top-Siders and head to the **Jacob K. Javits Convention Center** for the boat show, which promises a leviathan fleet of boats and marine products from the world's leading manufacturers. Call ℂ **212/984-7007** or visit **www.boatshows.com, www.nyboatshow.com,** or **www.javits center.com.** January 2012.

Winter Restaurant Week. Twice a year some of the best restaurants in town offer three-course prix-fixe meals at *almost* affordable prices. In 2010, Winter Restaurant Week was officially from January 25 to February 7, which, of course means it really should be renamed Restaurant *Weeks.* And if it goes down like years past, it could be extended by some restaurants through all of February, and into March! In 2011, the deal was $24.07 for lunch and $35 for dinner—both three-course meals. Some restaurants participating in 2010 included standouts like A Voce, Devi, and Molyvos. Call ℂ **212/484-1222** for info, or visit **www.nycgo.com.** You can make reservations starting 2 weeks in advance. Late January/early February.

Chinese New Year. Every year, Chinatown rings in its own New Year (based on a lunar calendar) with 2 weeks of celebrations, including parades with dragon and lion dancers, plus vivid costumes of all kinds. The parade usually winds throughout Chinatown along Mott, Canal, and Bayard streets, and along East Broadway. Call the **NYCVB hot line** at ℂ **212/484-1222** or the **Asian American Business Development Center** at ℂ **212/966-0100.** Chinese New Year falls on January 23 in 2012, and it's the Year of the Rabbit.

FEBRUARY

Westminster Kennel Club Dog Show. The ultimate purebred-pooch fest. Some 30,000 dog fanciers from the world over congregate at **Madison Square Garden** for the annual "World Series of Dogdom." All 2,500 dogs are American Kennel Club Champions of Record, competing for the Best in Show trophy. Check the website **www.westminster kennelclub.org** for further info. Tickets are available after January 1 via **Ticketmaster** (ℂ **212/307-7171;** www.ticket master.com). February 13–14, 2012.

MARCH

The Pier Antiques Show. During the city's largest and most comprehensive antiques show, 500 dealers exhibit their treasures, ranging from jewelry to home furnishings, at **Pier 94** on the Hudson River at 55th Street. The weekend-long event also hosts restorers, appraisers, and vintage fashions. Call ℂ **212/255-0020** or visit **www.stellashows.com** for this year's dates, plus a calendar of additional shows. Usually mid-March, and again in mid-November.

St. Patrick's Day Parade. More than 150,000 marchers join in the world's largest civilian parade, as Fifth Avenue, from 44th to 86th streets, rings with the sounds of bands and bagpipes. The parade usually starts at 11am, but go extra early if you want a good spot. Call ℂ **212/484-1222.** March 17.

APRIL

New York International Auto Show. Here's the irony: You don't need a car in New York, yet this is the largest car show in the U.S. Held at the Javits Center, many concept cars show up that will never roll off the assembly line but are fun to dream about. Call ℂ **800/282-3336** or visit **www.autoshowny.com** or **www.javitscenter.com.** April 6–15, 2012.

Easter Parade. This isn't a traditional parade, per se: There are no marching bands, no baton twirlers, and no protesters. Once upon a time, New York's gentry came out to show off their tasteful but discreet toppings. Today, if you were planning to slip on a tasteful little number—say, something delicately woven in straw with a simple flower or two that matches your gloves—you will *not* be the grandest lady in this springtime hike along Fifth Avenue, from 48th to 57th streets. It's more about flamboyant exhibitionism, with hats and costumes that get more outrageous every year, and anybody can join in for free. The parade generally runs Easter Sunday from about 10am to 3 or 4pm. Call ℂ **212/484-1222.** April 8, 2012.

TriBeCa Film Festival. Conceived in 2002 by the unofficial mayor of TriBeCa, Robert De Niro, the festival has grown in popularity and esteem every year. In 2010, the 12-day festival featured about 130 films and included such special events as a Family Festival Street Fair, music performances and an art exhibition, and outdoor "drive-in" films. Call ℂ **212/941-2400** or visit **www.tribeca filmfestival.org.** Last week in April/early May.

MAY

Bike New York: The Five Boro Bike Tour. The largest mass-participation cycling event in the United States attracts about 30,000 cyclists from all over the world. After a 42-mile ride through the five boroughs, finalists are greeted with a traditional New York–style celebration of food and music. Call ℂ **212/932-BIKE** (2453), or visit **www.bikenewyork.org** to register. First or second Sunday in May.

Ninth Avenue International Food Festival. Street fairs are part of the New York landscape each summer, but this is one of the best. You can spend the day sampling Italian sausages, homemade pierogi, spicy curries, and other ethnic dishes. Street musicians, bands, and vendors add to the festive atmosphere stretching along Ninth Avenue from 37th to 57th streets. Call ℂ **212/484-1222.** Mid-May.

Fleet Week. About 10,000 Navy and Coast Guard personnel are "at liberty" in New York for the annual Fleet Week at the end of May. Usually from 1 to 4pm daily, you can watch the ships and aircraft carriers as they dock at the piers on the west side of Manhattan, tour them with on-duty personnel, and watch some dramatic exhibitions by the U.S. Marines. Even if you don't take in any of the events, you'll know it's Fleet Week because those 10,000 sailors invade Midtown in their starched white uniforms. It's wonderful—just like *On the Town* come to life. Call ℂ **212/245-0072,** or visit **www.intrepidmuseum. org.** Late May.

JUNE

Belmont Stakes. The third jewel in the Triple Crown is held at **Belmont Park Race Track** in Belmont, Long Island. If a Triple Crown winner is to be named, it will happen here. For information, call ℂ **516/488-6000** or visit **www.nyra. com.** Early June.

Museum Mile Festival. Fifth Avenue, from 82nd to 104th streets, is closed to cars from 6 to 9pm as 20,000-plus strollers enjoy live music, from Broadway tunes to string quartets; street entertainers; and free admission to nine Museum Mile institutions, including the Metropolitan Museum of Art and the Guggenheim. Call ☏ **212/606-2296** or any of the participating institutions for details. Usually the second Tuesday in June.

Parades, parades, parades. During the summer there is a parade for almost every holiday, nationality, or ethnicity. June is the month for (among others) the sometimes raucous but colorful **Puerto Rican Day Parade** and the **Lesbian, Gay, Bisexual, and Transgendered Pride March,** where Fifth Avenue goes wild as the LGBT community celebrates with bands, marching groups, floats, and plenty of panache. The parade starts on upper Fifth Avenue in Midtown and continues into the Village, where a street festival and a waterfront dance party with fireworks cap the day. Call ☏ **212/807-7433** or check **www.hopinc.org**. Mid- to late June.

SummerStage. A summer-long festival of outdoor performances in **Central Park,** featuring world music, pop, folk, and jazz artists, ranging from Steve Earle to Craig David to Basement Jaxx to the New York Grand Opera to the Chinese Golden Dragon Acrobats. Shows are often free, but some big-name shows (called "fundraisers") require tickets. Call ☏ **212/360-2756,** or visit **www. summerstage.org**. June through August.

Shakespeare in the Park. The Delacorte Theater in **Central Park** is the setting for first-rate free performances under the stars—including at least one Shakespeare play each season—most often with stars on the stage. For details, see "Park It! Shakespeare, Music & Other Free Fun," in chapter 9. Call ☏ **212/539-8500,** or visit **www.publictheater.org**. June through August.

Restaurant Week. Late June (see "January," above).

Macy's Fourth of July Fireworks. Start the day amid the crowds at the Great July 4th Festival in lower Manhattan, and then catch Macy's fireworks extravaganza. Taking place off the waters surrounding Manhattan, it's the country's largest pyrotechnic show on Independence Day. Call ☏ **212/484-1222** or the Macy's Visitor Center at 212/494-3827. July 4.

Lincoln Center Festival. This festival celebrates the best of the performing arts from all over—theater, ballet, contemporary dance, opera, nouveau circus performances, even puppet and media-based art. Recent editions have featured performances by Le Théâtre du Soleil, the Royal Opera, the Royal Ballet, and actors Ralph Fiennes, Liam Neeson, and Alan Cumming. Schedules are available in mid-March, and tickets go on sale in May or early June. Call ☏ **212/875-5456,** or visit **www.lincolncenter.org/festival**. Throughout July.

Midsummer Night's Swing. Dancing duos head to the **Lincoln Center Plaza** for evenings of big-band swing, salsa, and tango under the stars to the sounds of top-flight bands. Dance lessons are offered with purchase of a ticket. Call ☏ **212/875-5456,** or visit **www.lincoln center.org**. July and August.

Mostly Mozart Festival. World-renowned ensembles and soloists (Alicia de Larrocha and André Watts have performed in the past) are featured at this month-long series at venues like **Avery Fisher Hall** and **Walter Reade Theater.** Schedules are available in mid-April, and tickets go on sale in early May. Call ☏ **212/875-5456** for information, or 212/721-6500 to order tickets through Center Charge; or visit **www.lincolncenter.org/mostly mozart**. Late July through August.

Lincoln Center Out of Doors. This series of free music and dance performances is held outdoors on the plazas of **Lincoln**

Center. Call ☎ **212/875-5456,** or visit **www.lincolncenter.org/outofdoors** for the schedule (usually available in mid-July). Throughout August.

Harlem Week. The world's largest black and Hispanic cultural festival actually spans almost the entire month, to include the Harlem Jazz and Music Festival and the New York City Children's Festival. Expect a full slate of music, from gospel to hip-hop, and lots of other festivities. Call ☎ **212/484-1222,** or visit **http://harlemweek.com.** Throughout August.

New York International Fringe Festival (FringeNYC). Held in a variety of downtown venues and park spaces for a crowd looking for the next underground hit (as in *Urinetown,* which went from the Fringe to Broadway), this arts festival presents alternative as well as traditional theater, musicals, comedy, and all manner of performance. Hundreds of events are held at all hours over about 10 days. The quality can vary wildly (lots of performers use Fringe as a workshop to develop their acts and shows), and some performances really push the envelope. Nonetheless, you'd be surprised at how many shows are actually *good.* Call ☎ **212/279-4488** for information, or 866/468-7619 to purchase tickets; or visit **www.fringenyc.org**. Mid- to late August.

U.S. Open Tennis Championships. The final Grand Slam event of the tennis season is held at the Arthur Ashe Stadium at the USTA National Tennis Center, the largest public tennis center in the world, at **Flushing Meadows Park** in Queens. Tickets go on sale in May or early June. The event sells out immediately because many tickets are held by corporate sponsors who hand them out to customers. (It's worth it to check the list of sponsors to determine if anyone you know has a ticket connection.) You can usually buy scalped tickets outside the complex (an illegal practice, of course), which is next to Citi Field, the new home of the New York Mets. The last few matches of the tournament are the most expensive, but you'll see more tennis early on, when your ticket allows you to wander the outside courts and view several matches. Call ☎ **866/OPEN-TIX** (673-6849; it's always busy) or 718/760-6200 well in advance; visit **www.usopen.org** or **www.usta.com** for information. Two weeks around Labor Day.

SEPTEMBER

West Indian–American Day Parade. This annual Brooklyn event is New York's largest and best street celebration. Come for the extravagant costumes, pulsating rhythms (soca, calypso, reggae), bright colors, folklore, food (jerk chicken, oxtail soup, Caribbean soul food), and two million hip-shaking revelers. The route can change from year to year, but it usually runs along Eastern Parkway from Utica Avenue to Grand Army Plaza (at the gateway to Prospect Park). Call ☎ **718/467-1797,** or visit **www.wiadca.com**. Labor Day.

Broadway on Broadway. This free alfresco afternoon show features the songs and casts from nearly every Broadway show on a stage in the middle of Times Square. Call ☎ **888/BROADWAY** (276-2392), or visit **www.timessquarenyc.org**. Sunday in mid-September.

New York Film Festival. Legendary hits *Pulp Fiction* and *Mean Streets* both had their U.S. premieres at the Film Society of Lincoln Center's 2-week festival, a major stop on the film-fest circuit. Schedules in recent years have included advance looks at *No Country for Old Men, Volver,* and *The White Ribbon.* Screenings are held in various Lincoln Center venues; advance tickets are a good bet always, and a necessity for certain events (especially evening and weekend screenings). Call ☎ **212/875-5600** (for recorded information), or 212/875-5050 for box office information; or check out **www.filmlinc.com/nyff**. Two weeks from late September to early October.

BAM Next Wave Festival. One of the city's most important cultural events takes place at the **Brooklyn Academy of Music.** The months-long festival showcases experimental new dance, theater, and music by both renowned and lesser known international artists. Recent performances have included *In-I,* a dance performance by Oscar-winning actress Juliette Binoche; Douglas J. Cuomo's cross-cultural chamber opera, *Arjunas's Dilemma,* based on the Bhagavad Gita; and the U.S. premier of *Kepler,* a concert staging of an opera presented by composer Philip Glass. Call ☏ **718/636-4100,** or visit **www.bam.org**. September through December.

OCTOBER

Feast of St. Francis. Animals from goldfish to elephants are blessed as thousands of *Homo sapiens* look on at the **Cathedral of St. John the Divine.** A magical experience—pets, of course, are welcome. A festive fair follows the blessing and music events. Tickets are only available the morning of the event, on a first-come, first-served basis. For information, call **212/316-7490,** or visit **www.stjohndivine.org**. First Sunday in October.

Ice-Skating. Show off your skating style in the limelight at the diminutive **Rockefeller Center** rink (☏ **212/332-7654;** www.rockefellercenter.com), open from mid-October to mid-March or early April (you'll skate under the magnificent Christmas tree for the month of Dec). In Central Park, try **Wollman Rink,** on the east side of the park between 62nd and 63rd streets (☏ **212/439-6900;** www.wollmanskatingrink.com), and **Lasker Rink,** midpark between 106th and 108th streets (☏ **917/492-3857**). Both Central Park skating rinks usually close in early April. There's also **The Pond in Bryant Park.** The season here is a short one—from October to mid-January—but the skating is free. Call ☏ **866/221-5157,** or visit **www.thepondatbryantpark.com**.

Big Apple Circus. New York City's homegrown, not-for-profit performing-arts circus is a favorite with children and anyone who's young at heart. Big Apple is committed to maintaining the classical circus tradition with sensitivity, and only features animals that have a traditional working relationship with humans. A tent is pitched in **Damrosch Park** at **Lincoln Center.** Call ☏ **800/922-3772,** or visit **www.bigapplecircus.org**. Late October through January.

Greenwich Village Halloween Parade. This is Halloween at its most outrageous. You may have heard Lou Reed singing about it on his classic album *New York*—he wasn't exaggerating. Drag queens and assorted other flamboyant types parade through the Village in wildly creative costumes. The parade route has changed over the years, but most recently it has started after sunset at Spring Street and marched up Sixth Avenue to 23rd Street or Union Square. Call the *Village Voice* parade hot line at ☏ 212/475-3333, ext. 14044; visit **www.halloween-nyc.com**; or check the papers for the exact route so you can watch—or participate—if you have the threads and the imagination. October 31.

NOVEMBER

New York City Marathon. Some 30,000 runners from around the world participate in the largest U.S. marathon, and more than a million fans cheer them on as they follow a route that touches all five New York boroughs and finishes at Central Park. Call ☏ **212/423-2249** or 212/860-4455, or visit **www.nyrr.org**, where you can find applications. First Sunday in November. November 7, 2010.

The Chocolate Show. This burgeoning 4-day event devoted to chocolate is at the Metropolitan Pavilion in Chelsea and features booths representing over 50 of the world's best chocolate makers with tastings, demonstrations, and activities for children. Call **866/CHOC-NYC** (246-2692) for info or Ticketmaster at

800/745-3000 for tickets, or visit **www. chocolateshow.com**. Late October/early November.

Radio City Christmas Spectacular. A rather gaudy extravaganza, but lots of fun, this event stars the Radio City Rockettes and a cast that includes live animals (just try to picture the camels sauntering into the Sixth Ave. entrance!). For information, call ✆ **212/307-1000,** or visit **www.radiocity.com**; you can also buy tickets at the box office or via Ticketmaster's **Radio City Hot Line** (✆ **212/307-1000**), or visit **www.ticketmaster. com**. Throughout November and December.

The Pier Antiques Show. Mid-November (see "March," above).

Macy's Thanksgiving Day Parade. The procession from Central Park West and 77th Street and down Broadway to Herald Square at 34th Street continues to be a national tradition. Huge hot-air balloons in the forms of Rocky and Bullwinkle, Snoopy, the Pink Panther, Bart Simpson, and other cartoon favorites are the best part. The night before, you can usually see the big blow-up on Central Park West at 79th Street; call in advance to see if it will be open to the public. Call ✆ **212/484-1222** or Macy's Visitor Center at 212/494-2922. November 22, 2010.

The Nutcracker. Tchaikovsky's holiday favorite is performed by the New York City Ballet at **Lincoln Center.** The annual schedule is available beginning in mid-July, and tickets usually go on sale in early October. Call ✆ **212/870-5570,** or go online to **www.nycballet.com**. Late November through early January.

Lighting of the Rockefeller Center Christmas Tree. The annual lighting ceremony is accompanied by ice skaters, singing, entertainment, and a *huge* crowd. The tree stays lit 24/7 until after the New Year. Call ✆ **212/332-6868,** or visit **www.rockefellercenter.com**. Late November or early December.

Holiday Trimmings. Stroll down festive Fifth Avenue and you'll see a 27-foot sparkling snowflake floating over the intersection outside **Tiffany's,** the **Cartier** building beribboned with red bows, wreaths warming the necks of the **New York Public Library**'s lions, and fanciful figurines in the windows of **Saks Fifth Avenue** and **Lord & Taylor.** Madison Avenue between 55th and 60th streets is also a good bet; **Sony Plaza** usually displays something fabulous, as does **Barneys New York.** Throughout December.

Christmas Traditions. In addition to the *Radio City Christmas Spectacular* and the New York City Ballet's staging of *The Nutcracker* (see "November," above), traditional holiday events include the National Chorale's singalong performances of Handel's *Messiah* at **Avery Fisher Hall** (✆ **212/875-5030;** www. lincolncenter.org) for a week before Christmas. The *Messiah* is also staged in many churches and other venues throughout the city during December. Check local listings.

Lighting of the Hanukkah Menorah. Everything is done on a grand scale in New York, so it's no surprise that the world's largest menorah (32 ft. high) is at Manhattan's **Grand Army Plaza,** Fifth Avenue and 59th Street. Hanukkah celebrations begin at sunset, with the lighting of the first of the giant electric candles. December 20-28, 2011.

New Year's Eve. The biggest party of all is in **Times Square,** where raucous revelers count down the year's final seconds until the ball drops at midnight at 1 Times Sq. This one, in the cold surrounded by thousands of drunks, is a masochist's delight. Call ✆ **212/768-1560** or 212/484-1222, or visit **www. timessquarenyc.org**. December 31.

Runner's World Midnight Run. Enjoy **fireworks** followed by the New York

Road Runners Club's annual run in **Central Park,** which is fun for runners and spectators alike; call ✆ **212/860-4455,** or visit **www.nyrr.org**. December 31.

Brooklyn's fireworks celebration. Head to Brooklyn for the city's largest New Year's Eve **fireworks** celebration at Prospect Park. Call ✆ **718/965-8999,** or visit **www.prospectpark.org**. December 31.

New Year's Eve Concert for Peace. The Cathedral of St. John the Divine is known for its annual concert, whose past performances have included folk singer Judy Collins, Forces of Nature Dance Company, and the world premiere of *Songs of War, Remembrance, and Hope* by Glen Cortese. The evening culminates in the passing of a candle flame while the audience of thousands sings "This Little Light of Mine." For tickets, call ✆ **212/316-7540** or go online to **www.stjohndivine.org**. December 31.

RESPONSIBLE TOURISM

"Green" travel in New York City? That seems like an odd combination, yet there's a lot that New York does that makes it (in some ways) an environmentally friendly destination, not the least of which is its highly useful (and much-used) mass transit system.

While much of the focus of ecotourism is about reducing impacts on the natural environment, ethical tourism concentrates on ways to preserve and enhance local economies and communities, regardless of location.

In New York City? You can embrace ethical tourism by using mass transit, staying at a hotel or B&B that makes an effort to be "green," shopping at a locally owned store, and eating at a diner, coffee shop, or mom-and-pop eatery instead of at a fast-food chain.

New York recycles its bottles and cans (including bottled water); look for containers for recyclables when you are discarding your litter.

You can even contribute to sustaining the environment by going to a baseball game. The new home of the New York Mets, Citi Field, was built with 95% recycled steel, has ultraefficient field lighting that cuts energy consumption by as much as 50%, and has an on-site irrigation system and low-flow plumbing fixtures such as waterless urinals and sensor-activated faucets that help save an estimated 4 million gallons of water a year.

See **www.frommers.com/planning** for more tips on responsible travel.

3

NEW YORK CITY NEIGHBORHOODS & SUGGESTED ITINERARIES

T here are a lot of neighborhoods on the (relatively) small island of Manhattan, and more to explore in the other boroughs. Each has its own vibe, and here we'll lay out a thumbnail description of the major parts of town, as well as mentioning how they rank in terms of places to stay, eat, and see the sights.

Once we've given you the lay of the land, we'll give you some itineraries that make the most of your time in New York City, whether you're here for just a day or a bit longer than that.

NEW YORK CITY NEIGHBORHOODS IN BRIEF

Because they grew up over the course of hundreds of years, Manhattan neighborhoods have multiple, splintered personalities and fluid boundaries. Still, it's relatively easy to agree upon what they stand for in general terms—so if you stop New Yorkers on the street and ask them to point you to, say, the Upper West Side or the Flatiron District, they'll know where you want to go. From south to north, here is how we've defined Manhattan's neighborhoods throughout this book.

Downtown

LOWER MANHATTAN: SOUTH STREET SEAPORT & THE FINANCIAL DISTRICT At one time, this was New York—period. Established by the Dutch in 1625 (hence the city's original name, Nieuw-Amsterdam, or New Amsterdam), the first settlements sprang up on the southern tip of Manhattan island; everything uptown was farm country and wilderness. This is the best place in the city to search for the past.

Lower Manhattan constitutes everything south of Chambers Street. **Battery Park,** the point of departure for the Statue of Liberty, Ellis Island, and Staten Island, is on the southern tip. The **South Street Seaport,** touristy but still a reminder of times when shipping was the lifeblood of the city, is a bit north on the East Side; it's south of the Brooklyn Bridge, which stands proudly as the ultimate achievement of New York's 19th-century industrial age.

The rest of the area is considered the **Financial District,** but may be more famous now as **Ground Zero.** Until September 11, 2001, the Financial District was anchored by the **World Trade Center,** with the World Financial Center complex and Battery Park City to the west, and **Wall Street** running crosstown a little south and to the east. Construction has begun on the new complex, but it will take years to complete. What won't take so long to build are the hundreds of new condo developments in the area (whether they will be able to sell them with the current economic downturn remains to be seen).

FACING PAGE: **New York's past, present and future are all reflected downtown on its waterfront.**

Downtown

For those New Yorkers who live Uptown, lower Manhattan is practically a different planet, but one which has much to offer. The website for the **Alliance for** **Downtown New York** (www.downtown ny.com), updated daily, is a trusty source to keep abreast on new developments and exciting downtown events.

City Hall remains the northern border of the district, abutting Chambers Street (look for City Hall Park on the map). Most of the streets around here are narrow concrete canyons, with Broadway serving as the main uptown-downtown artery.

Just about all of the major subway lines congregate here before they either end or head to Brooklyn.

TRIBECA Bordered by the Hudson River to the west, the area north of Chambers Street, west of Broadway, and south of Canal Street is the *Tri*angle *Be*low *Ca*nal Street, or TriBeCa. Since the 1980s, as SoHo became saturated with chic, the spillover has been transforming TriBeCa into one of the city's more cutting-edge, exclusive neighborhoods, where celebrities and families coexist in cast-iron warehouses converted into expensive apartments. Artists' lofts and galleries as well as hip antiques and design shops pepper the area, as do some of the city's best restaurants.

Robert De Niro gave the neighborhood a huge boost when he established the TriBeCa Film Center, and Miramax headquarters gave the area further capitalist-chic cachet. Still, such historic streets as White (especially the Federal-style building at no. 2) and Harrison (the stretch west from Greenwich St.) evoke a bygone, more human-scale New York, as do a few holdout businesses and pubs.

The main uptown-downtown drag is **West Broadway** (2 blocks west of Broadway). Consider the Franklin Street subway station on the 1 line to be your gateway to the action.

CHINATOWN New York City's most famous ethnic enclave has burst past its 19th- and 20th-century boundaries and has encroached on Little Italy. The former marshlands northeast of City Hall and below Canal Street, from Broadway to the Bowery, are where Chinese immigrants arriving from San Francisco were forced to live in the 1870s. This booming neighborhood is a conglomeration of Asian populations. It offers tasty cheap eats from Szechuan to Hunan to Cantonese to Vietnamese to Thai. Exotic shops offer strange foods, herbs, and souvenirs; bargains on clothing and leather are plentiful. It's a blast to walk down Canal Street, peering into the stores and watching crabs escape from their baskets at the fish markets.

The Canal Street (J, Z, N, R, 6, Q) station will get you to the heart of the action. The streets are crowded during the day and empty out after around 9pm; they remain quite safe, but the neighborhood is more enjoyable during the bustle.

LITTLE ITALY Little Italy, traditionally the area east of Broadway between Houston and north of Canal streets, is a shrinking community, due to the encroachment of thriving Chinatown. It's now limited mainly to **Mulberry Street,** where you'll find most restaurants. With rents going up in the

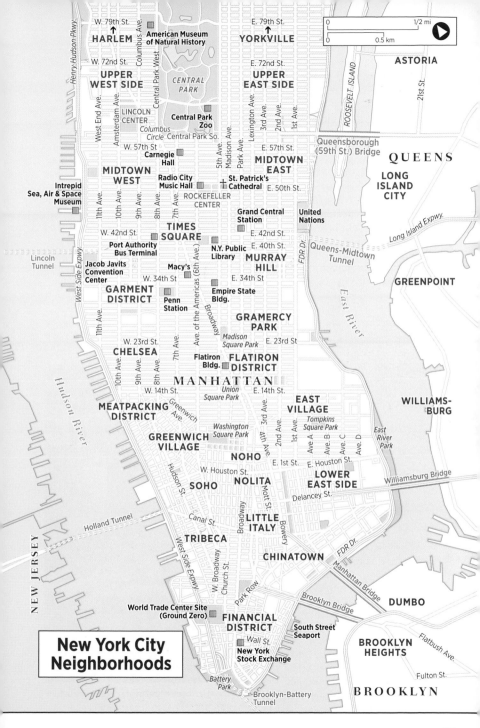

New York City Neighborhoods

trendy Lower East Side, the chic spots are moving in, further intruding upon the old-world landscape. The best way to reach Little Italy is to walk east from the Spring Street station (on the no. 6 line) to Mulberry Street; turn south for Little Italy (you can't miss the year-round red, green, and white street decorations).

THE LOWER EAST SIDE   The Lower East Side (or LES) boasts the best of both old and new New York—though the new is eking out what is left of the old. But still, witness the stretch of Houston between Forsyth and Allen streets, where Yonah Shimmel's Knish Shop sits shoulder to shoulder with the Sunshine Theater, an art-house cinema. Some say the Lower East Side has come full circle: Self-important hipsters with well-honed senses of entitlement (and trust funds) have come back to the neighborhoods their immigrant grandparents worked to escape.

Of all the successive waves of immigrants and refugees who passed through this densely populated tenement neighborhood from the mid–19th century to the 1920s, Eastern European Jews left the most lasting impression. The Jewish communities, which popped up between Houston and Canal streets east of the Bowery, are now just part of history. The neighborhood has experienced quite a renaissance over the last few years and makes a fascinating stop for both nostalgists and nightlife hounds.

There are some remnants of what was once the largest Jewish population in America along **Orchard Street,** where you'll find great bargain hunting in its old-world fabric and clothing stores still thriving between the club-clothes boutiques and lounges. Keep in mind these shops close early on Friday afternoon and all day on Saturday (the Jewish Sabbath). The exponentially expanding trendy set can be found in the blocks between Allen and Clinton streets south of Houston and north of Delancey, with more new shops, bars, and restaurants popping up every day.

This area is not well served by the subway system (one cause for its years of decline), so your best bet is to take the F train to Second Avenue (you can get off closer to First) and walk east on Houston; when you see Katz's Deli, you've arrived. You can also reach the LES from the Delancey Street station on the F line, and the Essex Street station on the J, M, and Z lines.

Patrons enjoy a corned beef sandwich at Katz's Deli on the Lower East Side.

Visiting the Lower East Side

The **Lower East Side Business Improvement District** operates a neighborhood visitor center at 54 Orchard St., between Hester and Grand streets (*©* **866/224-0206** or 212/226-9010), that's open weekdays from 9:30am to 5:30pm and weekends from 9:30am to 4pm. Stop in for a *GO EAST!* shopping and restaurant guide (which you can also download online or request in advance), plus other information on this historic yet freshly hip 'hood. You can also find shopping, dining, and nightlife directories at **www.lowereastsideny.com.**

SOHO & NOLITA   No relation to the London neighborhood of the same name, **SoHo** got its moniker as an abbreviation of **So**uth of **Ho**uston Street. This fashionable neighborhood extends down to Canal Street, between Sixth Avenue to the west and Lafayette Street (1 block east of Broadway) to the east. It's easily accessible by subway: Take the N or R to the Prince Street station; the C, E, or 6 to Spring Street; or the F, B, D, or M train to the Broadway/Lafayette stop.

An industrial zone during the 19th century, SoHo retains the impressive cast-iron architecture of the era, and in many places, cobblestone peeks out from beneath the street's asphalt. In the early 1960s, artists began occupying the drab, deteriorating buildings, turning this into the trendiest neighborhood in the city. SoHo is now a prime example of urban gentrification and a major New York attraction thanks to its restored buildings, fashionable restaurants, and stylish boutiques. On weekends, the cobbled streets and narrow sidewalks are packed with shoppers, with the prime action between Broadway and Sullivan Street north of Grand Street.

Some critics claim that SoHo is a victim of its own popularity—witness the departure of art galleries and boutiques that have fled to TriBeCa and Chelsea as well as the influx of mall-style stores such as J. Crew and Victoria's Secret. Still, SoHo is one of the best shopping neighborhoods in the city, and few are more fun to browse. High-end street peddlers set up along the boutique-lined sidewalks, hawking jewelry, books, and their own art. At night the neighborhood is transformed into a terrific (albeit pricey) dining and barhopping neighborhood.

In recent years SoHo has been crawling east, taking over Mott and Mulberry streets—and Elizabeth Street—north of Kenmare Street, an area now known as **Nolita** for **No**rth of **Li**ttle **Ita**ly. Nolita is becoming known for its hot shopping prospects, which include a number of pricey antiques and home-design stores. Taking the no. 6 train to Spring Street will get you closest by subway, but it's just a short walk east from SoHo proper.

THE EAST VILLAGE & NOHO   The **East Village,** which extends between 14th and Houston streets, from Broadway east to First Avenue and beyond to Alphabet City—avenues A, B, C, and D—is where you can still find some of the city's real bohemians. Once, flower children tripped along St. Marks Place and listened to music at the Fillmore East; now the East Village is a mix of affordable ethnic and trendy restaurants, clothing designers and kitschy boutiques, some music clubs, and Ukrainian dive bars. Several Off- and Off-Off Broadway theaters also call this place home.

The gentrification that has swept the city has made a huge impact on the East Village, but there's still a seedy element some won't find appealing—and some will. It's here where you can spend an afternoon at the sparkling new New Museum of Contemporary Art, and then have a drink at the celebrity-magnet bar of the Bowery Hotel, while around the corner you'll see a line of homeless people making their way to a nearby soup kitchen. It's here where yuppies and other ladder-climbing types make their homes alongside old-world Russian immigrants, who have lived in the neighborhood forever, and the drag queens and squatters who settled here in between. The neighborhood still embraces ethnic diversity, with strong elements of its Ukrainian and Irish heritages, while 6th Street, between First and Second avenues, is referred to as Little India.

The East Village isn't very accessible by subway unless you're traveling along 14th Street (the L line will drop you off at Third and First aves.) or take the 4, 5, 6, N, Q, or R to 14th Street/Union Square; the N or R to 8th Street; or the 6 to Astor Place and walk east.

Until the 1990s, **Alphabet City** resisted gentrification and remained a haven of drug dealers and other unsavory types—no more. Bolstered by a major real-estate boom, this way-east area of the East Village has blossomed. French bistros and smart shops have popped up on every corner, not to mention some terrific pubs where you can soak up some atmosphere.

The southwestern section of the East Village, around Broadway and Lafayette between Bleecker and 4th streets, is called **NoHo** (for **No**rth of **Ho**uston), and has a completely different character. As you might have guessed from its name, this area has developed much more like its neighbor to the south, SoHo. Here you'll find a crop of trendy lounges, stylish restaurants, cutting-edge designers, and upscale antiques shops. NoHo is fun to browse; the Bleecker Street stop on the no. 6 line will land you in the heart of it, and the Broadway/Lafayette stop on the F and D lines at all times (and B and M trains on weekdays) will drop you at its southern edge.

GREENWICH VILLAGE Tree-lined streets crisscross and wind, following ancient streams and cow paths. Each block reveals yet another row of Greek Revival town houses, a well-preserved Federal-style house, or a peaceful courtyard or square. This is "the Village," from Broadway west to the Hudson River, bordered by Houston Street to the south and 14th Street to the north. It defies Manhattan's orderly grid system with streets that predate it, virtually every one chockablock with activity, and unless you live here, it may be impossible to master the lay of the land—so be sure to take a map along as you explore.

The Seventh Avenue line (1, 2, 3) is the area's main subway artery, while the West 4th Street station (where the A, C, and E lines meet the B, D, F, and M lines) serves as its central hub.

Nineteenth-century artists such as Mark Twain, Edgar Allan Poe, Henry James, and Winslow Homer first gave the Village its reputation for embracing the unconventional. Groundbreaking artists such as Edward Hopper and Jackson Pollock were drawn in, as were writers such as Eugene O'Neill, e. e. Cummings, and Dylan Thomas. Radical thinkers from John Reed to Upton Sinclair basked in the neighborhood's liberal ethos, and beatniks Allen Ginsberg, Jack Kerouac, and William Burroughs dug the free-swinging atmosphere.

Now, like so many neighborhoods, gentrification and escalating real estate values have just about pushed out the artistic element, but culture and counterculture still rub shoulders in cafes, renowned jazz clubs, neighborhood bars, Off- and Off-Off Broadway theaters, and an endless variety of tiny shops and restaurants.

The Village is probably the most chameleonlike of Manhattan's neighborhoods. Some of the highest-priced real estate in the city runs along lower Fifth Avenue, which dead-ends at **Washington Square Park.** Serpentine **Bleecker Street** stretches through most of the neighborhood and is emblematic of the area's historical bent. The anything-goes attitude in the Village has fostered a large gay community, still in evidence around **Christopher Street** and Sheridan Square (including the landmarked Stonewall Bar). The streets west of Seventh Avenue, the **West Village,** boast some of the city's most charming, historic brownstones. Three colleges—New York University, Parsons School of Design, and the New School for Social Research—keep the area thinking young.

Streets are often crowded with weekend warriors and teenagers, especially on Bleecker, West 4th, 8th, and surrounding streets, and have been known to become increasingly sketchy west of Seventh Avenue in the very late hours, especially on weekends. Keep an eye on your wallet when navigating the weekend throngs.

Midtown

CHELSEA & THE MEATPACKING DISTRICT **Chelsea** has come on strong in recent years as a trendy address, especially for gay urban professionals. A low-rise composite of town houses, tenements, lofts, and factories (though a lot of high-rise apartment buildings have replaced some of the former in the last several years), the neighborhood comprises roughly the area west of Sixth Avenue from 14th to 30th streets. (Sixth Ave. itself below 23rd St. is considered part of the Flatiron District; see below.) Its main arteries are Seventh and Eighth avenues, and it's primarily served by the C or E and 1 subway lines.

The **Chelsea Piers** sports complex to the far west and a host of shops (both unique boutiques and big names such as Williams-Sonoma), well-priced bistros, and thriving bars along the main drags have contributed to the area's rebirth. Even the Hotel Chelsea—the neighborhood's most famous architectural and literary landmark, where Thomas Wolfe, Edgar Lee Masters, and Arthur Miller wrote; Bob Dylan composed "Sad-Eyed Lady of the Lowlands"; Viva and Edie Sedgwick of Andy Warhol fame lived

---

Free New York City Tours

If you'd like to tour a specific neighborhood with an expert guide, call **Big Apple Greeter** (© **212/669-8159;** www.bigapplegreeter.org) at least 4 weeks ahead of your arrival. You can also go to the website and fill out a visit request form. This nonprofit organization has specially trained volunteers who take visitors around town for a free 2- to 4-hour visit (with a $20 suggested donation) of a particular neighborhood. And they say New York isn't friendly!

The High Line has become one of New York City's most popular parks.

(and filmed parts of Warhol's "Chelsea Girls"); and Sid Vicious killed Nancy Spungeon—has been renovated. Chelsea is also the home of the Joyce Theater, New York's principal modern-dance venue.

One of the most influential trends in Chelsea has been the establishment of far **West Chelsea** (from Ninth Ave. west) and the adjacent **Meatpacking District** (south of West Chelsea, roughly from 17th St. to Little W. 12th St.) as the style-setting neighborhoods for the 21st century. What SoHo was in the 1960s, this industrial west world (dubbed "the Lower West Side" by *New York* magazine) is today. New restaurants, shopping, and superhot restaurants pop up daily in the Meatpacking District (dubbed "MePa" by ironic wags), while the area from West 22nd to West 29th streets, between Tenth and Eleventh avenues, is home to numerous dance clubs and the cutting edge of today's New York art scene. This area is still in transition and continually evolving. Like much of Manhattan, sleek glass condo towers are rising and the ambitious "High Line" project, a park along Tenth Avenue—between 30th and Gansevoort streets in the remains of an old elevated railway—first opened in spring 2009. This park is a great example of how New York keeps reinventing itself. It's well worth a visit.

THE FLATIRON DISTRICT, UNION SQUARE & GRAMERCY PARK These adjoining and at places overlapping neighborhoods are some of the city's most appealing. Their streets have been rediscovered by New Yorkers and visitors alike, largely thanks to the boom-to-bust dot-com revolution of the late 1990s; the Flatiron District served as its geographical heart and earned the nickname "Silicon Alley" in the process. These neighborhoods boast great shopping and dining opportunities and a central-to-everything location that's hard to beat. A number of impressive new hotels have been added to the mix over the last few years. The commercial spaces are often large, loftlike expanses with witty designs and graceful columns.

The **Flatiron District,** south of 23rd Street to 14th Street, between Broadway and Sixth Avenue, and centered on the historic Flatiron Building on 23rd (so named for its clothes-iron shape) and Park Avenue South, is littered with celebrity-chef-run restaurants. Below 23rd Street along Sixth Avenue (once known as the Ladies' Mile shopping district), mass-market discounters and others have moved in. The shopping gets classier on Fifth Avenue, where you'll find a mix of national names and hip boutiques. Lined with Oriental-carpet dealers and high-end fixture stores, Broadway is becoming the city's home-furnishings alley; its jewel is the justifiably famous ABC Carpet & Home, with eight floors of gorgeous textiles, housewares, and gifts on one side of Broadway, and an equally dazzling display of floor coverings on the other.

Union Square is the hub of the entire area; the N, Q, R, 4, 5, 6, and L trains stop here, making it easy to reach from most other city neighborhoods. Long in the shadows of the more bustling (Times and Herald) and high-toned (Washington) city squares, Union Square has experienced a major renaissance. Local businesses joined forces with the city to rid the park of drug dealers a decade or so back, and now it's a delightful place to spend an afternoon. Union Square is best known as the setting for New York's premier Greenmarket every Monday, Wednesday, Friday, and Saturday from 8am to 6pm. In-line skaters take over the market space in the after-work hours. A number of hip restaurants rim the square, as do superstores such as the city's best Barnes & Noble superstore, Whole Foods supermarket, and a W Hotel.

From about 16th to 23rd streets, east from Park Avenue South to about Second Avenue, is the leafy, largely residential district known as **Gramercy Park.** The pity of the Gramercy Park district is that so few can enjoy the actual park: Built by Samuel Ruggles in the 1830s to attract buyers to the area, it is the only private park in the city and is locked to all but those who live on its perimeter (the rule is that your windows have to overlook the park in order for you to have a key). At the southern endpoint of Lexington Avenue (at 21st St.), it is one of the most peaceful spots in the city. If you know someone who has a magic key, go there. Even if you don't, it's fun to stroll around its perimeter and soak in the pretty architecture.

At the northern edge of the area, fronting the Flatiron Building on 23rd Street and Fifth Avenue, is another of Manhattan's lovely little parks, **Madison Square.** Across from its northeastern corner once stood Stanford White's original Madison Square Garden (in whose roof garden White was murdered in 1906 by possibly deranged, but definitely jealous, millionaire Harry K. Thaw). It's now majestically presided over by the massive New York Life Insurance Building, the masterful New York State Supreme Court, and the Metropolitan Life Insurance Company, whose tower in 1909 was the tallest building in the world at 700 feet. Madison Square is also the home of Danny Meyer's insanely popular Shake Shack, a modern day "roadside burger stand."

TIMES SQUARE & MIDTOWN WEST **Midtown West,** the vast area from 34th to 59th streets west of Fifth Avenue to the Hudson River, encompasses several famous names: Madison Square Garden, the Garment District, Rockefeller

Center, the Theater District, and Times Square. This is New York's tourism central, where you'll find the bright lights and bustle that draw people from all over. As such, this is the city's biggest hotel neighborhood, with options running the gamut from cheap to chic.

The 1, 2, 3 subway line serves the massive neon-lit station at the heart of Times Square, at 42nd Street between Broadway and Seventh Avenue, while the F, M, B, D line runs up Sixth Avenue to Rockefeller Center. The N, R, Q line cuts diagonally across the neighborhood, following the path of Broadway before heading up Seventh Avenue at 42nd Street. The A, C, E line serves the west side, running along Eighth Avenue.

If you haven't been here in a few years, you'll be surprised by the "new" **Times Square.** Longtime New Yorkers like to *kvetch* nostalgic about the glory days of the old peep-show-and-porn-shop Times Square that this cleaned-up, Disneyfied version supplanted. And there really is not much here to offer the native New Yorker. The revival, however, has been nothing short of an outstanding success for tourism. Grand old theaters have come back to life as Broadway and children's playhouses, and scores of new family-friendly restaurants and shops have opened. Plenty of businesses have moved in—MTV studios overlook Times Square at 1515 Broadway, and *Good Morning America* has its own street-facing studio at Broadway and 44th Street. The neon lights have never been brighter, and Middle America has never been more welcome. Expect dense crowds, though; it's often tough to make your way along the sidewalks. **Note:** What began as an experiment has now become reality: Mayor Bloomberg has permanently closed parts of Times Square (and Herald Square) to automobile traffic. Pedestrians, rejoice.

> ## Impressions
>
> *I'm opposed to the redevelopment. I think there should be one neighborhood in New York where tourists are afraid to walk.*
> —Fran Leibowitz, on the "new" Times Square

Most of the great Broadway theaters light up the streets off Times Square, in the west 40s, just east and west of Broadway. At the heart of the **Theater District,** where Broadway meets Seventh Avenue, is the TKTS booth, where crowds line up daily to buy discount tickets for that day's shows.

To the west of the Theater District, in the 40s and 50s between Eighth and Tenth avenues, is **Hell's Kitchen,** an area that is much nicer than its ghoulish name and one of our favorites in the city. The neighborhood resisted gentrification until the mid-1990s but has grown into a charming, less touristy adjunct to the neighboring Theater District. Ninth Avenue, in particular, has blossomed into one of the city's finest dining avenues; just stroll along and you'll have a world of dining to choose from, ranging from American diner to sexy Mediterranean to traditional Thai. Stylish boutiques and bars have also popped up in this area in the last several years. Realtors have tried to rename the area Clinton, but locals have held fast to the Hell's Kitchen moniker with delight. In the last couple of years, it's become one of Manhattan's more popular gay neighborhoods, as rents in first the West Village, then Chelsea, have caused a northward migration.

Unlike Times Square, gorgeous **Rockefeller Center** has needed no renovation. Situated between 46th and 50th streets, from Sixth Avenue east to Fifth, this Art Deco complex contains some of the city's great architectural gems, which house hundreds of offices, a number of NBC studios (including *Saturday Night Live, Late Night with Jimmy Fallon,* and the famous glass-walled *Today* show studio at 48th St.), and some pleasing upscale boutiques (attention, shoppers: Saks Fifth Avenue is just on the other side of Fifth). If you can negotiate the crowds, holiday time is a great time to be here, as ice skaters take over the central plaza and the huge Christmas tree twinkles against the night sky.

Along Seventh Avenue, south of 42nd Street, is the **Garment District,** of little interest to tourists except for its sample sales, where some great new fashions are sold off cheap to serious bargain hunters willing to scour the racks. That part of town plays host to many small theater companies if you're venturing into the Off-Off Broadway scene. Other than that, it's a pretty commercial area. Between Seventh and Eighth avenues and 31st and 33rd streets, **Penn Station** sits beneath unsightly behemoth **Madison Square Garden,** where the Rangers, Liberty, and the Knicks play. Taking up all of 34th Street, between Sixth and Seventh avenues, is **Macy's,** the world's largest department store; exit Macy's at the southeast corner and you'll find more famous-label shopping around **Herald Square.** The blocks around 32nd Street just west of Fifth Avenue have developed into a thriving Koreatown, with midprice hotels and bright, bustling Asian restaurants offering some of the best-value stays and eats in Midtown.

Midtown West is also home to some of the city's most revered museums and cultural institutions, including **Carnegie Hall,** the **Museum of Modern Art,** and **Radio City Music Hall,** to name just a few.

MIDTOWN EAST & MURRAY HILL **Midtown East,** the area including Fifth Avenue and everything east from 34th to 59th streets, is the more upscale side of the Midtown map. This side of town is short of subway trains, served primarily by the Lexington Avenue 4, 5, 6 line.

Midtown East is where you'll find the city's finest collection of grand hotels, mostly along Park Avenue and near the park at the top of Fifth. The stretch of **Fifth Avenue** from Saks at 49th Street, extending to the 24-hour Apple Store and FAO Schwarz at 59th Street, is home to the city's most high-profile *haute* shopping, including Tiffany & Co. and Bergdorf Goodman, but more midprice names, such as Banana Republic and Gap, have moved their stores in over the last few years. The stretch of 57th Street between Fifth and Lexington avenues is also known for high-fashion boutiques (Chanel, Dior) and high-ticket galleries, but change is underway since names like Niketown have squeezed in. You'll find plenty of spillover along **Madison Avenue,** a great strip for shoe shopping in particular.

Magnificent architectural highlights include the recently repolished **Chrysler Building,** with its stylized gargoyles glaring down on passersby; the Beaux Arts tour de force that is **Grand Central Terminal; St. Patrick's Cathedral;** and the glorious **Empire State Building.**

Far east, swank Sutton and Beekman places are enclaves of beautiful town houses, luxury living, and pocket parks that look out over the East River. Along this river is the **United Nations,** which isn't officially in New

Visitors stop by the United Nations complex on the East River.

York City, or even the United States, but on a parcel of international land belonging to member nations.

Claiming the territory east from Madison Avenue, **Murray Hill** begins somewhere north of 23rd Street (the line btw. it and Gramercy Park is fuzzy), and is most clearly recognizable north of 30th Street to 42nd Street. This brownstone-lined quarter is largely a quiet residential neighborhood, most notable for its handful of good budget and midprice hotels. The stretch of Lexington Avenue in the high 20s is known as Curry Hill and has usurped the East Village's Little India as the destination for inexpensive, high-quality Indian and Pakistani food.

Uptown

UPPER WEST SIDE   North of 59th Street and encompassing everything west of Central Park, the Upper West Side contains **Lincoln Center,** arguably the world's premier performing-arts venue; the **Time Warner Center** with its upscale shops such as **Hugo Boss, A/X Armani,** and **Sephora; Jazz at Lincoln Center;** the **Mandarin Oriental Hotel;** the gargantuan **Whole Foods Market,** and possibly the most expensive food court in the world, with restaurants such as **Masa** and **Per Se.** The Upper West Side is also the home of the **American Museum of Natural History,** whose Dinosaur Halls and magnificent Rose Center for Earth and Space garner rave reviews. You'll also find a growing number of midprice hotels, whose larger-than-Midtown rooms and nice residential location make them some of the best values—and some of our favorite places to stay—in the entire city.

Unlike the more stratified Upper East Side, the Upper West Side is home to an egalitarian mix of middle-class yuppiedom, laid-back wealth (lots of celebs and media types call the grand apartments along Central Park West home), and ethnic families here from before gentrification.

The neighborhood runs all the way up to Harlem, around 125th Street, and encompasses **Morningside Heights,** where you'll find **Columbia University** and the perennial construction project known as the **Cathedral of St. John the Divine.**

But prime Upper West Side—the part you're most likely to explore— is the area running from Columbus Circle at 59th Street into the 80s, between the park and Broadway. North of 59th Street is where Eighth Avenue becomes Central Park West, the eastern border of the neighborhood (and the western border of Central Park); Ninth Avenue becomes Columbus Avenue, lined with attractive boutiques and cafes; and Tenth Avenue becomes Amsterdam Avenue, less charming than Columbus to the east and less trafficked than bustling Broadway (whose highlights are the gourmet megamarts Zabar's and Fairway) to the west; still, Amsterdam has blossomed into quite a happening restaurant-and-bar strip over the last couple of years. You'll find Lincoln Center in the mid-60s, where Broadway crosscuts Amsterdam.

Two major subway lines service the area: The 1, 2, 3 line runs up Broadway, while the B and C trains run up Central Park West, stopping at the Dakota apartments (where John Lennon was shot and Yoko Ono still lives) at 72nd Street, and at the Museum of Natural History at 81st Street.

The Museum of the City of New York is on the Upper East Side's "Museum Mile."

UPPER EAST SIDE North of 59th Street and east of Central Park is some of the city's most expensive residential real estate. This is New York at its most gentrified: Walk along Fifth and Park avenues, especially between 60th and 80th streets, and you're sure to encounter some of the wizened WASPs and Chanel-suited socialites that make up the most rarefied of the city's population. Madison Avenue, from 60th Street well into the 80s, is the moneyed crowd's main shopping strip, recently vaunting ahead of Hong Kong's Causeway Bay to become the most expensive retail real estate *in the world*—so bring your platinum card. You can also use it to stay at one of the neighborhood's luxurious hotels, such as the Carlyle or the Plaza Athénée, or to dine at four-star wonders such as Caravaggio and Daniel.

The main attraction of this neighborhood is **Museum Mile,** the stretch of Fifth Avenue fronting

In Harlem, 125th Street is the vibrant heart of the neighborhood.

Central Park that's home to no fewer than 10 terrific cultural institutions, including Frank Lloyd Wright's **Guggenheim,** and anchored by the mind-boggling **Metropolitan Museum of Art.** But the elegant rows of landmark town houses are worth a look alone: East 70th Street, from Madison east to Lexington, is one of the world's most charming residential streets. If you want to see where real people live, move east to Third Avenue and beyond; that's where affordable restaurants and active street life start popping up.

A second subway line is under construction on and underneath Second Avenue, but years away from completion. For now, the Upper East Side is served solely by the crowded Lexington Avenue line (4, 5, 6 trains), so wear your walking shoes (or bring taxi fare) if you're heading up here to explore.

HARLEM   Harlem has benefited from a dramatic image makeover in the last few years, and, with new restaurants, condos, clubs, and stores, is becoming a neighborhood in demand.

Harlem is actually several areas. **Harlem proper** stretches from river to river, beginning at 125th Street on the West Side, 96th Street on the East Side, and 110th Street north of Central Park. East of Fifth Avenue, **Spanish Harlem (El Barrio)** runs between East 100th and East 125th streets. Harlem proper, in particular, is benefiting greatly from the revitalization that has swept so much of the city, with national-brand retailers moving in, restaurants and hip nightspots opening everywhere, and visitors arriving to tour historic sites related to the golden age of African-American culture, when great bands such as the Count Basie and Duke Ellington orchestras played the Cotton Club and Sugar Cane Club, and literary giants such as Langston Hughes and James Baldwin soaked up the scene.

Some houses date from a time when the area was something of a country retreat, and represent some of the best brownstone mansions in the city. On **Sugar Hill** (from 143rd to 155th sts., btw. St. Nicholas and Edgecombe aves.) and **Striver's Row** (W. 139th St., btw. Adam Clayton Powell Jr., and Frederick Douglass blvds.) are a significant number of fine town houses. For cultural visits, there's the Morris-Jumel Mansion, the Schomburg Center, the Studio Museum, and the Apollo Theater.

You'll find 125th Street a fun place to shop, with its mix of such national chains as Old Navy standing side by side with emporiums of hip-hop fashion.

By all means, come see Harlem—it's one of the city's most vital, historic neighborhoods, and no other feels quite so energized right now. Your best bet for seeing all the sights is to take a guided tour (see "Organized Sightseeing Tours," in chapter 6); if you head up on your own, come in daylight. Don't wander thoughtlessly, especially at night. If you head up after dark to a restaurant or nightspot, be clear and confident about where you're going, and stay alert.

WASHINGTON HEIGHTS & INWOOD   At the northern tip of Manhattan, Washington Heights (the area from 155th to Dyckman sts., with adjacent Inwood running to the tip) is home to a large segment of Manhattan's Latino community, plus an increasing number of yuppies who don't mind trading

The Cloisters looms high above the northern tip of Manhattan.

a half-hour subway commute to Midtown for lower rents. **Fort Tryon Park** and **the Cloisters** are the two big reasons for visitors to come up this way. The Cloisters houses the Metropolitan Museum of Art's stunning medieval collection, in a building perched atop a hill, with excellent views across the Hudson to the Palisades. Committed off-the-beaten-path sightseers might also want to visit the **Dyckman Farmhouse,** a historic jewel built in 1783 and the only remaining Dutch Colonial structure in Manhattan.

The Outer Boroughs

Manhattan is just one of the five boroughs that make up the very Big Apple. The others are Brooklyn, the Bronx, Queens, and Staten Island. People who live in the outer boroughs are sometimes (insultingly) referred to by Manhattanites as "B&T" (bridge &

tunnel), because they have to cross a bridge or go through a tunnel to get to Manhattan.

It's an outmoded attitude, because while Manhattan remains the capital (at least in its own mind) of all that is cool and hip, its rents are too high for most people who aren't independently wealthy or with very high-paying jobs, so the hipsters may hang in Manhattan, but are more likely to live in (and establish scenes in) Brooklyn and Queens, in neighborhoods ranging from Williamsburg and DUMBO to Astoria and Long Island City. And, they have the best views of Manhattan.

There are a lot of things to see (and great places to eat) in B&T-land, and see if you can find the time to cross the waters and take a look.

BROOKLYN   Brooklynites are quick to tell you that their borough is the fourth-largest city in the United States. That's because this borough is about pride and attitude. And though it has been over 50 years since the team left, don't even talk about the Dodgers.

Brooklyn is also about neighborhoods and diversity; the borough is a pleasure to explore, though gentrification is creeping into many of the once diverse neighborhoods. Some highlights include New York's first historic district, **Brooklyn Heights,** with its elegant brownstones; the Promenade, with its spectacular view of Manhattan; and the romantic River Cafe. Truman Capote lived here in the 1950s and wrote a wonderful essay about the experience, *A House on the Heights.* Luckily, it has now been reissued in book form, published by the Little Bookroom. He captures much of the magic of the place. (In fact, the novels and stories about, and set in, Brooklyn are legion—from *A Tree Grows in Brooklyn* to *The Fortress of Solitude.* If you have time, check out a few. A guidebook—even one as good as this one—can only take you so far.) To get to Brooklyn Heights, take the A or C to Jay Street; the 2 or 3 to Clark Street; or the M (during rush hours) and R to Court Street.

One of the first Brooklyn neighborhoods to undergo major gentrification was **DUMBO** (**D**own **U**nder the **M**anhattan **B**ridge **O**verpass). What was once a scattering of warehouses is now a thriving (far from starving) artist's colony, with those warehouses now converted into expensive lofts, and just about impossible for most artists to afford. The main drag is **Washington Street,** and businesses are beginning to populate the area. It's here where you'll find **Jacques Torres Chocolate,** the **Brooklyn Ice Cream Factory,** and **Grimaldi's Pizza.** The best way to get to DUMBO is the F train to York Street or the A or C to High Street.

Brooklyn's now-way-past-hip neighborhood (though the very hippest say it's "over") is **Williamsburg.** In the early 1990s, artists began to flee Manhattan's high rents to live here among the Hispanic and Hasidic communities already there. Now, though, the pioneers have seen their once independent and inexpensive enclave being transformed into Brooklyn's version of SoHo. There are a number of funky, youth-oriented boutiques along the neighborhood's main drag, **Bedford Avenue,** but Williamsburg is also the home of that venerable red-meat institution, **Peter Luger.** The best train to take to get to Williamsburg from Manhattan is the L to Bedford Avenue.

Other emerging neighborhoods are **Carroll Gardens, Cobble Hill,** and **Boerum Hill. Smith Street** cuts through all three and has become a

Williamsburg's streets are a colorful mix of old and new.

booming restaurant destination. To get to Smith Street, the best train is the F, with stops at either Carroll Street or Bergen Street.

Downtown Brooklyn off Flatbush Avenue is probably best known for **BAM,** the **Brooklyn Academy of Music.** You'll also find a number of department stores and one of the borough's most beloved landmarks, **Junior's,** the diner noted for its cheese-cakes. Many subway lines con-verge in downtown Brooklyn at the Pacific Street/Atlantic Avenue station, including the 2, 3, 4, 5, B, D, N, Q, and R, as well as the LIRR commuter railroad (you can catch a train at Penn Station in Manhattan).

Park Slope is probably the heart of Brooklyn; it is here and in nearby Prospect Heights where you find the **Brooklyn Museum,** the **Brooklyn Botanical Gardens,** and **Prospect Park** and the **Richard Meier** glass condos, symbolic of the change that is enveloping Brooklyn. The 2 and 3 trains to Grand Army Plaza will land you close to all of the above.

In its heyday during the early 20th century, **Coney Island** was to New York what South Beach is to Miami. This was where everyone flocked to escape the heat and grime of a New York summer day. Few remnants of Coney Island's past remain, such as the long-defunct parachute ride; but during the summer, you can still ride on one of the best roller coasters any-where, the famous **Cyclone.** After several fits and starts, Astroland, the famous amusement park, closed in the fall of 2008, though the city took over the property and opened Luna Park in the spring of 2010. For an idea of what the place was like in its heyday, have a look at Ric Burns's film, *Coney Island.* Coney Island is also the home of the **New York Aquarium** and the Mets' minor-league baseball team, the Cyclones. To get to Coney Island, take the F or Q to West 8th Street, Brooklyn.

THE BRONX   Perhaps the most famous destination in the Bronx, and next to Rome's Colosseum maybe one of the most celebrated sports arenas in the world, is **Yankee Stadium**—although 2008 was the old stadium's last sea-son. Even if you are a Yankee hater, you will be awed by the new Yankee Sta-dium, a modernized replica of the House that Ruth Built (some are calling the new stadium the House that Jeter Built). The 4, B, or D trains all stop there.

The Bronx is also the home of the United States' largest metropolitan animal park, the **Bronx Zoo,** and the **New York Botanical Garden.** Both are wonders worthy of an excursion. To get to the Bronx Zoo, you can take the 2 or 5 train to East Tremont Ave/West Farms Square and walk to the zoo's Asia gate entrance (Gate A). To get to the Botanical Garden, you can take Metro-North Harlem local line from Grand Central Station to the Botanical Garden station.

While visiting the Bronx Zoo or the Botanical Garden, stop at the Little Italy of the Bronx, **Arthur Avenue,** for a mouthwatering walk past meat markets, delis, vegetable stands, fish markets, cafes, and restaurants. To get to Arthur Avenue, take the 4, B, or D train to Fordham Road and transfer to the no. 12 bus east, or the no. 2 or 5 train to Pelham Parkway and the no. 12 bus west.

QUEENS Queens is the largest borough in New York and it's also the city's most ethnically diverse. There are more languages spoken in its 109 square miles than anywhere else on the planet. All that ethnicity translates into an adventurous eater's paradise. We've dined on Thai, Peruvian, Indian, Guyanese, Greek, Colombian, and Brazilian here, and we've barely scratched the surface. But there's more to Queens than just food.

Astoria, with its large Greek community, is also the home of the newly reopened **Museum of the Moving Image,** dedicated to the movies—film, television, and digital. To get there, take the R to Steinway Street or the N or Q to 36th Avenue.

With former warehouses and factories being converted to expensive condos, **Long Island City,** directly across the river from Manhattan's Upper East Side, is becoming Queens's version of DUMBO. It is also where you will find a number of museums, including the **Noguchi Museum, Socrates Park,** and the **P.S. 1 Contemporary Art Center.** The best train to take to get to Long Island City is the no. 7, also known as the International Express, running through one ethnic community after another; get off at just about any spot and you'll see signs in an assortment of languages. The no. 7 train will also take you to Flushing, where you'll find the new **Citi Field,** home of the Mets, replacing the old Shea Stadium; the Louis Armstrong Stadium and the Arthur Ashe Stadium at **Flushing Meadow Park,** where the **U.S. Open** is held each September; and the **Queens Museum of Art** on the grounds of the 1964 World's Fair.

STATEN ISLAND Staten Island is the most remote of the boroughs and most enjoyably reached by ferry. There is a suburban feel to the borough, making it a haven for commuters. The free **Staten Island Ferry** gets you to the borough. If you decide to spend time in Staten Island, take in a **Staten Island Yankees** minor-league baseball game. The stadium is within walking distance of the ferry and has lovely views of downtown Manhattan.

SUGGESTED NEW YORK CITY ITINERARIES

I've lived in New York for more than half my life and I still haven't seen it all. That's not because I don't want to; it's just there is so much to see. So it's understandable if you feel a bit overwhelmed by all the options. Seeing the best of New York requires endurance, patience, perseverance, good walking shoes, a Metro-Card, and a subway map. For some attractions—such as the Empire State Building or a Broadway play—you should score tickets *before* you come to New York to avoid long lines or a shutout. Besides your own two feet, the subway will be your best bet to cover the most ground. I also recommend a few bus routes that will not only get you to some of New York's best attractions, but will also act as your own tour bus on which you'll see sights on the way.

THE BEST OF NYC IN 1 DAY

If you want to have any chance of seeing the best of New York in just 1 day, you need to get an early start. You also need a plan of attack. You don't want to waste time zigzagging around the city to various attractions. So we recommend taking on New York by thirds. On the first third, we will concentrate on the best of midtown Manhattan. **Start:** *Pier 83 on 42nd Street.*

1   Circle Line Sightseeing Cruise ★★

By starting your day on the water on a 2-hour half-island "Semi-Circle" cruise, or the 75-minute Liberty Cruise, you'll get a good overview of Manhattan. You'll pass by the Statue of Liberty and Ellis Island; see the lower Manhattan skyline; head up the East River, where you will go under the Brooklyn, Manhattan, and Williamsburg bridges; and view the United Nations and the East Side skyline, including the Empire State and Chrysler buildings. See p. 299.

Afterward, take the M42 42nd Street crosstown bus to Fifth Avenue, where you'll come to the:

2   New York Public Library ★★

You'll recognize this building by the lion sculptures guarding its gates. Step inside for more grandeur, especially the incredible **Main Reading Room,**

The New York Public Library's glorious Reading Room is open to all.

where you might want to take a break and read the paper (if you have time). While you're here, take a look at the library's backyard, **Bryant Park.** Between end of October and February, the **Pond** ice-skating rink will be up. You can also go round and round on **Le Carrousel.** See p. 273.

3 Grand Central Terminal ★★

Before stepping into this magnificent working train station, take a look east toward Lexington Avenue and then crane your neck up. You'll see my favorite skyscraper, the **Chrysler Building ★★**. Okay, now enter Grand Central, where approximately 500,000 commuters dash through daily. I hope it's not rush hour . . . but even if it is, you really won't have to worry about colliding with a commuter: The building and the stupendous main concourse were constructed so cleverly that despite the perceived chaos, people rarely bump into each other. You'll want to spend hours examining the beautiful detail throughout the terminal, but you don't have hours to spare. A walk through the main concourse and a look at the sky ceiling will be evidence enough. See p. 233.

Grand Central Terminal ☕

You're hungry now and the choices in the Grand Central Terminal dining concourse are plentiful and good. Chow down on anything from Indian food to pizza. Or opt for a heartier (and more expensive!) lunch at the legendary Oyster Bar & Restaurant, or upstairs overlooking the concourse at Michael Jordan's the Steak House N.Y.C.

4 Empire State Building ★★★

It's an 8-block walk down Fifth Avenue from Grand Central Station to the Empire State Building. Let's hope it's a beautiful day because I want your view from the top of this historic structure, the tallest building in New York, to be pristine. You already have your tickets (don't you?), so you don't have to wait at the ticket booth (see box "Empire State Building Ticket Buying" on p. 231 for details). The elevator will zip you up to the 86th story, where you will get a panoramic view of Manhattan. See p. 232.

Take the B or D train uptown to Seventh Avenue. Walk east across 53rd Street to the:

5 Museum of Modern Art ★★

Yes, the $20 admission is outrageous, but this is New York and you are getting used to outrageous. And you'll forget about the admission charge once you peruse the exhibits in this beautiful museum. Airy and expansive, with sky-lit, open galleries along with smaller, intimate rooms, the museum is one of a kind. See p. 237.

6 Rockefeller Center ★★

A short walk from MoMA is the Rockefeller Center complex. If you are here during the Christmas holidays, you'll fight the crowds for a glimpse of the Christmas tree and the skaters in the small rink. If your timing is right, you might be able to squeeze in the 70-minute NBC Studio Tour. If not, you'll see **Radio City Music Hall ★** and **30 Rockefeller Plaza ★**. If you did not have advance tickets for the Empire State Building and the line was

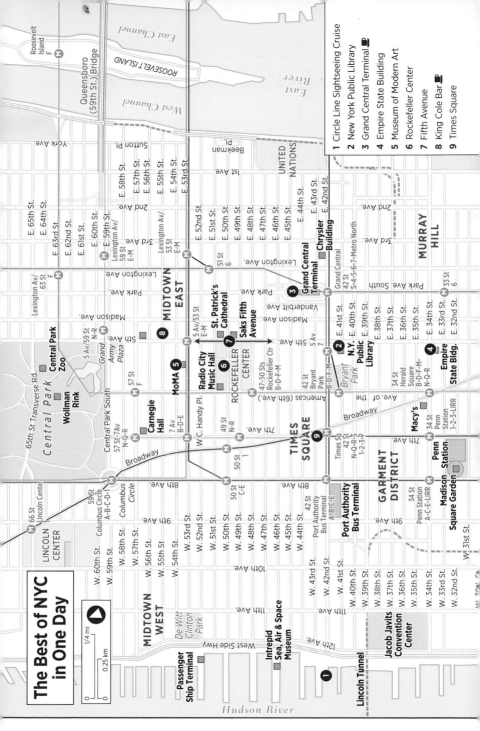

The Best of NYC in One Day

1 Circle Line Sightseeing Cruise
2 New York Public Library
3 Grand Central Terminal 🍴
4 Empire State Building
5 Museum of Modern Art
6 Rockefeller Center
7 Fifth Avenue
8 King Cole Bar 🍷
9 Times Square

much too long, take the elevator up 70 floors to **Top of the Rock ★★** for, arguably, as good a view as you would have at the Empire State Building. Across the street (Fifth Ave.) you'll see **St. Patrick's Cathedral.** See p. 280.

7 Fifth Avenue

Is a street an attraction? When it's one of the most famous in the world, it is. Walk north up Fifth Avenue from Rock Center and pass such big-name stores as Saks Fifth Avenue, Henri Bendel, the NBA Store, Tiffany & Co., Cartier, Bergdorf Goodman, FAO Schwarz, and the Apple Store. You'll also see Trump Tower from the popular *Apprentice* TV series. At 59th Street, you'll see the ornate Plaza Hotel. Across the street you'll see the southern end of Central Park. See p. 349.

8 King Cole Bar ☕

Now would be a good time to rest your legs as well as your senses. Head back down Fifth Avenue a few blocks to the lounge at the St. Regis Hotel. This is where the bloody mary was supposedly invented, and it's the perfect place for a late-afternoon or early-evening cocktail. 2 E. 55th St., at Fifth Avenue. ✆ 212/753-4500. See p. 434.

9 Times Square ★

You've got tickets for a Broadway show, so before you head into the theater, this is your chance to see what Times Square is all about. The lights are blinding, the crowds are thick, and the noise is infernal, but that's Times Square. There's nowhere like it in the world. But don't linger too long! Broadway curtains rise promptly! See p. 244.

THE BEST OF NYC IN 2 DAYS

On your second day, you'll head downtown and explore the city where it began. You'll wander through streets that are as old as any in New York, and some that are curiously towered by ultramodern, gleaming steel-and-glass skyscrapers. Again, you'll want to get a very early start because there is so much to see and always too little time. *Start: Subway: 1 to South Ferry or 4 or 5 to Bowling Green.*

1 Statue of Liberty ★★★

You saw Lady Liberty on your Circle Line half-island tour yesterday, but now you want to get up close and personal with her. Ferries leave from Battery Park (check the online schedule, which changes seasonally). On Liberty Island, you can take one of two tours. The Pedestal/Museum Ticket takes visitors to the base of the Statue and the Pedestal Observation Deck, while the Crown Ticket incorporates the pedestal/museum tour and makes a visit to the Crown of the Statue of Liberty. See p. 243.

2 Ellis Island ★★

Your Statue of Liberty ferry ticket also includes a stop at Ellis Island on your way back from Liberty Island; ferries leave every 15 to 20 minutes, depending on the season. (They will leave less frequently in the dead of winter.)

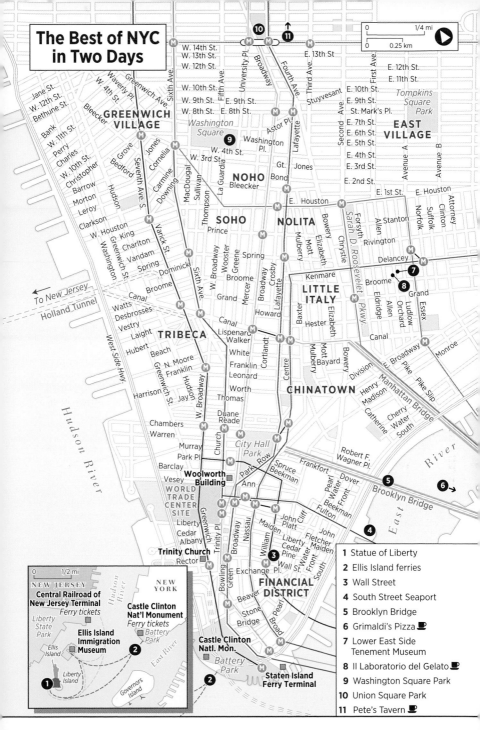

The Best of NYC in Two Days

GREENWICH VILLAGE

Washington Square

NOHO

Bleecker

SOHO

NOLITA

LITTLE ITALY

TRIBECA

CHINATOWN

EAST VILLAGE

Tompkins Square Park

St. Mark's Pl.

To New Jersey

Holland Tunnel

Hudson River

WORLD TRADE CENTER SITE

Woolworth Building

City Hall Park

FINANCIAL DISTRICT

Trinity Church

Brooklyn Bridge

East River

Robert F. Wagner Pl.

NEW JERSEY

Central Railroad of New Jersey Terminal
Ferry tickets

Liberty State Park

Ellis Island Immigration Museum

Ellis Island

NEW YORK

Castle Clinton Nat'l Monument
Ferry tickets

Battery Park

Castle Clinton Natl. Mon.

Battery Park

Liberty Island

Governors Island

Staten Island Ferry Terminal

1 Statue of Liberty
2 Ellis Island ferries
3 Wall Street
4 South Street Seaport
5 Brooklyn Bridge
6 Grimaldi's Pizza
7 Lower East Side Tenement Museum
8 Il Laboratorio del Gelato
9 Washington Square Park
10 Union Square Park
11 Pete's Tavern

The Immigration Museum is one of the most touching in the city. Incredible, personal details of the immigrant experience are on display, from letters and jewelry to battered valises. You could spend all day there, but you don't have time! Wander through the Registry room and you'll hear the echoes of hundreds of different languages of immigrants who came through these doors to a better life. See p. 230.

3 Wall Street

Back in Manhattan, the walk up to the Financial District is not long. Along the way you'll see structures such as **Castle Clinton National Monument,** the remnants of a fort built in 1808 to defend New York Harbor against the British, and the impressive **U.S. Customs House,** which houses the Museum of the American Indian, part of the Smithsonian Institution. Once on Wall Street, stop for a photo op at the **Federal Hall National Memorial,** with the statue of George Washington in front, and the **New York Stock Exchange,** across the street. Unfortunately, the exchange is no longer open for tours, but if you are a person of some significance, they might let you ring the opening day's bell. See p. 245.

Take the free Downtown Connection bus that travels from Battery Park to South Street Seaport, with stops along the way including one at Wall Street. See the "Take a Free Ride" box in chapter 9 for details.

4 South Street Seaport

Here the streets are really old—so old they are rough with cobblestones. This is a 17th-century historic district with restored 18th- and 19th-century buildings still standing. The interesting South Street Seaport Museum will fill you in on more of the 11 square blocks of seafaring history. Also part of the seaport complex is Pier 17, a historic barge that now is the home to various stores that you are probably very familiar with. See p. 339.

Take the A or C train at Broadway–Nassau Street toward Brooklyn and get off at High Street, the first stop in Brooklyn.

5 Brooklyn Bridge ★★

You have been well fed, so now you have the energy to make the approximately half-hour stroll back to Manhattan across one of the greatest suspended bridges in the world. The view of the Manhattan skyline is spectacular—make sure you have plenty of room in the card of your digital camera. See p. 228.

6 Grimaldi's Pizzeria 🍽

You are now in Brooklyn and probably very hungry. You'll need nourishment for your next adventure, and where better than this famed pizzeria, in the shadow of the Brooklyn Bridge? 19 Old Fulton St., between Front and Water streets. 𝄢 718/858-4300. See p. 178.

7 Lower East Side Tenement Museum ★

When you visited Ellis Island, you learned about the immigrants' struggles to gain entry into this country. Now visit the prototype of a Lower East Side tenement where many of those immigrants lived. The only way to see the museum is by guided tour, which takes place frequently between 10am and 6pm. See p. 255.

8 Il Laboratorio del Gelato ☕

Just across the street from the Lower East Side Tenement Museum is a wonderful ice-cream-and-gelato shop where you can experience a multitude of homemade ice cream and sorbet flavors. Pick up a cone or cup for the walk to the subway. 95 Orchard St., between Broome and Delancey streets. ✆ 212/343-9922.

Take the F train at Second Avenue and Houston Street two stops uptown to West 4th Street.

9 Washington Square Park

Welcome to the center of Greenwich Village. This neighborhood's bohemian tradition is best represented by this park and the characters in it. It recently went through a major renovation and so is looking the best it has in years. On the north end of the park, you'll see a row of elegant late-19th-century town houses and Washington Square Arch, patterned after the Arc de Triomphe in Paris. See p. 296.

10 Union Square Park

About 10 blocks north of Washington Square Park, you'll find this small but welcome bit of park. And if it is a Monday, Wednesday, Friday, or Saturday, you'll be in for a treat because the city's best greenmarket, the **Union Square Greenmarket ★★**, will be buzzing with activity. See p. 295.

11 Pete's Tavern ☕

A few blocks east of Union Square Park is Pete's Tavern, the city's oldest continually operating drinking establishment. Look familiar? You may have seen it in an episode of Seinfeld, Sex and the City, or Law & Order, or else on the big screen. Stop in for a pint to quench your thirst after that full day of walking. 129 E. 18th St. (at Irving Place). ✆ 212/473-7676. www.petestavern.com. Subway: L, N, R, Q, 4, 5, or 6 to 14th St./Union Sq. See p. 429.

THE BEST OF NYC IN 3 DAYS

You've seen a sizable chunk of the best of Manhattan, but there's still plenty left to fill up a day. We haven't even gotten to some of the city's great museums or that urban oasis called Central Park. We'll do all that and maybe even escape to the wilds of the Bronx before the day is done. If the weather's nice, plan on a picnic in Central Park. *Start: B or C to 72nd Street.*

1 The Dakota

We'll start our day in front of this 1884 apartment building. This was standing when the only thing around it was greenery. The building has a dubious past: It was here where John Lennon lived (and where Yoko Ono still lives), and where he was shot and killed. Across the street in Central Park is **Strawberry Fields ★**, named in honor of the former Beatle; fans gather here every year on the anniversary of his death, December 8. See p. 271.

It's feeding time at the Central Park Zoo.

2 American Museum of Natural History ★★★

Don't try to cover too much ground at this 4-square-block museum; you'll be here all day. Pick a few of the highlights, like the Fossil Halls where the dinosaurs reside, the Hall of Biodiversity, and the Culture Halls. On the 81st Street side of the building, you'll find the **Rose Center for Earth and Space,** where you can marvel at the beauty of the cosmos in the grand Hayden Planetarium. See p. 220.

3 Central Park ★★★

From the Museum of Natural History, cross the street to Central Park and enter at 81st Street. Follow the path east, and just south of the Delacorte Theater, you'll see Belvedere Castle. Climb to the top and soak in the view of the park. To the north, you'll see the Great Lawn, sight of so many concerts, and beyond that the Jacqueline Kennedy Onassis Reservoir. To the south you'll see the lake with its rowboats (rent one if you have time) and the skyline of Manhattan. See p. 282.

A Picnic in the Park ☕

If you didn't pack a lunch, stop in the Zabar's (at 80th and Broadway), and get your lunch to go. Head to the park and grab a bench, or spread out a blanket and take in the sunshine.

4 Metropolitan Museum of Art ★★★

Continuing east across Central Park, you'll hit Fifth Avenue and the Met. As with the Museum of Natural History, there is no way you can see all the Met has to offer in one visit, but stop by the renovated Greek and Roman Galleries, and the museum's collection of European paintings—including 5 Vermeers (more than any other museum in the world) and 38 Monets. There are various free museum highlight tours. They last an hour and will give you a pretty good overview of this great museum. See p. 234.

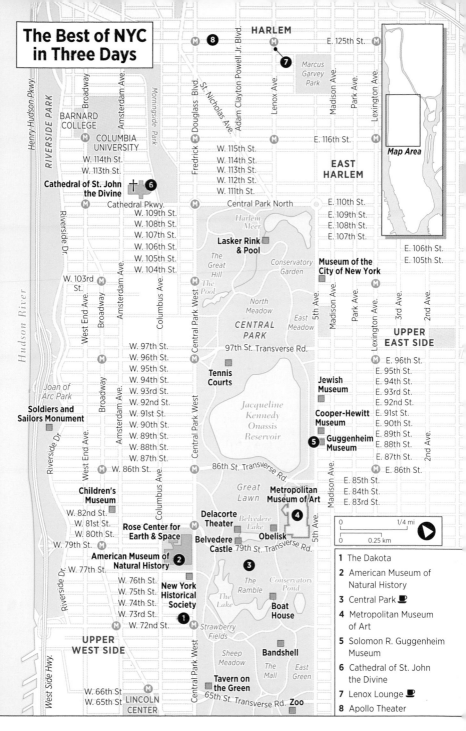

The Best of NYC in Three Days

HARLEM

E. 125th St.

Marcus Garvey Park

Morningside Park

BARNARD COLLEGE

COLUMBIA UNIVERSITY

W. 114th St.
W. 113th St.

Cathedral of St. John the Divine

Cathedral Pkwy.
W. 109th St.
W. 108th St.
W. 107th St.
W. 106th St.
W. 105th St.
W. 104th St.

W. 103rd St.

RIVERSIDE PARK

Riverside Dr.

W. 97th St.
W. 96th St.
W. 95th St.
W. 94th St.
W. 93rd St.
W. 92nd St.
W. 91st St.
W. 90th St.
W. 89th St.
W. 88th St.
W. 87th St.

West End Ave.

Broadway

Amsterdam Ave.

Columbus Ave.

Central Park West

W. 115th St.
W. 114th St.
W. 113th St.
W. 112th St.
W. 111th St.

Central Park North

Harlem Meer

Lasker Rink & Pool

The Great Hill

The Pool

North Meadow

CENTRAL PARK

97th St. Transverse Rd.

Conservatory Garden

East Meadow

E. 116th St.

EAST HARLEM

Map Area

E. 110th St.
E. 109th St.
E. 108th St.
E. 107th St.

E. 106th St.
E. 105th St.

Museum of the City of New York

5th Ave.

Madison Ave.

Park Ave.

Lexington Ave.

3rd Ave.

2nd Ave.

UPPER EAST SIDE

E. 96th St.
E. 95th St.
E. 94th St.
E. 93rd St.
E. 92nd St.
E. 91st St.
E. 90th St.
E. 89th St.
E. 88th St.
E. 87th St.

E. 86th St.

E. 85th St.
E. 84th St.
E. 83rd St.

Jewish Museum

Cooper-Hewitt Museum

Guggenheim Museum

Madison Ave.

Tennis Courts

Jacqueline Kennedy Onassis Reservoir

86th St. Transverse Rd.

Joan of Arc Park

Soldiers and Sailors Monument

Riverside Dr.

West End Ave.

Broadway

Amsterdam Ave.

Columbus Ave.

Hudson River

Henry-Hudson-Pkwy.

Broadway

Amsterdam Ave.

St. Nicholas Ave.

Fredrick Douglass Blvd.

Adam Clayton Powell Jr. Blvd.

Lenox Ave.

Madison Ave.

Park Ave.

Lexington Ave.

Children's Museum

W. 82nd St.
W. 81st St.
W. 80th St.
W. 79th St.

Rose Center for Earth & Space

American Museum of Natural History

W. 77th St.
W. 76th St.
W. 75th St.
W. 74th St.
W. 73rd St.
W. 72nd St.

New York Historical Society

Great Lawn

Metropolitan Museum of Art

Delacorte Theater

Belvedere Lake

Belvedere Castle

Obelisk

79th St. Transverse Rd.

The Ramble

The Lake

Strawberry Fields

UPPER WEST SIDE

Sheep Meadow

Tavern on the Green

65th St. Transverse Rd.

W. 66th St
W. 65th St

LINCOLN CENTER

Central Park West

West Side Hwy.

Riverside Dr.

Conservatory Pond

Boat House

The Mall

East Green

Bandshell

Zoo

5th Ave.

2nd Ave.

| 0 | | 1/4 mi |
| 0 | 0.25 km | |

1 The Dakota

2 American Museum of Natural History

3 Central Park

4 Metropolitan Museum of Art

5 Solomon R. Guggenheim Museum

6 Cathedral of St. John the Divine

7 Lenox Lounge

8 Apollo Theater

HERE ARE SOME THINGS not to do IN NYC

New York has so much going for it, the good overwhelms the bad. But there is bad, and I'm not talking about the obvious. I'm talking about experiences that might be perceived as good, but take my word for it: They are not. So, despite what you have heard, the following are a few experiences you can avoid:

New Year's Eve in Times Square: You see it on television every year, and now you're here. This is your chance to be one of the thousands of revelers packed together in the frigid cold to watch the ball drop. *Don't do it!* Despite the happy faces you see on TV, the whole thing is a miserable experience and not worth the forced elation of blowing on a noisemaker at midnight with half a million others. You won't find many New Yorkers here; we know better.

Three-Card Monte: When you see a crowd gathered around a cardboard box with one man flipping cards, madly enticing innocent rubes into his game, while another guy scans the crowd for undercover cops, keep on walking. Don't stop and listen to the dealer's spiel or think you can be the one to beat him at his game. You can't. Buy a lottery ticket instead; your odds are much better.

Horse-Drawn Carriage Rides: Pity those poor beasts of burden. They get dragged out in the heat (though not extreme heat) and cold (though not extreme cold) with a buggy attached just to give passengers the feel of an old-world, romantic buggy ride through Central Park. But the horses look so forlorn, as if it's the last thing they want to do. And they don't even get a cut of the generous take: It's generally $50 for a 20-minute ride, excluding tip. There is also a periodic effort to totally ban these rides, but it hasn't taken hold—yet. If you want a slow, leisurely ride through Central Park, minus the ripe and frequent smell of horse poop, consider an alternative called **Manhattan Rickshaw Company** (© **212/ 604-4729;** www.manhattanrickshaw.com). The beast of burden has two legs, and pedals you and a companion in the back of a pedicab, where the rate is negotiable

5 Solomon R. Guggenheim Museum ★

Continuing on our minitour of Museum Mile, that stretch of artistic real estate that runs on upper Fifth Avenue, is the Guggenheim. You'll know it when you see it; there's nothing else like this Frank Lloyd Wright–designed museum, and now you have the chance to walk the spiraling rotunda. But get off the rotunda and take a look at some of the permanent collection that includes works by Picasso, Chagall, and Klee. Or wander into the Kandinsky Gallery for a dose of the master's eye-opening works. See p. 241.

Take the M96 crosstown bus at Fifth Avenue and 97th Street West. Get off at Amsterdam Avenue and 96th Street and transfer to an uptown M11 bus. Get off at 110th Street.

6 Cathedral of St. John the Divine ★

On the east side of Amsterdam, you will see the world's largest Gothic cathedral. Construction began in 1892 and is still not finished. You can explore the inside of the cathedral on your own or opt for a tour. If you're but is usually $15–$30 for a street hail ride; call to arrange a guided tour.

Chain Restaurants: Oh yes; they're here, probably to stay—and most likely with more to come. I'm referring to those restaurants with familiar names like Olive Garden, Applebee's, Red Lobster, and Domino's. When you begin to feel the pangs of hunger, ask yourself: Did I come to New York to eat what I can eat in every city or town in this country? Or did I come here to experience what makes New York so unique? Well, that includes the amazing variety of unchained restaurants, from the coffee shops and diners to the bargain-priced ethnic cuisine and higher-end dining experiences. So bypass the old standards, and try something different and exciting. You won't regret it.

The Feast of San Gennaro: At one time this was a genuine Italian feast (see the films *Godfather II* and *Mean Streets* for the feast in the good old days). Its decline has pretty much coincided with the decline of Little Italy, a neighborhood that is just a shell of what it once was. Now the feast, held annually for 11 days in September, is just an overblown and overcrowded street fair with bad food, cheap red wine, and games of chance you have no chance of winning.

Driving in the City: Do you really want to have to maneuver your car in heavy traffic, battling yellow cabs, and searching fruitlessly for a legal parking spot? With its subways and buses (and your feet), New York has the best and fastest public transportation. A car is a luxury you want no part of.

Waiting on Lines for Breakfast: (And please note, New Yorkers wait *on* line, not *in* line). Sometimes New Yorkers can be masochistic—and silly. They hear about a restaurant that serves a great breakfast, and they begin lining up on weekend mornings to eat. Sometimes they wait for over an hour, standing outside, winter or summer, to order pancakes, omelets, or whatever else the breakfast menu offers. They do this even though many coffee shops and diners are serving patrons the same foods at much less cost and without more than a minute's wait. Now what would you do?

here at Easter or during the Feast of St. Francis in October, don't miss the blessing of animals—where the creature congregation has been known to include an elephant or camel. See p. 278.

Take the M7 uptown bus to 125th Street.

7 Lenox Lounge ☕
Stop at this classic (circa 1930s) Harlem bar for a beer or cocktail. You might get lucky and Patience Higgins and the Sugar Hill Quartet will be playing some straight ahead bebop when you're there. 288 Lenox Ave., between 124th and 125th streets. ☎ 212/427-0253.

8 Apollo Theater ★
Here's a city landmark that is as well known as La Scala or the Taj Mahal. And if it's Wednesday, make sure you have tickets, because Amateur Night

at the Apollo is an experience not to be missed. There would be no *American Idol* without this Harlem institution. But even if it's not Wednesday, you can tour this historic theater where Bessie Smith, James Brown, Stevie Wonder, and so many other greats played. See p. 402.

MMMM . . . THE ESSENTIAL NEW YORK EATING ITINERARY

New York has countless restaurants of quality and variety. If you want a sampling of true New York cuisine, follow the "required eating" itinerary below. Whether you jam the stops below into 1, 2, or 3 days, a gargantuan appetite is required. For full reviews of the places listed below, see chapter 5, "Where to Dine."

1 Bagels with Lox

Start your food tour at **Barney Greengrass, the Sturgeon King,** 541 Amsterdam Ave. (✆ **212/724-4707**), where they have been making that famous combination, bagels and lox, since 1908. If there is anything more satisfying than a fresh out-of-the-oven bagel with a schmear of cream cheese and a slice of lox, I don't know what it is. This might be one of the most popular breakfast items in New York.

2 Cuban/Chinese

There used to be dozens of Cuban/Chinese restaurants in Manhattan, most on the Upper West Side. The boom began in the late 1950s after the Cuban revolution and the beginning of the Castro regime. Chinese-Cubans emigrated to New York and opened up restaurants serving both Cantonese-style Chinese food and traditional Cuban food. A few are left, and my favorite is **Flor de Mayo,** 2651 Broadway (✆ **212/663-5520**). Here I can order a big bowl of wonton soup followed by a huge plate of yellow rice and black beans.

3 Chicken & Waffles

You're out late, maybe listening to jazz at one of Harlem's many clubs, it's getting near dawn, and you can't decide whether you want dinner or breakfast. You can't resist the fried chicken, but waffles sound good, too. So you try both—maple syrup melding with the hot sauce, sweet with savory. The birthplace of this dish is said to be Wells Chicken and Waffles in Harlem in 1938. Wells is long gone, but chicken and waffles live on. For the best rendition, as well as for grits and fish cakes—another outstanding combo—go to **Amy Ruth's,** 113 W. 116th St. (✆ **212/280-8779**).

4 The New York Oyster

There was a time when New York was more the Big Oyster than the Big Apple. The local harbor beds overflowed with oysters, and the mollusk helped feed the city. You can recall those glory days at the **Oyster Bar & Restaurant** in Grand Central Station (✆ **212/490-6650**) where, since 1913, oysters have been the specialty. Order them on the half-shell from Long Island, Washington State, Maine, Virginia, or Canada, with the Metro-North commuter trains rumbling in the background. It's a true New York eating experience if there ever was one.

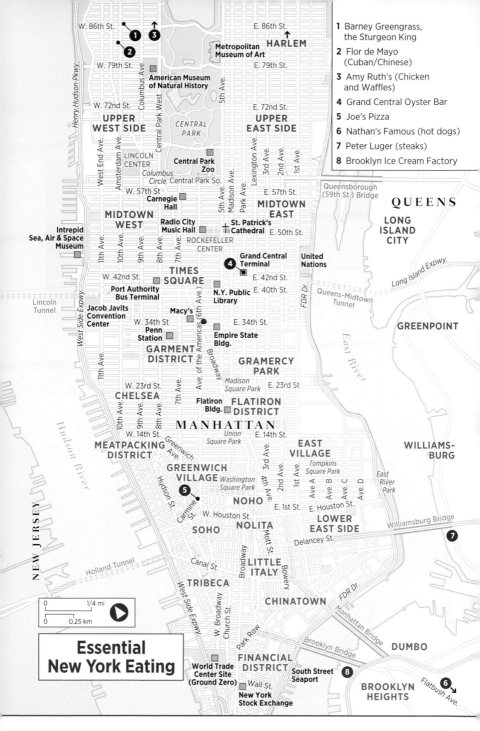

Essential New York Eating

1 Barney Greengrass, the Sturgeon King
2 Flor de Mayo (Cuban/Chinese)
3 Amy Ruth's (Chicken and Waffles)
4 Grand Central Oyster Bar
5 Joe's Pizza
6 Nathan's Famous (hot dogs)
7 Peter Luger (steaks)
8 Brooklyn Ice Cream Factory

5   A Slice of Pizza

Toss on some red pepper or garlic, fold it in half lengthwise, and eat it standing up to capture the grease before it stains your clothes. That's the way we've been eating pizza in New York for years. The classic New York slice, however, has been on the decline ever since the chain pizzerias have corrupted the landscape. For the best slice, head to **Joe's Pizza,** 7 Carmine St. (℃ **212/255-3946**) in the Village, open late to satisfy your cravings.

6   The Hot Dog

This might be an obvious choice, but I don't think so. You can find carts selling cheap hot dogs throughout the city. You might be tempted to try one just to say you did. And I think you should; it definitely is a New York experience. But even better, take the train out to Coney Island and sample a **Nathan's Famous** dog right on the boardwalk, at 1310 Surf Ave. (℃ **718/946-2705**). Maybe it's the salty sea air. Maybe it's the crisp skin of the hot dog, or the way it's perfectly fried. Whatever it is, you won't forget your Nathan's hot dog on Coney Island.

Nathan's Famous at Coney Island.

7   The New York Strip

Some of New York's oldest restaurants are steakhouses, and for good reason. They keep it simple. Some might have sawdust on the floors, others clay pipes on the ceiling or photos of celebrities on the walls, but that is about as fancy as they get. What they do is serve quality, properly aged meat cooked to perfection and presented in a no-nonsense, no-frills manner. And no one does that better than **Peter Luger** in Williamsburg, Brooklyn, 178 Broadway (℃ **718/387-7400**).

8   Ice Cream with a View

If you've been able to sample the above essential New York eating experiences into 1, 2 or 3 days, finish your tour off at the **Brooklyn Ice Cream Factory,** 1 Water St. at the Fulton Ferry Landing Pier (℃ **718/246-3963**), where the homemade ice cream is absolutely delicious and the view at river's edge of Manhattan, just below the Brooklyn Bridge, is equally stunning.

WHERE
TO STAY

4

t's no doubt that New York City hotels are among the finest in the world. From high-design luxury icons like the Mandarin Oriental and hip, modern towers like the Gansevoort Hotel to grand dames like the Carlyle and The Plaza, the range of New York City hotels is staggering. And though high-end hotels abound here, the city also provides a plethora of equally stunning and affordable options. We've provided a range of recommendations from which to choose.

best SPLURGE HOTELS IN MANHATTAN

- **Ritz-Carlton New York, Central Park,** 50 Central Park South (www.ritz carlton.com; ✆ **212/308-9100**): The combination of a great location across from Central Park, large well-outfitted rooms, and excellent Ritz-Carlton service is as good as it gets. See p. 105.

- **The Mercer,** 147 Mercer St. (www.mercerhotel.com; ✆ **888/918-6060** or 212/966-6060): The best of the hip, downtown hotels, the Mercer is in the heart of SoHo. The high-ceilinged, loftlike rooms and suites, some with fireplaces, all with ceiling fans and luxurious bathrooms, are spectacular. See p. 94.

- **The Peninsula New York,** 700 Fifth Ave. (www.peninsula.com; ✆ **800/262-9467** or 212/956-2888): The combination of old-world elegance and 21st-century technology is best realized in this practically perfect hotel. See p. 117.

- **The Pierre,** Fifth Avenue at 61st Street (www.tajhotels.com/pierre; ✆ **800/838-8000**): After a 2-year, $100-million renovation, new owners Taj Hotels, Resorts, and Palaces have restored the Pierre to its former grande dame elegance and status. See p. 117.

- **Inn New York City,** 266 W. 71st St. (www.innnewyorkcity.com; ✆ **212/580-1900**): I wouldn't call it a hotel, more like your own home away from home complete with fireplace

The sumptuous Pierre Hotel is one of New York's grand dames. PREVIOUS PAGE: The unique exterior of the Gershwin Hotel.

and a fully stocked kitchen, all in a charming Upper West Side brownstone. See p. 126.

o **The Carlyle, a Rosewood Hotel,** 35 E. 76th St. (www.thecarlyle.com; ✆ 800/227-5737 or 212/744-1600): You are in rarefied territory when you stay in the Carlyle. Service is white gloved and rooms are sumptuous. Many have incredible views of the city and Central Park. And don't forget Café Carlyle for cabaret and Bemelmans Bar for a cocktail. See p. 129.

o **The Mark,** Madison Avenue, at 77th Street (www.themarkhotel.com; ✆ 866/744-4300): After a $150 million renovation, the Mark has not rejoined the elite hotels in the city. Huge rooms, great service, a Jean-Georges run restaurant, and just a block from Central Park. What more could you ask for? See p. 130.

best MODERATELY PRICED HOTELS

o **Casablanca Hotel,** 147 W. 43rd St. (www.casablancahotel.com; ✆ 888/922-7225 or 212/869-1212): In the Theater District, the Casablanca offers clean, well-outfitted rooms at value rates, as well as nice extras such as complimentary breakfast, bottled water, free high-speed Internet, and a roof deck perfect for a cocktail on a balmy evening. See p. 109.

o **Hotel Metro,** 45 W. 35th St. (www.hotelmetronyc.com; ✆ 800/356-3870 or 212/947-2500): You'll find good deals and lots of extras at this Midtown hotel that's popular with Europeans. See p. 111.

o **Inn on 23rd Street,** 131 W. 23rd St. (www.innon23rd.com; ✆ 877/387-2323 or 212/463-0330): You cannot do better than this charming inn for top-notch quality and extras. Rooms are rustic and uniquely designed, but all have up-to-date amenities. Breakfast is complimentary and served in a lovely library. See p. 98.

The Sofitel New York exudes elegance.

o **The Lucerne,** 201 W. 79th St. (www.thelucernehotel.com; ✆ 212/875-1000): A great Upper West Side location, proximity to Central Park and the Museum of Natural History, and in a classic Beaux Arts building all combine to make this a top moderate choice. See p. 127.

o **Nu Hotel,** 85 Smith St., Brooklyn (www.nuhotelbrooklyn.com; ✆ 718/852-8585): Hotel construction is booming in Brooklyn, and the best of the few that have already arrived is the Nu Hotel. Close to downtown Brooklyn, residential nabes Brooklyn Heights, Cobble Hill, Boerum Hill, and Carroll Gardens, and the restaurant row of Smith Street . . . and near to all major subway lines that can get you to

Manhattan quickly, the Nu Hotel, with its in-room hammocks and bunk beds, is the perfect Brooklyn location. See p. 132.

o **Sofitel New York,** 45 W. 44th St. (www.sofitel.com; © **212/354-8844**): This relatively new hotel exudes old-world (French) elegance. And you should be able to score some good weekend packages on the Internet. See p. 109.

best HOTELS FOR FAMILIES

o **Hotel Beacon,** 2130 Broadway (www.beaconhotel.com; © **800/572-4969** or 212/787-1100): Not only is this hotel a great deal—you can get good-size suites for much less than in Midtown—the Upper West Side, with its parks, the Museum of Natural History, and fun, inexpensive restaurants, is a great neighborhood for children. See p. 125.

o **Doubletree Guest Suites Times Square,** 1568 Broadway (www.doubletree. com; © **800/222-TREE** [222-8733] or 212/719-1600): This hotel boasts an entire floor of childproof suites, complete with living rooms for spreading out and kitchenettes for preparing light meals. It's also just a block from kid-friendly chain restaurants and the Toys "R" Us superstore. See p. 106.

best INCENTIVES FOR HOTEL-HOPPING

o **Best Hotel Suite: Town-House Suite in the Kitano New York,** 66 Park Ave. (http://kitano.com; © **800/548-2666** or 212/885-7000). Each of the three one-bedroom suites in the town house that is part of this hotel features a hallway leading to a sunken living room with original art, a state-of-the-art stereo system, and a tea maker with green tea. See p. 119.

o **Best Inexpensive Hotel Restaurant: Burger Joint in Le Parker Meridien,** 118 W. 57th St. (www.parkermeridien.com; © **800/543-4300** or 212/245-5000). Hidden off the lobby, this joint has been discovered by locals, so the lines are long, but worth it. The burgers are fabulous (see "Best Burger," below) and under $6. See p. 176.

o **Best Hotel Bar: Bemelmans Bar,** in the Carlyle, 35 E. 76th St. (www.the carlyle.com; © **800/227-5737** or 212/744-1600). Named after illustrator Ludwig Bemelmans, who created the *Madeline* books and painted the mural, this romantic, charming bar features white-gloved service and classic cocktails. See p. 434.

o **Best Hotel for a Romantic Tryst: Hotel Elysée,** 60 E. 54th St. (www.elysee hotel.com; © **800/535-9733** or 212/753-1066). This lovely old hotel, a favorite of mid-20th-century writers and actors, is discreetly ensconced between two mammoth office buildings and is the perfect romantic hideaway in the middle of Manhattan. See p. 118.

o **Best Hotel Swim-Up Bar: Room Mate Grace Hotels,** 125 W. 45th St. (www.room-matehotels.com; © **212/354-2323**). There is much to like about the Grace, but I love the fact that it has a swimming pool—in the lobby—with a swim-up bar. You can't ask for much more in the middle of Manhattan. See p. 112.

- **Best Hotel Pool: The Greenwich Hotel,** 377 Greenwich St (www.the greenwichhotel.com; ☏ **212/941-8900**). Robert DeNiro's baby features a Japanese-inspired pool housed under a bamboo roof from a 250-year-old farmhouse. See p. 91.

- **Best New Hotel: The Setai,** 400 Fifth Avenue (http://setaififthavenue.com; ☏ **212/695-4005**): In a 60-story tower, this combination residences and hotel offers five star service, large modern rooms, views galore, a Michael White-run restaurant, and one of the top spas and salons in the city. See p. 118.

- **Best Hotel View of New Jersey: Ink48,** 653 11th Ave. (www.ink48.com; ☏ **212/757-0088**) This new Kimpton property on the far west side of Manhattan offers typically good Kimpton service and unobstructed views of the USS *Intrepid* battleship, the Hudson River, and the hills of New Jersey beyond. See p. 112.

- **Best Hotel View not in Manhattan: Hotel Le Bleu,** 370 Fourth Ave., Brooklyn (www.hotellebleu.com; ☏ **718/625-1500**). Look past the nearby U-Haul

WHAT'S NEW IN accommodations

New York added 6,600 hotel rooms in 2010. In 2011 there are even more to come. Some of the early openings of 2011 include the 55-room **Nolitan** (www.nolitanhotel.com) in, where else, but NoLita, at 30 Kenmare Street, the first major hotel to open in that small slice of cutely named, expensive real estate.

Also opened in spring 2011 was the **Mondrian Soho,** a member of the Morgan's Hotel Group. The 270-room **Mondrian Soho,** is the second hotel to open on tiny Crosby Street in the past few years. **The Crosby Street Hotel** (p. 93) being the other.

Moving a bit further uptown to the Flatiron District, is the cleverly named, 64-room **Flatiron Hotel.** At Broadway and 26th Street, the Flatiron Hotel, which at press time had not opened yet, will be across from Madison Square Park and very close to the penultimate food court, **Eataly** (see chapter 5) and will feature a two-story aquarium in its lobby. In the Rockefeller Center Area, the **Cassa Hotel and Residences** at 70 W. 45th St. finally made its much-postponed opening in late 2010.

Besides the Hyatt openings of their Wall Street and Fifth Avenue boutique branch, Andaz Hotels, the **Grand Hyatt New York** underwent a $130 million renovation transforming the hotel's 1,311-rooms into a more sleek, modern "Manhattan" look.

Also in the works from Hyatt is a new property called **Hyatt48Lex.** Guess where it's located?

Another big hotel brand, Hilton, as in Conrad, has plans to transform the Embassy Suites, at 102 North End, in New York's Financial District into a **Conrad Hotel.** No dates for the transformation were given at press time.

Finally, the biggest news in the New York hotel scene was that the legendary **Hotel Chelsea** was up for sale. The home for a time for luminaries such as playwright Arthur Miller, singers Janis Joplin and Patti Smith, has been immortalized in songs by Bob Dylan and Leonard Cohen, and even in a film, *Chelsea Girls,* made by Andy Warhol. The sale price is around $100 million if anyone is interested in picking up a New York icon for a souvenir.

garage and the murky Gowanus Canal just below and you'll see the skyline of lower Manhattan, the Statue of Liberty, the F train as it snakes into Manhattan, and, looking east, the rooftops and churches of Park Slope.

SOUTH STREET SEAPORT & THE FINANCIAL DISTRICT

Though you are far away from the bustle of midtown and most of the attractions uptown, there are benefits to staying in the Financial District. Busy during the day, the Financial District empties at night creating an almost serene calm to the neighborhood. Weekends are also quiet and as a result there are some substantial savings to be found when staying at a Financial District hotel on a weekend.

Very Expensive

Ritz-Carlton New York, Battery Park ★★★   Perfect on almost every level, the only drawback to this Ritz-Carlton is that it's so far downtown. But the location, on the extreme southern tip of Manhattan, is also one of its strengths. Where else can you get, in most rooms anyway, magnificent views of New York Harbor from your bedroom—complete with telescope for close-ups of Lady Liberty? And where else can you have a cocktail in your hotel bar and watch the sun set over the harbor? This modern, Art Deco–influenced high-rise differs from the English-countryside look of most Ritz-Carltons, including its sister hotel on Central Park (p. 105), but that's where the differences end. You'll find the full slate of comforts and services typical of Ritz-Carlton, from Frette-dressed feather beds to the chain's signature **Bath Butler,** who will draw a scented bath in your own deep soaking tub. If you don't mind the location and the commute to Midtown and beyond, you won't find a more luxurious choice.

2 West St., New York, NY 10004. www.ritzcarlton.com/batterypark. ✆ **800/241-3333** or 212/344-0800. Fax 212/344-3801. 298 units. $315–$545 double; from $625 suite. Check website for weekend packages. AE, DC, DISC, MC, V. Valet parking $60. Subway: 4 or 5 to Bowling Green. Pets under 20 lbs. accepted. **Amenities:** Restaurant; bar; lobby lounge for light meals and cocktails; Ritz-Carlton Club Level w/five food presentations daily; concierge; state-of-the-art health

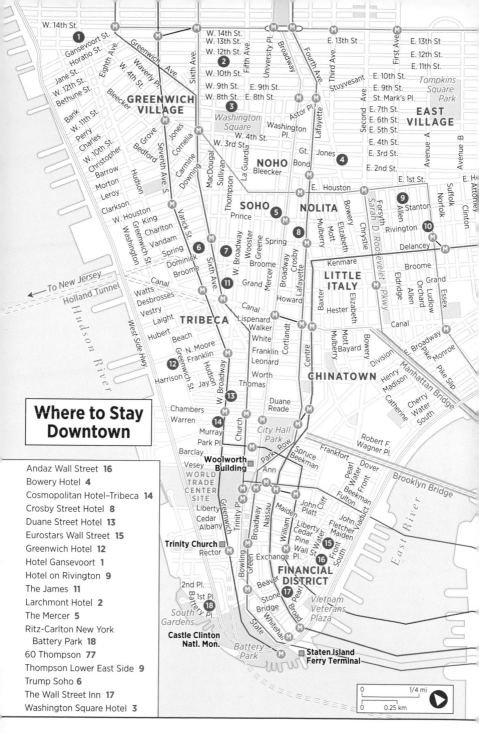

Where to Stay Downtown

club w/panoramic views; room service; technology butler and bath butler services. *In room:* A/C, TV w/pay movies and video games, DVD w/surround sound in suites and Club rooms, CD player, fridge, hair dryer, minibar, Wi-Fi.

Expensive/Moderate

Andaz Wall Street ★★   The first of Hyatt Hotel & Resorts' new Andaz collection to open in New York debuted with a Wall Street address in early 2010. Offering a more personal, less corporate alternative to the Hyatt brand, Andaz delivers with stellar results: personalized check-in; a communal living room–like lobby where wine and coffee are complimentary daily; a state-of-the-art spa and fitness facility; and spacious rooms, many with bathrooms where huge soaking tubs peek into the bedroom. Like its neighborhood, the Andaz is high tech-y; rooms are economical in their use of space, with a rotating wall that includes a full-size mirror, closet, and minibar. Floor-to-ceiling soundproof windows offer plenty of light, including some with panoramic downtown views. The Andaz is a welcome new addition to an area that doesn't offer much boutique lodging.

75 Wall St. (at Water St.), New York, NY 10005. www.andazwallstreet.com. ☏ **212/590-1234.** Fax 212/590-1238. 253 units. AE, DISC, MC, V. From $275 double. Parking from $35. Subway: 2 or 3 to Wall St. **Amenities:** Restaurant; bar; concierge; fitness center and spa; room service. *In room:* A/C, TV, hair dryer, complimentary snacks and nonalcoholic-beverage minibar, Geneva sound system, unlimited local calls, Wi-Fi (free).

Eurostars Wall Street ★   This cozy hotel is a solid midpriced choice if you are looking for a downtown location. A short walk from Wall Street, the South Street Seaport, Brooklyn Bridge, and Chinatown, the Eurostars Hotel features personalized service and a few perks such as free Wi-Fi and a complimentary continental breakfast. Recently renovated in a sleek, contemporary style, standard and deluxe guest rooms are on the small size, but are outfitted nicely, including plasma televisions. The suites are roomy with a separate living room, black-leather furniture, and a full-size kitchen. Bathrooms are tight in both the guest rooms and suites, and sadly include those very fashionable marble bowl sinks that look good, but don't leave much space for any of your toiletries.

129 Front St. (btw. Wall and Pine sts.), New York, NY 10005. www.exchangehotel.com. ☏ **212/742-0003.** Fax 212/742-0124. 53 units. AE, DC, MC, V. $129–$389 double; $310–$469 suite. Parking $25. Subway: 2 or 3 to Wall St. **Amenities:** Lounge; access to nearby fitness club; complimentary continental breakfast. *In room:* A/C, TV/VCR, full-size kitchens in suites, microwave, minifridge, Wi-Fi (free).

The Wall Street Inn ★ 🛏   This intimate hotel is a good, moderate choice for those working or not working on the Street. This intimate, seven-story hotel is ideal for those who want a lower Manhattan location without corporate blandness. The lovely early American interiors boast a pleasing freshness. The hotel is warm, comforting, and serene, and the friendly, professional staff offers the kind of personalized service you won't get from a chain. Rooms aren't huge, but the bedding is top quality and all the conveniences are at hand. Rooms ending in "01" are smallest; seventh-floor rooms are best, as the bathrooms have extra counter space and whirlpool tubs.

9 S. William St. (at Broad St.), New York, NY 10004. www.thewallstreetinn.com. ☏ **800/747-1500** or 212/747-1500. Fax 212/747-1900. 46 units. $269–$450 double. Rates include continental breakfast. Ask about corporate, group, and/or deeply discounted weekend rates (as low as

$265 at press time). AE, DC, DISC, MC, V. Parking $36 nearby. Subway: 2 or 3 to Wall St.; 4 or 5 to Bowling Green. **Amenities:** Babysitting; concierge; well-outfitted exercise room w/sauna and steam; common guest kitchen w/microwave. *In room:* A/C, HDTV, fax, fridge, Wi-Fi (free).

TRIBECA & THE LOWER EAST SIDE

Arguably the most expensive real estate in New York, TriBeCa is a mostly residential neighborhood with numerous good restaurants. The hotel options, though limited, offer a taste of life on the far west side. The Lower East Side's resurgence in the past decade has been remarkable. What once was just housing projects and tenements is now home to some of the city's most vibrant clubs and hippest restaurants. Both TriBeCa and the Lower East Side are a little off the beaten track in terms of touring the city, but offer a taste of New York neighborhood living.

To locate the hotels in this section, see the map on p. 89.

Very Expensive

The Greenwich Hotel ★★★   Built from the ground up, the Greenwich Hotel, like the **Bowery Hotel** (p. 95), is a combination of modern meets rustic in design. The building was crafted with handmade bricks, reclaimed wood, and furniture from antique stores and flea markets throughout the world. Each tile of the lobby terra cotta–and-marble floors is hand-molded, and the courtyard features Turkish travertine. No guest room is alike, whether it is a Tibetan silk rug in one or the Moroccan tile used in the bathrooms. The uniqueness does not automatically make a great hotel. First and foremost for are comfort and service, and the Greenwich provides both. The rooms are airy and quiet; some have Hudson River views. The hotel has a Japanese-inspired spa, including a pool surrounded by a 250-year-old Japanese farmhouse assembled without using a single nail. You might find the location a bit too far away from the heart of the city, but maybe in this case, that's the point.

> ### Pet Policies
>
> I've indicated in the listings in this chapter those hotels that accept pets. However, understand that these policies may have limitations, such as weight and breed restrictions; may require a deposit and/or a signed waiver against damages; and may be revoked at any time. Always inquire when booking if you're bringing Fluffy or Spike—*never* just show up with a pet in tow.

377 Greenwich St. (btw. N. Moore and Franklin sts.), New York, NY 10013. www.thegreenwich hotel.com. (℗ **212/941-8900.** Fax 212/941-8600. 88 units. $450–$725 double. Valet parking $55. AE, DC, DISC, MC, V. Subway: 1 to Franklin St. **Amenities:** Restaurant; bar; lobby lounge and outdoor courtyard; concierge; fitness center; pool; room service; spa. *In room:* A/C, TV, hair dryer, complimentary minibar (alcoholic beverages excluded), MP3 docking stations, Wi-Fi (free).

Expensive

The Hotel on Rivington ★★   The contrast of a 21-story, glass-tower luxury hotel in the midst of 19th- and early-20th-century Lower East Side tenement buildings is a striking, but accurate, representation of what that neighborhood has become. From the floor-to-ceiling windows of your room, surrounded by amenities such as flatscreen TVs, Japanese soaking tubs in the bathrooms, and Tempur-Pedic mattresses, not only do you have incredible, unobstructed city views, but you also can look down and spot Lower East Side landmarks such as the sign for the Schapiro Kosher wine factory. You will be in a location where old-world customs and institutions coexist with the new and the supercool. Along with the views, most of the rooms have terraces, the option of in-room spa services, and heated, tiled floors in the bathrooms where you can enjoy your view of the city as you bathe.

107 Rivington St. (btw. Ludlow and Essex sts.), New York, NY 10002. www.hotelonrivington.com. ℂ 212/475-2600. Fax 212/475-5959. 110 units. From $395 double. AE, DC, MC, V. Parking $50. Subway: F to Delancey St. **Amenities:** Restaurant; concierge; fitness center; room service. *In room:* A/C, TV, CD players and JBL On Stage iPod speaker system available, fridge, hair dryer.

Thompson LES ★   Of all the Thompson properties, none better embody the Thompson urban chic trademark "industrial" look than this 18-story glass tower in the now chicly urban industrial-looking Lower East Side. I had no problem getting comfortable in my sizable (most average 425-sq.-ft. or larger) room, with a Lee Friedlander photograph illuminated above the bed's headboard. The art throughout the hotel comes from Andy Warhol and his circle of artists, and no disrespect to them, but I spent more time staring out my floor-to-ceiling window (all rooms have them) at the magnificent view it offered of lower Manhattan and beyond. On the rooftop is an outdoor pool with a portrait of Andy Warhol on the bottom, and a bar; just above the lobby is the highly rated restaurant, **Shang.**

190 Allen St. (btw. Houston and Ludlow sts.), New York, NY 10002. www.thompsonhotels.com. ℂ 212/460-5300. Fax 212/542-8685. 141 units. $329–$429 double; $500–$2,500 suite. AE, DC, DISC, MC, V. Parking $46. Subway: F to Second Ave. **Amenities:** Restaurant; 2 bars; concierge; fitness club; outdoor heated pool; spa services. *In room:* A/C, TV, minibar, MP3 docking stations, Wi-Fi (free).

Moderate

Duane Street Hotel ★ 🏨   Small and cozy, the Duane Street Hotel is a perfect fit for vibrant TriBeCa. The rooms are on the small size and designed with IKEA-ish furnishings, but like the loft apartments in the neighborhood, the walls are hardwood, the ceilings are high, and the windows are large, providing more of a sense of space. Bathrooms are spacious and well outfitted, with showers equipped with rain shower heads. Every room has a good-size desk and a 32-inch plasma HDTV. Best of all is the personable, extremely helpful staff that seems to enjoy doing the little extras to improve your stay.

130 Duane St. (at Church St.), New York, NY 10013. www.duanestreethotel.com. ℂ 212/964-4600. Fax 212/964-4800. 45 units. $259–$799 double. AE, DC, DISC, MC, V. Subway: A or C to Chambers St. **Amenities:** Restaurant; concierge. *In room:* A/C, TV, CD player, hair dryer, spa services, Wi-Fi (free).

Inexpensive

Cosmopolitan Hotel–Tribeca ★ 🏨   Behind a plain-vanilla TriBeCa awning is one of the best hotel deals in Manhattan for budget travelers who prefer a private bathroom. Everything is strictly budget but nice: The modern IKEA-ish furniture includes a work desk and an armoire (a few rooms have a dresser and hanging rack instead); for a few extra bucks, you can have a love seat, too. Beds are comfy, and sheets and towels are of good quality. Rooms are small but make the most of the limited space, and the entire place is pristine. The two-level minilofts have lots of character, but expect to duck on the second level. Management does a great job of keeping everything fresh. The TriBeCa location is safe, superhip, and subway convenient. Services are kept at a bare minimum to keep costs down, so you must be a low-maintenance guest to be happy here.

95 W. Broadway (at Chambers St.), New York, NY 10007. www.cosmohotel.com. ℂ **888/895-9400** or 212/566-1900. Fax 212/566-6909. 105 units. $200–$270 double (Internet specials as low as $129). AE, DC, MC, V. Subway: 1, 2, 3, A, or C to Chambers St. *In room:* A/C, ceiling fan, TV.

SOHO

Despite numerous chain stores moving into SoHo, the area is still the heart and soul of downtown fashion. But at these prices, you'll find no grunge in SoHo. The neighborhood is strictly high end now. A stay in the SoHo area offers close proximity to Chinatown, designer-name shopping, and some very fine restaurants.

To locate the hotels in this section, see the map on p. 89.

Very Expensive

Crosby Street Hotel ★★   Following the trend of the Gramercy Park Hotel, the Bowery, and the Greenwich, the Crosby Street Hotel features individually designed rooms complete with hand-picked art and furniture combined with the newest in high-tech amenities. London-based Firmdale Hotels, constructed the 11-story hotel on quiet, cobblestoned Crosby Street in the heart of SoHo; the hotel, recessed somewhat from the street, blends in with the neighborhood's distinctive cast-iron architecture. The rooms all feature floor-to-ceiling warehouse-style windows—some with amazing downtown Manhattan views, especially from the upper floors. Designed with bright colors, including some in pink and violet and unusual furniture, the spacious rooms are quirky yet cozy. The lavish bathrooms feature heated towel racks and bidets. A courtyard and garden, screening room, and "drawing room" add to the hotel's wonderfulness. And knowing that the hotel is environmentally responsible and aims for a GOLD LEED certification makes indulging in all that extravagance almost guilt-free.

79 Crosby St. (btw. Prince and Spring sts.), New York, NY 10012. www.crosbystreethotel.com. ℂ **212/226-6400.** Fax 212/226-0055. 86 units. From $495 double; from $815 suite. AE, DC, DISC, MC, V. Parking $55–$65. Subway: N or R to Prince St. **Amenities:** Restaurant; bar; concierge; fitness center; room service; screening room. *In room:* A/C, TV, Bose iPod docking stations, minibar, Wi-Fi (free).

The James   Built new in 2010, the tall and slender James has its own little niche of space just off Canal at the juncture of TriBeCa and SoHo. As a result, views abound from the big windows of the guest rooms and the hotel's very trendy rooftop bar, the **Jimmy.** The downtown location, which might be a bit remote for some, attracts hipsters from the fashion, film, and art. Though check-in is a bit clumsy; the lobby is a floor above the entrance, the rooms are nicely appointed, flowing with light and with big bathrooms, some with windows that peek out into the rooms. I wouldn't have minded a desk as opposed to the small round table that was in my room. A rooftop outdoor pool and an urban garden and herb garden off the second floor lobby add to the James's appeal. At press time, a restaurant was in the works.

27 Grand Street (at Sixth Avenue), New York, NY 10013. www.jameshotels.com. ℂ **888/526-3778.** 114 units. $599–$899 double. Check website for specials. AE, DISC, MC, V. Subway: 1 to

Canal St. **Amenities:** Restaurant; bar; concierge; rooftop pool; fitness center with complimentary training sessions; pet friendly; room service. *In room:* A/C, iPod docking station, Wi-Fi (free).

The Mercer ★★★   One of the first and the best of the downtown hip and trendy hotels, the Mercer is a place where even those who represent the antithesis of hip (and I'm speaking personally) can feel at home. Though SoHo can be a bit over the top with its high-end boutiques, restaurants, and a constant parade of too-serious fashionistas, it is still an exciting place. And the hotel's location at the corner of Mercer and Prince streets is probably the epicenter of SoHo. Yet once inside, there is a pronounced calm—from the postmodern library lounge and the relaxed Mizrahi-clad staff, to the huge soundproof loftlike guest rooms; the hotel is a perfect complement to the scene outside your big window. The Mercer is one of the few New York hotels with ceiling fans, and even if you don't need them, they look nice whirring above your comfortable bed. The tile-and-marble bathrooms have a steel cart for storage, and an oversize shower stall or oversize two-person tub (state your preference when booking).

147 Mercer St. (at Prince St.), New York, NY 10012. www.mercerhotel.com. ✆ **888/918-6060** or 212/966-6060. Fax 212/965-3838. 75 units. $495–$695 double; $710–$895 studio; from $1,600 suite. AE, DC, DISC, MC, V. Parking $55 nearby. Subway: N or R to Prince St. **Amenities:** Restaurant; lounge; food and drink service in lobby; concierge; free access to nearby Equinox fitness center; book, magazine, video, DVD, and CD libraries; room service. *In room:* A/C, ceiling fan, TV/DVD, CD player, minibar, MP3 docking stations, Wi-Fi (free).

Trump SoHo ★★   The 21st century rendition of the prototypical brooding Trump monolith debuted in early 2010 in a slightly more edgy SoHo location. What makes the 46-story hotel somewhat different than other Trump efforts is that it actually tries to incorporate some of the neighborhood's artistic tradition in its design. Despite those efforts, Trump bigness prevails—and in this case, that's not a bad thing. The lobby, created by the renowned Rockwell group, features soft chocolate tones, vertical screens, and slender columns that reflect the obvious verticality of space. Rooms are typically spacious, ranging from 420 to 540 square feet while one-bedroom suites are positively jumbo-sized, peaking at over 900 square-feet. Views are spectacular and unobstructed in all directions. The hotel also features an outdoor pool, indoor/outdoor bar, and an 11,000 square-foot spa. At a Trump hotel, service is impeccable and the guests are always the boss, never the apprentice.

246 Spring Street (at Varick St.) New York, NY 10013. www.trumpsohohotel.com. ✆ **212/842-5500.** Fax 212/842-5501. 391 units. AE, DC, DISC, MC, V. Rates from $459 double. Parking $65. Subway: C, E to Spring St. **Amenities:** Restaurant, 2 bars, concierge, fitness center, 24 hr. room service, pool, spa, Trump attaché services. *In room:* A/C, TV, MP3 player, Control 4 interface system, Wi-Fi (free).

THE VILLAGE & MEATPACKING DISTRICT

Greenwich Village, despite the influx of big name stores, still has that romantic appeal with its winding, narrow streets, charmingly expensive brownstones, and intimate dining spots. The Meatpacking District has become a hotbed for celebrities and wannabes, with its plethora of fashionable clubs and restaurants, while the East Village, once a hippie outpost, is now the bastion of NYU students and youngsters on trust funds. Still, the streets are exciting and the food options probably the most varied in the city.

To locate the hotels in this section, see the map on p. 89.

Expensive

The Bowery Hotel ★★   Despite the history associated with its name and location, the Bowery Hotel is about as far from a flophouse as you could imagine. Standing alone in the heart of NoHo, the Bowery Hotel has that burnished, dark-wood look inside, most evident in the expansive lobby with a fireplace, comfy velvet draperies and furniture, vintage paneling, Moroccan tiles, and an adjoining outdoor area complete with plush lounge chairs. The rooms—and no two are the same—are very large and airy by New York standards with high ceilings and ceiling fans, many with huge terraces, and all with spectacular views. What the Gansevoort Hotel did for the Meatpacking District, the Bowery Hotel is doing for the Bowery—making a once-desolate area a hip destination.

335 Bowery (at 3rd St.), New York, NY 10003. www.theboweryhotel.com. ⓒ **212/505-9100.** Fax 212/505-9700. 135 units. From $375 double; from $675 suite. AE, DISC, MC, V. Parking $31 self-parking, $45 valet. Subway: 4, 6 to Bleecker St. **Amenities:** Restaurant; bar; concierge; room service. *In room:* A/C, HDTV/DVD, hair dryer, iPod stereo and MP3 docking system, minibar, Wi-Fi (free).

Gansevoort Meatpacking Hotel ★★   Despite its potentially excessive trendiness, the 14-floor, zinc-colored Gansevoort offers excellent, personable service. As well, rooms are a good size with comfortable furnishings in soft tones and high-tech amenities such as plasma televisions. Suites have a living room and separate bedroom, and some have small balconies and bay windows. Corner suites offer adjoining guest rooms for families or larger parties. The generous-size bathrooms are done up in ceramic, stainless steel, and marble and are impeccably appointed. In all the guest rooms and throughout the hotel, original art by New York artists is on display. The **G Spa,** a 5,000-square-foot spa and fitness center, and the indoor/outdoor **O Bar** are destinations unto themselves.

18 Ninth Ave. (at 13th St.), New York, NY 10014. www.hotelgansevoort.com. ⓒ **877/426-7386** or 212/206-6700. Fax 212/255-5858. 187 units. From $425 double; from $675 suite. Parking $40. Subway: A, C, or E to 14th St. Pet-friendly floors. **Amenities:** Restaurant; 2 bars; 2 lounges; concierge; fitness center; indoor/outdoor rooftop pool; rooftop garden; room service; spa. *In room:* A/C, TV, hair dryer, minibar, Wi-Fi (free).

Inexpensive

Larchmont Hotel ⚑   If you're willing to share a bathroom, it's hard to do better for the money at this wonderful European-style hotel. Each bright guest room is tastefully done in rattan and outfitted with a writing desk, a minilibrary of books, an alarm clock, a wash basin, and a few extras that you normally have to pay a lot more for, such as cotton bathrobes, slippers, and ceiling fans. Every floor has two shared bathrooms (with hair dryers) and a small, simple kitchen. The management is constantly renovating, so everything feels clean and fresh. What's more, those looking for a hip downtown base couldn't be better situated, because some of the city's best shopping, dining, and sightseeing—plus your choice of subway lines—are just a walk away. This hotel has devoted followers who recommend it to all their friends, so book *well* in advance (the management suggests 6–7 weeks' lead time).

When you think of accommodations in New York, you usually think big—tall monoliths with hundreds of rooms. You don't think of quaint antiques-laden guesthouses or inns where a home-cooked breakfast is served. But New York is a diverse city, and that diversity can be found in its accommodations, too. If you want an alternative to the quintessential huge hotel and would prefer a taste of urban hominess, here are a few options.

On the steep end of the economic scale, but worth the price (if 19th-century Victorian romance is what you are seeking), is the fabulous **Inn at Irving Place** ★★ (pictured at the right). Housed in a 170-year-old town house, its lodgings range from $445 to $645 a night and the rooms are named after late-19th- or early-20th-century New Yorkers, some inspired by the works of Edith Wharton and Henry James. Complimentary breakfast is served in Lady Mendl's parlor, where, if the weather is nippy, you'll find a comforting fire roaring. See p. 103 for a detailed review.

Breakfast prepared by culinary students of the New School is one of the highlights of the **Inn on 23rd Street** ★★★. Each of the inn's 14 rooms, which range from $219 to $359 a night, is distinctly decorated by the personable owners, Annette and Barry Fisherman, with items they've collected from their travels over the years. See p. 98 for a detailed review.

Now 25 years old, the first home of the Gay Men's Health Crisis, an 1850 brownstone in the heart of Chelsea, is now the charming **Colonial House Inn,** 318 W. 22nd St., between Eighth and Ninth avenues (www.colonialhouseinn. com; ✆ **800/689-3779** or 212/243-9669). This 20-room four-story walk-up

caters to a largely GLBT clientele, but everybody is welcome, and straight couples are a common sight. Some rooms have shared bathrooms; deluxe rooms have private bathrooms, and some have working fireplaces. There's a roof deck with a clothing-optional area. Breakfast is included in the rates, which range from $130 to $150 a night for a room with a shared bathroom or $180 for a deluxe room with private bath.

On the increasingly popular, yet still residential, Upper West Side is the very special **Inn New York City** ★★★, 266 W. 71st St., between Amsterdam and West End avenues (www.innnewyorkcity. com; ✆ **212/580-1900**), where there are just four unique, rustic self-contained units so comfortable you will be hard pressed to leave and see much of the city. See p. 126 for a detailed review.

Also on the Upper West Side is the aptly named **Country Inn the City** ★, 270 W. 77th St., between Broadway and West End Avenue (www.countryinnthe city.com; ✆ **212/580-4183**). This 1891 town house has only four rooms, but all are spacious, quaintly decorated, and equipped with full kitchens. Rates range from $210 to $350 a night (check for last-minute specials as low as $200 per night), and include breakfast items in your refrigerator. But you're on your

27 W. 11th St. (btw. Fifth and Sixth aves.), New York, NY 10011. www.larchmonthotel.com. ✆ **212/989-9333.** Fax 212/989-9496. 62 units, all with shared bathroom. $90–$125 single; $119–$165 double. Rates include continental breakfast. Children 12 and under stay free in parent's room. AE, MC, V. Parking $25 nearby. Subway: A, B, C, D, E, F, or M to W. 4th St. (use 8th St. exit). **Amenities:** Common kitchenette; MP3 docking stations. *In room:* A/C, ceiling fan, TV, hair dryer.

4

WHERE TO STAY | The Village & Meatpacking District

own in many respects; there is no resident innkeeper and a maid services your room only every few days. Still, if you are the independent sort, the inn's charm makes it an excellent choice.

If you want the genuine New York brownstone experience, go to Harlem. It's anything but a flophouse, but that's what they call **Harlem Flophouse,** 242 W. 123rd St., between Adam Clayton Powell and Frederick Douglass boulevards (www.harlemflophouse.com; ✆ **212/662-0678**). Owner René Calvo has restored the historic row house to Harlem Renaissance splendor, when the "flophouse" was frequented by top musicians and artists of that era. If you visit in the summer, you just might get invited to one of Calvo's impromptu barbecues. Rates ($100–$175 a night) include Wi-Fi; for $15 extra you get a full breakfast.

Like Harlem, Brooklyn boasts a number of historic districts with restored brownstones, some of which have been converted to inns. One of the most interesting is **Akwaaba Mansion,** 347 MacDonough St. (www.akwaaba.com; ✆ **866/INN-DULJ** [466-3855] or 718/455-5958), a restored 1860s Italianate villa in Bedford-Stuyvesant, outfitted with Afro-centric elegance. Four suites are available in the 18-room home, each with private bathroom with either a claw-foot or a Jacuzzi tub ($160–$175 double)—including a hearty, Southern-style breakfast.

The historic neighborhood of Park Slope is the heart of brownstone Brooklyn and home to **Bed & Breakfast on the Park,** 113 Prospect Park West (www.bbnyc.com; ✆ **718/499-6115**). In an 1895 Victorian town house across the street from Prospect Park, this inn has two beautifully outfitted units (from $295). A sumptuous breakfast is served in the formal dining room. Six more rooms with private bathrooms are available for guests who are willing to splurge.

Washington Square Hotel Popular with a young international crowd, this affordable hotel sits behind a pretty facade facing Washington Square Park (historically Henry James territory, now the midst of NYU) in the heart of Greenwich Village. The lobby is a pleasant place for tea in the afternoon and cocktails in the evening. The rooms are tiny and each comes with a firm bed, a private bathroom, and a small closet. It's worth paying a few extra dollars for a south-facing room on a high floor, since the others can be a bit dark. Bathrooms were also renovated, with the addition of granite counters.

103 Waverly Place (btw. Fifth and Sixth aves.), New York, NY 10011. www.wshotel.com. © **800/ 222-0418** or 212/777-9515. Fax 212/979-8373. 160 units. $199–$250 single; $210–$400 double; $225–$450 quad. Rates include continental breakfast. Inquire about special rates and jazz packages. AE, MC, V. Parking $30 nearby. Subway: A, B, C, D, E, F, or M to W. 4th St. (use 3rd St. exit). **Amenities:** Restaurant and lounge; exercise room. *In room:* A/C, TV, hair dryer, free high-speed Internet.

CHELSEA

Now the center of modern art in Manhattan, Chelsea has also surpassed the West Village as the most prominent gay community in the city. You'll find some great dining in Chelsea, and it's just a short walk to the shopping of Herald Square, Union Square, Madison Square Garden, and the Empire State Building.

Expensive

Eventi ★ Kimpton Hotel's (Ink 48, the Muse, 70 Park) newest (2010) New York property is also its most ambitious and offers probably the only luxury lodging in an otherwise barren (of hotels) stretch of Sixth Avenue north of Chelsea and south of Herald Square. Despite the pioneering location, close to the Garment District, the sprawling 59-story Eventi features the spacious food court **FoodParc** (p. 166); an outdoor plaza with a 20-foot wide multimedia screen; and 16 rooms of meeting space including a screening room which attract a large business, fashion, and arts clientele. Equally spacious are the well-outfitted rooms, many of which have open city views and touches like the Kimpton standard nightly complimentary wine reception. A comfortable choice for both business and leisure travelers.

851 Sixth Ave. (btw. 29th & 30th sts.), New York, NY, 10001. www.eventihotel.com. © **212/564-4567.** Fax 212/564-6825. 292 units. $349–$549 double. Check website for specials. AE, DISC, MC, V. Subway: B, D, F, M, N, R, Q to 34th Street. **Amenities:** Restaurant; food court; concierge; fitness center; room service; spa. *In room:* A/C, TV, mini-bar, iHome sound system, Wi-Fi (free).

Moderate

Inn on 23rd Street ★★★ 🎁 Behind an unassuming entrance on bustling 23rd Street is one of New York's lodging treasures: a real urban bed-and-breakfast with as personal a touch as you will find. All 14 guest rooms are spacious. Each has a king or queen bed outfitted with a comfy pillow-top mattress and top-quality linens, satellite TV, a private bathroom with Turkish towels, and a roomy closet. Rooms have themes: There's the Rosewood Room, with '60s built-ins; the elegantly Asian Bamboo Room; and Ken's Cabin, a lodgelike room with cushy, well-worn leather furnishings and wonderful Americana relics. The inn features a library where the complimentary breakfast is served, and a (cheap!) honor bar, and where wine and cheese are served on Friday and Saturday. The only drawback is that the inn is so comfortable, you might be tempted to lounge around instead of getting out on the town.

131 W. 23rd St. (btw. Sixth and Seventh aves.), New York, NY 10011. www.innon23rd.com. © **877/387-2323** or 212/463-0330. Fax 212/463-0302. 14 units. $199–$300 double; $359 suite.

Rates include continental breakfast. Extra person $25. Children 11 and under stay free in parent's room. AE, DC, DISC, MC, V. Parking $20 nearby. Subway: F or 1 to 23rd St. **Amenities:** Fax and copy service; complimentary computer to do e-mail and print boarding passes; cozy library w/ stereo and VCR. *In room:* A/C, TV, hair dryer, free local and long-distance calling, Wi-Fi (free).

Inexpensive

Also consider the intimate **Colonial House Inn** (✆ 800/689-3779 or 212/243-9669). For more information, see the sidebar "Plenty of Room at the Inn," above.

Chelsea Lodge ★ 🏠   In a lovely brownstone on a landmark block in the heart of Chelsea, this small hotel is charming and a terrific value. Impeccable renovations have restored original woodwork to mint condition. The beds are the finest I've seen in this price category. The only place with a similar sensibility for the same money is the **Larchmont Hotel** (p. 95), but there, all bathroom facilities are shared; at Chelsea Lodge, each room has its own sink and in-room shower stall, so you only have to share a toilet room with your neighbors. The rooms are petite, the open closets are small, and beds are full size (queens wouldn't cut it). Considering the stylishness, the amenities, and the neighborhood, you'd be hard-pressed to do better for the money. It's best for couples rather than shares. *Tip:* Try to book no. 2A, which is bigger than most, or one of the first-floor rooms, whose high ceilings make them feel more spacious.

318 W. 20th St. (btw. Eighth and Ninth aves.), New York, NY 10011. www.chelsealodge.com. ✆ **800/373-1116** or 212/243-4499. Fax 212/243-7852. 22 units, all with semiprivate bathroom. $119 single; $129 double. AE, DC, DISC, MC, V. Parking about $27 nearby. Subway: 1 to 18th St.; C or E to 23rd St. *In room:* A/C, ceiling fan, TV, Wi-Fi (free).

UNION SQUARE, FLATIRON DISTRICT & GRAMERCY PARK

Located in the center of Manhattan, the gateway to the Flatiron District is Union Square Park with Madison Square Park, home of the original Shake Shack, bordering the neighborhood's northern extremities. Close to numerous subway lines and within easy walking distance of both Midtown and Greenwich Village downtown make the Flatiron District a convenient location. A bit further east is Gramercy Park, where you can still find very visible remnants of New York's Gilded Age.

Very Expensive

The Gansevoort Park Hotel ★★   Tamer than its Meatpacking District older sister, **Gansevoort Meatpacking Hotel** (p. 95), the Gansevoort Park, which opened in 2010, still retains much of big sister's cool glamour feel. There's the indoor/outdoor rooftop bar and plunge pool, an Exhale spa and gym, and transportation to various city locations on a first come, first serve basis in a chauffeur-driven Panamera Porsche. Rooms average a spacious 475 square feet with suites topping out at an enormous 1,500 square feet, including some with landscaped terraces and many with open midtown views. All the rooms have big desks and glass-tiled bathrooms with deep soaking tubs.

420 Park Ave. S (at 29th Street), New York, NY, 10016. www.gansevoortpark.com. ✆ **888/702-9348.** 249 units. From $495 double; from $725 suites. AE, DISC, MC, V. Parking $50. Subway: 6 to

Where to Stay in Midtown

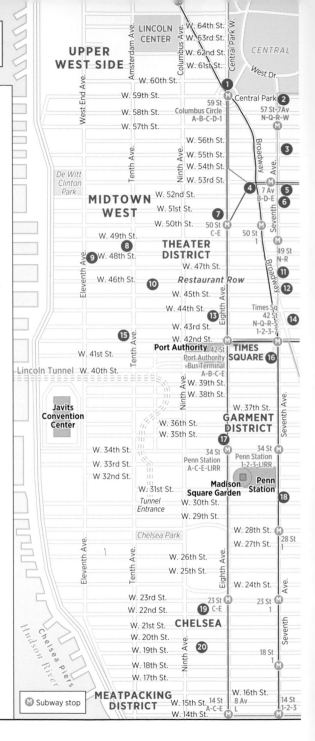

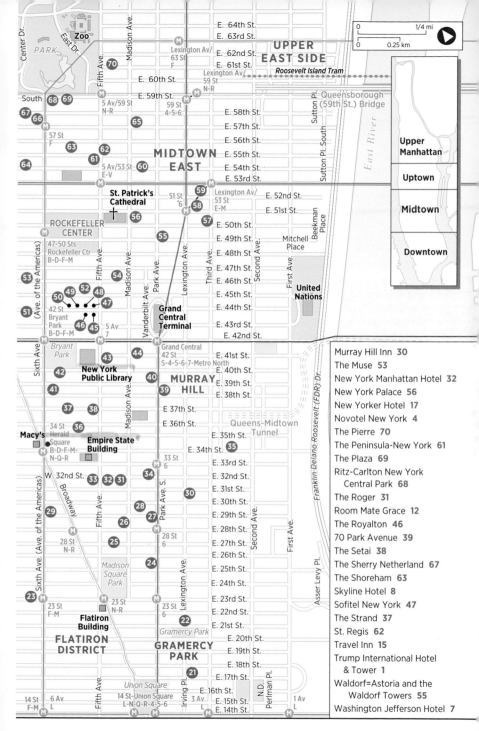

Murray Hill Inn **30**
The Muse **53**
New York Manhattan Hotel **32**
New York Palace **56**
New Yorker Hotel **17**
Novotel New York **4**
The Pierre **70**
The Peninsula-New York **61**
The Plaza **69**
Ritz-Carlton New York
  Central Park **68**
The Roger **31**
Room Mate Grace **12**
The Royalton **46**
70 Park Avenue **39**
The Setai **38**
The Sherry Netherland **67**
The Shoreham **63**
Skyline Hotel **8**
Sofitel New York **47**
The Strand **37**
St. Regis **62**
Travel Inn **15**
Trump International Hotel
  & Tower **1**
Waldorf=Astoria and the
  Waldorf Towers **55**
Washington Jefferson Hotel **7**

28th Street. **Amenities:** Restaurant; 2 bars; concierge; gym; plunge pool; room service; Exhale Spa; Cutler salon; pet friendly. *In room:* A/C, TV, iPod docking stations, hair dryer, Wi-Fi (free).

Gramercy Park Hotel ★★★ More than half of the rooms are suites at this 1925-built legend, some with views overlooking Gramercy Park. All rooms are appointed with mahogany English drinking cabinets where the minibar and DVD player are hidden, some variation of the overstuffed lounge chair, and a portrait of Schnabel's friend, the late Andy Warhol. Beds are velvet upholstered, tables feature leather tops, and photos by world-famous photojournalists adorn the walls. Bathrooms are large and feature wood-paneled walls. If you choose to leave your room, the hotel's magnificent **Rose Bar** is where you should venture first, followed by the Danny Meyer-run restaurant, **Maialino**.

2 Lexington Ave. (at 21st St.), New York, NY 10010. www.gramercyparkhotel.com. ℭ **212/920-3300.** Fax 212/673-5890. 185 units. From $595 double; from $700 suite. AE, DC, DISC, MC, V. Parking $55. Subway: 6 to 23rd St. **Amenities:** Restaurant; 2 bars; concierge; fitness center and spa; room service. *In room:* A/C, TV/DVD, CD player, hair dryer, minibar, MP3 docking station, Wi-Fi (free).

Expensive

Carlton Hotel on Madison Avenue ★★ This 1904 Beaux Arts hotel was hotel was getting worn around the edges when it was rescued by architect David Rockwell and refurbished magnificently a few years ago. The highlight is the grand, sweeping lobby complete with a marble curving staircase and a cathedral-like high ceiling. The Hotel Carlton has tried to recapture the majestic glory of the past blended with New Age nods such as contemporary furnishings in the lobby along with a bubbling, two-story waterfall. Rooms are a generous size and retain that Beaux Arts motif with the addition of modern amenities. The marble bathrooms offer plenty of counter space; some rooms have bathtubs, while others just have showers. The fine restaurant **Millesime** (p. 168) also offers room service.

88 Madison Ave. (btw. 28th and 29th sts.), New York, NY 10016. www.carltonhotelny.com. ℭ **800/601-8500** or 212/532-4100. Fax 212/889-8683. 316 units. $295–$550 double; from $750 suite. AE, DC, DISC, MC, V. Valet parking $40. Subway: 6 to 28th St./Lexington Ave. **Amenities:** Restaurant; 2 bars; concierge; gym; room service. *In room:* A/C, TV, MP3 docking station/clock radio, Wi-Fi (free).

Hotel Giraffe ★★ In the fashionable Madison Park area, this hotel is a real charmer with a calm, intimate feel. Guest rooms are stylish, evoking an urban European character, with high ceilings, velveteen upholstered chairs, and black-and-white photographs from the 1920s and 1930s. All the rooms are good size, with high ceilings, while deluxe rooms and suites feature French doors that lead to small balconies with large windows and remote-controlled blackout shades. Bathrooms are spacious, with plenty of marble counter space and glass-paneled doors. But what really separates this hotel from so many others are its services: A continental breakfast is included in the rate and served in the hotel's lobby, where coffee, cookies, and tea are available all afternoon, and wine, cheese, and piano music are offered each evening. There is also a lovely rooftop garden.

365 Park Ave. South (at 26th St.), New York, NY 10016. www.hotelgiraffe.com. ℭ **877/296-0009** or 212/685-7700. Fax 212/685-7771. 73 units. $350–$421 double; from $460 1- or 2-bedroom suite; from $2,500 penthouse suite. Rates include continental breakfast and evening wine and

cheese accompanied by piano music. Check website or ask about reduced rates (as low as $269 at press time). AE, DC, MC, V. Parking $28. Subway: 6 to 28th St. **Amenities:** Restaurant; 2 bars; concierge; complimentary access to nearby gym; room service; video and CD libraries; rooftop garden. *In room:* A/C, TV/VCR, CD player, hair dryer, minibar, Wi-Fi (free).

Inn at Irving Place ★★   This 170-year-old town house offers antique charm more easily found in the Berkshires than in the heart of what used to be Silicon Alley. All rooms are spacious, with period antique furniture and art, nonworking fireplaces, and big bathrooms with pedestal sinks and brass fixtures, while the junior suites feature small but luxurious sitting areas. The rooms are named for famous 19th-century New Yorkers such as Edith Wharton, O. Henry, and Washington Irving. The Madame Olenska (bonus points if you know who she was) junior suite features a king bed and a window nook overlooking Irving Place where you can curl up with a glass of sherry or a cup of tea. Breakfast in bed, tea served in your room, or in-room massages can all be easily arranged by the inn's helpful staff.

56 Irving Place (btw. 17th and 18th sts.), New York, NY 10003. www.innatirving.com. © **800/685-1447** or 212/533-4600. Fax 212/533-4611. 12 units. From $415 double; from $545 suite. Extra person $25. Rates include continental breakfast. 2-night minimum on weekends. AE, DC, MC, V. Parking $25–$30 nearby. Subway: N, R, 4, 5, or 6 to 14th St./Union Sq. No children 11 or under. **Amenities:** 2 restaurants; lounge; concierge; access to nearby health club; room service; video and CD libraries. *In room:* A/C, TV/VCR, CD player, fax machines and laptops on request, hair dryer, minibar, MP3 docking station.

Inexpensive

Gershwin Hotel ★ ☺   This Warholesque hotel caters to up-and-coming artistic types—and well-established names with an eye for good value—with its bold modern-art collection and wild style. The standard rooms are clean and bright, with Picasso-style wall murals and Philippe Starck-ish takes on motel furnishings. Superior rooms are best, as they're newly renovated, and well worth the extra $10; all have a queen bed, two twins, or two doubles, plus a newish private bathroom with cute, colorful tile. If you're bringing the brood, two-room suites (or family rooms), are a good option. For the *very* low budget traveler, the Gershwin also offers hostel-style accommodations (called "Bunkers") from $39 a night in 10-bed or 6-bed rooms. The hotel is more service-oriented than you usually see at this price level, and the staff is professional.

7 E. 27th St. (btw. Fifth and Madison aves.), New York, NY 10016. www.gershwinhotel.com. © **212/545-8000.** Fax 212/684-5546. 150 units. $109–$355 double; $329–$405 Family Room. Extra person $20. Check website for discounts or other value-added packages. AE, MC, V. Parking $25 3 blocks away. Subway: N, R, or 6 to 28th St. **Amenities:** Bar; coffee bar; babysitting. *In room:* A/C, TV, hair dryer, Wi-Fi (free).

TIMES SQUARE & MIDTOWN WEST

Times Square might be the heart of Manhattan, but also the city's most congested neighborhood (if you can really call it a neighborhood). Corporate Midtown West is centrally located, but as a result, high in demand for both business and leisure travelers. Hotels here are almost always fill up fast thus prices tend to me substantially higher than most other areas.

Very Expensive

The Chatwal ★ In a restored 1905-built, Stanford White-designed building that once housed the famous Lamb's professional theater club in the heart of Times Square until the 1970s, the Chatwal Hotel, like the colorized-version of the movie *Miracle on 34th Street* that was continuously playing in the elevator when I visited, is a recreation of 1930s New York Art Deco glamour, but with a modern gloss to it. Bellboys in traditional uniforms greet you in the sleek, but small lobby and whisk you to your well-equipped, though somewhat dimly-lit, dark leather and oak decorated room. The rooms average around 400 square-feet and feature backgammon and cocktail sets. The complimentary butler service is a treat, but I think you would have to be from another era to actually know how to best use this service. **The Lamb's Club** restaurant (p. 172), Kashwere spa and a fitness center round out some of the Chatwal's many amenities.

130 W 44th St (btw. Sixth and Seventh aves.), New York, NY 10036. www.chatwalny.com. ℂ **212/764-6200.** Fax 212/764-6222. 83 units. $695–$859 double; $989–$1,659 suite. Check website for specials. AE, DC, DISC, MC, V. Subway: 1, 2, 3, 7, N, R, Q, S to 42nd Street-Times Square. **Amenities:** Restaurant; bar; complimentary butler service; concierge; fitness club including lap pool; room service; spa. *In room:* A/C, TV, Blueray DVD, iPod docking station, mini-bar, Wi-Fi (free).

Jumeirah Essex House ★★★ Managed by the Dubai-based Jumeirah Group, this Central Park icon oozes Art Deco, with black-and-white marble floors, white banquettes where afternoon tea is served, and historic photos of New York lining its corridors. Of the guest rooms many attributes are the wall-to-wall wooden cabinetry, leather-framed mirrors, and window blinds that mirror the leaf patterns you might see across the street in the park as well as state-of-the art technology, such as "stumble lights" underneath nightstands so your path to a late-night bathroom engagement won't be totally in the dark. You won't find tiny rooms here, nor should you; suites are magnificent, especially those overlooking the park.

160 Central Park South (btw. Sixth and Seventh aves.), New York, NY 10019. www.jumeirah.com. ℂ **888/645-5697** or 212/247-0300. Fax 212/315-1839. 515 units. From $709 double; from $959 suite. AE, DC, DISC, MC, V. Valet parking $55. Subway: N, Q, or R to 57th St. **Amenities:** Restaurant; bar; concierge; lobby lounge; afternoon tea; fitness center; room service; spa. *In room:* A/C, TV, minibar, speaker phones, Wi-Fi (free).

Le Parker Meridien ★★ ☺ Consider the many attributes of this hotel: Its location on 57th Street is not too far from Times Square and a short walk from Central Park and Fifth Avenue shopping; there's a 17,000-square-foot fitness center, **Gravity,** featuring basketball and racquetball courts, a spa, and a rooftop pool; three excellent restaurants, including **Norma's** (p. 175), for breakfast, and the aptly named **Burger Joint** (p. 182), rated by many as the best burger in the city; a gorgeous lobby that also serves as a public space off where **Knave,** the hotel's excellent espresso bar is located, and elevators with TVs that show *Tom and Jerry* and Charlie Chaplin shorts. The spacious rooms, though a bit on the IKEA side, have a fun feel, with hidden drawers and twirling television platforms, making an economical use of space. Many have fantastic Central Park views. Rooms have wood platform frames with feather beds, built-ins that include large work desks, and Aeron chairs; the bathrooms are large but come with shower only.

119 W. 56th St. (btw. Sixth and Seventh aves.), New York, NY 10019. www.parkermeridien.com. ℂ **800-/543-4300** for reservations, or 212/245-5000. Fax 212/307-1776. 727 units. $300–$600 double; from $750 suite. Extra person $50. Excellent packages and weekend rates often available

(as low as $225 at press time). AE, DC, DISC, MC, V. Parking $53. Subway: F, N, Q, or R to 57th St. Pets accepted. **Amenities:** 3 restaurants; espresso/cocktail bar; concierge (2 w/Clefs d'Or distinction); fitness center and spa w/Wii studio; rooftop pool; room service; sun deck. *In room:* A/C, TV w/DVD/CD player, hair dryer, high-speed Internet, minibar.

Ritz-Carlton New York, Central Park ★★★ ☺

There's a lot to like about this hotel—from its location overlooking Central Park to the impeccable, personable service—but what I like best is that this luxury hotel manages to maintain a homey elegance and does not intimidate you with an overabundance of style. Rooms are spacious and decorated in English-country style. Suites are larger than most New York apartments. Rooms facing Central Park come with telescopes, and the marble bathrooms are oversize and feature a choice of bathrobes. For families who can afford the steep prices, the hotel is extremely kid-friendly. Suites have sofa beds, and cribs and rollaway beds can be brought in. Children are given in-room cookies and milk. The adults can be pampered with services at the Switzerland-based **La Prairie Spa** or dine at the hotel's restaurant, **BLT Market** (p. 170).

50 Central Park South (at Sixth Ave.), New York, NY 10019. www.ritzcarlton.com/centralpark. ☏ **212/308-9100.** Fax 212/207-8831. 259 units. $595–$1,195 double; from $995 suite. Package and weekend rates available. AE, DC, DISC, MC, V. Parking $55. Subway: N or R to Fifth Ave.; F to 57th St. Pets under 60 lbs. accepted. **Amenities:** Restaurant; bar; babysitting; concierge; lobby lounge for tea and cocktails; Ritz–Carlton Club Lounge; fitness center; room service; La Prairie spa and facial center; butler and bath butler services. *In room:* A/C, TV/DVD, hair dryer, high-speed Internet, minibar.

Expensive

One of New York's iconic skyscrapers, the **New Yorker Hotel,** 481 Eighth Ave., at 34th St. (☏ **212/244-0719;** www.newyorkerhotel.com), in the first half of the 20th century was one of Manhattan's biggest hotels with 2,500 rooms. It now has 912 rooms and its location, across the street from Madison Square Garden, 1 block from Herald Square shopping, and 2 blocks from the Empire State Building make it a good Midtown option.

Affinia Manhattan ★

You'll never forget you are in New York when you stay at the Affinia Manhattan. The large lobby is sort of a miniversion of the Waldorf=Astoria's, where a Grand Central Station–like information booth in its center features a series of televisions with video images of New York landmarks. Though the New York theme is fun, all you really need to do is look out your window, where you just might see the Empire State Building, and you'll know very well what city you are in. All rooms are suites with full kitchens. The room decor here is old school—no edgy furniture or amenities, but there is plenty of space. Bathrooms are small by comparison but include details such as black-and-white-tiled floors. In addition to this property and the Affinia Dumont (p. 116), there's another Affinia on the East side, the Affinia 50 at 155 E. 50th St.

371 Seventh Ave. (at 31st St.), New York, NY 10001. www.affinia.com. ☏ **212/563-1800.** Fax 212/643-8028. 526 units. From $225 suite. Check website for specials, which were as low as $199 at press time. AE, DC, MC, V. Parking $40. Subway: 1, 2, or 3 to 34th St. **Amenities:** Restaurant; bar; concierge; fitness center; room service. *In room:* A/C, TV, kitchen, Wi-Fi (free).

AKA Central Park ★

With four extended-stay residences with hotel-like amenities in locations such as Times Square, Sutton Place, the United Nations area, and Central Park, AKA offers combination apartment/hotel accommodations where your stay can be as brief as just 1 night. The rooms, from spacious studios to two bedrooms, feature full modern kitchens, marble bathrooms, two televisions, and a complimentary weekday breakfast. I found the Central Park location, 1 block from Central Park South, the homiest of the group. It's a very attractive and more calming alternative to the nearby hotel hysteria.

42 W. 58th St. (btw. Fifth and Sixth aves.), New York, NY 10019. www.stayaka.com. ℂ **646/744-3100** or 888/aka-1500. Fax 646/744-3120. 134 units. Rates from $395. AE, DC, MC, V. Parking $50 per day. Subway: N, Q, or R to 57th St. **Amenities:** Complimentary breakfast (weekdays); concierge; health club and spa services; room service. *In room:* A/C, 2 TVs, CD/DVD player, hair dryer, full kitchen, 2-line cordless phone w/complimentary local phone services, Wi-Fi (free).

The Blakely New York ★★   The Blakely has a clubby yet modern feel to it, making it a more intimate Midtown-hotel option. The rooms are all generously sized: None are smaller than 300 square feet and, if it matters to you, some have views of the City Center dome across the street. The dark cherrywood furniture helps perpetuate the clubhouse aura that is contrasted, happily, by modern amenities such as flatscreen TVs. Marble bathrooms are well sized and appointed; bathroom suites have separate tubs and showers. The lobby, though redesigned after the renovation, remains small and can get hectic at times, but the staff is helpful and efficient.

136 W. 55th St. (btw. Sixth and Seventh aves.), New York, NY 10019. www.blakelynewyork.com. ℂ **212/245-1800.** Fax 212/582-8332. 118 units. $305–$495 double; $395–$595 suite. Check the website for packages and seasonal specials. AE, DISC, MC, V. Parking $33. Subway: N or R to 57th St. **Amenities:** Restaurant; concierge; complimentary access to nearby health club; room service. *In room:* A/C, TV, CD/DVD player, fridge, microwave, minibar, Wi-Fi (free).

Bryant Park Hotel ★   Despite being housed in the stately 1924-built American Radiator Building, the Bryant Park Hotel falls into that hip/boutique category, with its whitewashed rooms filled with high-tech goodies like Bose Wave radios, iPod docking stations, and stacks of fashion magazines. The location overlooking Bryant Park is an enviable one and the reason for the fashion emphasis (Bryant Park was the home of the twice-yearly Fashion Week before it moved on to Lincoln Center). A screening room adds appeal to visitors with cinematic aspirations and movie mogul wannabes. Rooms are not grand but they are a good size and, because many have spectacular Bryant Park and Midtown views, bright.

40 W. 40th St. (btw. Fifth and Sixth aves.), New York, NY 10018. www.bryantparkhotel.com. ℂ **212/642-2200** or 212/861-0100. Fax 212/869-4446. 128 units. $395–$695 double; from $595–$1,000 suite. Parking $40. AE, DISC, MC, V. Subway: B, D, F, or M to 42nd St. **Amenities:** Restaurant; bar; concierge; fitness center; room service; screening room. *In room:* A/C, TV, CD, hair dryer, iPod docking station, Wi-Fi (free).

Doubletree Guest Suites Times Square ★ ☺   For many, the location of this 43-story Doubletree—in the heart of darkness known as Times Square, where the streets are constantly gridlocked, the neon burns holes into your eye sockets, and the noise level is ear-splitting—might offer a more Vegas-like experience than a true New York one. But at times we all must make sacrifices for our children, and this Doubletree, location and all, is perfect for the kids. From the fresh-baked chocolate-chip cookies served upon arrival, the spacious, affordable and the all-day children's room-service menu to the proximity to the gargantuan Toys "R" Us, the TKTS booth, and other kid-friendly Times Square offerings, this

Doubletree is hard to beat for families. Bathrooms have two entrances so the kids don't have to traipse through the parent's room.

1568 Broadway (at 47th St. and Seventh Ave.), New York, NY 10036. www.doubletree.com. ✆ **800/222-TREE** (222-8733) or 212/719-1600. Fax 212/921-5212. 460 units. From $349 suite. Extra person $20. Children 17 and under stay free in parent's suite. Ask about senior, corporate, and AAA discounts and special promotions. AE, DC, DISC, MC, V. Parking $35. Subway: N or R to 49th St. **Amenities:** Restaurant; lounge; babysitting; concierge; fitness center; room service. *In room:* A/C, 2 TVs w/pay movies and video games, fridge, hair dryer, high-speed Internet, microwave, minibar, wet bar.

Flatotel ★★ ☺ 🎁 🛍 In the heart of midtown Manhattan and surrounded by Sheratons and other brand name hotels, the Flatotel (Flat, like an apartment in London combined with hotel amenities) offers something those brands do not: space. All the hotel's sleek, apartment-like rooms, especially the suites, are large by New York standards and all feature refrigerators and microwaves, while suites have kitchenettes or full kitchens, two flatscreen TVs, and generous desks. The marble bathrooms are spacious and well equipped. The hotel also features 60 one- to three-bedroom family suites with dining areas and full kitchens in each. In some suites on higher floors—the hotel is 47 stories—you have spectacular, river-to-river views. Though the hotel has the appearance of a corporate refuge, with its dark marble and metal tones, its services are personable and more like a boutique than the Midtown monolith it appears to be.

132 W. 52nd St. (btw. Sixth and Seventh aves.), New York, NY 10019. www.flatotel.com. ✆ **800/ FLATOTEL** [352-6835] or 212/887-9400. Fax 212/887-9795. 288 units. From $399 double; from $549 suite. AE, DC, DISC, MC, V. Parking $30 self-parking, $47 valet. Subway: B, D, or E to Seventh Ave. **Amenities:** Restaurant; bar; concierge; fitness center; room service. *In room:* A/C, TV, CD player, fridge, hair dryer, high-speed Internet, microwave.

The London NYC ★ Its un-New York name aside, the London is the quintessential midtown Manhattan hotel. It features a sleek, airy look starting in the lobby, high-ceilinged and bright with white marble, and attended by black-coated, derby-wearing porters. The rooms are spacious, with big windows providing spectacular views—the hotel, with 54 floors, is one of the New York's tallest. Electronic amenities include flatscreen LCD televisions and iHome MP3 docking stations. The addition of oak-parquet floors gives the hotel's cool feel more of a rustic homey touch. The white-tiled bathrooms have been designed by the bathroom purveyor Waterworks and feature their amenities. The hotel's suites include two televisions, a separate parlor, some with French doors, and bathrooms with two shower heads.

151 W. 54th St. (btw. Sixth and Seventh aves.), New York, NY 10019. www.thelondonnyc.com. ✆ **866/690-2029** or 212/468-8856. Fax 212/468-8747. 562 units. $499–$1,199 double. Check the website for specials; prices as low as $249 at press time. AE, DC, MC, V. Parking $55. Subway: B, D, or E to Seventh Ave. **Amenities:** Restaurant; bar; concierge; fitness center; room service. *In room:* A/C, TV, hair dryer, minibar, MP3 docking stations, Wi-Fi (free).

The Michelangelo ★★ 🛍 Owned by the Italian-based Starhotel, this is the group's only U.S. property, and it offers a welcome dose of Italian hospitality in the heart of New York. From the moment you enter the spacious lobby, adorned with Italian marble, you feel you've left behind the rapid-fire sight-and-sound assault of nearby Times Square. Off the lobby is a lounge where coffee and cappuccino are served all day and a complimentary Italian breakfast of pastries and fruit is offered each morning. The recently renovated rooms come in various sizes, all of which are more than adequate by New York standards. Among other things, they feature marble foyers, Italian fabrics, king beds, and two television sets (one in the bathroom). The bathrooms are well maintained and feature deep whirlpool bathtubs.

152 W. 51st St. (btw. Sixth and Seventh aves.), New York, NY 10019. www.michelangelohotel.com. ✆ **800/237-0990** or 212/765-0505. Fax 212/581-7618. 179 units. From $395 double; from $625 suite. Rates include Italian breakfast. Visit website for (sometimes substantial) discounts. AE, DC, DISC, MC, V. Parking (1 block away) $32 per day self-park, $40 per day valet. Subway: N or R to 49th St. **Amenities:** Restaurant; lounge; concierge; fitness center; room service. *In room:* A/C, TV, fax, hair dryer, high-speed Internet, minibar.

The Muse ★   The beauty of the Muse is that it is a Times Square hotel that feels like it's miles away, an inspired oasis in the bustle and noise that is Times Square. All the rooms are good sized, with feather beds and custom linens. There was a Muse statue in my room, but I'm not sure if it inspired me to do anything but get a good night's sleep. And for that I can't complain. The bathrooms are sumptuous and well outfitted. Service is solid and anticipatory. Like other Kimpton hotels, the Muse offers a complimentary wine reception in the lobby each afternoon.

130 W. 46th St. (btw. Sixth and Seventh aves.), New York, NY 10036. www.themusehotel.com. ✆ **877/692-6873** or 212/485-2400. Fax 212/485-2789. 200 units. $309–$399 double; from $399 suite. AE, DC, DISC, MC, V. Parking $43. Subway: B, D, F, or M to 42nd St. Pets accepted. **Amenities:** Restaurant; concierge; good fitness room; room service. *In room:* A/C, TV w/pay movies, CD player, hair dryer, high-speed Internet.

Royalton Hotel ★★   The Royalton toned down its, fashion-trendy look and style a few years back and now has an understated elegance and sophistication to it. Once you locate the very unassuming entrance (for a hotel), you enter what is a marvel of a lobby. Dark and narrow with check-in counters that appear more like coat-check closets, a sprawling lounge area accentuated by a blazing two-sided glass-enclosed fireplace, a very lively bar just off the front entrance, and a restaurant in the rear. Rooms still retain the hotel's original cool Phillipe Starck minimalist feel with categories vary ranging from the standard (no tub but decent sized) to deluxe standards with fireplaces and soaking tubs, to alcove suites with long couches and big Jacuzzi tubs, to penthouse suites. Despite the bustle of hotel heavy 44th Street and the action in the lobby, rooms are, thankfully, quiet and comfortable making the Royalton a very worthy Hotel Row (see the sidebar "Checking In on Hotel Row," below) option.

44 W. 44th St (btw. Fifth and Sixth aves.), New York, NY 10036. www.royaltonhotel.com. ✆ **800/697-1781** or 212/869-4400. Fax 212/869-8965. 169 units. $249–$599. AE, DC, DISC, MC, V. Subway: B, D, F, or M to 42nd Street–Bryant Park. **Amenities:** Restaurant; 2 bars; concierge; fitness room; room service. *In room:* A/C, TV, iPod docking stations, Wi-Fi (free).

The Shoreham ★ 🛏   No, it's not on the luxury level of the Peninsula or the St. Regis down the block, but with added amenities such as champagne or sparkling water upon check-in and a 24-hour self-service coffee bar, and a charge of about half the price, the Shoreham is a more than worthy, less expensive alternative to those other hotels down the block. Rooms vary in size and amenities, and though all have been upgraded or totally renovated, it's better to spring for a deluxe or a suite where you will get a bigger bathroom, some with five-head rainshowers and

Jacuzzis. The hotel offers the little extras that give you value, such as a complimentary shoeshine, *New York Times,* two bottles of Voss water, and, for fashionistas, a complimentary daily copy of *Women's Wear Daily.*

33 W. 55th St. (btw. Fifth and Sixth aves.), New York, NY 10019. www.shorehamhotel.com. © **800/553-3347** or 212/247-6700. Fax 212/765-9741. 174 units. $309–$609 double. Check website for specials. AE, MC, V. Parking nearby $45 with in/out privileges. Subway: B, D, or E to Seventh Ave. **Amenities:** Restaurant; bar; cappuccino and coffee; fitness club; room service; complimentary shoeshine. *In room:* A/C, TV, VCR/DVD/CD player, hair dryer, minifridge.

Sofitel New York ★★★ 🛍 There are many fine hotels on 44th Street between Fifth and Sixth avenues (see the sidebar "Checking In on Hotel Row," p. 110), but the best, in my estimation, is the soaring Sofitel. Upon entering the hotel and the warm, inviting lobby with check-in tucked off to the side, you wouldn't think you were entering a hotel that is this young, which is one of the reasons why the hotel is so special. The designers have successfully melded modern, new-world amenities with European old-world elegance. The rooms are spacious and ultra-comfortable, adorned with art from New York and Paris. The lighting is soft and romantic, the walls and windows soundproofed. Suites are extra special, equipped with king beds, two televisions, and pocket doors separating the bedroom from a sitting room. Bathrooms in all rooms are magnificent, with separate showers and soaking tubs.

45 W. 44th St. (btw. Fifth and Sixth aves.), New York, NY 10036. www.sofitel.com. © **212/354-8844.** Fax 212/354-2480. 398 units. $235–$599 double; from $700 suite. 1 child stays free in parent's room. AE, DC, MC, V. Parking $45. Subway: B, D, F, or M to 42nd St. Pets accepted. **Amenities:** Restaurant; bar; concierge; exercise room; room service. *In room:* A/C, TV w/pay movies, CD player, hair dryer, minibar, Wi-Fi (free).

Moderate

Casablanca Hotel ★★ 🌿 Just off Broadway in the middle of Times Square, the Casablanca Hotel is an oasis in the middle of all that mayhem, where, in **Rick's Café,** the Casablanca's homey lounge, you can sit by a fire, read a paper, check your e-mail, watch television on the big screen TV, or sip a cappuccino from the serve-yourself machine. Or, if it's balmy, you can lounge on the rooftop deck or second-floor courtyard. The rooms might not be the biggest around, but they are well outfitted with ceiling fans, free bottles of water, and beautifully tiled bathrooms. The Casablanca is an HK Hotels property (the Library, Elysée, and Giraffe), and like those hotels, service is top-notch. Because of its location, moderate prices, and size (only 48 rooms), the Casablanca is in high demand, so book early.

147 W. 43rd St. (just east of Broadway), New York, NY 10036. www.casablancahotel.com. © **888/922-7225** or 212/869-1212. Fax 212/391-7585. 48 units. $249–$299 double; from $399 suite. Rates include continental breakfast, all-day cappuccino, and weekday wine and cheese. Check website for specials. AE, DC, MC, V. Parking $25 next door. Subway: N, R, 1, 2, or 3 to 42nd St./Times Sq. **Amenities:** Cyberlounge; concierge; free access to New York Sports Club; room service; video library. *In room:* A/C, ceiling fan, TV/VCR, CD player, hair dryer, minibar.

414 Hotel ★ 🛍 A block from Times Square and close to Hell's Kitchen, this place offers 37-inch flatscreen TVs in every room, spacious, well-equipped bathrooms, complimentary bottled water, continental breakfast, Wi-Fi, in-room refrigerators, a newly renovated lobby, and a lovely courtyard. It all sounds too

CHECKING IN ON hotel row

There are hundreds of hotels in Manhattan, but most are spread out over a good chunk of real estate. There is, however, 1 block—West 44th Street, between Fifth and Sixth avenues—where the hotels stand practically side by side.

The block has a sophisticated, urbane, and literary feel to it, emanating from the legendary **Algonquin ★**, 59 W. 44th St. (www.algonquinhotel.com; ✆ **646/744-3100**), where the *New Yorker* was born, where Lerner and Loewe wrote *My Fair Lady,* and—most famously—where some of the biggest names in 1920s literati, among them Dorothy Parker, met to trade boozy quips at the celebrated Algonquin Round Table. The hotel was recently purchased by Marriott hotels to become what is now called the "Marriott Autograph Collection."

Next to the Algonquin, at 55 W. 44th St., sits the 65-room Jeffrey Bilhuber–designed **City Club** (www.cityclubhotel.com; ✆ **212/921-5500**). The structure started out in 1904 as a gentlemen's club and saw many incarnations, but its latest life, as the ultrafashionable City Club, casts aside the usual style of the New York "boutique" property—cramped and minimalist decor that make a virtue of discomfort. City Club's modernist elements are tempered with touches like Queen Anne chairs, natural Frette linens, vintage books, chocolate marble, and Hermès bath products you'd be afraid to steal. This haven for mavens of fashion also is the home of one of Daniel Boulud's restaurants, **db Bistro Moderne.**

For many years there was a barbershop adjacent to the lobby of the **Iroquois Hotel,** 49 W. 44th St. (www.iroquoisny.com; ✆ **212/840-3080**), called the Dumont Barbershop and Shoeshine. The shop's principal barber, Louis Fontana, used to notice a young man hanging out on the stoop of the hotel, which, at the time, was a men's residence. When Louie asked the kid why he was hanging around the barbershop, the kid stuttered that he needed a haircut but couldn't afford one; he was an actor looking for work. "Kid, what's your name?" the legend goes. The kid answered, "James Dean." Big-hearted Louis gave him a free haircut that day. That's a true story and part of the legend of the Iroquois. The 114-room hotel, after a full renovation some years ago, is now a member of the Small Luxury Hotels of the World and features a suite named after its former most famous resident.

Just next to the Iroquois, at 45 W. 44th St., is the **Sofitel New York ★★★** (p. 109); from the appearance of the lobby and entrance, you might think you have entered a hotel built in the same era as the others. But take a look from across the street; the glittering curved tower was built less than 6 years ago. Despite its newness, the hotel blends in perfectly on historic Hotel Row.

Closer to Fifth Avenue and on the south side of the block at 12 W. 44th St. is the **Mansfield ★** (www.mansfieldhotel.com; ✆ **800/255-5167**), which was built as a bachelor's residence in 1905 and, in keeping with the block's literary and artistic tradition, was once the home of poet W. B. Yeats's father.

Closer to Sixth Avenue, at 44 W. 44th St., is the newly renovated **Royalton ★★** (p. 108). Redesigned from a minimalist Starck look, the Royalton now has an understated sophistication worthy of the street where it is located. In an homage to the past is the presence of working fireplaces in 40 of the hotel's 169 rooms.

Times Square & Midtown West

WHERE TO STAY

good for a budget hotel. But if you want all that and don't want to pay anything close to what hotels offering much less are asking, then you also have to endure the 414's thin walls; if stomping above you is a problem ask for a top-floor room, which would mean you would have to walk the four floors: There's no elevator. Despite these inconveniences, the 414 Hotel has comfortable, clean rooms, and all the perks make it a very good Midtown moderate choice.

414 W. 46th St. (btw. Ninth and Tenth aves.), New York, NY 10036. www.hotel414.com. © **866/414-HOTEL** [414-4683] or 212/399-0006. Fax 212/957-8710. 22 units. $169–$259 double. Subway: A, C, E, or 7 to 42nd St. **Amenities:** Complimentary continental breakfast; complimentary coffee, juice, and tea; concierge. *In room:* A/C, TV, fridge, hair dryer, MP3 docking stations, Wi-Fi (free).

Hotel 41 ★ 🎁   Like the **Casablanca Hotel** (p. 109) a few blocks up, Hotel 41 offers a stylish, comfortable, and moderate alternative to the many gleaming, glittering, and more pricey hotels that tower over Times Square. Just seven floors, the Hotel 41 features minimalist modern decor in the guest rooms. Rooms, for these prices, are of decent size, but what sets the hotel apart are the freebies: Wi-Fi, continental breakfast, and all-day espresso or cappuccino. Rooms also come equipped with DVD players with the hotel's DVD library available for viewing, plush bathrobes, double-paned windows (a necessity in Times Square), and refrigerators. If you plan to stay for more than a few days, go for one of the junior suites or, for a splurge, Penthouse no. 2, which features a large outdoor deck. Service is boutique-friendly, and off the lobby is **Bar 41,** a lively bar/restaurant (where breakfast is served) that draws a local after-work crowd.

206 W. 41st St. (btw. Seventh and Eighth aves.), New York, NY 10036. www.hotel41nyc.com. © **212/703-8600.** Fax 212/302-0895. 47 units. $149–$399 double; $239–$899 suite. Check website for specials. AE, DISC, MC, V. Parking $32–$42. Subway: 1, 2, 3, 7, A, C, E, N, Q, R, or S to Times Sq. Pets accepted. **Amenities:** Restaurant; bar; continental breakfast; access to nearby fitness center; room service. *In room:* A/C, TV/DVD, fridge, hair dryer, Wi-Fi (free).

Hotel Metro ★ ☺   The Metro is the choice in Midtown for those who don't want to sacrifice style or comfort for affordability. This Art Deco–style jewel has larger rooms than you'd expect for the price. They're outfitted with retro furnishings and smallish but beautifully appointed marble bathrooms. Only about half the bathrooms have tubs, but the others have shower stalls big enough for two (junior suites have whirlpool tubs). The Family Room is a two-room suite that has a second bedroom in lieu of a sitting area; families on tighter budgets can opt for a roomy double/double. Premier rooms featuring new bathrooms and iPod docking stations were recently renovated.

The comfy, firelit library/lounge area, where a complimentary buffet breakfast is laid out and the coffeepot's on all day, is a popular hangout. Service is attentive, and the rooftop terrace boasts a breathtaking view of the Empire State Building and makes a great place to order up room service from the **Metro Grill.**

45 W. 35th St. (btw. Fifth and Sixth aves.), New York, NY 10001. www.hotelmetronyc.com. © **800/356-3870** or 212/947-2500. Fax 212/279-1310. 179 units. $179–$365 double; $245–$420 triple or quad; $255–$425 Family Room; $275–$475 suite. Extra person $25. Check website for specials, rates as low as $180 at press time; check with airlines and other package operators for great-value package deals. 1 child 12 or under stays free in parent's room. Rates include continental breakfast. AE, DC, MC, V. Parking $20 nearby. Subway: B, D, F, N, R, or M to 34th St. **Amenities:**

Restaurant; alfresco rooftop bar in summer; good fitness room; room service. *In room:* A/C, TV, fridge, hair dryer, high-speed Internet.

Ink48 ★ Located in Midtown on the far west side, 1 block from the Hudson River, is Kimpton Hotels' (the Muse, 70 Park Avenue, p. 108 and 122) newest New York property, Ink48. And if you don't mind the long walk (and sometimes windy, and cold in the winter, conditions) from the subway, the hotel is an intriguing, more serene alternative than those a few blocks east. Being next to car dealers and behind a Verizon truck depot may not seem very serene, but if your room faces west, with floor-to-ceiling windows of the Hudson River and the U.S.S. *Intrepid* or the east, with spectacular city views, you might just discover that serenity. The rooms, featuring standard Kimpton, minimalist furniture, are generously proportioned by New York City standards and offer now basic, high-tech amenities like iHome sound systems and flatscreen televisions with WebTV. Though it prides itself as a "boutique" hotel, the term and the design seem outdated. Still, what Ink48 lacks in in-room and design aesthetics it more than makes up for in service and in those amazing views.

653 11th Ave. (btw. 47th and 48th sts.), New York, NY 10036. www.ink48.com. ✆ **212/757-0088.** Fax 212/757-2088. 222 units. AE, DC, DISC, MC, V. Rates from $279. Parking $55–$75. Subway: C or E to 50th Street. Pet-friendly. **Amenities:** Restaurant; bar; concierge; fitness center; room service; spa; wine reception daily. *In room:* A/C, TV, wireless and high-speed Internet, iHome sound systems.

Novotel New York ★ ☺ Run expertly by the French company Accor (**Sofitel,** p. 109), this towering hotel on the northern fringe of Times Square, with its bilingual staff and a selection of international newspapers, attracts an international crowd. But domestic visitors shouldn't neglect what is a good moderate option in one of the busiest parts of the city. The vast, sunny lobby on the seventh floor, with open views of Times Square, is the hotel's pride and joy; it is also the location of the underrated **Café Nicole,** where a breakfast buffet is offered. Guest rooms, though pleasant and of a decent size, are more motel-like in decor. Rooms were recently renovated and many have spectacular views of Times Square and/or the Hudson River. All are soundproof.

226 W. 52nd St. (at Broadway), New York, NY 10019. www.novotel.com. ✆ **212/315-0100.** Fax 212/765-5365. 480 units. From $189 double. 2 children 15 and under eat for free and stay free in parent's room. Check website for specials, which were as low as $159 at press time. AE, DC, DISC, MC, V. Parking $30. Subway: B, D, or E to Seventh Ave. Pets accepted. **Amenities:** Restaurant; bar; concierge; fitness room; room service. *In room:* A/C, TV, hair dryer, minibar, Wi-Fi (free).

Room Mate Grace Hotel ★ ✦ From its Midtown location to its many extras, such as a swimming pool in the lobby, steam room and sauna, complimentary continental breakfast, and good-size rooms, including a number with bunk beds, Grace Hotel is one of the better moderate options in the Times Square area. Upon entering, you check in at a kiosk/front desk where you pick up periodicals or essentials to stock your minibar. Making your way to the elevators, you might see guests swimming in the lobby pool or having a drink at the swim-up bar, an unusual sight in the Big Apple. The rooms are sparse in tone, but the queen- and king-size platform beds are plush and dressed with Egyptian cotton sheets. The biggest drawback is the bathrooms: There are no doors on the bathrooms—sliding doors conceal the shower (none of the rooms have tubs) and the toilet.

WHERE TO STAY | Times Square & Midtown West

125 W. 45th St. (btw. Sixth Ave. and Broadway), New York, NY 10036. www.room-matehotels. com. ✆ **212/354-2323.** Fax 212/302-8585. 139 units. $179–$350 double. AE, DC, MC, V. Parking nearby $25. Subway: B, D, F, or M to 47th–50th sts./Rockefeller Center. **Amenities:** Bar; complimentary Spanish-inspired breakfast; gym; pool; sauna; steam room. *In room:* A/C, flatscreen TV, CD/DVD players, hair dryer, iHome docking port, free high-speed Internet, minifridge, 2-line speakerphones w/free local calls, blackout drapes.

The Strand   Sandwiched between fashion wholesale outlets on the fringe of the Garment District, the Strand is a good moderate Midtown option. Though the neighborhood is not the most vibrant, it is close to Times Square, Macy's and the shopping of Herald Square, and to a conglomeration of subway lines which will speedily take you anywhere you need to go. The lobby is sleek with a wall waterfall while the rooms, equipped with Condé Nast photos from the 1930s, conveys the glamour of that era. The overall design notwithstanding, I found the decor of the rooms, which are nicely sized, to have more of an executive feel. They all have expansive desks, iPod docking systems, and computer hookups. But welcome amenities like a sumptuous complimentary buffet, a fitness center with massage services, and a beautiful rooftop bar with amazing views of the Empire State Building will please even nonexecutives.

33 W. 37th Street (btw. Fifth and Sixth aves.), New York, NY 10018. www.thestrandnyc.com. ✆ **212/448-1024.** Fax 212/448-0811. 177 units. AE, DISC, DC, MC, V. $249–$359 superior rooms. Check website for specials. Parking $33–$40. Subway: B, D, F, M, N, R, Q to 34th St. **Amenities:** Restaurant; complimentary breakfast buffet; bar; concierge; fitness center; room service. *In room:* A/C, TV, iPod docking systems, VoIP phone system, Wi-Fi (free).

Washington Jefferson Hotel ★   This is one of the few affordable hotels in the heart of my favorite Manhattan neighborhood for dining, Hell's Kitchen. The lobby has a warm and welcoming ambience, with a friendly, snappily attired staff and more than a dash of designer style. Snazzy blue-carpeted halls lead to rooms that are *small*—don't say I didn't warn you—but attractively outfitted in a palette of soft grays. Nice touches include platform beds with generous cushioned headboards and fluffy goose-down comforters. The limestone-and-slate bathrooms are stylish and relatively spacious, although some have showers only.

318 W. 51st St. (btw. Eighth and Ninth aves.), New York, NY 10019. www.wjhotel.com. ✆ **888/567-7550** or 212/246-7550. Fax 212/246-7622. 135 units. $130–$320 double. Ask about special deals. AE, DC, DISC, MC, V. Parking $35 nearby. Subway: C or E to 50th St. **Amenities:** Restaurant; exercise room; room service. *In room:* A/C, TV w/pay movies/video games, hair dryer, Wi-Fi (free).

Inexpensive

Americana Inn ★ 🍴   In the budget-basic category, the hotel is professionally run and immaculately kept. Rooms are mostly spacious, with good-size closets, private sinks, and an alarm built into the TV; the beds are the most comfortable I've found at this price. Most rooms come with a double bed or two twins; a few can accommodate three guests in two twin beds and a pullout sofa, or in three twins. One hall bathroom accommodates every three rooms or so; all are spacious and spotless. Every floor has a common kitchenette with microwave, stove, and fridge (BYO cooking utensils, or go plastic). The five-story building has an elevator, and four rooms are accessible for travelers with disabilities. The Garment District location is convenient for Midtown sightseeing and shopping; ask for a back-facing room away from the street noise.

69 W. 38th St. (at Sixth Ave.), New York, NY 10018. www.theamericaninn.com. ☏ **888/HOTEL-58** (468-3558) or 212/840-6700. Fax 212/840-1830. 50 units, all with shared bathroom. $65–$150 double. Extra person $20. Check website for specials (winter rates as low as $60 double). AE, MC, V. Parking $30 nearby. Subway: B, D, F, or M to 34th St. **Amenities:** Common kitchen. *In room:* A/C, TV, hair dryer (ask reception).

La Quinta Inn Manhattan 🔥 The first and only La Quinta Inn in Manhattan is another top Midtown budget choice. Housed in a 1904 Beaux Arts structure on the block known as Little Korea, La Quinta Inn offers standard motel amenities along with motel-like prices. Like the other Apple Core properties, including the New York Manhattan Hotel across the street, service is friendly and a continental breakfast adds to the value. The rooms are basic in motel-room decor and size, but there's nothing wrong with that, especially at these prices. Bathrooms are small but clean and well equipped. There's even a cozy rooftop bar that offers indoor and outdoor seating in the shadow of the majestic Empire State Building. And if you like Korean barbecue and dumplings, you won't have to travel far: The block is packed with some good Korean restaurants.

17 W. 32nd St. (btw. Fifth and Sixth aves.), New York, NY 10001. www.lq.com. ☏ **800/551-2303** or 212/736-1600. 181 units. $109–$329 double (usually less than $189). Rates include continental breakfast. Children 12 and under stay free in parent's room. AE, DC, DISC, MC, V. Parking $26. Subway: B, D, F, N, R, or M to 34th St. **Amenities:** Bar; breakfast room; concierge; exercise room. *In room:* A/C, TV w/pay movies and video games, Wi-Fi (free).

New York Manhattan Hotel ★ 🔥 This hotel, formerly a Red Roof Inn, occupies a building that was once an office space, which was gutted and laid out fresh, allowing for more spacious rooms and bathrooms than you'd usually find at this price. The lobby feels smart, and elevators are quiet and efficient. In-room amenities—including coffeemakers and TVs with on-screen Web access—are better than most competitors', and furnishings are new and comfortable. Wi-Fi is available throughout the property. The location—on a bustling block lined with nice hotels and affordable Korean restaurants, a stone's throw from the Empire State Building and Herald Square—is excellent. Be sure to compare the rates offered by Apple Core Hotel's reservation line (the management company) and those quoted on Red Roof's national reservation line and website, as they can vary significantly. Complimentary continental breakfast adds to the good value.

6 W. 32nd St. (btw. Broadway and Fifth Ave.), New York, NY 10001. http://applecorehotels.com/the-new-york-manhattan-hotel. ☏ **800/755-3194,** 800/RED-ROOF (733-7663), or 212/643-7100. Fax 212/643-7101. 171 units. $109–$329 double (usually less than $189). Rates include continental breakfast. Children 12 and under stay free in parent's room. AE, DC, DISC, MC, V. Parking $26. Subway: B, D, F, N, R, or M to 34th St. **Amenities:** Breakfast room; wine-and-beer lounge; concierge; exercise room. *In room:* A/C, TV w/pay movies, fridge, hair dryer, video games, Wi-Fi (free).

Skyline Hotel ☺ 🔥 This fairly recently renovated motor hotel offers predictable comforts and some uncommon extras—inexpensive parking ($10 per day) and a lovely indoor pool—that make it a good value. A pleasant lobby leads to motel-standard rooms that are bigger than most in this price range. There are two room categories: standard, with two twin beds, and deluxe, with either a king bed with sofa or a queen bed. The deluxe with king and sofa is best for families. They boast decent-size closets, small work desks (in most), and double-paned windows that open to let fresh air in and shut out a surprising amount of street noise when closed. Everything is well kept. Another plus for the family is the pool,

Lugging the kids to New York City can be a daunting experience. Finding a hotel that makes that experience (whether in the accommodations or in the amenities), a bit less overwhelming can be a huge help. Here are some of the city's best accommodations for families:

Doubletree Guest Suites Times Square (Times Sq.; p. 106)   An entire floor of childproof suites, plus a Kids Club for ages 3 to 12.

Flatotel (Midtown West; p. 107)   With one- to three-bedroom suites equipped with full kitchens, this is a great Midtown option for the family.

Gershwin Hotel (Flatiron District; p. 103)   High space-to-dollar ratio with the Family Room, a two-room suite.

Hotel Beacon (Upper West Side; p. 125)   In-room kitchenette, on-site laundromat, and spacious rooms in a kid-friendly neighborhood—what more do you want?

Hotel Metro (Midtown West; p. 111) The sitting rooms of the hotel's Family Room suites are smartly converted into second bedrooms.

Le Parker Meridien (Midtown West; p. 104)   Cartoons playing in the elevators, a great swimming pool (pictured at right), a kid-friendly burger joint in the lobby, and spacious rooms and suites.

The Lowell (Upper East Side; p. 129) Total *luxe*, but with the feel of a residential dwelling. Most units are equipped with a kitchenette or full kitchen.

Novotel New York (Midtown West; p. 112)   Kids 16 and under stay free in their parent's room and eat free at the hotel's beautiful Café Nicole.

Ritz-Carlton New York, Central Park (Midtown West; p. 105)   You'll pay dearly for it, but kids love the in-room cookies and milk.

Skyline Hotel and Travel Inn (Midtown West; p. 114)   Inexpensive ($10) to free parking at the Skyline and Travel Inn, respectively, oversize rooms, and swimming pools (a rarity in affordable hotels).

which has a tiled deck and plush deck chairs, but it's only open limited hours, so call ahead.

725 Tenth Ave. (at 49th St.), New York, NY 10019. www.skylinehotelny.com. ℭ **800/433-1982** or 212/586-3400. Fax 212/582-4604. 232 units. $209–$389 standard; $219–$409 deluxe. Extra person $20. Children 14 and under stay free in parent's room. Check website or inquire about specials. AC, DC, DISC, MC, V. Parking $10 (no in/out privileges). Subway: A, C, E to 50th St. **Amenities:** Restaurant; fitness center; Internet access in lobby; indoor pool. *In room:* A/C, TV w/ pay movies/video games/high-speed Internet, dataport, hair dryer.

Travel Inn 😊 ✦   Extras such as a huge outdoor pool and sun deck, a sunny and up-to-date fitness room, and *free* parking (with in and out privileges!) make the Travel Inn another terrific deal, similar to the one offered by the **Skyline Hotel** (see above). Like the Skyline, the Travel Inn may not be loaded with personality, but it does offer the clean, bright regularity of a good chain hotel. Rooms are oversize and comfortably furnished, with extra-firm beds and work desks; even the smallest double is sizable and has a roomy bathroom, and double/doubles make great affordable shares for families. A total renovation over the last couple

4

WHERE TO STAY

Times Square & Midtown West

years has made everything feel like new, even the tiled bathrooms. Though a bit off the track, Off-Broadway theaters and affordable restaurants are at hand, and it's a 10-minute walk to the Theater District.

515 W. 42nd St. (just west of Tenth Ave.), New York, NY 10036. www.thetravelinnhotel.com. *©* **888/HOTEL58** (468-3558), 800/869-4630, or 212/695-7171. Fax 212/967-5025. 160 units. $105–$250 double. Extra person $10. Children 15 and under stay free in parent's room. AAA discounts available; check website for specials. AE, DC, DISC, MC, V. Free self-parking. Subway: A, C, or E to 42nd St./Port Authority. **Amenities:** Coffee shop; fitness center; terrific outdoor pool w/deck chairs and lifeguard in season; room service. *In room:* A/C, TV, hair dryer.

MIDTOWN EAST & MURRAY HILL

This is "Mad Men" territory, where the barons of advertising and big business reside. As a result, you'll find some of the grandest hotels—and also the most expensive. To find the hotels described in this section, see map on p. 100.

Apart from those listed below, consider two of New York City's grandest dames, the 282-room **Plaza,** at Fifth Avenue and Central Park South (www. fairmont.com/theplaza; *©* **212/759-3000**) and the 1904 Beaux Arts classic build by John Jacob Aster, the **St. Regis,** 2.E 55th Street (www.stregis.com; *©* **212/753-4500**).

Very Expensive

Affinia Dumont ★ The Affinia Dumont is the perfect choice for fitness-focused guests: When you book a room, you can request a complimentary "Fit Kit" that will be prepared based on your needs for an in-room workout. The hotel also has a terrific fitness spa, with weights, cardio equipment, and massage and skin treatments. But even if you don't want to break a sweat, the hotel features amenities that make it an attractive option. The suites range from studios to two bedrooms, and all include full kitchens, at least one TV, a large desk with an ergonomic chair, the "Affinia Bed" with a custom-designed mattress and "pillow menu." The hotel is away from the center of Midtown, but still within easy walking distance of Herald Square shopping, the Empire State Building, Madison Square Garden, and Grand Central Terminal.

150 E. 34th St. (btw. Third and Lexington aves.), New York, NY 10016. www.affinia.com. *©* **212/ 481-7600.** Fax 212/889-8856. 241 units. From $350 studio suite; from $450 1-bedroom suite; from $650 2-bedroom suite. AE, DC, MC, V. Valet parking $45 per car, $55 per SUV. Subway: 6 to 33rd St. **Amenities:** Restaurant; concierge; health club and spa; room service; grocery-shopping service. *In room:* A/C, TV/VCR, Fit Kit, hair dryer, high-speed Internet, full kitchen, minibar.

The Benjamin ★★★ From the retro sign and clock on Lexington Avenue to the high-ceilinged marble lobby, when you enter the Benjamin, it's as if you've stepped into the Jazz Era of 1920s New York. But the in-room amenities are definitely 21st-century high-tech. All rooms are airy, but the deluxe studios and one-bedroom suites are extra large. There are a few one-bedroom suites with terraces. The hotel features a "sleep concierge" who *guarantees* a good night's sleep, and a pillow menu with 11 options, including buckwheat and Swedish Memory. I chose the standard down pillow and did not have to exercise the guarantee. If you are a light sleeper, book a room off Lexington Avenue, which can get busy most weeknights and mornings. The hotel also features a good fitness center and the Wellness Spa.

125 E. 50th St. (at Lexington Ave.), New York, NY 10022. www.thebenjamin.com. © **888/4-BEN-JAMIN** (423-6526) or 212/715-2500. Fax 212/715-2525. 209 units. From $429 superior guest room; from $449 deluxe studio; from $489 suite. Call or check website for specials. AE, DC, DISC, MC, V. Parking $45. Subway: 6 to 51st St.; E or F to Lexington Ave–53rd Street. Pets accepted. **Amenities:** Restaurant; concierge; exercise room; room service; full-service spa; valet service; sleep concierge. *In room:* A/C, TV w/pay movies/video games, high-speed Internet, kitchenette, microwave, minibar.

Four Seasons Hotel New York ★★ Designed by überarchitect I. M. Pei, this modernist tower of honey-hued limestone rises 52 stories, making it the city's tallest hotel and providing hundreds of rooms with a view. Enter via the soaring lobby, with its marble floors and backlit onyx ceiling. From the stellar service—only surpassed by the Ritz-Carlton hotels and Trump International—to the fantastic facilities, including a luxurious spa, this is a stunner. The soundproof guest rooms are among the city's largest, averaging 600 square feet, and feature massive windows (50% of which boast Central Park views). About two dozen of the priciest rooms also have terraces. The mammoth Florentine marble bathrooms have soaking tubs that fill in 60 seconds, and separate showers with pressure controls.

57 E. 57th St. (btw. Park and Madison aves.), New York, NY 10022. www.fourseasons.com. © **800/819-5053,** 800/487-3769, or 212/758-5700. Fax 212/758-5711. 368 units. $725–$925 double; from $1,550 suite. Extra rollaway bed $50. Check website for specials. AE, DC, DISC, MC, V. Parking $60. Subway: N, R, 4, 5, or 6 to 59th St. **Amenities:** Restaurant; bar w/evening entertainment; lobby lounge for afternoon tea and light fare; babysitting; children's program; concierge; 5,000-sq.-ft. fitness center and spa w/whirlpool, steam, and sauna; room service. *In room:* A/C, TV w/pay movies, hair dryer, high-speed Internet, minibar.

The Peninsula New York ★★★ Housed in a beauty of a landmark Beaux Arts building, the Peninsula is the perfect combination of old-world charm and modern, state-of-the-art technology. Rooms are huge with plenty of closet and storage space. The huge marble bathrooms all have soaking tubs with televisions so you can watch while taking your bubble bath. The Peninsula also features one of the best and biggest New York hotel health clubs and spas, the rooftop **Pen-Top Bar,** and a faultless concierge desk.

700 Fifth Ave. (at 55th St.), New York, NY 10019. www.peninsula.com. © **800/262-9467** or 212/956-2888. Fax 212/903-3949. 239 units. $975–$1,175 double; from $1,375 suite. Extra person rollaway charge $75. Children 18 years and under stay free in parent's room. Winter weekend package rates from $795 at press time. AE, DC, DISC, MC, V. Valet parking $55. Subway: E or M to Fifth Ave. Pets accepted. **Amenities:** Restaurant; rooftop bar; library-style lounge for afternoon tea and cocktails; babysitting; room service; tri-level rooftop health club and spa w/exercise classes, heated pool, sauna, sun deck, treatment rooms, and whirlpool. *In room:* A/C, TV w/pay movies, fax, hair dryer, minibar, complimentary "water bar" w/5 choices of bottled water, Wi-Fi (free).

The Pierre ★★★ A property of India-based Taj Hotels, the Pierre, along with the St. Regis and the Plaza, is one of New York's grandest of grand dame hotels. The elegant white-glove service, elevator operators, sprawling hallways, and high-ceilinged, sumptuous rooms remain, but now are meshed with a more contemporary feel. Rooms are apartment-like, many with Central Park views, and now feature amenities like Bose wave studio music systems and 40-inch plasma televisions. The marble-clad bathrooms were redesigned, adding glass-walled showers and, in some rooms, tubs decadently equipped with flat-panel televisions. As part of the renovation, high tea is now served, along with cocktails at

2E, the new lobby lounge off the hotel's 61st Street entrance. A stay at the Pierre, if you can afford it, is a one-of-a-kind New York experience.

Fifth Ave. (at 61st St.), New York, NY 10021. www.tajhotels.com/pierre. ☎ **800/838-8000.** Fax 212/940-8109. 189 units. AE, DC, DISC, MC, V. From $495 double. Parking $60. Subway: N, R to 59th St./Fifth Ave. **Amenities:** Restaurant; 2 bars; concierge; fitness center and spa; room service. *In room:* A/C, TV, Bose Wave studios systems, fax machine, Wi-Fi (free).

The Setai ★★★ Contemporary grandeur in the form of a steep, limestone 60-floor tower debuted on Fifth Avenue in late 2010 in the form of The Setai. A combination hotel/condo, the Setai offers some of the largest rooms I've seen along with five-star service, a Michael White-helmed restaurant called **Ai Fiori**, a spa with over 11,000 square feet featuring four "lunar" treatments, and a Julien Farel salon offering styling for both women and men. Just a few blocks from the Empire State Building, Bryant Park, and Herald Square just adds to the appeal of the Setai. Most guest rooms are larger than 700 square feet and have deep soaking tubs, televisions inset into the bathroom mirrors, and expansive windows. If you want to splurge, book an apartment suite, which includes a state-of-the-art kitchens that might even tempt you to cook something during your stay. The only problem at the Setai is that all this wonderfulness will make it very hard to venture out.

400 Fifth Ave. (btw, 36th and 37th sts). www.setaififthavenue.com. ☎ **212/695-4005.** 214 units. From $595. AE, DC, DISC, MC, V. Valet parking $80. Subway: B, D, F, M, N, R, Q to 34th St. **Amenities:** Restaurant; bar; fitness center; personal assistants; 24-hour room service; spa; salon; complimentary pressing service upon arrival. *In room:* A/C, TV, iPod docking stations, espresso machines, minibar, kitchens in apartment suites, washer/dryer in apartment suites, Wi-Fi (free).

Expensive

Andaz Fifth Avenue ★★ 🎁 In mid-2010 the second Andaz hotel (the first was Andaz Wall Street, p. 90), a boutique brand of Hyatt hotels, opened in New York at what couldn't be a more central location on Fifth Avenue—across from the New York Public Library. But it's not just the location that makes the property desirable. Upon arrival, you're greeted with a personal check-in, in which roving staff members with hand held computers complete the business and then escort you to your room. And those rooms are all spacious with high ceilings, high tech controls, complimentary snack and beverage bar (excluding alcohol), enormous bathrooms with a foot soaking basin (a first in any New York hotel I've visited), and original art by Uruguayan artist, Carlos Capelan. Other perks include New York-centric art in the hallways by students at local New York public schools, a subterranean bar, a restaurant featuring local and organic produce, and virtual concierge services.

485 Fifth Ave. (at 41st St.) New York, NY, 10017. www.andaz.com. ☎ **212/601-1234.** Fax 212/601-8888. 194 units. AE, MC, V. From $465 double. Parking $60. Subway: B, D, F, M to 42nd Street. **Amenities:** Restaurant; bar; concierge; fitness center; room service. *In room:* A/C, TV, iPod docking stations, hair dryer, Wi-Fi (free).

Hotel Elysée ★★ This romantic gem in the heart of Midtown might be easy to miss: It's dwarfed by glass towers on either side of it. But that it is so inconspicuous is part of the Elysée's immense appeal. Built in 1926, the hotel has a storied past as the preferred address for artists and writers, including Tennessee Williams, Jimmy Breslin, Maria Callas, and Vladimir Horowitz (who donated a Steinway, which still resides in the Piano Suite). The hotel retains that sexy, discreet feel. Rooms have many quirky features; some have fireplaces, others have kitchens or solariums, and all are decorated in country-French furnishings. Good-size bathrooms are done up in Italian marble and well outfitted. Off the gorgeous black-and-white marble-floored lobby is the legendary **Monkey Bar.** On the second floor is the Club Room, where a free continental breakfast is offered daily, along with complimentary wine and cheese weekday evenings.

60 E. 54th St. (btw. Park and Madison aves.), New York, NY 10022. www.elyseehotel.com. ⓒ **800/535-9733** or 212/753-1066. Fax 212/980-9278. 103 units. From $249 double; from $409 suite. Check website for seasonal specials. Rates include continental breakfast and evening wine-and-cheese reception. AE, DC, DISC, MC, V. Parking $30. Subway: E or M to Fifth Ave. **Amenities:** Restaurant; bar; concierge; free access to nearby gym; room service. *In room:* A/C, TV/VCR, DVD on request, iPod docking stations/radio/alarm clock, hair dryer, minibar, Wi-Fi (free).

The Kitano New York ★   Owned by the Kitano Group of Japan, this elegant Murray Hill gem offers a unique mix of East and West sensibilities. The marble and mahogany lobby, with its Y-shaped staircase and Botero bronze *Dog,* is one of the most attractive in New York. If you're a lucky (and wealthy) individual, you'll get the opportunity to stay in one of three one-bedroom town-house suites, each with sunken living room, bay windows, and original, eclectic art. Or if your sensibilities are Eastern-oriented, the hotel offers the Tatami suite, with tatami mats, rice paper screens, and a Japanese tea ceremony room. All rooms include mahogany furniture, soundproof windows, and, for a real taste of Japan, green tea upon arrival; marble bathrooms are large and have heated towel racks and removable shower heads. On the mezzanine-level is a bar, where Wednesday through Saturday you can hear the acclaimed **Jazz at the Kitano.**

66 Park Ave. (at 38th St.), New York, NY 10016. www.kitano.com. ⓒ **800/548-2666** or 212/885-7000. Fax 212/885-7100. 149 units. $249–$605 double; from $450–$750 junior suite. Check website for specials, which were as low as $235 at press time. AE, DC, DISC, MC, V. Parking $40. Subway: 4, 5, 6, 7, or S to Grand Central. **Amenities:** 2 restaurants; bar w/live jazz; concierge; complimentary access to a nearby health club; room service. *In room:* A/C, TV, fax, hair dryer, high-speed Internet.

The Library Hotel ★★ 🛍   Located 1 block from the New York Public Library, the Library Hotel has a pleasing, informal feel. Each of the Library Hotel's 10 guest-room floors is dedicated to 1 of the 10 major categories of the Dewey Decimal System. When I visited the hotel, I was appropriately booked into a "Geography and Travel" room. Guest rooms, which come in three categories—petite (really small), deluxe, and junior suites—feature mahogany built-ins, generous desks, and immaculate marble bathrooms; all are extremely comfortable. The Library's public spaces—a reading room where weekday wine and cheese and a complimentary daily breakfast are served, a writer's den with a fireplace and flatscreen TV, and a rooftop terrace—all help make it a welcome refuge in the heart of the city.

299 Madison Ave. (at 41st St.), New York, NY 10017. www.libraryhotel.com. ⓒ **877/793-7323** or 212/983-4500. Fax 212/499-9099. 60 units. $239–$289 double; $329 Love Room or junior suite; $619 2-room family suite. Rates include continental breakfast buffet, all-day snacks, and wine and cheese nightly. Check the website for packages and weekend rates (as low as $329 at press time). AE, DC, MC, V. Parking $30 nearby. Subway: 4, 5, 6, 7, or S to 42nd St./Grand Central. **Amenities:** Restaurant; roof garden lounge; free access to nearby health club; room service; video library of American Film Institute's Top 100 films. *In room:* A/C, TV/VCR, CD player, iPod docking station/radio/alarm, hair dryer, minibar, Wi-Fi (free).

HOTEL pet peeves

In my research for this book, I spend a lot of (perhaps *too* much) time in hotels trying to weed out the good from the bad. Many think it's a glamorous job: staying at luxury New York hotels, indulging in room service, spa services, and lounging in plush robes while I do my "research." Yet, it is still a *job*, and while I certainly enjoy the fun parts, I have compiled an extensive list of things that bug me about hotels, little irritants that make me shake my head when they occur (particularly when it's an expensive room in New York City!). So here is my top 10 (. . . well, 11) list of hotel pet peeves, things that you should look out for next time you book a room . . . if you can.

1. **Noisy hallways:** Why is it that the storage rooms for housekeeping are always right next to my room? Or are they on every floor? The opening and closing of doors, chattering of housekeepers, rattling of carts—and it goes on well into the night and begins first thing in the morning.

2. **Temperature control:** I'll be the first to admit that I'm not very technologically savvy, but why can't I ever get the right temperature in any of my rooms? It's always too hot or too cold, no matter what I do.

3. **Smoking rooms:** I always request a smoke-free room. Why, then, sometimes, when I check into a room, is there often that stale barroom smell, like a sense memory of the days when smoking was allowed in bars? If a two-pack-a-day smoker was staying in your suite before you, an air-purifying ionizer should be provided to you at no charge (and used to treat the room before you arrive).

4. **An extra charge to use the fitness facilities:** It seems that the hotels that practice this outrageous policy are the ones whose rates are equally outrageous. I can accurately call this greed.

5. **Charging extra for Wi-Fi:** See above. (In fact, it's the budget hotels that are usually the best at offering free Internet service.)

The New York Palace ★★　In perhaps the most prime of prime locations, in the absolute heart of Midtown, a block from Rockefeller Center, St. Patrick's Cathedral, fashionable Fifth Avenue, and adorned by the magnificent, 19th-century Villard Mansion on Madison Avenue and 50th Street, the New York Palace has undergone many transformations in the past decade. Now a member of the prestigious, London-based Dorchester Collection of Hotels (the Beverly Hills Hotel, Hotel Plaza Athéneé in Paris, and Principe di Savoia in Milan), the Palace has been spruced up in appearance and service to match that company's esteemed reputation. Rooms have always been grand, some with amazing views of Rockefeller Center and St. Patrick's, but now they have added a sleeker, more contemporary look along with high-tech amenities such as iPod docking stations and high-definition flatscreen televisions. Still, for a hotel this opulent, better window soundproofing should have been part of the renovations; I could hear, clearly, trucks and construction from my room on the 49th floor.

455 Madison Ave. (at 50th St.), New York, NY 10022. www.newyorkpalace.com. © **800/804-7035** or 212/888-7000. Fax 212/303-6000. 899 units. AE, DC, DISC, MC, V. $349–$1,199 double.

6. **Overstuffed minibars:** You bought a beer at a local deli that you would like to drink while watching a game on the enormous HDTV in your room. You want to keep the beer cold, but, no matter how hard you try, you cannot squeeze it into that minibar . . . and if you take something out, sensors that monitor removal of items will record it and charge you, even if you didn't drink it.

7. **Complimentary bottled water, or lack thereof:** Many hotels now provide a bottle or two when you check in, yet, those same culprits who charge for Wi-Fi and using the fitness facilities make you take it out of the overstuffed minibar and charge you several bucks for it. (Or they put it by the bed or in the bathroom with a note that tells you how much it costs.)

8. **Lack of bathroom counter space:** Many hotels now feature big glass or porcelain tub–like sinks, and they look great and are perfect for scooping big handfuls of water onto your face. But when I unpack my toiletries, I would like to keep my toothbrush, toothpaste, shaving cream, and razor close to the sink instead of on top of the toilet tank.

9. **Single-paned windows:** You might get away with them at a beachside resort, but in New York City it is *essential* to have double- or, better yet, triple-paned windows, especially if your room happens to overlook a busy street. *(WHAT? I COULDN'T HEAR YOU OVER THE GARBAGE TRUCK OUTSIDE!)*

10. **Showers without shower curtains or shower doors:** I know, designers think a half-pane of Plexiglas is sufficient to keep water from spilling onto the bathroom floor and it looks very hip. Why, then, do I think something is missing when I take a shower? (Well, except for a puddle on the floor. That's there.)

11. **Pounding dance music in the elevators:** Am I in a hotel or a nightclub? I would almost prefer catatonic Muzak to the monotonous "beat" of the bass in the comfy confines of an elevator.

From $772 suite. Parking $51. Subway: 6 to 51st Street. E or M to 53rd Street–Fifth Avenue. **Amenities:** 2 restaurants; bar; concierge; fitness center and spa; room service. *In room:* A/C, TV, hair dryer, iPod docking stations, Wi-Fi (free).

The Roger ★★   Starting from the welcoming lobby with its odd assortment of mod yet comfortable seating to the many different varieties of rooms—some small, some generous, some with huge landscaped terraces, others with views of the Empire State building, and all with impressive amenities such as quilts, flatscreen TVs, and good-size marble bathrooms—the Roger is one of the top choices in what is a quiet yet convenient Midtown location. A floating granite staircase leads from the lobby to a mezzanine lounge, where you can have breakfast in the morning and drink cocktails by candlelight at night.

131 Madison Ave. (at E. 31st St.), New York, NY 10016. www.hotelrogerwilliams.com. ✆ **888/448-7788** or 212/448-7000. Fax 212/448-7007. 193 units. From $319 double. AE, DC, DISC, MC, V. Subway: 6 to 28th St./Lexington Ave. **Amenities:** Lounge; concierge; fitness center. *In room:* A/C, flatscreen TV, minibar, Wi-Fi (free).

70 Park Avenue ★ New York's first Kimpton property, and in keeping with that company's New Age trademark, this hotel encourages environmental awareness (including guest recycling and water-saving programs); guests even get a yoga channel on their TVs. The lobby is a beauty, with a long wooden table that serves as the concierge station and a 14-foot limestone-and-sandstone fireplace. Guest rooms, though not overly large, are efficiently constructed with an economical use of space: Note the minibar tucked into a dresser and the mahogany armoire that serves as the closet. In the room where I stayed, there were five huge mirrors, which could be a good thing or a bad thing depending on your self-esteem. Bathrooms in standard rooms are a bit tight but well outfitted, while a number of guest rooms offer two-person whirlpool spa tubs.

70 Park Ave. (btw. 37th and 38th sts.), New York, NY 10016. www.70parkave.com. © **877/707-2752** or 212/973-2400. Fax 212/973-2401. 205 units. $275–$525 double; from $1,000 suites. Check website for specials. AE, DC, DISC, MC, V. Valet parking $42. Subway: 4, 5, 6, 7, or S to Grand Central. Pets accepted. **Amenities:** Restaurant; bar; complimentary wine reception, concierge; access to nearby fitness center; room service. *In room:* A/C, TV, DVD/CD player, hair dryer, high-speed Internet, minibar, phone.

Waldorf=Astoria and the Waldorf Towers ★★ If you are looking for the epitome of old-school elegance, stop at the Waldorf=Astoria. This 1-square-block Art Deco masterpiece is not only a hotel icon, but also a New York City landmark. Here you'll find a lobby so big and grand, it's reminiscent of Grand Central Terminal, and with its own signature clock. With over 1,000 rooms, the pace can be hectic, and at times the lines for checking in might remind you of the post office. And what rooms they are; no two the same, yet all are airy, with high ceilings, traditional decor, comfortable linens and beds, and spacious marble bathrooms. For even more opulence, try a suite in the **Waldorf Towers,** where most rooms are bigger than most New York City apartments. Tower rooms include butler service, and Clefs d'Or concierge service.

　　Peacock Alley, off the main lobby, is open for breakfast, lunch, and dinner, and is also famous for the sumptuous Sunday brunch.

301 Park Ave. (btw. 49th and 50th sts.), New York, NY 10022. www.waldorfastoria.com. © **800/WALDORF** (925-3673), 800/774-1500, or 212/355-3000. Fax 212/872-7272 (Astoria) or 212/872-4875 (Towers). 1,245 units (180 in the Towers). Waldorf=Astoria $259–$585 double; from $549 suite. Waldorf Towers $419–$959 double; from $799 suite. Extra person $35. Children 17 and under stay free in parent's room. Corporate, senior, seasonal, and weekend discounts may be available (as low as $189 at press time), as well as attractive package deals. AE, DC, DISC, MC, V. Parking $55. Subway: 6 to 51st St. **Amenities:** 4 restaurants; 4 bars; concierge and theater desk; executive-level rooms; 3,000-sq.-ft. fitness center and excellent spa; room service. *In room:* A/C, TV w/pay movies, hair dryer, high-speed Internet (in executive-level rooms and suites), minibar. Waldorf Towers suites include kitchenette or wet bar w/fridge.

Moderate

Also consider the sliver-like, 66-room **Gotham Hotel,** 16 E. 46th Street (www.thegothamhotelny.com; © **212/490-8500**) which opened in late 2010 on the location of the famous Gotham Book Mart and pays homage to that literary past by providing books in every room, along with terraces where you might want to step out and read one.

Doubletree Metropolitan Hotel 🎐 With its retro 1960s look, this Doubletree brand hotel features a lobby stocked with mod furniture on which guests can lounge and surf the Internet on their laptops (the public spaces have Wi-Fi). Guest rooms are on the smallish side, and even with the renovations (including LCD televisions), they still have a cookie-cutter, motel feel to them. The beds, however, are like other Doubletree properties: extremely comfortable, guaranteeing the "Sweet Dreams by Doubletree Sleep Experience."

569 Lexington Ave. (at 51st St.), New York, NY 10022. www.dtnewyork.com. ✆ **800/836-6471** or 212/752-7000. Fax 212/758-6311. 755 units. $250–$350 single; $300–$450 double. Check website for specials as low as $199. AE, DC, MC, V. Parking $30 nearby. Subway: 6 to 51st St.; E or M to Lexington Ave. **Amenities:** Restaurant; bar; concierge; fitness center; room service. *In room:* A/C, TV, hair dryer, high-speed Internet, 2-line phone.

Inexpensive

Hotel Grand Union 🍴 This centrally located hotel is big with budget-minded international travelers. A pleasant white-on-white lobby leads to clean and spacious rooms with nice extras that are uncommon in this price category, such as hair dryers and free HBO. Fluorescent overhead lighting, unattractive colonial-style furniture, and an utter lack of natural light dampen the mood—but considering the roominess, low rates, and central-to-everything location, the Grand Union is a good deal. Room no. 309, a nicely configured quad with two twins and a queen in a separate alcove, is great for families. The staff is helpful, and there's a pleasant sitting room off the lobby and an adjacent coffee shop for morning coffee or a quick burger.

34 E. 32nd St. (btw. Madison and Park aves.), New York, NY 10016. www.hotelgrandunion.com. ✆ **212/683-5890.** Fax 212/689-7397. 95 units. $150–$225 single or double; $225–$300 twin or triple; $245–375 quad. Call or check website for special rates (as low as $90 at press time). AE, DC, DISC, MC, V. Parking $22 nearby. Subway: 6 to 33rd St. **Amenities:** Coffee shop; fax service. *In room:* A/C, TV, fridge, hair dryer, high-speed Internet (free).

Hotel Thirty Thirty ★ 🍴 Thirty Thirty is just right for bargain-hunting travelers looking for a splash of style with an affordable price tag. The design-conscious tone is set in the loftlike industrial-modern lobby. Rooms are mostly on the smallish side but do the trick for those who intend to spend their days out on the town rather than holed up here. Configurations are split between twin/twins (great for friends), queens, and queen/queens (great for triples, budget-minded quads, or shares who want more spreading-out room). A few larger units have kitchenettes, great if you're staying for a while, as you'll appreciate the extra room and the fridge. There's no room service, but delivery is available from nearby restaurants.

30 E. 30th St. (btw. Madison and Park aves.), New York, NY 10016. www.thirtythirty-nyc.com. ✆ **800/804-4480** or 212/689-1900. Fax 212/689-0023. 243 units. $139–$349 double; $259–$599. Call for last-minute deals, or check website for special promotions (as low as $101 at press time). AE, DC, DISC, MC, V. Parking $30 1 block away. Subway: 6 to 28th St. Pets accepted with advance approval. **Amenities:** Restaurant; concierge. *In room:* A/C, TV, hair dryer.

Murray Hill Inn In a renovated five-story walk-up in a quiet residential neighborhood, the Murray Hill Inn is shoestring basic—but there's no arguing with its cleanliness. Rooms are tiny and outfitted with not much more than either one or two beds with motel-standard bedspread and furnishings, a wall rack, a phone, and a small TV; most rooms with shared bathroom also have private sinks (request one when booking). These Euro-style rooms share in-hall bathrooms that are new and spotless. Some of the doubles have alcoves that can accommodate third travelers on cots if you're on an extra-tight budget. Rooms with private bathrooms are the nicest; most also have pullout sofas that can accommodate an extra traveler or two. Don't expect much in terms of facilities beyond a pleasant (if tiny) lobby, plus a downstairs sitting area with a vending machine, an ATM, and a luggage-storage area.

143 E. 30th St. (btw. Lexington and Third aves.), New York, NY 10016. www.murrayhillinn.com. ℭ **888/996-6376** or 212/545-0879. Fax 212/545-0103. 45 units, 3 with shared bathroom. $89 double with shared bathroom; $109–$159 double with private bathroom; $95–$169 private deluxe. Extra person $15. Children 11 and under stay free in parent's room. AE, MC, V. Parking about $25 nearby. Subway: 6 to 28th St. *In room:* A/C, TV, high-speed Internet.

UPPER WEST SIDE

Probably the most residential neighborhood in the city, the Upper West Side, compared to the other neighborhoods, has the homiest feel to it. Close to Lincoln Center, Central Park, Riverside Park, and the Museum of Natural History, the Upper West Side also offers many subway routes to midtown and downtown.

To find the hotels described in this section, see map on p. 100.

Very Expensive

Trump International Hotel & Tower ★★★   From the outside, it's a tall, dark monolith, hovering over Columbus Circle and lower Central Park. But go inside and spend a night or two, and experience services such as your own "Trump Attaché," a personal concierge who will provide comprehensive services; take advantage of such first-class facilities as the 6,000-square-foot health club with lap pool and a full-service spa; or order room service from the hotel's signature restaurant, the four-star **Jean-Georges.**

Guest rooms are surprisingly understated, with high ceilings and floor-to-ceiling windows, some with incredible views of Central Park and all with telescopes for taking in the view, and marble bathrooms with Jacuzzi tubs. But if that's not enough—it certainly was for me—you also get two complimentary bottles of Trump water, complete with a picture of the Donald on each one. For a hotel this well run, you can forgive the man for his excesses.

1 Central Park West (at 60th St.), New York, NY 10023. www.trumpintl.com. ℭ **212/299-1000.** Fax 212/299-1150. 176 units. From $765 double; from $1,200 1- or 2-bedroom suite. Children stay free in parent's room. Check website for special rates and package deals; also try booking through www.travelweb.com for discounted rates. AE, DC, DISC, MC, V. Parking $48. Subway: A, B, C, D, or 1 to 59th St./Columbus Circle. Pets allowed. **Amenities:** Restaurant; babysitting; butler (personal attaché); concierge; health club w/spa and pool; DVD Library. *In room:* A/C, TV/VCR w/pay movies and video games, DVD/CD player, iPod docking stations, fax/copier/printer, hair dryer, high-speed Internet, minibar.

Expensive

The Empire Hotel ★   If the Upper West Side needs a gateway symbol, the Empire Hotel and its beaconlike neon sign is, and has been, that symbol for more than 50 years. Situated where Broadway and Columbus (9th) Avenue intersect at 63rd Street, across the street from Lincoln Center, and 1 block from Central Park, the Empire Hotel's location is as good as it gets. After a renovation, the rooms were enlarged and designed in rich earth tones while the bathrooms feature showers (no tubs) with rain shower heads. The rooftop bar and pool and a big neighborhood attraction as well. Though there is much to like about the new Empire Hotel, why, during the room renovations, were not double- or triple-paned windows installed to keep out the noise of what is a very busy intersection?

44 W. 63rd St (btw. Broadway and Columbus Ave.), New York, NY 10023. www.empirehotelnyc. com. ☏ **212/265-7400.** Fax 212/265-7401. 420 units. From $229 double. Check website for specials. AE, DC, DISC, MC, V. Parking $60. Subway: 1 to 66th St.; A, B, C, D, or 1 to 59th St./ Columbus Circle. **Amenities:** Restaurant; 2 bars; concierge; fitness center and spa; rooftop pool. *In room:* A/C, TV, minibar, iPod docking stations, Wi-Fi (free).

Moderate

In addition to the hotels below, also consider the romantic **Country Inn the City ★**, 270 W. 77th St., between Broadway and West End Avenue (www.country innthecity.com; ☏ **212/580-4183**), comprised of four self-contained units in a charming 1891 town house (see "Plenty of Room at the Inn," p. 96).

Excelsior Hotel Located across from the Museum of Natural History and steps from Central Park, the Excelsior couldn't ask for a better address. Freshly done in an attractive traditional style, the guest rooms boast high-quality furnishings. The two-bedded rooms are large enough to accommodate budget-minded families (a few even have two queens), and suites feature pullout sofas and trouser presses. The museum-facing rooms are only worth the extra dough if a park view is important to you, as all rooms are relatively bright and quiet. On the second floor is a library-style lounge with working fireplace, books, games, leather seating, writing desks, and a large flatscreen TV.

45 W. 81st St. (btw. Columbus Ave. and Central Park West), New York, NY 10024. www.excelsior hotelny.com. ☏ **212/362-9200.** Fax 212/580-3972. 198 units. $150–$499 double; $399–$699 1-bedroom suite; $499–$899 2-bedroom suite. Extra person $20. Children 12 and under stay free in parent's room. Inquire about seasonal rates and specials (winter rates can go as low as $199 double). AE, DC, DISC, MC, V. Parking $27 nearby. Subway: B or C to 81st St./Museum of Natural History. **Amenities:** Restaurant; breakfast room w/2 open-air decks and daily breakfast buffet; concierge; exercise room. *In room:* A/C, TV w/pay movies/video games, fax/copier, hair dryer, Wi-Fi (free).

Hotel Beacon ★★ ☺ ✦ For families, you won't find a better location—or value. Close to Central Park and Riverside Park, the Museum of Natural History and Lincoln Center, and major subway lines, the Beacon's location is ideal. Rooms were recently updated and are generously sized, featuring a kitchenette, a roomy closet, and a marble bathroom. Nearly all standard rooms have two double beds, and they're plenty big enough to sleep a family on a budget. The large one- and two-bedroom suites are some of the best bargains in the city; each has two closets and a pullout sofa in the well-furnished living room. The two-bedroom suites have a second bathroom, enough to house a small army—including my own. There's no room service, but a wealth of good budget dining options that deliver, along with such excellent markets as Fairway, Trader Joe's, and Citarella, make the Beacon even more of a home away from home.

2130 Broadway (at 75th St.), New York, NY 10023. www.beaconhotel.com. ☏ **800/572-4969** or 212/787-1100. Fax 212/724-0839. 265 units. Double from $205; 1-bedroom suite suites from $250. Extra person $15. Children 12 and under stay free in parent's room. Check website for specials. AE, DC, DISC, MC, V. Parking $55 1 block away. Subway: 1, 2, or 3 to 72nd St. **Amenities:** Coffee shop adjacent; concierge; access to nearby health club; Internet center. *In room:* A/C, TV w/pay movies, hair dryer, fully stocked kitchenette.

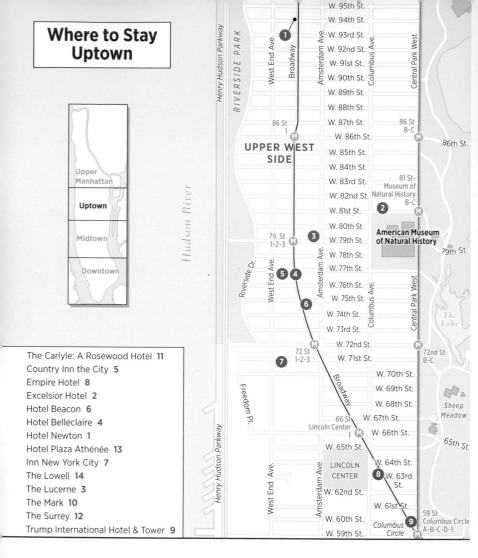

Where to Stay Uptown

Upper Manhattan

Uptown

Midtown

Downtown

Hudson River

RIVERSIDE PARK

UPPER WEST SIDE

American Museum of Natural History

The Lake

Sheep Meadow

LINCOLN CENTER

Columbus Circle

Inn New York City ★★★ 🎁 Tucked away in an Upper West Side brownstone in is a quaint, almost rustic retreat located, ironically, in the shadow of Donald Trump's mammoth and unrustic Trump Place. Featuring four delicious, self-contained units—each has a full kitchen—Inn New York City offers a very different experience than one you will find at your standard New York City hotel. Here, after a day of touring, you can relax in the huge Jacuzzi in the Spa Suite, or sip coffee on the terrace overlooking the tranquil backyard from the Inn's Opera Suite. If you have a family, the very spacious Library Suite comes equipped with a sofa bed and a pocket door that separates the sleeping areas. Along with all the rustic—the quilts, stained glass, and antique furnishings—you also get modern amenities like plasma televisions. A stay at the romantic Inn New York City is as special as it gets.

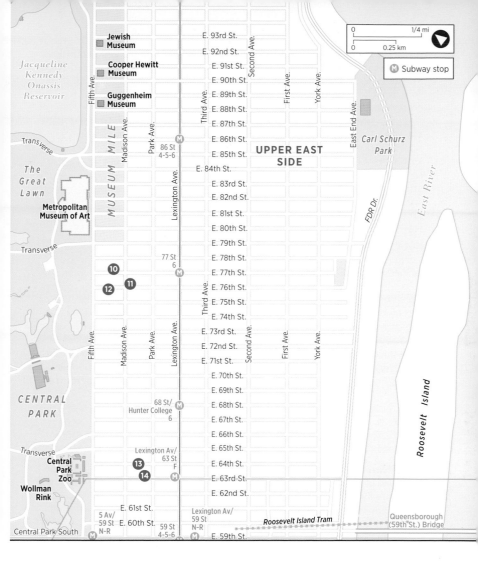

266 W. 71st St. (btw. Amsterdam and West End aves.), New York, NY 10023. www.innnewyorkcity. com. ☎ **212/580-1900.** Fax 212/580-4437. 4 units. AC, MC, V. $475–$645 double. Check website for specials. Parking $38. Subway: 1, 2, 3 to 72nd St. *In room:* A/C, TV, CD/DVD players, kitchen, complimentary snacks, wine and cheese on arrival, Wi-Fi (free).

The Lucerne ★★ As a longtime resident of the Upper West Side, I can easily say the Lucerne, in a magnificent 1903 landmark building, best captures the feel of this special neighborhood. Service is impeccable, especially for a moderately priced hotel, and everything is fresh and immaculate. The rooms are comfortable and big enough for kings, queens, or two doubles, with attractive bathrooms complete with travertine counters. Some of the rooms have views of the Hudson

River. The suites are extra special and include kitchenettes, stocked minifridges, microwaves, and sitting rooms with sofas and extra TVs. The highly rated **Nice Matin** (p. 193) offers room service for breakfast, lunch, and dinner. But if you don't want to dine there, you can sample some of the neighborhood food at nearby Zabar's or H&H Bagels.

201 W. 79th St. (at Amsterdam Ave.), New York, NY 10024. www.thelucernehotel.com. © **800/ 492-8122** or 212/875-1000. Fax 212/362-7251. 250 units. $200–$440 superior queen; $310– $470 superior double; $330–$490 superior king or deluxe double; $360–$520 deluxe king; $390–$600 1-bedroom suite. Extra person $20. Children 15 and under stay free in parent's room. AAA discounts offered; check website for deals as low as $189 at press time. AE, DC, DISC, MC, V. Parking $29 nearby, valet parking $42. Subway: 1 to 79th St. **Amenities:** Restaurant; fitness center; room service. *In room:* A/C, TV w/Nintendo, hair dryer, Wi-Fi (free).

Inexpensive

Hotel Belleclaire ★   This Beaux Arts hotel boasts a great Upper West Side location and renovated, stylish guest rooms that are larger than most. The accommodations, though simple, do the job, and the management seems intent on pleasing. The rooms have small, freshly tiled bathrooms with tub/shower combos (six have roll-in showers to accommodate travelers with disabilities). Beds have cushioned headboards, and there are nice fabric-covered cubes for modular seating; closets are small. The shared-bathroom units are the same but have in-room sinks and share hall bathrooms at a ratio of three to one. The family suite features two attached, semiprivate bedrooms with a bathroom, a minifridge, and a big walk-in closet. This is a decent choice in a first-class residential neighborhood.

250 W. 77th St. (at Broadway), New York, NY 10024. www.hotelbelleclaire.com. © **877/HOTEL-BC** (468-3522) or 212/362-7700. Fax 212/362-1004. 189 units, 39 with shared bathroom. $109– $269 double with shared bathroom; $169–$469 double with private bathroom; $229–$569 family suite. Ask about AAA, group, and other discounts. AE, DC, DISC, MC, V. Parking $25 nearby. Subway: 1 to 79th St. **Amenities:** Access to nearby health club. *In room:* A/C, TV w/pay movies and games, fridge, hair dryer, Wi-Fi (free).

Hotel Newton ★ ✔   On the northern edge of the Upper West Side, the Newton is one of the best choices in the city in the inexpensive category. As you enter the pretty lobby, you're greeted by a uniformed staff that's attentive and professional. The rooms are generally large, with good, firm beds, a work desk, and a sizable bathroom, plus roomy closets in most (a few of the cheapest have wall racks only). Some are big enough to accommodate families, with two doubles or two queen beds. The suites feature two queen beds in the bedroom, a sofa in the sitting room, plus niceties such as a microwave, minifridge, and iron, making them well worth the few extra dollars. The bigger rooms and suites have been upgraded with cherrywood furnishings, but even the older laminated furniture is much nicer than I usually see in this price range.

2528 Broadway (btw. 94th and 95th sts.), New York, NY 10025. www.thehotelnewton.com. © **888/HOTEL58** (468-3558) or 212/678-6500. Fax 212/678-6758. 110 units. $75–$175 double or junior suite. Extra person $25. Children 14 and under stay free in parent's room. AAA, corporate, senior, and group rates available; check website for special Internet deals. AE, DC, DISC, MC, V. Parking $27 nearby. Subway: 1, 2, or 3 to 96th St. **Amenities:** Room service. *In room:* A/C, TV, hair dryer, Wi-Fi ($4.95 per day).

UPPER EAST SIDE

Madison Avenue is showing its age, but if you want old time splendor and a location close to Central Park, a stay in this tony stretch will not disappoint.

To find the hotels described in this section, see map on p. 126.

Very Expensive

The Carlyle, a Rosewood Hotel ★★★　This 34-story grande dame towers over Madison Avenue, perfectly epitomizing the old-world, moneyed neighborhood where it stands. Service is white glove (literally) and doormen wear bowler hats; many celebrities and dignitaries, some with faces obscured by silk scarves, sip tea in the hotel's cozy Gallery. Guest rooms range from singles to seven-room suites, some with terraces and full dining rooms. All have marble bathrooms with whirlpool tubs and all the amenities you'd expect from a hotel of this caliber. The English manor–style decor is luxurious but not excessive, creating the comfortably elegant ambience of an Upper East Side apartment. Many apartments have breathtaking views of downtown or the West Side and Central Park.

The marble-floored lobby with Piranesi prints and murals is a beauty. The hotel's supper club, **Cafe Carlyle** (p. 422), offers first-rate cabaret. Charming **Bemelmans Bar,** named after illustrator Ludwig Bemelmans, who created the *Madeleine* books and painted the mural (see "Checking into Hotel Bars," in chapter 8), is a great spot for cocktails.

35 E. 76th St. (at Madison Ave.), New York, NY 10021. www.thecarlyle.com. ℂ **800/227-5737** or 212/744-1600. Fax 212/717-4682. 180 units. $650–$950 double; from $950 1- or 2-bedroom suite. AE, DC, DISC, MC, V. Parking $48. Subway: 6 to 77th St. Pets under 25 lbs. accepted. **Amenities:** 3 restaurants (including one of the city's best cabaret rooms); bar; tearoom; concierge; high-tech fitness room w/sauna, Jacuzzi, and spa services; room service; video library. *In room:* A/C, TV/ VCR, CD player, fax/copier/printer, hair dryer, high-speed Internet, pantry kitchenette or full kitchen w/minibar.

Hotel Plaza Athénée New York ★★★　This hideaway in New York's most elegant neighborhood (the stretch of Madison Ave. in the 60s) is elegant, luxurious, and oozing with sophistication. With antique furniture, hand-painted murals, and the Italian-marble floor that adorns the lobby, the Plaza Athénée has a European feel. In that tradition, service here is as good as it gets, with personalized check-in and attentive staff at every turn. The rooms come in a variety of shapes and sizes, and are all high ceilinged and spacious; entrance foyers give them a residential feel. Many of the suites have terraces large enough to dine on. The Portuguese-marble bathrooms are outfitted with thick robes made for the hotel. The lush, leather-floored lounge is called **Bar Seine** and is a welcome spot for a pre-dinner cocktail.

37 E. 64th St. (btw. Madison and Park aves.), New York, NY 10021. www.plaza-athenee.com. ℂ **800/ 447-8800** or 212/734-9100. Fax 212/772-0958. 142 units. $790–$825 double; from $1,620 suite. Check for packages and seasonal specials (as low as $495 at press time). AE, DC, DISC, MC, V. Parking $53. Subway: F to Lexington Ave.–63rd St. **Amenities:** Restaurant; bar; Clefs d'Or concierge; fitness center; room service; spa. *In room:* A/C, TV, fax, hair dryer, high-speed Internet, minibar.

The Lowell ★★★ ☺　The Lowell's style of luxury is best described as elegant, sophisticated 20th-century opulence. It has the feel of a residential dwelling; the lobby is small and clubby with first-rate European, old-world service. The rooms are the real treasures, each unique and all a good size. About two-thirds are suites with kitchenettes or full kitchens; some have terraces and most have working

STAYING ACROSS THE EAST RIVER IN queens

A construction boom in Long Island City (LIC) in Queens, directly across the East River from Midtown Manhattan, has led to a number of new chain hotels within viewing distance of the East Side. Should you consider staying at one of them? You might want to cross the river if:

○ You find a better price than at an equivalent Manhattan hotel, or can stay free with frequent-flier miles or a chain's reward program.

○ You are planning on some Queens-based activities, such as Mets games or the U.S. Open; LIC hotels are somewhat closer to those venues, but Manhattan is a short hop away. LIC and the next neighborhood over, Astoria, also have an interesting restaurant and bar scene.

○ You feel comfortable on the subway, and having to ride two or three stops out of Manhattan isn't going to faze

you. That said, make sure your hotel really *is* steps from the train; for example, the Holiday Inn in LIC, and soon to open Sheraton Four Points (with fabulous Manhattan views) are a block from the 39th Avenue stop on the N or Q train, while the trendy Raval Hotel (which has popular parties on its roof) is 6 long blocks from the nearest subway stop.

○ If it's the sort of thing that matters to you, the new hotels will likely have larger rooms than you'd find in Manhattan, and newer fixtures and furniture, along with extras like exercise rooms and hot tubs.

HERE ARE A FEW OF THE NEWER LIC CHOICES:

Best Western Plaza Hotel
39–34 21st St., Long Island City
(www.bestwesternnewyork.com;

℡ **718/880-3853;** Subway: F to Queensbridge/21st St). This brand-new Best Western is a no-smoking hotel,

fireplaces. In the rooms you'll also find nice big, cushy armchairs, lots of leather, interesting artwork, and porcelain figurines scattered about. Bathrooms are Italian marble and outfitted with Bulgari amenities. On a quiet, tree-lined street 1 block from Central Park and right in the middle of Madison Avenue shopping, the Lowell's location is ideal for those who want (and can afford) an urban retreat away from the Midtown madness.

28 E. 63rd St. (btw. Madison and Park aves.), New York, NY 10021. www.lowellhotel.com. ℡ **212/838-1400.** Fax 212/319-4230. 70 units. From $735 doubles; from $935 suites. Ask about packages and weekend and seasonal rates. AE, DC, DISC, MC, V. Parking $49. Subway: F to Lexington Ave.–63rd St. Pets under 15 lb. accepted. **Amenities:** 2 restaurants; tearoom; babysitting; concierge; well-outfitted fitness room; room service; video library. *In room:* A/C, TV/VCR/DVD, CD player, fax/copier, hair dryer, minibar, Wi-Fi (free).

The Mark ★★★   After a spectacular $150 million top-to-bottom renovation, the Mark Hotel has once again established itself, along with the Carlyle (p. 129) across the street, as the height in luxury in the already luxurious stretch of Madison Avenue real estate. Gone is the frumpy, grand dame, replaced by a contemporary, art-centric look along with the prerequisite high tech amenities, a Frederic Fekkai salon, and a restaurant helmed by master chef, Jean Georges Vongerichten offering 121 units, including 6 handi-capped accessible rooms. Continental breakfast is included, and there's a 24-hour exercise room, a business center, and free Wi-Fi. The street is busy and not very attractive, but you're steps from the train, and you're probably staying here for the good rates. The place is especially popular with European visitors. Rates ranged from under $100 to around $130 in spring 2011, with various Internet specials and discounts (from AARP and AAA, for example).

Quality Inn   30-03 40th Ave., Long Island City (www.qualityinn.com; ℭ **718/391-0202;** Subway: N or Q to 39th Ave.). The new-in-2009 Quality Inn offers 48 rooms two stops into LIC; rates include continental breakfast, free Wi-Fi, and a business center. Rates were running from about $100 to about $160 a night in spring 2011.

Verve Hotel   (an Ascend Collection Hotel), 40-03 29th St., Long Island City (www.ascendcollection.com; ℭ **718/786-4545;** Subway: N or Q to 39th Ave.).

Calling itself a "boutique hotel" with 87 units, the Verve is a no-smoking hotel, and rates include continental breakfast, free Wi-Fi, and an exercise and game room. Rates were as low as $119 for a double, to about $229 for a suite with a hot tub in spring 2011.

Fairfield Inn by Marriott New York Long Island City Manhattan View   52-34 Van Dam St., Long Island City (www.mariott.com; ℭ **718/389-7700;** Subway: 7 to 33rd/Rawson). The mouthful of a name is the reason for this hotel's popularity: It has a lovely view of Manhattan from many of the rooms as well as an outdoor patio/deck area. It's off the "International Express" (no. 7 train), and a complimentary shuttle runs to and from the hotel from the subway and nearby restaurants and attractions. The 154 rooms are no-smoking, and rates include an "expanded continental breakfast." Rates in spring 2010 ranged from $149–$201 for doubles, with last-minute specials dropping the price on some weekend stays.

(p. 197). There is nothing not to like here, with the exception of the steep rates: this kind of luxury does not come cheap. But for your money you get space; no rooms are less than 400 square feet and suites start at 700 square feet. Rooms are outfitted with Bang & Olufsen LCD televisions, subzero refrigerators and freezer drawers, marble bathrooms with deep soaking tubs, and maid service twice daily. A stay at The Mark is most definitely a splurge, but one you most likely never forget, and might even worth the money.

Madison Ave. (at 77th St.), New York, NY, 10075. www.themarkhotel.com. ℭ **212/744-4300,** 866/744-4300. Fax 212/606-3100. 150 units. $875–$1,025 superior rooms; from $1,590 suites. Check website for specials. AE, DISC, MC, V. Parking $55. Subway: 6 to 77th Street. **Amenities:** Restaurant; bar; fitness center; business center; concierge; room service; pet friendly. *In room:* A/C, TV, MP3, cordless phones, touch screen room control panel, Wi-Fi (free).

Expensive

The Surrey ★   Set among town houses between Madison and Fifth avenues, the Surrey has always reeked of classic Upper East Side elegance. But after a $60-million "re-creation," when you step inside the Art Deco gray-marble lobby and notice graffiti splattered on a large dresser near the elevators, you understand the "re-creation" was to offer elegance with an edge. Along with the Beaux Arts grandeur of the building, the rooms and public spaces are adorned with art by Jenny Holzer, Richard Serra, and William Kentridge. Rooms vary in size from cozy to spacious suites that offer private terraces. All are very well equipped though most standard rooms do not have tubs and, unfortunately, the re-creation did not soundproof the walls; I could clearly hear incessant Caribbean patois coming from a next-door maid's room. Still, the hotel offers a beautiful rooftop garden; a new, intimate bar; and room service by the very good **Café Boulud.**

20 E. 76th St. (btw. Fifth and Madison aves), New York, NY 10021. www.thesurrey.com. © **212/288-3700.** 190 units. AE, DC, DISC, MC, V. $450–$575 salon; from $899 suite. Subway: 6 to 77th St. Pet-friendly. **Amenities:** Restaurant; 2 bars; concierge; fitness center and spa; room service; rooftop garden. *In room:* A/C, TV, high-speed and wireless Internet, iPod docking station, minibar.

HARLEM

Consider a stay on what is called Harlem's Gold Coast in the new Starwood brand, **Aloft,** 2296 Frederick Douglass Blvd. (at 124th St.) (www.starwoodhotels. com/alofthotels; © **212/749-4000**), 1 block from the bustle of 125th Street, or at the **Harlem Flophouse** (p. 97).

BROOKLYN

The properties mentioned here are in vibrant neighborhoods and within an easy subway commute into Manhattan and also offer substantial discounts as compared to what you would pay across the river. Along with what's listed below, consider the new Starwood brand **Aloft,** 216 Duffield St. (www.starwoodhotels. com/alofthotels; © **718/256-3833**), in downtown Brooklyn.

Hotel Le Bleu ★ ✦   Curiously located on raw, industrial Fourth Avenue sits a modern, steel-and-cobalt-blue structure that claims to be Brooklyn's first luxury boutique hotel (it opened in late 2007). And if you are looking for a genuine Brooklyn experience—the hotel is a block from bustling Fifth Avenue in Park Slope with its many restaurants, bars, and shops—with unobstructed views of lower Manhattan, the Statue of Liberty, and the rooftops and churches of Brooklyn, as well as comforts and amenities you would pay much more for in Manhattan and just a few blocks from a subway stop to "the city," then Hotel Le Bleu is a solid value option. Rooms are well equipped with either king or double/doubles though the glass showers and bathrooms bleed into the living area—tastefully. All of the rooms have small terraces and the hotel provides a number of freebies, including a minibar, continental breakfast, and first-come, first-served parking in the hotel's small lot.

370 Fourth Ave. (btw. 3rd and 4th sts.), Brooklyn, NY 11215. www.hotellebleu.com. © **718/625-1500.** Fax 718/625-2600. 48 units. AE, DC, DISC, MC, V. $129–$219 double. Check the website for packages and specials. Complimentary parking. Subway: F, M, or R to 9th St./Brooklyn. **Amenities:** Restaurant; bar; complimentary continental breakfast; concierge; discount to local fitness clubs; room service. *In room:* A/C, TV, Bose integrated music system, CD player, hair dryer, free high-speed Internet, complimentary minibar, MP3 docking station.

Nu Hotel ★★ 🎁   A few blocks from downtown Brooklyn and subway lines leading quickly into Manhattan, and across the street from Brooklyn's restaurant row, Smith Street, the Nu Hotel couldn't have found a better location. This eco-friendly hotel uses cork flooring in the guest rooms, organic Baltic linen, and recycled teak-wood furnishings. Eco-friendly doesn't always translate to guest friendly; however, I'm happy to report that the Nu Hotel was more than friendly to me. Rooms, though not enormous, have high ceilings and windows that allow an abundance of light; mine had a view of the iconic Williamsburg Savings Bank. The larger rooms, including the "friends suites," have queens and bunk beds for families, while the "urban suites" feature a sitting area and your own personal hammock, making the Nu Hotel the only hotel in New York City that I know of that has hammocks. A well-equipped gym, complimentary breakfast, and business center add to the hotel's enormous appeal.

85 Smith St. (at Atlantic Ave.), Brooklyn, NY 11201. www.nuhotelbrooklyn.com. © **718/852-8585**. 93 units. $199–$249 double. AE, DC, DISC, MC, V. Parking $25. Subway: F to Bergen/Smith St.; A or C to Hoyt/Schermerhorn. **Amenities:** Lounge; complimentary continental breakfast; concierge; fitness club. *In room:* A/C, TV, jack packs to dock audio, video and computer electronics, Sangean radio, Sonus Satellite music systems in some rooms.

PRACTICAL INFORMATION
The Big Picture

In his annual assessment of New York City tourism in January 2011, Mayor Bloomberg proudly announced that the city attracted 48.7 million tourists in 2010, a record even more impressive because of continuing tough economic conditions. And to help all those tourists have a comfortable place to stay, the city added 6,600 rooms in 2010.

For this book, I have covered 10 new hotels, and as the book goes to press, many more are scheduled to open. The average rate in 2010 was $250 per night; still probably the highest in the country. And with the added rooms, deals can be found, though a deal in New York is far from a deal anywhere else. In terms of value, you're likely to get more *luxe* for your buck if you have the money to spend. Keep an eye out for specials, bargains, and packages designed to get you to NYC and to fill up the rooms at a much lower cost than last year.

And, keep in mind, that even at a lot of the luxury places, New York hotel rooms give everybody a new perspective on "small." Space is the city's biggest asset, and getting some will cost you. If you're on a tight budget, don't be surprised if your room isn't much bigger than the bed that's in it and your bathroom has a sink so small you'll have difficulty spitting out your toothpaste without spilling it. Even expensive rooms can be on the small side, lack closet space, or have smallish bathrooms.

Getting the Best Deal

In the listings above, I've tried to give you an idea of the kind of deals that may be available at particular hotels: which ones have the best packages, which ones offer AAA and other discounts, which ones allow kids to stay with Mom and Dad for free, and so on. But there's no way of knowing what the offers will be when you're booking, so also consider these general tips:

- **Ask about special rates or other discounts.** Always ask whether a room less expensive than the first one quoted is available, or whether any special rates apply to you. You may qualify for corporate, student, military, senior, or other discounts. Mention membership in AAA, AARP, frequent-flier programs, or if you are in the military, or a government or union worker, which may entitle you to special deals. Find out the policy on children—do kids stay free or is there a special rate?

o **Choose your season carefully.** Room rates can vary dramatically—by hundreds of dollars in some cases—depending on what time of year you visit. Winter, from January through March, is best for bargains, with summer (especially July–Aug) second best. Fall is the busiest and most expensive season after Christmas, but November tends to be quiet and rather affordable, as long as you're not booking a parade-route hotel on Thanksgiving weekend. All bets are off at Christmastime—expect to pay top dollar for everything.

o **Go uptown or downtown.** The advantages of a Midtown location are overrated, especially when saving money is your object. The subway can whisk you anywhere you want to go in minutes; even if you stay on the Upper West Side, you can be at the ferry launch for the Statue of Liberty in about a half-hour. You'll get the best value for your money by staying outside the Theater District, in the residential neighborhoods where real New Yorkers live, such as the Upper West Side, or even Brooklyn. Residential neighborhoods like TriBeCa, Greenwich Village, and the Lower East Side have slowly creeped up in price to near midtown-levels, so bargains in those neighborhoods might be harder to find.

o **Visit over a weekend.** If your trip includes a weekend, you might be able to save big. Business hotels tend to empty out, and rooms that go for $300 or more Monday through Thursday can drop dramatically, as low as $150 or less, once the execs have headed home. These deals are prevalent in the Financial District, but they're often available in tourist-friendly Midtown, too. Also, you'll find that Sunday nights are the least expensive. Check the hotel's website for weekend specials. Or just ask when you call.

o **Shop online.** Hotels often offer "Internet only" deals that can save you 10% to 20% or more over what you'd pay if you booked over the telephone. Also, hotels often advertise all of their available deals on their websites, so you don't have to rely on a reservation agent to fill you in. What's more, some of the discount reservations agencies (see below) have sites that allow you to book online. And consider joining the **Playbill Online Theater Club** (www.playbillclub.com), a free service that offers some excellent members-only rates at select city hotels, in addition to discounts on theater tickets. American Automobile Association members can often score the best discounts by booking at **www.aaa.com**. Travel search sites such as **Expedia** (www.expedia.com), **Priceline** (www.priceline.com), and **Travelocity** (www.travelocity.com) offer other discount options. Shop around. And if you have special needs—a quiet room, a room with a view—call the hotel directly and make your needs known after you've booked online.

o **Dial direct.** When booking a room in a chain hotel, you'll often get a better deal by calling the specific hotel's reservation desk rather than the chain's main number.

o **Make deals with the budget chains.** With a few exceptions, I have not listed budget chains in this chapter. In my opinion, they tend to lack the character and local feel that most independently run hotels have. And it's that feel, I believe, that is so much a part of the travel experience. Still, when you're looking for a deal, they can be a good option. Most hotels—particularly such chains as Comfort Inn and Best Western—are market sensitive. Because they hate to see rooms sit empty, they'll often negotiate good rates at the last minute and in slow seasons.

You can also pull out all the stops for discounts at a budget chain, from auto-club membership to senior status. You might be able to take advantage of corporate rates or discounted weekend stays. Most chain hotels let the kids stay with parents for free. Ask for every kind of discount; if you find that you get an unhelpful reservation agent, call back. Of course, there's no guarantee.

Two chains with franchises in Manhattan include **Best Western** (© **800/780-7234;** www.bestwestern.com), though their rack rates for New York hotels are higher than you'd expect, and **Howard Johnson** (© **800/446-4656;** www.hojo.com). There's a Best Western at South Street Seaport and at two Midtown locations, and a Howard Johnson in Queens. Check their websites for all the details.

At these and other franchised hotels—such as the ones run by **Apple Core Hotels** (www.applecorehotels.com), a management company that handles the **Comfort Inn Midtown,** the **Ramada Inn Eastside,** the **New York Manhattan Hotel** (p. 114), the **Hotel Times Square,** and **La Quinta** (p. 114)—doubles can go for as little as $109. Check with the franchiser if you're not quoted a good advance-booking rate or through the management company's online reservations system; their global 800 and online reservations systems will often garner you a better rate, which might include a promotion—or, at minimum, an "Internet user's rate" that's 10% lower than the standard.

A good source for deals is **Choice Hotels** (© **877/424-6423;** www. hotelchoice.com), which oversees Comfort Inn, Quality Hotel, and Clarion Hotel chains, all of which have Manhattan branches.

Another hotel to try is the **Hilton Garden Inn,** 790 Eighth Ave., at 48th Street (© **212/581-7000;** www.hiltongardeninn.com).

○ **Investigate reservations services.** These outfits usually work as consolidators, buying up or reserving rooms in bulk, and then dealing them out to customers at a profit. You can get 10% to 50% off; but remember, these discounts apply to rack rates—inflated prices that people rarely end up paying. You may get a decent rate, but always call the hotel directly to see if you can do better.

Quikbook (© **800/789-9887,** or 212/779-7666 outside the U.S.; www.quikbook.com) is the best of the bunch. You might also try the **Hotel Reservations Network,** also known as HotelDiscount.com (© **800/715-7666;** www.hoteldiscount.com).

Note: Never just rely on a reservations service or an online-booking site. Do a little homework; compare the rack rates to the discounted rates being offered to see what kind of deal they're actually offering. If you're being offered a stay in a hotel I haven't recommended, do more research on it, especially if it isn't a reliable chain name such as Holiday Inn or Hyatt. It's not a deal if you end up at a dump.

○ **Avoid excess charges and hidden costs.** When you book a room, ask whether the hotel charges for parking. Use your own cellphone, pay phones, or prepaid phone cards instead of dialing direct from hotel phones, which usually have exorbitant rates. And don't be tempted by minibar offerings: Most hotels charge through the nose for water, soda, and snacks. Finally, ask about local taxes and service charges, which can increase the cost of a room by 15% or more. If a hotel insists upon tacking on an "energy surcharge" that wasn't mentioned at check-in, you can often make a case for getting it removed.

o **Buy a money-saving package deal.** A travel package that combines your airfare and your hotel stay for one price may just be the best bargain of all. In some cases, you'll get airfare, accommodations, transportation to and from the airport, plus extras—maybe an afternoon sightseeing tour or restaurant and shopping discount coupons—for less than the hotel alone would have cost had you booked it yourself. Most airlines and many travel agents, as well as the usual booking websites (Priceline, Travelocity) offer good packages to New York City.

Alternative Accommodations

o **Consider B&B accommodations or an apartment.** If Big Apple hotels seem too expensive, or you'd just like something a little more like home, consider renting a room in a genuine New York apartment—or even an entire apartment. These accommodations can range from spartan to splendid, from a hosted bedroom in a private home to an unhosted, fully equipped apartment with multiple bedrooms. No matter what, you can pretty much guarantee that you'll get more for your money than if you book into a regular hotel. However, you need to be rather independent-minded to enjoy this option. For more, see the sidebar "Plenty of Room at the Inn," later in this chapter.

The place to start with is **Manhattan Getaways** (✆ **212/956-2010;** www.manhattangetaways.com) which maintains a beautifully kept and managed network of bed-and-breakfast rooms (from $110 nightly) and unhosted apartments (from $150) around the city. There's a 3-night minimum stay, and credit cards are accepted. Another decent bet is **Metro Home** (✆ **646/274-1505;** www.elitecitystays.com), which owns and manages 300 apartments around Manhattan starting at $99 a night, or $850 weekly for a basic studio. These are rather sparsely furnished apartments, and the company offers little in the way of service (it took me 5 days to get my TV fixed when I was displaced from my home by renovation), but the apartments are clean and do the trick. There's no minimum stay, and credit cards are accepted. Cleaning services are available for longer stays.

Additional agencies that can book you into a B&B room or a private apartment, with prices starting at $90 nightly, include **Abode Apartment Rentals** (✆ **800/835-8880** or 212/472-2000; www.abodenyc.com); **City Sonnet** (✆ **212/614-3034;** www.citysonnet.com); **Manhattan Lodgings** (✆ **212/677-7616;** www.manhattanlodgings.com); and **New York Habitat** (✆ **212/255-8018;** www.nyhabitat.com). Be sure to get all details in writing and an exact total upfront to avoid disappointments.

4

WHERE TO STAY | Practical Information

WHERE
TO DINE

O kay, I'm a bit prejudiced, but I am sure that New York is the best restaurant town in the country, and maybe the top food destination in the world. In Boston, you think of seafood; New Orleans, Creole and Cajun; Paris and Rome—you get what you expect you would get. But you cannot define a specific "local food" of New York because there really isn't any—the city is an amalgamation of global cuisines that you won't find anywhere else. And this amazing variety ranges from hole-in-the-wall ethnic joints to the most hallowed (and wallet-draining) temples of food. One thing you will not do in New York: Go hungry.

THE most unforgettable
DINING EXPERIENCES

- **Aquavit,** 65 E. 55th St. (☏ **212/307-7311;** www.aquavit.org): Though its new digs are not nearly as charming as its former town house setting, the service and the food are as good as ever. See p. 181.
- **Oceana,** 1221 Sixth Ave. (☏ **212/759-5941;** www.livanosrestaurantgroup.com): Now in a huge Rockefeller Center location, Oceana not only got bigger, it got better. The assortment of seafood, offered raw or prepared best simply, is as fresh as you will find anywhere in the city. See p. 173.
- **Big Wong King,** 67 Mott St. (☏ **212/964-0540**): Come here for the true Chinatown experience. You'll share tables with Chinese families, order bowls of *congee* with fried crullers, plates of stir-fried vegetables, and platters of roast pork and duck—all served by brusque no-nonsense waiters. I guarantee it will be unforgettable. See p. 145.
- **DiFara Pizza,** 1424 Ave. J, Brooklyn (☏ **718/258-1367**): Spend an hour in nondescript, often grimy DiFara and watch as Domenico DeMarco slowly, laboriously makes one pizza at a time until finally he is making yours, and you have the supreme privilege of tasting the most sublime pie you'll ever have. See p. 178.

best NEW RESTAURANTS

- **Locanda Verde,** 377 Greenwich St. (☏ **212/925-3797;** www.locandaverde nyc.com). Formerly the chef of A Voce, Andrew Carmellini found a home in the Greenwich Hotel's Locanda Verde. The restaurant's sheep's milk ricotta with herbs is one of the city's absolute must-haves. See p. 142.

- **Keste Pizzeria & Vino,** 271 Bleecker St. (✆ **212/243-1500;** www.keste pizzeria.com). The authentic Neopolitan pizzeria abides by the standards of *Associazione Pizzaiuoli Napoletani* (the Association of Neapolitan Pizza), with mouthwatering results. See p. 178.

- **Prime Meats,** 465 Court St. (✆ **718/254-0327;** www.frankspm.com). The newest venture from the owners of Frankie's Spuntino, this Carroll Gardens, Brooklyn, meat palace features many locally sourced ingredients, including vegetables straight from local farms, as well as local and imported meats, prepared to perfection. See p. 206.

best BITES FOR ALL APPETITES

- **Best Barbecue: RUB,** 208 W. 23rd St. (✆ **212/524-4300;** www.rubbbq. net). Co-owner Paul Kirk brings his Kansas City pit prowess to New York, with mouthwatering results. Try the Taste of the Baron, a little bit of everything for a big crowd. See p. 162.

- **Best for Breakfast: Good Enough to Eat,** 483 Amsterdam Ave. (✆ **212/ 496-0163;** www.goodenoughtoeat.com). They've been lining up on Amsterdam Avenue every weekend for over 20 years for chef/owner Carrie Levin's bountiful home-cooked breakfasts. But why wait in line? You're on vacation; go during the week. See p. 195.

- **Best for Brunch: Norma's,** at Le Parker Meridien Hotel, 118 W. 57th St. (✆ **212/708-7460;** www.normasnyc.com). Though I am not a devotee of brunch, I make an exception for Norma's. Skip the traditional breakfast items and go for creative interpretations such as the asparagus-and-seared-rock-lobster omelet. See p. 175.

- **Best Jewish Deli: Katz's Delicatessen,** 205 E. Houston St. (✆ **212/254-2246;** www.katzdeli.com). This is the choice among those who know their kreplach, knishes, and pastrami. No cutesy sandwiches named for celebrities here, just top-notch Jewish classics. See p. 149.

- **Best Burger: Burger Joint,** at Le Parker Meridien Hotel, 118 W. 57th St. (✆ **212/708-7414;** www.parkermeridien.com). Who woulda thunk that a fancy hotel such as Le Parker Meridien would be the home to a "joint" that serves great burgers at great prices? See p. 182.

- **Best Pizzeria Old Style: Patsy's Pizzeria,** 2287 First Ave. (✆ **212/534-9783;** www.patsyspizzeriany.com). This great east Harlem pizzeria has been cranking out coal-oven pizza since 1932. You can also order by the slice here, but only do so if the pie is fresh out of the oven. See p. 178.

- **Best Pizzeria New Style: Trattoria Zero Otto Nove,** 2357 Arthur Ave., the Bronx (✆ **718/220-1027;** www.roberto089.com). The best pizza in the Bronx uses ingredients from local Arthur Avenue establishments cooked perfectly in a wood-burning oven, resulting in an authentic Neapolitan pie. See p. 179.

- **Best 20th-Century Steakhouse: Frankie & Johnnie's,** 32 W. 37th St. (✆ **212/947-8940;** and 269 W. 45th St., ✆ 212/997-9494; www.frankies andjohnnies.com). Whether you choose the former speakeasy that is the original location in the Theater District or the newer branch in John Barrymore's former town house, your steak, particularly the house sirloin, will remind you why Frankie & Johnnie's has been around since 1926. See p. 171.

5

WHERE TO DINE

Best Bites for All Appetites

- **Best 21st-Century Steakhouse: Porter House New York,** 10 Columbus Circle (📞 212/823-9500; www.porterhousenewyork.com). New steakhouses sprout every year with much hype; this one in the Time Warner Center, helmed by chef Michael Lomonaco, distinguished itself far ahead of the pack of new steakhouses. See p. 163.

- **Best Mutton Chop: Keens Steakhouse,** 72 W. 36th St. (📞 212/947-3636; www.keens.com). Of course, it might be the *only* restaurant in New York that offers a mutton chop, but that's not the only reason to head to Keens. The other "chops" are first rate, and the rooms—there are several—are like museum pieces without the stuffiness. See p. 172.

- **Best Greek Restaurant: Kefi,** 505 Columbus Ave. (📞 212/873-0200; www.kefirestaurant.com). In a new and expanded space and now taking reservations and credit cards, Kefi is not only the best Greek restaurant in Manhattan, but also one of the least expensive. You won't believe basic Greek taverna food could be so good. See. p. 193.

- **Best Japanese Izakaya: En Japanese Brasserie,** 435 Hudson St. (📞 212/647-9196; www.enjb.com). Like a Japanese pub, this *izakaya* features a staggering selection of sake and *shochu* while you can munch on small plates like house-made warm tofu prepared three times each evening and short ribs grilled on a hot stone. See p. 154.

- **Best for Families: Virgil's Real BBQ,** 152 W. 44th St. (📞 212/921-9494; www.virgilsbbq.com). In Times Square, Virgil's, in a sense, is a theme restaurant, the theme being barbecue, but they do an excellent job of it. It's loud, colorful, and has great options for children. See p. 176.

- **Best Cheap Meal: Gray's Papaya,** 2090 Broadway (📞 212/799-0243). Though the $4.45 Recession Special—two hot dogs and a fruit drink—is almost a $1 increase from last year, it's still a bargain. But is it any good? Witness the lines out the door every day for lunch. See p. 144.

- **Best Ice Cream: Brooklyn Ice Cream Factory,** Fulton Ferry Landing Pier, Brooklyn (📞 718/246-3963). The perfect reward after a brisk walk across the Brooklyn Bridge. Rich homemade ice cream, with a view of the Manhattan skyline: it's a tough combination to beat. See p. 207.

- **Best Bagel: Absolute Bagels,** 2788 Broadway (📞 212/932-2052). They're not huge like some bagels these days, but they are always hot and baked to perfection. See p. 169.

FINANCIAL DISTRICT & TRIBECA

To find the restaurants reviewed below, see the map on p. 141.

Expensive

Capsouto Frères ★ FRENCH   In 1980, before the triangle below Canal Street was given the acronym TriBeCa, and before the neighborhood became rife with celebrities and hip restaurants, Capsouto Frères opened. And now, after TriBeCa's amazing growth, the restaurant has thrived with a loyal following. What accounts for the longevity? Is it the simple, home-style French cuisine: the famous soufflés; the spicy *saucisson;* the always reliable sole meunière, steak frites, or cassoulet; the warm, wood-floored, high-ceilinged always-festive dining

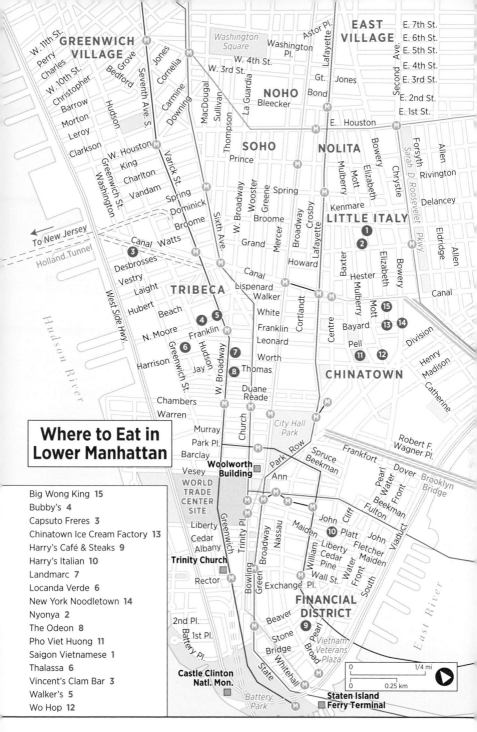

Where to Eat in Lower Manhattan

room; the gregarious and engaging hosts; the *freres* Jacques and Sammy? Or is it a combination of all of the above? Sturdy and reliable Capsouto Frères offers a literal taste of what it was like before Robert De Niro "discovered" TriBeCa.

451 Washington St. (at Watts St.). ☎ **212/966-4900.** www.capsoutofreres.com. Reservations recommended. Lunch prix fixe $24, main courses $12–$24; dinner prix fixe $35, main courses $16–$29. AE, DC, MC, V. Tues–Fri noon–3:30pm; Sun–Thurs 6–10:30pm; Fri–Sat 6–11pm; brunch Sat–Sun noon–3:30pm. Subway: 1, A, C, or E to Canal St.

Harry's Café & Steak ★★ 🎁 STEAK Harry's is a steakhouse, with all the accoutrements of your traditional red-meat joint, dry-aged beef with hearty sides; it's a cafe, with a bountiful original menu; and it's a lively bar with a well-stocked spirits and wine selection. Down a few steps from the cafe is the steakhouse, carved out of an old stone wine cellar. But it doesn't matter where you eat, the kitchen is the same and you can order from either menu. When I visited, I chose to mix and match from both menus. I started with a superb Greek salad topped with white anchovies from the cafe menu, followed by the grilled triple-cut pork chops on a bed of sauerkraut, accompanied by a Mason jar of fresh apple sauce with a chili pepper embedded in it. The side of escarole with white beans and prosciutto was almost a meal itself. The dry-aged rib steak is as good as you'll find anywhere west of Peter Luger's.

1 Hanover Sq. (at Pearl St.). ☎ **212/785-9200.** www.harrysnyc.com. Reservations recommended. Main courses $15–$46. AE, DC, DISC, MC, V. Cafe daily 11:30am–midnight; steakhouse Mon–Fri 11am–11pm. Subway: 2 or 3 to Wall St.

Landmarc ★★ ☺ FRENCH/ITALIAN/MEDITERRANEAN This intimate TriBeCa restaurant is too good to be considered just a neighborhood joint. Chef/owner Marc Murphy has put his own spin on this Italian/French rendition of a bistro. You'll find excellent smoked mozzarella and ricotta fritters alongside escargots bordelaise. You can mix and match cuisines. Try the pasta of the day accompanied by mussels with a choice of sauce—Provençal, Dijonnaise, or the comforting blend of shallots, parsley, and white wine. Steaks and chops are cooked over an open fire and the steaks are offered with a variety of sauces; I had the hangar with a shallot bordelaise that complemented the meat perfectly. What keeps the neighbors pouring in, along with the excellent food, are the affordable wines sold, not by the glass, but by the bottle or half-bottle. Desserts are simple, small, and priced that way, with none more than $4. For a special treat, ask for the cotton candy. Landmarc also has an **uptown** location, at the Time Warner Center, 10 Columbus Circle (☎ **212/823-6123**).

179 W. Broadway (btw. Leonard and Worth sts.). ☎ **212/343-3883.** www.landmarc-restaurant.com. Reservations recommended. Main courses $15–$34. AE, DC, DISC, MC, V. Mon–Fri noon–2am; Sat–Sun 9am–4pm and 5:30pm–2am. Subway: 1 to Franklin St.

Locanda Verde ★★★ ITALIAN It's just simple sheep's milk ricotta sprinkled with herbs and sea salt and served over crostini. Doesn't sound like much, does it? But that simple starter is the one dish everyone raves (deservedly) about after dining at Locanda Verde, the fun and delicious restaurant in the Greenwich Hotel helmed by Daniel Boulud–trained chef Andrew Carmellini. I think what makes Locanda Verde so good is that Carmellini eschews the fancy and sticks with hearty family dishes like "My Grandmother's Ravioli" rigatoni with lamb ragu, or the other "must-try" dish, the porchetta sandwich, thin-sliced roast pork served on hearty bread with vinegar peppers. It's a scene at Locanda

Verde—loud, crowded, always busy—but know that going in and hurry up and order that sheep's milk ricotta, and all that background buzz will soon be just a minor irritation.

377 Greenwich St (at N. Moore St.). ℭ **212/925-3797.** www.locandaverdenyc.com. Reservations highly recommended. Main courses $17–$28. AE, DISC, MC, V. Mon–Fri 11:30am–3pm; Mon–Sun 5:30–11pm; Sat–Sun 10am–3pm. Subway: 1 to Franklin St.

Thalassa ★★ GREEK Greek food is best when prepared simply with the freshest ingredients, especially fish, and Thalassa does a remarkable job of that. The variety of seafood is staggering: When I visited, the options included fresh langoustines from Scotland, pound-and-a-half shrimp from Mexico, and a number of oyster selections. For starters, the zucchini-and-eggplant chips were addictive, while the octopus, simply grilled with a red-wine vinaigrette, was as good as I've had west of Astoria (the Greek neighborhood in Queens). The main courses won't disappoint: Seafood *Thalassina,* a stew of shellfish including those aforementioned Gulf shrimp, was a standout, while the grilled branzino, simply prepared with a touch of olive oil and lemon, was exceptional. The knowledgeable sommelier can help you select a Greek wine from the restaurant's cellar, where a number of unusual and good Greek cheeses are also stored. The restaurant is large; tables are spaced well enough apart for intimacy, and service is attentive and pleasant.

179 Franklin St. (btw. Greenwich and Hudson sts.). ℭ **212/941-7661.** www.thalassanyc.com. Reservations recommended. Prix-fixe lunch $24; main courses dinner $28–$42. AE, DC, DISC, MC, V. Mon–Fri noon–3pm; Mon–Thurs 6–11pm; Fri–Sat 6pm–midnight; Sun 5–10pm. Subway: 1 to Franklin St.

Moderate

If you are wandering the canyons of Wall Street and crave a good pizza, **Harry's Italian,** 2 Gold St. (ℭ **212/747-0797;** www.harrysitalian.com), will more than suffice. Related to **Harry's Café & Steak** (p. 142), this Harry's also serves traditional family-style pastas and mains.

Bubby's Pie Company ★ ☺ AMERICAN You might have to wait in line to eat at Bubby's. You might get squeezed in at a table perilously close to another couple, and have to talk loudly to maintain a conversation with your dining companion. But this all pales when you get your Bubby's comfort food. Whether it is the slow-cooked pulled barbecue pork, the lighter-than-air meatloaf, or the buttermilk-fried half-chicken, coupled with such sides as collard greens, sautéed spinach, macaroni and cheese, or baked beans, Bubby's dishes define comfort. Save room for the desserts, especially the homemade pies; one taste of the chocolate peanut-butter pie brought on happy childhood flashbacks. Breakfast is big here and lasts well into the middle of the day. On weekends, though, the wait for brunch can be lengthy. Celebrities need comfort, too, and you might spot one or two at Bubby's. Bubby's also has a branch across the river in the DUMBO neighborhood of Brooklyn.

120 Hudson St. (at N. Moore St.). ℭ **212/219-0666.** www.bubbys.com. Reservations recommended for dinner (not accepted for brunch). Main courses $10–$15 breakfast, brunch, and lunch; $10–$21 dinner. DC, DISC, MC, V. Mon–Thurs 8am–11pm; Fri 8am–midnight; Sat 9am–4:30pm and 6pm–midnight; Sun 9am–10pm. Subway: 1 to Franklin St. Bubby's Brooklyn: 1 Main St. (at Water St.). ℭ **718/222-0666.** Subway: A or C to High St.; F to York St.

FOOD IN A N.Y. MINUTE

I do my best in this chapter to not mention the fast-food chain options in the city. They are here and, unfortunately, here to stay. But why eat the same fast food you can get anywhere else when you're in the cuisine-enriched city of New York? Here are a few original options you should consider before parting the golden arches:

New York is a hot dog town. You can buy them from street vendors all over the city, and doing so is something everyone should experience. But once might be enough. If you want an original New York dog, **Nathan's Famous ★**, established in 1916, is the best example. There are Nathan's Famous hot dogs all over the city now, but though the hot dogs are the same, they just don't taste as good as the ones served in its original location on the **Coney Island boardwalk** in Brooklyn, 1310 Surf Ave., at Stillwell Avenue (✆ **718/946-2202**).

For the cheapest quick meal, nothing can match **Gray's Papaya.** This 24-hour hot dog stand is a New York institution. The Recession Special, two hot dogs and a drink (overly sweetened papaya, piña colada, or orange juice), is a whopping $4.45 (up recently from $3.50). The hot dogs are delicious, though for your own good, don't be tempted to eat more than two, despite the low prices. There are three Gray's Papayas around the city, but the best is the original at the corner of 72nd Street and Broadway, at 2090 Broadway (✆ **212/799-0243**).

Like the hot dog, pizza is also a New York staple. I discuss the best pizza in New York in the box "The Pizza Capital of the United States" (p. 178), but most of the places mentioned require sitting down and ordering a whole pie. For a quick slice, my personal favorite is **Joe's Pizza ★**, 7 Carmine St., at Bleecker Street (✆ **212/255-3946**). Joe's offers the epitome of what a slice is supposed to taste like: thin-crusted with the proper balance of sauce, which actually has flavor, and cheese that doesn't taste like something you could bounce off a wall.

Be prepared to wait in line during busy evening hours and then take your slice outside and eat it like a real New Yorker—folded in half lengthwise, standing up.

In Philadelphia, arguments rage over who makes the best cheesesteak. But we are in New York, and of the Philly-style cheesesteak establishments, my pick is **Shorty's ★**, formerly known as Tony Luke's, 576 Ninth Ave., between 41st and 42nd streets (✆ **212/967-3055**). On the edge of the Theater District, in the shadow of the Port Authority Bus Terminal, Shorty's location is about as gritty as it gets. But that just adds to the appeal of Shorty's gargantuan sandwiches. The cheesesteak, with your choice of cheese—Provolone, American, or Whiz (go for the Whiz, of course)—melting into the fresh Italian roll, is hard to resist, but if you can, order the roast pork Italian: roast pork with peppers, onions, and broccoli rabe.

Chinatown offers a plethora of quick food options, but one of my new favorites in that neighborhood is the *banh mi* sandwich. A Vietnamese creation combining that country's Asian and French influences between a freshly baked baguette. My personal favorite is a small take-out shop called **Saigon Vietnamese Sandwich,** 369 Broome St., between Mott and Elizabeth streets (✆ **212/219-8341;** www.vietnamese-sandwich.com), and I'm not alone. Lines form outside the shop just before lunch, so plan accordingly. At Saigon they make 12 different types of *banh mi,* including several vegetarian, but the house special with grilled pork, cilantro, pickled vegetables, and homemade pâté is the best place to start.

The Odeon ★ AMERICAN/BRASSERIE   For 3 decades, the Odeon has been a symbol of the TriBeCa sensibility; in fact, the restaurant can claim credit for the neighborhood's cachet—it was the first to lure artists, actors, writers, and models to the area below Canal Street before it was given its moniker. Why did they come? They came to drink, schmooze, and enjoy the hearty no-frills brasserie grub such as the country frisée salad with bacon, Roquefort cheese, and pear vinaigrette; the truffled poached egg; steak frites; and pan-roasted cod. Though the restaurant is not quite the celebrity magnet it was in its heyday of the 1980s, the food, drink, and that inviting, open, Art Deco–ish room have withstood the test of time and have surpassed trendy to claim well-deserved New York establishment status.

145 W. Broadway (at Thomas St.). ✆ **212/233-0507.** www.theodeonrestaurant.com. Reservations recommended. Main courses $13–$35 lunch, $19–$35 dinner (most less than $21); fixed-price lunch $27. AE, DC, DISC, MC, V. Mon–Fri noon–11pm; Sat 10am–midnight; Sun 10am–11pm. Subway: 1, 2, or 3 to Chambers St.

Inexpensive

For an inexpensive alternative in TriBeCa, consider the pub **Walker's** (p. 424), 16 N. Moore St., at Varick Street (✆ **212/941-0142**), where you can get a good burger and fries for less than $10.

CHINATOWN

To find the restaurants reviewed below, see the map on p. 147.

Inexpensive

Also consider two restaurants that have stood the test of time, **Wo Hop,** 17 Mott St., between Worth and Mosco streets (✆ **212/962-8617**), and **Vincent's Clam Bar,** 119 Mott St., at Hester Street (✆ **212/226-8133;** www.original vincents.com). For more on both, see the box "Hello, Old Friends" on p. 152.

Big Wong King ★ CHINESE/CANTONESE   For over 30 years, Big Wong (recently called New Big Wong) has been an institution for workers from the nearby courthouses and Chinese families who come to feast on *congee* (rice porridge) and fried crullers for breakfast (see "Breakfast, Not Brunch!" p. 195). They also come for the superb roasted meats, the pork and duck seen hanging in the window, the comforting noodle soups, and the terrific barbecued ribs. This is simple, down-home Cantonese food—lo mein, chow fun, bok choy in oyster sauce—cooked lovingly, and so cheap. If you don't mind sharing a table, and brusque service at best, Big Wong is a must at any time of day.

67 Mott St. (btw. Canal and Bayard sts.). ✆ **212/964-0540.** Appetizers $1.50–$5; *congee* $1.50–$6; soups $3–$5; Cantonese noodles $5.25–$11. No credit cards. Daily 8:30am–9pm. Subway: N or R to Canal St.

Great New York Noodletown ★★ CHINESE/SEAFOOD   So what if the restaurant has all the ambience of a school cafeteria? I'm wary of an overadorned dining room in Chinatown; the simpler the better. New York Noodletown is simple, but the food is the real thing. Seafood-based noodle soups are spectacular, as is the platter of chopped roast pork. Those two items alone would make me happy. But I'm greedy and wouldn't leave the restaurant without one of its perfectly prepared shrimp dishes, especially the salt-baked shrimp. If your hotel room has a fridge, take the leftovers home—they'll make a great snack the next day. New York Noodletown keeps very long hours, which makes it one of the best late-night bets in the neighborhood, too.

28½ Bowery (at Bayard St.). ☎ **212/349-0923.** Reservations accepted. Main courses $4–$15. No credit cards. Daily 9am–3am. Subway: N, R, or 6 to Canal St.

Nyonya ★ 🎒 ASIA/PACIFIC RIM/MALAYSIAN   One of the few, and one of the best, Malaysian restaurants in Manhattan is Chinatown's Nyonya. This spacious, bustling restaurant designed like a tiki hut offers efficient, friendly service, but it's the huge portions of spicy food that are the real treat. Coconut milk, curry, and chili pepper–laden dishes are staples of Malaysian cuisine. The Malaysian national dish, *roti canai* (an Indian pancake with a curry-chicken dipping sauce), is outstanding. The noodle soups are meals in themselves; *prawn mee* (egg noodles, shredded pork, and large shrimp in a spicy shrimp broth) is sinus clearing, while the curry spareribs are spectacular. The drinks and desserts include *sooi pooi* drink (sour plum) and *pulut hitam* (creamy black glutinous rice with coconut milk). But vegetarians beware: There's not much on the menu for you here; most dishes are prepared in either a meat or fish broth.

194 Grand St. (btw. Mulberry and Mott sts.). ☎ **212/334-3669.** www.ilovenyonya.com. Appetizers $2.25–$8; noodle soups $4.25–$6; main dishes $5.95–$23. No credit cards. Sun–Thurs 11am–11:30pm; Fri–Sat 11am–midnight. Subway: 6 to Spring St.

Pho Viet Huong ★ 🍴 VIETNAMESE   The best Vietnamese restaurant in Chinatown is Pho Viet Huong. The menu is vast and needs intense perusing, but your waiter will help you. The Vietnamese know soup, and *pho,* a beef-based soup served with many ingredients, is the most famous, but the hot-and-sour *canh* soup is the real deal. The small version is more than enough for two to share. The odd pairing of barbecued beef wrapped in grape leaves is another of the restaurant's specialties and should not be missed, while the *bun,* various meats and vegetables served over rice vermicelli, is simple, hearty, and inexpensive. All of the above is best washed down with an icy cold Saigon beer.

73 Mulberry St. (btw. Bayard and Canal sts.). ☎ **212/233-8988.** Appetizers $3–$8.50; soups $6–$7; main courses $10–$25. AE, MC, V. Daily 10:30am–10:30pm. Subway: 6, N, Q, or R to Canal St.

LOWER EAST SIDE

Expensive

Rayuela ★★ NUEVO LATINO   The menu at Rayuela features a hodgepodge of Latino foods; a little Peruvian here, a dash of Mexican there, maybe a dollop of Cuba with a scoop of Spain. I'm a traditionalist when it comes to ethnic cuisine,

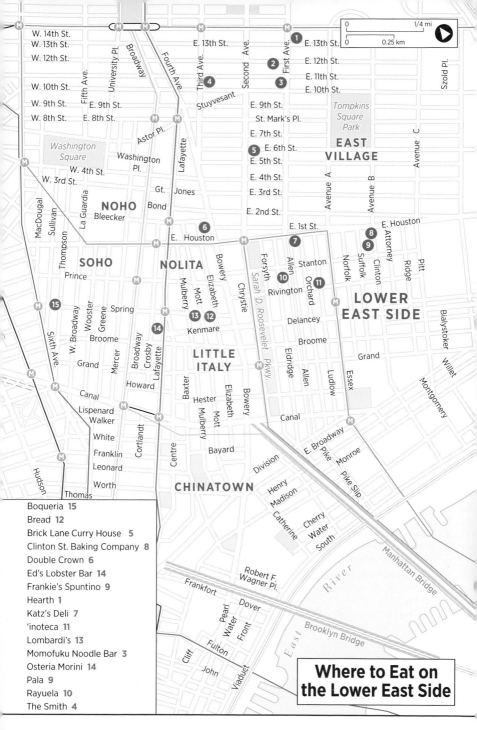

Boqueria **15**
Bread **12**
Brick Lane Curry House **5**
Clinton St. Baking Company **8**
Double Crown **6**
Ed's Lobster Bar **14**
Frankie's Spuntino **9**
Hearth **1**
Katz's Deli **7**
'inoteca **11**
Lombardi's **13**
Momofuku Noodle Bar **3**
Osteria Morini **14**
Pala **9**
Rayuela **10**
The Smith **4**

Where to Eat on the Lower East Side

but once I tasted the corvina ceviche, 1 of 10 on the menu, I was a convert. The classic Peruvian ceviche of kingfish marinated in blood-orange juice, lime, cilantro, garlic, and onions was refreshingly tart. At Rayuela, you can make your meal from various small plates; the appetizer of *camarones con chorizo,* shrimp in a spicy salsa with *fufu,* a root vegetable, and thin yucca fries, is a worthy nod to the cuisine of the Dominican Republic and an excellent complement to the ceviche. Rayuela offers two levels; a bustling downstairs lounge and small-bites scene, where a live olive tree grows; and more intimate dining on the upstairs level.

165 Allen St. (btw. Rivington and Stanton sts.). ℂ **212/253-8840.** www.rayuelanyc.com. Reservations recommended. Ceviches $12–$17; main courses $22–$31. AE, DC, DISC, MC, V. Sun–Thurs 5:30–11pm; Fri–Sat 5:30pm–midnight; brunch Sat–Sun 10am–5pm. Subway: F to Second Ave.

Moderate

Don't forget the Manhattan outpost of **Frankie's Spuntino** ★★★, 17 Clinton St., between Houston and Stanton streets (ℂ **212/253-2303;** www.frankies spuntino.com), where the food is as good as you'll get on the other side of the East River.

'inoteca ★★ 🍴 ITALIAN   The Lower East Side was once the home to many kosher wine factories, but you'll find only Italian wines at cozy 'inoteca. The list is over 250 bottles long, but even better are the exquisitely prepared small plates that complement the wines. Though the Italian-language menu is a challenge, servers are helpful. The panini stand out in their freshness and their delicacy, with the *coppa* (a spicy cured ham) with hot peppers and *rucola* (arugula) being the standout. The *tramezzini,* a crustless sandwich, is nothing like the crustless sandwiches served at high tea. Here, you can have yours stuffed with tuna and chickpeas or with *pollo alla diavola,* spicy shredded pieces of dark-meat chicken. The "Fritto" section includes a mozzarella *in corroza,* breaded mozzarella stuffed with a juicy anchovy sauce and lightly fried. 'inoteca is a place to go slow, to savor both wine and food.

98 Rivington St. (at Ludlow St.). ℂ **212/614-0473.** www.inotecanyc.com. Reservations accepted for parties of 6 or more. Panini $8–$17; *piatti* (small plates) $8–$11. AE, MC, V. Daily noon–3am; brunch Sat–Sun 10am–4pm. Subway: F, J, M, or Z to Delancey St. Also at 323 Third Ave. (at 24th St.). ℂ **212/614-0473.** Subway: 6 to 23rd St.

Inexpensive

Clinton St. Baking Company ★ 🎁 AMERICAN   Though they are open all day, breakfast and desserts are the best offerings here. The blueberry pancakes with maple butter and the buttermilk-biscuit egg sandwich are worth braving the morning lines for, while the desserts, all homemade and topped with a scoop or two of ice cream from the Brooklyn Ice Cream Factory, are good any time of day.

4 Clinton St. (at Houston St.). ℂ **646/602-6263.** www.clintonstreetbaking.com. Main courses $8–$14. No credit cards. Mon–Fri 8am–4pm and 6–11pm; Sat 10am–11pm; Sun 10am–4pm. Subway: F to Second Ave.

Katz's Delicatessen ★ 🗡 DELICATESSEN   Founded in 1888, this cavernous, brightly lit place is suitably *Noo Yawk,* with dill pickles, Dr. Brown's cream soda, and old-world attitude to spare. Take the ticket they give you when you come in and either head for the cafeteria-style line, or seat yourself in the "waiter service" area. But one word of caution: Katz's has become a serious tourist destination, so if you see a big tour bus parked in front, you might be in for a long wait. (And remember to tip your carver, who gives you a sample of the succulent pastrami or corned beef as he prepares your sandwich!)

205 E. Houston St. (at Ludlow St.). ℂ **212/254-2246.** www.katzdeli.com. Reservations not accepted. Sandwiches $3–$10; main courses $5–$18. AE, DC, DISC, MC, V ($20 minimum). Sun–Tues 8am–10pm; Wed 8am–11pm; Thurs 8am–midnight; Fri–Sat 8am–3am. Subway: F to Second Ave.

SOHO & NOLITA

To locate the restaurants reviewed below, see the map on p. 147.

Expensive

Boqueria ★★ SPANISH/TAPAS   We can thank the Spanish and their tapas for initiating the small plate craze that has hit New York City during these tougher economic times. At Boqueria, Spanish in name, traditional tapas are taken to new level—the fried quail egg with chorizo on toast as an example—with very pleasing results. But this is not to say that Boqueria ignores the traditional; the *patatas bravas,* crispy potatoes roasted in garlic and olive oil, is, thankfully, a constant on an ever-changing menu and a must-have, while the *pimientos de pardon* (blistered shishito peppers with coarse sea salt) are an addictive accompaniment to the restaurant's extensive wine list and sangria. Boqueria makes its own chorizo and it can be found in many of the restaurant's dishes, including the very good paella. There are two branches of Boqueria, the tiny original in the Flatiron District and a somewhat more roomy, though still cramped and loud, SoHo outpost. Reservations are taken only for groups of six or more, so expect a wait.

171 Spring St. (btw. Thompson and West Broadway). ℂ **212/343-4255.** www.boquerianyc.com. Reservations for groups of 6 or more. Tapas $5–$14; *raciones* (main courses) $19–$29. AE, DISC, MC, V. Daily noon–midnight. Subway: C, E to Spring St. Also at 53 W. 19th St. (btw. 5th–6th aves.). ℂ **212/255-4160.** Subway: F, M to 23rd St.

Osteria Morini ★★ ITALIAN   From the prolific chef, Michael White (**Marea, Ai Fiori**) comes his take on the cuisine of Emilia-Romagna in northern Italy. That translates to much hearty fare, including lots of pork. Examples include a hockey puck-sized disc of spit roasted *porchetta,* meat protected by a generous layer of fat on the outside while seasoned with sage and rosemary, and an enormous grilled pork chop resting on a bed of polenta and flavored with balsamic vinegar and sweet cipollini onions. Either of the pork entrees will sustain you through a very cold winter's night as it did me, especially if you begin with an antipasto of marinated sardines or a platter of cured meats. Follow that with heavenly *cappelletti,* little raviolis filled with truffled mascarpone and prosciutto, or the *tagliatelle* with a ragu and you'll be very challenged to find room for one of pastry chef, Heather Bertinetti's dessert creations. Rustic with lots terra cotta tiles and rough wood, the restaurant is riotously loud, so don't expect conversation. But do expect stick-to-your ribs, Italian fare.

218 Lafayette St. (btw. Spring and Broome sts.). ✆ **212/965-8777.** www.osteriamorini.com. Reservations recommended. Main courses: $17–$29. Mon–Fri 11:30am–3:30pm; Sat–Sun 11:30am–4pm; Tue–Sat 5pm–1am; Sun–Mon 5pm–midnight. Subway: 6 to Spring St.

Moderate

Ed's Lobster Bar ★★ AMERICAN/SEAFOOD
You may be a long way in distance (and price) from a roadside shack in Maine when dining at Ed's Lobster Bar, but take a seat at the white marble counter and bite into Ed's signature lobster roll (prepared cold with mayonnaise), and you might think that it's the rocky Atlantic coast outside the window rather than bustling Lafayette Street. After you've tried the overstuffed lobster roll, if you still have room, try the oysters, raw or delicately fried. Or the fried Ipswich clams, or the steamers, or the chowder. Thankfully unpretentious, Ed's is straight-ahead New England seafood served in a casual, laid-back dining room and whitewashed bar. They even have paper bibs, homemade pickles, and Belfast Bay Lobster Ale on tap. What more could you want in a seafood "shack" in New York City?

222 Lafayette St. (btw. Spring and Kenmare sts.). ✆ **212/343-3236.** www.lobsterbarnyc.com. Main courses $15–$30 (lobster and oysters at market price). Tues–Thurs noon–3pm and 5–11pm; Fri noon–3pm and 5pm–midnight; Sat noon–4pm and 5pm–midnight; Sun noon–9pm. Subway: 6 to Spring St.

Inexpensive

Also consider **Lombardi's Pizza,** 32 Spring St., between Mott and Mulberry streets (✆ **212/941-7994;** see "The Pizza Capital of the United States" p. 178).

Bread ★ ITALIAN/LIGHT FARE
Bread does bread like no other sandwich shop. The bread comes from Balthazar Bakery down the street, but it's what they do with it that makes it so special. They might take a rustic ciabatta loaf, slather it with Sicilian sardines, Thai mayonnaise, tomato, and lettuce, and then turn it over to their panini press. The result is a gooey convergence of flavors that you will attempt to gobble gracefully. It *will* fall apart, but that's okay; someone will be along shortly with more napkins. Besides the spectacular sardine sandwich, the Italian tuna with mesclun greens and tomatoes in a lemon dressing, and the fontina with grilled zucchini, eggplant, arugula, and tomato in a balsamic vinaigrette are also standouts. The menu also includes salads, pastas, and "plates." The 32-seat restaurant is in chic Nolita, and you may even see a model wrapping herself around one of their sandwiches.

20 Spring St. (btw. Mott and Elizabeth sts.). ✆ **212/334-1015.** Reservations not accepted. Breads $7–$9.50; plates $6–$16. AE, MC, V. Sun–Thurs 10:30am–midnight; Fri–Sat 10:30am–1am. Subway: 6 to Spring St.

THE EAST VILLAGE & NOHO

To locate the restaurants reviewed below, see the map on p. 147.

Expensive

Double Crown ★ ASIAN/ENGLISH Who would have thought that a restaurant that draws its inspiration from the food of the former British colonies in Asia would work (and work well) as a concept? It came from Britain . . . and was reinvented in Asia. In the now-trendy Bowery, Double Crown's presence with its eclectic AVROK-designed front and back dining areas, adds to the neighborhood's appeal. And at Double Crown, the food is as good as the look. The menu is inventive and of the entrees, the wild striped bass in a sesame broth with prawn dumplings, was simple perfection. The dining room in the front of the restaurant can get very loud. If you prefer a bit less commotion, try for a table in the back.

316 Bowery (at Bleecker St.). ✆ **212/254-0350.** www.doublecrown-nyc.com. Reservations recommended. Main courses $17–$30. AE, DISC, MC, V. Sun–Wed 6–11pm; Thurs–Sat 6pm–midnight; Sat–Sun 11am–3:30pm. Subway: 6 to Bleecker St.

Hearth ★★ 🏠 AMERICAN/ITALIAN If you're in the East Village, you will be doing yourself a great service if you decide to spend some of that time at aptly named Hearth. The restaurant is as welcoming as its name, and the food and drinks even more so. The owners proclaim that their menu is American with hints of the Italian origins. It's those hints that make Hearth so distinct, and if you are in the mood for humble Italian food, Hearth's three-course *cucina povera* with its robust *ribollita,* a soup of cabbage, beans, Parmesan, and far-from-humble braised lamb shank, will definitely satisfy that mood. But if you want haughty instead of humble, try the chef's rabbit ballotine or snapper *crudo* (raw). Or, because Hearth lets you mix and match, you can have both. Along with an excellent wine selection, Hearth features an impressive wine and tequila list. Service is knowledgeable and seating is comfortable, confirming the restaurant's public philosophy that "ALL the needs of the guest have been met and exceeded."

403 E. 12th St. (at 1st Ave.). ✆ **646/602-1300.** www.restauranthearth.com. Reservations recommended. *Cucina povera* $35; seasonal tasting menu $70; main courses $25–$29. AE, MC, V. Sun–Thurs 6–10pm; Fri–Sat 6–11pm. Subway: L to 14th St.–1st Ave.

Moderate

Brick Lane Curry House ★ INDIAN The vibrancy of the traditional Indian restaurants on the block of East 6th Street, known as "Little India," has diminished over the years; Brick Lane has added some welcome vigor. **Beware:** They might just have the hottest dish in the city. It's a curry called *phaal* that requires a verbal disclaimer from the customer to not hold the restaurant liable for any physical or emotional damage incurred from eating it. If you are able to finish it, the restaurant promises a bottle of beer on the house. The other, less hazardous, curries will bring on a good enough sweat, including the excellent Madras

HELLO, OLD FRIENDS!

New York has many restaurants that are institutions, places that have been around forever and are known all over. When you think of classic New York restaurants that have survived for decades, you might think of the **Carnegie Deli** (see the box "The New York Deli News," p. 180), Grand Central Terminal's **Oyster Bar** (p. 187), or the **Peter Luger Steakhouse** (p. 205). But there are countless lesser-known restaurants that have a storied past and are well loved by their customers. The menus remain pretty much the same; not succumbing to the ever-changing food trends, the service is usually old school; turnover is low, and your waiter will probably recognize you from your last visit, which might have been a year or two earlier. At these places, it's not about the quality of the food, which will likely not be four-star; it's more about being part of the family.

I first experienced Chinatown's **Wo Hop,** 17 Mott St., between Worth and Mosco streets (*©* **212/962-8617**), established in 1938, when I was in college. You couldn't find a cheaper restaurant in New York. It was open 24 hours—I have fond memories of dining late at night and then ascending the stairs from the subterranean restaurant to a sunny dawn; portions were huge and the food was dense. Time has stood still at Wo Hop (pictured at right), and though the prices have gone up, it's still one of the cheapest eateries in the city, and open from 10am to 7pm daily, and still dishing out huge portions of dense food. Here you'll find those Chinese-American classics you might remember from your youth: egg drop soup, chow mein, egg foo young, and subgum vegetables.

At around the same time, I was introduced to **Vincent's Clam Bar,** 119 Mott St., at Hester Street (*©* **212/226-8133;** www.originalvincents.com), a few blocks up in Little Italy. At the time, there was still a remnant of what Little Italy used to be that is now gone. But Vincent's has been around since 1904, and though, like the rest of Little Italy, there is a touristy, theme-restaurant atmosphere to it, where else can you actually still order that old Italian-American favorite, scungilli? Like the shrinking Italian presence in Little Italy, scungilli (sliced conch) has practically disappeared from the menus of Italian restaurants. Here they pile it high on top of your linguine. Vincent's tomato sauce is unique and tastes exactly as I remember it from my first visit: rich and tomato-paste thickened. It comes in three flavors: sweet, medium, and hot. The hot is fiery, and the best way to experience it is with a semistale biscuit and as an accompaniment to fried seafood.

I admit, I'm a relative newcomer to **El Faro ★**, 823 Greenwich St., at Horatio Street (*©* **212/929-8210;** www.elfaro nyc.com), one of the oldest Spanish restaurants in New York, which celebrated its 84th birthday in 2011. But one visit and you will feel like you are a

and the tangy Goan. Brick Lane's signature *boti* rolls (chicken tikka served in fresh-baked bread) are special, while the *rassam* soup of the day, a thin, clear soup that changes daily, will help clear your sinuses even before you touch a curry. There are also a number of vegan items. 306–308 E. 6th St. (btw. First and Second aves.). *©* **212/979-2900.** www.bricklane curryhouse.com. Reservations recommended. Appetizers $6–$10; curries $12–$19. AE, DC, DISC, MC, V. Sun–Thurs 1–11pm; Fri–Sat 1pm–1am. Subway: 6 to Astor Place.

signature sangria, also known as "truth serum."

We all know how hard it is to make it on Broadway, and to make it as a pre-theater restaurant and survive for almost 50 years is a feat. But that's what **Chez Napoleon,** 365 W. 50th St., between 8th and 9th avenues (© **212/ 265-6980;** www.cheznapoleon.com), has done. In the shadow of Worldwide Plaza, the Bruno family, led by matriarch *"Grandmere"* Marguerite, has run Chez Napoleon since 1960, serving traditional Gallic cuisine. The presentation and preparation of the restaurant's *coq au vin* and the beef bourguignon remain today exactly as it was before Marguerite was a *grandmere.*

People ask me for recommendations for a "real deal" diner. My answer is always **Eisenberg's Coffee Shop,** 174 Fifth Ave., at 22nd Street (© **212/675- 5096).** This luncheonette has been dishing up eggs/bacon/burgers/sandwiches since 1929, at pretty much the same prices—adjusted slightly for inflation, of course. The waiters and cooks have seemingly been working there since the Eisenhower era. More likely than not, you'll be greeted with a growled "Hiya, sweetheart," or a gravelly "What'll it be, love?" If a tuna sandwich were on a "best of" list, Eisenberg's version would win. Feel a little run down? A bowl of matzo-ball soup will perk you up. Or sit at the counter and order an egg cream with real, from-the-bottle seltzer.

longtime friend of the Lurgis family, who have owned the place since 1959. Maybe you'll get to sit in James Baldwin's favorite corner table—the restaurant is mentioned in his biography—the table off the bar, where a resident ghost is rumored to occasionally sit. The menu features dishes from Spain that are now familiar, such as *paella a la Valenciana,* shrimp *al ajillo,* and *mariscada* (mixed seafood) with green sauce. All this is complemented with El Faro's potent

Momofuku Noodle Bar ★ ASIAN   Practically unclassifiable, Momofuku might be put in the Asian noodle category. But you will also find such items as fried veal sweetbreads, spicy honeycomb tripe, grilled beef tongue, country ham and hash browns, and grits and shrimp. Despite the seemingly contradictory menu, the Southern-style Asian noodle combo works. Still, unless you have a craving for offal, come to Momofuku for the noodles, the ramen in particular. And in the Momofuku Ramen, a big bowl brimming with rich broth, noodles, shredded smoky pulled pork, and a poached egg, you actually can get a taste of the South and Asia in one bowl. Of the hot items, the roasted Brussels sprouts with a kimchee purée, bacon, and carrots is a revelation, while the steamed pork bun is stuffed with a side of pork belly. Service is brisk, but try to get to Momofuku early or for lunch, before the few communal tables fill up and lines begin to form.

171 First Ave. (btw. 10th and 11th sts.). 📞 **212/777-7773.** www.momofuko.com. Reservations not accepted. Main courses $10–$17. AE, DISC, MC, V. Daily noon–4pm; Sun–Thurs 5:30–11pm; Fri–Sat 5:30pm–midnight. Subway: L at Third Ave.

The Smith AMERICAN   This big, high-ceilinged American brasserie is loud and, at times, swarming with NYU students and visiting parents. Don't let the collegiate atmosphere stop you from enjoying the comfortingly conventional menu, where you can munch on crawfish hush puppies or crispy calamari while sipping a beer from the impressive selection. There are a few more ambitious main courses, but it's best to stick with the more simple items such as the pot of mussels steamed in a chardonnay broth or the hangar steak; both come with very good fries. Add a side of the caramelized Brussels sprouts—you'll be glad you did. If you are in the neighborhood on Sunday morning, the hearty brunch offerings will sustain you the rest of the day.

55 Third Ave. (btw. 10th and 11th sts.). 📞 **212/420-9800.** www.ctrnyc.com/THESMITH. Main courses $16–$29. AE, DISC, MC, V. Mon–Tues 8:30am–midnight; Wed–Thurs 8:30am–1am; Fri 8:30am–2am; Sat 10am–2am; Sun 10am–midnight. Subway: 6 to Astor Place, or R to 8th St.

GREENWICH VILLAGE & THE MEATPACKING DISTRICT

Very Expensive

Mas ★★ 🍴 FRENCH   This "farmhouse" is in the West Village, and though there are nods to the rustic in the decor, there is also an atmosphere of sophistication. A glass-enclosed wine cellar is visible from the small dining room, the restaurant stays open late, and you'll find hipsters as well as folks in power suits. The dishes are innovative and the ingredients are fresh, many supplied by upstate New York farms. The tender, perfectly prepared braised pork belly is served with polenta and a stew of escargot and lima beans; the duck breast melds magically with apple purée, sautéed Brussels sprouts, and chestnuts; and the trout Piscator, rainbow trout, is stuffed with watercress and smoked trout and topped with a tangy apple-and-horseradish dressing. Service is low key but attentive, and the seating, though somewhat cramped, is not enough to dim the romantic aura.

39 Downing St. (btw. Bedford and Varick sts.). 📞 **212/255-1790.** www.masfarmhouse.com. Reservations recommended. 4-course tasting menu $68, 6-course $95; main courses $32–$36. AE, DC, DISC, MC, V. Mon–Sat 6pm–4am (small-plate tasting menu after 11:30pm). Subway: 1 to Houston St.

Expensive

En Japanese Brasserie ★★★ JAPANESE   At En they bill themselves as a "modern *izakaya*," a kind of Japanese pub where diners share small plates along with beer, sake, or *shochu* (a vodkalike drink made from various ingredients like

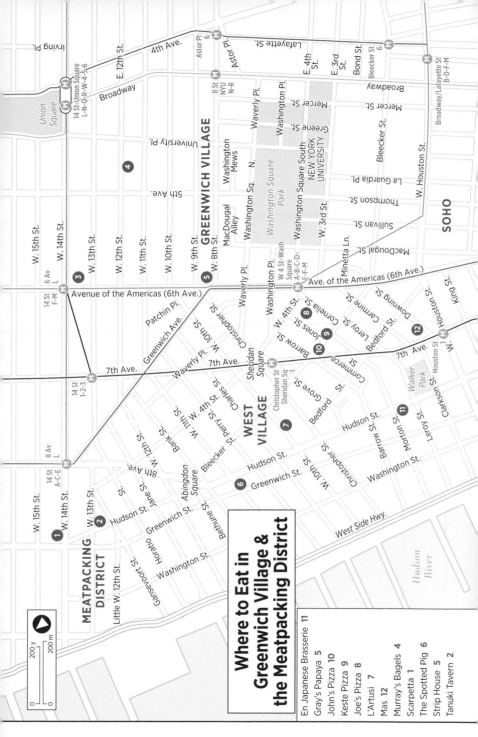

Where to Eat in Greenwich Village & the Meatpacking District

En Japanese Brasserie 11
Gray's Papaya 5
John's Pizza 10
Keste Pizza 9
Joe's Pizza 8
L'Artusi 7
Mas 12
Murray's Bagels 4
Scarpetta 1
The Spotted Pig 6
Strip House 5
Tanuki Tavern 2

barley, sweet potato, and buckwheat). And as a fan of pubs in general, I can truly appreciate this one, where I can sample numerous sakes along with amazing dishes: warm, freshly scooped tofu (at En they make their own tofu at hour-and-a-half intervals each evening); Japanese mountain vegetables in spicy soy sauce; black cod marinated in miso; grilled, thinly sliced Kobe-style short ribs grilled on a hot stone; and razor-thin yellowtail served with hot water so you can give it its own bath before devouring it. At En, ordering can be overwhelming, so there are *kaiseki* menus where a selection of dishes are put together by the chef and accompanied with sake and *shochu*. The room is cavernous and seats, with the exception of a granite fountain with communal dining around it, are spread out, giving you the elbow room needed to properly consume your feast.

435 Hudson St. (at Leroy St.). © **212/647-9196.** www.enjb.com. Reservations recommended. Main courses $15–$35; *kaiseki* $65–$85 per person. AE, DC, MC, V. Mon–Thurs noon–2:30pm and 5:30–11:30pm; Fri–Sat noon–2:30pm and 5:30pm–midnight; Sun 5:30–11pm. Subway: 1 to Christopher Street.

Scarpetta ★★ ITALIAN Don't be fooled by the unassuming, dimly lit exterior—the Scarpetta dining experience is anything but. Scarpetta and its skylight-ceilinged dining room is a grand arena to showcase the famed chef, Scott Conant's talents with Italian cuisine. Starting with two *crudo*, or raw seafood appetizers, a thinly sliced yellowtail sprinkled simply with sea salt and olive oil, and the Italian take on sushi, called here "tuna susci," a roll with marinated vegetables and truffle oil, is the way to begin. When pondering the pasta choices, my waiter advised that the duck and foie gras ravioli was "just a small portion." What arrived was a substantial platter sprinkled with ravioli so good and so rich that continuing to a *piatti*, or entrée, was a challenge. I was up to it, and able to experience the Mediterranean *orata* (sea bass), coated lightly with a fresh puttanesca sauce. Desserts are as good as the entrees and do not leave without trying one, in particular, the chocolate and vanilla parfait. The restaurant is busy and bustling, yet service is unflappable.

355 W. 14th St. (at Ninth Ave.). © **212/691-0555.** www.scarpettanyc.com. Reservations highly recommended. Main courses $22–$38. AE, DISC, MC, V. Mon–Thurs 5:30–11pm; Fri–Sat 5:30pm–midnight; Sun 5:30–10:30pm. Subway: A, C, E, or L to 14th St.–8th Ave.

Tanuki Tavern ★ JAPANESE Just off the lobby of the Meatpacking District's Gansevoort Hotel is Tanuki Tavern. Billing itself as a Japanese gastropub (as opposed to an *izakaya*, kind of a Japanese gastropub featuring beer, sake, cocktails, and small plates, usually not sushi or sashimi), Tanuki Tavern includes an extensive list of sushi and sashimi on its menu. But, though the sashimi and sushi I sampled was very good, what makes the place stand out are those small plates: the addictive crispy baby bok choy with lemon pepper, broiled Japanese mushrooms in parchment, *tebayaki*, grilled chicken wings with citrus salt, or the decadent, miso-braised beef marrow bone. All are perfect companions to something from the vast sake list or with a pint of Hitachino white ale. The ramen noodles are homemade and a bowl of *cha shu* ramen, brimming with sliced pork belly in a ginger pork broth, and one of the hibachi offerings such as the miso-marinated black cod are worthy detours from the small plates. The atmosphere is loud, almost raucous; it's a nightclub-slash-restaurant, not unlike so many others in the trendy Meatpacking District.

EATING CHINESE OUTSIDE OF CHINATOWN

Don't get me wrong—I love Chinatown. But you don't have to traverse Mott, Mulberry, Bayard, and the Bowery, to name a few of Chinatown's congested streets, to find authentic and exotic Chinese food. In particular, there has been a mini-explosion of Szechuan restaurants, and I don't mean the generic "Szechuan" featuring the much abused General Tso and his take on shrimp, pork, and chicken or watered down, cold sesame noodles. No, the Szechuan restaurants I'm suggesting might offer the above selections, but also, maybe, the "thousand year old egg" with chili jam, or stir fried intestines with chili and snake beans, or even rabbit with pickled chili pepper. Do you see a pattern here? Yes, it's the use of chilies. The Szechuan food offered at the restaurants below do not skimp on heat and, personally, I would have it no other way.

Who would have known that 39th Street, between Fifth and Sixth Avenues, would have two of the best of said Szechuan restaurants? At 21 W. 39th St. you will find the appropriately named, **Szechuan Gourmet** (✆ 212/921-0233; www.szechuangourmetnyc.com), where I enjoyed the crispy lamb filets with chili cumin, the braised eel with baby eggplant, and the beef brisket noodle soup.

Down the block a bit from Szechuan Gourmet at 60 W. 39th St. is **Lan Sheng** (✆ 212/575-8899; www.lansheng restaurant.food.officelive.com). At Lan Sheng there are items similar to Szechuan Gourmet's, some done better like the

Dan Dan noodles and the braised beef filets with Napa cabbage. Best of all is the fish filet with pickled mustard green in broth; an enormous soup that serves at least two.

The bi-level, grand **Legend Bar & Restaurant** at 88 Seventh Ave., btw. 15th and 16th sts. (✆ 212/929-1778; www.legend restaurant88.com) in Chelsea, lives up to its name by churning out legendary Szechuan food. You want hot? Try the "Tears in the Eyes" noodles with spicy mung. You want exotic? Go for the bamboo fungus and chicken soup. If you just want real good, the braised whole fish with hot bean sauce will more than suffice.

18 Ninth Ave. (at 13th St). ✆ **212/660-6766.** www.chinagrillmgt.com. Reservations recommended. AE, DC, DISC, MC, V. Snacks and small plates $5–$12; main courses $16–$38. Daily noon–3pm Mon–Tues 6pm–midnight; Wed–Sat 6pm–1am; Sun 6pm–11pm. Subway: A, C, E to 14th St.–8th Ave.

Moderate

L'Artusi ★★ ITALIAN   Offering a staggering range of small plates from *crudo* (raw) to *carne* (meat), L'Artusi has something for everyone, and most of it very good. Seating is a bit cramped at the long, narrow restaurant that features an open kitchen and dining at the bar and at the *crudo* bar, and L'Artusi is noisy and busy. The menu changes frequently, but if you are lucky, the chicory with lemon-anchovy dressing will be available, along with the combination pork belly with cockles under the *carne* section. L'Artusi's cavatelli with sausage is perfectly spiced, while the side of sunchokes with Calabrian chilies is a worthy complement to the grilled octopus. The restaurant features a 2,500-bottle walk-in wine cellar and the servers go out of their way to find the right pairings for your selections.

228 W. 10th St. (btw. Bleecker and Hudson sts.). ✆ **212/555-5757.** www.lartusi.com. Reservations recommended. Main courses $10-$24. AE, DISC, MC, V. Sun-Thurs 5:30-11pm; Fri-Sat 5:30pm-midnight. Subway: 1 to Christopher St.

Inexpensive

The downtown branch of **Gray's Papaya** is at 402 Sixth Ave., at 8th Street (✆ **212/260-3532**). The original **John's Pizzeria** is at 278 Bleecker St., near Seventh Avenue (✆ **212/243-1680;** see "The Pizza Capital of the United States," p. 178). For one of the best slices of pizza, go to **Joe's Pizza,** 7 Carmine St., at Bleecker Street (✆ **212/255-3946**). Also, you'll find **Murray's Bagels** at 500 Sixth Ave., between 12th and 13th streets (✆ **212/462-2830;** see "The Hole Truth: N.Y.'s Best Bagels," p. 169).

A great neighborhood hangout that serves vegetarian/vegan food, is **'sNice,** 45 Eighth Ave., at West 4th Street (✆ **212/645-0310**). You don't have to be vegetarian to enjoy the hearty, homemade sandwiches, wraps, salads, desserts, and tea and coffee. There are board games, Wi-Fi, shared tables, and an all-ages crowd that appreciates the ambience. It's open Sunday to Thursday 7:30am to 10pm, and Friday and Saturday 8am to 10pm.

CHELSEA

To locate the restaurants in this section, see the map on p. 160.

Expensive

Bar Basque SPANISH   Set in a futuristic, rich red and black venue on the second floor of the **Eventi Hotel** (p. 158), Bar Basque seems an unlikely venue to present the traditional food of that historic region of Spain. But even if you are dining under the retractable roof overlooking the outdoor **FoodParc** (another China Grill Management creation) dining area with the movie "My Man Godfrey" showing on one of New York's largest television screens, your enjoyment of, say, the crispy farm egg with olive oil crushed potatoes, pepper, and Serrano ham in a cheese broth shouldn't be diminished. And even if the retractable roof happens to be open, which it wasn't when I visited, you wouldn't be able to hear the movie, much less the conversation across from you. Bar Basque is one of many of the current nightclubs that also pose as restaurants. The foods best experienced are the small plates, or tapas, like slow-baked piquillo peppers, Cantabric anchovies, and the assorted Basque charcuterie plate.

839 Sixth Ave. (btw. 29th and 30th sts.). ✆ **646/600-7150.** www.chinagrillmgt.com. Reservations recommended. Tapas $4-$26; main courses: $28-$36. AE, MC, V. Subway: B, D, F, M, N, Q, R to 34th Street. Sun-Wed 6pm-11pm; Thurs-Sat 6pm-12am.

Buddakan ★ ASIAN   Is Buddakan a bus depot disguised as a nightclub with a restaurant inside, or is it a restaurant with a nightclub persona inside a sort of Buddhist-decor bus depot? My expectations were of a loud dance club scene in a large space where the food would be showy, but flavorless. I was right about the loud scene, but wrong about the food. The Brasserie is the main dining room on the lower level, and the steps can seem steep after a few cocktails in the upstairs lounge. To fortify yourself, don't hesitate to order some of Buddakan's superb appetizers, such as the edamame dumplings. You could make a meal out of appetizers—the extensive menu at Buddakan works best for large parties and has the now obligatory "communal" table. But if you order one entree, make sure it's the sizzling short rib, tender and removed from the bone and sitting on top of a bed of mushroom chow fun.

75 Ninth Ave. (at 16th St.). ℭ **212/989-6699.** www.buddakannyc.com. Dim sum appetizers $9–$13; main courses $17–$35. AE, DC, MC, V. Sun–Wed 5:30pm–midnight; Thurs–Sat 5:30pm–1am. Subway: A, C, or E to 14th St.

Cookshop ★★ AMERICAN   On far west Tenth Avenue, Cookshop is brawny and boisterous, with food to match. Seating can be tight, and you would hear your neighbor's conversation if the whole place weren't so loud. But nevermind: Enjoy the chef's creations. A pizza with shaved king oyster mushrooms and *stracchino* cheese or the grilled Montauk squid in a *salsa verde* make good starters to complement the restaurant's innovative cocktails. Or combine a few snacks, like the fried spiced hominy or the smoked pork tacos as starters for the table. Cookshop offers entree options in four categories: sauté, grill, wood oven, and rotisserie. The whole roasted porgy, head and all, cooked in the wood oven, is moist and full of flavor, while the chili-braised beef short ribs, served over cheddar grits, from the sauté section, are tender to the bone. Service is casually efficient and helpful.

156 Tenth Ave. (at 20th St.). ℭ **212/924-4440.** www.cookshopny.com. Reservations recommended. Main courses $21–$36. AE, DC, MC, V. Mon–Sat 5:30–11:30pm; Sun 11am–3pm and 5:30–10pm. Subway: C or E to 23rd St.

Morimoto ★★ JAPANESE   The Morimoto experience is like a theme park for foodies. You've seen him on television, but here, in this 12,000-square-foot bi-level space in Chelsea, you can sample Iron Chef Masaharu Morimoto's creations. The problem, however, is how to decide amongst all the treasures. The tuna pizza, spicy with jalapeño peppers and with anchovy aioli, is a good start while the "duck, duck, duck" entree, a foie gras croissant, roast duck, and a soft duck egg in a red miso sauce, is out of the Iron Chef playbook. If it's all too overwhelming, leave it to the chef and order the Morimoto Omasake tasting menu. Whatever path you choose, accompany your meal with one of the many sake options and don't skip dessert; the soft chocolate ganache with black-and-white sesame ice cream is memorable. The cavernous space can get noisy, and when I visited a fire alarm from the adjoining Chelsea Market kept going off, but the army of chefs in the open kitchen, used to false alarms, were unfazed and went about their business without missing a beat.

88 Tenth Ave. (btw. 15th and 16th sts.). ℭ **212/989-8883.** www.morimotonyc.com. Reservations recommended. Main courses $14–$48; Omasake tasting menu $120 per person. AE, DISC, MC, V. Lunch: Mon–Fri noon–2:30pm; dinner: Mon–Wed 5:30–11pm, Thurs–Sat 5pm–midnight. Subway: A, C, E, or L to 14th St.–8th Ave.

Moderate

La Nacional ★★ 🍴 SPANISH/TAPAS   It's not easy to find the oldest Spanish restaurant in New York. But once you find it, your perseverance will be rewarded. Founded in 1868 as a gathering spot for the Benevolent Spanish Society, La Nacional, a social club, is a hidden treat. At one time, Spanish expatriates congregated here, filling the room with smoke and talk of Spanish politics and football. Gabriel Garcia Lorca spent countless hours here, documenting his New York City experience. The cigarette smoke has been replaced by the smoke of the grill, which turns out tasty tapas with sardines, octopus, and shrimp. There is a

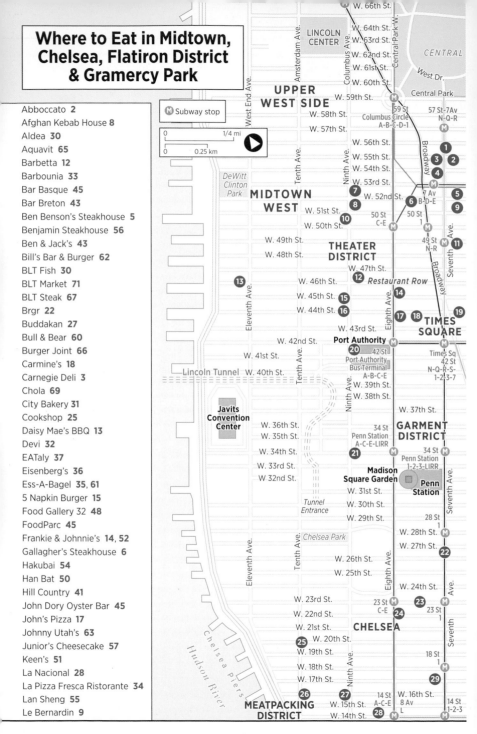

Where to Eat in Midtown, Chelsea, Flatiron District & Gramercy Park

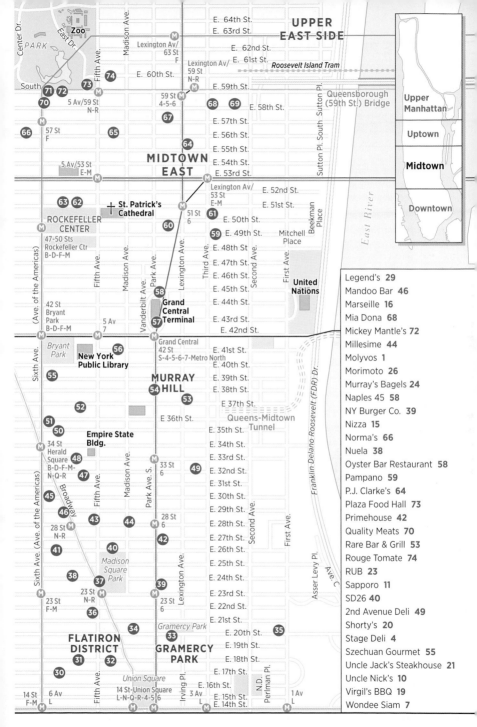

E. 64th St.
E. 63rd St.

**UPPER
EAST SIDE**

E. 62nd St.

Lexington Av/
63 St
F

E. 61st St.

Roosevelt Island Tram

Lexington Av/
59 St
N-R

E. 60th St.

Zoo

Center Dr.
East Dr.

PARK

Fifth Ave.
Madison Ave.

⑦④

South

㉛㉒㉓
⑦⓪

5 Av/59 St
N-R

59 St
4-5-6

E. 59th St.

㉖㉘㉙

E. 58th St.

Queensborough
(59th St.) Bridge

Sutton Pl. South
Sutton Pl.

**Upper
Manhattan**

Uptown

㉗

E. 57th St.

⑥⑥

57 St
F

⑥⑤

E. 56th St.

E. 55th St.

㉔

E. 54th St.

Midtown

5 Av/53 St
E-M

**MIDTOWN
EAST**

E. 53rd St.

East River

Downtown

Lexington Av/
53 St
E-M

E. 52nd St.

㉓㉒

† **St. Patrick's
Cathedral**

E. 51st St.

Beekman
Place

**ROCKEFELLER
CENTER**

51 St
6

㉑

E. 50th St.

㉖

47-50 Sts
Rockefeller Ctr
B-D-F-M

㉙

E. 49th St.

Mitchell
Place

E. 48th St.

Fifth Ave.
Madison Ave.
Park Ave.
Lexington Ave.
Third Ave.
Second Ave.
First Ave.

(Ave. of the Americas)

42 St
Bryant
Park
B-D-F-M

E. 47th St.

E. 46th St.

E. 45th St.

**United
Nations**

5 Av
7

E. 44th St.

㉘

**Grand
Central
Terminal**

E. 43rd St.

㉗

E. 42nd St.

*Bryant
Park*

Grand Central
42 St
S-4-5-6-7-Metro North

㉖

**New York
Public Library**

E. 41st St.

Sixth Ave.

㉕

E. 40th St.

E. 39th St.

**MURRAY
HILL**

E. 38th St.

㉒

㉔

E 37th St.

㉓

㉕

E 36th St.

Franklin Delano Roosevelt (FDR) Dr.

㉑

Empire State
Bldg.

E. 35th St.

*Queens-Midtown
Tunnel*

㉚

E. 34th St.

34 St
Herald
Square
B-D-F-M
N-Q-R

㊽

E. 33rd St.

Madison Ave.

33 St
6

E. 32nd St.

㊾

㊼

E. 31st St.

Fifth Ave.

E. 30th St.

㊺

E. 29th St.

Park Ave. S.

㊻

28 St
N-R

㊸

㊹

28 St
6

E. 28th St.

E. 27th St.

㊷

㊶

Sixth Ave. (Ave. of the Americas)

Broadway

Madison Ave.

㊵

E. 26th St.

E. 25th St.

Lexington Ave.

Second Ave.

First Ave.

㊳

*Madison
Square
Park*

㊲

E. 24th St.

㊴

E. 23rd St.

23 St
N-R

23 St
6

E. 22nd St.

㊱

23 St
F-M

E. 21st St.

㉞

Gramercy Park

E. 20th St.

㉟

**FLATIRON
DISTRICT**

㉛

㉜

㉝

**GRAMERCY
PARK**

E. 19th St.

E. 18th St.

E. 17th St.

Asser Levy Pl.

Ave. C

㉚

6 Av
Fifth Ave.

Union Square

14 St-Union Square
L-N-Q-R-4-5-6

Irving Pl.
3 Av

E. 16th St.

E. 15th St.

*N.D.
Perlman Pl.*

1 Av
L

14 St
F-M

L

E. 14th St.

THE PRIME CUT: STEAKS! STEAKS! STEAKS!

The number of prime-cut palaces in New York continues to mushroom like . . . mushrooms. **Peter Luger Steakhouse** ★★ (p. 205) has been the steakhouse standard for years, Beginning the steak-as-style trend a few years back was **BLT Steak** ★★★ (p. 183), which proves there is substance with the style., Wall Street traders and financial bigwigs often have carnivorous reputations and at **Harry's Café & Steak** ★★ (p. 142), they don't have to go far to satisfy their cravings. Some of the city's oldest restaurants are steakhouses, and two of the oldest of those are **Frankie & Johnnie's** ★★ (p. 171) and **Keens Steakhouse** ★★★ (p. 172), which was formerly known as a chophouse for their selection of such chops as their acclaimed mutton chop.

Most entrees at the following steakhouses tend to fall in the $22 to $38 range. Always book ahead and inquire about dress codes, especially at the old-school spots.

One of the best of the traditional old-world steakhouses is the clubby, fun **Bull and Bear,** in the Waldorf=Astoria, 301 Park Ave., between 49th and 50th streets (✆ **212/872-1275**), which serves the best New York strip I've had in the city. You can also call **the Post House** ★★ (p. 196), where seats are claimed by VIPs; clubby, but that won't deter me from enjoying their Cajun-rubbed rib-eye.

Another oldie but goodie is the venerable Theater District institution **Gallagher's Steakhouse** ★, 228 W. 52nd St., between Broadway and Eighth Avenue (✆ **212/245-5336;** www.gallaghers nysteakhouse.com). Since 1927, big

hunks of aging prime beef in the restaurant's glass-enclosed aging room have been visible from the street. Long a hangout for athletes, sportswriters, and other celebrities, Gallagher's still remains the only steakhouse in the city that grills over hickory coals. There aren't many better steakhouses than **Ben Benson's Steakhouse,** 123 W. 52nd St., between Sixth and Seventh avenues (✆ **212/581-8888;** www.benbensons.com). Smack in the middle of Midtown, Ben Benson's is loud and large, and though it's definitely a man's world at Ben's, women are treated with respect here.

Uncle Jack's Steakhouse ★, 440 Ninth Ave., at 34th Street (✆ **212/244-0005;** www.unclejacks.com), is also testosterone fueled, and the decor is plush and bawdy with huge banquettes. Portions are monstrous; the 48-ounce

somewhat formal dining room in front, while in the back, next to the open kitchen, there are a few tables and TVs usually tuned to soccer matches. Come and share a bottle of Spanish wine and make a meal out of the tapas—the *albondigas* (Spanish meatballs), *boquerones* (white anchovy filets), and aforementioned octopus are my favorites—or you can order the restaurant's excellent paella. Tapas range from $7 to $9, while no entree is more than $18.

239 W. 14th St. (btw. Seventh and Eighth aves.). ✆ **212/243-9308.** www.lanacionaltapas.com. Tapas $7–$9; main courses $16–$18. AE, DC, DISC, MC, V. Sun–Wed noon–10pm; Thurs–Sat noon–11pm. Subway: A, C, E, 1, 2, or 3 to 14th St.

RUB ★★ BARBECUE   It stands for "Righteous Urban Barbecue," but when was barbecue an urban thing—not to mention righteous? But the name is cool;

porterhouse, Uncle Jack's signature dish, is large enough for a big family.

Despite its bawdy name, **Strip House ★★**, 13 E. 12th St., between University Place and Fifth Avenue (*℃* **212/328-0000;** www.striphouse. net) serves no-nonsense steaks.

Restaurateur Stephen Hansen's contribution to the New York steakhouse universe is the Flatiron located, **Primehouse ★** 381 Park Ave. S., at 27th Street (*℃* **212/824-2600;** www. brguestrestaurants.com), where they have their own salt room to dry their special slabs of beef.

Chef Michael Lomonaco and his amazing chili-rubbed strip steak can be had in the stylish Time Warner Center at **Porter House New York ★★** 10 Columbus Circle, 4th Floor, in the Time Warner Center, at 60th Street (*℃* **212/823-9500;** www.porterhousenewyork.com).

There are steakhouses that claim to rival Peter Luger all over the city, a few started by ex-Luger waiters. But the **Benjamin Steakhouse ★**, 52 E. 41st St., in the Dylan Hotel (*℃* **212/297-9177;** www.benjaminsteakhouse.com), is the only one to feature an ex-chef from Luger's, Arturo. The result is not quite Luger's-quality steaks, but it does have better service and a dramatic room highlighted by a huge walk-in fireplace.

Ex-Luger waiters are everywhere and like the Benjamin above, two Luger refugees moved on to bigger and better things when they opened **Ben & Jack's Steakhouse ★★** at two locations in Manhattan: 219 E. 44th St., between Second and Third avenues (*℃* **212/682-5678;** www.benandjackssteakhouse. com) and 255 Fifth Avenue, between 28th and 29th streets (*℃* **212/532-7600;** www.benandjackssteakhouse.com).

Set in a stunning, bi-level space designed by the famous team of AvroKO is **Quality Meats ★**, 57 W. 58th St., between Fifth and Sixth avenues (*℃* **212/371-7777;** www.qualitymeats nyc.com). And the quality of the food matches the quality of the design, with some nontraditional steakhouse menu items such as pan-roasted lamb T-bones with figs and mint, and a flatiron steak with blackberries.

If you're up around Museum Mile on the Upper East Side and you get a craving for red meat, drop by the **Parlor Steakhouse ★** 1600 Third Ave., at 90th Street (*℃* **212/423-5888;** www.parlor steakhouse.com), where their filet mignon steals the show.

and after tasting some of the barbecue that comes out of the restaurant's custom-made, New York City Health Department–approved smoker, "righteous" is an apt description. RUB is co-owned by Kansas City pit master Paul Kirk, who has won seven World Barbecue Championships and is a member of the Barbecue Hall of Fame. The smoked turkey and barbecued chicken are the best I've had—moist inside with a distinctive smoked flavor—and the ribs, St. Louis–style, were delicate and crispy, yet tender and meaty. The "burnt ends," the fatty part of the brisket, were a bit tough. The best way to get a taste of all of RUB's barbecue is the humongous Taste of the Baron, where a little of everything is piled high on a platter. The restaurant is cramped and loud and the prices urban (meaning high), but the food at RUB will provide all the comfort you need.

208 W. 23rd St. (btw. Seventh and Eighth aves.). ☏ **212/524-4300.** www.rubbbq.net. Sandwiches $9–$12; platters $15–$23; Taste of the Baron $46. AE, MC, V. Tues–Thurs noon–11pm; Fri–Sat noon–midnight. Subway: 1 to 23rd St.

Inexpensive

Paradise Café, 141 Eighth Ave. (btw. 16th and 17th sts.; ☏ **212/647-0066**), is a neighborhood gem in so-trendy-it's-exhausting Chelsea, where it's hard to find a good meal for under $10 at most places. A sign behind the counter reads, "If you insist on ordering using Starbucks terms, we will be forced to charge you Starbucks prices." So don't order a "venti," but do order all kinds of free-trade teas and coffees, sandwiches, wraps, smoothies, and homemade desserts. The narrow storefront has French doors that are left open in good weather, and you can sit on a bench out front or lounge at one of the indoor tables, surfing with your laptop on the free Wi-Fi, reading the papers and magazines, and enjoying the original art on the walls. It's open daily from 6am to 9pm.

UNION SQUARE, FLATIRON DISTRICT & GRAMERCY PARK

To locate the restaurants in this section, see the map on p. 160.

Expensive

Aldea ★★ 🎁 AMERICAN/PORTUGUESE   Chefs sometimes get carried away with their own ambitions and distract from the food. At the very pleasant, low-key Aldea, I'm glad to report, chef George Mendes keeps it simple, letting the fresh, first-rate ingredients shine without too much accompaniment. Though he is Portuguese American, only traces of Portuguese cooking can be found in his appetizers and *petiscos* (small bites), where bits of *bacalao* (salt cod) are added to a simple farm egg or the addition of *pimenton* (Portuguese hot pepper) is included in the preparation of shrimp *alhinho*. The main dishes—original creations like the *arroz de pato,* duck confit, chorizo, duck cracklings and olive, and the monk-fish in a stew of fennel, potato, leeks and mussels over black rice—would be unusual, but very welcome, on any menu east (or west) of the Azores. Narrow with an open kitchen, you would think Aldea would be loud and jarring, but everything proceeds orderly and conversation is, remarkably, attainable.

31 W. 17th St. (btw. 5th and 6th aves.) ☏ **212/675-7223.** www.aldearestaurant.com. Reservations recommended. Main courses $24–$29; chef's tasting menu $85. AE, DC, DISC, MC, V. Mon–Fri 11:30am–2pm; Mon–Thurs 5:30–11pm; Fri–Sat 5:30pm–midnight. Subway: 4, 5, 6, N, R, Q, L to 14th St.–Union Sq.

Barbounia ★ GREEK/MEDITERRANEAN/MIDDLE EASTERN   The countries of Greece and Israel, separated by the Mediterranean, represent the cradle of civilization, so it should be no surprise that their cuisines, with a detour to another ancient land, Turkey, mesh as well as they do at Barbounia. This ornate, high-ceilinged restaurant complete with Moorish columns is gorgeous, but those same cavernous features make for a loud experience. If you go, proceed happily to the chef's creations beginning with his fresh Israeli salad combined with *lachma hajuan,* fresh-baked flatbread with Turkish lamb, pine nuts, and tahini. If you opt for a main course instead of just gorging on mezes like "married"

APRIL'S TRIO BLOOMS IN NYC

Chef April Bloomfield and her partner, Ken Friedman, made their initial mark on New York's dining scene over 5 years ago when, in a small space in the West Village, they opened something that was new to the city at the time: a gastropub. They called it **The Spotted Pig** ★, 314 W. 11th St., at Greenwich Street (✆ **212/620-0393;** www. thespottedpig.com), and with its cask beers like Spotted Pig bitters, small plates to accompany them, like crispy pigs ears, deviled eggs like you've never had before, and a now legendary burger with Roquefort cheese, the restaurant was an immediate sensation and celebrity magnet.

Flash forward to 2010 and Bloomfield and Friedman repeated their Spotted Pig success with another pub-like restaurant they called **The Breslin,** 16 W. 29th St., off the lobby of the **Ace Hotel** (✆ **646/214-5780;** www.thebreslin.com). Open for breakfast, lunch, and dinner, it's the evening crowd where the mobs begin to descend for the classic cocktails and, of course, the meat-heavy menu. The lamb burger with feta has already been christened by many publications as the city's best burger while the pig foot for two makes the Breslin a worthy destination for the growing numbers of adventurous foodies out there.

Across the busy lobby of the Ace, is the third Bloomfield and Friedman venture; their newest which opened in early 2011 they call **The John Dory Oyster Bar** ★★, 1196 Broadway at 29th Street in the Ace Hotel (✆ **212/792-9000;** www.thejohndory.com). The space is small with bar-like tables and counter space along the windows and the no-reservations policy makes for a maddening scene, but none of those discomforts matter once you settle in and begin feasting on the John Dory's delicious offerings. Oysters vary daily and, as the restaurant's name suggests, are a must to start with. There are also several "crudo" (raw fish lightly seasoned) items on the menu including the revelatory Australian *hiramasa*. Of the small plates, the escarole salad with anchovies is an amazing variation of the Caesar, while the piquant oyster pan roast, seemingly small, but bursting with flavor and the chorizo-stuffed squid with smoked tomatoes are so good that even before you finish, will have you plotting your next visit to the John Dory Oyster Bar.

sardines with spicy harissa and cilantro or falafel, the grilled whole branzino is prepared to simple perfection with a drizzling of olive oil and herbs. There is a lively bar scene here, which adds to the noise level, but after sampling cocktails like the Greek mojito (made with ouzo instead of rum), I was able to block out the noise and enjoy all Barbounia has to offer.

250 Park Ave. South (at 20th St.). ✆ **212/995-0242.** www.barbounia.com. Reservations recommended. Main courses $19–$33; mezes $6.50–$18. AE, DISC, MC, V. Mon–Fri 11:30am–4pm; Sat–Sun 11am–4pm; Mon–Thurs 5–11pm; Fri–Sat 5pm–midnight. Subway: 6 to 23rd St.

BLT Fish ★★ SEAFOOD   The seafood branch of the **BLT** (Bistro Laurent Tourondel, BLT Steak, BLT Prime, BLT Market, BLT Burger) empire, is actually two restaurants with two kitchens. The downstairs is a moderately priced faux-seafood shack with a raw bar, fried fare, and the much-in-demand lobster roll. Upstairs (you can walk the steps or take a glass elevator) is the elegant (and

FOODIE FOOD COURTS IN THE BIG APPLE

One of the new trends in New York's foodie mania, along with gourmet food trucks, is the emergence of diverse, sometimes ethnic, always non-chain food booths within food courts. And, as opposed to eating from a truck, you can actually sit and eat. It's difficult enough for me to stuff my face standing; sitting just makes it that much easier.

Restaurateur Jeffrey Chodorow (**Bar Basque, Tanuke Tavern,** p. 158) got into the food court business in 2010 when he opened **FoodParc** ★ on the ground level of the **Eventi Hotel** (p. 166) at 845 Sixth Ave., at 29th Street (**www.foodparc.com**). The four-venue food court features indoor and outdoor seating. The outdoor seating includes an enormous television screen where independent short films and classics are often running. The attraction, however, is not the seating but the fresh goods offered at the restaurants. **Red Farm Stand** specializes in dumplings and noodles, plus a delicious twist on Asian appetizers—their Katz's pastrami egg roll (yes, an egg roll stuffed with Katz's Deli world famous salami). Also in Food-Parc you'll find **3B's,** which means burgers, bacon, and brews. The burgers are a hanger steak blend, the bacon, artisanal, and the brews from domestic micro-breweries.

Not far from FoodParc, in Koreatown, is **Food Gallery 32,** an Asian food emporium at 11 W. 32nd St., between Sixth and Fifth avenues, where vendors sell snacks from Korea, Japan, China, and Vietnam. The two levels of seating make the experience not only tasty, but convenient.

Having a food court named after you must qualify you as a "Top Chef," and Todd English has that distinction with the upscale **The Plaza Food Hall by Todd English** (**www.theplazafoodhall.com**). In the 5,400 square foot eating emporium, you will find such venues as the Grill, the Wine Bar, Sushi Bar, Ocean

higher-priced) dining room. Here you can sit under a skylight or near the open kitchen and watch an army of servers move from the kitchen with huge platters, where whole fish sit, dressed up beautifully, ready for consumption. Check out the crispy red snapper, Cantonese style, that is filleted tableside. Another is the sea-salt-crusted New Zealand pink snapper, which you'll have to crack to get to the tender, juicy flesh underneath. Of the smaller dishes, the Maine Day boat sea scallops stand out, along with the Alaskan black cod in a honey-reduction sauce. Like BLT Steak and BLT Prime, don't expect quiet conversation.

21 W. 17th St. (btw. Fifth and Sixth aves.). © **212/691-8888.** www.bltfish.com. Reservations recommended. Prices $25–$35. BLT Fish Mon–Thurs 5:30–11pm; Fri–Sat 5:30–11:30pm. BLT Fish Shack Mon–Fri 11:45am–2:30pm; Mon–Thurs 5:30–11pm; Fri–Sat 5:30–11:30pm; Sun 5–10pm. Subway: 4, 5, 6, L, N, Q, or R to 14th St.–Union Sq.

Dévi ★★ INDIAN   Few of the many Indian restaurants in the city are like this one. Dévi offers $45 to $85 tasting menus (vegetarian and nonvegetarian), and that's really the way to go. The menu features small courses that will let you sample much of what the restaurant has to offer. Some of the highlights include tender tandoori chicken stuffed with spicy herbs; halibut coated in a cilantro rub accompanied with mint-coconut chutney and lemon rice; *zimikand koftas* (meatballs); delicate yam *koftas* in a creamy tomato-onion sauce; and the addictive,

Grill & Oyster Bar, "Pizza," the Dumpling Bar, Bakery, and a demo kitchen. All are very self-explanatory and all very rudimentary . . . though not for a food court, especially one located in the Plaza Hotel.

Finally, there is the monster that is **Eataly** (pictured below), at 200 Fifth Ave., between 23rd and 24th streets (**212/229-2560;** www.eatalyny.com). Encompassing a full city block, this Mario Batali and Joe and mother Lydia Bastianich (**Babbo, Del Posto**) enterprise is a food court like no other—a true nirvana to the Italian foodie in particular. Here you will find 12 different "eateries," an Italian-accented steakhouse called Manzo; Il Pesce, for fresh fish; La Pizza and Pasta; and a Paninoteca, for Italian sandwiches to name just a few of the eating options. Along with the eateries, you can browse various Italian foodstuffs like salumi and cheese, fresh and dry pasta, meat, seafood, vegetables, wine, coffee, and much more.

Eataly is a wonderland for sure, but only if you can negotiate the crowds and the enormous maze-like room. I admit to having been intimidated by the scale of it all the few times I have visited, but that probably says more about me than about the wildly successful Eataly. You can download a PDF of Eataly's floor plan from the website that might come in handy when visiting.

crispy okra, the Indian equivalent of french fries. With the tasting menus, you get a choice of desserts; I recommend the fabulous *falooda,* an Indian sundae that's a refreshing combination of noodles with honey-soaked basil seeds, mango, and strawberry sorbet in lemon grass–infused coconut milk. Seating is comfortable and service is knowledgeable and helpful.

8 E. 18th St. (btw. Fifth Ave. and Broadway). *212/691-1300.* www.devinyc.com. Reservations recommended. AE, DISC, MC, V. Main courses $15–$30; tasting menus $45–$85. Mon-Sat noon–2:30pm and 5:30–11pm; Sun 5–10pm. Subway: N, Q, R, 4, 5, or 6 to 14th St.–Union Sq.

Nuela ★ LATIN New in 2010, this sprawling, raucous restaurant is more a nightclub than a dining room. The music pounds, the crowd is young and lively, and the mojitos flow nonstop. Yet despite the sideshow, you will eat well especially if your inclination is toward ceviches. Here there are a minimum of 10 offered daily and they are the perfect accompaniment to said mojito. Throughout the menu, the chef melds hints of Asia with the predominately Latin menu, and the tuna ceviche with Thai flavors and coconut milk is a good example. Of the many ceviches, the hamachi, bathed in sour orange juice and dabbed with dots of pungent black garlic, is my favorite. If ceviche is not enough and you need something even more substantial, try one of the *platos* or main courses; the lobster *chupe,* a lobster chowder with turnips, celery, purple potato, and a tiny quail egg will put you over the edge. For a group—and Nuela is definitely a group place—the *cochinillo* (suckling pig) served either in quarters, half, or whole, will more than suffice.

43 W. 24th St. (btw. Fifth–Sixth aves) ☎ **212/929-1200.** www.nuelany.com. Reservations recommended. Ceviches $10–$18; main courses $25–$35. AE, MC, V. Sun–Thurs 5pm–11pm; Fri–Sat 5pm–12am. Subway: F, M to 23rd Street.

SD26 ★ ITALIAN   From the former owners of the now-closed, very formal, Central Park South standard San Domenico, SD26 is less formal, but still elegant, in a downtown way, a *new* San Domenico. Gone are the required jackets for men and hedge-fund-size tabs. In its new home facing Madison Square Park is a lively front-of-restaurant wine bar where there is a self-service dispensing system offering 1-, 2-, and 4-ounce pours, a salumeria station, and an open kitchen complete with chef's table. In this case, the change was definitely for the better. Like so many other current restaurants, SD26 features numerous small plates, the best of which I sampled was the polenta with wild mushrooms while the salad of bottarga (tuna roe) with blood orange was the perfect mix of salt, sweet, and tart. The pastas are homemade; mine was *candele,* a thick ziti with spicy sausage that, unfortunately, took "al dente" to the extreme. An old favorite from the original San Domenico, soft egg yolk–filled raviolo with truffled butter, has made the trek downtown as well and no one is complaining. The owners work the room enthusiastically, greeting each customer as if they were an old friend and, in my case, that effort went a long way in me forgiving a few missteps by the serving staff.

19 E. 26th St. (btw. Madison and Fifth aves.). ☎ **212/265-5959.** www.sd26ny.com. Reservations recommended. Main courses $15–$36. AE, DC, DISC, MC, V. Mon–Sat 11:30am–2:30pm and 5:30–11pm; Sun 5pm–10pm. Subway: 6 to 23rd St.

Moderate

Bar Breton FRENCH   In the shadow of the Empire State Building and open for breakfast, lunch, and dinner, Bar Breton is a welcome refuge in an area somewhat devoid of decent dining. Bar Breton offers a casual spin on classic French cuisine. But the twist here is the restaurant's *galettes,* buckwheat crepes stuffed with any number of delicacies. The *galette* with lamb shank made for a hearty entree, while the Quimper, a *galette* with blue cheese and topped with honey and pecans, was more of an appetizer. If you are not in the mood for a pancake with your wine, Bar Breton offers good burgers and numerous fish options. Though it is a bit noisy and has unforgiving wooden seating, you could do a lot worse in the immediate neighborhood than Bar Breton and it's a solid choice especially for breakfast or lunch. Some friends proudly related they were there the night former President Bill Clinton stopped in to say "hi" to daughter Chelsea, who was having a drink at the bar.

254 Fifth Ave. (btw. 28th and 29th sts.). ☎ **212/213-4999.** www.barbreton.com. Galettes $12–$15; entrees $16–$28. AE, MC, V. Breakfast: 7–11:30am Mon–Fri; lunch: 11:30am–4pm Mon–Fri; dinner: 4–11pm Mon–Thurs; 4:30pm–midnight Fri–Sat; 4:30–11pm Sun; brunch: 10:30am–4:30pm Sat–Sun. Subway: N, R to 28th St.

Millesime ★★ FRENCH/SEAFOOD   On the lush mezzanine lobby of the Carlton Hotel (p. 102), replete with wondrous skylights, an open kitchen, comfortable seating, and a raw bar, is Millesime. Despite the occasional intrusion from the live music from the downstairs lounge, this intimate and romantic spot

THE HOLE TRUTH: N.Y.'S BEST BAGELS

Not many things are more "New York" than a bagel, and New Yorkers are loyal to their favorite bagel purveyors. In fact, discussions about who makes the best bagel can lead to heated arguments. Following are the top contenders:

Absolute Bagels 2708 Broadway, between 107th and 108th streets (𝄐 **212/932-2052**). A new player on the scene, their egg bagels, hot out of the oven, melt in your mouth, and their whitefish salad is perfectly smoky, not overpowering.

Ess-A-Bagel 359 First Ave., at 21st Street (𝄐 **212/260-2252;** www.ess-a-bagel.com). When it comes to size, Ess-a-Bagel's are the best of the biggest; plump, chewy, and *oh* so satisfying. Also at 831 Third Ave., between 50th and 51st streets (𝄐 **212/980-1010**).

H&H Bagels 639 W. 46th St., at Twelfth Avenue (𝄐 **212/595-8000;** www.hhbagels.com). These are long reputed to be the best bagels in New York, which may have resulted in the arrogant price hike to $1 a bagel. Some complain they are a bit too sweet, but I disagree. And they are always fresh and warm, the bagel aficionado's prerequisite. Takeout only.

Kossar's Bialys 367 Grand St., at Essex St. (𝄐 **877/4-BIALYS** [424-2597]; www.kossarsbialys.com). We know about their bialys, but don't forget about their bagels. Also hand rolled, the result is a slightly crunchy exterior with a tender, moist middle. Sure, you came for the bialys, but you will leave with both.

Murray's Bagels 500 Sixth Ave., between 12th and 13th streets (𝄐 **212/462-2830**), and 242 Eighth Ave., at 23rd Street (𝄐 646/638-1335; www.mbchelsea.com). There's nothing like a soft, warm bagel to begin your day, and Murray's does them beautifully. Their smoked fish goes perfectly on their bagels.

---

serves very good, very fresh seafood. The raw bar is the best place to start, especially the oysters, both east coast and west coast selections. Of the hors d'oeuvres, Milliesime's take on the Caesar salad—featuring grilled romaine, smoked black cod with parmesan cheese, and lime—is a revelation. The fish is prepared simply, either grilled or on a wood plank. My choice was grilled cod and then I had to make another decision: which of the five sauces would best accompany my fish. I went with the sauce vierge, made of olives, tomato, and basil, and it was the perfect complement to the flaky fish. The wine list is extensive and impressive and service is casual not snooty.

92 Madison Ave. (at 29th St.). 𝄐 **212/889-7100.** www.millesimerestaurant.com. Reservations recommended. AE, DC, DISC, MC, V. $15–$24. Daily 11:30am–2:00pm; Tue–Sat 5:30pm–11pm; Sun–Mon 5:30pm–10pm. Subway: 6 to 28th St.

Inexpensive

Don't forget **Eisenberg's Coffee Shop,** 174 Fifth Ave., at 22nd Street (𝄐 **212/675-5096**), for the New York diner experience. For more, see "Hello, Old Friends" on p. 152.

For healthy burgers, try either outlet of the **New York Burger Co.,** 303 Park Ave. South, between 23rd and 24th streets (𝄐 **212/254-2727**), and 678 Sixth Ave., between 21st and 22nd streets (𝄐 **212/229-1404**). For a burger

5

with boutique quality meat, try **Brgr,** 287 Seventh Ave., at 26th Street (© **212/488-7500**). For more on all three, see the sidebar "Where to Find Your (Burger) Bliss in NYC," on p. 182.

City Bakery ★ ☺ AMERICAN/ORGANIC   City Bakery offers comfort food that manages to be delicious, nutritious, *and* eco-friendly. Its salad bar is unlike any other in the city, where the integrity of the ingredients is as important as the taste. This is health food, all right—roasted beets with walnuts, glistening sautéed greens, lavender eggplant tossed in miso—but with heart and soul, offering such favorites as French toast with artisanal bacon, flavorful mac 'n' cheese, tortilla pie, and smoked salmon with all the trimmings on Sunday. The "bakery" refers to the plethora of sinful desserts; kids love the spinning wheel of chocolate and the homemade marshmallows.

3 W. 18th St. (btw. Fifth and Sixth aves.). © **212/366-1414.** www.thecitybakery.com. Salad bar $13 per lb.; soups $4–$7; sandwiches $5–$10. AE, MC, V. Mon–Fri 7:30am–7pm; Sat 7:30am–6:30pm; Sun 9am–6pm. Subway: N, Q, R, 4, 5, or 6 to 14th St.–Union Sq.

TIMES SQUARE & MIDTOWN WEST

To locate the restaurants in this section, see the map on p. 160.

Very Expensive

In addition to the choices below, consider the *New York Times* four-star winner **Le Bernardin,** 155 W. 51st St., between Sixth and Seventh avenues (© **212/554-1515;** www.le-bernardin.com).

And consider the following steakhouses in the box "The Prime Cut: Steaks! Steaks! Steaks!," on p. 162: **Uncle Jack's Steakhouse** ★, 440 Ninth Ave., at 34th Street (© **212/244-0005;** www.unclejacks.com); **Ben Benson's Steakhouse** ★, 123 W. 52nd St., between Sixth and Seventh avenues (© **212/581-8888;** www.benbensons.com); **Benjamin Steakhouse,** 52 E. 41st St., in the Dylan Hotel (© **212/297-9177;** www.benjaminsteakhouse.com); and **Quality Meats** ★, 57 W. 58th St., between Fifth and Sixth avenues (© **212/371-7777**).

BLT Market ★★ CONTEMPORARY AMERICAN   In the Ritz-Carlton Central Park and across from Park is a perfect setting for the "market" cuisine served here. Other restaurants have chimed in on the market-fresh food trend, but few do it as well. The ingredients change seasonally, sometimes daily, depending on what's fresh at the market. Each month, the menu lists what is peak in that particular season. In November, sunchokes, pumpkin, black cod, Bosc pear, chestnut, and a variety of mushrooms were some of the items used in that day's dishes. Matsutake mushrooms and sunchokes could be found in the meaty roasted langoustine appetizer, while the flaky and moist entree of black cod sat atop a delicious celeriac purée. The Bosc pear was used in a perfectly made *tarte tatin,* while chestnuts were found in a floating island accompanied by orange-blossom madeleines. Even my cocktail, a spin on the Brazilian caipirinha, displayed seasonal ingredients with the addition of Concord grapes. Service is professional and helpful, and the room tries to re-create a rustic, farmhouselike ambience, with water served in milk bottles and an old plow at the restaurant's entrance.

1430 Ave. of the Americas (at 59th St., in the Ritz-Carlton Central Park). ℂ **212/521-6125.** www.
bltmarket.com. Reservations recommended. Main courses $32–$45. AE, DC, DISC, MC, V. Daily
11:45am–2pm and 5:30–10pm. Subway: N, Q, or R to 57th St.

Expensive

Abboccato ★ ITALIAN   This is the Italian entry from the Livanos family,
owners of **Molyvos** (p. 173) and **Oceana** (p. 173), and no ordinary Italian at
that! The menu is ambitious and hearty, with offerings that include such appetizers as the *affetati misti* (a platter of cured meats), *pesce crudo* (raw fish marinated
in olive oil), and grilled tripe; unusual, rustic pastas such as spaghettini with razor
clams and mullet roe and orecchiette with cuttlefish; plus such staples as
tagliatelle Bolognese and spaghetti carbonara. Rich meat mains include braised
(in chocolate and port wine) beef short ribs and crispy veal sweetbreads. Service
is good, but not up to Oceana's level. The room is a throwback; its round yellow
booths are reminiscent of 1960s New York Italian.

136 W. 55th St. (btw. Sixth and Seventh aves.). ℂ **212/265-4000.** www.livanosrestaurantgroup.
com. Reservations recommended. Pasta $23–$26; main courses $32–$42. AE, DC, MC, V. Mon-
Sat noon–3pm; Mon–Tues and Fri–Sat 5–11pm; Sun 4–10pm; breakfast Sat–Sun only 7:30–
10:30am. Subway: N, Q, or R to 57th St.

Barbetta ★★ ITALIAN   The debate over which is New York's oldest restaurant rages on, and Barbetta (est. 1906) is in the thick of it. But there is no debate
over Barbetta's sustained excellence. The first, and still one of the few, New York
restaurants to serve cuisine from Piemonte (the Piedmont), Italy's northwestern-
most region, Barbetta's food, like the decor, is richly elegant. At Barbetta, if you
dine in the autumn or winter, you might have the pleasure of white truffles, flown
in from Piemonte, and shaved over your already decadent *gnochetti ai formaggi*,
freshly made gnochi in an unforgettable cheese sauce, or the stunning creation
of an edible quail's nest filled with *fonduta* cheese and surrounded by three tiny,
speckled quail's eggs. On the menu you can choose from one of the restaurant's
1906 creations such as the *bolliti misti*, a mix of boiled meats and broth served
from an antique silver cart (order 48 hr. in advance). Barbetta also features an
impressive Italian wine list and, in the warmer months, one of the city's most
romantic outdoor gardens. Though this is a Theater District restaurant, and
many come for the pre-theater prix fixe, Barbetta is best experienced at a relaxed,
leisurely pace.

321 W. 46th St. (btw. Eighth and Ninth aves.). ℂ **212/246-9171.** www.barbettarestaurant.com.
Reservations recommended. Prix-fixe dinner $58; main courses lunch $22–$29, dinner $28–$36.
AE, DC, MC, V. Mon–Sat noon–2:30pm and 5pm–midnight. Subway: C or E to 50th St.

Frankie & Johnnie's ★★ STEAK   When restaurants spin off other branches,
red flags go up. Does that mean the restaurant has become a chain and quality
has eroded? In the case of Frankie & Johnnie's, the legendary former speak-easy
turned steakhouse in the Theater District, the answer is "no!" There are now two
other outlets, one in Westchester and the other in a two-story town house once
owned by actor John Barrymore. Just try their signature sirloin. It also helps that
the dining room on the second floor of the town house is gorgeous, especially the
Barrymore room, the actor's former study with stained-glass ceiling panels, dark-
wood walls, and a working fireplace. Not only are Frankie & Johnnie's steaks
underrated in the competitive world of New York steakhouses, but the other

options are also superb. The crab cake appetizer had a high crab-to-cake ratio, while the sides of hash browns were the best I've had. Service is steakhouse old school, and if you are staying in Midtown, the restaurant provides complimentary stretch limo service to and from the restaurant.

32 W. 37th St. (btw. Fifth and Sixth aves.). © **212/947-8940.** www.frankieandjohnnies.com. Reservations recommended. Main courses $25–$36. Mon–Fri noon–2:30pm; Mon–Thurs 4–10:30pm; Fri–Sat 4–11pm. Subway: B, C, D, N, Q, R, or M to 34th St./Herald Sq. Also at 269 W. 45th St. (at Eighth Ave.). © **212/997-9494.** Subway: 1, 2, 3, 7, A, C, E, N, Q, R, or S to 42nd St.

Hakubai ★ 🍴 JAPANESE   In the basement of the Japanese-owned, **Kitano Hotel** (p. 416), lies what is now a rarity in Manhattan; a traditional, old-style Japanese restaurant complete with Tatami rooms, kimono-clad servers, and chef-prepared *Kaiseki* dinners (a multi-course tasting dinner where the chef creates a meal based on the daily ingredients). Forget that there are no windows in the small, much-too-bright restaurant and enjoy the parade of platters, impeccably designed, as they are brought to your table by one of the aforementioned kimono-clad servers; they are so pretty (the platters) that you might hesitate before eating thinking, "this couldn't be real." But real, and delicious, it is including the amazingly fresh sashimi, delicate noodles, marinated fish, and perfectly fried tempuras. It's a true Tokyo-like experience in the heart of Midtown.

66 Park Ave. (in the Kitano Hotel, at 38th St.). © **212/885-7111.** Reservations recommended. Main courses: $22–$70; *kaiseki* dinners $85–$130. AE, MC, V. Mon–Fri 11:30am–2pm and 6–10pm; Sat–Sun 6–10pm. Subway: 4, 5, 6, 7, S to 42nd St.–Grand Central.

Keens Steakhouse ★★★ STEAK   Until the latter part of the 20th century, Keens, which was established in the same location in 1885, referred to itself as a "chop house." They are now known as a steakhouse, but I wish they had remained true to their roots. To their credit, they are a steakhouse in name only. They serve the basics of a steakhouse—the porterhouse for two, aged T-bone, and filet mignon with requisite sides such as creamed spinach and hash browns—but they still serve chops: lamb chops, prime rib, short ribs, and most notably, mutton chops. It is the mutton chop that has made Keens famous. The monstrous cut has two flaps of long, thick, rich, subtly gamy meat on either side of the bone that look kind of like mutton-chop sideburns. So which came first, the sideburns or the chop? Keens is no gussied-up remake of old New York: It's the real thing, from the thousands of ceramic pipes on the ceiling (regular diners were given their own personal pipes, including such celebrities as Babe Ruth, George M. Cohan, and Albert Einstein) to the series of rooms on two floors with wood paneling, leather banquettes, fireplaces, a clubby bar with a three-page menu of single malts, and even the framed playbill Lincoln was reading at the Ford Theater that infamous evening in 1865. Keens has been there, done that, got the playbill.

72 W. 36th St. (at Sixth Ave.). © **212/947-3636.** www.keens.com. Reservations recommended. Main courses $26–$45. AE, DC, DISC, MC, V. Mon–Fri 11:45am–10:30pm; Sat 5–10:30pm; Sun 5–9pm. Subway: B, D, F, N, Q, R, or M to 34th St./Herald Sq.

The Lamb's Club ★ AMERICAN   In 2010 the Lamb's Club—a gathering spot for thespians, writers, and other literati in the 1920s and 1930s—was reincarnated in the same Stanford White-designed 1905-landmark building where it was originally located. And the creators of the restaurant have done their best to recreate that clubby feel with lush red leather banquettes, oak walls, a huge fireplace, and a wraparound mezzanine bar. The photos of the former members of the famous club hang on the wall in the dining room are further reminders of the ghosts of the past Now, thankfully, you don't have to be a member of the club, an actor, or even a "literati" to enjoy Chef Geoffrey Zakarian's food. Cocktails are prepared by the famous mixologist Sasha Petraske and what better to accompany one than with the Chef's beef tartare or raw marinated hamachi to start. The appetizers will ease you toward an entrée and the runaway best of those is the Chatham cod with slow roasted pork belly, leeks and clams. Whatever your entrée choice, add a either "Beans and Greens" or mashed potatoes—they are both that good. Service is informal, yet professional and by the time dessert is offered, you might actually feel as if you are actually a member of a club.

132 W. 44th St. (btw. Sixth Ave. and–Broadway). www.thelambsclub.com. ☏ **212/997-5262.** Reservations recommended. Main courses: $26–$46. AE, MC, V. Mon–Fri 11:45–2:30; Sat–Sun 11am–2:30pm; Mon–Thurs 5:30pm–11pm; Fri–Sat 5:30pm–12am; Sun 5:30pm–10pm. Subway: B, C, D, F, M to 42nd Street.

Molyvos ★★ GREEK   A trailblazer of upscale and innovative Greek dining, Molyvos's success is based on its ability to please those who want traditional Greek food as well as exciting, original Greek-accented creations. For those who like their Greek unadulterated, you won't go wrong with cold mezes, such as the *tzatziki, melitzanosalata,* and *taramosalata,* and hot mezes such as spinach pie or grilled octopus. For Greek food with an edge, there is ouzo-cured salmon on a chickpea fritter or the seafood Cretan bread salad. Just a sampling of the mezes alone should be enough for anyone, but with entrees as good as grilled *garides,* wild head-on prawns barbecued souvlaki-style, and the *chios* pork and *gigante* bean stew, not ordering one would be a mistake. The knowledgeable sommelier will pair your choices with a Greek wine, of which there are many. Or, skip the wine and sample one or two of the dozens of ouzos; but don't skip the desserts. Sure you've had baklava before, but have you ever had chocolate baklava? Yes, it's as good as it sounds.

871 Seventh Ave. (btw. 55th and 56th sts.). ☏ **212/582-7500.** www.molyvos.com. Reservations recommended. Main courses $17–$29 at lunch (most less than $20); $20–$36 at dinner (most less than $25); fixed-price lunch $24; pre-theater 3-course dinner $37 (5:30–6:45pm). AE, DC, DISC, MC, V. Mon–Thurs noon–11:30pm; Fri–Sat noon–midnight; Sun noon–11pm. Subway: N or R to 57th St.; B, D, or E to Seventh Ave.

Oceana ★★★ SEAFOOD   In 2009 Oceana moved from its longtime yacht-like home on the east side to a luxury liner of a space in the McGraw-Hill building across the street from Rockefeller Center. The move to pre-theater, expense-account territory could have been a culinary misstep, but I'm happy to report that the new Oceana is as good as or better than its previous incarnation. At Oceana, as its name implies, it all starts with extremely fresh seafood, and no better than to sample that than with the restaurant's very good raw bar comprised of a variety of oysters, clams, crab, and mussels. The marinated appetizers—ceviches, crudos, and smoked fish—are delicately flavorful and a few of them would make a fine meal in itself. But if you have the stamina (and the deep pockets) to continue, the whole branzino, roasted and stuffed with mushrooms, spinach, and olives will reward you for your grit. With fish this fresh, you can't go wrong with any of the "simply prepared" items offered on the menu, in particular the wild striped bass. Service for such a large restaurant is exceptional and the sommelier and his crew are especially attentive to proper pairings with your selections.

WHERE TO DINE

Times Square & Midtown West

URBAN BBQ: THE best 'CUE IN NEW YORK CITY

New York is known for many cuisines, but barbecue is not traditionally one of them. But the hankering for slow-cooked, charred meat has made its way to the big city. And, really, what is more primal and satisfying than the sensation of tearing slow-smoked meat from bone, eating the meat with your fingers and then, of course, licking that sweet and savory sauce off your own natural utensils?

The appropriately named **RUB** ★★ (p. 162), is helmed by Kansas City pit master Paul Kirk. The smoked turkey and chicken were as close to perfection as I've found. Close to the West Side Highway, **Dinosaur Bar-B-Que** (p. 200), a Syracuse transplant barbecue joint, is like a roadhouse in atmosphere, and the pulled pork is as good as it gets north of 125th Street. In the heart of tourist trap mecca Times Square lies a kitschy, themed barbecue joint, **Virgil's Real BBQ** ★★ (p. 176), which, especially for a theme restaurant, serves remarkably good 'cue.

French-trained, and a former chef at Daniel, Adam Perry Lang gave up the haute French cuisine to open his own joint: **Daisy May's BBQ**, 623 11th Ave., at 46th Street (☎ **212/977-1500;** www.daisymaysbbq.com), with stellar results. Daisy May carts can be found in locations around the city, but if you can't find a cart, squeeze into his cafeteria-style restaurant for Memphis-style dry-rub ribs.

For Texas-style barbecue, visit **Hill Country** ★, 30 W. 26th St., between Broadway and Sixth Avenue (☎ **212/255-4544;** www.hillcountryny.com), for the amazing beef short ribs, and **Johnny Utah's** ★, 25 W. 51st St., between Fifth and Sixth avenues (☎ **212/265-UTAH** [265-8824]; www.johnnyutahs.com), where you can have your steak and watch inebriated Texan-wannabes get tossed from a mechanical bull.

Restaurateur Danny Meyer, a St. Louis native, wanted to replicate the barbecue he remembered growing up, so he opened **Blue Smoke,** 116 E. 27th St., between Lexington and Park avenues (☎ **212/447-7733;** www.jazzstandard.net), as part of the jazz club, the **Jazz Standard** (p. 417). Blue Smoke offers the usual array of barbecue, made in Meyer's custom-built smoker, but with a few quirks such as a fried bologna sandwich.

Brooklyn is honing its 'cue skills with the recent addition of two joints, including the appropriately named **The Smoke Joint,** 87 S. Elliot Place (☎ **718/797-1011;** www.thesmokejoint.com), in Fort Greene, where the "Baby Got Back" baby backs fall off the bone. **Fette Sau** ★★, in Williamsburg (p. 206), means "fat pig" in German, but though there is plenty of good fat in the pig served at Fette Sau, there is nothing German about that down-home smoky taste. Also in Williamsburg, the non-traditional, but great 'cue just the same can be found at the Asian accented **Fatty 'Cue** ★★ (p. 205).

Rack & Soul, 2818 Broadway, at 109th Street (☎ **212/222-4800;** www.rackandsoul.com), not only offers pan-fried chicken by chicken master Charles Gabriel (see **Charles' Pan Fried Chicken** on p. 202), but also barbecued baby back ribs that are so good you might have to pass on his chicken; or go for a combo platter where you can get a taste of both.

1221 Sixth Ave. (btw. 48th and 49th sts.). ☎ **212/759-5941.** www.livanosrestaurantgroup.com. Reservations recommended. Main courses $28–$34. AE, DC, DISC, MC, V. Mon–Sun 11:30am–3pm; Mon–Sat 5–11pm; Sun 4–10pm. Subway: B, D, F, M to 47th–50th sts./Rockefeller Center.

Moderate

The family-style Italian restaurant **Carmine's** has a Times Square branch at 200 W. 44th St., between Broadway and Eighth Avenue (☎ **212/221-3800;** www. carminesnyc.com).

Becco ★ 👜 ITALIAN   If you're a fan of Lidia Bastianich's PBS cooking shows, you can sample her simple, hearty Italian cooking here. Becco, on Restaurant Row, is designed to serve her meals "at a different price point" (read: cheaper) than her East Side restaurant, Felidia. The prices are not rock bottom, but in terms of service, portions, and quality, you get great bang for your buck. The main courses can head north of the $20 mark, but take a look at the prix-fixe **Sinfonia de Pasta** menu ($18 at lunch, $23 at dinner), which includes a Caesar salad or an antipasto plate, followed by unlimited servings of the three fresh-made daily pastas. There's also an excellent selection of Italian wines at $25 a bottle. If you can't make up your mind about dessert, have them all: A tasting plate includes gelato, cheesecake, and whatever else the dessert chef has whipped up that day.

355 W. 46th St. (btw. Eighth and Ninth aves.). ☎ **212/397-7597.** www.becco-nyc.com. Reservations recommended. Main courses lunch $13–$25, dinner $19–$35. AE, DC, DISC, MC, V. Mon noon–3pm and 5–10pm; Tues noon–3pm and 5pm–midnight; Wed 11:30am–2:30pm and 4pm–midnight; Thurs–Fri noon–3pm and 5pm–midnight; Sat 11:30am–2:30pm and 4pm–midnight; Sun noon–10pm. Subway: C or E to 50th St.

Marseille ★ FRENCH   Lively and casual with open, high ceilings and a tiled floor that creates a Casablanca-like ambience, this restaurant, named after the port city in France, features the food of that city, including its North African influences. That means you'll find such entrees as Moroccan chicken, couscous, and tagine on the menu, along with Provençal specialties such as bouillabaisse, which comes in three varieties (chicken, vegetarian, and traditional, made with fish—stick with the traditional), short-rib daube, salad Niçoise, and soup *au pistou.* You can make a meal of the mezes (small plates), which feature a tangy grilled *merguez* sausage, anchovies, and roasted peppers; *brandade* (whipped salt cod); tapenade; and broiled sardines wrapped in *lardo* (thick bacon). In the Film Center building on Ninth Avenue, this is a good pre-theater choice, but even better when the pre-theater rush is over.

630 Ninth Ave. (at 44th St.). ☎ **212/333-2323.** www.marseillenyc.com. Mezes $4–$13; main courses $16–$28. AE, DC, MC, V. Mon–Fri 11:30–3pm; Sat–Sun 11am–3pm; Sun–Mon 5:15–11pm; Tues–Sat 5:15pm–midnight. Subway: A, C, E, or 7 to 42nd St./Times Sq.

Norma's ★★ AMERICAN   Nowhere is breakfast treated with such reverence, and decadence, as at Norma's, a soaring, ultramodern ode to the ultimate comfort food. There's something for everyone on the huge menu. Classics come in styles both simple and haute: Blueberry pancakes come piled high with fresh Maine berries and Devonshire cream, while buttermilks are topped with fresh Georgia peaches and chopped walnuts. Even oatmeal is special: Irish McCann's, dressed with sautéed green apples and red pears and brûléed for a flash of sugary sweetness. Don't pass on the applewood-smoked bacon, so good it's worth blowing any diet. Norma's can even win over breakfast foes with creative sandwiches, a generous Cobb salad with seared ahi, and a terrific chicken potpie. Not cheap for breakfast, but definitely worth the splurge.

At Le Parker Meridien hotel, 118 W. 57th St. (btw. Sixth and Seventh aves.). ☎ **212/708-7460.** www.normasnyc.com. Reservations accepted. Main courses $8–$23 (most $13–$18). AE, DC, DISC, MC, V. Mon–Fri 6:30am–3pm; Sat–Sun 7am–3pm. Subway: B, N, Q, or R to 57th St.

Virgil's Real BBQ ★★ ☺ BARBECUE/SOUTHERN In the heart of Times Square is a theme restaurant that actually has good food. The theme is Southern barbecue, and the restaurant is made to look and feel like a Southern roadhouse with good-ol'-boy decorations on the walls and blues on the sound system. Virgil's does an admirable job in recreating that authentic flavor. The spice-rubbed ribs are slow cooked and meaty, but it's the Owensboro lamb (smoked slices of lamb) and the Texas beef brisket that are the standouts. Both are melt-in-your-mouth tender; the lamb is sprinkled with a flavorful mustard sauce, while the brisket is perfect with a few dabs of Virgil's homemade spicy barbecue sauce. For starters, the corn dogs with poblano mustard are something New Yorkers rarely have the pleasure of experiencing, while the barbecue nachos—tortilla chips slathered with melted cheese and barbecued pulled pork—are a meal in themselves. Desserts are what you would expect from a restaurant emulating a Southern theme: big and sweet. Try the homemade ice-cream sandwich, made with the cookie of the day. Virgil's is a great place to bring the kids; if they're noisy, no one will notice.

152 W. 44th St. (btw. Sixth and Seventh aves.). ✆ **212/921-9494.** www.virgilsbbq.com. Reservations recommended. Sandwiches $10–$13; main courses and barbecue platters $15–$24 (most less than $19). AE, DC, DISC, MC, V. Sun–Mon 11am–11pm; Tues–Fri 11:30am–midnight; Sat 11am–midnight. Subway: 1, 2, 3, 7, N, or R to 42nd St./Times Sq.

Inexpensive

If you're looking for the quintessential New York deli, you have a choice between the **Stage Deli,** 834 Seventh Ave., between 53rd and 54th streets (✆ **212/245-7850**), known for its massive celebrity-named sandwiches, and the **Carnegie Deli,** 854 Seventh Ave., at 55th Street (✆ **800/334-5606**), the place to go for the best pastrami, corned beef, and cheesecake in town. For more, see the sidebar "The New York Deli News," on p. 180.

There is a nice outlet of **John's Pizzeria** in Times Square, 260 W. 44th St., between Broadway and Eighth Avenue (✆ **212/391-7560;** Subway: 1, 2, 3, 7, A, B, C, E, N, Q, R, or S to 42nd St./Times Sq.; see the box "The Pizza Capital of the United States," p. 178). Also consider the aptly named **Burger Joint** ★★, in the lobby of Le Parker Meridien Hotel, 118 W. 57th St. (✆ **212/708-7414**), for cheap yet excellent no-frills burgers (see the box "Where to Find Your [Burger] Bliss in NYC," p. 182).

For the New York version of the Philadelphia cheesesteak, try **Shorty's** ★, at 576 Ninth Ave., between 41st and 42nd streets (✆ **212/967-3055**).

Afghan Kebab House ⚔ MIDDLE EASTERN You'll find Afghan Kebab Houses all over the city. Are they related? Who knows, but I like this one best for its heaping plates of first-rate Middle Eastern fare. Kebabs are the first order of business: All are pleasing, but my favorite is the *sultani,* chunks of ground lamb marinated in aromatic spices and broiled over wood coals with green peppers and tomatoes. The *tikka kebab,* in lamb or beef, is impressive, as is the chicken korma, slow-cooked with onions, tomatoes, peppers, and fresh herbs. All plates come with amazingly aromatic brown Indian basmati rice and flat Afghan bread. The room is simple and well worn but evocative, with Oriental carpets serving as table runners. Service is attentive.

764 Ninth Ave. (btw. 51st and 52nd sts.). ✆ **212/307-1612** or 212/307-1629. Reservations accepted. Main courses $10–$16 (most under $12). AE, DC, DISC, MC, V. Daily 11am–11pm. Subway: C or E to 50th St.

Han Bat ★ 🍴 KOREAN   A few blocks from 33rd Street's Koreatown, a block from the Empire State Building, and open 24/7, Han Bat serves authentic Korean food as good as you'll find anywhere. If you are familiar with Korean food, Han Bat offers the standards, but Korean standards can be exotic. On the menu are items like "ox-knee" meat; "jello extracted from ox-leg"; broiled meat, tongue, and spleen; beef intestines; and something called *yook hoe*, shredded raw beef marinated in seasoned sesame oil. For the standards, the *bibimbab*, a do-it-yourself concoction of rice, marinated meat, egg, and vegetables in a sizzling hot stone bowl, is a meal unto itself. The clientele is mostly Korean, which is always a good sign of authenticity, and Han Bat can get very busy—don't take the brusque, almost pushy service personally.

53 W. 35th St. (btw. 5th–6th aves.). ☎ **212/629-5588.** Main courses $9–$22. AE, MC, V. Daily 24 hr. Subway: B, D, F, N, Q, R, M to 34th St.

Mandoo Bar ★ 🎁 KOREAN   The heart of Manhattan's Koreatown is 32nd Street between Fifth and Sixth avenues—and the number of Korean restaurants on that 1 block is dizzying. You'll know you've found Mandoo Bar when you see the two women in the window rolling and stuffing fresh *mandoo* (dumplings). The dumplings, stuffed with a variety of ingredients, are always incredibly fresh. There's the *mool mandoo* (basic white dumplings filled with pork and vegetables), the *kimchee mandoo* (steamed dumplings stuffed with potent kimchi [Korean spiced cabbage], tofu, pork, and vegetables), the green vegetable *mool mandoo* (boiled dumplings filled with mixed vegetables), and the *goon mandoo* (pan-fried dumplings filled with pork and vegetables). You really can't go wrong with any of these, so sample them all with a Combo Mandoo. With seating that is nothing more than wooden benches, Mandoo Bar is better suited for quick eats rather than a lingering meal—a perfect lunch break from shopping in Herald Square or visiting the nearby Empire State Building.

2 W. 32nd St. (just west of Fifth Ave.). ☎ **212/279-3075.** Reservations not accepted. Main courses $7–$17. AE, MC, V. Daily 11:30am–10pm. Subway: B, D, F, N, Q, R, M to 34th St./Herald Sq.

Nizza ★★ 🍴 FRENCH/ITALIAN   You won't do much better for pre- or post-theater dining than Nizza. Nizza offers the cuisine of the French Mediterranean, the city of Nice specifically, and its Ligurian-Italian influence. It's a restaurant where you can fill up on appetizers and salads, starting with the tangy tapenade of black olives served with freshly baked focaccia chips and *socca*, a chickpea pancake cooked in a brick oven and sprinkled with fresh herbs. Or savor a glass of wine with a plate of *salumi,* a selection of cured meats such as *coppa, mortadella,* prosciutto, and a variety of salamis, including duck. The romaine salad I had in a garlic vinaigrette with anchovies and shaved pecorino cheese made me swear off Caesar salad forever—well, almost. From that same brick oven come pizzas, including a Provençal pie with ratatouille, goat cheese, and pesto; entrees such as the delicate *polpette* (meatballs), served on a bed of polenta and garnished with a hot green pepper; and wild-boar lasagna that is much less ferocious than it sounds. The restaurant is loud and seating is tight, but you'll love the memorable food and the easy-on-your-wallet prices.

630 Ninth Ave. (at 45th St.). ☎ **212/956-1800.** www.nizzanyc.com. Main courses $12–$20. AE, MC, V. Tues–Sat 11:30am–2am; Sun–Mon 11:30am–midnight. Subway: A, C, E, or 7 to 42nd St.

THE pizza CAPITAL OF THE UNITED STATES

You just won't find a city with better pizza than New York. And in recent years, with the emergence of many new, authentic Neopolitan places, it's gotten even better. Here I've separated the old-school New York pizzerias from the new kids on the block. You won't go wrong with any of the choices below.

OLD SCHOOL

DiFara Pizza ★   1424 Ave. J, Brooklyn, at E. 15th Street (© **718/258-1367;** Subway: Q to Ave. J/16th St.). Some claim it's the best pizza in the city. And DiFara's lives up to its reputation, thanks to the zeal of owner Dominic DeMarco, who, for over 40 years, has made every pizza himself. DeMarco uses top ingredients to craft each pizza, finishing with hand-grated Parmesan cheese, a few dollops of extra-virgin olive oil, and then hand-cutting fresh basil onto the pie. The result is a work of art, but one that might test your patience. And for that art, a slice is a city-high $5. Expect to wait an hour for a pie, maybe a bit less for a slice. But it's worth it!

Grimaldi's Pizzeria   19 Old Fulton St., between Front and Water streets (© **718/858-4300;** www.grimaldis.com; Subway: 2 or 3 to Clark St., A or C to Clark St., F to York St.). If you need incentive to walk across the Brooklyn Bridge, Grimaldi's, in Brooklyn Heights, easily provides it. In fact, the pizza is so good, made in a coal oven with a rich flavorful sauce and homemade mozzarella, you might run across the bridge to get to it. **Be warned:** It can get very crowded at dinnertime.

John's Pizzeria   278 Bleecker St., near Seventh Avenue South (© **212/243-1680**). Since it has expanded from this original location, the once-gleaming luster of John's has faded slightly, but the pizza is still a cut above the rest. Thin crusted and out of a coal oven with the proper ratio of tomato sauce to cheese, John's pizza has a loyal following. The original Bleecker Street location is my favorite. Also at 260 W. 44th St., between Broadway and Eighth Avenue (© **212/391-7560**), and 408 E. 64th St.,

between York and First avenues (© **212/ 935-2895**).

Lombardi's   32 Spring St., between Mulberry and Mott streets (© **212/941-7994;** www.firstpizza.com; Subway: 6 to Spring St.). Claiming to be New York's first "licensed" pizzeria, Lombardi's opened in 1905 and still uses a generations-old Neapolitan family pizza recipe. The coal oven kicks out perfectly cooked pies, some topped with ingredients such as pancetta, homemade sausage, and even fresh-shucked clams. A garden makes it even more inviting during warm weather.

Patsy's Pizzeria ★   2287 First Ave., between 117th and 118th streets (© **212/ 534-9783;** www.patsyspizzeriany.com; Subway: 6 to 116th St.). My favorite, and the favorite of Frank Sinatra, who had its pies flown out to Las Vegas. The coal oven here has been burning since 1932. Try the marinara pizza, a pie with fresh marinara sauce but no cheese, that's so good you won't miss the mozzarella. Unlike the other pizzerias mentioned here, you can order by the slice at Patsy's. Don't be fooled by imitators using Patsy's name; this is the original and the best.

Totonno's Pizzeria Napolitano
1524 Neptune Ave., between West 15th and West 16th streets, Coney Island, Brooklyn (© **718/372-8606;** Subway: D to Stillwell Ave./Coney Island). This unassuming little pizzeria (pictured at right) has been at the same spot since 1924, and it makes pizzas almost exactly as it did 80 years ago—thin crust, fresh sauce, and mozzarella, and that's about it.

NEW SCHOOL

Keste Pizzeria & Vino ★★   271 Bleecker St., near Seventh Avenue South

(☎ **212/243-1500;** www.kestepizzeria. com). Keste, new in 2009, set up its brick oven across the street from John's (see above) with glowing results. A member of the *Associazione Pizzaiuoli Napoletani* (the Association of Neapolitan Pizza), Keste maintains strict ingredient and cooking guidelines. How does the pizza taste? At Keste it's so fresh, so authentically Neopolitan, that, I'm sad to say, you may not again venture across the street, even for old time's sake.

La Pizza Fresca Ristorante ★

31 E. 20th St., between Park Ave. and Broadway (☎ **212/598-0141;** www.la pizzafresca.com). Those who have sampled the genuine Neapolitan pizza swear by its quality. To achieve certification they must use a wood-burning oven, San Marzano tomatoes, bufala mozzarella, hand-pressed dough, and all the ingredients must be cooked with the pizza in the oven. You can have your pizza many different ways, including *Quattro Formaggi,* a combination of four cheeses and a hint of pancetta (Italian bacon); but for the unadulterated Neapolitan flavor, try the tomato, bufala mozzarella, and basil pie.

Motorino ★ 319 Graham Ave., at

DeVoe Street, Williamsburg, Brooklyn (☎ **718/599-8899;** www.motorinopizza. com). Can one borough have too many good pizzerias? In the case of Brooklyn—with gems like Totonnos, DiFara, and Grimaldi's, to name just a few—apparently not. I'm a purist, but I was convinced to try Motorino's special creation the day I visited, a fingerling potato pie, and very glad I did. Still, how can you really resist the Margherita D.O.C. pie, with mozzarella *di bufala?* In Motorino's case, the pie more than adequately passed my stringent taste test. In 2009, Motorino's success led to expansion to Manhattan at 349 E. 12th St. (☎ **212/777-2644**).

Naples 45 200 Park Ave., at 45th Street (☎ **212/972-7001;** www.patina group.com). Made in a wood-burning brick oven, the pizzas are created with flour from Southern Italy, spring water, *Fior de Latte* mozzarella, and San Marzano tomatoes. The Margherita D.O.C pizza with the San Marzano tomatoes and mozzarella is close to perfection.

Trattoria Zero Otto Nove ★★

2357 Arthur Ave., at 186th Street, the Bronx (☎ **718/220-1027;** www. roberto089.com). Taking its name from the Salerno, Italy, area code, you'll think you're in Salerno when you bite into one of Roberto Paciullo's Neapolitan pizzas. The mozzarella is made at nearby Casa de Mozzarella, the tomatoes are San Marzano, the pies cooked in a wood-burning brick oven, the basil from the Arthur Avenue Market across the street—the result pure pizza perfection. One of the best at Zero Otto Nove is the butternut squash purée with smoked mozzarella, pancetta, and basil. And the good news is that the pizzeria has opened a branch at 16 W. 21st St. in Manhattan.

THE NEW YORK DELI NEWS

There's nothing more Noo Yawk than hunkering down over a mammoth pastrami on rye at an authentic Jewish deli, where anything you order comes with a bowl of lip-smacking sour dills and a side of attitude. Here are some of the best:

Artie's New York Delicatessen 2290 Broadway, between 82nd and 83rd streets (✆ **212/579-5959;** www.arties. com). Compared to the legends below, Arties, which has been around since 1999, is the new kid on the deli block but can hold its own on the playground with the big boys, thank you very much (especially in the wiener department).

Barney Greengrass, the Sturgeon King 541 Amsterdam Ave., between 86th and 87th streets on the Upper West Side (✆ **212/724-4707**). This unassuming, daytime-only deli has become legendary for its high-quality salmon (sable, gravlax, Nova Scotia, kippered, lox, pastrami—you choose), whitefish, and sturgeon (of course).

Carnegie Deli 854 Seventh Ave., at 55th Street (✆ **800/334-5606** or 212/757-2245; www.carnegiedeli.com). It's worth subjecting yourself to surly service, tourist-targeted overpricing, and elbow-to-elbow seating for some of the best pastrami and corned beef in town. Even big eaters may be challenged by mammoth sandwiches with such names as "Fifty Ways to Love Your Liver" (chopped liver, hard-boiled egg, lettuce, tomato, and onion).

Katz's Delicatessen ★ Katz's (pictured at right) remains fabulously old world despite its hipster-hot Lower East Side location at 205 E. Houston St., at Ludlow Street (✆ **212/254-2246**). For more on Katz's, see p. 149.

Lansky's 235 Columbus Ave., between 70th and 71st streets (✆ **212/787-0400**), is the newest addition to the world of deli on the Upper West Side and New York. And a welcome one, especially for its foot-long, deep-fried, garlicky hot dogs, and friendly service.

2nd Avenue Deli ★ 162 E. 33rd St., between Lexington and Third avenues (✆ **212/689-9000;** www.2ndavedeli. com). After the original closed suddenly and to great angst, the 2nd Avenue Deli has returned, but now it's just off Third Avenue, about 20 blocks north of its former location. The East Village feel is gone, but not the quality Kosher deli specialties. The standards: Corned beef, pastrami, and brisket are as good as you'll get, while such guilty pleasures as *gribenes* (fried chicken skin) and chicken liver, despite their artery-clogging qualities, are almost impossible to resist. Unlike other delis, you might even get a smile from your waiter!

Stage Deli 834 Seventh Ave., between 53rd and 54th streets (✆ **212/245-7850;** www.stagedeli.com). Noisy and crowded and packed with tourists, it's still as authentic as they come. The celebrity sandwiches, ostensibly created by the personalities themselves, are massive mountains of top-quality fixings: The Tom Hanks is roast beef, chopped liver, onion, and chicken fat, while the Dolly Parton is (drum roll, please) twin rolls of corned beef and pastrami.

Sapporo ★ 🍴 JAPANESE   Peruse the community bulletin board as you enter Sapporo and you might find yourself a deal on an apartment—that is, if you can read Japanese. Thankfully, the menu is in English in this longtime Theater District Japanese noodle shop. If the mostly Japanese clientele doesn't convince you of Sapporo's authenticity, the din of satisfied diners slurping huge bowls of steaming ramen (noodle soup with meat and vegetables) will. And though the ramen is Sapporo's specialty, the *gyoza* (Japanese dumplings) and the *donburi* (pork or chicken over rice with soy-flavored sauce) are also terrific. Best of all, nothing on the menu is over $10, and that's not easy to find in the oft-overpriced Theater District.

152 W. 49th St. (btw. Sixth and Seventh aves.). ☎ **212/869-8972.** Reservations not accepted. Main courses $6–$9. No credit cards. Mon–Sat 11am–11pm; Sun 11am–10pm. Subway: N or R to 49th St.

Uncle Nick's GREEK   For stupendous portions of good traditional Greek food at good prices, come to Uncle Nick's. It's a bit LOUD for conversation, but how can you talk if your mouth is filled with one or more of Nick's Greek dips such as *taramosalata* or *tzatziki,* or his tender grilled baby octopus? If you haven't filled up on appetizers, order one of Nick's grilled specialties: The lamb kabob is a winner and guaranteed for leftovers, while the gyro plate is a challenge for those with even the heartiest appetites. Seafood is also good, especially the swordfish kabobs. Desserts are standard; you won't have room for them anyway. Service is friendly and matches the rollicking atmosphere here. Next door is the slightly more intimate **Uncle Nick's Ouzeria,** specializing in mezes, Greek small dishes like tapas.

747 Ninth Ave. (btw. 50th and 51st sts.). ☎ **212/245-7992.** www.unclenicksgreekrestaurant.com. Appetizers $8–$15; main courses $15–$25. Sun–Thurs noon–11pm; Fri–Sat noon–11:30pm. Nick's Ouzeria: 749 Ninth Ave. ☎ **212/397-2892.** Subway: C or E to 50th St.

Wondee Siam ★ 🍴 THAI   Hell's Kitchen offers countless ethnic culinary variations, and one of the most prevalent is Thai—there are at least six Thai restaurants in a 5-block radius. My favorite among these is the tiny, zero-ambience Wondee Siam. I don't need colorful decorations or a fish tank to enjoy authentic, uncompromisingly spicy Thai food, and that's what I get at Wondee Siam. Here you don't have to worry that your waiter will assume you want a milder form of Thai. If there is a little red asterisk next to your item, you can be sure it is appropriately spicy. The soups are terrific, especially the sinus-clearing *tom yum.* In fact, there is an entire section of *yum* (chilies) dishes on the menu, my favorite being the *larb gai,* minced ground chicken with ground toasted rice. The curries are first rate, as are the noodles, including the mild pad Thai. This is BYOB and you'll want to do so to complement the spicy food. If you want a bit more comfort, try Wondee Siam II 1 block up. But make sure you ask your waiter not to dumb down the spice, but rather to serve up the food authentic Thai style.

792 Ninth Ave. (btw. 52nd and 53rd sts.). ☎ **212/459-9057.** Reservations not accepted. Main courses $8.50–$18 (most under $10). No credit cards. Mon–Sat 11am–11pm; Sun 11am–10:30pm. Wondee Siam II: 813 Ninth Ave. (btw. 53rd and 54th sts.). ☎ **917/286-1726.** Subway: C or E to 50th St.

MIDTOWN EAST & MURRAY HILL

To locate the restaurants in this section, see the map on p. 160.

Expensive

Aquavit ★★★ SCANDINAVIAN   The restaurant, in the bottom of a glass tower on East 55th Street, is designed in sleek Scandinavian style with modernist furniture. In the front of the restaurant is an informal and less expensive cafe,

WHERE TO FIND YOUR (burger) BLISS IN NYC

New York is hamburger happy. And that happiness has nothing to do with Mickey D's or BK. It's about real, solid, locally made burgers, and there are plenty of places to find them without resorting to supersizing yourself. Here are some:

Bill's Bar and Burger 16 W. 51st Street (☎ **212/705-8510;** www.billsbar andburger.com) is restaurateur Stephen Hanson's entrée into the competitive world of New York City burgers with very successful results. His "classic" burger is, simply put, classical with very little frills. The Rockefeller Center outlet makes a great, budget-saving lunch spot in the heart of expense-account New York. There is also another location in the Meat-packing District at 22 Ninth Avenue (☎ **212/414-3003**).

Brgr ★ 287 Seventh Ave., at 26th Street (☎ **212/488-7500;** www.brgr.us). The hook here is top-quality meats and homemade toppings. The beef is natural Angus from Montana Legend beef, but just as good are the turkey burgers made from Plainville Farms all-natural turkeys. Some of the toppings include Roquefort cheese, sweet-onion marmalade, and homemade burger sauce.

Burger Joint ★★ Located discreetly behind a curtain in the lobby of Le Parker Meridien Hotel, 118 W. 57th St.

(☎ **212/708-7414**), is like the burger joint you might remember in college—only the burgers are better. And for a place off the lobby of a fancy hotel, it's downright cheap.

5 Napkin Burger ★ 630 Ninth Ave., at 45th Street (☎ **212/757-2277;** www.fivenapkinburger.com), and 2315 Broadway, at 84th Street (☎ **212/333-4488**). The burger, topped with Comté cheese, caramelized onions, and rosemary aioli that was made famous at Nice Matin (p. 193), has been awarded its own restaurant. Now, however, it's not the only burger sold at 5 Napkin; you can try the veggie, turkey, or lamb *kofta*.

New York Burger Co. 303 Park Ave. South, between 23rd and 24th streets (☎ **212/254-2727**), and 678 Sixth Ave., between 21st and 22nd streets (☎ **212/229-1404**). Here you won't feel guilty as you devour the burgers (pictured at right) at this "healthy" fast-food alternative. The beef is all-natural Coleman beef, devoid of hormones or antibiotics and served on a fresh-baked brioche. What do they taste like? The burgers have plenty of

while past a long bar is the dining room. The smoked fish—all the fish—is prepared perfectly. I daydream about the herring plate: four types of herring accompanied by a tiny glass of *aquavit*, distilled liquor not unlike vodka flavored with fruit and spices, and a frosty Carlsberg beer. The hot smoked Arctic char on the main a la carte menu, served with clams and bean purée in a mustard green broth, is also a winner. Most fixed-price menus offer a well-chosen beverage accompaniment option.

65 E. 55th St. (btw. Park and Madison aves.). ☎ **212/307-7311.** www.aquavit.org. Reservations recommended. Cafe main courses $9–$32; 3-course fixed-price meal $24 at lunch, $35 at dinner; main dining room fixed-price meal $45 at lunch, $85 at dinner ($39 for vegetarians); 3-course pre-theater dinner (5:30–6:15pm) $55; tasting menus $58 at lunch, $105 at dinner ($90 for vegetarians); supplement for paired wines $30 at lunch, $80 at dinner. AE, DC, MC, V. Mon–Fri noon–2:30pm; Sun–Thurs 5:30–10:30pm; Fri–Sat 5:15–10:45pm. Subway: E or F to Fifth Ave.

Midtown institution for over 50 years, and its hamburger, like the restaurant's old wood walls, broken telephone booth, and hidden dining nook for two, has been blessedly preserved. Nothing more than a slab of chopped meat cooked to order, on a bun; and for the curious price of $8.90, the hamburger is a simple masterpiece. There is a Clarke's in the Financial District downtown at 4 World Financial Center (𝄞 **212/285-1500**) and a new location off Lincoln Center, 44 W. 63rd St. (𝄞 **212/957-9700**).

Rare Bar & Grill ★   303 Lexington Ave., between 37th and 38th streets (𝄞 **212/481-1999;** www.rarebarandgrill.com). You might pay a little more for your burger at Rare Bar & Grill—they range from $9 to $21—but you are paying for 8 ounces of Grade A American chuck beef that is ground daily at the restaurant. Rare has a number of interesting varieties; my favorites are the T-Bone, a blend of strip and sirloin that will almost have your forgetting about the steak the meat came off of, and the restaurant's classic M&M Burger, with caramelized shallots, cheddar cheese, and apple-smoked bacon.

flavor and come in a number of varieties, from a classic New York burger to the Chicago burger (bacon, Cheddar and Thousand Island sauce); Dallas burger (Monterey Jack cheese, onions, BBQ sauce); and so on.

P.J. Clarke's ★   915 Third Ave., at 55th Street (𝄞 **212/317-1616;** www.pjclarkes.com). P.J. Clarke's has been a

BLT Steak ★★★ STEAK   Steakhouses are often stereotyped as bastions of male bonding—testosterone fueled with red meat and hearty drinks. But BLT (Bistro Laurent Tourendel) Steak breaks that mold; on the night I visited, I noticed more women—slinky and model-like—chomping on thick cuts of beef than men. That doesn't mean men can't also enjoy the beef here; it's served in cast-iron pots and finished in steak butter with a choice of sauces—Béarnaise, red wine, horseradish, and bleu cheese, to name a few. The signature is the porterhouse for two (a whopping $84), but I recommend the New York strip or the short ribs braised in red wine. Both can be shared, which may be a good idea, especially after devouring the complimentary popovers and sampling an appetizer such as the tuna tartare or a side of onion rings, potato gratin, or creamy spinach. Even after sharing one of the meats, you might not have room for the chestnut-chocolate sundae or peanut-butter chocolate mousse, and that would be a shame. It's not a restaurant for quiet conversation, but then, it's a steakhouse.

106 E. 57th St. (btw. Park and Lexington aves.). ℂ **212/752-7470.** www.bltsteak.com. Reservations highly recommended. Main courses $29–$45. AE, DC, MC, V. Mon–Fri 11:45am–2:30pm; Mon–Thurs 5:30–11pm; Fri–Sat 5:30–11:30pm. Subway: 4, 5, 6, N, or R to 59th St.

Mia Dona ★★ ITALIAN/GREEK   The cuisine of Mia Dona is a celebration of mostly rustic Italian dishes, with a few nods to Greece. The marriage is a natural one, and best of all, easy on the wallet. The appetizer of grilled calamari and caponata salad (a combination of sweet [from currants] and sour from the pickled eggplant) works terrifically, the calamari grilled to perfection; the crispy rabbit with salt and fingerling chips is a starter you likely won't find anywhere else. Another original is the fresh fettuccia with roasted tomato sauce; it's the standout in a selection of very good pastas. Of the entrees, the olive oil–poached cod with broccoli rabe in a sun-dried tomato pesto tasted as good as its description, while the hearty braised veal breast with escarole and cannellini beans is Italian comfort food at its best. The rather high noise level is the only negative.

206 E. 58th St. (btw. Second and Third aves.). ℂ **212/750-8170.** www.miadona.com. Reservations recommended. Pastas $15–$16; entrees $17–$24. AE, DC, DISC, MC, V. Mon–Fri noon–2:30pm; Sat–Sun 11am–2pm; Mon–Thurs 5–10:30pm; Fri–Sun 5–11pm. Subway: 4, 5, 6, N, or R to 59th St./Lexington Ave.

Pampano ★★ MEXICAN/SEAFOOD   I'm usually wary of overly presented and overpriced Mexican food, much preferring the stuff I can buy from the taco trucks in east Harlem. Pampano, however, does things with Mexican ingredients, especially seafood, that no taco truck has ever done—and the lovely, lush town house location is much more comfortable. The fish is the highlight of the menu. Start with the tasting of either three or four ceviches; they are all spectacular, especially the halibut bathed in lemon juice, cilantro, chilies, and mango. For a rare and special treat, try a lobster taco—you won't find that at your local *taqueria.* Of the entrees, it would be difficult to order anything but the fantastic *camarones pompano,* shrimp in a pepper-tomato sauce resting on an Anaheim chili stuffed with goat cheese, but you won't suffer too much if you settle for the tuna with cilantro-ginger pico de gallo, in a *chile de arbol* sauce. Save room for chocolate flan and maybe a cleansing shot of one of the restaurant's many excellent tequilas. Pampano is a scene, but a festive one with a lively bar and a beautiful upstairs dining area.

209 E. 49th St. (at Third Ave.). ℂ **212/751-4545.** www.modernmexican.com. Reservations recommended. Main courses $23–$30. AE, DC, MC, V. Mon–Fri 11:30am–2:30pm; Mon–Wed 5–10pm; Thurs–Sat 5–11pm; Sun 5–9:30pm. Subway: E or M to Lexington Ave./53rd St.; 6 to 51st St.

Rouge Tomate ★ AMERICAN   For a restaurant that prides itself on not grilling or frying its food and that uses no cream and—gasp—no butter, I immediately lower the expectations. The restaurant, an import from Brussels, is stunning to look at with lots of glass and mirrors, tables that give diners room to move their elbows and actually talk with their companions, is S.P.E.–approved (*Sanitas Per Escam:* Health Through Nutrition; a nutritional charter developed by chefs and dieticians) and has a nutritionist to make sure the menu items are properly nutritionally balanced. The "no butter" thing made me skeptical. But when my first course arrived, a delicious celery and almond panna cotta topped with grapefruit and sprinkled with crab, my skepticism vanished. With my second course,

😊 FAMILY-FRIENDLY RESTAURANTS

While it's always smart to call ahead to make sure a restaurant has kids' menus and highchairs, you can count on the following to be especially accommodating. And what kid doesn't love pizza? See the sidebar "The Pizza Capital of the United States," on p. 178, for suggestions.

Here are some other options for the entire family:

Big Nick's Burger and Pizza Joint ★ (p. 194). In the unlikely event that your kids can't find anything they like on the 27-page menu, they can just tune in to the nonstop *Three Stooges* marathon playing on the restaurant's TVs.

Bubby's Brooklyn ★ (p. 205). Larger than the TriBeCa branch, this Bubby's has a tremendous view of Manhattan and is across the street from a playground. In Manhattan, check out **Bubby's Pie** for sweet treats for the kids (and yourself) as well (p. 143).

Carmine's ★ (p. 192). This rollicking family-style Italian restaurant was created with kids in mind. You won't have to worry about them making too much noise here.

City Bakery ★ (p. 170). What child wouldn't be taken with the chocolate spinning wheel and homemade marshmallows? As a bonus, the organic fare is nutritious *and* delicious.

Dinosaur Bar-B-Que (p. 200). Kids come away from this loud and casual space with dinosaur tattoos to go with the barbecue-sauce stains that they will undoubtedly wear on their clothes.

Good Enough to Eat ★ (p. 195). This spot offers comfort food for kids, such as macaroni and cheese, pizza, and great desserts.

Landmarc ★★ (p. 142). With a kids' menu featuring pigs in a blanket, PB and Nutella, and green eggs and ham pesto, not to mention cotton candy for dessert, Landmarc will keep the kiddies entertained while the old folks enjoy the restaurant's extensive wine list and first-rate steaks and seafood.

Mickey Mantle's 42 Central Park South (btw. Fifth and Sixth aves.; 🕾 **212/ 688-7777;** www.mickeymantles.com). As a player, the Mick had a reputation for being testy with autograph hounds and children, but he more than made up for it in retirement when he opened his extremely kid-friendly restaurant located just across the street from Central Park.

Nick's Family-Style Restaurant and Pizzeria ★ (p. 198). With locations in both Queens and Manhattan, Nick's has been wowing families for over a decade with its praiseworthy pizza and Italian specialties.

Serendipity 3 (p. 199). Kids will love this whimsical restaurant and ice-cream shop, which serves up a huge menu of American favorites, followed up by colossal ice-cream treats.

Virgil's Real BBQ ★★ (p. 176). This pleasing Times Square barbecue joint welcomes kids with open arms—and Junior will be more than happy, I'm sure, to be *expected* to eat with his hands.

an enormous brook trout *a la plancha* (roasted on a wood plank) stuffed with mustard greens and served with Indian lentils, I was pretty much convinced that the words "flavor" and "healthy eating" can actually co-exist. The staff is knowledgeable about the restaurant's unique concept and will help guide you through the unusual menu, making Rouge Tomate worth the adventure sans guilt.

12 E. 60th St. (btw. Fifth and Madison aves.). © **646/237-8977.** www.rougetomatenyc.com. Reservations recommended. Main courses $21–$39. AE, DC, DISC, MC, V. Daily noon–4pm and 5:30–10:30pm. Subway: N, or R to Fifth Ave./59th St.

Tulsi ★★ 🍴 INDIAN   Chef Hemant Mathur, formerly of **Devi** (p. 166), has taken his considerable talents to a new, sleek venue in the heart of Midtown. Like at Devi, Mathur has created original spins on traditional Indian cuisine, but here he takes the creativity even further with innovations like shrimp and crab stuffed *pappadum,* the amazing Manchurian cauliflower, or the lamb kebabs (spiced with cardamom and mace, accented with a basil yogurt dip). And those are just the starters. Mathur's signature entrée is the remarkable tandoor-grilled lamb chops; on the vegetarian side, the masala-stuffed baby eggplant is not to be missed. To best experience Tulsi's creations, I recommend the chef's vegetarian or omnivorous tasting menu. Service is efficiently casual, and seating is surprisingly intimate.

211 E. 46th St (btw. Second and Third aves; © **212/888-0820.** www.tulsinyc.com. Reservations recommended. AE, DC, DISC, MC, V. Starters $7–$14; main courses $22–$30; 7-course chef's tasting menu $65. Mon–Sat 12pm–3pm; Mon–Sat 5:30pm–10:30pm, Sun 5pm–10pm. Subway: 4, 5, 6, 7, S to 42nd St.-Grand Central.

Moderate

Chola ★★ 🍴 INDIAN   The food of Chola, which includes a number of hard-to-find dishes from India's southern regions, is as good as you will find anywhere in Manhattan. The menu is extensive and features many vegetarian and vegan options. Of the starters, the *kurkuri bhindi* (crispy okra and red onions flavored by a lime and *chaat* marsala) is not to be missed, while the Cochin lamb chops, rubbed with southern spices and served with onions and garlic, is so good that it might tempt a vegetarian to cross over to the dark side. Long, crispy *dosas* (thin crepes stuffed with spiced potatoes and peas) are also available, and, according to the menu, a favorite of Martha Stewart's. After a few bites, I concurred with Martha. Of the "Southern Specialties," *savitri amma's avail,* vegetables in a yogurt sauce, was unlike anything I had tasted in an Indian restaurant, but I'll definitely have it again. Chicken *korma,* seemingly a conventional Indian dish, was anything but, with the tender roasted chicken coated in a rich cashew sauce. Probably the best way to experience Chola and to sample a wide variety of its dishes is to visit to take advantage of the popular weekend "maharaja" buffet—just don't expect to eat again for a long time.

225 E. 58th St. (btw. Second and Third aves.). © **212/688-4619.** wwwfineindiandining.com. Main courses $14–$23; lunch buffet $14. AE, DC, DISC, MC, V. Mon–Fri noon–3pm; Sat–Sun 11am–3pm; daily 5–11pm. Subway: 4, 5, 6, N, or R to 59th St.

Inexpensive

The lower concourse of **Grand Central Terminal** ★★, 42nd Street at Park Avenue, has developed into a quick-bite bonanza that is an ideal choice for lunch—and the setting is an architecture-lover's delight. Head downstairs and choose from among the many outlets, offering everything from bratwurst to sushi. Standouts include **Junior's,** an offshoot of the Brooklyn stalwart, serving deli sandwiches, terrific steak burgers, and their world-famous cheesecake in their own waiter-serviced dining area.

WHERE TO DINE | Midtown East & Murray Hill

WHERE THE EDITOR EATS . . .

After a long day of shepherding Frommer's Travel Guides from manuscript to publication, this editor can use a good meal, a stiff drink, and a kind word. Here are some places where I can find them:

In the West Village, I like to swing by **Cowgirl,** 519 Hudson St., at West 10th Street (✆ **212/633-1133;** www.cowgirl nyc.com; Subway: 1 to Christopher St.) for a frozen blood-orange margarita (served in a Mason jar) or the Bible Belt (sort of a bourbon margarita), especially at happy hour, and enjoy some not-too-expensive Tex-Mex-style snacks or entrees (from chicken-fried chicken and chicken-fried steak, to Frito pie and veggie options). The staff is friendly and sassy and part of the show.

Zuni, 598 Ninth Ave., just below 43rd Street (✆ **212/765-7626;** www.zuniny. com) is Off-Off Broadway central; each evening waves of actors, directors, techies, and audiences flood the place from various theaters in the neighborhood. They make the bar a fun scene, with the booths in the back quiet enough to hear yourself talk, but with enough room to table-hop if you see friends. The menu is American/eclectic with a tilt

toward Mexican (ask about the quesadilla of the day). Also recommendable are the sandwiches (grilled salmon with wasabi aioli, an excellent burger) and solid entrees with daily specials and soups.

In often-expensive (and sometimes snippy) Chelsea, I enjoy the scrumptious, reasonably priced food and the cute, charming staff at **Pad Thai,** 114 Eighth Ave., at 16th Street (✆ **212/691-9266**). The generic name belies a lovely little restaurant (one of five run by the same owners, serving traditional Thai food in Manhattan), beautifully decorated, with French doors that open onto the sidewalk in good weather. There's a well-chosen menu of noodles, soups, salads, and entrees, none of which are much over $10, and lunch and dinner "box" specials. I try to swing by for happy hour, when it's $2 off all drinks, including my favorite: a frozen mango-lime margarita.

—*Kathleen Warnock*

For a glorious meal, dining under an impressive curved and tiled ceiling, try the New York landmark **Oyster Bar & Restaurant** ★ (✆ 212/490-6650; www.oysterbarny.com). Excellent soups and sandwiches (most for under $10) fall into the inexpensive category, but you will head on up into moderate and expensive for full meals of the fresh, well-prepared seafood. For a complete list of vendors, check out **www.grandcentralterminal.com.**

In addition to the listings below, there's also **Ess-A-Bagel** (see "The Hole Truth: N.Y.'s Best Bagels," p. 169) at 831 Third Ave., at 51st Street (✆ **212/ 980-1010**).

UPPER WEST SIDE

To locate the restaurants in this section, see the map on p. 188.

Very Expensive

Also consider the four-star-rated restaurant on Columbus Circle: **Jean-Georges,** in the Trump International Hotel & Tower, 1 Central Park West, at 60th Street/ Columbus Circle (✆ **212/299-3900;** www.jean-georges.com).

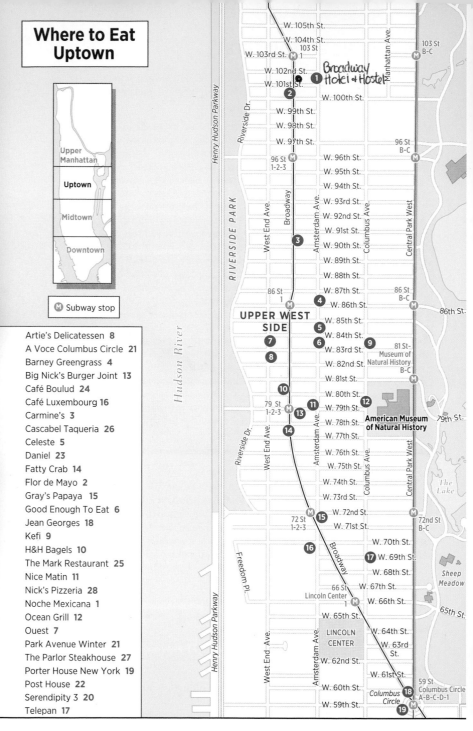

Where to Eat Uptown

Upper Manhattan

Uptown

Midtown

Downtown

Ⓜ Subway stop

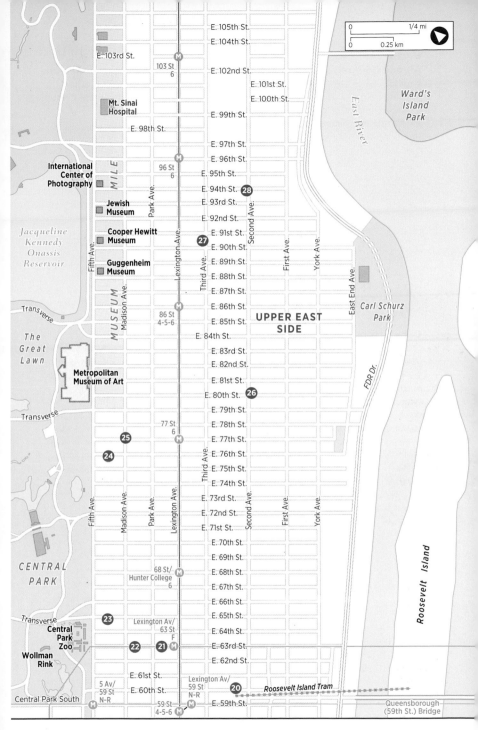

Expensive

A Voce Columbus Circle ★★★ ITALIAN   The original A Voce off Madison Park has always been popular, but this one, which opened in 2009, in the Time Warner Center, with picture windows overlooking Columbus Circle and Central Park, is even better and a grand experience on every level. The room is big, sparkling and convivial with to-die-for views, but take all that away and you still have the food. And if it were served in a coat check closet, I wouldn't be complaining. The menu changes periodically, each new menu focusing on a different Italian region; when I visited, the emphasis was on Sicily and the south. The housecured baccala with pine nuts and raisins was the perfect mix of salt and sweet and a wonderful first course. A pasta course is a must; I still dream about the cavatelli with Brussels sprouts, almonds, and whipped sheep's milk ricotta. With Sicily in mind, I sampled the *pesce spada,* or swordfish, with fennel, olives, and a chickpea fritter that was cooked to moist perfection. A Voce makes their own gelato, sorbet, and granite (Italian ice), and either or all are irresistible as an accompaniment to any of the restaurant's amazing desserts.
10 Columbus Circle, 3rd Floor. ℭ **212/823-2523.** www.avocerestaurant.com. Reservations recommended. Pastas $19–$25; main courses $22–$38. AE, DC, DISC, MC, V. Mon–Fri 11:30am–3pm; Sun–Wed 5–10pm; Thurs–Sat 5–11:30pm; Sat–Sun 11am–3pm. Subway: A, B, C, D, 1 to 59th St./Columbus Circle.

Café Luxembourg ★ FRENCH/AMERICAN   Located on the Upper West Side on an unassuming side street, Café Luxembourg opened its doors in 1983. And who knew then that crowds from all over the city—many of them celebrities—would flock to the unassuming side street on the Upper West Side and cramp into a pretty neighborhood bistro? Even more baffling is that they have been doing so for now over 27 years. It's loud and seats can be a little too close together, but Café Luxembourg is reliable—the food consistently solid and the space, despite the noise and elbow-to-elbow seating, offers a certain old-school comfort that never goes out of style. Start with a country salad replete with bacon lardons, a poached egg, and Fourme d'Ambert cheese followed by steak tartare or steak frites, all perfectly and not fussily prepared, and you really can't go wrong. All that is accompanied by an always excellent wine list and finished with one of the restaurant's classic desserts like crème brûlée or the addictive profiteroles. After 27 years, there are no surprises at Café Luxeumbourg, and really, that's the secret of their success.
200 W. 70th St. (btw. Amsterdam and West End aves.). ℭ **212/873-7411.** www.cafeluxembourg. com. AE, MC, V. Main courses $22–$35. Mon–Fri noon–3pm; Sun–Tues 5:30pm–11pm; Wed–Sat 5:30pm–midnight; Sat–Sun 9am–4pm. Subway: 1, 2, 3 to 72nd St.

Ocean Grill ★★ SEAFOOD   The Stephen Hanson/BRGuest Restaurant empire (Primehouse, Blue Water Grill, and Dos Caminos, to name a few) is vast, and sometimes its brawny restaurants can be a wee bit impersonal. But Ocean Grill, despite its considerable size, defies that generalization. Maybe it's because the restaurant is across the street from the Museum of Natural History and feeds off that building's wondrous vibe? Or maybe because it is in the heart of the family-friendly Upper West Side that Ocean Grill feels more like an intimate neighborhood joint. At Ocean Grill you go for the always fresh seafood, usually prepared without too many frills, which complements that relaxed good feeling. There are numerous menu options, including a touch of Asian in the preparation of the seafood, specifically Japanese, with a generous selection of house-made maki rolls—the creamy wasabi tuna is so good you will immediately forget any mercury warnings you've read about. Or try one of the fish entrees such as the sublime Chilean sea bass in a violet mustard emulsion served with polenta fries, or any of the fish grilled with a choice of sauces, such as black-olive tapenade or a soy-ginger vinaigrette, and sides such as bok choy or broccoli rabe. Most of the desserts change seasonally, but, if you are lucky, the caramelized banana ice-cream tower will be on the menu when you visit.

384 Columbus Ave. (btw. 79th and 80th sts.). *(C)* **212/579-2300.** www.brguestrestaurants.com. Reservations recommended. Main courses $20–$33. AE, DC, DISC, MC, V. Mon–Tues 11:30am–11pm; Wed–Thurs 11:30am–11:30pm; Fri–Sat 11:30am–midnight; Sun 10:30am–11pm. Subway: B or C to 81st St.

Ouest ★★★ CONTEMPORARY AMERICAN   When chef/restaurateur Tom Valenti opened Ouest in 2001, it signaled a renaissance in the Upper West Side dining scene. With red banquettes and an intimate balcony area, Ouest is both cozy and clubby. Service is personable but also professional—so good you'll need to keep reminding yourself that you are on the Upper West Side. But what really draws the crowds is Valenti's mastery in the kitchen, especially with such meats as his signature braised lamb shank or his melt-in-your-mouth braised beef short ribs. The quality suffers not one iota when you switch to seafood. The sautéed skate is perfectly prepared, with a simple sauce of parsley and olive oil, while the baby calamari in a spicy tomato-sopressata sauce appetizer was so good I actually smiled as I ate it.

2315 Broadway (at 84th St.). *(C)* **212/580-8700.** www.ouestny.com. Reservations required well in advance. Main courses $23–$36. AE, DC, DISC, MC, V. Mon–Thurs 5:30–10:30pm; Fri–Sat 5–11:30pm; Sun 5–9:30pm. Subway: 1 or 2 to 86th St.

Telepan ★★ AMERICAN   The venue for Telepan, named for chef/owner Bill Telepan, is an Upper West Side town house with a dining room painted in soothing lime green. The cool design complements the menu, which changes seasonally but always features farm-fresh products. In spring I was greeted with fresh ramps, fiddleheads, and young peas in many of the dishes I sampled. There was no fresh produce, however, in the foie gras donuts listed as a "share." The "donuts" are dusted with cocoa and cinnamon and might work as well with a cup of java as with a cocktail. Of the appetizers, the standout was the wild green frittata, which came with in-season ramps. Telepan offers "Mid Courses," and of them, the pea pancakes with pea agnolotti looked and, more importantly, tasted green-market fresh. Save room for an entree, specifically the haddock with a sweet lobster sauce. Whatever you choose to eat, you'll have no problem finding a complementary wine from the restaurant's long and impressive list. Telepan has become a pre–Lincoln Center favorite; so if you want to avoid the crush, make a reservation for after curtain.

72 W. 69th St. (at Columbus Ave.). © **212/580-4300.** www.telepan-ny.com. Reservations recommended. Main courses $29–$36; 4-course tasting menu $55; 5-course tasting menu $65. AE, DC, MC, V. Lunch Wed–Fri 11:30am–2:30pm; dinner Mon–Thurs 5–11pm, Fri–Sat 5–11:30pm, Sun 5–10:30pm; brunch Sat–Sun 11am–2:30pm. Subway: B or C to 72nd St.

Moderate

Also consider **Rack & Soul,** 2818 Broadway, at 109th Street (© **212/222-4800**), for the unbeatable combination of barbecued ribs and Southern-style pan-fried chicken.

Carmine's ★ ☺ ITALIAN   Everything is B-I-G at this family-style mainstay with two locations, on the Upper West Side (the original) and in Times Square. Carmine's, with a dining room vast enough to deserve its own zip code and massive portions, turns out better pasta and entrees than most 20-table Italian restaurants. I've never had pasta here that wasn't al dente, and the marinara sauce is as good as any I've had in Manhattan. The salads are always fresh and the fried calamari tender. Rigatoni marinara, linguini with white-clam sauce, and ziti with broccoli are pasta standouts, while the best meat entrees include veal parmigiana, broiled porterhouse steak, shrimp scampi, and the remarkable chicken *scarpariello* (chicken pan-broiled with a lemon-rosemary sauce). The tiramisu is pie size, thick, creamy, and bathed in Kahlúa and Marsala. Order half of what you think you'll need. Don't expect intimate conversation; in fact, it's downright loud. Unless you come early, expect to wait.

2450 Broadway (btw. 90th and 91st sts.). © **212/362-2200.** www.carminesnyc.com. Reservations recommended. Family-style main courses $19–$65 (most $23 or less). AE, DC, DISC, MC, V. Sun–Thurs 11:30am–11pm; Fri–Sat 11:30am–midnight. Subway: 1, 2, or 3 to 96th St. Also at 200 W. 44th St. (btw. Broadway and Eighth Ave.). © **212/221-3800.** Subway: A, C, E, N, R, S, 1, 2, 3, or 7 to 42nd St./Times Sq.

Fatty Crab MALAYSIAN   The loud, busy, somewhat rushed ambience complements the chef's pull-no-punches spicy Malaysian cuisine. If you don't want to venture to Chinatown or Queens for family-run, inexpensive, and authentic Malaysian, Fatty Crab is a pricier but worthy alternative, with a few innovations like the funky Fatty Dog, a pork sausage seasoned with chilies and shrimp paste and served in a potato hot-dog bun. The restaurant's signature dish, chili Dungeness crab, is lip-searing good, but a project that requires intricate surgery to remove the delicate crabmeat, not to mention numerous napkins and additional wet wipes. If you don't want to bother, the noodle and rice dishes are exceptional especially the Lo Si Fun, rice noodles with Chinese sausage and shitake mushrooms. All the dishes are for sharing and you can make a substantial meal out of the snacks alone.

2170 Broadway (btw. 76th and 77th sts.). ℂ **212/496-CRAB** (496-2722). www.fattycrab.com. Reservations recommended. $7-$22. AE, DISC, MC, V. Daily 5pm-midnight; brunch Sat-Sun 11am-4pm. Subway: 1, 2, or 3 to 72nd St. Also at 643 Hudson St. (btw. Gansevoort and Horatio sts.). ℂ **212/352-3590.** Mon-Wed noon-midnight; Thurs-Fri noon-2am; Sat-Sun 11am-midnight. Subway: A, C, E, or L to 14th St.

Kefi ★★★ 🏠 GREEK   Kefi is like your Greek mother's kitchen (if you had a Greek mother), and, in fact, the restaurant was inspired by chef Michael Psilakis's mother and her traditional recipes. Greek standards such as moussaka, spinach pie, Greek salad, and grilled fish are featured. But, oh, what Psilakis does with the standards! The mezes (Greek appetizers) are good enough to make up a meal; it's hard to resist the selection of spreads accompanied by pita, the warm feta, tomatoes, capers, and anchovies, and especially the very good grilled octopus salad. But something's gotta give if you want to save room for such entrees as the flat noodles with braised rabbit; the grilled whole branzino with potatoes, olives, tomatoes, and feta; or the slow-cooked, comforting lamb shank on a bed of orzo. If it is humanly possible after indulging in all of the above, don't miss out on the desserts, most notably the walnut cake with maple walnut ice cream. Service is casual and the bi-level space much roomier than its original location, but still, because of its popularity, always crammed, though never enough to deter you from the many pleasures of Kefi.

505 Columbus Ave. (at 84th St.). ℂ **212/873-0200.** www.kefirestaurant.com. Reservations recommended. Main courses $10-$20. AE, DISC, MC, V. Tues-Fri noon-2:30pm; Sun-Thurs 5-10pm; Fri-Sat 5-11:30pm; Sat-Sun noon-4pm. Subway: B or C to 86th St.

Nice Matin ★ FRENCH   This restaurant is named after Nice's major newspaper, and appropriately you'll find such Provençal classics as *pistou, pissaladiere,* and *velouté* of mussels on the menu. You'll also find innovations such as the creamy, delicious fava-bean tortellini, moist grilled sea bass with artichokes stewed in olive oil, and a rich daube of beef short ribs with chickpea fries. There are specials daily; and on Monday, normally not a great day to dine out, the *aioli monstre* is featured—salt cod, shrimp, meats, and vegetables accompanied by a tangy, fresh aioli. On any day you can order the five-napkin burger (so good they named a restaurant after it; p. 182), also accompanied by that pleasingly persistent aioli. If cholesterol is no concern, opt for the decadently dense dark-chocolate pot au creme for dessert.

201 W. 79th St. (at Amsterdam Ave., in the Lucerne Hotel). ℂ **212/873-NICE** (873-6423). www.nicematinnyc.com. Reservations recommended. Main courses $9.25-$20 at lunch, $16-$25 at dinner. AE, DC, MC, V. Breakfast Mon-Fri 7-11:30am, Sat-Sun 7-10:30am; lunch Mon-Sat 11:30am-3:30pm; dinner Mon-Sat 5:30pm-midnight, Sun 5-11pm; brunch Mon-Sat 7am-3:30pm, Sun 7am-2:30pm. Subway: 1 to 79th St.

Inexpensive

For breakfast or lunch, also consider **Artie's Delicatessen,** 2290 Broadway, between 82nd and 83rd streets (ℂ **212/579-5959;** www.arties.com); **Lansky's,** 235 Columbus Ave., between 70th and 71st streets (ℂ **212/787-0400;** www.lanskysnyc.com); and **Barney Greengrass, the Sturgeon King,** 541 Amsterdam Ave., between 86th and 87th streets (ℂ **212/724-4707**), three of the best Jewish delis in town. See "The New York Deli News" sidebar on p. 180 for further details.

You'll find some of the best bagels in New York on the Upper West Side, including **H&H Bagels,** 2239 Broadway, at 80th Street (📞 **212/595-8003**), and **Absolute Bagels,** 2788 Broadway, between 106th and 107th streets (📞 **212/932-2052**). For more information, see the box "The Hole Truth: N.Y.'s Best Bagels," on p. 169.

For nonvegetarians and the non-health-minded, consider the cheapest, yet in some ways most comforting, indulgence: **Gray's Papaya,** 2090 Broadway, at 72nd Street (📞 **212/799-0243**). This 24-hour hot-dog stand is a New York institution. See the box "Food in a N.Y. Minute" on p. 144 for more.

Big Nick's Burger and Pizza Joint ★ ☺ AMERICAN/PIZZA A neighborhood landmark since 1962, Big Nick's has a menu that seems to have grown each year of its existence—it's now a whopping 27 pages long. Trying to decide if you want the Madrid burger, with olives, feta, and pimentos, with or without buffalo meat; a slice of Hawaiian pizza; or just an order of the spinach pie, can be exhausting. If reading the menu is too much for you, peruse the numerous photos of celebrities who have supposedly chowed down at Big Nick's over the years, or just keep your eyes on the nonstop *Three Stooges* marathon playing on the restaurant's televisions. Whatever you do, you'll never forget your Big Nick's experience. With all those diversions, it's a great place to take the kids; they'll never be bored.

2175 Broadway (at 77th St.). 📞 **212/362-9238.** www.bignicksnyc.com. Reservations not accepted. Main courses $3.50–$19 (most less than $10). Cash only. Daily 24 hrs. Subway: 1 to 79th St.

Celeste ★★ 🍴 ITALIAN Tiny but charming Celeste features its own woodburning pizza oven, which churns out thin-crusted, simple, but delicious pizzas. But pizza is not the only attraction here; the *"fritti"* (fried) course is unique; the *fritto misto de pesce* (fried mixed seafood) is delectable, but the fried zucchini blossoms, usually available in the summer and fall, are amazing. The fresh pastas are better than the dried pasta; I never thought the fresh egg noodles with cabbage, shrimp, and sheep's cheese would work, but it was delicious. Not on the menu, but usually available, are plates of rare, artisanal Italian cheeses served with homemade jams. Though the main courses are also good, stick with the pizzas, antipasto, *frittis,* and pastas. For dessert, try the gelato; the pistachio was the best I've ever had in New York. The restaurant has been "discovered," so go early or late or expect a wait.

502 Amsterdam Ave. (btw. 84th and 85th sts.). 📞 **212/874-4559.** Reservations not accepted. Pizza $10–$12; antipasto $7–$10; pasta $10; main courses $14–$16. No credit cards. Mon–Sat 5–11pm; Sun noon–10:30pm. Subway: 1 to 86th St.

Flor de Mayo 🍴 CUBAN/CHINESE Cuban/Chinese cuisine is a New York phenomenon that started in the late 1950s when Cubans of Chinese heritage immigrated to New York after the revolution. Most of the immigrants took up residence on the Upper West Side, and Cuban/Chinese restaurants flourished. Many have disappeared, but the best one, Flor de Mayo, still remains and is so popular that a new branch opened farther south on Amsterdam Avenue. The kitchen excels at both sides of the massive menu, but the best dish is the *la brasa* half-chicken lunch special—beautifully spiced and slow roasted until it's fork tender and falling off the bone, served with a giant pile of fried rice, bounteous with roast pork, shrimp, and veggies. Offered Monday through Saturday until 4:30pm, the entire meal is just $6.95, and it's enough to fortify you for the day.

BREAKFAST, NOT BRUNCH!

Brunch has always been a pet peeve of mine. I mean, what is it really but a slightly fancier version of breakfast at inflated prices? And it's not even served until midmorning—and only on weekends. I'll take breakfast any day over brunch—*especially* on weekends. Here are some of my favorite breakfast spots:

Big Wong King ★ 67 Mott St., between Canal and Bayard streets *Dim Sum* (☎ **212/964-0540**). No eggs. No coffee. No pancakes. Can this be breakfast? You bet it is! Not much is more satisfying in the morning than a hot bowl of *congee* (rice porridge with pork, beef, or shrimp), accompanied with a fried cruller and tea served in a glass. It might sound a little unusual, but you won't be alone; Big Wong is a favorite for breakfast among the residents of Chinatown. Opens daily at 8:30am. For more on Big Wong King, see p. 145.

Bubby's Pie Company ★ 120 Hudson St., at North Moore Street (☎ **212/219-0666;** www.bubbys.com). I don't usually order grits north of the Mason-Dixon line, but I make an exception at Bubby's. They are the perfect complement to Bubby's Breakfast: two eggs, toast, bacon, and a cup of joe. Open at 8am Monday through Friday and 9am Saturday and Sunday. For more on Bubby's, see p. 143.

Clinton St. Baking Company ★ $$ 4 Clinton St., at Houston Street *Best pancakes ever but a little more expensive*

(☎ **646/602-6263**). The lines are long on weekend mornings, but you can get breakfast all day here. Meaning you can eat their unbelievable pancakes at 4 in the afternoon—if that's breakfast time for you.

Good Enough to Eat ★ 483 *Bakery* Amsterdam Ave., between 83rd and 84th streets (☎ **212/496-0163**). The wait for breakfast at this Upper West Side institution on the weekends is ridiculous, so try to go during the week when you can gorge on Pumpkin French Toast; the Wall Street Omelet, with honey-mustard-glazed ham with Vermont cheddar; or Peter Paul Pancakes, filled with Belgian chocolate chips, coconut, and topped with coconut. I'm getting hungry writing this. Opens at 8am Monday through Friday and 9am Saturday and Sunday. See p. 195.

Norma's ★★ At Le Parker Meridien Hotel, 118 W. 57th St., between Sixth and Seventh avenues (☎ **212/708-7460**). An ode to the ultimate comfort food. It's pricey, but worth it for classics done with style and creativity. See p. 175.

Service and atmosphere are reminiscent of Chinatown: efficient and lightning-quick. My favorite combo: the hearty Chinese soup, laden with noodles, greens, shrimp, and pork, with yellow rice and black beans.

2651 Broadway (btw. 100th and 101st sts.). ☎ **212/663-5520** or 212/595-2525. Reservations not accepted. Main courses $4.50–$19 (most under $10); lunch specials $5–$7 (Mon–Sat to 4:30pm). AE, MC, V ($15 minimum). Daily noon–midnight. Subway: 1 to 103rd St. Also at 484 Amsterdam Ave. (btw. 83rd and 84th sts.). ☎ **212/787-3388.** Subway: 1 to 86th St.

Good Enough to Eat ★ ☺ 🎒 AMERICAN   For over 25 years the crowds have been lining up on weekends outside Good Enough to Eat to experience chef/owner Carrie Levin's incredible breakfasts (see "Breakfast, Not Brunch!," above). As a result, lunch and dinner have been somewhat overlooked. Too bad, because these meals can be just as great as the breakfasts. The restaurant's cow motif and farmhouse knickknacks imply hearty, home-cooked food, and that's what's done best here. Stick with the classics: meatloaf with gravy and mashed potatoes; turkey with cranberry relish, gravy, and cornbread stuffing; macaroni and cheese; and the barbecue sandwich, roast chicken with barbecue sauce and homemade potato chips. And save room for the homemade desserts; I can never resist the coconut cake. This is food you loved as a kid, which is one reason why the kids will love it today. There are only 20 tables, so expect a wait on weekends during the day or for dinner after 6pm.

483 Amsterdam Ave. (btw. 83rd and 84th sts.). ℂ **212/496-0163.** www.goodenoughtoeat.com. Breakfast $5.25–$12; lunch $8.50–$15; dinner $8.50–$23 (most under $18). AE, MC, V. Breakfast Mon–Fri 8am–4pm, Sat–Sun 9am–4pm; lunch Mon noon–4pm, Tues–Fri 11:30am–4pm; dinner Mon–Thurs 5:30–10:30pm, Fri–Sat 5:30–11pm, Sun 5:30–10pm. Subway: 1 to 86th St.

Noche Mexicana ★ 🎁 MEXICAN   This Mexican restaurant serves some of the best tamales in New York. Wrapped in cornhusks, as a good tamale should be, they come in two varieties: in a red mole sauce with shredded chicken, or in a green tomatillo sauce with shredded pork. There are three tamales in each order, which costs only $6, making it a cheap and almost perfect lunch. The burritos are authentic and meals unto themselves. The *tinga* burrito, shredded chicken in a tomato-and-onion chipotle sauce, is my favorite. Each is stuffed with rice, beans, and guacamole. Don't get fancy here; stick with the tamales, burritos, and soft tacos, the best being the taco *al pastor,* a taco stuffed with pork marinated with pineapple and onions.

852 Amsterdam Ave. (btw. 101st and 102nd sts.). ℂ **212/662-6900** or 212/662-7400. www. noche-mexicana.com. Burritos $6.50–$8.50; tacos $2; tamales $6; Mexican dishes $9.50–$11. AE, DISC, MC, V. Sun–Thurs 10am–11pm; Fri–Sat 10am–midnight. Subway: 1 to 103rd St.

UPPER EAST SIDE

To locate the restaurants in this section, see the map on p. 188.

Very Expensive

Also consider elegant *New York Times'* four-star winner, **Daniel,** 60 E. 65th St., between Madison and Park avenues (ℂ **212/288-0033;** www.danielnyc.com).

The Post House ★★ STEAK   Yes, I know I've categorized the Post House as a steakhouse, and I know it is owned by the Smith & Wollensky group (see the box "The Prime Cut: Steaks! Steaks! Steaks!" on p. 162), and the windowless restaurant off the Lowell Hotel has a clubhouse (my seat was adorned with Ron Perelman's bronzed commemorative inscription) alpha-male feel, but the Post House is not your traditional meat-and-potatoes steakhouse. There are as many non–meat items on the menu as there are steak and chops. Most of the appetizers come from the sea, and the cornmeal fried oysters layered on a potato chip with cole slaw is something I've never had in a steakhouse before. Dover Sole, lobster, and grilled chicken are just a few of the nonsteak options you'll find at the Post House, but I've categorized the restaurant as one because you need to forget those other options and order the Cajun rib-eye steak, broiled in a subtle cayenne rub that perfectly melds with the richness of the meat. The starchy side dishes are traditional and served family-style (meaning large), so make sure you are eating with a family before ordering a platter of hash browns or onion rings. For dessert it will be worth your while to wait the extra 10 minutes it takes to prepare the restaurant's classic chocolate soufflé.

28 E. 63rd St. (btw. Park and Madison aves.). ✆ **212/935-2888.** www.theposthouse.com. Reservations recommended. Main courses $26–$70; three-course lunch daily $24.07. AE, DC, DISC, MC, V. Mon–Fri noon–5pm; Mon–Thurs 5–11pm; Fri–Sun 5pm–midnight. Subway: 4, 5, 6, N, R, or W at Lexington Ave./59th St.

Expensive

The Mark Restaurant ★★★ CONTINENTAL Everything comes together, as it usually does for chef/restaurateur Jean Georges Vongerichten at his newest New York City venture in the Mark Hotel. Opened in 2010, The Mark Restaurant offers perfection on every level. The long, flowing dining room is airy, with ample comfortable seating including many tables in a recessed glass solarium. Service is low key, not overly formal, but always attentive while the food, of course, is hard to beat. A simple Caesar salad becomes a memorable taste with just the right combination of lemon, cheese, and aioli in the dressing. A pasta offering of fettuccine with parmesan, black pepper, and lemon relies on the freshness of the ingredients to get it right, while a veal Milanese with spicy sweet potatoes, dried cranberries, and arugula tastes is as good (probably better) than anything similar you might find at your favorite Italian restaurant. Best of all, the Mark Restaurant, despite its elegant Madison Avenue location, serves a far-from-stuffy selection of pizzas, burgers (albeit with black truffle dressing and brie), fried calamari, and simply cooked meats and fish. The Mark Restaurant is a treat and an indulgence, but not one that will either bankrupt you or overwhelm you with excessive highbrow attitude.

25 E. 77th St. (at Madison Ave., in the Mark Hotel). ✆ **212/606-3030.** www.themarkrestaurant nyc.com. Reservations highly recommended. Main courses: $21–$48. AE, MC, V. Mon–Fri 11:30am–2:30pm; Sat–Sun 11:30am–3pm; Mon–Sun 5:30pm–11pm. Subway: 6 to 77th St.

Café Boulud ★ 🍴 FRENCH Dying to try the stellar cuisine of Daniel Boulud, New York's best French chef, but can't quite afford **Daniel?** Then head to Café Boulud, Boulud's more casual playground for new ideas and culinary cross-pollinations. Daniel's high style has been pleasingly laid back and toned down here. With the food, Boulud has gone eclectic, offering four menus: La Tradition, featuring Boulud's signature French-country classics; Le Potager, a vegetarian menu; La Saison, focusing on seasonal dishes; and Le Voyage, a monthly globe-hopping menu highlighting Tuscany, Thailand, or somewhere in between. The experimental nature of the wide-ranging menu makes choosing a thrill, and even the most inventive dishes tend to dazzle the palate. But in true Boulud tradition, La Tradition and La Saison are where the kitchen really excels. The poached Dover sole with baby leeks and sauce vin blanc is truly memorable. All in all, a first-rate dining experience at more palatable prices than cuisine this memorable usually costs. Don't be in a rush, though, especially at lunch.

20 E. 76th St. (btw. Madison and Fifth aves.). ✆ **212/772-2600.** www.danielnyc.com. Reservations recommended. Main courses $25–$40 at lunch, $26–$43 at dinner; 2- or 3-course prix-fixe lunch $28–$35. AE, DC, DISC, MC, V. Daily 5:45–11pm; Tues–Sat noon–2:30pm (no lunch Sat July–Aug). Subway: 6 to 77th St.

Park Avenue Winter ★★ CONTEMPORARY AMERICAN/MEDITERRA-NEAN Not only might the name of this restaurant be different when you visit, but the look (created by award-winning design firm AvroKO) and the menu will be totally changed as well. The gimmick here is that the restaurant transforms itself each season. And though a restaurant with a gimmick is sometimes, well, gimmicky, in this case, it works: Park Avenue Winter (the season I happened to visit it) is first rate. For the winter look, the large, high-ceilinged dining room was a snowy, glacial white and the menu reflected the season. Starters included the hearty porcini ravioli with Swiss chard in a flavorful Gorgonzola cream sauce, while you might not find a more comforting cold-weather dish than the entree of filet mignon on a bed of shredded short ribs accompanied by root vegetables. But surprisingly, the winter fare has a welcome light touch, as evidenced in the delicate cornbread-crusted red snapper on a citrus salad. Even the side of potato latkes was light and airy. Those same words, however, would definitely describe the chocolate cube I had for dessert. Stuffed with chocolate bits and chocolate mousse, the cube was incredibly dense—and I would have it no other way.

100 E. 63rd St. (at Park Ave.). (Ⓒ **212/644-1900.** www.parkavenyc.com. Reservations recommended. Main courses $26–$48. AE, DC, DISC, MC, V. Mon–Fri 11:30am–3pm; Sat–Sun 11am–3pm; Mon–Thurs 5:30–11pm; Fri–Sat 5:30–11:30pm; Sun 5:30–10pm. Subway: F to Lexington Ave./63rd St.

Inexpensive

Cascabel Taqueria ★ 🎁 MEXICAN A real deal taqueria in the heart of the Upper East Side's Frat row? Now who would've ever believed that? But it's true. Cascabel serves up some of the tastiest tacos south of Spanish Harlem. Sure, you need to fight through the throngs of aforementioned frat brothers and their sorority sisters to get in, but it's worth the raucous scene to sample Cascabel's take on the crab cake with *piquillo* pepper aioli or the zesty guacamole, made very spicy if so desired. The *pescado* taco, a soft corn tortilla stuffed with crispy tuna belly with hearts of palm is a wondrous mess while the *carnitas,* slow roasted Berkshire pork butt, pickled red onion, and roasted chile *de arbol* is an absolute must. The beer and cocktail list is extensive, the televisions are plentiful, and the tables are cramped, but you won't go wrong with the grub.

1538 Second Ave. (at 80th St.) (Ⓒ **212/717-8226.** www.nyctacos.com. Reservations recommended. AE, MC, V. Starters: $5–$8; tacos $9. Sun–Thurs 11:30am–12am. Fri–Sat 11:30am–1am. Subway: 6 to 77th Street.

Nick's Family-Style Restaurant and Pizzeria ★ ☺ ITALIAN Since 1994, Nick Angelis has wowed them in Forest Hills, Queens, with his pizza. In 2003, he took his act to Manhattan, where the pizza is garnering high praise. The pizza is thin crusted, with the proper proportions of creamy, homemade mozzarella and fresh tomato sauce. But this is much more than a pizzeria: Try the light, lemony baked clams or Josephine's (perfectly breaded) Eggplant Parmigiana. If you dare combine pizza with a calzone, this is the place; Nick's Calzone, stuffed with ricotta and mozzarella cheese, is spectacular. The orecchiette with broccoli rabe and sausage is the pasta winner, while the filet of *sole oreganato Livornese* with mussels is the standout main course. Save room for an extra-large cannoli for dessert; the shell perfectly flaky, the filling ultracreamy. Full orders are enough to feed two or three and are a great bargain for a group, but half orders are also available. The room is comfortable and far from fancy. Go early or be prepared to wait.

1814 Second Ave. (at 94th St.). *C* **212/987-5700.** www.nicksnyc.com. Pizza $12–$14; macaroni half orders $6–$12, full orders $12–$24; entree half orders $8.50–$12, full orders $17–$24. AE, DC, DISC, MC, V. Daily 11:30am–10pm. Subway: 6 to 96th St.

Serendipity 3 ★ ☺ AMERICAN You'd never guess that this whimsical place was once a top stop on Andy Warhol's itinerary. Wonders never cease—and neither does the confection at this delightful restaurant and sweets shop. Tucked into a cozy brownstone a few steps from Bloomingdale's, happy people gather here at marble-topped ice-cream-parlor tables for burgers and foot-long hot dogs, country meatloaf with mashed potatoes and gravy, and salads and sandwiches with such cute names as the Catcher in the Rye (their own twist on the BLT, with chicken and Russian dressing—on rye, of course). The food isn't great, but the main courses aren't the point—they're just an excuse to get to the desserts. The restaurant's signature is frozen hot chocolate, a slushy version of everybody's cold-weather favorite, but other crowd-pleasers include Dark Double Devil Mousse, Celestial Carrot Cake, Lemon Icebox Pie, and anything with hot fudge. So cast that willpower aside and come on in—Serendipity is an irony-free charmer to be appreciated by adults and kids alike.

225 E. 60th St. (btw. Second and Third aves.). *C* **212/838-3531.** www.serendipity3.com. Reservations accepted for lunch and dinner (not dessert only). Main courses $7.50–$20; sweets and sundaes $6–$20 (most under $10). AE, DC, DISC, MC, V. Sun–Thurs 11:30am–midnight; Fri 11:30am–1am; Sat 11:30am–2am. Subway: N or R to Lexington Ave.; 4, 5, or 6 to 59th St.

HARLEM

To locate these restaurants, see the map on p. 201.

Expensive

Red Rooster ★★ AMERICAN/SOUTHERN The buzz surrounding the opening of one of Harlem's most anticipated restaurants became deafening until, in early 2011, famed chef Marcus Samuelsson (Aquavit, p. 181) quieted it when the restaurant, after numerous delays, finally opened. Now the sounds you hear are the ooohs and ahhhs over the refined down home comfort food presented by Chef Samuelsson. Exploring the diversity of Harlem in the menu with nods to Latino, African, West Indian, and, most prominently, the South, Red Rooster is the most exciting and dynamic restaurant to open north of 110th Street. The boisterous, large dining room is highlighted by an open kitchen where, even over the din, you can hear chefs barking out their orders to the waiters. On my first visit, I stuck mostly to the south, sampling the succulent and spicy fried yard bird, with white mace gravy on a bed of collard greens along with the rich, heartily satisfying oxtails braised in stout and served with plantains. The bar scene is lively and Red Rooster also features live music in their downstairs lounge. Best of all, for this type of quality and scene, the prices are more Harlem-friendly than what you would find for the comparable experience downtown.

310 Lenox Ave. (btw. 125th–126th sts.) *C* **212/792-9001.** www.redroosterharlem.com. Reservations recommended. AE, MC, V. Main courses: $14–$32. 11:30am–3pm daily; 5:30pm–10:30pm daily. Subway: 2, 3 to 125th Street.

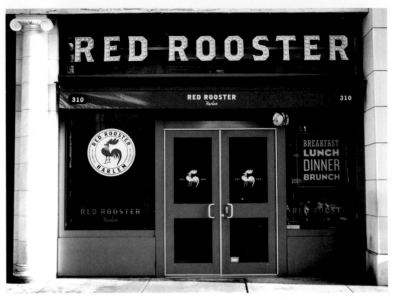

Celebrity chef Marcus Samuelsson's Red Rooster made its debut in Harlem in 2011.

Inexpensive

Also consider **Patsy's Pizzeria** ★ (see "The Pizza Capital of the United States," p. 178); and see the box "The Soul of Harlem," on p. 202, for great soul-food restaurants.

Covo Trattoria & Pizzeria ★ ITALIAN/PIZZA   *Covo* means "cave" in Italian, and coincidentally the location of Covo, under the West Side Highway and down steep steps from Riverside Park, can be considered very cavelike. But this *covo* has a wood-burning pizza and bread oven manned by a trained Neapolitan pizza maker, along with a very affordable menu of rustic Italian dishes. If you want to put that Neapolitan to the test, try the *paesana* pizza, a pie made with tomato sauces, Pecorino cheese, and black olives, or an antipasti of bruschetta slathered with tomato and chickpeas. Of the pastas, the homemade pappardelle with a honey-braised short rib ragu is addictive, while the *rigatoni alla norma* (pasta with tomato sauce, eggplant, basil, and fresh ricotta cheese) is the restaurant's signature dish. The list of Italian wines is decent and easy on the wallet, but because you are in a *covo,* the sound level when the restaurant is busy can be deafening. Be prepared.

701 W. 135th St. (at 12th Ave.). (✆ **212/234-9573.** www.covony.com. Pizza $8–$13; main courses $10–$19. AE, DC, DISC, MC, V. Daily noon–midnight. Subway: 1 to 137th St.

Dinosaur Bar-B-Que ☺ BARBECUE   It's one thing for a genuine Southern barbecue joint to infiltrate Manhattan, but it's quite another when the barbecue interloper is from up north. Now *that's* chutzpah! The popular Syracuse-based barbecue chain that built its reputation with bikers entered the New York City market with a roadhouselike restaurant on the outskirts of west Harlem. What can Syracuse know about barbecue, you ask? Well, they know pulled pork, which

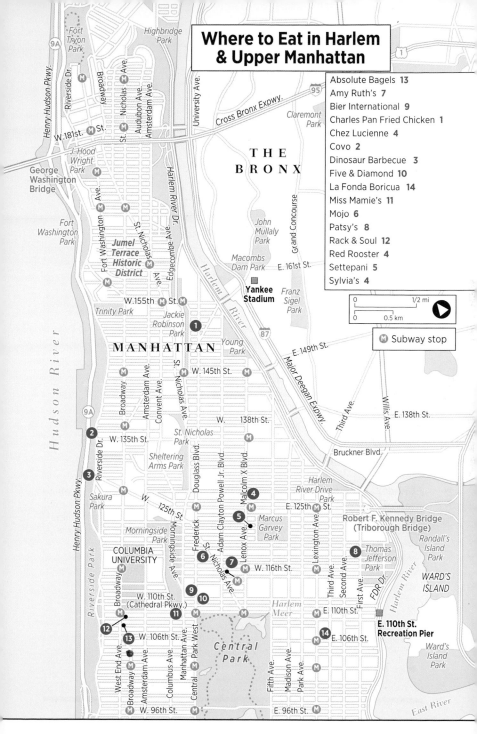

Where to Eat in Harlem & Upper Manhattan

Absolute Bagels **13**
Amy Ruth's **7**
Bier International **9**
Charles Pan Fried Chicken **1**
Chez Lucienne **4**
Covo **2**
Dinosaur Barbecue **3**
Five & Diamond **10**
La Fonda Boricua **14**
Miss Mamie's **11**
Mojo **6**
Patsy's **8**
Rack & Soul **12**
Red Rooster **4**
Settepani **5**
Sylvia's **4**

Subway stop

is slow-cooked till it's tender. And they know Texas brisket for the same reasons. The ribs I sampled didn't fare as well, but two out of three ain't bad—especially for a Yankee. Sides are standard: coleslaw, macaroni salad, collard greens, and standout barbecue beans. The restaurant is loud, but if you're lucky, you might be able to catch some of the good blues playing over the din. There's a lively bar and service is as down home as an upstate restaurant can be. Though its location is seemingly remote—close to the West Side Highway—it's only a 3-block walk from the no. 1 train.

700 W. 125th Street. (at Twelfth Ave.). ☎ **212/694-1777.** www.dinosaurbarbque.com. Main courses $13–$22. AE, MC, V. Tues–Thurs 11:30am–11pm; Fri–Sat 11:30am–midnight; Sun noon–10pm. Subway: 1 to 125th St.

THE SOUL OF HARLEM

There is much soul in Manhattan, but Harlem seems to possess the mother lode when it comes to food, though recently many old favorites have become victims of the recession. Here is one man's primer to what is left of Harlem's soul food:

Amy Ruth's   113 W. 116th St., between Lenox and Seventh avenues (☎ **212/280-8779;** www.amyruthsharlem.com). Claiming to be authentic soul, Amy Ruth's has become a mecca for Harlem celebs, with the kitschy gimmick of naming platters after some of them, such as the Rev. Al Sharpton (chicken and waffles) and the Rev. Calvin O. Butts III (chicken wings and waffles). The celebrities have recently deserted Amy Ruth's and have been replaced mostly by foreign tourists seeking soul after Sunday gospel tours.

Charles' Pan Fried Chicken ★ 2839–2841 Frederick Douglass Blvd., between 151st and 152nd streets (☎ **212/281-1800**). One of the saddest days of 2008 was when I learned Charles's Southern Style Kitchen had closed. It was the best soul fool restaurant in Harlem, mainly because of chef/owner Charles Gabriel's pan-fried chicken. Imagine my happiness when the news arrived that Gabriel was reopening in late 2009 under a new name but with the same perfect fried chicken. It's out of the way, but worth the visit.

Miss Mamie's Spoonbread Too 366 W. 110th St., between Columbus and Manhattan avenues (☎ **212/865-6744;** www.spoonbreadinc.com). Entering this strawberry-curtained charmer is like stepping into South Carolina. But you are in Harlem, or at least the southern fringe of Harlem, and you won't be paying South Carolina soul prices, or Harlem soul prices, either. Still, despite the cost, Miss Mamie's is the real deal, especially the barbecued ribs, falling off the bone in a sweet peppery sauce, and the smothered chicken, fried and then covered with thick pan gravy.

Sylvia's   328 Lenox Ave., between 126th and 127th streets (☎ **212/996-0660;** www.sylviassoulfood.com). Sylvia is the self-proclaimed queen of not only Harlem soul food but all soul food. In reality, Sylvia is queen of self-promotion. Sylvia's now has become a franchise, with canned-food products, beauty and hair products, and fragrances and colognes. With all that attention to merchandising, the food at her original Harlem restaurant has suffered and now has regressed into a tourist trap. If you plan to go, however, make it on Sunday for the gospel brunch, which is an absolute joy.

HARLEM RESTAURANT RENAISSANCE

It's not just soul food and fast food up in Harlem anymore. A spate of new, exciting restaurants have opened since the last edition of this book, hopefully ushering in a new era of Harlem eating.

Leading the way is celebrity chef Marcus Samuelsson's **Red Rooster** ★★ (p. 199), bringing his take on Harlem comfort foods from Africa to the American South. If the wait is too long to get into Red Rooster, an authentic, very friendly French bistro, **Chez Lucienne** ★, at 308 Lenox Ave., between 125th and 126th streets (✆ **212/289-5555;** www.chezlucienne.com), located right next door, is a worthy alternative. At Chez Lucienne, *moules* (mussels), French onion soup, and coq au vin are just some of the traditional options offered along with, on certain nights, African music and jazz.

Chef Samuelsson is a Harlem resident and before opening Red Rooster could be found dining at one of his self-proclaimed favorite restaurants, **Settepani,** 196 Lenox Avenue, at 120th Street (✆ **917/492-4806;** www.settepani.com). Specializing in the cuisine of Southern Italy and Sicily, Settepani was first a local bakery and cafe but in 2010 converted into a full-fledged restaurant. The breads are made in house and serve as a nice complement to the fragrant pastas like pasta *con sarde* (perciatelli with sardines, pine nuts, fennel, and currants) and pasta *alla norma* (rigatoni with tomato sauce, eggplant, and aged ricotta).

They now call Frederick Douglass Boulevard the "Gold Coast" of Harlem. Much of the gold can be found in a number of new condos, but also in many good restaurants. The innovative and casually elegant **5 and Diamond,** at 2072 Frederick Douglass Boulevard, between 112th and 113th streets (✆ **646/684-4662;** www.5anddiamondrestaurant.com) serves contemporary American fare like phyllo wrapped cod, organic hanger steak, and local, Senat farm chicken.

Even more casual, but no less innovative is **Bier International** ★, 2099 Frederick Douglass Boulevard, at 113th Street (✆ **212/280-0944;** www.bierinternational.com), where the beer list is as varied as the selection of wursts. Family-friendly, Bier International will make you feel at home no matter what your nationality in the best Harlem tradition.

A short block from Frederick Douglass Boulevard is where you can find the Harlem hip **Mojo,**186 St. Nicholas Ave, at 119th Street (✆ **212/280-1923;** www.mojo-harlem.com), where a live DJ, extensive cocktail list, and upscale munchies like sexy grits, cornbread panzella, and Harlem fried chicken sliders add to the cool vibe.

La Fonda Boricua ★ 🎒 SPANISH TAPAS/PUERTO RICAN   The food of Puerto Rico is vastly underrated, and the best of that cuisine can be found in the heart of El Barrio at La Fonda Boricua. This former diner is a hangout for leaders of the local Latino community, including ballplayers, politicians, musicians, and artists. They come for the succulent octopus salad, the "Bobby Flay's Throwdown" winning *arroz con pollo,* garlic-laden *lechon asado* (roasted pork shoulder) thinly pounded, citrus-marinated steak smothered with onions, and that artery-clogging favorite, *mofongo* (twice-fried and pounded plantains with garlic and crispy pork skin). The portions are more than generous and prices very affordable. It's loud and raucous, and the owners and clientele would have it no other way.

169 E. 106th St. (btw. Third and Lexington aves.) ✆ **212/410-7292.** www.fondaboricua.com. Main courses $10–$16. AE, MC, V. Daily 11am–10pm. Subway: 6 to 103rd St.

THE OUTER BOROUGHS
The Bronx

If you are looking for old-fashioned, Italian-American food—the kind you used to get before waiters began asking if you want your water tap or sparkling—look no further than the Bronx. The best concentration of Italian-American "red-sauce" restaurants can be found in the Little Italy of the Bronx, on and around **Arthur Avenue.** One of my favorites is **Mario's Restaurant,** 2342 Arthur Ave., between Crescent Avenue and East 187th Street (✆ **718/584-1188**), where the Neapolitan pizza is magnificent and the ziti with broccoli unforgettable. Reservations are accepted, as are American Express, Discover, Diners Club, MasterCard, and Visa. Wonderful **Dominick's,** on the same block at 2335 Arthur Ave. (✆ **718/733-2807**), is the inspiration behind family-style re-creations such as Carmine's. There's no menu here, but trust your waiter to ramble off what is on the day's menu, which almost always includes tender calamari marinara and luscious veal Francese. There's always a crowd, so go early or expect to wait for a communal table. Reservations are not accepted and please, cash only.

To get to Arthur Avenue, take the no. 4 or D train to Fordham Road and then the no. 12 bus east; the no. 2 or 5 train to Pelham Parkway, and the no. 12 bus west; or the Metro-North Harlem line to Fordham Road, and the shuttle bus to Belmont and the Bronx Zoo.

A few miles east of Arthur Avenue you'll find another classic Italian "red-sauce" restaurant. This one, **Frankie and Johnnie's Pine Restaurant,** 1913 Bronxdale Ave., between Matthews and Muliner avenues (✆ **718/792-5956**), has been around so long, I remember watching the Times Square ball drop on a black-and-white television in the dining room while devouring a bowl of *zuppa di pesce* one lonely New Year's Eve many years ago. I remember that New Year's, though lonely, very fondly mainly because of that *zuppa di pesce*. Now the Pine, as it's known, has become popular as a hangout for New York Yankees who crave pasta after their games at Yankee Stadium. As a result, you'll find plenty of

The Best Pizza in the Bronx?

Head for **Trattoria Zero Otto Nove ★★,** 2357 Arthur Ave., at 186th Street, the Bronx (✆ 718/220-1027; www.roberto089.com). Taking its name from the Salerno, Italy, area code, you'll think you are in Salerno when you bite into one of chef Roberto Paciullo's Neapolitan pizzas. The mozzarella is made at nearby Casa de Mozzarella, the tomatoes are San Marzano, the pies cooked in a wood-burning brick oven, the basil fresh from the Arthur Avenue Market across the street—the result pure pizza perfection. There are numerous variations but, surprisingly, one of the best at Zero Otto Nove is the butternut squash purée with smoked mozzarella, pancetta, and basil.

baseball memorabilia on the walls. Reservations are not accepted, and it's cash only. Take the no. 2 or 5 train to Bronx Park East.

Brooklyn

VERY EXPENSIVE

At the foot of the Brooklyn Bridge, with spectacular views of the New York skyline, the **River Café**, 1 Water St. (☎ 718/522-5200), could possibly be the most romantic special-occasion restaurant in New York. Service is good, prices are steep, and the contemporary Continental cuisine is more than adequate, but nothing can top that view.

EXPENSIVE

Peter Luger Steakhouse ★★ STEAK   If you love steak, then book a table here and hop a cab to Williamsburg. Expect loads of attitude and nothing in the way of decor or atmosphere (beer hall is the theme)—but this 114-year-old institution is porterhouse heaven. The first-rate cuts—the only ones they serve—are dry-aged on the premises and come off the grill dripping with fat and butter, crusty on the outside and tender pink within. It's the best steak in the five boroughs. Nonbelievers can order sole or lamb chops, but don't bother if you're not coming for the cow. The $5.95 Peter Luger burger is a little-known treasure. As sides go, the German fried potatoes are crisp and delicious, and the creamed spinach is everything it should be. Bring wads of cash because this place is expensive but doesn't take credit cards (other than their own house account). And call far, far in advance, especially during the holiday seasons.

178 Broadway (at Driggs Ave.), Williamsburg, Brooklyn. ☎ **718/387-7400.** www.peterluger. com. Reservations essential; call a month in advance for weekend bookings. Main courses $5–$20 lunch, $20–$32 dinner. No credit cards (Peter Luger accounts only). Mon–Thurs 11:45am–9:45pm; Fri–Sat 11:45am–10:45pm; Sun 12:45–9:45pm. Subway: J, M, or Z to Marcy Ave. (or take a cab).

MODERATE

Consider **Bubby's Brooklyn,** 1 Main St., at Water Street (☎ 718/222-0666), the DUMBO outpost of the comforting, comfort-food **Bubby's** (p. 143).

Fatty 'Cue ★★ 🍴 ASIAN/BARBECUE   It's worth the trek over (or under) the river to Williamsburg to experience the newest of the Fatty Crew's (**Fatty Crab,** p. 192) venture. This one specializes in barbecue with a heavy Asian slant. I'm not one for fusion; I like my 'cue straight up, but after sampling the offerings at Fatty Cue, I'm a happy convert. Sure the space may be cramped, loud, and grungy, but the food here is anything but grunge. How about coriander cured bacon, dragon Pullman toast with a side of "fat," or the amazing Heritage pork ribs to snack on while imbibing in one of the restaurant's many cocktails. Of the many outstanding entrees, the hand-pulled lamb shoulder is perfectly gamey and pungent with garlic, while the Brandt ranch beef brisket bathed in a bone broth adorned with chili jam was so good, I didn't even care that I had no idea where Brandt ranch was. The only problem with Fatty Cue is that you can't have it all in one sitting. You'll just have to cross the river again. I know I will.

91 South 6th St., Williamsburg. ☎ **718/599-3090.** www.fattycue.com. Reservations recommended. Snacks: $4–$14; entrees: $19–$35. Daily 12pm–12am. Subway: L to Bedford.

Fette Sau ★★ 🏮 BARBECUE   I learn something new every day. Now I know that Fette Sau means "fat pig" in German. And could there be a more clever name for a barbecue joint? And Fette Sau is as good as any cutesy-named barbecue place you will find in the New York area. Housed in a former garage in Williamsburg, Fette Sau is rustic; seating is wooden picnic tables—in the warmer months there are tables outside in the small driveway leading to the restaurant. Service is from a counter; you order your meats by the weight, making it tough to control your intake. The meats, pork and beef, are organic and from local farms. Not all the cuts of meat are available daily. When I went, I was fortunate that barbecue pork belly (thicker, fattier bacon) was available. It was the first time that I ever experienced barbecue pork belly and it's one I want to repeat. The boneless beef ribs were perfectly smoked, charred on the outside and tender within, while the Berkshire rib chop, coated with fat to keep the thick, other white moist meat was flavorful. The barbecue is so good here, don't bother with the sauces, but do try the burnt-end baked beans, a meal in itself. Fette Sau also has a remarkable beer and bourbon list worth traveling for even if you are a vegetarian.

354 Metropolitan Ave. (btw. Havermeyer and Roebling sts.), Williamsburg. ℂ **718/963-3404.** www.fettesaubbq.com. Main courses $10–$25. MC, V. Sun–Thurs 5pm–2am; Fri–Sat 5pm–4am. Subway: L to Lorimer St.

Frankie's Spuntino 457 ★★★ 🍴 ITALIAN   *Spuntino* means an informal meal or snack in Italian. Why then, whenever I snack informally at Frankie's, either at the original Carroll Gardens location or the Manhattan Lower East Side restaurant, do I feel like I've done much more than just snack? I could swear I've had an almost three-plus-course meal beginning with, maybe, a salad; the escarole with sliced red onions and walnuts is tough to resist—but then I can't have the roasted beets and avocado. If I have both then maybe I should refrain from the cured meat-tasting menu which would make me kick myself the next day. Of course, no matter what, I must have one of Frankie's amazing specials, which are really entrees, like the pork braciola in a perfect marinara sauce or the delicate Sicilian-style meatballs with raisins and pine nuts. If I'm with a hungry group, even better, we can all share a plate of homemade cavatelli with hot sausage or the house-made gnocchi with ricotta and marinara. After all that snacking, dessert cannot be denied, especially the old standby, tiramisu, here made as good as anywhere I've sampled it. The confines at both locations are cozy (the Brooklyn restaurant features garden dining in warm weather), and with these prices, the waits can be long, but service is never harried and return customers know the wait will be well worth it.

457 Court St. (btw. 4th Pl. and Luquer St.). ℂ **718/403-0033.** www.frankiesspuntino.com. No reservations. Main courses $9–$18. No credit cards. Sun–Thurs 11am–11pm; Fri–Sat 11am–midnight. Subway: F or G to Carroll St. Also at 17 Clinton St. (btw. Houston and Stanton sts.). ℂ **212/253-2303.** AE, MC, V. Sun–Thurs 11am–midnight; Fri–Sat 11am–1am. Subway: F or M to Delancey St.

Prime Meats ★★ 🏮 AMERICAN/STEAKS   From the creators of Frankie's Spuntino 457 (see above) is their newest venture, an ode to the restaurants and food of New York at the turn of the 20th century—though after sampling Prime Meats, I'm pretty sure what I tasted was probably much better than anything you could have imagined back in the day. The relevance to early New York cuisine is that at Prime Meats just about all the food and drinks are locally and seasonally sourced. And that freshness comes out in the simplicity of the dishes; the steaks, using grass-fed beef from upstate farms, is as good as you might find at any Manhattan steakhouse. An Alpine tasting board of house-cured meats is the perfect accompaniment to a pint of Brooklyn-brewed Sixpoint Mason's Black Wheat beer. Prime Meats also features a number of German dishes as tribute to that era when German restaurants dominated the New York cuisine and the sauerbraten (beef brisket brined for 3 days) and braised red cabbage is so good here that it would be a hit in any era. Service is professional and helpful in explaining the restaurant's mission, but Prime Meats' no reservation policy is the only drawback, especially if you are venturing from Manhattan.

465 Court St. (at Luquer St.). ☏ **718/254-0327.** www.frankspm.com. No reservations. No credit cards. Small plates $7–$14; main courses $13–$23. Mon–Wed 1pm–1am; Thurs 1pm–2am; Fri–Sat 3pm–2am; Sun 3pm–1am. Subway: F, G to Smith St.

INEXPENSIVE

The fabulous **Grimaldi's Pizzeria** is at 19 Old Fulton St., between Front and Water streets (☏ **718/858-4300**). Out in Coney Island, the 1924-established and little-changed **Totonno's** is at 1524 Neptune Ave., between West 15th and West 16th streets (☏ **718/372-8606**). While in Williamsburg, don't miss **Motorino** 319 Graham Ave., at DeVoe Street, Williamsburg, Brooklyn (☏ **718/ 599-8899;** www.motorinopizza.com). For more information on both, see "The Pizza Capital of the United States" on p. 178.

Also in Coney Island is the famous **Nathan's Famous,** 1310 Surf Ave., at Stillwell Avenue (☏ **718/946-2202**), for hot dogs by the beach. See how many you can eat.

If you are traveling to BAM to see a show, you'll be tempted to have either your pre- or post-theater meal at **Junior's,** 386 Flatbush Ave., at DeKalb Avenue (☏ **718/852-5257**). Everyone knows about Junior's world-famous cheesecake, the epitome of New York cheesecake, but don't miss the opportunity to experience the authentic Brooklyn atmosphere here, complete with old-school waiters you'll not soon forget. Don't expect anything fancy, but do expect great cheesecake.

The best ice cream in New York can be found right over the Brooklyn Bridge at the **Brooklyn Ice Cream Factory,** 1 Water Street at the Fulton Ferry Landing Pier, Brooklyn (☏ **718/246-3963**). Everything is freshly made, including the hot fudge for your sundae.

Ferdinando's Focacceria ★ 🏠 ITALIAN/SICILIAN   You might think that focaccia, that wonderful Italian bread coated with olive oil, herbs, and tomato sauce, is a recent culinary innovation. Think again. They've been making focaccia at Ferdinando's since 1904. But the focaccia they make at this Sicilian restaurant, in the increasingly trendy neighborhood of Carroll Gardens, is nothing like the focaccia you've tasted. Here the specialty focaccia is *panelle,* a deep-fried pancake made of chickpea flour. You can have your *panelle* plain or you can have it topped with ricotta and grated cheese. The restaurant also features Sicilian specials such as marinated octopus, stuffed calamari, tripe in tomato sauce, and a magnificent *caponatina* (eggplant salad).

151 Union St. (btw. Columbia and Hicks sts.), Cobble Hill. ☏ **718/855-1545.** Panelle $4; main courses $15–$22. No credit cards. Mon–Thurs 11am–7pm; Fri–Sat 11am–10pm Subway: F or G to Carroll St.

Queens

EXPENSIVE

Water's Edge ★★ CONTEMPORARY AMERICAN   When it comes to dining with the best views of the Manhattan skyline, many consider the River Café tops. But the view from Water's Edge, where the lights of the Citicorp, Chrysler, United Nations, and Empire State buildings flicker right across the river, gives the River Café a run for its money. Throw in free ferry service from Manhattan (a 10-min. ride) to the restaurant, the possibility of watching a family of swans frolicking in the river as you dine, and succulent seasonal cuisine, and the Water's Edge experience becomes memorable. In the spirit of autumn, the season I visited the restaurant, the hearty, tender pomegranate-marinated venison stew came served inside a minipumpkin served with figs, cranberries, and chestnuts, while the decadently rich seared duck *foie gras* was accompanied by delicious blackmission-fig chutney. For a real splurge, Water's Edge offers tasting menus and wine pairings with the course. But this is Queens and the splurge won't hit you quite as hard in the wallet as it would if you went to that other restaurant on the river in Brooklyn.

East River and 44th Dr., Long Island City, Queens. ℂ **718/482-0033.** www.watersedgenyc.com. Main courses $26–$36; 4-course tasting menu $75. AE, DC, DISC, MC, V. Mon–Fri noon–3pm and 5:30–11pm; Sat 5:30–11pm. Subway: E or V to 23rd St./Ely Ave.

INEXPENSIVE

The no. 7 train is sometimes known as the International Express (p. 332). Take it out of Manhattan and through the borough of Queens and you will pass one ethnic neighborhood after another. You could write a book on all the different restaurants located around the no. 7 train in Queens. Here are a few of my favorites:

Get off at the 69th Street stop in Woodside, walk 1 block north, and you might begin to detect the aroma of barbecued meats. That smell is coming from **Ihawan,** 40–06 70th St. (ℂ **718/205-1480**), which claims to be home of the best barbecue in town. But unless you've been to the Philippines, Ihawan's country of origin, this is barbecue unlike any you've tasted before. Here you can sample barbecued pork on bamboo skewers, grilled marinated pork chops, and the local favorite, grilled marinated pork belly. The menu here also includes other Filipino specialties such as *dinuguan,* pork stewed in pork-blood gravy, and *lapulapu,* a whitefish, served in tamarind soup.

If you get off the train at the 82nd Street/Jackson Heights stop, a few steps from the elevated tracks, you'll find **Arunee Thai,** 37–68 79th St., off Roosevelt Avenue (ℂ **718/205-5559**). Here, the Thai food is so authentic (and the clientele mostly Thai) that the menus are written in Thai and English. Everything is delicious, and the spice level is not toned down for delicate palates. The fish, served whole on the bone, with chili, garlic, and hot-and-sour sauce, will either take the chill off a cold winter's day or, if it's summer, the chilies will cool down your overheated body and soul.

Exit the last stop of the no. 7 train, Flushing/Main Street, and you might think you're in downtown Beijing. Where you are is Flushing's Chinatown, bigger than Manhattan's and crammed with teahouses, noodle shops, banquet halls, bakeries, and Asian supermarkets. The food choices are staggering and you won't go wrong at just about any of the countless restaurants. For a Flushing Chinatown experience like no other, try **Minni's Shabu Shabu,** 136–17 38th Ave.

WHERE TO DINE | The Outer Boroughs

WHERE THE EDITOR EATS (QUEENS VERSION)

Queens may not be the dining destination that Brooklyn is becoming, but there's lots of good, eclectic cuisine, usually much less expensive than across the East River. Combine a trip to one or more of the western Queens attractions (see chapter 6) with a meal at one of my favorite spots off the N or Q train.

If you're headed to the Museum of the Moving Image (p. 330), walk a few blocks down 36th Avenue for lunch or dinner at **Malagueta** at 25–35 36th Ave., at 28th Street (© **718/937-4821**). Chef Herbert Gomes combines his Brazilian background with his training at the French Culinary Institute to create a menu that has made his corner storefront into a favorite. (It's regularly cited as one of the city's best in *Time Out New York*'s annual "Cheap Eats" issue). It's small, but classy, with original art on the walls and Brazilian music playing in the background. Such appetizers as linguiça sausage with yucca fries and cilantro mayo lead up to a menu of main courses rarely topping $15 (except for specials). My favorite regular entree is the *picanha* steak, served with rice and beans, and a delicate vinaigrette and farofa. There's wine by the glass and bottle, and some scrumptious desserts (I like the passion-fruit mousse). It's open Tuesday to Thursday noon to 10pm; Friday noon to 11pm; Saturday 1 to 11pm; and Sunday 1 to 10pm. Subway: N or Q to 36th Ave/Washington Avenue.

Combine a visit to the Noguchi Museum (p. 68) and Socrates Sculpture Park (p. 333) with a stop at **Sanford's Restaurant,** just off the Broadway stop on the N or Q line at 30–13 Broadway, in Astoria (© **718/935-9269;** www.sanfordsnyc.com), which has been serving the neighborhood since 1930. Closed in late 2008 after a fire, its loyal clientele peered in the windows each day during renovation as the restaurant made itself over into a classy-looking Euro-style cafe. But when it reopened, under the stylish decor you could still find such favorites as "build your own" omelets and a fantastic chicken orzo soup, as well as excellent burgers. The buffed-up menu now features more entrees, ranging from a three-mushroom truffle risotto to a penne with smoked salmon and applewood bacon in a cream sauce. There's also a well-chosen (and reasonable) beer and wine menu. Burgers and omelets generally run under $10, with dinner entrees (which include soup or salad) from $12 up, and popular prix-fixe brunch on weekends for $13. It's open 24/7/365, and you might spot locals lingering over meals at any hour with their laptops using the Wi-Fi.

One of the few restaurants in the city serving pizza in a coal-fired oven (it cooks very quickly, and adds a crispness to the thin crust) is a couple blocks farther down Broadway at **Sac's Place** at 25–41 Broadway (© **718/204-5002;** www.sacsplace.com). Brothers Domenico and Anthony Sacramone have a full Italian menu, but it's the pizza, made with homemade mozzarella and San Marzano tomatoes imported from Italy, that gets the love from Astoria and beyond. Pizzas range from $9.95 to $20 for a cheese pizza, and there's a long list of toppings, ranging from homemade meatballs to sautéed portobello mushroom in white wine. *Mmm.* It's open Sunday to Thursday noon to 11pm, and Friday to Saturday noon to midnight.

—*Kathleen Warnock*

(© **718/762-6277**), where in front of each setting at each table there is a built-in soup pot complete with heat source. You order what you want to cook in the broth, including raw sliced beef or pork or a variety of seafood, add sauces, condiments, and vegetables, and put it into the pot, letting it cook right in front of you. It takes a bit of practice, but by the end of your meal, you'll have the procedure down for the perfect, and hearty, Chinese soup.

PRACTICAL INFORMATION
The Big Picture

New Yorkers can be fickle. One moment a restaurant is hot, the next it's passé. So, restaurants close with a frequency we wish applied to the arrival of subway trains. Always call ahead or check websites for the most up-to-date news.

Wherever you're from, particularly if you hail from the reasonably priced American heartland, New York's restaurants will seem *expensive*. Yet good value abounds, especially if you're willing to try ethnic cuisine (including types you may not have had before), and if you venture beyond tourist zones into such neighborhoods as Chinatown, Harlem, upper Manhattan, the East Village, the Upper West Side, and the boroughs. I include inexpensive restaurants in every neighborhood, including some of the city's best-kept secrets, so you'll know where to get good value for your money no matter where you are in Manhattan.

Reservations

Reservations are always a good idea in New York, and a necessity for popular restaurants if your party is bigger than two. Do yourself a favor and always call ahead so you won't be disappointed. If you're booking dinner on a weekend night, it's a good idea to call a few days in advance if you can.

Call *far* ahead for any special meal you don't want to miss—a month in advance is a good idea. Most top places start taking reservations 30 days in advance, so if you want to eat at a hot restaurant at a popular hour—Saturday at 8pm, say, at Aquavit—be sure to mark your calendar and start dialing 30 days prior at 9am. If you're booking a holiday dinner, call even earlier, or head to **OpenTable.com** (see below) as soon as you decide on the date of your dinner.

But if you didn't call well ahead and your heart's set on dinner at Red Rooster or Osteria Morini, don't despair. Often, early or late hours—between 5:30 and 6:30pm or after 9pm—are available, especially on weeknights. Try calling the day before or first thing in the morning, when you may be able to take advantage of a last-minute cancellation. Or go for lunch, which is usually much easier to book without lots of advance notice. If you're staying at a hotel with a concierge, don't be afraid to use him or her—a well-connected concierge can often get you into hot spots that might otherwise be booked.

Smoking Policy

You cannot light up in any restaurant in the city. Some restaurants entice smokers with back gardens or patios where smoking is permitted, but otherwise, you'll have to step out to the sidewalk (or "Bloomberg Lounge") for a cigarette. Some restaurants provide benches, chairs, and ashtrays, but it gets mighty cold out there in the winter.

OpenTable (www.opentable.com) allows you to book a reservation—and get an instant confirmation—over the Internet at about 150 restaurants throughout Manhattan (and in more than 20 other cities in the U.S. and Canada). You may need to hold the reservation with a credit card. You'll also find that an increasing number of restaurants offer online reservations through their own websites.

But what if they don't take reservations? Lots of restaurants, especially at the affordable end of the price continuum, don't take reservations at all. One of the ways they keep prices down is by packing people in as quickly as possible. Thus, the best cheap and mid-price restaurants often have a wait. Again, your best bet is to go early. Often you can get in more quickly on a weeknight. Or just go, knowing that you're going to have to wait if you head to a popular spot; hunker down with a cocktail at the bar and enjoy the festivities around you.

Tipping

Tipping is easy in New York. The way to do it: Double the 8.75% sales tax and *voilà*, happy waitstaff. In fancier venues, another 5% is appropriate for the captain. If the wine steward helps, hand him or her 10% of the bottle's price.

Leave $1 per item, no matter how small, for the checkroom attendant.

More Sources for Serious Foodies

Of course, New York has far more fabulous dining than I have room to discuss here—although the listings here are enough to keep you fat and happy for a year, much less the length of a vacation. But if you'd like a wider selection, a few good sources are available online or from your local bookstore.

Your best online sources are the online arm of the weekly *New York* magazine (**www.nymag.com**), which also features a daily food blog; New York Today (**www.nytoday.com**), the *New York Times'* arts and lifestyle site, where you can access a database of the paper's stellar restaurant reviews and blogs; the *Village Voice* (www.villagevoice.com), especially for the cheap-eats reviews by Robert Sietsema, and the national **www.eater.com** which has a New York section For a good online source with readers' reviews and menus, try **www.menupages.com**, which has more than 6,000 menus online.

Without a doubt, the best online source for the serious foodie is **www. chowhound.com**, a national website with message boards in local areas, including New York, where you can make an inquiry about a certain restaurant, type of food, location, and so on, and within a few hours, you might have several informative responses. For the not-so-serious foodie, but for someone who likes to eat, check out this author's own blog, **www.friedneckbones.wordpress.com**.

The *Zagat Survey,* which has made a name for itself rating restaurants based on extensive diner surveys, maintains a searchable database of city restaurants at **www.zagat.com**, so if you're willing to do your research before you leave home (or if you're toting a laptop), there's no need to acquire a hard copy of the no-frills guide. They do, however, charge a fee to access the online information. At press time, a year's subscription of Zagat online was $24.95 and a 30-day

5

WHERE TO DINE

Practical Information

subscription was $4.95. In my opinion, with so many similar food sources online for free, paying for a subscription is not worth it.

The slick weekly *Time Out New York* has an "Eat Out" section in every issue, as well as coverage of new openings and dining trends. Weekly *New York* magazine also maintains extensive restaurant listings in its listings section at the back of the magazine.

RESTAURANTS BY CUISINE

AMERICAN

See also "Contemporary American"
Aldea ★★ ($$$, p. 164)
Artie's New York Delicatessen ($, p. 180)
Big Nick's Burger and Pizza Joint ★ ($, p. 194)
Bill's Bar & Burger ★ ($, p. 182)
Brgr ★ ($, p. 182)
Bubby's Pie Company ★ ($$, p. 143)
Burger Joint ★★ ($, p. 182)
Café Luxembourg ($$$, p. 190)
City Bakery ★ ($, p. 170)
Clinton St. Baking Company ★ ($, p. 149)
Cookshop ★★ ($$$, p. 159)
Ed's Lobster Bar ★★ ($$, p. 150)
5 Napkin Burger ★ ($$, p. 182)
Good Enough to Eat ★ ($, p. 195)
New York Burger Co. ($, p. 182)
Norma's ★★ ($$, p. 175)
The Odeon ★ ($$, p. 145)
P.J. Clarke's ★ ($$, p. 183)
Prime Meats ★★ ($$, p. 206)
Rare Bar & Grill ★ ($$, p. 183)
Red Rooster ★★ ($$$, p. 199)
Rouge Tomate ★ ($$$, p. 184)
Serendipity 3 ★ ($, p. 199)
The Lamb's Club ★ ($$$, p. 172)
The Smith ($$, p. 154)
Telepan ★★ ($$$, p. 191)
Walker's ($, p. 424)

ASIA/PACIFIC RIM
Buddakan ★ ($$$, p. 158)
Double Crown ★ ($$$, p. 151)

Momofuku Noodle Bar ★ ($$, p. 153)
Nyonya ★ ($, p. 146)

BARBECUE/SOUTHERN
Blue Smoke ($$, p. 174)
Charles' Pan Fried Chicken ★ ($, p. 202)
Daisy May's BBQ ($$, p. 174)
Dinosaur Bar-B-Que ($, p. 200)
Fatty 'Cue ★★ ($$, p. 205)
Fette Sau ★★ ($$, p. 206)
Hill Country ★ ($$, p. 174)
Johnny Utah's ★ ($$, p. 174)
Rack & Soul ($$, p. 174)
RUB ★★ ($$, p. 162)
The Smoke Joint ($$, p. 174)
Virgil's Real BBQ ★★ ($$, p. 176)

BREAKFAST & BRUNCH
Absolute Bagels ($, p. 169)
Artie's New York Delicatessen ($, p. 180)
Barney Greengrass, the Sturgeon King ($, p. 180)
Big Wong King ★ ($, p. 145)
Bubby's Pie Company ★ ($$, p. 143)
Clinton St. Baking Company ★ ($, p. 149)
Ess-A-Bagel ($, p. 169)
Good Enough to Eat ★ ($, p. 195)
Katz's Delicatessen ★ ($, p. 149)
Lansky's ($, p. 180)
Murray's Bagels ($, p. 169)
Norma's ★★ ($$, p. 175)
Sylvia's ($, p. 202)

KEY TO ABBREVIATIONS:
$$$$** = Very Expensive   **$$$** = Expensive   **$$** = Moderate   **$ = Inexpensive

CHINESE

Big Wong King ★ ($, p. 145)
Great New York Noodletown ★★
 ($, p. 145)
Lan Sheng ($$, p. 157)
Szechuan Gourmet ($$, p. 157)
Wo Hop ($, p. 152)

CONTEMPORARY AMERICAN

BLT Market ★★ ($$$$, p. 170)
5 and Diamond ($$$, p. 203)
Ouest ★★★ ($$$, p. 191)
Park Avenue Winter ★★
 ($$$, p. 198)
The Mark Restaurant ★★★
 ($$$, p. 197)
The River Café ($$$$, p. 205)
Water's Edge ★★ ($$$, p. 208)

DELICATESSEN

Artie's New York Delicatessen
 ($, p. 180)
Barney Greengrass, the Sturgeon
 King ($, p. 180)
Carnegie Deli ($, p. 180)
Junior's ($, p. 207)
Katz's Delicatessen ★ ($, p. 149)
Lansky's ($, p. 180)
Stage Deli ($, p. 180)

FILIPINO

Ihawan ($, p. 208)

FRENCH

Bar Breton ($$, p. 168)
Café Boulud ★ ($$$, p. 197)
Café Luxembourg ★($$$, p. 190)
Capsouto Frères ★ ($$$, p. 140)
Landmarc ★★ ($$$, p. 142)
Le Bernardin ($$$$, p. 170)
Marseille ★ ($$, p. 175)
Mas ★★ ($$$$, p. 154)
Millesime ★★ ($$, p. 168)
Nice Matin ★ ($$, p. 193)
Nizza ★★ ($, p. 177)

GERMAN

Bier International ★ ($$, p. 203)
Prime Meats ★★ ($$$ p. 206)

GREEK

Barbounia ★ ($$$, p. 164)
Kefi ★★★ ($$, p. 193)
Mia Dona ★★ ($$$, p. 184)
Molyvos ★★ ($$$, p. 173)
Thalassa ★★ ($$$, p. 143)
Uncle Nick's ($, p. 181)

INDIAN

Brick Lane Curry House ★
 ($$, p. 151)
Chola ★★ ($$, p. 186)
Dévi ★★ ($$$, p. 166)

ITALIAN

Abboccato ★ ($$$, p. 171)
A Voce Columbus Circle ★★★
 ($$$, p. 190)
Barbetta ★★ ($$$, p. 171)
Becco ★ ($$, p. 175)
Bread ★ ($, p. 150)
Carmine's ★ ($$, p. 192)
Celeste ★★ ($, p. 194)
Covo Trattoria & Pizzeria ★
 ($, p. 200)
Dominick's ($$, p. 204)
Ferdinando's Focacceria ★
 ($, p. 207)
Frankie and Johnnie's Pine Restaurant
 ($$, p. 171)
Frankie's Spuntino ★★★ ($$, p. 148)
Harry's Italian (p. 143)
Hearth ★★ ($$$, p. 151)
'inoteca ★★ ($$, p. 148)
Landmarc ★★ ($$$, p. 142)
La Pizza Fresca Ristorante ★★
 ($$, p. 179)
L'Artusi ★★ ($$, p. 157)
Locanda Verde ★★★($$$, p. 142)
Mario's Restaurant ($$, p. 204)
Mia Dona ★★ ($$$, p. 184)
Motorino ★ ($, p. 179)
Naples 45 ★ ($$, p. 179)
Nick's Family-Style Restaurant and
 Pizzeria ★ ($, p. 198)
Nizza ★★ ($, p. 177)
Osteria Morini ★★ ($$$, p. 149)
SD26 ★($$$, p. 168)
Scarpetta ★★ ($$$, p. 156)

JAPANESE

En Japanese Brasserie ★★★ ($$$, p. 154)
Hakubai ★ ($$$, p. 172)
Morimoto ★★ ($$$, p. 159)
Sapporo ★ ($, p. 180)
Tanuki Tavern ★ ($$$, p. 156)

KOREAN

Han Bat ★ ($, p. 177)
Mandoo Bar ★ ($, p. 177)

LATIN AMERICAN/SOUTH AMERICAN/NUEVO LATINO

Flor de Mayo ($, p. 194)
Nuela ★ ($$$, p. 167)
Rayuela ★★ ($$$, p. 146)

LIGHT FARE/TAKEOUT

Absolute Bagels ($, p. 169)
Artie's New York Delicatessen ($, p. 180)
Barney Greengrass, the Sturgeon King ($, p. 180)
Bread ★ ($, p. 150)
Carnegie Deli ($, p. 180)
Eisenberg's Coffee Shop ($, p. 153)
Ess-A-Bagel ($, p. 169)
Gray's Papaya ($, p. 144)
H&H Bagels ($, p. 169)
Junior's ($, p. 207)
Katz's Delicatessen ★ ($, p. 149)
Kossar's Bialys ($, p. 169)
Lansky's ($, p. 180)
Murray's Bagels ($, p. 169)
Nathan's Famous ($, p. 207)
2nd Avenue Deli ★ ($, p. 180)
Shorty's ★ ($, p. 144)
'sNice ($, p. 158)
Stage Deli ($, p. 180)

MALAYSIAN

Fatty Crab ($$, p. 192)
Nyonya ★ ($, p. 146)

MEDITERRANEAN

Barbounia ★ ($$$, p. 164)
Landmarc ★★ ($$$, p. 142)
Park Avenue Winter ★★ ($$$, p. 198)

MEXICAN/TEX-MEX/SOUTHWESTERN

Cascabel Taqueria ★ ($, p. 198)
Noche Mexicana ★ ($, p. 196)
Pampano ★★ ($$$, p. 184)

MIDDLE EASTERN

Afghan Kebab House ($, p. 176)
Barbounia ★ ($$$, p. 164)

PIZZA

Big Nick's Burger and Pizza Joint ★ ($, p. 194)
Covo Trattoria & Pizzeria ★ ($, p. 200)
DiFara Pizza ★ ($, p. 178)
Grimaldi's Pizzeria ($, p. 178)
Joe's Pizza ($, p. 144)
John's Pizzeria ($, p. 178)
Keste Pizzeria & Vino ★★ ($$, p. 178)
La Pizza Fresca Ristorante ★ ($$, p. 179)
Lombardi's ($, p. 178)
Motorino ★ ($, p. 179)
Naples 45 ($$, p. 179)
Patsy's Pizzeria ★ ($, p. 178)
Totonno's Pizzeria Napolitano ($, p. 178)
Trattoria Zero Otto Nove ★★ ($$, p. 179)

PORTUGUESE

Aldea ★★ ($$$, p. 164)

SCANDINAVIAN

Aquavit ★★★ ($$$, p. 181)

SEAFOOD

BLT Fish ★★ ($$$, p. 165)
Ed's Lobster Bar ★★ ($$, p. 150)
Great New York Noodletown ★★ ($, p. 145)
Le Bernardin ($$$$, p. 170)
Millesime ★★ ($$, p. 168)
Oceana ★★★ ($$$, p. 173)
Ocean Grill ★★ ($$$, p. 190)
Oyster Bar & Restaurant ★ ($$, p. 187)
Pampano ★★ ($$$, p. 184)
Vincent's Clam Bar ($, p. 152)

SOUL FOOD

Amy Ruth's ($, p. 202)
Miss Mamie's Spoonbread Too
($$, p. 202)
Rack & Soul ($$, p. 174)
Sylvia's ($, p. 202)

SPANISH/TAPAS

Bar Basque ★ ($$$, p. 158)
Boqueria ★★ ($$$, p. 149)
El Faro ★ ($$, p. 152)
La Fonda Boricua ★ ($, p. 203)
La Nacional ★★ ($$, p. 159)
Nuela ★ ($$$, p. 167)
Rayuela ★★ ($$$, p. 146)

STEAK

Ben & Jack's ★($$$, p. 163)
Ben Benson's Steakhouse
($$$$, p. 162)
Benjamin Steakhouse ★
($$$$, p. 163)
BLT Steak ★★★ ($$$, p. 183)
Bull and Bear ($$$, p. 162)
Frankie & Johnnie's ★★
($$$, p. 171)

Gallagher's Steakhouse ($$$, p. 162)
Harry's Café & Steak ★★
($$$, p. 142)
Keens Steakhouse ★★★
($$$, p. 172)
The Parlor Steakhouse ★
($$$, p. 163)
Peter Luger Steakhouse ★★
($$$, p. 205)
Porter House New York ★★
($$$$, p. 163)
The Post House ★★ ($$$$, p. 196)
Primehouse ★ ($$$, p. 163)
Prime Meats ★★ ($$$, p. 206)
Quality Meats ★ ($$$$, p. 163)
Strip House ★★ ($$$$, p. 163)
Uncle Jack's Steakhouse ★
($$$$, p. 162)

THAI

Arunee Thai ($, p. 208)
Wondee Siam ★ ($, p. 181)

VIETNAMESE

Pho Viet Huong ★ ($, p. 146)

5

WHERE TO DINE

Restaurants by Cuisine

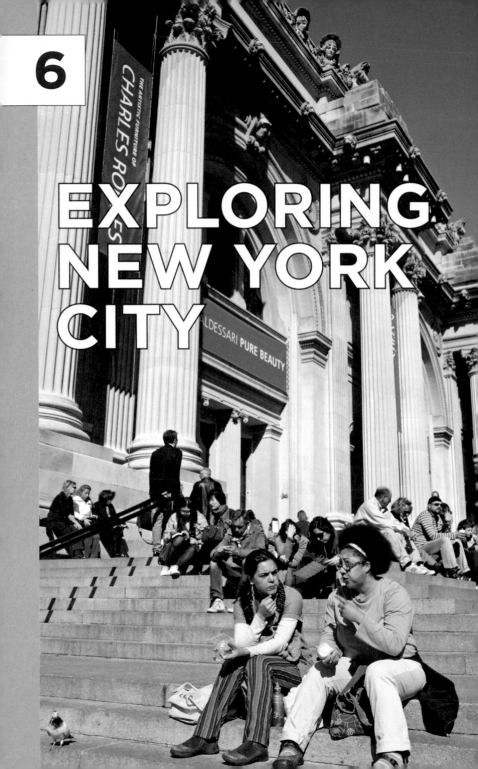

6

EXPLORING NEW YORK CITY

f this is your first trip to New York, face the facts: It will be impossible to take in the entire city—this time. Because New York is almost unfathomably big and constantly changing, you could live your whole life here and still make fascinating daily discoveries—we New Yorkers do. This chapter is designed to give you an overview of what's available in this multifaceted place so you can narrow your choices to an itinerary that's digestible for the amount of time you'll be here—be it a day, a week, or something in between.

So don't try to tame New York—you can't. Decide on a few must-see attractions, then let the city take you on its own ride. See chapter 3, "New York City Neighborhoods & Suggested Tours," for suggestions on what to see and how to cram it all into 1, 2, or 3 days. But inevitably, as you make your way around the city, you'll be blown off course by unplanned diversions that are as much fun as what you meant to see.

After all, the true New York is in the details. As you dash from sight to sight, take time to admire a cornice on a prewar building, linger over a cup of coffee at a sidewalk cafe, or just idle away a few minutes on a bench watching New Yorkers parade through their daily lives.

SIGHTS & ATTRACTIONS BY NEIGHBORHOOD

Manhattan

CHELSEA

Bateaux New York (p. 299)
Chelsea Piers Sports & Entertainment Complex (p. 297)
Rubin Museum of Art (p. 267)
Spirit Cruises (p. 300)

EAST VILLAGE

Merchant's House Museum ★ (p. 274)

THE FLATIRON DISTRICT/ UNION SQUARE

Center for Jewish History (p. 248)
Flatiron Building (p. 273)

Union Square Greenmarket ★★ (p. 296)
Union Square Park (p. 295)

GREENWICH VILLAGE

Washington Square Park (p. 296)

HARLEM

Abyssinian Baptist Church ★ (p. 278)
Astor Row Houses (p. 271)
Dwyer Cultural Center (p. 250)
Jumel Terrace Historic District (p. 271)
Morris-Jumel Mansion ★ (p. 274)
Mother A.M.E. Zion Church (p. 280)
Schomburg Center for Research in Black Culture (p. 268)
Strivers' Row (p. 271)

FACING PAGE: Visitors take a break from exploring (as you should, too!) on the steps of the Metropolitan Museum of Art.

Subway Access Alert

On almost every weekend, and throughout the year, changes in normal subway service tend to occur. I *strongly* recommend you check with the **Metropolitan Transit Authority** at ✆ **718/330-1234** or **www.mta.info** before you plan your travel routes; your hotel concierge or any token-booth clerk should also be able to assist you. ***Note:*** The MTA website is excellent and easy to maneuver.

LOWER EAST SIDE

LOWER MANHATTAN/THE FINANCIAL DISTRICT/NEW YORK HARBOR

MIDTOWN EAST

SOHO

TIMES SQUARE & MIDTOWN WEST

Circle Line Sightseeing Cruises ★★
(p. 299)
Gray Line New York (p. 301)
International Center of Photography
★ (p. 253)
Liberty Helicopters (p. 301)
Madison Square Garden (p. 337)
Museum of Arts and Design (formerly
American Craft Museum) ★
(p. 257)
Museum of Modern Art ★★
(p. 237)
New York Waterway ★★ (p. 299)
The Paley Center for Media (p. 266)
Radio City Music Hall ★ (p. 240)
Rockefeller Center ★★ (p. 238)
Times Square (p. 244)
Intrepid Sea, Air & Space Museum
★★ (p. 253)

UPPER EAST SIDE

Asia Society (p. 247)
Central Park ★★★ (p. 282)
Central Park Zoo ★ (p. 287)
Cooper-Hewitt National Design
Museum ★ (p. 250)
El Museo del Barrio (p. 251)
The Frick Collection ★★ (p. 251)
The Grolier Club (p. 252)
The Institute for the Study of the
Ancient World (p. 252)
The Jewish Museum (p. 254)
Metropolitan Museum of Art ★★★
(p. 234)
Museum of the City of New York
(p. 259)
Neue Galerie New York (p. 260)
Solomon R. Guggenheim Museum ★
(p. 264)
Temple Emanu-El (p. 280)
Tisch Children's Zoo ★ (p. 287)
Whitney Museum of American Art
★★ (p. 245)

UPPER MANHATTAN

The Cloisters ★★ (p. 249)
Dyckman Farmhouse Museum
(p. 274)
The Little Red Lighthouse
(p. 298)

UPPER WEST SIDE

American Museum of Natural History
★★★ (p. 220)
The Ansonia (p. 271)
Cathedral of St. John the Divine ★
(p. 278)
Central Park ★★★ (p. 282)
Children's Museum of Manhattan ★
(p. 309)
The Dakota (p. 271)
New-York Historical Society ★
(p. 265)
Riverside Park ★★ (p. 294)
Rose Center for Earth and Space ★
(p. 220)
Wollman Rink ★ (p. 289)

Outer Boroughs
THE BRONX

The Bronx Museum of the Arts
(p. 319)
Bronx Zoo Wildlife Conservation Park
★★★ (p. 312)
City Island (p. 318)
Edgar Allan Poe Cottage (p. 274)
New York Botanical Garden ★ (p. 315)
Pelham Bay Park (p. 318)
Wave Hill ★ (p. 317)
Woodlawn Cemetery (p. 319)
Yankee Stadium (p. 334)

BROOKLYN

Brooklyn Botanic Garden ★ (p. 320)
Brooklyn Children's Museum (p. 309)
Brooklyn Heights Historic District
(p. 326)
Brooklyn Lyceum (p. 328)
Brooklyn Museum of Art ★★
(p. 321)
Brooklyn Tabernacle ★ (p. 322)
Coney Island ★★ (p. 322)
Coney Island Museum (p. 323)
Dime Savings Bank (p. 328)
Grand Army Plaza (p. 326)
New York Aquarium (p. 323)
New York Transit Museum ★ (p. 324)
Pratt Institute (p. 328)
Prison Ship Martyrs Monument
(p. 328)

THE TOP ATTRACTIONS

In addition to the choices below, don't forget **Central Park** ★★★, the great green swath that is, just by virtue of its existence, New York City's greatest marvel. Central Park is so big and multifaceted that it earns its own section, starting on p. 282.

American Museum of Natural History ★★★ ☺ This is one of the hottest museum tickets in town, thanks to the **Rose Center for Earth and Space** ★, whose four-story-tall planetarium sphere hosts the show *Journey to the Stars*, narrated by Whoopi Goldberg, about the lives and deaths of stars. Prepare to be blown away by this astounding, literally earth-shaking short film.

Buy your tickets in advance for the Space Show in order to guarantee admission (they're available online); I also recommend buying tickets in advance for a specific IMAX film or special exhibition, such as the Butterfly Conservatory (see below), especially during peak seasons (summer, autumn, holiday time) and for weekend visits; otherwise, you might miss out. Other must-sees include the **Big Bang Theater,** which re-creates the theoretical birth of the universe; the **Hall of the Universe,** with its very own 16-ton meteorite; and the terrific **Hall of Planet Earth,** which focuses on the geologic processes of our home planet (great volcano display!). All in all, you'll need a minimum of 2 hours to fully explore the Rose Center.

The rest of the 4-square-block museum is nothing to sneeze at, either. Founded in 1869, it houses the world's greatest natural-science collection in a group of buildings

See the planets and stars up close at the Rose Center for Earth and Space.

WHAT'S new THIS YEAR AROUND TOWN

The **National September 11 Memorial** is scheduled to open on September 11, 2011. Ten years after the event that is seared permanently in our memories took place, this long-awaited memorial is realized. The Memorial consists of two massive pools set within the footprints of the Twin Towers, with the largest manmade waterfalls in the country cascading down their sides. The Plaza is shaded by 400 white oak trees. **Note:** The September 11th Memorial Museum, located beneath the Memorial, will open in 2012.

Pier 25, the newest section of Hudson River Park, opened to the public in 2010. Located at N. Moore Street in TriBeCa, Pier 25 is the longest pier in Hudson River Park and includes an 18-hole miniature golf course, snack bar, sand volleyball court, and children's playground. The adjoining upland section includes a basketball court, a skate park, natural lawns, and seating areas.

The **Museum of Moving Image** reopened in January 2011 after a $67 million expansion and renovation. It's the only museum in America that explores all aspects anything that moves across a screen, including film, television, video and digital media. This is not just a walk down memory lane, it *is* memory lane. Located in Astoria, Queens, the museum is well worth a visit. It may be one of the few museums in New York—along with the Museum of Natural History—that is equally appealing to children and to adults.

made of towers and turrets, pink granite, and red brick. The diversity of the holdings is astounding: some 36 million specimens, ranging from microscopic organisms to the world's largest cut gem, the Brazilian Princess Topaz (21,005 carats). Rose Center aside, it would take you all day to see the entire museum, and then you *still* wouldn't get to everything. If you don't have a lot of time, you can see the best of the best on free highlights tours offered daily every hour at 15 minutes after the hour from 10:15am to 3:15pm. Free daily spotlight tours, thematic tours that change monthly, are also offered; stop by an information desk for the day's schedule. High-tech audio tours that allow you to access narration in the order you choose are also available to help you make sense of it all.

If you only see one exhibit, see the **dinosaurs ★**, which take up the fourth floor.

The Hall of Biodiversity is an impressive multimedia exhibit, but its doom-and-gloom story about the future of rainforests and other natural habitats might be too much for the little ones. Kids 5 and up should head to the Discovery Room, with lots of hands-on exhibits and experiments. (***Parents, be prepared:*** There seems to be a gift shop overflowing with stuffed animals at every turn.) The Anne and Bernard Spitzer Hall of Human Origins traces the evolution of man and even offers children's workshops where kids can compare skull casts of early humans.

The museum excels at special exhibitions, so check to see what will be on while you're in town in case any advance planning is required. The magical **Butterfly Conservatory ★**, a walk-in enclosure housing nearly 500 free-flying tropical butterflies, has developed into a can't-miss fixture from October through May; check to see if it's in the house while you're in town.

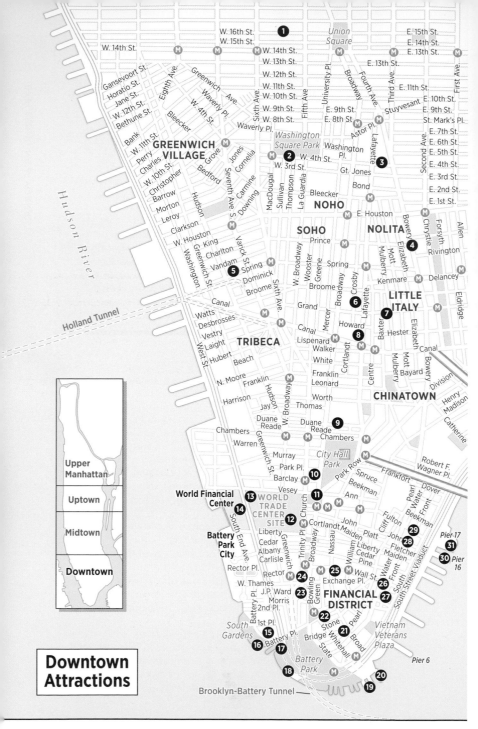

Downtown Attractions

Midtown Attractions

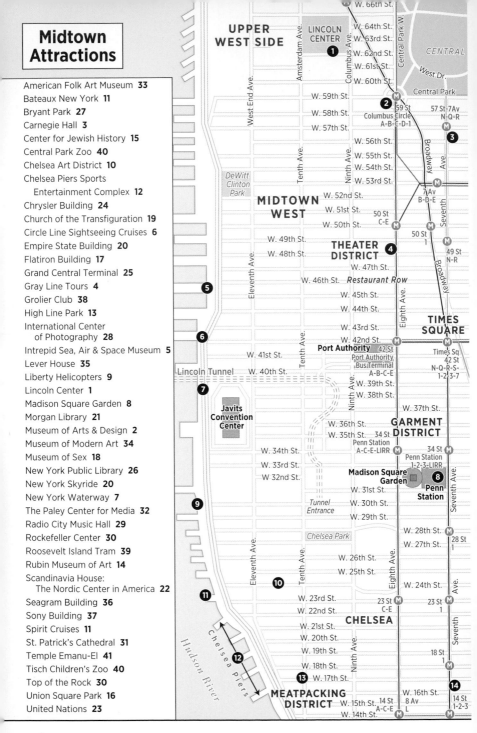

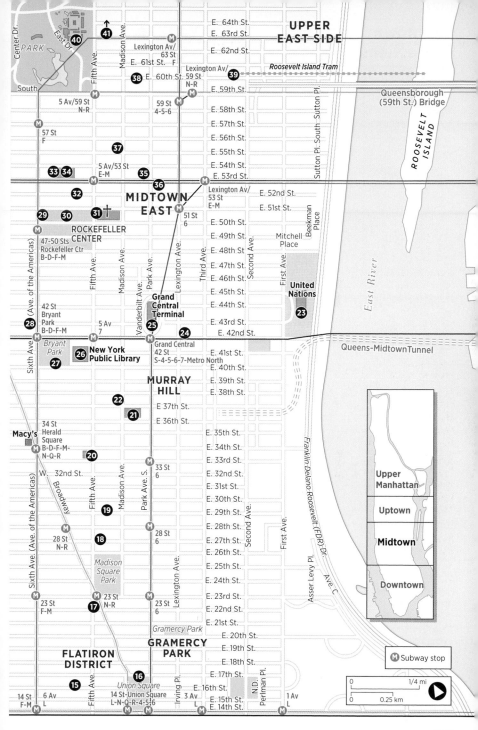

Uptown Attractions

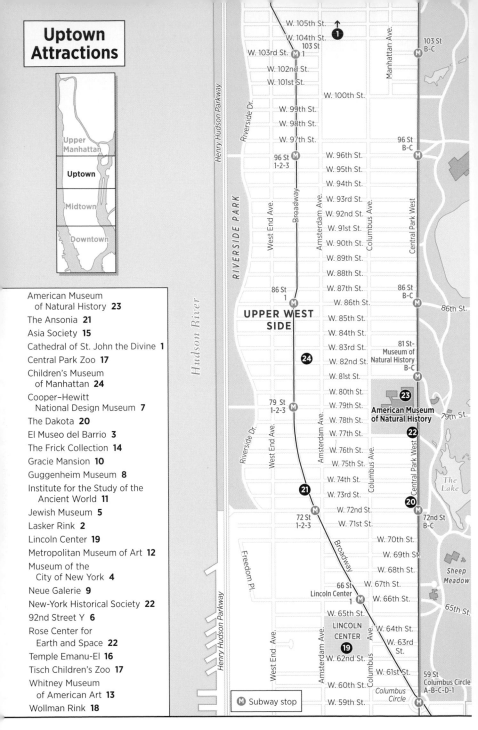

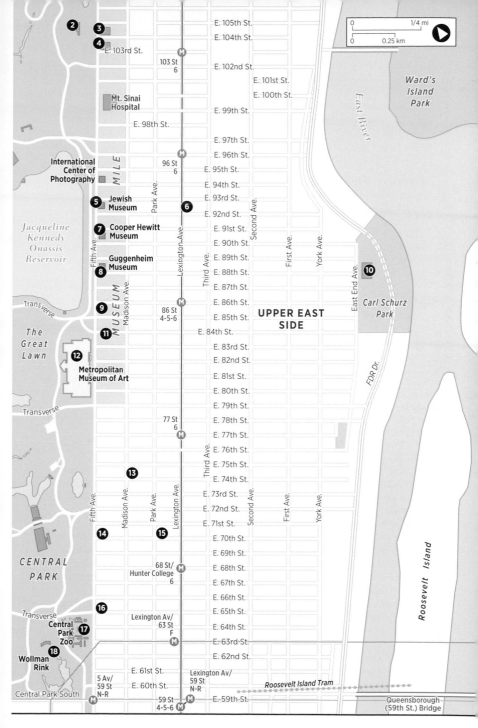

E. 105th St.
E. 104th St.
E. 103rd St.

103 St
6

E. 102nd St.
E. 101st St.
E. 100th St.
E. 99th St.

Mt. Sinai
Hospital

E. 98th St.
E. 97th St.
E. 96th St.

96 St
6

E. 95th St.
E. 94th St.
E. 93rd St.
E. 92nd St.
E. 91st St.
E. 90th St.
E. 89th St.
E. 88th St.
E. 87th St.
E. 86th St.

International
Center of
Photography

Jewish
Museum

Cooper Hewitt
Museum

Guggenheim
Museum

Jacqueline
Kennedy
Onassis
Reservoir

MUSEUM MILE

Park Ave.
Lexington Ave.
Third Ave.
Second Ave.
First Ave.
York Ave.
East End Ave.

Carl Schurz
Park

Ward's
Island
Park

East River

86 St
4-5-6

E. 85th St.
E. 84th St.
E. 83rd St.
E. 82nd St.
E. 81st St.
E. 80th St.
E. 79th St.
E. 78th St.
E. 77th St.
E. 76th St.
E. 75th St.
E. 74th St.
E. 73rd St.
E. 72nd St.
E. 71st St.
E. 70th St.
E. 69th St.
E. 68th St.
E. 67th St.
E. 66th St.
E. 65th St.
E. 64th St.
E. 63rd St.
E. 62nd St.

UPPER EAST
SIDE

The
Great
Lawn

Transverse

Metropolitan
Museum of Art

77 St
6

Fifth Ave.
Madison Ave.
Park Ave.
Lexington Ave.
Third Ave.
Second Ave.
First Ave.
York Ave.

CENTRAL
PARK

Transverse

68 St/
Hunter College
6

Lexington Av/
63 St
F

Central
Park
Zoo

Wollman
Rink

Central Park South

5 Av/
59 St
N-R

E. 61st St.
E. 60th St.

59 St
4-5-6

Lexington Av/
59 St
N-R

E. 59th St.

Roosevelt Island Tram

Queensborough
(59th St.) Bridge

Roosevelt Island

FDR Dr.

Madison Ave.

Fifth Ave.

0   1/4 mi
0   0.25 km

227

Note: The Museum's website is a trip in itself, and well worth a visit. It's got all sorts of interactive things going on for kids (click on the "Kids & Families" tab) as well as cool—and free—apps for iPad and iPhone (**www.amnh.org/apps**).

Central Park West (btw. 77th and 81st sts.). ℂ **212/769-5100** for information, or 212/769-5200 for tickets (tickets can also be ordered online for an additional $4 charge). www.amnh.org. Suggested admission $16 adults, $12 seniors and students, $9 children 2–12; Space Show admission $24 adults, $18 seniors and students, $14 children 2-12. Additional charges for IMAX movies and some special exhibitions. Daily 10am–5:45pm; Rose Center also 1st Fri of every month until 8:45pm. Subway: B, C to 81st St.; 1 to 79th St.

Brooklyn Bridge ★★ 📷 Its Gothic-inspired stone pylons and intricate steel-cable webs have moved poets such as Walt Whitman and Hart Crane to sing the praises of this great span, the first to cross the East River and connect Manhattan to Brooklyn. Begun in 1867 and ultimately completed in 1883, the Brooklyn Bridge is now the city's best-known symbol of the age of growth that seized the city during the late 19th century. Walk across the bridge and imagine the awe that New Yorkers of that age felt at seeing two boroughs joined by this span. It's still astounding.

Walking the bridge: Walking the Brooklyn Bridge is one of my all-time favorite New York activities, although there's no doubt that the lower Manhattan views from the bridge now have a painful resonance as well as a joyous spirit. A wide wood-plank pedestrian walkway is elevated above the traffic, making it a relatively peaceful, and popular, walk. It's a great vantage point from which to contemplate the New York skyline and the East River.

There's a sidewalk entrance on Park Row, just across from City Hall Park (take the 4, 5, or 6 train to Brooklyn Bridge/City Hall). But why do this walk *away*

A Money & Time-Saving Tip

CityPass may be New York's best sightseeing deal. Pay one price ($79, or $59 for kids 6–17) for admission to six major attractions: The American Museum of Natural History (including the Space Show), the Guggenheim Museum or Top of the Rock, the Empire State Building, the Museum of Modern Art, the Metropolitan Museum of Art and the Cloisters, Statue of Liberty and Ellis Island, or a 2-hour Circle Line harbor cruise. Individual tickets would cost more than twice as much (though I should point out that the Met and Museum of Natural History are "suggested" admission fees).

More important, CityPass is not a coupon book. It contains actual tickets, so you can bypass lengthy lines. This can save you hours, as sights such as the Empire State Building often have ticket lines of an hour or more.

CityPass is good for 9 days from the first time you use it. It's sold at all participating attractions and online at **www.citypass.com/city/ny**. To avoid online service and shipping fees, you may buy the pass at your first attraction (start at an attraction that's likely to have the shortest admission line, such as the Guggenheim, or arrive before opening to avoid a wait at such spots as the Empire State Building). However, if you begin your sightseeing on a weekend or during holidays, when lines are longest, online purchase may be worthwhile.

For more information, call CityPass at ℂ **888/330-5008** (note, however, that CityPass is not sold over the phone).

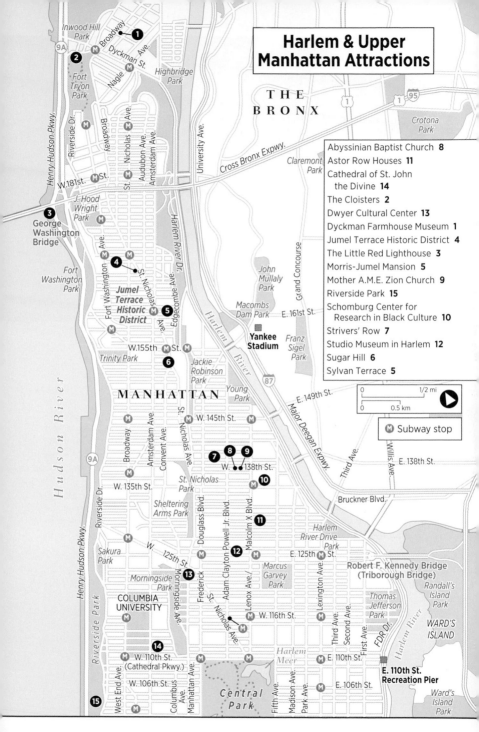

Harlem & Upper Manhattan Attractions

Abbyssinian Baptist Church **8**
Astor Row Houses **11**
Cathedral of St. John
  the Divine **14**
The Cloisters **2**
Dwyer Cultural Center **13**
Dyckman Farmhouse Museum **1**
Jumel Terrace Historic District **4**
The Little Red Lighthouse **3**
Morris-Jumel Mansion **5**
Mother A.M.E. Zion Church **9**
Riverside Park **15**
Schomburg Center for
  Research in Black Culture **10**
Strivers' Row **7**
Studio Museum in Harlem **12**
Sugar Hill **6**
Sylvan Terrace **5**

Ⓜ Subway stop

The Brooklyn Bridge.

from Manhattan, toward the far less impressive Brooklyn skyline? Instead, for Manhattan skyline views, take an A or C train to High Street, one stop into Brooklyn. From there, you'll be on the bridge in no time: Come above ground, then walk through the little park to Cadman Plaza East and head downslope (left) to the stairwell that will take you up to the footpath. (Following Prospect Place under the bridge, turning right onto Cadman Plaza East, will also take you directly to the stairwell.) It's a 20- to 40-minute stroll over the bridge to Manhattan, depending on your pace, the amount of foot traffic, and the number of stops you make to behold the spectacular views (there are benches along the way). The footpath will deposit you right at City Hall Park.

Tasty tips: The perfect complement to your stroll over the Brooklyn Bridge is a stop for pizza at **Grimaldi's** (p. 178), followed by homemade ice cream at the **Brooklyn Ice Cream Factory** (© **718/246-3963**), at the Fulton Ferry Fire Boat House on the river and in the shadow of the bridge. The pizza and ice cream will fortify you for your stroll into Manhattan.

Subway: A, C to High St.; 4, 5, 6 to Brooklyn Bridge–City Hall.

Ellis Island ★★   One of New York's most moving sights, the restored Ellis Island opened in 1990, slightly north of Liberty Island. Roughly 40% of Americans (myself included) can trace their heritage back to an ancestor who came through here. For the 62 years when it was America's main entry point for immigrants (1892–1954), Ellis Island processed some 12 million people. The greeting was often brusque—especially in the early years of the century (until 1924), when as many as 12,000 came through in a single day. The statistics can be overwhelming, but the Immigration Museum skillfully relates the story of Ellis Island and immigration in America by placing the emphasis on personal experience.

Visitors can learn about the immigrant experience at Ellis Island.

It's difficult to leave the museum unmoved. Today you enter the Main Building's baggage room, just as the immigrants did, and then climb the stairs to the Registry Room, with its dramatic vaulted tiled ceiling, where millions waited anxiously for medical and legal processing. A step-by-step account of the immigrants' voyage is detailed in the exhibit, with haunting photos and touching oral histories. What might be the most poignant exhibit is "Treasures from Home," 1,000 objects and photos donated by descendants of immigrants, including family heirlooms, religious articles, and rare clothing and jewelry. Outside, the American Immigrant Wall of Honor commemorates the names of more than 500,000 immigrants and their families, from Myles Standish and George Washington's great-grandfather to the forefathers of John F. Kennedy, Jay Leno, and Barbra Streisand. You can even research your own family's history at the interactive American Family Immigration History Center. You might also make time to see the award-winning short film *Island of Hope, Island of Tears,* which plays on a continuous loop in two theaters. Short live theatrical performances depicting the immigrant experience are also often part of the day's events.

Touring tip: Ferries run daily to Ellis Island and Liberty Island from Battery Park and Liberty State Park at frequent intervals; see the **Statue of Liberty** listing (p. 243) for details.

Empire State Building Ticket Buying

Lines can be long, with a wait of up to 90 minutes during high season at the concourse-level ticket booth, so consider purchasing advance tickets online using a credit card at **www.esbnyc.com**. Tickets to the ESB are also included in your **CityPass** (see box, p. 228). You'll pay slightly more—tickets were priced $2 higher on the website at press time—but it's well worth it, especially if you're visiting during busy seasons, when the line can be hours long. You're not required to choose a time or date for your tickets in advance; they can be used on any regular open day. Print them out at home and proceed directly to the turnstiles—past everyone who didn't plan as well as you did!

Now you can call in advance to get an estimate of your wait in line, along with a report on the visibility from the observatory. Dial ℂ 877/692-8439 for the service.

The Empire State Building.

In New York Harbor. ℂ **212/363-3200** (general info), or 877/LADY-TIX (523-9849; ticket/ferry info). www.nps.gov/elis/index.htm, www.ellisisland.org, or www.statuecruises.com. Free admission (ferry ticket charge). Daily 9:30am–5pm (last ferry departs around 2pm), with extended hours in the summer. For subway and ferry details, see the Statue of Liberty listing on p. 243 (ferry trip includes stops at both sights).

Empire State Building ★★★ It took 60,000 tons of steel, 10 million bricks, 2.5 million feet of electrical wire, 120 miles of pipe, and 7 million man-hours to build. King Kong climbed it in 1933—and again in 2005. A plane slammed into it in 1945. The World Trade Center superseded it in 1970 as the island's tallest building. And in 1997, a gunman ascended it to stage a deadly shooting. On that horrific day of September 11, 2001, it once again regained its status as New York City's tallest building, after 31 years of taking second place. And through it all, the Empire State Building has remained one of the city's favorite landmarks and its signature high-rise. Completed in 1931, the limestone-and-stainless-steel Streamline Deco dazzler climbs 102 stories (1,454 ft.) and now harbors the offices of fashion firms, and, in its upper reaches, a jumble of high-tech broadcast equipment.

Always a conversation piece, the Empire State Building glows every night, bathed in colored floodlights to commemorate events of significance—red, white, and blue for Independence Day; green for St. Patrick's Day; red, black, and green for Martin Luther King Day; blue and white for Hanukkah; even blue and white for the Yankees' World Series victory in 2009 (you can find a complete lighting schedule online). The familiar silver spire can be seen from all over the city.

The best views, and what keeps the nearly three million visitors coming every year, are the ones from the 86th- and 102nd-floor observatories. The lower

Vanderbilt Lobby in Grand Central Terminal.

one is best—you can walk out on a windy deck and look through coin-operated viewers (bring quarters!) over what, on a clear day, can be as much as an 80-mile visible radius. The citywide panorama is magnificent. One surprise is the flurry of rooftop activity, an aspect of city life that thrives unnoticed from our everyday sidewalk vantage point. The higher observation deck is glass-enclosed and cramped.

Light fog can create an admirably moody effect, but it goes without saying that a clear day is best. Dusk brings the most remarkable views and the biggest crowds. Consider going in the morning, when the light is still low on the horizon, keeping glare to a minimum. Starry nights are pure magic.

In your haste to go up, don't rush through the three-story-high marble lobby without pausing to admire its features, which include a wonderful Streamline mural and a recently restored ceiling mural etched in gold leaf.

350 Fifth Ave. (at 34th St.). ✆ **212/736-3100.** www.esbnyc.com. 86th Floor Observatory admission $20 adults, $18 seniors, $14 children 6–12, free for children 5 and under. Daily 8am–2am (last elevator at 1:15am). Subway: B, D, F, N, Q, R, M to 34th St.; 6 to 33rd St.

Grand Central Terminal ★★ Even if you're not catching one of the subway lines or Metro-North commuter trains that rumble through Grand Central Terminal, come for a visit; it's one of the most magnificent public places in the country. And even if you arrive and leave by subway, be sure to exit the station, walking a couple of blocks south, to about 40th Street, before you turn around to admire Jules-Alexis Coutan's neoclassical sculpture *Transportation* hovering over the south entrance, with a majestic Mercury, the Roman god of commerce and travel, as its central figure.

The greatest visual impact comes when you enter the vast majestic main concourse. The high windows allow sunlight to penetrate the space, glinting off the half-acre Tennessee marble floor. The brass clock over the central kiosk gleams, as do the gold- and nickel-plated chandeliers piercing the side archways. The masterful sky ceiling, a brilliant greenish blue, depicts the constellations of the winter sky above New York. They're lit with 59 stars, surrounded by dazzling 24-carat gold and emitting light fed through fiber-optic cables, their intensities roughly replicating the magnitude of the actual stars as seen from Earth. Look carefully and you'll see a patch near one corner left unrestored as a reminder of the neglect once visited on this splendid overhead masterpiece. On the east end of the main concourse is a grand marble staircase.

This dramatic Beaux Arts splendor serves as a hub of social activity as well. Excellent-quality retail shops and restaurants have taken over the mezzanine and lower levels. The highlights of the West Mezzanine are **Michael Jordan's the Steak House N.Y.C.**, a gorgeous Art Deco space that allows you to dine within view of the sky ceiling as well as the gorgeously restored **Campbell Apartment** (p. 435), which serves cocktails. Off the main concourse at street level, there's a nice mix of specialty shops and national retailers, as well as the truly grand Grand Central Market for gourmet foods. **The New York Transit Museum Store** (p. 380), in the shuttle passage, houses city transit–related exhibitions and a terrific gift shop that's worth a look for transit buffs. The lower **dining concourse** ★ houses a stellar food court and the famous **Oyster Bar & Restaurant** (see chapter 5 for details on both).

During the Christmas holidays, Grand Central Terminal is even more special, with laser shows every 30 minutes on the ceiling of the main concourse, a toy train exhibit at the New York Transit Museum Store, and a crafts fair off the Main Concourse.

The **Municipal Art Society** (✆ **212/935-3960;** www.mas.org) offers a walking tour of Grand Central Terminal on Wednesday at 12:30pm, which meets at the information booth on the Grand Concourse (for a $10 "suggested donation"). An audio tour is available on headsets or for download.

42nd St. at Park Ave. ✆ **212/532-4900.** www.grandcentralterminal.com. Subway: S, 4, 5, 6, or 7 to 42nd St./Grand Central.

Metropolitan Museum of Art ★★★   Home of blockbuster after blockbuster, the Metropolitan Museum of Art attracts some five million people a year, more than any other spot in New York City. And it's no wonder—this place is magnificent. At 1.6 million square feet, this is the largest museum in the Western Hemisphere. Nearly all the world's cultures are on display through the ages—from Egyptian mummies to ancient Greek statuary to Islamic carvings to Renaissance paintings to Native American masks to 20th-century decorative arts—and masterpieces are the rule. You could go once a week for a lifetime and still find something new on each visit.

So unless you plan on spending your entire vacation in the museum (some people do), you cannot see the entire collection on one visit. My recommendation is to give it a good day—or better yet, 2 half-days so you don't burn out. One good way to get an overview is to take advantage of the little-known **Museum Highlights Tour,** offered every day at various times throughout the day (usually btw. 10:15am and 3:30pm; tours also offered in French, Spanish, Italian, Japanese, German, and Korean). Even some New Yorkers who've spent many hours

Cocktails & Art: Evenings at the Met

On Friday and Saturday evenings, the Met remains open late not only for art viewing but also for cocktails in the Great Hall Balcony Bar (4–8:30pm) and classical music from a string ensemble. A slate of after-hours programs (gallery talks, walking tours, family programs) changes by the week; call for the current schedule. The restaurant at Petrie Court Café and Wine Bar stays open until 10:30pm (last reservation at 8:30pm), and dinner is usually accompanied by piano music.

Temple of Dendur, from the outside in.

in the museum could profit from this once-over. Visit the museum's website for a schedule of this and subject-specific walking tours (Old Masters Paintings, American Period Rooms, Arts of China, Islamic Art, and so on); you can also get a schedule of the day's tours at the Visitor Services desk when you arrive. A daily schedule of Gallery Talks is available as well.

The least overwhelming way to see the Met on your own is to pick up a map at the round desk in the entry hall and choose to concentrate on what you like, whether it's 17th-century paintings, American furniture, or the art of the South Pacific. Highlights include the American Wing's Garden Court, with its 19th-century sculpture; the terrific ground-level Costume Hall; and the Frank Lloyd Wright room. The beautifully renovated Roman and Greek galleries are overwhelming, but in a marvelous way, as are the collections of Byzantine Art and later Chinese art. The highlight of the Egyptian collection is the Temple of Dendur, in a dramatic, purpose-built glass-walled gallery with Central Park views. The Greek Galleries, which at last fully realize McKim, Mead & White's grand neoclassical plans of 1917, and the Ancient Near East Galleries, are particularly of note. But it all depends on what your interests are. Special exhibitions can range from "Orazio and Artemisia Gentileschi: Father and Daughter Painters in Baroque Italy" to "Earthly Bodies: Irving Penn's Nudes, 1949–50." The Met now offers **podcasts** about current exhibitions at www.metmuseum.org/podcast/index.asp. The speakers can be surprising. For example: *New York Times* food columnist Mark Bittman and restaurateur Danny Meyer discussed John Sloan's painting *Chinese Restaurant,* as part of the exhibition "American Stories: Paintings of Everyday Life, 1765–1915."

The Greek and Roman galleries reopened after a $220-million renovation redesigned and expanded the galleries to 57,000 square feet. The galleries now exhibit ancient artifacts that had been in storage, including 30,000 feet of the square footage devoted to Roman collections.

The Met now opens on "holiday Mondays." On those Mondays, such as Memorial Day or President's Day, the museum is open from 9:30am to 5:30pm.

To purchase **tickets** for concerts and lectures, call (C) **212/570-3949** (Mon–Sat 9:30am–5pm, Sun noon–5pm). The museum contains several dining

Publisher's Choice: *The Heart of the Andes*

Frommer's Associate Publisher Ensley Eikenburg is a docent at the Metropolitan Museum of Art. We asked her to choose a favorite artwork and comment on it. Ensley replies: *"The Heart of the Andes* by Frederic Edwin Church, one of the mainstays of the Met's sizable Hudson River School collection, is back on view in the newly renovated American Wing Galleries. Take your time with this epic landscape and you'll notice that Church has crammed every type of natural element he can think of into his canvas—from the monumental Mount Chimborazo in the background to the infinitesimal spider's nest in the lower-right-hand corner. When the painting was first exhibited in 1859, 13,000 New Yorkers paid 25 cents to see what Ecuador looked like in full color. Think of it as the 19th century's answer to the Discovery Channel. Today it's an American masterpiece that you can spend hours traveling through."

facilities, including a full-service restaurant serving Continental cuisine (© **212/570-3964** for reservations). The roof garden is worth visiting if you're here from spring to autumn, offering peaceful views over Central Park and the city. I think its gift shop—though "shop" seems a bit pedestrian here—is the best of any museum in New York—by a long shot. The Met sells wonderful reproductions of its jewelry, statuettes, and fabrics (for scarves) among many other items that are not only elegant but also quite fairly priced. (The prices can be high in the Boutique, which is separate from the main gift shop. But all the jewelry is stunning.) The bookstore, which is part of the gift shop, is equally wonderful. It's chock-full of books on every artist, era, and style of art imaginable. It also has a superb, wide-ranging array of books about New York City. Stop in. You won't regret it. And you don't need to pay admission to the museum to get in to the gift shop/book store.

The Met's medieval collections are in upper Manhattan at the **Cloisters ★★**; see the full listing on p. 249.

Fifth Ave. at 82nd St. ☎ **212/535-7710.** www.metmuseum.org. Suggested admission (includes same-day entrance to the Cloisters) $20 adults, $15 seniors, $10 students, free for children 11 and under when accompanied by an adult. Sun, holiday Mon (Memorial Day, President's Day, and so forth), and Tues-Thurs 9:30am-5:30pm; Fri-Sat 9:30am-9pm. Strollers are permitted in most areas—inquire at Information Desks for gallery limitations. Oversize and jogging strollers are prohibited. Subway: 4, 5, 6 to 86th St.

Museum of Modern Art ★★

After a 2-year renovation completed in 2004, MoMA grew to almost twice the size of the original. The renovation, designed by Yoshio Taniguchi, highlights space and light, with open rooms, high ceilings, and gardens—a beautiful work of architecture and a perfect complement to the art within. This is where you'll find van Gogh's *Starry Night,* Cezanne's *Bather,* Picasso's *Les Demoiselles d'Avignon,* and the

Explore the best of modern art at MoMA.

great sculpture by Rodin, *Monument to Balzac.* Whenever I visit, I like to browse the fun "Architecture and Design" department, with examples of design for appliances, furniture, and even sports cars. MoMA also features edgy new exhibits and a celebrated film series that attracts serious cinephiles. But the heart of the museum remains the **Abby Aldrich Rockefeller Sculpture Garden,** which has been enlarged; the museum's new design affords additional views of this lovely space from other parts of the museum. And MoMA has installed a museumwide Wi-Fi network so that visitors can access a mobile website on their wireless devices. They can then load up audio tours and commentary; content is available in eight languages as well as in specialized versions for children, teenagers, and the visually impaired. MoMA is one of the most expensive museums in New York, but it does have a "free" day: Fridays from 4 to 8pm. Don't miss its gift shop, either. It has a good range of posters from its collection for starters. Can't afford to buy the real van Gogh *Starry Night?* Get the poster here. MoMA has a blog called "Inside/Out," which is a joint effort with its hip affiliate, P.S.1: **www. moma.org/explore/inside_out**.

11 W. 53rd St. (btw. Fifth and Sixth aves.). ☎ **212/708-9400.** www.moma.org. Admission $20 adults, $16 seniors, $12 students, children 16 and under free if accompanied by an adult. Sat-Mon and Wed-Thurs 10:30am-5:30pm; Fri 10:30am-8pm. Subway: E, M to Fifth Ave.; B, D, F to 47th-50th sts./Rockefeller Center.

Brave New World: Facebook, YouTube, Twitter, and the Rest

It's not just your teenager who uses Facebook, YouTube, or the many new forms of social media to communicate with one another. New York's finest museums, for example (not to mention restaurants, sports teams, and Broadway shows), have their own Facebook pages and tweet on Twitter and even post on YouTube. They simply have recognized that these media have become the ways they can spread the word about their attraction. Which means, of course, that you can join their pages, or follow their tweets, to see what's happening at their houses. I have to admit, though, that it's a bit strange to see an ad for "AARP Medicare Supplement" on the Metropolitan Museum of Art's Facebook page. Still, there's much to recommend. The Met's FB page (www.facebook.com/metmuseum) is appealingly informal yet chock-full of good stuff. I especially like their YouTube page (www.youtube.com/metmuseum). Here, for instance, you might see and hear the head of the museum, Thomas Campbell, talk about the discovery of a Velázquez in the museum's collection, with two senior curators standing next to him spelling out the details. Most people have no idea who runs the Met, much less what he looks and sounds like. YouTube posts also elaborate on current exhibitions, which can mean interviews with the artist whose work is on display. *Note:* Sometimes these media can be hard to find on an institution's website; that's the case with the New-York Historical Society, for example. Its terrific podcasts are buried in a hard-to-find "Media Center" section of their website. It's almost as if some of these institutions are parents who haven't come to terms with a child who has gone Goth. Use the site map.

Rockefeller Center ★★ A Streamline Moderne masterpiece, Rockefeller Center is one of New York's central gathering spots for visitors and New Yorkers alike. A prime example of the city's skyscraper spirit and historic sense of optimism, it was erected mainly in the 1930s, when the city was deep in the Depression—as well as in its most passionate Art Deco phase. Designated a National Historic Landmark in 1988, it's now the world's largest privately owned business-and-entertainment center, with 18 buildings on 21 acres.

For a dramatic approach to the entire complex, start at Fifth Avenue between 49th and 50th streets. The builders purposely created the gentle slope of the Promenade, known here as the Channel Gardens because it's flanked to the south by La Maison Française and to the north by the British Building (the Channel, get it?). You'll also find a number of attractive shops along here, including a big branch of the Metropolitan Museum of Art Store, a good stop for elegant gifts. The Promenade leads to the Lower Plaza, home to the famous ice-skating rink in winter (see next paragraph) and alfresco dining in summer in the shadow of Paul Manship's freshly gilded bronze statue *Prometheus.* All around, the flags of the United Nations' member countries flap in the breeze. Just behind *Prometheus,* in December and early January, towers the city's official and majestic Christmas tree.

Even noble Rockefeller Center is not without its share of controversy. In 1934, workmen, under orders from John D. Rockefeller, Jr., destroyed Diego Rivera's mural, "Man at the Crossroads," at the Center—which had, in fact, been commissioned by Rockefeller—because Rivera had inserted the figure of Lenin

The beautiful Art Deco lobby of Radio City Music Hall.

and refused to take it out. This event is uncompromisingly dramatized in the 2002 movie, *Frida*.

The Rink at Rockefeller Center ★ (② **212/332-7654;** www.rockefeller center.com) is tiny but positively romantic, especially during the holidays, when the giant Christmas tree's multicolored lights twinkle from above, the rink is open from mid-October to April, and you'll skate under the magnificent tree for the month of December. The focal point of this "city within a city" is the building at **30 Rockefeller Plaza** ★, a 70-story showpiece towering over the plaza. It's still one of the city's most impressive buildings; walk through for a look at the granite-and-marble lobby, lined with monumental sepia-toned murals by José Maria Sert. You can pick up a walking-tour brochure on the center's art and architecture at the main information desk in this building.

NBC television maintains studios throughout the complex. *Saturday Night Live* and *Late Night with Jimmy Fallon* originate at 30 Rock—but not *30 Rock,* which is filmed mostly in Queens. NBC's *Today* show is broadcast live on weekdays from 7 to 11am from the glass-enclosed studio on the southwest corner of 49th Street and Rockefeller Plaza; come early if you want a visible spot, and bring your HI MOM! sign.

The 70-minute **NBC Studio Tour** (② **212/664-3700;** www.nbcuniversal store.com) will take you behind the scenes at the Peacock network. The tour changes daily but might include the *Today* show, *NBC Nightly News, Late Night with Jimmy Fallon,* and/or *Saturday Night Live* sets. Who knows? You may even run into Brian Williams or Kathie Lee Gifford. Tours run every 15 minutes Monday through Thursday from 8:30am to 5:30pm, Friday and Saturday from 8:30am to 6:30pm, Sunday from 8:30am to 4:30pm (later on certain summer days); of course, you'll have a better chance of encountering some real live action on a weekday. Tickets are $19 for adults, $16 for seniors and children 6 to 12. **Note:** Children 5 and under are not admitted. You can reserve your tickets in advance

HEADING FOR THE TOP OF THE ROCK

Giving the Empire State Building some friendly competition when it comes to spectacular views is the observation deck of 30 Rockefeller Plaza, known as the **Top of the Rock ★★**. The deck, which comprises floors 67 to 70, which had been closed since 1986, reopened in 2005. The stately deck was constructed in 1933 to resemble the grandeur of a luxury ocean liner, and unlike the Empire State Building, the observation deck here is more spacious and the views, though not quite as high, are just as stunning. You might have just as much fun getting up there as you will on the deck itself; the sky-shuttle elevators with glass ceilings project images from the 1930s through the present day as it zooms its way up. Reserved-time tickets help minimize the lines and are available online. The observation deck is open daily from 8am to midnight; admission rates are $21 for adults, $19 for seniors 62 and older, $14 for ages 6 to 12, and free for children 5 and under. For more information, call ℂ **877/NYC-ROCK** (692-7625) or 212/698-2000, or visit **www. topoftherocknyc.com**.

(reservations are recommended) or buy them right up to tour time at the NBC Experience store, on Rockefeller Plaza at 49th Street. They also offer a 60-minute Rockefeller Center tour Monday to Saturday on the hour from 10am to 5pm, and Sunday 10am to 4pm. Tickets are $12 for adults, $10 for seniors and children 6 to 12; two-tour combination packages are available for $21. Call ℂ **212/ 664-7174.**

Other notable buildings throughout the complex include the International Building, on Fifth Avenue between 50th and 51st streets, worth a look for its Atlas statue out front; and the McGraw-Hill Building on Sixth Avenue, between 48th and 49th streets, with its 50-foot sun triangle on the plaza.

Radio City Music Hall ★, 1260 Sixth Ave., at 50th Street (ℂ **212/247-4777**; www.radiocity. com), is perhaps the most impressive architectural feat of the complex. Designed by Donald Deskey and opened in 1932, it's one of the largest indoor theaters, with 6,200 seats. But its true grandeur derives from its magnificent Art Deco appointments. The crowning touch is the stage's great proscenium arch, which from the distant seats evokes a faraway sun setting on the horizon of the sea. The men's and women's lounges are also splendid. The

Take a peek at the city from the Top of the Rock.

theater hosts the annual "Christmas Spectacular," starring the Rockettes. The illuminating 1-hour **Stage Door Tour** is offered daily from 11am to 3pm; tickets are $19 for adults, $10 for children 11 and under, and $15 for seniors. Btw. 48th and 50th sts., from Fifth to Sixth aves. ✆ **212/247-4777** (tour info). www.radiocity. com. Subway: B, D, F, M to 47th–50th sts./Rockefeller Center.

Solomon R. Guggenheim Museum ★

It's been called a bun, a snail, a concrete tornado, and even a giant wedding cake; bring your kids, and they'll probably see it as New York's coolest opportunity for skateboarding. Whatever description you choose to apply, Frank Lloyd Wright's only New York building, completed in 1959, is best summed up as a brilliant work of architecture—so consistently brilliant that it competes with the art for your attention. If you're looking for the city's best modern art, head to MoMA or the Whitney first; come to the Guggenheim to see the house. The museum underwent a $29-million restoration that was completed in 2008.

It's easy to see the bulk of what's on display in 2 to 4 hours. The museum's spiraling rotunda circles over a slowly inclined ramp that leads you past changing exhibits that, in the past, have ranged from "Matthew Barney: The Cremaster Cycle" to "Norman Rockwell: Pictures for the American People," said to be the most comprehensive exhibit ever of the beloved painter's works. Usually the progression is counterintuitive: from the first floor up, rather than from the sixth floor down. If you're not sure, ask a guard before you begin. Permanent exhibits of 19th- and 20th-century art, including strong holdings of Kandinsky, Klee, Picasso, and French Impressionists, occupy a stark annex called the Tower Galleries, an addition (accessible at every level) that some critics have claimed made the entire structure look like a toilet bowl backed by a water tank. (Judge for yourself—I think there may be something to that view.)

The Guggenheim Museum.

Roosevelt Island Tram

Want to take in a little-known but spectacular view of the New York skyline? Take a ride on the **Roosevelt Island Tram** (✆ **212/832-4555;** http://www.rioc.com/transportation.htm). This is the tram you have probably seen in countless movies, most recently *Spider-Man*. The tram originates at 59th Street and Second Avenue, costs $2.25 each way ($1 for seniors), and takes about 5 minutes to traverse the East River to Roosevelt Island, where there are a series of apartment complexes and parks. During those 5 minutes you will be treated to a gorgeous view down the East River and the East Side skyline, with views of the United Nations and four bridges: the Queensboro, Williamsburg, Manhattan, and Brooklyn. On a clear day you might even spot Lady Liberty. And don't worry; despite what you've seen in the movies, the tram is safe, and your friendly neighborhood Spider-Man has everything under control. The tram operates daily from 6am until 2am and until 3:30am on weekends.

The Guggenheim runs some special programs, including free docent tours daily at 11am and 1pm, a limited schedule of lectures, free family films, and avant-garde screenings for grown-ups.

1071 Fifth Ave. (at 89th St.). ✆ **212/423-3500.** www.guggenheim.org. Admission $18 adults, $15 seniors 65 and older and students, free for children 11 and under; pay-what-you-wish Sat 5:45–7:45pm. Sun–Wed and Fri 10am–5:45pm; Sat 10am–7:45pm. Subway: 4, 5, 6 to 86th St.

Staten Island Ferry ★ 🐟 In 2006, the Staten Island Ferry celebrated its 100th anniversary. Over the years it has been one of New York's best bargains—sometimes costing a nickel and most of the time, like now, a free ride. It's New York's best freebie—especially if you just want to glimpse the Statue of Liberty and not climb her steps. You get an hour-long excursion (round-trip) into the world's biggest harbor. This is not strictly a sightseeing ride but commuter transportation to and from Staten Island. As a result, during business hours, you'll share the boat with working stiffs reading papers and drinking coffee inside, blissfully unaware of the sights outside.

You, however, should go on deck and enjoy the harbor traffic. The old orange-and-blue boats usually have open decks along the sides or at the bow and stern; try to catch one of these if you can, since the newer white boats don't have decks. Grab a seat on the right side of the boat for the best view. On the way out of Manhattan, you'll pass the Statue of Liberty (the boat comes closest to Lady Liberty on the way to Staten Island), Ellis Island, and from the left side of the boat, Governors Island; you'll see the Verrazano-Narrows Bridge spanning from Brooklyn to Staten Island in the distance.

When the boat arrives at St. George, Staten Island, if you are required to disembark, follow the boat-loading sign on your right as you get off; you'll circle around to the next loading dock, where there's usually another boat waiting to depart for Manhattan. The skyline views are simply awesome on the return trip. Well worth the time spent.

Departs from the Whitehall Ferry Terminal at the southern tip of Manhattan. ℂ **718/727-2508.** http://home2.nyc.gov/html/dot/html/ferrybus/statfery.shtml#info. Free admission. 24 hr.; every 15 min. during rush hour, every half hour or hour during nights and weekends. Subway: N, R to Whitehall St.; 4, 5 to Bowling Green; 1 to South Ferry (ride in one of the 1st 5 cars).

Statue of Liberty ★★★ ☺ For the millions who came by ship to America in the last century—either as privileged tourists or needy, hopeful immigrants— Lady Liberty, standing in the Upper Bay, was their first glimpse of America. No monument so embodies the nation's, and the world's, notion of political freedom and economic potential. Even if you don't make it out to Liberty Island, you can get a spine-tingling glimpse from Battery Park, from the New Jersey side of the bay, or during a ride on the Staten Island Ferry (see above). It's always reassuring to see her torch lighting the way.

Proposed by French statesman Edouard de Laboulaye as a gift from France to the United States, commemorating the two nations' friendship and joint notions of liberty, the statue was designed by sculptor Frédéric-Auguste Bartholdi with the engineering help of Alexandre-Gustave Eiffel (who was responsible for the famed Paris tower) and unveiled on October 28, 1886. (Americans in Paris have sometimes become disoriented when they see the 40-ft.-high replica on the Île des Cygnes in the Seine.) ***Touring tips:*** Ferries leave daily every hour from 9am to about 2pm, with extended hours in summer. Try to go early on a weekday to avoid the crowds that swarm in the afternoon, on weekends, and on holidays.

A stop at **Ellis Island** ★★ (p. 230) is included in the fare, but if you depart after 2pm, you can only visit the statue or Ellis Island, not both.

You can buy ferry tickets in advance via **www.statuecruises.com**, which will allow you to board without standing in the ticket line (often more than 90

The Staten Island Ferry offers a (free) ride across New York Harbor.

The Statue of Liberty.

minutes long). Even if you've already purchased tickets, arrive as much as 30 minutes before your desired ferry time to allow for increased security procedures prior to boarding. The ferry ride takes about 20 minutes.

Once on Liberty Island, you'll start to get an idea of the statue's immensity: She weighs 225 tons and measures 152 feet from foot to flame. Her nose alone is 4½ feet long, and her index finger is 8 feet long.

After September 11, 2001, access to the base of the statue was prohibited until 2004, and it wasn't until July 2009 that the crown was reopened. No more than 10 people will be allowed in the crown at a time, and you'll have to make reservations through Statue Cruises website to have a chance to ascend the statue. You can also explore the Statue of Liberty Museum, peer into the inner structure through a glass ceiling near the base of the statue, and enjoy views from the observation deck on top of a 16-story pedestal.

On Liberty Island in New York Harbor. ✆ **212/363-3200** (general info), or 877/523-9849 (ticket/ ferry info). www.nps.gov/stli or www.statuecruises.com. Free admission; ferry ticket to Statue of Liberty and Ellis Island $12 adults, $10 seniors 62 and older, $5 children 4–12. Daily 9:30am–5pm (last ferry departs around 2pm); extended hours in summer. Subway: 4, 5 to Bowling Green; 1 to South Ferry. Walk south through Battery Park to Castle Clinton, the fort housing the ferry ticket booth.

Times Square 👆 There's no doubting that Times Square has evolved into something much different than it was well over a decade ago, when it had a deservedly sleazy reputation. There is much debate among New Yorkers about which incarnation was better. Even the *New York Times,* which gave Times Square its name, has moved. For the natives, Times Square is a place we go out of our way to avoid. The crowds, even by New York standards, are stifling; the restaurants, mostly national chains, aren't very good; the shops, also mostly national chains, are unimaginative; and the attractions, such as Madame Tussaud's New York wax museum and Ripley's Believe it or Not, are kitschy. I suppose it's a little too Vegas for me. Still, you've come all this way; you've got to at least take a peek, if only for the amazing neon spectacle of it.

Most of the Broadway theaters are around Times Square, so plan your visit before or after the show you're going to see. For your pre-theater meal, walk 2 blocks west to Ninth Avenue where you'll find a number of relatively inexpensive, good restaurants. If you are with the kids, the Ferris wheel in the Toys "R" Us store makes a visit to Times Square worthwhile. Mayor Bloomberg has decreed part of Times

Times Square: the crossroads of the world (or New York City).

Square (and Herald Square as well) to be permanently vehicle-free. What was an 8-month experiment has been fully embraced by the city. Pull up a chair (literally: there are chairs and tables on formerly heavily trafficked streets) and watch the world go by.

Subway: 1, 2, 3, 7, N, Q, R, S to Times Sq.; A, C, E to 42nd St./Port Authority.

Wall Street & the New York Stock Exchange   Wall Street—it's an iconic name, and the world's prime hub for bulls and bears everywhere (mostly bears recently . . . oww!). There was once an actual wall here hundreds of years ago, hence the name. This narrow 18th-century lane (you'll be surprised at how little it is) is appropriately monumental, lined with neoclassical towers that reach as far skyward as the dreams and greed (never more evident than in 2008) of investors who built it into the world's most famous financial market.

At the heart of the action is the New York Stock Exchange (NYSE), the world's largest securities trader, where billions change hands. The NYSE came into being in 1792, when merchants met daily under a nearby buttonwood tree to try to pass off to each other the U.S. bonds that had been sold to fund the Revolutionary War. By 1903, they were trading stocks of publicly held companies in this Corinthian-columned Beaux Arts "temple" designed by George Post. About 3,000 companies are now listed on the exchange, trading nearly 314 billion shares valued at about $16 trillion. Unfortunately, the NYSE is no longer open to the public for tours.

11 Wall St. (𝐶 **212/656-3000.** www.nyse.com. Subway: J, Z to Broad St.; 2, 3, 4, 5 to Wall St.

Whitney Museum of American Art ★★   What is arguably the finest collection of 20th-century American art in the world belongs to the Whitney, thanks to the efforts of Gertrude Vanderbilt Whitney. A sculptor herself, Whitney organized exhibitions by American artists shunned by traditional academies, assembled a sizable personal collection, and founded the museum in 1930 in Greenwich Village.

Today's museum is an imposing presence on Madison Avenue—an inverted three-tiered pyramid of concrete and gray granite with seven seemingly random windows designed by Marcel Breuer, a leader of the Bauhaus movement. The

Bullish on Wall Street.

Explore the art of the 20th century (and beyond) at The Whitney.

WORLD TRADE CENTER SITE (GROUND ZERO)

Do you call a place where over 3,000 people lost their lives an "attraction"? Or do you now call it a shrine? This is the quandary of the World Trade Center site. Construction began in early 2006 on the proposed "Freedom Tower" to be built at the site (now called One World Trade Center). The new design retains essential elements of the original—soaring 1,776 feet into the sky, its illuminated mast evoking the Statue of Liberty's torch. From the square base, the tower will taper into eight tall isosceles triangles, forming an octagon at its center. An observation deck will be located 1,362 feet above ground. It is now scheduled to be completed in 2013.

The **National September 11 Memorial** was scheduled to open on September 11, 2011, the 10th anniversary of the destruction of the Twin Towers. The Memorial will consist of two massive pools set within the footprints of the Twin Towers with the largest manmade waterfalls in the country cascading down their sides. The Plaza will be shaded by 400 white oak trees. The almost 3,000 names of the men, women, and children killed in the attacks of September 11, 2001, and February 26, 1993, will be inscribed on bronze parapets surrounding the pools. **Note:** The site will be administered under a timed-admission system, so check **www.national911memorial.org** for details about tickets.

This has been long coming, and we New Yorkers are especially relieved and proud to have the Memorial ready on this solemn day. The site is bounded by Church, Barclay, Liberty, and West streets. Call ℂ **212/484-1222,** or go to **www.nycgo.com** for viewing information; go to **www.downtownny.com** for lower-Manhattan area information and rebuilding updates. The Tribute Center gives guided tours of the site. Call ℂ **866/737-1184,** or visit **www.tributewtc.org** for more information. Tours are given daily at 11am, noon, 1, and 3pm; there are two additional tours on Saturday at 2 and 4pm. The fee is $10 for adults, and free for children 11 and under.

permanent collection consists of an intelligent selection of major works by Edward Hopper, George Bellows, Georgia O'Keeffe, Roy Lichtenstein, Jasper Johns, and other significant artists. A second-floor space is devoted exclusively to works from its permanent collection from 1900 to 1950, while the rest is dedicated to rotating exhibits. Shows are usually well curated and more edgy than what you'd see at MoMA or the Guggenheim (though not as left of mainstream as what you'll find at the New Museum). Topics range from topical surveys, such as "American Art in the Age of Technology" and "The Warhol Look: Glamour Style Fashion" to in-depth retrospectives of famous or lesser known movements (such as Fluxus, the movement that spawned Yoko Ono, among others) and artists (like Mark Rothko, Keith Haring, Duane Hanson, and Bob Thompson). Free gallery tours are offered daily, and music, screenings, and lectures fill the calendar.

Note: 2012 is the next Whitney Biennial, a special 4-month long exhibition that is a major event in the contemporary American art world. Reputations are made and lost here. Curators Elisabeth Sussman and Jay Sanders will literally scour the country, visiting artists' studios to make their picks of what they think is the best new art around. There is inevitably some controversy about the choices—some of the work is beyond original—and that's all part of the fun. If you're here between March and the end of June, you might want to have a look and offer up your own opinion as well. As the name indicates, it only happens every 2 years.

945 Madison Ave. (at 75th St.). ℂ **212/570-3600.** www.whitney.org. Admission $18 adults, $12 seniors, free full-time students and ages 19–25, free children 18 and under; pay-what-you-wish Fri 6–9pm. Wed–Thurs and Sat–Sun 11am–6pm; Fri 1–9pm. Subway: 6 to 77th St.

MORE MANHATTAN MUSEUMS

For the **Brooklyn Museum of Art** ★★, the **New York Transit Museum,** the **American Museum of the Moving Image** ★, the **Queens Museum of Art,** the **Isamu Noguchi Garden Museum** ★, the **P.S. 1 Contemporary Art Center,** and the **Louis Armstrong House Museum** ★, see "Highlights of the Outer Boroughs," later in this chapter.

If you're traveling with the kids, also consider the museums listed under "Especially for Kids," on p. 309, which include the **Children's Museum of Manhattan** ★, the **Sony Wonder Technology Lab,** and the **New York Hall of Science** ★.

If you're interested in historic house museums, see the box called "In Search of Historic Homes," on p. 274.

Also, don't forget to see what's on at the monumental **New York Public Library** ★★, which regularly holds excellent exhibitions. See p. 273.

American Folk Art Museum ★★ This gorgeous, ultramodern boutique museum is not only a stunning structure, but it also heralds American folk art's entry into the top echelon of museum-worthy art. The modified open-plan interior features an extraordinary collection of traditional works from the 18th century to the self-taught artists and artisans of the present, reflecting the breadth and vitality of the American folk-art tradition. A splendid variety of quilts, in particular, makes the textiles collection the museum's most popular. The book-and-gift shop is outstanding, filled with one-of-a-kind objects.

45 W. 53rd St. (btw. Fifth and Sixth aves.). ℂ **212/265-1040.** www.folkartmuseum.org. Admission $12 adults, $8 seniors and students, free for children 11 and under; free to all Fri 5:30–7:30pm. Tues–Sun 10:30am–5:30pm; Fri 11am–7:30pm. Subway: B, D, F to 47th–50th sts./Rockefeller Center; E, M to Fifth Ave.

Asia Society The Asia Society was founded in 1956 by John D. Rockefeller III with the goal of increasing understanding between Americans and Asians through art exhibits, lectures, films, performances, and international conferences. The society is a leader in presenting contemporary Asian and Asian-American art. After a $30-million renovation that doubled the exhibition space, the society's headquarters is bigger, smarter, and better than ever. Never has so much of the core collection, which comprises Rockefeller's Pan-Asian acquisitions dating from 2000 B.C. to the 19th century, been on display before. Well-curated temporary exhibits

---

📎 Be an Early Bird

New York is the city that never sleeps, and you shouldn't either—at least not too much. Get an early start on your day. Check opening times for museums and attractions and be there as soon as they open to avoid the crowds. It's no fun waiting on lines or peering over throngs of people to view exhibits. So, remember: The early bird gets the worm, and the uncrowded attraction!

run the gamut from "The New Way of Tea," exploring Japan's elaborate tea ceremony, to "Through Afghan Eyes: A Culture in Conflict, 1987–95," a study in photographs and video. Additionally, the mammoth calendar of events ranges from film screenings to arts lectures to discussion panels featuring experts in Pan-Asian and global politics, business, and more; call or check the website for a current schedule.

You can follow a lot of the goings on via YouTube at www.youtube.com/user/asiasociety.

725 Park Ave. (at 70th St.). ✆ **212/288-6400.** www.asiasociety.org. Gallery admission $10 adults, $7 seniors, $5 students with ID, free for children 15 and under; free to all Fri 6–9pm. Tues–Sun 11am–6pm (Fri to 9pm; except July 4–Labor Day). Subway: 6 to 68th St./Hunter College.

Center for Jewish History 🏛 This 125,000-square-foot complex is the largest repository of Jewish history, art, and literature in the Diaspora. It unites five of America's leading institutions of Jewish scholarship: the **American Jewish Historical Society** (www.ajhs.org), the national archives of the Jewish people in the Americas; the **Leo Baeck Institute** (www.lbi.org), which documents the robust history of German-speaking Jewry from the 17th century until annihilation under the Nazis; the **Yeshiva University Museum** (www.yumuseum.org), with general-interest exhibits, plus a renowned collection of Judaica objects confiscated by the Nazis; the **YIVO Institute for Jewish Research** (www.yivoinstitute.org), which focuses on exhibits exploring the diversity of the Jewish experience; and the **American Sephardi Federation** (www.americansephardifederation.org), representing the spiritual, cultural, and social traditions of the American Sephardic communities (Jews from southern Europe, North Africa, and the Middle East). Together, this union represents about 100 million archival documents, 500,000 books, and thousands of objects of art and ephemera, ranging from Thomas Jefferson's letter denouncing anti-Semitism to memorabilia of famous Jewish athletes.

The main gallery space is the **Yeshiva Museum,** which comprises four galleries, an outdoor sculpture garden, and a children's workshop; a range of exhibits also showcase various holdings belonging to the other institutions as well. A central

FROM TOP: **Arts and crafts at the American Folk Art Museum; explore the world of Asian art at the Asia Society.**

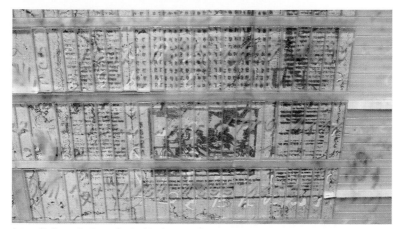

Art on display at the Center for Jewish History.

feature is the **Reading Room,** home to open stacks accessible by serious researchers and lay historians alike, as well as the **Center Genealogy Institute,** which offers assistance in family-history research. Another huge component of the center is its 250-seat state-of-the-art auditorium, home to a packed schedule of lectures, music, and film presentations. If you get hungry, a **kosher cafe** is on-site.

15 W. 16th St. (btw. Fifth and Sixth aves.). © **212/294-8301.** www.cjh.org. Admission to Yeshiva University Museum $8 adults, $6 seniors and students, free children 4 and under; free to all Mon, Wed 5–8pm, and Fri. Free admission to all other facilities. Yeshiva University Museum Sun, Tues, and Thurs 11am–5pm; Mon 3:30–8pm; Wed 11am–8pm; Fri 11am–2:30pm. Reading Room and Genealogy Institute Mon 9:30am–7:30pm, Tues–Thurs 9:30am–5:00pm; Fri 9:30am–1:30pm Sun 11am–4pm. All other exhibition galleries Sun 11am–5pm; Mon and Wed 9:30am–8pm; Fri 9am–3pm.; Sun 11am–5pm. Subway: L, N, R, 4, 5, 6 to 14th St./Union Sq.; F, M to 14th St.

The Cloisters ★★ 📷 If it weren't for this branch of the Metropolitan Museum of Art, many New Yorkers would never get to this northernmost point in Manhattan. This remote yet lovely spot is devoted to the art and architecture of medieval Europe. Atop a cliff overlooking the Hudson River, you'll find a 12th-century chapter house, parts of five cloisters from medieval monasteries, a Romanesque chapel, and a 12th-century Spanish apse brought intact from Europe. Surrounded by peaceful gardens, this is the one place on the island that can approximate the kind of solitude suitable to such a collection. Inside you'll find extraordinary works that include the Unicorn tapestries, sculpture, illuminated manuscripts, stained glass, ivory, and precious metal work.

Modern times have even come to the Cloisters. There is an official blog—and one of the best I've ever seen by an institution—devoted to their wonderful **medieval garden, http://blog.metmuseum.org/cloistersgardens**. Garden lovers will love to peruse its postings. By the way, even in the dead of winter and without flowers, the garden—which is inside the museum in the center of a courtyard—has a magical quality, especially when it snows.

Despite the remoteness, the Cloisters are quite popular, especially in fine weather, so try to schedule your visit during the week rather than on a crowded weekend afternoon. A free guided Highlights Tour is offered Sundays and

Enjoy a respite from the city at The Cloisters.

Tuesday through Friday at 3pm; gallery talks are also a regular feature. Additionally, Garden Tours are offered Tuesday through Sunday at 1pm May to October, and medieval music concerts are regularly held in the stunning 12th-century Spanish chapel. For an extra-special experience, you may want to plan your visit around one.

At the north end of Fort Tryon Park. (© **212/923-3700.** www.metmuseum.org/cloisters. Suggested admission (includes same-day entrance to the Metropolitan Museum of Art) $20 adults, $15 seniors, $10 students, free for children 11 and under. Nov–Feb Tues–Sun 9:30am–4:45pm; Mar–Oct Tues–Sun 9:30am–5:15pm. Subway: A to 190th St., then a 10-min. walk north along Margaret Corbin Dr., or pick up the M4 bus at the station (1 stop to Cloisters). Bus: M4 Madison Ave. (Fort Tryon Park/the Cloisters).

Cooper-Hewitt National Design Museum ★ Part of the Smithsonian Institution, the Cooper-Hewitt is housed in the Carnegie Mansion, built by steel magnate Andrew Carnegie in 1901, and undergoing a renovation of the Fox and Miller town houses and the Museum Mansion, which will create a third floor and expand gallery space by 80%. The renovation is scheduled to be completed in 2011. During the renovations, the museum remains open and galleries will continue to be devoted to changing exhibits that are invariably well conceived, engaging, and educational. Shows are both historic and contemporary in nature, and topics range from "The Work of Charles and Ray Eames: A Legacy of Invention" to "Russell Wright: Creating American Lifestyle" to "The Architecture of Reassurance: Designing the Disney Theme Parks." Many installations are drawn from the museum's own vast collection of industrial design, drawings, textiles, wall coverings, books, and prints.

On your way in, note the fabulous Art Nouveau–style copper-and-glass canopy above the entrance. And be sure to visit the garden, ringed with Central Park benches from various eras. Once back home, you can keep in touch via the museum's blog at http://blog.cooperhewitt.org.

2 E. 91st St. (at Fifth Ave.). (© **212/849-8400.** www.cooperhewitt.org. Admission $15 adults, $10 seniors and students with ID, free for children 11 and under. Mon–Fri 10am–5pm; Sat 10am–6pm; Sun 11am–6pm. Subway: 4, 5, 6 to 86th St.

Dwyer Cultural Center 🎒 While technically not a museum, this new addition to what could be called the latest Harlem Renaissance has enough going for it in terms of exhibitions and other delights to more than warrant its inclusion here. Occupying three floors of what used to be a huge warehouse, the center's very existence in this era of extreme budget cutbacks is a kind of miracle. The ongoing exhibit, "Harlem Is…," explores the various aspects of what has made Harlem a name synonymous with art, music, and literature. In 2010, the center hosted trombonist and composer Craig Harris and the Tailgaters Tales for their performance of a score based on the physical language of Muhammad Ali, as well

The Cooper-Hewitt's exhibits are displayed in the Carnegie Mansion.

as an exhibition of work by the seminal Weusi Collective. The center is not far from the Schomburg Center for Research in Black Culture, so you might well combine the two in a single visit.

258 St. Nicholas Ave. (at 123rd St.). ✆ **212/222-3060.** www.dwyercc.org. Admission free to exhibitions; check website for prices for theater and music events. Wed–Fri noon–5pm; Sat 1–5pm. Subway: A, B, C, D to 125th St.

El Museo del Barrio   What started in 1969 with a small display in a classroom in east Harlem is today the only museum in America dedicated to the art and culture of Puerto Ricans, Latin Americans, and all Latino communities throughout the U.S. The northernmost Museum Mile institution has a permanent exhibit ranging from pre-Columbian artifacts to photographic art and video. The display of *santos de palo* (wood-carved religious figurines) is noteworthy, as is "Taíno, Ancient Voyagers of the Caribbean," dedicated to the highly developed cultures that Columbus encountered when he landed in the New World. The well-curated exhibitions tend to focus on 20th-century artists and contemporary subjects.

1230 Fifth Ave. (at 104th St.). ✆ **212/831-7272.** www.elmuseo.org. Suggested admission $9 adults, $5 seniors (free Wed) and students, free for children 11 and under. Tues–Sun 11am–6pm. Subway: 6 to 103rd St.

The Frick Collection ★★   Henry Clay Frick could afford to be an avid collector of European art after amassing a fortune as a pioneer in the coke and steel industries at the turn of the 20th century. To house his treasures and himself, he hired architects Carrère & Hastings to build this 18th-century French-style mansion (1914), one of the most beautiful remaining on Fifth Avenue.

Most appealing about the Frick is its intimate size and setting. This is a living testament to New York's vanished Gilded Age—the interior still feels like a private home (albeit a really, really rich guy's home) graced with beautiful paintings, rather than a museum. Come here to see the classics by some of the world's most famous painters: Titian, Bellini, Rembrandt, Turner—his large canvases are especially stunning—Vermeer, El Greco, and Goya, to name only a few. A highlight of the collection is the Fragonard Room, graced with the sensual rococo series "The Progress of Love." The portrait of Montesquieu by Whistler is also stunning. It's worth going to see Velázquez's portrait of King Philip IV alone.

El Museo del Barrio features classic and new Latino art.

Included in the price of admission, the Acoustiguide audio tour is particularly useful because it allows you to follow your own path rather than a prescribed route. A free 11-minute video presentation is screened in the Music Room every 20 minutes from 10:20am to 5pm; starting with this helps to set the tone for what you'll see.

In addition, chamber music concerts ($30 per ticket) are held fall through spring, Sunday at 5pm; once-a-month lectures are offered select Wednesdays at 6pm. Call or visit the website for the current schedule and ticket information.

1 E. 70th St. (at Fifth Ave.). ✆ **212/288-0700.** www.frick.org. Admission $18 adults, $12 seniors, $5 students. Children 9 and under not admitted. Tues–Sat 10am–6pm; Sun 11am–5pm. Closed all major holidays. Subway: 6 to 68th St./Hunter College.

The Grolier Club ★★   Book lovers, take note. Founded in 1884, the Grolier Club is America's oldest and largest society for bibliophiles and enthusiasts in the graphic arts. The club has organized exhibitions on topics ranging from William Blake to murder mysteries to Art Nouveau posters. There are four shows a year in the main ground-floor gallery, all open to the public free of charge. Not too long ago, I went to a fascinating exhibition of Cuban book artists, men and women who produce books and art out of anything and everything they can lay their hands on, all with the same pluck enterprise that keeps those old 1950s American automobiles running year after year. This is a small, calm, relaxed space, and could be a perfect break for you from the Midtown crowds, which can be overwhelming.

47 E. 60th St. ✆ **212/838-6690.** www.grolierclub.org. Free admission. Mon–Fri 10am–5pm. Closed in August. Subway: 6 to 59th St.; N, R to 59th St./Fifth Ave.

The Institute for the Study of the Ancient World ★★   Part of a graduate program at New York University, the ISAW also offers free exhibitions that typically stay around for 5 or 6 months. One such exhibit was "The Lost World of Old Europe: The Danube Valley, 5000–3500 B.C." It was an eye-opener, especially if, like me, you thought of Old Europe as, well, inhabited by people in bad fur coats. In fact, their potters developed striking designs, and the coppersmiths were, in their day, the most advanced metal artisans in the world. Who knew?

The Fragonard Room is one of the highlights of the Frick.

15 E. 84th St. (℃) **212/992-7843.** www.nyu.edu/isaw. Free admission. Tues–Sun 11am–6pm. Subway: 6 to 86th St.

International Center of Photography ★ 🎁   The ICP is one of the world's premier educators, collectors, and exhibitors of photographic art. The state-of-the-art gallery space is ideal for viewing rotating exhibitions of the museum's 50,000-plus prints as well as visiting shows. The emphasis is on contemporary photographic works, but historically important photographers aren't ignored. This is a must-see on any photography buff's list. Check out ICP's excellent blog, **http://fansinaflashbulb.wordpress.com**.

1133 Sixth Ave. (at 43rd St.). (℃) **212/857-0000.** www.icp.org. Admission $12 adults, $8 seniors and students, 11 and under free. Tues–Thurs and Sat–Sun 10am–6pm; Fri 10am–8pm. Subway: B, D, F, M to 42nd St.

Intrepid Sea, Air & Space Museum ★★ 😊   The most astonishing thing about the aircraft carrier Intrepid is how it can be simultaneously so big and so small. It's a few football fields long, weighs 40,000 tons, holds 40 aircraft, and sometimes doubles as a ballroom for society functions. But stand there and think about landing an A-12 jet on the deck and suddenly it's minuscule. Furthermore, in the narrow passageways below, you'll find it isn't quite the roomiest of vessels. Now a National Historic Landmark, the exhibit also includes the submarine Growler, the only intact strategic missile submarine open to the public anywhere in the world, as well as a collection of vintage and modern aircraft, including the A-12 Blackbird, the world's fastest spy plane, and a retired British Airways Concorde jet.

Kids can explore vintage aircraft at the Intrepid Museum.

Kids just love this place. They, and you, can climb inside a replica Revolutionary War submarine, sit in an A-6 Intruder cockpit, and follow the progress of America's astronauts as they work in space. There are even Navy flight simulators—including a "Fly with the Blue Angels" program—for educational thrill rides in the Technologies Hall.

The program "All Hands on Deck" teaches children and adults how things work on ships, plus there's an AH-1 Cobra attack helicopter. The action-packed *Intrepid Wings* shows aircraft carrier take-offs and recoveries in the new Allison and Howard Lutnick Theater; the film runs continuously throughout the day. The grand visitor center makes for an impressive entrance, and the massive museum store is well stocked; goods include NYPD and FDNY logo gear.

Each year, in February, the museum presents **Kids Week,** which takes advantage of so much New York has to offer for kids. This may include a performance by the Alvin Ailey dance troupe, a kids fashion show, or some Broadway acts. If you're in town with your family—in 2011 Kids Week was February 19 to 27—come on board. If that isn't enough, the museum presents various moving exhibitions. For 4 months in 2010, you could see "Snoopy as the World War I Flying Ace," with 29 high-resolution prints made from Charles M. Schulz's original drawings.

Dress warmly for a winter visit—it's almost impossible to heat an aircraft carrier. **Note:** It was just a few blocks north of the *Intrepid* where Captain Sully Sullenberger landed US Airways Flight 1549 in the Hudson River on January 15, 2009, without a soul lost. When you're on the flight deck, you can gaze out and imagine the miraculous event. After landing, the plane floated right by the aircraft carrier, much to the astonishment of those tourists on board.

Pier 86 (W. 46th St. at Twelfth Ave.). ☎ **877/957-7447** or 212/245-0072. www.intrepidmuseum. org. Admission $22 adults; $18 seniors and students; $17 children 3–17 and veterans; free for active military, retired U.S. military, and children 2 and under. Nov–Mar Tues–Sun 10am–5pm; Apr–Oct Mon–Fri 10am–5pm; Sat–Sun 10am–6pm. Closed Christmas and Thanksgiving. Subway: A, C, E to 42nd St./Port Authority. Bus: M42 Crosstown.

Italian American Museum   This intimate storefront museum on the corner of Mulberry and Grand Streets, in the heart of Little Italy, once housed "Banca Stabile," which was a bank founded by Francesco Stabile in 1885. During its heyday, the bank offered the newly arrived immigrants from Italy much more than financial services. It also provided telegraph, travel via steam ships, import-export, notary public, and post office—a kind of all-in-one immigrant community service center. The museum is chockfull of mementos from that immigrant life, from a genuine knife grinder's pushcart to florid child-sized Punch-and-Judy-like marionettes. The director and founder, Dr. Joseph Scelsa, is often there, and if you're lucky, he'll play the restored hand organ for you. Past exhibitions have included "Prisoners in Our Own Home: The Italian American Experience As America's Enemy Aliens" and "Italian Americans in Law Enforcement; Petrosino, Serpico, Sprizzo."

155 Mulberry St. (corner of Mulberry and Grand). ☎ **212/965-9000.** www.italianamerican museum.org. Admission $5 (suggested). Sat–Sun 11am–6pm; Mon–Fri open for groups of 12 or more by appointment. Closed Christmas Day and New Years Day. Subway: N or R to Prince St.; F, B, D to Broadway/Lafayette.

The Jewish Museum   Housed in a Gothic-style mansion renovated in 1993 by AIA Gold Medal winner Kevin Roche, this wonderful museum now has the world-class space it deserves to showcase its remarkable collections, which chronicle 4,000 years of Jewish history. The two-floor permanent exhibit, "Culture and Continuity: The Jewish Journey," tells the story of the Jewish experience from ancient times through today, and is the museum's centerpiece. Artifacts include daily objects that might have served the authors of the books of Genesis, Psalms, and Job, and a great assemblage of intricate torahs. A wonderful collection of classic TV and radio programs is available for viewing through the Goodkind Resource Center (as any fan of television's golden age knows, its finest comic moments were Jewish comedy). The scope of the exhibit is phenomenal, and its story an enlightening—and intense—one. The museum has also put on other landmark exhibitions. I *still* recall the amazing "The Dreyfus Affair: Art, Truth & Justice," from 1987. In spring 2011, the museum welcomed the public to "Houdini: Art and Magic." (He was born Ehrich Weiss.) Audio guides and daily docent-led tours are free with admission. In addition to the in-house shop, don't miss Celebrations—The Jewish Museum Design Shop, housed in the adjacent brownstone.

1109 Fifth Ave. (at 92nd St.). © **212/423-3200.** www.thejewishmuseum.org. Admission $12 adults, $10 seniors, $7.50 students, free for children 11 and under; free for all Sat. Sun–Tues and Sat 11am–5:45pm; Thurs 11am–8pm; Fri 11am–4pm. Subway: 4, 5, 6 to 86th St.; 6 to 96th St.

Lower East Side Tenement Museum ★ ☺

This museum is the first-ever National Trust for Historic Preservation site that was not the home of someone rich or famous. It's something quite different: a five-story tenement that 10,000 people from 25 countries called home between 1863 and 1935—people who had come to the United States looking for the American dream and made 97 Orchard St. their first stop. The tenement museum tells the story of the immigration boom of the late 19th and early 20th centuries, when the Lower East Side was considered the "Gateway to America." A visit here makes a good follow-up to an Ellis Island trip.

The only way to see the museum is by guided tour. Two primary tenement tours, held on all open days and lasting an hour, offer a satisfying exploration of the museum: "Piecing It Together: Immigrants in the Garment Industry," which

Immigrant life is re-created at the Lower East Side Tenement Museum.

focuses on the restored apartment and the lives of its turn-of-the-20th-century tenants, an immigrant Jewish family named Levine from Poland; and "Getting By: Weathering the Great Depressions of 1873 and 1929," featuring the homes of the German-Jewish Gumpertz family and the Sicilian-Catholic Baldizzi family, respectively. A knowledgeable guide leads you into each dingy urban time capsule, where several apartments have been restored to their lived-in condition, and recounts the real-life stories of the families who occupied them in fascinating detail. You can pair them for an in-depth look at the museum, since the apartments and stories are so different; however, one tour serves as an excellent introduction if you don't want to invest an entire afternoon here. In addition to "Piecing It Together" and "Getting By," the museum offers "The Moores: An Irish Family in America"; "Confino Family"; and two Lower East Side walking tours.

Most of these tours are not really for kids. The best one for them is the hour-long Confino Family Apartment tour, a living-history program geared to families, which allows kids to converse with an interpreter who plays teenage immigrant Victoria Confino (ca. 1916); kids can also handle whatever they like and try on period clothes.

Small permanent and rotating exhibits, including photos, videos, and a model tenement, are housed in the visitor center and exhibition space in the tenement building at 97 Orchard St. Special tours and programs are sometimes on the schedule. Tours are limited in number and sell out quickly, so it pays to buy tickets in advance, which you can do online or by calling ℂ **866/606-7232.** You might want to check out their blog as well: http://tenement-museum.blogspot.com.

108 Orchard St. (btw. Delancey and Broome sts.). ℂ **212/431-0233.** www.tenement.org. All tours $20 adults, $15 seniors and students. There are 6 different tours leaving at various hours daily 10:00am–6pm (the schedule is complicated and varies by month, so check the website or call). **Note:** The "Immigrant Soles" walking tour does not include a visit to a tenement. Subway: F to Delancey St.; J, M to Essex St.

The Morgan Library & Museum ★★ 🎫 This New York treasure—boasting one of the world's most important collections of original manuscripts, rare books and bindings, master drawings, and personal writings—has become newly popular since extensive renovations and an addition designed by architect Renzo Piano were completed in 2006. Those renovations include a welcoming entrance on Madison Avenue; new and renovated galleries, so that more of the library's holdings can be exhibited; a modern auditorium; and a new Reading Room with greater capacity and electronic resources and expanded space for collections storage. The permanent collection is nothing but astounding, including not one but *three* Gutenberg Bibles; letters and manuscripts of Jane Austen, Balzac, Byron, Dickens, James Joyce, and Alexander Pope; and a sumptuous, eye-boggling collection of medieval illuminated manuscripts. **Note:** The collection is too vast for it to be all exhibited at one time, and the displays change periodically. Some of the library's exhibitions have included one on the life of Bob Dylan through music, letters, memorabilia; "On the Money: Cartoons for *The New Yorker*"; and "The Modern Stage: Set Designs, 1900–1970." You can lunch in the intimate **Morgan Dining Room** as if you were dining in JP's own quarters. If you want more of the Morgan experience, be sure to check out the museum's website, which has some of the finest online exhibitions of any museum.

225 Madison Ave. (btw. 36th and 37th sts.). ℂ **212/685-0008.** www.themorgan.org. $12 adults, $8 seniors and students, free for children 11 and under; free for all Fri 7–9pm. Tues–Thurs 10:30am–5pm; Fri 10:30am–9pm; Sat 10am–6pm; Sun 11am–6pm. Subway: 6 to 33rd St.

Museum of Arts and Design ★

🎁 Formerly called the American Craft Museum, this museum is the nation's top showcase for contemporary crafts. The collection focuses on objects that are prime examples of form and function, ranging from jewelry to baskets to furniture. You'll see a strong emphasis on material as well as craft, whether it be fiber, ceramics, or metal. Special exhibitions can range from expressionist clay sculpture to fine bookbinding, and can celebrate movements or single artisans. Stop into the gorgeous shop even if you don't make it into the museum. In 2008, the museum moved to a quirky and controversial building designed by modernist architect Edward Durrell Stone in 1963 at 2 Columbus Circle, doubling its exhibition space.

2 Columbus Circle. ☏ **212/299-7777.** www. madmuseum.org. Admission $15 adults, $12 students and seniors, free for high school students with ID and children 11 and under; pay-what-you-wish Thurs 6–9pm. Tues–Sun 11am–6pm; Thurs 11am–9pm. Subway: 1, 2, 3, A, B, C, D to 59th St./Columbus Circle.

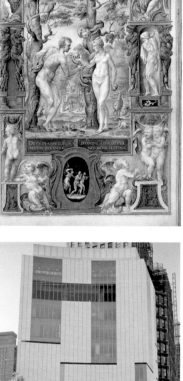

FROM TOP: Rare and unusual manuscripts are on display at the Morgan Library; people are MAD about the Museum of Art and Design at Columbus Circle.

Museum of Chinese in America ★   In the heart of Chinatown, this museum is dedicated to "reclaiming, preserving, and presenting the history and culture of Chinese people in the United States." Past exhibitions include "Have You Eaten Yet? The Chinese Restaurant in America" and "Fly to Freedom," a collection of 123 paper sculptures made by passengers of the ill-fated ship *Golden Venture*, which ran aground in 1993 and most of whose passengers were detained by immigration officials for up to 4 years. In 2009, the museum moved into a new, larger space at 215 Centre St., designed by Vietnam Veteran's Memorial creator, Maya Lin. Don't miss her fascinating video tour of the museum at **www.mocanyc.org/visit**.

215 Centre St. ℂ **212/619-4785.** www.mocanyc.org. Admission $7 adults, $4 students and seniors, free on Thurs and for children 11 and under. Mon and Fri 11am–5pm; Thurs 11am–9pm; Sat–Sun 10am–5pm. Subway: 6, N, R, Q, J, M to Canal St.

Museum of Jewish Heritage—A Living Memorial to the Holocaust ★
In the south end of Battery Park City, the Museum of Jewish Heritage occupies a strikingly spare six-sided building designed by award-winning architect Kevin Roche, with a six-tier roof alluding to the Star of David and the six million murdered in the Holocaust. The permanent exhibits—"Jewish Life a Century Ago," "The War Against the Jews," and "Jewish Renewal"—recount the daily prewar lives, the unforgettable horror that destroyed them, and the tenacious renewal experienced by European and immigrant Jews in the years from the late 19th century to the present. The museum's power derives from the way it tells that story: through the objects, photographs, documents, and, most poignantly, through the videotaped testimonies of Holocaust victims, survivors, and their families, all chronicled by Steven Spielberg's Survivors of the Shoah Visual History Foundation.

While advance tickets are not usually necessary, you may want to purchase them to guarantee admission; call ℂ **646/437-4202.** Audio tours narrated by Meryl Streep and Itzhak Perlman are available at the museum for an additional $5. You might also want to check out the museum staff's very good blog at **www. mjhstaff.blogspot.com**. It offers behind-the-scenes looks at the museum's comings and goings.

36 Battery Place (at 1st Place), Battery Park City. ℂ **646/437-4200.** www.mjhnyc.org. Admission $12 adults, $10 seniors, $7 students, free for children 11 and under and for everyone Wed

Famed architect Maya Lin designed the new home of the Museum of Chinese in America.

4–8pm. Sun–Tues and Thurs 10am–5:45pm; Wed 10am–8pm; Fri and eves of Jewish holidays 10am–3pm (10am–5pm Fri during daylight saving time). Subway: 4, 5 to Bowling Green.

Museum of Sex 🎁   How many cities can claim their own Museum of Sex? Not many in the U.S., that's for sure! This one, despite its provocative title, offers a studied, historical look at the history of sex in our culture. Past exhibits include "Action: Sex and the Moving Image" and "Rubbers: The Life, History, and Strug-

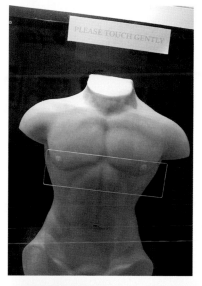

gle of the Condoms." **Note:** Many of the displays are very graphic, so the museum may not be for everyone.

233 Fifth Ave. (at 27th St.). ℂ **212/689-6337.** www.museumofsex.com. Admission adults $17; students and seniors $15. At press time, there was a $3 coupon available on its website. No one 17 and under admitted. Sun–Thurs 10am–8pm; Fri and Sat 10am–9pm. Subway: N, R, 6 to 28th St.

Museum of the City of New York A wide variety of objects—costumes, photographs, prints, maps, dioramas, and memorabilia—trace the history of New York City from its beginnings as a humble Dutch colony in the 16th century to its present-day prominence. Two outstanding permanent exhibits are the re-creation of John D. Rockefeller's master bedroom and dressing

FROM TOP: **The Museum of Sex takes a look at the history of sex in our culture; it's all about NYC at the Museum of the City of New York.**

room, and the space devoted to "Broadway!," a history of New York theater. Kids will love "New York Toy Stories," a permanent exhibit showcasing toys and dolls owned and adored by centuries of New York children. The permanent "Painting the Town: Cityscapes of New York" explores the changing cityscape from 1809 to 1997, and carries new profundity in the wake of the September 11, 2001, terrorist attacks. In 2011, the museum featured "Denys Wortman Rediscovered," which included original cartoons created for the *World-Telegram and Sun* newspaper, depicting everyday life in New York in the early to mid-20th century.

1220 Fifth Ave. (at 103rd St.). ✆ **212/534-1672.** www.mcny.org. Suggested admission $10 adults, $6 seniors and students, $20 families, free children 12 and under. Tues–Sun 10am–5pm. Closed Thanksgiving, Christmas, and New Year's. Subway: 6 to 103rd St.

National Museum of the American Indian, George Gustav Heye Center

This impressive collection represents the Smithsonian Institution. The collection spans more than 10,000 years of Native heritage, gathered a century ago mainly by New York banking millionaire George Gustav Heye. About 70% of the collection is dedicated to the Natives of North America and Hawaii; the rest represents the cultures of Mexico and Central and South America. There's a wealth of material here, but it's not as well organized as it could be. The museum also hosts temporary themed exhibitions and interpretive programs, plus free storytelling, music, and dance presentations.

The museum is in the beautiful 1907 Beaux Arts **U.S. Customs House** ★, designed by Cass Gilbert, a National Historic Landmark worth a look in its own right.

1 Bowling Green (btw. State and Whitehall sts.). ✆ **212/514-3700.** www.nmai.si.edu. Free admission. 10am–5:30pm (Thurs until 8pm). Closed on Christmas. Subway: 4, 5 to Bowling Green; R to Whitehall; 1 to South Ferry.

Neue Galerie New York 📔

This museum is dedicated to German and Austrian art and design, with a particular focus on the early 20th century. Displayed on two floors, the collection features painting, works on paper, decorative arts, and other media from such artists as Klimt, Kokoschka, Kandinsky, Klee, and leaders of the Wiener Werkstätte decorative arts, and Bauhaus applied arts movements, such as Adolf Loos and Mies van der Rohe, respectively. The gallery made headlines in 2006 when it acquired Klimt's *Portrait of Adele Bloch-Bauer I*—dubbed the "Golden Adele"—for a record-setting $135 million (no, I didn't add an extra digit by mistake). The museum floated the idea of adding a high premium (up to $50) to view its new masterpiece, but the outcry caused the management to reconsider. You can see the Golden Adele for the $15 admission fee, without extra charge. "Birth of the Modern: Style and Identity in Vienna 1900" was

Art and artifacts from many native peoples can be found at the National Museum of the American Indian.

"Golden Adele" by Klimt is on display at the Neue Galerie.

The building is part of the art at the New Museum.

among the expositions in 2011. Once occupied by Mrs. Cornelius Vanderbilt III, the impeccably restored, landmark-designated 1914 Carrère & Hastings building (they built the New York Public Library as well) is worth a look itself. **Café Sabarsky** is modeled on a Viennese cafe, so museum-goers in need of a snack break can expect a fine Linzer torte.

1048 Fifth Ave. (at 86th St.). ℂ **212/628-6200.** www.neuegalerie.org. Admission $15 adults, $10 seniors and students. Children 11 and under not admitted, 12–16 must be accompanied by an adult. Thurs–Mon 11am–6pm. Subway: 4, 5, 6 to 86th St.

New Museum of Contemporary Art ★

Like boxes haphazardly piled upon one another, the seven-story New Museum of Contemporary Art, rising above the tenements of the Lower East Side, is one of New York's newest (2007) museum icons. But it's not only the exterior that catches the eye; the exhibits at the New Museum reflect the slightly offbeat, slanted look of the museum. The museum's debut exhibition, "Unmonumental," a four-part series displaying 21st-century sculptures, objects, video, and collages by 30 international artists, was a fitting beginning to what promises to be a bright future. On the first Saturday of each month, the museum offers programs for families with thematic tours, conversations with artists, and creative activities, all free of charge. You can stay in touch with the latest news via the museum's Facebook page, **www.facebook.com/newmuseum**.

235 Bowery (at Prince St.). ℂ **212/219-1222.** www.newmuseum.org. Admission $12 adult, $10 senior, $8 student, free 18 and under. Thurs 11am–9pm; Wed and Fri–Sun 11am–6pm. Subway: 6 to Spring St; N, R to Prince St.

New York City Fire Museum ★ ☺

Housed in a three-story 1904 firehouse, the former quarters of FDNY Engine Co. 30, this museum offers one of the country's most extensive collections of fire-service memorabilia from the 18th century to the present. It is also the best place to pay tribute to the 343 heroic firefighters who lost their lives blocks away in the World Trade Center disaster. Expect ongoing changing exhibits relating to the September 11, 2001, terrorist

ART FOR ART'S SAKE: THE GALLERY SCENE

Manhattan has more than 500 private art galleries, selling everything from old masters to tomorrow's news. Galleries are free to the public, generally Tuesday through Saturday from 10am to 6pm. Saturday afternoon gallery-hopping, in particular, is a favorite pastime—nobody will expect you to buy, so don't worry.

The best way to winnow down your choices is by perusing the back of the Sunday "Arts & Leisure" section of the *New York Times;* the listings section at the back of the weekly *New York* magazine, which I find to be particularly descriptive and user-friendly; the Art section in the weekly *Time Out New York;* or the *New Yorker*'s weekly "Goings on About Town" section. You can also find the latest exhibition listings online at **www.nymag.com/arts/art**, which will give you full access to *New York* magazine's listings; **www.artnet. com**; and **www.artinfo.com**. An excellent source—more for practicals on the galleries and the artists and genres they represent rather than current shows—is **www.artincontext.org**.

Keep in mind that uptown galleries tend to be more traditional and exclusive feeling, downtown galleries more high-ticket contemporary, and far-west Chelsea galleries the most cutting edge. Museum-quality works dominate uptown, while raw talent and emerging artists are most common in west Chelsea. But there are constant surprises in all neighborhoods.

Uptown   Uptown galleries are clustered in and around the glamorous crossroads of Fifth Avenue and 57th Street as well as on and off stylish Madison Avenue in the 60s, 70s, and 80s. Unlike their upstart Chelsea and SoHo

counterparts, these blue-chip galleries maintain a quiet white-glove demeanor. They include art-world powerhouses **Gagosian Gallery,** 980 Madison Ave. (✆ **212/744-2313;** www.gagosian.com), and **PaceWildenstein,** 32 E. 57th St. (✆ **212/421-3292;** www.pace wildenstein.com), whose focus is on classic modernism, representing such artists as Jim Dine, Barbara Hepworth, and Claes Oldenburg; and the **Richard Gray Gallery,** 1018 Madison Ave., Fourth Floor (✆ **212/472-8787;** www.richard graygallery.com), which features American and European contemporary works, with artists ranging from Josef Albers to David Hockney.

Chelsea   The area in the west 20s, between Tenth and Eleventh avenues, is home to the avant-garde of today's New York art scene, with W. 26th St. serving as the unofficial "gallery row." Most galleries are not in storefronts but in the large spaces of multistory former garages and warehouses. Galleries worth seeking out include **Paula Cooper,** 534 W. 21st St. (✆ **212/255-1105;** www.paulacoopergallery.com), a heavyweight in the modern-art world, specializing in conceptual and minimal art; one of Chelsea's biggest galleries, the **Matthew Marks Gallery,** 523 W. 24th St. (✆ **212/243-0200;** www.matthew marks.com); the **George Billis Gallery,** 521 W. 26th St. (✆ **212/645-2621;** www.

attacks. Other displays range from vintage fire marks to firetrucks (including the last-known example of a 1921 pumper) to the gear and tools of modern firefighters. Also look for leather hoses, fireboats, and Currier & Ives prints, plus a new exhibit on fire safety and burn prevention especially geared toward families. Best of all, real firefighters are almost always on hand to share stories and fire-safety

georgebillis.com), which shows works by talented emerging artists; **Barbara Gladstone Gallery,** 515 W. 24th St. (✆ **212/ 206-9300;** www.gladstonegallery.com); uptown powerhouse **Gagosian Gallery,** 555 W. 24th St. (✆ **212/741-1111;** www. gagosian.com), which shows such major modern artists as Richard Serra and John Currin; **Cheim & Read,** 547 W. 25th St. (✆ **212/242-7727;** www.cheimread.com), which often shows works by such high-profile popular artists as Diane Arbus and Robert Mapplethorpe; **Alexander and Bonin,** 132 Tenth Ave. (✆ **212/367-7474;** www.alexanderandbonin.com), which mounts excellent solo exhibitions; **James Cohan Gallery,** 533 W. 26th St. (✆ **212/ 714-9500;** www.jamescohan.com), particularly strong in modern photography; and **Lehmann Maupin,** 540 W. 26th St. (✆ **212/255-2923;** www.lehmannmaupin. com), whose roster runs the gamut from young unknowns to such contemporary masters as Ross Bleckner. For a

comprehensive listing of the Chelsea galleries, check the website **www.westchelseaarts.com.**

Downtown   SoHo remains colorful, if less edgy than it used to be, with the action centered around West Broadway and encroaching onto the edge of Chinatown. **Peter Blum Gallery,** (pictured above), 99 Wooster St. (✆ **212/343-0441;** www.peterblumgallery.com), which showcased the divine Kim Sooja, a Korean artist who uses traditional Korean bedcovers to comment on the promise of wedded bliss; **O. K. Harris,** 383 W. Broadway (✆ **212/431-3600;** www.okharris.com), which shows a fascinating variety of contemporary painting, sculpture, and photography; and **Louis K. Meisel,** 141 Prince St. (✆ **212/677-1340;** www.meiselgallery. com), which specializes in photo-realism and American pinup art (yep, Petty and Vargas girls).

information with kids. The retail store sells authorized FDNY logo wear and souvenirs. Call ahead for details on scheduling a guided tour.

278 Spring St. (btw. Varick and Hudson sts.). ✆ **212/691-1303.** www.nycfiremuseum.org. Suggested admission $7 adults; $5 seniors, students, and children. Tues–Sat 10am–5pm; Sun 10am–4pm. Subway: C, E to Spring St.; 1 to Houston St.

NIGHTS AT THE MUSEUM

No, the exhibits do not come alive once the sun goes down. But on certain nights the usually demure museum atmosphere changes into one of a slightly less-demure party scene. Here are a few museums that offer a variety of nighttime revelry.

Bronx Museum of the Arts 1040 Grand Concourse ((*C*) **718/681-6000;** www.bronxmuseum.org): Party in the house! Or, in this case, the museum. On the first Friday every month, from 6 until 10pm, the museum features live music, video screenings, and art performance. Free admission.

Brooklyn Museum 200 Eastern Pkwy. ((*C*) **718/638-5000;** www.brooklyn museum.org): **First Saturday** is the Brooklyn Museum of Art's ambitious and popular program that takes place on (you guessed it) the first Saturday of each month. It runs from 5 to 11pm and includes free admission and a slate of live music, films, dancing, curator talks, and other entertainment that can get pretty esoteric—think karaoke, lesbian poetry, silent film, experimental jazz, and disco.

Solomon R. Guggenheim Museum 1071 Fifth Ave., at 89th St. ((*C*) **212/423-3500;** www.guggenheim. org): In 2011, the Guggenheim began a new series of after-hours events called, "Art After Dark". Once the general public leaves for the day, the museum's landmark building resonates with music Frank Lloyd Wright never heard, while attendees mingle and possibly even look at some art. Event dates in 2011 included February 1, July 8, and December 8. Admission was $10, free for Guggenheim Members. Check the website to find dates for 2012.

Whitney Museum of Art 945 Madison Ave., at 75th St. ((*C*) **212/570-3600;** www.whitney.org): Most Friday evenings in the summer, it's "Whitney Live," dedicated to the performing arts and featuring concerts and a "pay-as-you-wish" admission (6–9pm year-round).

New York City Police Museum Located in the first precinct station house, built in 1901, the museum exhibits police equipment from throughout the years, such as pistols, uniforms, and vehicles, along with really fun stuff such as master burglar Willie Sutton's lock picks and a machine gun used by Al Capone. A permanent exhibit chronicling the role the NYPD played in the response to the September 11 terrorist attacks is located on the third floor.

100 Old Slip (btw. Water and South sts.). (*C*) **212/480-3100.** www.nycpolicemuseum. org. Admission $8 adults; $5 seniors, students, and children; free for children 1 and under. Mon–Sat 10am–5pm. Sun noon–5pm. Subway: 2, 3 to Wall St.

A firefighter's tools at the New York City Fire Museum.

√**New-York Historical Society ★**   Launched in 1804, the New-York Historical Society is a major repository of American history, culture, and art, with a special focus on New York and its broader cultural significance. The grand neoclassical edifice near the Museum of Natural History has finally emerged from the renovation tent. Now open on the fourth floor is the **Henry Luce III Center for the Study of American Culture,** a state-of-the-art study facility and gallery of fine and decorative arts, which displays more than 40,000 objects amassed over 200 years—including paintings, sculpture, Tiffany lamps, textiles, furniture, even carriages—that had been in storage for decades. The society's Audubon collection is the largest single repository of the works of the great naturalist and painter John James Audubon in the world, with 435 watercolors he made in preparation for *The Birds of America* (1827–38). Each year, the society exhibits a selection of around 40 different watercolors by Audubon revolving around different themes suggested by the legendary naturalist artist's work. Also look for paintings from Hudson River School artists Thomas Cole, Asher Durand, and Frederic Church, including Cole's five-part masterpiece *The Course of Empire*. Of interest to scholars and ephemera buffs are the extensive Library Collections, which include books, manuscripts, maps, newspapers, photographs, and documents chronicling the American experience. (An appointment may be necessary to view some or all of the Library Collections, so call ahead.)

An extensive, top-quality calendar of programs runs the gamut from exhibitions like 2011's "Making American Taste: Narrative Art for a New Democracy," to story hours, to music nights, to lectures by such luminaries as Ric Burns, to expert-led walks through Manhattan neighborhoods and self-guided interactive tours such as the remarkable "Hidden Sites of Slavery and Freedom" tour; call or check the website for schedules.

Take a ride into the past at the New-York Historical Society.

6

EXPLORING NEW YORK CITY

More Manhattan Museums

265

6 SACRED GROUND

In 1991, during the construction of a federal building on the corner of Duane Street and Broadway, workers unearthed human remains. Those remains, it turned out, were of enslaved people and free African slaves, and the site where they were discovered was part of the largest Colonial-era cemetery for blacks in the United States. Building on the site was halted and in 1993 declared a National Historic Landmark. In 2006, the site was designated a national monument and put under the jurisdiction of the National Parks Services. Finally, in late 2007, after almost 16 years, the **African Burial Ground Memorial** (at the corner of Duane and Elk sts.; ✆ **212/637-2019;** www.nps.gov/afbg) was constructed to honor the final resting place of an estimated 15,000 Africans.

The granite memorial (pictured below) sandwiched between towering glass-and-steel federal buildings has seven design elements, including a triangular structure that symbolizes the ship passage to the new world from Africa, and religious symbols from 20 countries of the African Diaspora on a spiral wall that leads down to a map of the world centered in West Africa. It's a moving memorial and well worth visiting while exploring downtown New York.

There is a small **visitor center** in the IRS building at 290 Broadway, adjacent to the memorial, but because it is a federal building, you have to go through a security check to enter. The memorial is open to the public, free of charge, from 9am until 5pm daily (4pm in the winter) except Thanksgiving, Christmas, and New Year's Day.

170 Central Park West (at 77th St.). ✆ **212/873-3400.** www.nyhistory.org. Admission $12 adults; $9 seniors, members of the military, and educators; $7 students; free for children 11 and under; pay-what-you-wish Fri 6–8pm. Tues–Sat 10am–6pm (Fri until 8pm); Sun 11am–5:45pm. Subway: B, C to 81st St.; 1 to 79th St.

The Paley Center for Media If you can resist the allure of this museum (formerly known as the Museum of Television and Radio), I'd wager you've spent the last 70 years in a bubble. You can watch and hear all the great personalities of TV and radio—from Uncle Miltie to Johnny Carson to Jerry Seinfeld—at a private console (available for 2 hrs.). You can also conduct computer searches to pick out the great moments of history, viewing almost anything that made its way onto the airwaves, from the Beatles' first appearance on *The Ed Sullivan Show* to the crumbling of the Berlin Wall (the collection consists of 75,000 programs and commercials). Selected programs are also presented in two theaters and two screening rooms, which can range from "Barbra Streisand: The Television Performances" to little-seen Monty Python episodes.

25 W. 52nd St. (btw. Fifth and Sixth aves.). 📞 **212/621-6600.** www.paleycenter.org. Admission $10 adults, $8 seniors and students, $5 children 13 and under. Wed–Sun noon–6pm (Thurs until 8pm) Subway: B, D, F, V to 47th–50th sts./Rockefeller Center; E, M to 53rd St.

Rubin Museum of Art 🎁 This subtle, lovely, and fascinating museum is in, of all places, the space once occupied by the Women's Department of Barneys. It is about as far from retail as you could imagine. The museum is dedicated to the art of the Himalayas, and in this case that term has a broad geographical reach, stretching all the way from India to Mongolia. You won't find such a wide array of art from Tibet, India, Nepal, Bhutan,

Delicate statues adorn the collection at the Rubin.

Pakistan, Afghanistan, and Burma in one place anywhere else in this hemisphere. The museum's permanent collection of over 2,000 works is enhanced and supplemented by a changing series of exhibits of art from other museums. The collection, which includes small brass and silver statues of deities, textiles, costumes, wall (or tent) hangings, and paintings is astonishing. The lighting and presentation of the art is elegant. I would recommend going through the museum with a guide. (Call ahead for times or to schedule.) The guide I had was wonderful. You may not walk out of this museum a Buddhist, but I would be very surprised if you didn't leave with *some* sense of enlightenment. The museum also has a stylish yet welcoming cafe that serves a selection of food from the countries of the Himalayan region. *Note:* On Friday evenings, the cafe becomes the **K2 Lounge,** where you can hang out, have a rotating special like the Dragon Eyes Mojito and, with a $7 bar minimum, see a movie at the museum for free.

150 W. 17th St. 📞 **212/620-5000.** www.rmanyc.org. Admission $10 adults; $7 seniors, artists, and neighbors; $2 students (with ID); free for children 11 and under; and free to all Fri 6–10pm. Mon and Thurs 11am–5pm; Wed 11am–7pm; Fri 11am–10pm; Sat–Sun 11am–6pm. Subway: A, C, or E to 14th St.; 1 to 18th St.; 2, 3 to 14th St.

Scandinavia House: the Nordic Center in America 🎁 Dedicated to both the shared and unique cultures of Denmark, Finland, Iceland, Norway, and Sweden, Scandinavia House features two floors of galleries and an outdoor sculpture terrace displaying art and design exhibits that can range from "Scandia: Important Early Maps of the Northern Regions" to "Strictly Swedish: An Exhibition of Contemporary Design." The rest of the space, including the 168-seat Victor Borge Hall, is dedicated to a full calendar of lectures, films, music and drama performances, and scholarly presentations, all of a Nordic ilk. The exquisite modern building—designed to showcase Scandinavian materials and aesthetics—is worth a look in itself, especially if you're a modern-architecture buff.

The shop is a riot of fine Scandinavian design, and the excellent **Smörgås Chef** at Scandinavia House serves up Swedish meatballs and other Scandinavian delicacies at reasonable prices, especially for this neighborhood.

58 Park Ave. (btw. 37th and 38th sts.). © **212/779-3587.** www.scandinaviahouse.org. Free. Exhibitions Tues–Sat noon–6pm; cafe Mon–Sat 11am–10pm, Sun 11am–5pm; store Mon–Sat noon–6pm (Wed until 7pm), Sun noon–5pm. Subway: 6 to 33rd St.; 4, 5, 6, 7, S to 42nd St./Grand Central.

Schomburg Center for Research in Black Culture Arturo Alfonso Schomburg, a black Puerto Rican, set himself to accumulating materials about blacks in America, and his massive collection—one of the largest collections of African-American materials in the world—is housed and preserved at this research branch of the New York Public Library in the heart of Harlem. The Exhibition Hall, the Latimer/Edison Gallery, and the Reading Room host changing exhibits related to black culture, such as "African Americans and American Politics," "Obama: The Historic Campaign and Victory in Photos," and a wonderful online exhibition, "In Motion: The African-American Migration Experience" (**www.inmotionaame.org**). A rich calendar of talks and performing-arts events is also part of the program. Make an appointment for a guided tour so you can see the 1930s murals by Harlem Renaissance artist Aaron Douglas; it'll be worth your while. Academics and others interested in a more complete look at the center's holdings can preview what's available online. Call to inquire about current exhibitions and information on tours and public programs. **Note:** Poet Maya Angelou announced recently that the Center will be the recipient of all her papers.

515 Malcolm X Blvd. (Lenox Ave., btw. 135th and 136th sts.). © **212/491-2200.** www.schomburgcenter.org. Free admission. Mon–Thurs noon–8pm; Fri 10am–6pm; Sat 10am–6pm. Subway: 2, 3 to 135th St.

Seaport Museum New York ☺ Dating back to the 17th century, this landmark historic district on the East River encompasses 11 square blocks of historic buildings, a maritime museum, several piers, shops, and restaurants.

You can explore most of the Seaport on your own. It's a beautiful but somewhat odd place. The mainly 18th- and 19th-century buildings lining the cobbled streets and alleyways are impeccably restored but nevertheless have a theme-park air about them, no doubt due to the mall-familiar shops housed within. The Seaport's biggest tourist attraction is Pier 17, a historic barge converted into a mall, complete with food court and cheap-jewelry kiosks.

Despite its rampant commercialism, the Seaport is well worth a look. There's a good amount of history to be discovered here, most of it around the Seaport Museum New York, a fitting tribute to the sea commerce that once thrived here.

In addition to the galleries—which house paintings and prints, ship models, scrimshaw, and nautical designs, as well as frequently changing exhibitions—there are a number of historic ships berthed at the pier to explore, including the 1911 four-masted *Peking* and the 1893 Gloucester fishing schooner *Lettie G. Howard*. A few of the boats are living museums and restoration works in progress; the 1885 cargo schooner *Pioneer* (© **212/748-8786**) offers 2-hour public sails daily from May through October, Tuesday through Friday 3 and 7pm, and Saturday and Sunday 1, 4, and 7pm for $40. If you'd rather keep those sea legs on dry land, the museum offers a number of guided walking tours; call or check the website for details.

The South Street Seaport & Museum offers many period ships and buildings.

Even Pier 17 has its merits. Head up to the third-level deck overlooking the East River, where the long wooden chairs will have you thinking about what it was like to cross the Atlantic on the *Normandie*. From this level you can see south to the Statue of Liberty, north to the Brooklyn Bridge, and Brooklyn Heights on the opposite shore.

At the gateway to the Seaport, at Fulton and Water streets, is the *Titanic* Memorial Lighthouse, a monument to those who lost their lives when the ocean liner sank on April 15, 1912. It was erected overlooking the East River in 1913 and moved to this spot in 1968, just after the historic district was so designated.

A variety of events take place year-round, ranging from street performers to concerts to fireworks; call or check the website.

At Water and South sts.; museum visitor center is at 12 Fulton St. © **212/748-8725** or 212/SEA-PORT (732-7678, for events). www.seany.org. Museum admission $15 adults; $12 students, seniors, and children; free for children 1 and under. Museum Apr–Dec Tues–Sun 10am–6pm; Jan–Mar Thurs–Sun 10am–5pm; ships open noon–4pm. Subway: 2, 3, 4, 5 to Fulton St. (walk east, or downslope, on Fulton St. to Water St.).

Skyscraper Museum   Wowed by the sheer verticality in this town? Awed by the architectural marvel that is the high-rise? You're not alone. If you'd like to learn more about the technology, culture, and muscle behind it all, seek out this formerly itinerant museum, which moved into its first permanent home in 2004 in the 38-story Skidmore, Owings & Merrill tower that also houses the Ritz-Carlton New York, Battery Park. The space comprises two galleries, one housing a permanent exhibition dedicated to the evolution of Manhattan's commercial skyline, the other for changing shows. In 2010 the museum featured "China Prophecy: Shanghai," an exhibition that explored that city's rapid urbanization and modernization.

39 Battery Place (Little West St. and 1st Place). © **212/968-1961.** www.skyscraper.org. Admission: $5 adults, $2.50 seniors and students. Wed–Sun noon–6pm. Subway: 4, 5 to Bowling Green.

Studio Museum in Harlem   This small but lovely museum is devoted to presenting 19th- and 20th-century African-American art, as well as 20th-century African and Caribbean art and traditional African art and artifacts. Rotating exhibitions are a big part of the museum's focus, such as "Smithsonian African-American Photography: The First 100 Years, 1842–1942"; an installation by the artist Shinique Smith as part of its ongoing "Project Space" program; and an annual exhibition of works by emerging artists as part of its Artists-in-Residence program. There's also a small sculpture garden, a good gift shop, and a full calendar of special events.

144 W. 125th St. (btw. Lenox Ave. and Adam Clayton Powell Blvd.). © **212/864-4500.** www. studiomuseum.org. Suggested admission $7 adults, $3 seniors and students, free for children 11 and under, free for all Sun. Thurs–Fri noon–9pm; Sat 10am–6pm; Sun noon–6. Subway: 2, 3 to 125th St.

SKYSCRAPERS & OTHER ARCHITECTURAL HIGHLIGHTS

For details on the **Empire State Building ★★★**, see p. 232; for **Grand Central Terminal ★★**, p. 233; for **Rockefeller Center ★★**, p. 238; for the **U.S. Customs House ★**, p. 276; and for the **Brooklyn Bridge ★★**, p. 228. You might also wish to check out "**Places of Worship,**" later in this chapter, for such treasures as St. Patrick's Cathedral, Temple Emanu-El, and the Cathedral of St. John the Divine ★. See also chapter 2, "New York City in Depth," for a look at the city's evolving architecture.

In addition to checking out the landmarks below, architecture buffs may also want to seek out these notable buildings: The **Lever House,** built in 1952 at 390 Park Ave., between 53rd and 54th streets, and the neighboring **Seagram Building** (1958), at 375 Park Ave., are the city's best examples of the form-follows-function, glass-and-steel International style, with the latter designed by master architect Mies van der Rohe. Also in Midtown East is the **Sony Building,** at 550 Madison Ave., designed in 1984 by Philip Johnson, with a pretty rose-granite facade and a playful Chippendale-style top that puts it a cut above the rest on the block.

The "wedding cake" Ansonia Building.

HARLEM'S ARCHITECTURAL TREASURES

Originally conceived as a bucolic suburbia for 19th-century Manhattan's moneyed set, Harlem has always had more than its share of historic treasures. To find them, pay a call on the **Astor Row Houses,** 130th Street between Fifth and Lenox avenues, a fabulous series of 28 redbrick town houses built in the early 1880s by the Astor family and graced with wooden porches, generous yards, and ornamental ironwork.

Equally impressive is **Strivers' Row,** West 139th Street between Adam Clayton Powell, Jr., and Frederick Douglass boulevards, where hardly a brick has changed among the gorgeous McKim, Mead & White neo–Italian Renaissance town houses since they were built in 1890. Once the original white owners had moved out, these lovely houses attracted the cream of Harlem, such "strivers" as Eubie Blake and W. C. Handy.

Handsome brownstones, limestone town houses, and row houses are atop **Sugar Hill,** 145th to 155th streets, between St. Nicholas and Edgecombe avenues, named for the "sweet life" enjoyed by its residents. In the early 20th century, such prominent blacks as W. E. B. DuBois, Thurgood Marshall, and Roy Wilkins lived in the now–landmark building at 409 Edgecombe Ave.

And if you're venturing this far uptown, don't miss the **Jumel Terrace Historic District,** west of St. Nicholas Avenue between 160th and 162nd streets. Of particular note is **Sylvan Terrace,** which feels more like an upstate Hudson River town than a part of Harlem—well worth seeking out for architecture lovers. A walk along it will lead you directly to the grand **Morris-Jumel Mansion ★**, which is open to the public for tours (see "In Search of Historic Homes," p. 274).

The Upper West Side is home to two of the city's prime examples of residential architecture. On Broadway, between 73rd and 74th streets, is the **Ansonia,** looking for all the world like a flamboyant architectural wedding cake. This splendid Beaux Arts building has been home to the likes of Stravinsky, Toscanini, and Caruso, thanks to its virtually soundproof apartments. (It was also the spot where members of the Chicago White Sox plotted to throw the 1919 World Series, a year before Babe Ruth moved in after donning the New York Yankees' pinstripes.) Even more notable is the **Dakota,** at 72nd Street and Central Park West. Legend has it that the angular 1884 apartment house—accented with gables, dormers, and oriel windows that give it a brooding appeal—earned its name when its developer, Edward S. Clark, was teased by friends that he was building so far north of the city that he might as well be building in the Dakotas. The building's most famous resident, John Lennon, was gunned down outside the 72nd Street entrance on December 8, 1980; Yoko Ono still lives there.

Chrysler Building ★★   Built as Chrysler Corporation headquarters in 1930 (they moved out decades ago), this is perhaps the 20th century's most romantic architectural achievement, especially at night when the lights in its triangular openings play off its steely crown. As you admire its facade, be sure to note the gargoyles reaching out from the upper floors, looking for all the world like Streamline-Gothic hood ornaments. You may recall the picture of Margaret Bourke-White, the famous photographer, perched on one of the gargoyles with her camera. Don't try this at home.

Harlem's elegant "Striver's Row" (see box on p. 271).

There's a fascinating tale behind this building. While it was under construction, its architect, William Van Alen, hid his final plans for the spire that now tops it. Working at a furious pace in the last days of construction, the workers assembled in secrecy the elegant pointy top—and then they raised it right through what people had assumed was going to be the roof, and for a brief moment it was the world's tallest building (a distinction stolen by the Empire State Building a few months later). Its exterior chrome sculptures are magnificent and spooky. The observation deck closed long ago, but you can visit its lavish ground-floor interior, which is Art Deco to the max. The ceiling mural depicting airplanes and other marvels of the first decades of the 20th century evince the bright promise of technology. The elevators are works of art, masterfully covered in exotic woods (especially note the lotus-shaped marquetry on the doors).

405 Lexington Ave. (at 42nd St.). Subway: S, 4, 5, 6, 7 to 42nd St./Grand Central.

An Art Deco spire tops the Chrysler Building.

The surrounding neighborhood is named after the Flatiron Building.

Linger awhile in the beautiful reading room at the New York Public Library.

Flatiron Building   This triangular masterpiece was one of the first skyscrapers. Its wedge shape is the only way the building could fill the triangular property created by the intersection of Fifth Avenue and Broadway, and that happy coincidence created one of the city's most distinctive buildings. (Once asked to compare herself to a famous building in New York City, Katharine Hepburn chose the Flatiron.) Built in 1902 and fronted with limestone and terra cotta (not iron), the Flatiron measures only 6 feet across at its narrow end. So-called for its resemblance to the laundry appliance, it was originally named the Fuller Building, then later "Burnham's Folly" because folks were certain that architect Daniel Burnham's 21-story structure would fall down. It didn't. There's no observation deck, and the building mainly houses publishing offices, but there are a few shops on the ground floor. The building's existence has served to name the neighborhood around it—the Flatiron District, home to a bevy of smart restaurants and shops. 175 Fifth Ave. (at 23rd St.). Subway: N, R to 23rd St.

New York Public Library ★★   The New York Public Library, adjacent to Bryant Park ★ (p. 292) and designed by Carrère & Hastings (1911), is one of the country's finest examples of Beaux Arts architecture, a majestic structure of white Vermont marble with Corinthian columns and allegorical statues. Before climbing the broad flight of steps to the Fifth Avenue entrance, note the famous lion sculptures—*Fortitude* on the right, and *Patience* on the left—so dubbed by whip-smart former mayor Fiorello La Guardia. At Christmastime they don natty wreaths to keep warm.

This library is actually the Humanities and Social Sciences Library, only one of the research libraries in the New York Public Library system. The interior is one of the finest in the city and features Astor Hall, with high-arched marble ceilings and grand staircases. Thanks to restoration and modernization, the main

IN SEARCH OF HISTORIC HOMES

The Historic House Trust of New York City preserves 23 sites, located in city parks in all five boroughs. Those particularly worth seeking out include the **Morris-Jumel Mansion ★** in Harlem at 65 Jumel Terrace, at 160th Street, east of St. Nicholas Avenue (℅ **212/923-8008;** www.morrisjumel.org; Wed–Sun 10am–4pm), a grand colonial mansion built in the Palladian style (in 1765) and now Manhattan's oldest surviving residential house.

Built around 1764, the **Dyckman Farmhouse Museum,** farther uptown at 4881 Broadway, at 204th Street (℅ **212/ 304-9422;** www.dyckmanfarmhouse.org; Wed–Sat 11am–4pm; Sun noon–4pm), is the only Dutch colonial farmhouse remaining in Manhattan, stoically and stylishly surviving the urban development that grew up around it.

The **Edgar Allan Poe Cottage,** 2460 Grand Concourse, at East Kingsbridge Road, the Bronx (℅ **718/881-8900;** www.bronxhistoricalsociety.org/poe cottage; Mon–Fri group tours by appointment, Sat 10am–4pm, Sun 1–5pm), was the last home (1846–49) of the brilliant but troubled poet and author, who moved his wife here because he thought the "country air" would be good for her tuberculosis. The house is outfitted as a memorial to the writer, with period furnishings and exhibits on his life and times. *Note:* The Cottage went through a major renovation in 2010-11 and is now ready to receive visitors once again.

The **Merchant's House Museum ★** (pictured below), 29 E. 4th St., between Lafayette Street and Bowery in NoHo (℅ **212/777-1089;** www.merchants house.org; Thurs–Mon noon–5pm), is a rare jewel: a perfectly preserved 19th-century home, complete with intact interiors, whose last resident is said to be the inspiration for Catherine Sloper in Henry James's *Washington Square.*

Each of the 19 other houses also has a fascinating story to tell. A brochure listing the locations and touring details of all 23 of the historic sites is available by calling ℅ **212/360-8282.** You'll also find information online at **www.historichouse trust.org**. Admission to each house is generally no more than $5 ($8 at Merchant's House).

Reading Rooms on the third floor have been returned to their stately glory and moved into the computer age (goodbye, card catalogs!). They are a must-see. *Note:* For those who just have to stay in touch, the library now provides Wi-Fi service for free in the reading rooms. After a $5-million restoration, what was once known only as Room 117, a Beaux Arts masterpiece with incredible views of Fifth Avenue and 42nd Street, is now known as the Lionel Pincus and Princess Firyal Map Division. Here you will find possibly the finest and most extensive collection of maps in the world. In 2008, the library's facade began a 3-year restoration, to be completed for the building's centennial in 2011.

Even if you don't stop in to peruse the periodicals, you may want to check out one of the excellent rotating exhibitions. Call or check the website to see what's on while you're in town. There's also a full calendar of lecture programs, with past speakers ranging from Tom Stoppard to Pico Iyer; popular speakers often sell out, so it's a good idea to purchase tickets in advance.

Fifth Ave. at 42nd St. ℂ **917/275-6975** (exhibits and events) or 212/930-0800 (general number). www.nypl.org. Free admission to all exhibitions. Mon and Thurs–Sat 10am–6pm; Tues–Wed 10am–8pm; Sun 1–5pm. Subway: 1, 2, 3 to 42nd St./Broadway; B, D, F, M to 42nd St./6th Ave.; S, 4, 5, 6 to Grand Central/42nd St.; 7 to Fifth Ave.

United Nations   In the midst of New York City is this working monument to world peace. The U.N. headquarters occupies 18 acres of international territory—neither the city nor the United States has jurisdiction here—along the East River from 42nd to 48th streets. Designed by an international team of architects (led by American Wallace K. Harrison and including Le Corbusier) and finished in 1952, the complex along the East River weds the 39-story glass slab Secretariat with the free-form General Assembly on beautifully landscaped grounds donated by John D. Rockefeller, Jr. The 180 member-nations use the facilities to arbitrate worldwide disputes.

During the 60-minute tour, your guide will take you to the General Assembly Hall and introduce the history and activities of the United Nations and its related organizations. Along the tour you'll see donated objects and artwork, including charred artifacts that survived the atomic bombs at Hiroshima and

Sculpture on the grounds of the United Nations.

HISTORIC DOWNTOWN STRUCTURES

To find a good sampling of "ancient" New York, head downtown, where it all began.

You might want to first stop at the southern tip of the island at Battery Park, where an old fort called **Castle Clinton National Monument** (✆ **212/344-7220;** www.nps.gov/cacl) still stands. The fort, or what remains of it, was built between 1808 and 1811 to defend New York Harbor against the British. In the mid–19th century the fort was the city's first immigration center. A small museum has exhibits that follow the evolution of the fort.

Not far from Castle Clinton, across the street from the northeast corner of Battery Park, at 1 Bowling Green, is the relatively modern 1907-built **U.S. Customs House** ★ (**www.oldnycustom house.gov**), which houses the National Museum of the American Indian (p. 260) and a federal bankruptcy court. Designed by Cass Gilbert and now a National Historic Landmark, the granite structure features giant statues carved by Daniel Chester French (of Lincoln Memorial fame) lining the front that personify Asia (pondering philosophically), America (bright eyed and bushy tailed), Europe (decadent and whose time has passed), and Africa (sleeping). Inside, the airy oval rotunda designed by Spanish engineer Raphael Guastavino was frescoed by Reginald Marsh to glorify the shipping industry (and, by extension, the Customs office once housed here).

One of Wall Street's most recognizable sights is the imposing **Federal Hall National Memorial,** 26 Wall St. (✆ **212/ 825-6990;** www.nps.gov/feha). Built in 1842, the memorial, with the 1883-built statue of George Washington on the steps directly across from the New York Stock Exchange, was erected on the site of New York's first City Hall. Inside, it's now a museum, with exhibits that elucidate the events surrounding the memorial and other aspects of American

history. The infrastructure of the memorial suffered from the massive shock of the nearby attack on the World Trade Center; as a result, it underwent a $16-million rehabilitation.

George Washington was a visible presence in 18th-century New York and he worshiped at **St. Paul's Chapel,** built in 1766 and part of the Trinity Church (p. 281) at 209 Broadway (✆ **212/233-4164;** www.saintpaulschapel.org). The chapel now serves as a memorial to the victims of 9/11.

So now we know where Washington worshiped, but where did he eat? At **Fraunces Tavern,** the same place where he bade farewell to his officers (as pictured below) at the end of the Revolution. This 1907-built tavern is a replica of the original 1717 tavern. It's now a museum, at 54 Pearl St., near Broad Street (✆ **212/425-1778;** www.fraunces tavernmuseum.org), and an actual restaurant (✆ **212/968-1776**).

Nagasaki, stained-glass windows by Chagall, a replica of the first *Sputnik,* and a mosaic called *The Golden Rule,* based on a Norman Rockwell drawing, which was a gift from the United States in 1985.

If you take the time to wander the beautifully landscaped grounds, you'll be rewarded with lovely views and some surprises. The mammoth monument *Good Defeats Evil,* donated by the Soviet Union in 1990, fashioned a contemporary St. George slaying a dragon from parts of a Russian ballistic missile and an American Pershing missile.

For an unusual treat, try a multiethnic meal while visiting the U.N. at the **Delegates' Dining Room** (*©* **212/963-7625;** www.aramark-un.com). Lunch is served from 11:30am to 2:30pm. Diners must be 12 years and over.

At First Ave. and 46th St. *©* **212/963-8687.** www.un.org/tours. Guided tours $16 adults, $11 seniors 60 and over and students 13 and over, $9 children 5–12. Children 4 and under not permitted. Weekday tours at 10:30am and 4pm. Guided tours might be canceled with short notice when heads of state and government are meeting. UN open weekdays 9:45am–4:45pm, weekends 10–4:15. Subway: S, 4, 5, 6, 7 to 42nd St./Grand Central.

Woolworth Building ★   This soaring "Cathedral of Commerce" cost Frank W. Woolworth $14 million worth of nickels and dimes in 1913. Designed by Cass Gilbert, it was the world's tallest edifice until 1930, when it was surpassed by the Chrysler Building. At its opening, President Woodrow Wilson pressed a button from the White House that illuminated the building's 80,000 electric light bulbs. Called the "Mozart of skyscrapers" by architectural critic Paul Goldberger, the neo-Gothic architecture is rife with spires, gargoyles, flying buttresses, vaulted ceilings, 16th-century-style stone-as-lace traceries, castlelike turrets, and a churchlike interior. Housing financial institutions and high-tech companies, the grand tower is still dedicated to the almighty dollar.

Step into the lofty marble entrance arcade to view the gleaming mosaic Byzantine-style ceiling and gold-leafed neo-Gothic cornices. The corbels (carved figures under the crossbeams) in the lobby include whimsical portraits of the building's engineer Gunvald Aus measuring a girder (above the staircase to the left of the main door), Gilbert holding a model of the building, and Woolworth counting coins (both above the left-hand corridor of elevators). Stand near the security guard's podium and crane your neck for a glimpse at Paul Jennewein's murals *Commerce* and *Labor,* half hidden up on the mezzanine. Cross Broadway for the best overview of the exterior.

233 Broadway (at Park Place, near City Hall Park). Subway: 2, 3 to Park Place; R to City Hall.

PLACES OF WORSHIP

New York has an incredible range of renowned religious institutions, notable for their history, architecture, and/or inspirational music. I've listed two of Harlem's premier gospel institutions below; if you would rather go to one of these gospel services in the company of a knowledgeable guide, see "Organized Sightseeing Tours," on p. 299 of this chapter. Additionally, if you would like to hear the rousing gospel of the four-time Grammy Award–winning **Brooklyn Tabernacle Choir** ★, see p. 322.

If you do plan to attend a gospel service, be prepared to stay for the entire 1½- to 2-hour service. It is impolite to exit early. (Services are extremely popular, so you'll find it just plain difficult to leave before the end anyway.)

Abyssinian Baptist Church ★
The most famous of Harlem's more than 400 houses of worship is this Baptist church, founded downtown in 1808 by African-American and Ethiopian merchants. It was moved uptown to Harlem back in the 1920s by Adam Clayton Powell, Sr., who built it into the largest Protestant congregation—white or black—in America. His son, Adam Clayton Powell, Jr. (for whom the adjoining boulevard was named), carried on his tradition, and also became the first-ever black U.S. congressman from New York. Abyssinian is now the domain of the fiery, activist-minded Rev. Calvin O. Butts, whom the chamber of commerce has declared a "living treasure." The Sunday morning services—at 9 and 11am—offer a wonderful opportunity to experience the Harlem gospel tradition.
132 Odell Clark Place (W. 138th St., btw. Adam Clayton Powell Blvd. and Lenox Ave.). ℭ **212/862-7474.** www.abyssinian.org. Subway: 2, 3, B, C to 135th St.

Abyssinian Baptist Church in Harlem.

Cathedral of St. John the Divine ★   The world's largest Gothic cathedral, St. John the Divine has been a work in progress since 1892. Its sheer size is amazing enough—a nave that stretches two football fields and a seating capacity of 5,000—but keep in mind that there is no steel structural support. The church is being built using traditional Gothic engineering—blocks of granite and limestone are carved out by master masons and their apprentices—which may explain why construction is still ongoing, more than 100 years after it began, with no end in sight. In December 2001, fire destroyed the north transept, which housed the gift shop. But this phoenix rose from the ashes quickly; the cathedral was reopened to visitors within a month, even though the scent of charred wood was still in the air. That's precisely what makes this place so wonderful: Finishing isn't necessarily the point. Though maybe it is; in late 2007 scaffolding was finally removed from the church's southwest tower exposing that magnificent structure for the first time in over 15 years. And in late 2008, after a $41-million cleaning and repair from the 2001 fire, the church was rededicated, its great nave open and its 8,500-pipe organ playing.

Though it's the seat of the Episcopal Diocese of New York, St. John's embraces an interfaith tradition. Internationalism is a theme found throughout the cathedral's iconography. Each chapel is dedicated to a different national, ethnic, or social group. The genocide memorial in the Missionary chapel—dedicated to the victims of the Ottoman Empire in Armenia (1915–23), of the Holocaust (1939–45), and in Bosnia-Herzegovina since 1992—moved me to tears, as did the FDNY memorial in the Labor chapel. Although it was originally

All the stonework is hand-carved at the Cathedral of St. John the Divine.

conceived to honor 12 firefighters killed in 1966, hundreds of personal notecards and trinkets of remembrance have evolved it into a moving tribute to the 343 firefighting heroes killed on September 11, 2001.

You can explore the cathedral on your own, or on the **Public Tour,** offered 6 days a week; also inquire about the **Vertical Tour** (offered twice every Sat), which takes you on a hike up the 11-flight circular staircase to the top, for spectacular views. St. John the Divine is also known for presenting outstanding workshops, musical events, and important speakers. The free New Year's Eve concert draws thousands of New Yorkers; so, too, does its annual **Feast of St. Francis** ★ (Blessing of the Animals), held in the first Sunday in October (see the "New York City Calendar of Events," in chapter 2). Call for event information and tickets. To hear the incredible pipe organ in action, attend the weekly recitals with visiting organists, which highlight one of the nation's most treasured pipe organs, Sunday at 5:15pm in the fall and spring.

1047 Amsterdam Ave. (at 112th St.). (C) **212/316-7490** or 212/932-7347 for tour information and reservations. www.stjohndivine.org. Public Tour $6 adults, $5 seniors and students; Vertical Tour $15 adults, $12 seniors and students. Mon–Sat 7am–6pm; Sun 7am–7pm. Public Tours offered Tues–Sat 11am and 1pm; Sun 1pm. Vertical Tours offered Sat noon and 2pm. Worship services daily 8am (morning prayer), Mon–Sat 5pm (evening prayer), Mon–Sat 8:30am and 12:15pm and Sun 8 and 9am (holy Eucharist), Sun 4pm (choral evensong); AIDS memorial service 4th Sat of the month at 12:15pm. Subway: B, C, 1 to Cathedral Pkwy.

The Church of the Transfiguration 📷 When you come upon this oddly beautiful historic structure amidst modern high-rise condos in the burgeoning Madison Square neighborhood, you will once again be awed at the diversity of New York. Also known as the Little Church Around the Corner, this Episcopalian house of worship, with its twists and turns, has been compared to a "holy cucumber vine." Built in 1849, the church was granted United States landmark status in 1973. Its history includes sheltering escaped slaves during the Civil War draft riots, being one of the first churches to hand out food for the poor at the start of the Depression, and, most significantly, for its close relationship to the theater. In 1923, the Episcopal Actor's Guild was formed at the church and some of the noted actors involved include Basil Rathbone, Mary Pickford, and Tallulah Bankhead, with Charlton Heston, Barnard Hughes, and, most recently Beth Holland serving as presidents.

1 E. 29th St. (btw. Fifth and Madison aves.). (C) **212/684-6770.** www.littlechurch.org. Subway: 6 to 28th St; R to 28th St.

Mother A.M.E. Zion Church   Another of Harlem's great gospel churches is this African Methodist Episcopal house of worship, the first black church to be founded in New York State. Established on John Street in lower Manhattan in 1796, Mother A.M.E. was known as the "Freedom Church" for the central role it played in the Underground Railroad. Among the escaped slaves the church hid was Frederick Douglass; other famous congregants have included Sojourner Truth and Paul Robeson. Mother A.M.E. relocated to Harlem in 1914 and moved into this grand edifice in 1925. Rousing Sunday services are at 11am.

140-6 W. 137th St. (btw. Adam Clayton Powell Blvd. and Lenox Ave.). ℭ **212/234-1544.** www. amez.org. Subway: 2, 3, B, C to 135th St.

St. Patrick's Cathedral   This incredible Gothic white-marble-and-stone structure is the largest Roman Catholic cathedral in the United States, as well as the seat of the Archdiocese of New York. Designed by James Renwick, begun in 1859, and consecrated in 1879, St. Patrick's wasn't completed until 1906. Strangely, Irish Catholics picked one of the city's WASPiest neighborhoods for St. Patrick's. Timothy Dolan was named archbishop of New York by Pope Benedict XVI in early 2009, upon the retirement of Cardinal Edward Egan. The vast cathedral seats a congregation of 2,200; if you don't want to come for Mass, you can pop in between services to get a look at the impressive interior. The St. Michael and St. Louis altar came from Tiffany & Co. (also located here on Fifth Ave.), while the St. Elizabeth altar—honoring Mother Elizabeth Ann Seton, the first American-born saint—was designed by Paolo Medici of Rome.

Fifth Ave. (btw. 50th and 51st sts.). ℭ **212/753-2261.** www.saintpatrickscathedral.org. Free admission. Daily 6:30am–8:45pm. Mass Mon–Fri 7, 7:30, and 8am, noon, and 12:30, 1, and 5:30pm; Sat 8am, noon, and 5:30pm; Sun 7, 8, 9, and 10:15am, noon, 1, 4 (in Spanish), and 5:30pm; holy days 7, 7:30, 8, 8:30, and 11:30am, noon, and 12:30, 1, 5:30, and 6:30pm. Subway: B, D, F, M to 47th–50th sts./Rockefeller Center.

Temple Emanu-El   Many of New York's most prominent and wealthy families are members of this Reform congregation—the first to be established in New York City—housed in the city's most famous synagogue. The largest house of Jewish worship in the world is a majestic blend of Moorish and Romanesque styles, symbolizing the mingling of Eastern and Western cultures. The temple houses a small but remarkable collection of Judaica in the Herbert & Eileen Bernard Museum, including a collection of Hanukkah lamps with examples ranging from the 14th to the 20th centuries. Three galleries also tell the story of the congregation Emanu-El from 1845 to the present. Abbreviated tours may be given after Friday night and Saturday morning

Beautiful altars line the walls of St. Patrick's Cathedral.

Temple Emanu-El features a blend of Moorish and Romanesque styles.

services; groups of 10 or more can reserve a tour for free (download the online form). Inquire for a schedule of lectures, films, music, symposiums, and other events.

1 E. 65th St. (at Fifth Ave.). © **212/744-1400.** www.emanuelnyc.org. Free admission. Self-guided tours Sun–Thurs 10am–4:30pm. Services Sun–Thurs 5:30pm; Fri 5:15pm; Sat 10:30am. Subway: N, R to Fifth Ave.; 6 to 68th St.

Trinity Church Serving God and mammon, this Wall Street house of worship—with neo-Gothic flying buttresses, beautiful stained-glass windows, and vaulted ceilings—was designed by Richard Upjohn and consecrated in 1846. At that time, its 280-foot spire dominated the skyline. Its main doors, embellished with biblical scenes, were inspired in part by Ghiberti's famed doors on Florence's Baptistery. The historic Episcopal church stood strong while office towers crumbled around it on September 11, 2001; however, a digital organ has replaced the historic pipe organ, which was severely damaged by dust and debris.

The church runs a brief **tour** daily at 2pm (a second Sun tour follows the 11:15am Eucharist); groups of five or more should call © **212/602-0872** to reserve. There's a small museum at the end of the left aisle displaying documents (including the 1697 church charter from King William III), photographs, replicas of the Hamilton-Burr duel pistols, and other items. Surrounding the church is a churchyard whose monuments read like an American history book: a tribute to martyrs of the American Revolution, Alexander Hamilton, Robert Fulton, and many more. Lined with benches, this makes a wonderful picnic spot on warm days.

Also part of Trinity Church is **St. Paul's Chapel,** at Broadway and Fulton Street, New York's only surviving pre-Revolutionary church, and a transition shelter for homeless men until it was transformed into a relief center after September 11, 2001; it returned to its former duties in mid-2002. Built by Thomas McBean, with a templelike portico and fluted Ionic columns supporting a massive pediment, the chapel resembles London's St. Martin-in-the-Fields. In the small graveyard, 18th- and early-19th-century notables rest in peace and modern businesspeople sit for lunch.

Trinity holds its renowned **Concerts at One** series of chamber music and orchestral concerts Thursday at 1pm.

At Broadway and Wall St. *℗* **212/602-0800** or 212/602-0872 for tour information. www.trinity wallstreet.org. Free admission and free tours at 2pm daily. Museum Mon–Fri 9am–5:30pm (closed during the 12:05pm service); Sat–Sun 9am–3:45pm. Services Mon–Fri 8:15am, 12:05, and 5:15pm (except Thurs); Sun 9 and 11:15am (also 8 and 10am Eucharist service at St. Paul's Chapel, at Broadway btw. Vesey and Fulton sts.); Daily Prayers for Peace service 12:30pm at St. Paul's Chapel. Subway: 4, 5 to Wall St.

CENTRAL PARK & OTHER PLACES TO PLAY

Without the miracle of civic planning that is **Central Park ★★★**, Manhattan would be a virtual unbroken block of buildings. Instead, smack in the middle of Gotham, an 843-acre natural retreat provides a daily escape valve and tranquilizer for millions of New Yorkers.

While you're in the city, be sure to take advantage of the park's many charms—not the least of which is its sublime layout. Frederick Law Olmsted and Calvert Vaux won a competition with a plan that marries flowing paths with sinewy bridges, integrating them into the natural rolling landscape with its rocky outcroppings, man-made lakes, and wooded pockets. Construction concluded in 1870 and designers predicted the hustle and bustle to come, and tactfully hid traffic from the eyes and ears of parkgoers by building roads that are largely hidden from the bucolic view.

Central Park is a year-round destination for New Yorkers.

On just about any day, Central Park is crowded with New Yorkers and visitors alike. On nice days, especially weekend days, it's the city's party central. Families come to play in the snow or the sun, depending on the season; in-line skaters come to fly through the crisp air and twirl in front of the band shell; couples come to stroll or paddle the lake; dog owners come to hike and throw Frisbees to Bowser; and just about everybody comes to sunbathe at the first sign of summer. On beautiful days, the crowds are part of the appeal—folks come here to peel off their urban armor and relax, and the common goal puts a general feeling of camaraderie in the air. On these days, the people-watching is more compelling than anywhere else in the city. But even on the most crowded days, there's always somewhere to get away from it all, if you just want a little peace and quiet and a moment to commune with nature.

ORIENTATION & GETTING THERE   Look at your map of the city—that great green swath in the center of Manhattan is Central Park.

It runs from 59th Street (also known as Central Park South) at the south end to 110th Street at the north end, and from Fifth Avenue on the east side to Central Park West (the equivalent of Eighth Ave.) on the west side. A 6-mile rolling road, Central Park Drive, circles the park, and has a lane set aside for bikers, joggers, and in-line skaters. A number of transverse (crosstown) roads cross the park at major points—at 65th, 79th, 86th, and 97th streets—but they're built down a level, largely out of view, to minimize intrusion on the bucolic nature of the park.

A number of subway stops and lines serve the park, and which one you take depends on where you want to go. To reach the southernmost entrance on the west side, take an A, B, C, D, or 1 to 59th Street/Columbus Circle. To reach the southeast corner entrance, take the N or R to Fifth Avenue; from this stop, it's an easy walk into the park to the **Information Center** in the Dairy (© **212/794-6564;** daily 10am–5pm), midpark at about 65th Street. Here you can ask questions, pick up park information, and purchase a good park map.

If your time for exploring is limited, I suggest entering the park at 72nd or 79th Street for maximum exposure (Subway: B, C to 72nd St. or 81st St./ Museum of Natural History). From here, you can pick up park information at the visitor center at **Belvedere Castle** (© **212/772-0210;** April–Oct Tues–Sun 10am–5pm, Nov–March Wed–Sun 10am-5pm), midpark at 79th Street. There's also a visitor center at the **Charles A. Dana Discovery Center** (© **212/860-1370;** Apr–Oct Tues–Sun 10am–5pm; Nov–Mar Wed–Sun 10am-5pm), at the northeast corner of the park at Harlem Meer, at 110th Street between Fifth and Lenox avenues (Subway: 2, 3 to Central Park North/110th St.). The Dana Center is also an environmental education center hosting workshops, exhibits, music, and park tours, and lends fishing poles for fishing in Harlem Meer (park policy is catch and release).

Food carts and vendors are set up at all of the park's main gathering points, so finding a bite to eat is never a problem. During the summer you'll also find a fixed food counter at the Conservatory Garden entrance at 105th and Fifth Avenue and on the east side of the park north of the 72nd Street entrance. Both casual snacks and more sophisticated New American dining is found at the **Boat House,** on the lake near 72nd Street and Park Drive North (© **212/517-2233;** www.thecentralparkboathouse.com).

GUIDED WALKS The Central Park Conservancy offers a slate of free walking tours of the park; call ☎ **212/360-2726** or check **www.centralparknyc. org** for the current schedule (click on "Visit" at the top, and then select "Tours."). The Dana Center hosts guided tours on occasion (call ☎ **212/ 860-1370,** or 311 for a schedule). Also consider a private walking tour; many of the companies listed in "Organized Sightseeing Tours," later in this chapter, offer guided tours of the park.

FOR FURTHER INFORMATION Call the main number at ☎ **212/310-6600** for recorded information, or 212/628-1036 to speak to a person. Call ☎ **888/ NY-PARKS** (697-2757) or go to www.nycgovparks.org/parks/centralpark for events information. The **Central Park Conservancy**'s comprehensive website is also worth checking out at **www.centralpark.org**, which features excellent maps and a far more complete rundown of park attractions and activities than I have room to include here. If you have an emergency in the park, dial ☎ **911,** or for a less pressing matter, call ☎ **311,** and you will be connected to the park rangers.

SAFETY TIP Even though the park has the lowest crime rate of any of the city's precincts, keep your wits about you, especially in the more remote northern end. It's a good idea to avoid the park entirely after dark, unless you're heading to one of the restaurants for dinner or to a SummerStage or Shakespeare in the Park event (see "Park It! Shakespeare, Music & Other Free Fun," p. 408), when you should stick with the crowds. For more safety tips, see "Safety," in chapter 9.

Exploring the Park

The best way to see Central Park is to wander along the park's 58 miles of winding pedestrian paths, keeping in mind the following highlights.

Before starting your stroll, stop by the **Information Center** in the Dairy (☎ **212/794-6564;** daily 10am–5pm), midpark in a 19th-century-style building overlooking Wollman Rink at about 65th Street, to get a good park map and other information on sights and events, and to peruse the kid-friendly exhibit on the park's history and design.

The southern part of Central Park is more formally designed and heavily visited than the relatively rugged and remote northern end. Not far from the Dairy are the **Carousel,** with 58 hand-carved horses (☎ **212/439-6900;** weather permitting; Apr–Oct Mon–Sun 10am–6pm; Nov–March Sat, Sun, and holidays 10am–dusk; rides are $2); the zoo (see below); and the Wollman Rink for roller- or ice-skating (see "Activities," below).

The Mall, a long formal walkway lined with elms shading benches and sculptures of sometimes forgotten writers, leads to the focal point of Central Park, **Bethesda Fountain ★** (along the 72nd St. transverse road). Bethesda Terrace and its grandly sculpted entryway border a large lake where dogs fetch sticks, rowboaters glide by, and early-morning anglers try their luck at catching carp, perch, catfish, and bass. You can rent a rowboat at or take a gondola ride from Loeb Boathouse, on the eastern end of the lake (see "Activities," below). Boats of another kind are at **Conservatory Water** (on the east side at 73rd St.), a stone-walled pond flanked by statues of both Hans Christian Andersen and Alice in Wonderland. On Saturday at 10am from April to November, die-hard yachtsmen race remote-controlled sailboats in fierce competitions that follow Olympic regulations.

Central Park

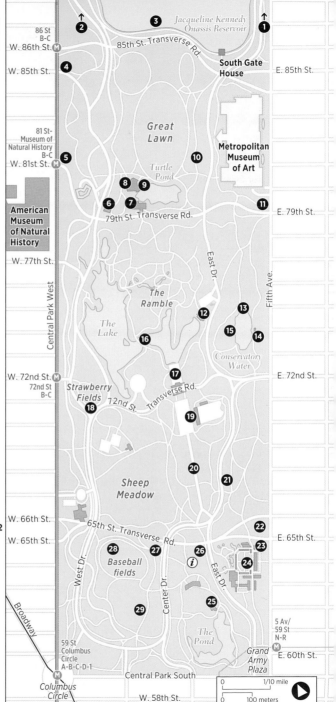

Strawberry Fields commemorates Beatle John Lennon in Central Park.

If the action there is too intense, Sheep Meadow on the southwestern side of the park is a designated quiet zone, where Frisbee throwing and kite flying are as energetic as things get. Another respite is **Strawberry Fields ★**, at 72nd Street on the west side. This memorial to John Lennon, who was murdered across the street at the Dakota apartment building (72nd St. and Central Park West, northwest corner), is a gorgeous garden centered on an Italian mosaic bearing the title of the lead Beatle's most famous solo song and his lifelong message: IMAGINE. In keeping with its goal of promoting world peace, the garden has 161 varieties of plants, donated by each of the 161 nations in existence when it was designed in 1985. This is a wonderful place for peaceful contemplation.

Bow Bridge, a graceful lacework of cast iron designed by Calvert Vaux, crosses over the lake and leads to the most bucolic area of Central Park, the Ramble. This dense 38-acre woodland with spiraling paths, rocky outcroppings, and a stream is the best spot for bird-watching and feeling as if you've discovered an unimaginably leafy forest right in the middle of the city.

North of the Ramble, **Belvedere Castle** (ⓒ **212/772-0210;** April–Oct Tues–Sun 10am–5pm, Nov–March Wed–Sun 10am–5pm), is worth a visit if you're with children. From the castle, set on Vista Rock (the park's highest point at 135 ft.), you can look down on the Great Lawn, where softball players and sun worshipers compete for coveted greenery, and the Delacorte Theater, home to Shakespeare in the Park (see "Park It! Shakespeare, Music & Other Free Fun," in chapter 8). The small Shakespeare Garden, south of the theater, is scruffy, but it does have plants, herbs, trees, and other greenery mentioned by the Bard. Behind the Belvedere Castle is the **Swedish Cottage Marionette Theatre ★** (ⓒ **212/988-9093;** tickets can be purchased online at www.city parksfoundation.org), hosting marionette plays for children throughout the year; call or go online to see what's on.

Continue north along the east side of the Great Lawn, parallel to East Drive. Near the glass-enclosed back of the **Metropolitan Museum of Art ★★★** (p. 234) is Cleopatra's Needle, a 69-foot obelisk originally erected in Heliopolis around 1475 B.C. It was given to the city by the khedive of Egypt in 1880. (The khedive bestowed to the city of London a similar obelisk, which sits on the embankment of the Thames.)

North of the 86th Street Transverse Road is the **Jacqueline Kennedy Onassis Reservoir,** renamed for the beloved first lady, who lived nearby and often enjoyed a run along the 1½-mile jogging track that circles the reservoir.

North of the reservoir is my favorite part of the park. It's much less traversed and in some areas absolutely tranquil. The North Meadow (at 96th St.) features 12 baseball and softball fields. Sadly, the North Meadow is circled by a not-very-attractive fence, and 6 months of the year that fence is locked and the meadow closed. An unfortunate recent trend in Central Park has been the proliferation of fences. They have become so prevalent that at times you get the feeling you are not really in a park but a museum.

North of the North Meadow, at the northeast end of the park, is the **Conservatory Garden ★** (at 105th St. and Fifth Ave.), Central Park's only formal garden, with a magnificent display of flowers and trees reflected in calm pools of water. (The gates to the garden once fronted the Fifth Ave. mansion of Cornelius Vanderbilt II.) The **Lasker Rink and Pool** (© **917/492-3857**) is the only swimming pool in Central Park, and in the winter it's converted to a skating rink that offers a less hectic alternative to Wollman Rink (see "Activities," below). Harlem Meer and its boathouse were recently renovated and look beautiful. The boathouse now berths the **Charles A. Dana Discovery Center,** near 110th Street between Fifth and Lenox avenues (© **212/860-1370;** April–Oct Tues–Sun 10am–5pm, Nov–March Wed–Sun 10am–5pm), where children learn about the environment and borrow fishing poles for catch-and-release at no charge. The Pool (at W. 100th St.), possibly the most idyllic spot in all of Central Park, was recently renovated and features willows, grassy banks, and a pond populated by some very well-fed ducks. You might even spot an egret and a hawk or two.

Central Park Zoo/Tisch Children's Zoo ★ ☺ Here is a pleasant refuge within a refuge, where lithe sea lions frolic in the central pool area with beguiling style, gigantic but graceful polar bears glide back and forth across a watery pool that has glass walls through which you can observe very large paws doing very smooth strokes, monkeys seem to regard those on the other side of the fence with knowing disdain, and in the hot and humid Tropic Zone, large colorful birds swoop around in freedom, sometimes landing next to nonplused visitors.

Because of its small size, the zoo is at its best with its displays of smaller animals. The indoor multilevel **Tropic Zone** is a real highlight, its steamy rainforest home to everything from black-and-white colobus monkeys to Emerald tree boa constrictors to a leaf-cutter ant farm; look for the new dart-poison-frog exhibit, which is very cool. So is the large penguin enclosure in the **Polar Circle,** which is better than the one at San Diego's SeaWorld. In the **Temperate Territory,** look for the Asian red pandas (cousins to the big black-and-white ones), which look like the world's most beautiful raccoons. Despite their pool and piles of ice, however, the polar bears still look sad.

The zoo is good for short attention spans; you can cover the entire thing in 1½ to 3 hours, depending on the size of the crowds and how long you like to linger. It's also very kid-friendly, with lots of well-written and -illustrated placards that older kids can understand. For the littlest ones, there's the $6-million **Tisch Children's Zoo ★**. With goats, llamas, potbellied pigs, and more, this petting zoo and playground is a real blast for the 5-and-under set.

830 Fifth Ave. (at 64th St., just inside Central Park). (© **212/439-6500.** www.central parkzoo.com. Admission $12 adults, $9 seniors, $7 children 3–12, free for children 2 and under. Apr–Oct Mon–Fri 10am–5pm, Sat–Sun and holidays 10am–5:30pm; Nov–Apr daily 10am–4:30pm. Last entrance 30 min. before closing. Subway: N, R to Fifth Ave; 6 to 68th St.

The Children's Zoo is just the right size for the young ones.

ACTIVITIES

The 6-mile rolling road circling the park, Central Park Drive, has a lane set aside for bikers, joggers, and in-line skaters. The best time to use it is when the park is closed to traffic: Monday to Friday 10am to 3pm (except Thanksgiving to New Year's). It's also closed from 7pm Friday to 7am Monday, but when the weather is nice, the crowds can be hellish.

BIKING   Off-road mountain biking isn't permitted; stay on Central Park Drive or your bike may be confiscated by park police. You can rent cruisers and 21-speed bikes as well as tandems in Central Park at the **Loeb Boathouse,** midpark near 72nd Street and Park Drive North, just in from Fifth Avenue (© **212/517-2233**), for $9 to $15 an hour, with a complete selection of kids' bikes, trailers, and the like ($200 cash or credit card deposit required); at **Metro Bicycles,** 1311 Lexington Ave., at 88th Street (© **212/427-4450;** www.metrobicycles.com), for about $9 an hour, or $45 a day; and at **Toga Bike Shop,** 110 West End Ave., at 64th Street (© **212/799-9625;** www.togabikes.com), for $35 a day. No matter where you rent, be prepared to leave a credit card deposit.

BIRD-WATCHING   Central Park is one of the great bird-watching sites in the U.S., believe it or not. Every spring, millions of birds migrate from their winter homes north to New England and Canada and many stop over for a few days in the park. About 230 species of birds can be found in Central Park each year, including owls and hawks, the most famous of which is Pale Male, whose illustrious life (including a brush with a Fifth Avenue co-op board that wanted to evict him from his nest on one of their ledges) has inspired not one, but *three* books. In the middle of May, you can see scores of bird-watchers with their binoculars in hand peering up at tree tops, hoping to catch a glimpse of their favorite warbler, nuthatch, or some rarely sighted species. They are friendly types, and it's usually very easy to fall in with one of the little groups that makes its way through the park. I am one of this breed of birders, and I tell you that on a sweet, warm spring day, all the trees in bloom, it's heaven to be in Central Park birding. I once saw 15 species of warblers in one afternoon! Visit **www.centralparknyc.org/visit/ things-to-do/sports/birding.html** for more information. There is also a good coffee-table book, *Birds of Central Park*. For those who can't make it in the spring, the whole process is repeated in reverse in the fall.

BOATING   From March through November, gondola rides and rowboat rentals are available at the **Loeb Boathouse,** midpark near 72nd Street and Park Drive North, just in from Fifth Avenue (ⓒ **212/517-2233;** www.thecentral parkboathouse.com). Rowboats cost $12 for the first hour, $2.50 for every quarter-hour thereafter, and a $20 (cash) deposit is required; reservations for gondola rides ($30 per half hour) are accepted.

HORSE-DRAWN CARRIAGE RIDES   At the entrance to the park at 59th Street and Central Park South, you'll see a line of horse-drawn carriages waiting to take passengers on a ride through the park or along certain of the city's streets. Horses belong on city streets as much as chamber pots belong in our homes. You won't need me to tell you how forlorn most of these horses look; if you insist, a ride is about $50 for 20 minutes (plus tip), but I suggest skipping it.

ICE-SKATING   Central Park's **Wollman Rink ★**, on the east side of the park between 62nd and 63rd streets (ⓒ **212/439-6900;** www.wollmanskating rink.com), is the city's best outdoor skating spot, more spacious than the tiny rink at Rockefeller Center. It's open for skating from mid-October to mid-April, depending on the weather. Rates are $11 for adults ($15 Fri–Sun), $4.75 for seniors ($8.25 Fri–Sun), and $5.50 for children 11 and under ($5.75 Sat–Sun), and skate rental is $6.25; lockers are available

Strolling Central Park in Spring is one of the great New York City activities.

Sailing away in Central Park.

(locks are $4.50, $6 deposit). **Lasker Rink** (℡ **917/492-3857** or 212/534-7639), on the east side around 106th Street, is a less expensive alternative to the more crowded Wollman Rink. It's open November through March. Rates are $6.50 for adults, $3.50 for children, $2.25 for seniors, and skate rental is $5.50; lockers are also available (locks are $3.25, $4 deposit).

IN-LINE SKATING   Central Park is the city's most popular place for blading. See the beginning of this section for details on Central Park Drive, the main drag for skaters. On weekends, head to West Drive at 67th Street, behind Tavern on the Green, where you'll find trick skaters weaving through a New York Roller Skating Association (NYRSA) slalom course, or to the mall in front of the band shell (above Bethesda Fountain) for twirling to tunes. In summer **Wollman Rink ★** converts to a hotshot roller rink, with half-pipes and lessons available (see "Ice-Skating," above).

You can rent skates for $20 a day (including pads and a helmet) from **Blades,** 156 W. 72nd St., between Broadway and Columbus Avenue (℡ **212/787-3911;** www.blades.com). Wollman Rink (see above) also rents in-line skates for park use at similar rates.

PLAYGROUNDS   Twenty-one playgrounds are scattered throughout the park, perfect for jumping, sliding, tottering, swinging, and digging. At Central Park West and 81st Street is the **Diana Ross Playground ★**, voted the city's best by *New York* magazine. Also on the west side is the Spector Playground, at 85th Street and Central Park West, and, a little farther north, the Wild West Playground, at 93rd Street. On the east side is the Billy Johnson Playground, at 67th Street and Fifth Avenue, a delightfully landscaped space rife with islands, bridges, and big slides; and the Pat Hoffman Friedman Playground, right behind the Metropolitan Museum of Art at East 79th Street, is geared toward older toddlers.

RUNNING   Marathoners and wannabes regularly run in Central Park along the 6-mile Central Park Drive, which circles the park (please run toward traffic to avoid being mowed down by wayward cyclists and in-line skaters). The **New York Road Runners** (℡ **212/860-4455;** www.nyrr.org), organizers of the New York City Marathon, schedules group runs (open to non-members) Monday through Friday at 6:30am and 6:30pm and Saturday and Sunday at 10am, leaving from the entrance to the park at 90th Street and Fifth Avenue. (For the NYRRC's list of the suggested running routes, see the box titled "Running the City," below.)

SWIMMING   The only pool in Central Park, **Lasker Pool** (on the east side at around 106th St.; ℡ **212/534-7639**), is open July through September 7. It's free. Bring a towel and other supplies, including a lock.

Other Parks

For parks in Brooklyn and Queens, see "Highlights of the Outer Boroughs," later in this chapter. For more information on these and other city parks, go online to **www.nycgovparks.org**. A new law (in effect May 2011) makes it a $50 fine to smoke in 43 square miles of parks, public plazas, beaches, and boardwalks.

Battery Park ★★   As you traverse Manhattan's concrete canyons, it's sometimes easy to forget that you're actually on an island. But here, at Manhattan's southernmost tip, you get the very real sense that just out past Liberty, Ellis, and Staten islands is the vast Atlantic Ocean.

RUNNING THE CITY

Here are the New York Road Runners' top picks for routes in Manhattan.

○ **Jacqueline Kennedy Onassis Reservoir:** Possibly the most famous running route in the world; presidential candidates have run this 1½-mile route, as well as the famous former first lady for whom it is now named.

○ **The Loop in Central Park:** I used to run past Madonna and her bodyguards when she was a frequenter of the 6-mile loop. Now I see Howard Stern jogging, no bodyguards in sight, but usually with a female companion or two.

○ **East River:** Entering on 63rd Street and York Avenue and running up to 125th Street and back is a 6-mile jog where you will pass Gracie Mansion,

high-rises overlooking the river, and fishermen testing the river waters.

○ **Hudson River South:** Enter at Chelsea Piers at West 23rd Street and continue down to Battery Park City and back for this approximately 5-mile run. In the warm months it's a carnival downtown, with in-line skaters, kayakers, musicians, and cyclists crowding the slim downtown park.

○ **Hudson River North:** This approximately 6-mile run starts at Riverbank State Park, at 145th Street on the Hudson River, and continues through lovely Riverside Park, passing the 79th Street Boat Basin, and ending at the Intrepid Sea, Air & Space Museum.

The 21-acre park is named for the cannons built to defend residents after the American Revolution. Castle Clinton National Monument (the place to purchase tickets for the Statue of Liberty and Ellis Island ferry; see listings earlier in this chapter) was built as a fort before the War of 1812, though it was never used as such.

Battery Park is a park of monuments and memorials, many paying tribute to tragedy and death. Here you will find the East Coast Memorial, dedicated to 4,601 servicemen who died in Atlantic coastal waters during World War II; the New York Korean War Veterans Memorial; the American Merchant Mariner's Memorial, dedicated to Merchant Mariners lost at sea; the Salvation Army Memorial; the Hope Garden, dedicated to those who live with HIV or have died from AIDS; the Irish Hunger Memorial, a tribute to those

The Battery Park Esplanade looks out over New York Harbor.

who died during the potato famine in Ireland; and the 22-ton bronze sphere by Fritz Koenig that was recovered from the rubble of the World Trade Center, where it stood on the plaza between the two Twin Towers as a symbol of global peace—severely damaged but still whole. Mingling throughout these memorials you will find the requisite T-shirt vendors, hot-dog carts, and Wall Streeters eating deli sandwiches on the many park benches. Pull up your own bench for a good view out across the harbor.

From State St. to New York Harbor. (C) **212/344-3491.** www.thebattery.org. Subway: R to Whitehall St.; 1 to South Ferry; 4, 5 to Bowling Green.

Bryant Park ★   Another success story in the push for urban redevelopment, Bryant Park is the latest incarnation of a 4-acre site that was, at various times in its history, a graveyard and a reservoir. Named for poet and *New York Evening Post* editor William Cullen Bryant (look for his statue on the east end), the park actually rests atop the New York Public Library's many miles of underground stacks. Another statue is also notable: a squat and evocative stone portrait of Gertrude Stein, one of the few outdoor sculptures of women in the city.

This simple green swath, just east of Times Square, is welcome relief from Midtown's concrete, taxi-choked jungle, and good weather attracts brown-baggers from neighboring office buildings. Just behind the library is **Bryant Park Grill** ((C) **212/840-6500**), a gorgeous, airy bistro with spectacular views but merely decent New American food. Still, brunch is a good bet, and the grill's summer alfresco restaurant—the casual **Cafe,** with small tables beneath a canopy of trees (open mid-Apr to Nov)—is extremely pleasant on a nice day. Laptop owners, take note: There is free Wi-Fi in the park.

Le Carrousel ★ complements the park's French classical style. It's not as big as the Central Park Carousel but utterly charming nonetheless, with 14 different animals that revolve to the sounds of French cabaret music. Le Carrousel is open daily all year, weather permitting (Aug–Oct 11am–8pm; Nov–Jan Sun–Thurs 11am–9pm, Fri–Sat 11am–10pm; February 11am–8pm; March–May 11am–7pm; June–Oct 11am–8pm), and costs $2 per ride.

From late October until late February, you can skate (for free!) on a seasonal ice rink called Citi **Pond.** Check **http://thepondatbryantpark.com** for the latest on the rink.

Behind the New York Public Library, at Sixth Ave. btw. 40th and 42nd sts. (C) **212/768-4242.** www.bryantpark.org. Subway: B, D, F, Q to 42nd St.; 7 to Fifth Ave.

Governors Island ★★   Situated a half-mile south of Manhattan, the 172-acre Governors Island, was, for many years, a Coast Guard installation. Before that, it was an army post for nearly 200 years and played a part in the Revolutionary War. In 2003, ownership was passed to the state of New York. In April 2010, New York City took over. It's actually a kind of miracle that this happened, given the often contentious city-state dealings, but it's all because the state's finances are so precarious it couldn't deal with the expenses of running the island. The city gladly pocketed the deed. Because it was a military base for so long, few New Yorkers, much less tourists, have ever visited Governors Island (though many a Coast Guard veteran can tell you stories about being stationed there). But that has changed. Mayor Bloomberg has already turned much of Governors Island into a public park. The city also plans to add a high school, some commercial development and potentially a satellite campus for New York University.

Governor's Island is a great place for families to explore.

Twenty-two acres on the island are already a national monument, centered around two 1812-era fortresses. The island is open to visitors from end of May to October. During that time, you can take a free ferry from the Battery Maritime Building adjacent to the Staten Island Ferry in lower Manhattan. (There is also a ferry from Pier 6 in Brooklyn Bridge Park.) On the island, you can walk or bicycle in a car-free environment and attend any number of activities from jazz concerts to table tennis demonstrations that occur over the summer and early fall. Visit the website for the latest news, events, and plans for the future of the park.

ⓒ **212/440-2200.** www.govisland.com. Free. Free ferries depart from Battery Maritime Building (a large green building right next to the Staten Island Ferry terminal), Slip #7, in Manhattan; in Brooklyn free ferries depart from Pier 6, at the foot of Atlantic Avenue; check the website for exact schedules. The island is open every Fri–Sun from end of May–Oct. Subway: 1 to South Ferry; 4/5 to Bowling Green. Bus: M1. 6, 15.

Hudson River Park Carousel & Skatepark ★★ ☺ Located at Pier 62 on the Hudson River next to Chelsea Piers, the carousel and skatepark are part of a 9-acre park (which includes the adjacent Pier 63) that is, without exaggerating, an urban miracle. With a Sheeps Meadow-like expanse of grass, marvelous landscaping and terrific views of the Hudson River, this is an ideal place to bring the kids for a sunny afternoon respite from the steel and concrete of the city. Opened in the spring of 2010, this park, which was built and is maintained by the nonprofit Hudson River Park Trust, is part of an enormous, revival of Manhattan's West Side waterfront. Its pride and joy is a custom-designed 36-passenger **carousel** with all the hand-carved animals indigenous to the greater New York City area. "Except for the unicorn," my guide informed me. It's hard to imagine a more joyful feeling than riding around and around with the soft breezes from the Hudson playing over you. Nearby is a state-of-the-art **Skatepark** where skateboarders can do their thing on 15,000 square feet of whorls, turns and dives designed by California's (where else?) Site design Group. The great Tony Hawk came to try it out and declared it one of the best he's ever experienced. After you've done your 180s, you can stroll over to Chelsea Piers and grab lunch or an early dinner and take the bus back to your hotel.

293

PARK RENAISSANCE IN LOWER MANHATTAN

For the last 10 years, New York City has slowly but most definitely surely been adding more park space to lower Manhattan—much of it absolutely wonderful. In fact, it's most often not only well-designed, but aesthetically gratifying—*beautiful,* why don't we just say it?—inventive, and plain fun.

A great example of this lower Manhattan park renaissance is the **High Line** (www.nycgovparks.org/parks/highline). Located in the old meatpacking district— once a desolate part of New York, now decidedly chic—the High Line is an elevated park where trains once rolled by. It runs from Gansevoort Street to West 30th Street, along Washington St. at the south end, then between Tenth and Eleventh avenues on the north end. Also on the west side is the newly opened **Pier 25,** not far from famed Stuyvesant High School, which features an 18-hole miniature golf course.

The east side of Lower Manhattan is having its own surge, as well. I took a walk recently from the Staten Island Ferry terminal up to the Brooklyn Bridge, and there was a flurry of activity. Much of the new construction is going on under the East River Drive—elevated at this point—where there will be public areas, landscaped with amenities for walkers. Near the South Street Seaport, **Pier 15** is being completely transformed and will feature a café and lots of green. In short, Lower Manhattan, in terms of park space, is getting better and better and better.

(f) **212/627-2020.** www.hudsonriverpark. org. Carousel $2 per ride. (Children under 42" tall must be accompanied by an adult 18 years or older.) Carousel open Sat–Sun, 11am–6pm, weather permitting. Skatepark free. Skatepark open from 8am to dusk. Subway: C, E to 23rd St. Bus: M23. **Note:** M23 bus will take you almost directly to the entrance of Pier 62.

Riverside Park ★★ 📖 I spent much of my time in my early years in New York in Riverside Park (*(f)* **212/408-0264;** www.nycgov parks.org/parks/riversidepark) staring at the New Jersey skyline, jogging along the wind-swept Hudson river, playing hoops at the courts on 77th Street (when I still could jump), taking strolls along the promenade on hot summer nights, and watching the comings or goings of the unusual community that lives in the boats at the 79th Street Boat

Riding a (large) indigenous creature on the Hudson River Park Carousel.

Basin. This underrated beauty, designed by Frederick Law Olmsted, the same man who designed Central Park, stretches 4 miles from 72nd Street to 158th Street. The serpentine route along the Hudson River offers a variety of lovely river vistas, 14 playgrounds, two tennis courts, softball and soccer fields, a skate park, beach volleyball, the aforementioned Boat Basin, two cafes—the **Boat Basin Café,** at 79th Street (☎ **212/496-5542;** www.boatbasincafe.com) open late March through October, and **Hurley's Hudson Beach Café,** at 105th Street (☎ **917/370-3448;** www.pdohurleys.com/hudson.htm), open April through October—and monuments such as the Eleanor Roosevelt statue at 72nd Street, the Soldiers and Sailors Monument at 90th Street, and **Grant's Tomb** at 122nd Street (☎ **212/666-1640;** www.grantstomb.org; daily 9am–5pm). But here's the best part: On a hot summer day, when Central Park is teeming with joggers, sunbathers, and in-line skaters, Riverside Park, just a few blocks from Central Park's western fringe, is comparatively serene. And if you're curious as to where now-famed airline pilot Sully Sullenberger landed US Airways Flight 1549 in the frigid Hudson River at 3:31pm on January 15, 2009, you can stroll or bike south of the Boat Basin to about 50th Street and gaze out and imagine the miraculous event. The **Riverside Park Fund** (☎ **212/870-3070;** www.riverside parkfund.org) has an excellent website with a comprehensive list of events and gives history with illustrations of the parkland.

Union Square Park   Here's a delightful place to spend an afternoon. Reclaimed from drug dealers and abject ruin in the late 1980s, Union Square Park is now one

POCKET PARKS IN MANHATTAN

When is a public space with trees and benches too small to be called a park? When it's a **pocket park.** They're also called **vest-pocket parks, mini-parks** and—gasp—**parkettes.** These spaces are too small for any of the traditional park activities—running, cycling, Frisbee-tossing, and so on. But because they're often located near big buildings and lots of pedestrian traffic, the parks provide a welcome respite from the sound and fury of New York City. None of them are probably worth a planned visit—not like their big brothers and sisters—but when you come across, pause and check out their assuming beauty.

Located at 53rd Street between Madison and Fifth Avenues—not far from Saks, Rockefeller Center and the Museum of Modern Art—**Paley Park** is one of New York's finest pocket parks. Here you can sit undisturbed and rest your tired dogs while thumbing through your trusty *Frommer's New York City.* Or simply close your eyes and take a catnap.

Other pocket parks are dotted within the city. If you're reading this and have access to the Internet, check out the very good list of New York pocket parks compiled by Jacquelin Carnegie on frommers.

com: **www.frommers.com/articles/6118. html**.

By the way, pocket parks are not to be confused with what the city is now calling **Public Plazas.** Defined by the City's Department of Transportation (which administers them) as "a public space in the city that provides a place for people to enjoy the public realm," the chief difference seems to be a lack of trees. Regardless, they're more places where you can sit and relax in the middle of it all. *Whatever* they're called, let's just be grateful.

Riverside Park is a great place for a run.

of the city's best assets and home of the New York's most famous **greenmarket** (see box below). The seemingly endless subway work should no longer be disturbing the peace by the time you're here. This patch of green remains, with or without the construction, the focal point of the Flatiron and Gramercy Park neighborhoods. Don't miss the grand equestrian statue of George Washington at the south end or the bronze statue (by Bartholdi, the sculptor of the Statue of Liberty) of the Marquis de Lafayette at the east end, gracefully glancing toward France.

From 14th to 17th sts. (btw. Park Ave. South and Broadway). www.nycgovparks.org/parks/union squarepark. Subway: 4, 5, 6, L, N, Q, R to 14th St./Union Sq.

Washington Square Park   You'll be hard-pressed to find much "park" in this mainly concrete square—a burial ground in the late 18th century—but it's undeniably the focal point of Greenwich Village. Chess players, skateboarders, street musicians, New York University students, couples, the occasional film crew, and

---

The Greening of New York

Whenever I travel to a city anywhere around the world, I make it a priority to visit that city's greenmarket, or farmers' market. I've been to some great ones, and I might be a bit prejudiced, but I haven't been to many better than the **Union Square Greenmarket ★★** in New York City. New York has greenmarkets throughout the city on different days of the week, but the biggest and best is at Union Square every Monday, Wednesday, Friday, and Saturday, 8am to 6pm.

You'll find fresh pickings from upstate and New Jersey farms, just-caught fish from Long Island,

homemade cheese and other dairy products, baked goods, plants, and organic herbs and spices. It's a true New York scene, with everyone from models to celebrated chefs poring over the bounty. The Union Square Greenmarket is open year-round but is at its peak August through October when the local harvest—tomatoes, corn, greens, grapes, peppers, and apples—flourishes. For more information and locations and schedules, see GrowNYC's website at **www.grownyc.org/unionsquaregreen market**, or call ✆ **212/788-7476.**

FROM TOP: **Union Square's Greenmarket draws crowds for the fresh produce and other treats; city dogs enjoy the run just for them at Washington Square Park.**

not a few homeless people compete for attention throughout the day and most of the night. (If anyone issues a friendly challenge to play you in the ancient and complex Chinese game of Go, don't take them up on it—you'll lose money.)

In the 1830s, elegant Greek Revival town houses on Washington Square North, known as "the Row" (note especially nos. 21–26), attracted the elite. Stanford White designed Washington Arch (1891–92) to commemorate the centenary of George Washington's inauguration as first president. The arch was refurbished in 2004 and now features exterior lighting. From 2007 to 2009, the park underwent a controversial, $16-million-plus renovation that added a perimeter fence, increased green space, and shrank the central plaza.

At the southern end of Fifth Ave. (where it intersects Waverly Place, btw. MacDougal and Wooster sts.). Subway: A, C, E, F, M to W. 4th St. (use 3rd St. exit).

Chelsea Piers

One of the city's biggest—and most successful—private urban-development projects is the 30-acre **Chelsea Piers Sports & Entertainment Complex** (© **212/336-6666;** www.chelseapiers.com). Jutting out into the Hudson River on four huge piers between 17th and 23rd streets, it's a terrific multifunctional recreational facility.

⟨ō⟩ The Little Red Lighthouse

Also known as Jeffrey's Hook Lighthouse, this little red lighthouse located under the George Washington Bridge in Fort Washington Park on the Hudson River was the inspiration for the 1942-children's book classic, *The Little Red Lighthouse and The Great Gray Bridge*, by Hildegarde Swift and Lynd Ward. Built in New Jersey in 1880 and reconstructed and moved to its current spot in 1921, it was operational until 1947. The lighthouse was to be removed in 1951, but because of its popularity there was a public outcry and it was saved. It's now a New York City landmark and on the list of National Register of Historic Places. It's a fun place for the kids to explore and scenic picnic spot in nice weather. It's open to the public, with guided tours by the **New York City Urban Park Rangers** (☎ 212/304-2365) from spring through fall.

The **Sports Center** (☎ 212/336-6000), a three-football-fields-long megafacility, does health clubs one better. It offers not only the usual cardiovascular training, weights, and aerobics, but also a four-lane quarter-mile indoor running track, a boxing ring, basketball courts, a sand volleyball court, a gorgeous 25-yard indoor pool with a whirlpool and sun deck, the world's most challenging rock-climbing wall plus a bouldering wall, and the Spa at Chelsea Piers, which offers massage, reflexology, facials, and the like. Day passes to the Sports Center are $50 for nonmembers; spa treatments are extra, of course.

The **Golf Club** (☎ 212/336-6400) has 52 all-weather fully automated hitting stalls on four levels and a 200-yard, net-enclosed, artificial-turf fairway jutting out over the water, making it the best place in the city to hit a few. Prices start at $25 for 90 balls (147 balls during off-peak hours), and club rentals are available.

The **Sky Rink** (☎ 212/336-6100) has twin indoor rinks for recreational skating and pickup hockey games with Hudson River views. General skating is $13 for adults, $11 for seniors and youth; skate rental is $7.50. Due to organized skating activities, general skating is limited, so call ahead to find out schedules of availability.

The **Field House** (☎ 212/336-6500) is mainly for team sports, but rock climbers will enjoy the 30-foot indoor climbing wall, designed for kids as well as grown-ups. Open climbs for adults 17 and older are $22, Tuesday through Thursday from 7:30pm to 9:30pm; same-day climb reservations start at 9am. Youth open rock climbing lessons ($30, ages 5–9, Tues–Thurs 3:30–4:30pm, Sat 9–10pm) are available. Batting cages are $2.50 per 10 pitches.

Feeling like a little 10-pin tonight? State-of-the-art **AMF Chelsea Piers Lanes** (☎ 212/835-BOWL [835-2695]; www.300newyork.com) offers 40 lanes of fun. Games are $8.25 to $11 per person, and shoe rental is $6 plus tax.

Beyond its athletics, the complex is a destination in and of itself. The 1¼-mile esplanade has benches and picnic tables with terrific river views; they serve as the perfect vantage point for watching a cruise ship head out to sea, or the Navy and Coast Guard ships sailing in for Fleet Week each May.

Getting there: Chelsea Piers is accessible by taxi and the M23 or M14 crosstown buses. The nearest subway is the C and E at 23rd Street and Eighth Avenue, then pick up the M23 or walk 4 long blocks west. Another option is to take the A, C, or E to 14th Street or the L train to Eighth Avenue, walk to the river, then follow the walking/riding/running path along the river north.

ORGANIZED SIGHTSEEING TOURS

Reservations are required for some of the tours listed below, but even if they're not, it's always best to call ahead to confirm prices, times, and meeting places.

Harbor Cruises

If you'd like to sail the New York Harbor aboard the 1885 cargo schooner *Pioneer*, see the listing for South Street Seaport & Museum on p. 268.

Note that some of the lines below may have limited schedules in winter, especially for evening cruises. Call ahead or check online for current offerings.

Bateaux New York The most elegant and romantic of New York's evening dinner cruises. Cruises are aboard the *Celestial*, designed to accommodate 300 guests with two suites, one dance floor, two outdoor strolling decks, a state-of-the-art sound system, and windows galore. Dinner is a three-course sit-down affair, with jackets and ties suggested for men, evening dresses for women. The food isn't what you'd get at Jean-Georges, but Bateaux (sister to egalitarian Spirit Cruises; see below) offers a very nice supper-club-style night on the town, and the views are fabulous. A live quartet entertains with jazz standards and pop vocal tunes.

Departs from Pier 61, Chelsea Piers, W. 23rd St. and Twelfth Ave. C **866/817-3463.** www. bateauxnewyork.com. 2-hr. brunch cruises around $56; 3-hr. dinner cruises around $116–$134 per person. Subway: C, E to 23rd St.

Circle Line Sightseeing Cruises ★★ A New York institution, the Circle Line is famous for its 3-hour tour around the entire 35 miles of Manhattan. This Full Island cruise passes by the Statue of Liberty, Ellis Island, the Brooklyn Bridge, the United Nations, Yankee Stadium, the George Washington Bridge, and more, including Manhattan's wild northern tip. The panorama is riveting, and the commentary isn't bad. The big boats are basic but fine, with lots of deck room for everybody to enjoy the view. Snacks, soft drinks, coffee, and beer are available onboard for purchase.

If 3 hours is more than you or the kids can handle, go for either the 2-hour Semi-Circle or the Harbor Lights cruise, both of which show you the highlights of the skyline. There's also a 75-minute Liberty version that sticks close to the south end of the island. But of all the tours, the kids might like the **Beast** best, a thrill-a-minute speedboat ride offered May through September only.

In addition, a number of adults-only live music and DJ cruises sail regularly from the seaport from May through September ($20–$40 per person). Depending on the night of the week, you can groove to the sounds of jazz, Latin, gospel, dance tunes, or blues as you sail along viewing the skyline.

Departing from Pier 83, at W. 42nd St. and Twelfth Ave. C **212/563-3200.** www.circleline42. com. Check the website or call for the most up-to-date schedule. Sightseeing cruises $27–$35 adults, $24–$30 seniors, $19–$22 children 12–3, free children 2 and under. Subway to Pier 83: A, C, E to 42nd St.

New York Waterway ★★ New York Waterway, the nation's largest privately held ferry service and cruise operator, does a 90-minute Skyline tour that takes in all the major sights, like the Empire State Building, Statue of Liberty, and Brooklyn Bridge. They also offer a staggering amount of different sightseeing options,

Seeing NYC from the Deck of a Historic Fireboat

The fireboat *John J. Harvey* served New York City from 1931 to 1994. Saved from the scrapyard by a group of boat lovers who purchased her in 1999, the *Harvey* (pictured below) is being lovingly and painstakingly preserved and restored, mostly by volunteer labor, and is now on the National Register of Historic Places. Currently docked at Pier 66 on the West Side of Manhattan (btw. 26th and 27th sts.), the boat offers occasional free tours around the harbor and up the Hudson River from May through autumn, periodically unleashing the "deck pipes" (water guns) to spray all around (at 18,000 gallons a minute). Expect to get soaked! Check the calendar at **www.fireboat.org** to see if you're lucky enough to be in town when one of these tours is offered, to learn more about the historic and heroic boat and its crew, or make a donation to help

fund its restoration. Even after starting its second life, the fireboat answered the call for New York City once more: on September 11, 2001, the *John J. Harvey* left its slip to head down to Ground Zero, and the crew rigged its pumps to draw water from the Hudson when downtown's fire hydrants weren't working after the attack on the World Trade Center. The boat and its crew pumped water for 80 hours. For more about the *John J. Harvey* and how New York Harbor and the Hudson River have shaped New York City and the United States from the Colonial era through today, pick up a copy of Jessica DuLong's *My River Chronicles: Rediscovering the Work that Built America* (Free Press, 2009), a personal memoir and history of the river and its times by the *Harvey's* acting chief engineer.

including a very good 90-minute Twilight Cruise, Shades of Autumn tour, and baseball cruises to Yankee games.

Most cruises departing from Pier 78, at W. 38th St. and Twelfth Ave. (Hudson River Park). (C) **800/533-3779.** www.nywaterway.com. Skyline and Twilight cruises $26 adults, $21 seniors, $15 children, free children 3 and under; Shades of Autumn cruise $45 adults, $40 seniors, $20 children 3–12. Free bus transportation from 57th, 49th, 42nd, and 34th sts. to 38th St. Terminal; you can flag down any of the big red buses labeled NY WATERWAY or wait at any of the bus stops along those streets.

Spirit Cruises Spirit Cruises' modern ships are floating cabarets that combine sightseeing in New York Harbor with freshly prepared meals, musical revues, and

The Attack of the Double-Decker Buses

They are everywhere. There is no escape. They clog up the already over-crowded streets, spewing exhaust, their red or blue exteriors splashed with a garish display of self-promotion and advertising, loudspeakers blaring as the people huddled on the upper deck (swathed in plastic ponchos when it rains) look down at the natives on the streets. I'm talking about double-decker buses. They run in the morning, they run at night, they run all day long. Can you tell I'm not a fan? I think New York is best appreciated on foot, or on public buses and subways. Sure these double-decker buses have guides but take the facts they dish out with a grain of salt; they aren't always accurate. If you insist, the top bus tour is **Gray Line New York** (*©* **800/669-0051** or 212/445-0848; www.newyorksightseeing.com). Tours depart from various locations. Hop-on, hop-off bus tours start at $49 adults, $39 children 3 to 11 (for 48 hours).

dancing to live bands. The atmosphere is festive, fun, and relaxed. The buffet meals are nothing special, but they're fine.

Departing from Pier 61 at Chelsea Piers, W. 23rd St. and Twelfth Ave. *©* **866/483-3866.** www. spiritcruises.com. 2-hr. lunch cruises around $41–46; 3-hr. dinner cruises around $75–$90 per person. Inquire about children's rates. Subway: C, E to 23rd St.

Air Tours

Liberty Helicopters   How about a bird's-eye view of Manhattan—literally? Fifteen- and 20-minute helicopter tours from lower Manhattan take in the Mid-town skyscrapers, Central Park, the Statue of Liberty. If you opt for the longest tour, you'll fly far enough uptown to take in the George Washington Bridge and Yankee Stadium. Flights leave every 15 minutes daily from 9am to 9pm, but note that at least a 24-hour advance reservation is required.

Departing from the Downtown Manhattan Heliport, Pier 6, 111 Wall St. *©* **212/967-6464** or 800/542-9933. www.libertyhelicopters.com. Pilot-narrated tours $150 and up, plus a $30 heli-port facility security fee. Subway: N, R to Whitehall St.; 1 to South Ferry.

Specialty Tours

In addition to the options below, for those interested in touring lower Manhattan, the **Municipal Art Society** ★ (𝄢 212/935-3960 or 212/453-0050; www.mas. org) offers a 90-minute **downtown tour** Tuesday at 12:30pm and a walking tour of Grand Central Terminal ★★ Wednesday at 12:30pm—though there is a $10 "suggested donation" for those tours (see below).

The **Downtown: Where New York Began** guided tour ★ explores the vivid history and amazing art and architecture of the nation's first capital and the world center of finance. Stops include the New York Stock Exchange, Trinity Church, Federal Hall National Monument, Cass Gilbert's gorgeous U.S. Customs House ★ (p. 276), and many other sites of historic and cultural importance. Tours begin at the **Downtown Information Center,** at 55 Exchange Place, Ste. 401 (Subway: J, M to Broad St.; 2, 3 to Wall St.). Reservations are not required (unless you're a group), but you can call 𝄢 212/935-3960 or 212/453-0050 or visit **www.mas.org** to confirm the schedule.

CULTURAL ORGANIZATIONS

The **Municipal Art Society** ★ (𝄢 **212/935-3960** or 212/453-0050; www. mas.org) offers excellent historical and architectural walking tours aimed at intelligent, individualistic travelers. Each is led by a highly qualified guide who offers insights into the significance of buildings, neighborhoods, and history. Topics range from the urban history of Greenwich Village to "Rockefeller Center: Art Deco Masterwork" to an examination of the Broadway theater district. Tours are $15. Reservations may be required depending on the tour, so it's best to call ahead. The full schedule is available online.

The **92nd Street Y** ★ (𝄢 **212/415-5500;** www.92ndsty.org) offers a wonderful variety of walking and bus tours, many featuring funky themes or behind-the-scenes visits. Subjects can range from "Carnegie Hall Tour and Tea" to "The Great Cupcake Challenge: Taste and Rate Tour," or from "Central Park West" to "Jewish Harlem." Prices range from $25 to $100, but many include ferry rides,

---

📎 Grabbing a (Pedi)cab

You really don't want to burden that nag with a carriage ride through Central Park in the middle of the summer, do you? Better you should hire a real beast of burden—a driver of a **pedicab** who probably really needs the money. Pedicabs are becoming common sights on the streets of New York. The drivers are friendly, informative, and don't poop in the street. The **Manhattan Rickshaw Company** (𝄢 212/604-4729; www. manhattanrickshaw.com) is one pedicab company, where fares range from $15–$30 for a street hail ride; call to arrange a guided tour.

Take the M5: A City Bus That Hits the Highlights

If your feet are worn out from walking, but you still want to see some sights, I suggest hopping on the **M5 bus.** Its route runs from Washington Heights down to the Staten Island Ferry terminal. If you board uptown, around 125th Street and Riverside Drive, and take it downtown, you'll pass landmarks such as Grant's Tomb, Riverside Church, Lincoln Center, Columbus Circle, St. Patrick's Cathedral, Rockefeller Center, the New York Public Library, Empire State Building, Flatiron Building, and Washington Square. And all you need is your MetroCard (or exact coin change) and your trusty *Frommer's New York City* guide with your maps in hand. The bus will move slowly enough where you will be able to consult your book and find the corresponding landmarks.

afternoon tea, dinner, or whatever suits the program. Guides are well-chosen experts on their subjects, ranging from historians to an East Village poet, mystic, and art critic (for "Allen Ginsberg's New York" and "East Village Night Spots"), and many routes travel into the outer boroughs; some day trips even reach beyond the city. Advance registration is required for all tours. Schedules are planned a few months in advance, so check the website for tours that might interest you.

INDEPENDENT OPERATORS

NYC Discovery Tours (② 212/465-3331; www.ny.com/sights/tours/nyc discovery) offers more than 80 walking tours of the Big Apple, divided into seven categories: neighborhood and architecture (such as "Brooklyn Bridge"), cultural theme ("Art History NYC"), biography ("John Lennon's New York"), tavern tours, food tasting ("Little Italy" and "Chinatown"), indoor ("U.S. Customs House"), and American history ("Civil War" and "American Revolution"). Tours are about 2 hours long and cost $18 per person ($25 per person for tasting tours; drinks cost extra for the tavern tours). Call for reservations and to receive a schedule.

All tours from **Joyce Gold History Tours of New York ★★** (② 212/242-5762; www.nyctours.com) are offered by Joyce Gold herself, an instructor of Manhattan history at New York University and the New School for Social Research, who has been conducting history walks around New York since 1975. Her tours can really cut to the core of this town; Joyce is full of fascinating stories about Manhattan and its people. Tours are arranged around such themes as "Wall Street: From Windmills to World Finance," "The Genius and Elegance of Gramercy Park," "Downtown Graveyards," "The Old Jewish Lower East Side," "Harlem: Keystone of African America," and "TriBeCa: New Diversity from an Industrial Past." Tours are offered most weekends March to December and last from 2 to 2½ hours, and the price is $15 per person ($12 for seniors); reservations are not required. Private tours can be arranged year-round, either for individuals or groups.

Myra Alperson, founder and lead tour guide for **NoshWalks** (② 212/222-2243; www.noshwalks.com), knows food in New York City and knows where to find it. Since 2000, Alperson has been leading adventurous, hungry walkers to some of the city's most delicious neighborhoods. From the Uzbek, Tadjik, and Russian markets of Rego Park, Queens, to the Dominican coffee shops of Washington Heights in upper Manhattan, Alperson has left no ethnic neighborhood unexplored. Tours are conducted on Saturday and Sunday, leaving between 11:30am and 1pm. The preferred means of transportation is subway and the

OFFBEAT NEW YORK TOURS

So maybe you've taken a harbor cruise or the bus tour, but you don't feel you got a taste of the gritty, quirky, neurotic elements that make New York unique. You want to see those sights that even many native New Yorkers have never seen. Here are a few alternatives to the conventional tours that might satisfy that need:

East Village Walking Tours

(*©* **347/465-7767;** www.leshp.org/walking-tours): Some of the quirky tours offered by East Village Visitors Center in conjunction with the Lower East Side History Project include the must-do "The Mafia" tour ($20), where you traverse the stomping grounds of such criminal luminaries as Charles "Lucky" Luciano, Bugsy Siegal, Al Capone, and Meyer Lansky; "Beat Writers and Poets" ($15), where you will discover the homes, hangouts, and galleries of the '50s counterculture literati; and their signature "Lower East Side" tour ($20), which travels through several ethnic enclaves and is offered several days a week.

Soundwalk (*©* **212/674-7407;**

www.soundwalk.com): This innovative company behind the self-guided audio tours debuted in 2003, offering insider's peeks at Chinatown, the Lower East Side, Times Square, DUMBO, and the Meatpacking District. All of these are great fun and will take you places no tour bus will, but my favorites are the two very authentic Bronx Soundwalks: "Graffiti," a tour of Hunts Point and the trail of some of the legendary graffiti artists, narrated by BG183 (also known as Sotero Ortiz), founding member of the TATS Cru and Mural Kings of the Bronx; and "Hip Hop," a Bronx River tour narrated by hip-hop DJ the Original Jazzy Jay, which takes you to the birthplace of hip-hop and the haunts of such rap pioneers as Afrika Bambataa and Cool Herc. For $5.99, download MP3s on the site or an app on Apple's iPhone store; all you need is an MP3 player or iPhone, map, MetroCard, walking shoes, and an adventurous spirit.

Wildman Steve Brill ★ (www.

wildmanstevebrill.com): If you ever get stranded in Central Park, a tour with Wildman Steve Brill (pictured at right) might

---

tours generally last around 3 hours and cost about $45 (including all tastes but not beverages; "Bronx Bites" and "New Bronx City" tours last longer and cost more). Space is limited, so book well in advance.

On Location Tours (*©* 212/209-3370; www.sceneontv.com) offers narrated minibus tours through screen history on their "NY TV and Movie Sites"; tickets are $38 for adults (plus a $2 ticket fee). Or, if you want to see Carrie Bradshaw's Big Apple, cut right to the chase and take the company's "Sex and the City Hotspots," which includes more than 40 show-related sights; tickets are $42 (plus the $2 fee). Schedules and departure points varies depending on what tour you take. There's also a 4-hour "Sopranos Tour" that will take you over to New Jersey for an afternoon of sights that range from Satriale's Pork Store to the Bada-Bing! club; this tour leaves near Seventh Avenue and 39th Street on Friday at 10am and Saturday at 2pm and costs $44 (plus $2). Reservations are required for all tours, as most sell out in advance; it also makes sense to confirm days and times and check for any additional offerings.

Harlem Spirituals (*©* **800/660-2166** or 212/391-0900; www.harlem spirituals.com) specializes in gospel and jazz tours of Harlem that can be help you survive. I've seen him in the park, raggedy beard, shorts, hiking boots, and pith helmet, leading groups of eager-eyed followers while instructing them on what flora and fauna they can forage—breaking off a stick of some edible tree and gnawing on it as an example. Brill's Central Park tours occur twice monthly and are not only hilarious, they are educational. If you're lucky, maybe he'll regale you with his tale of his arrest by a park ranger for eating a dandelion. Reservations must be made in advance; call ℅ **914/835-2153.** Suggested donation is

$15 ($12 for children 11 and under). Cash only, exact change.

Big Apple Jazz Tours (www.big applejazz.com): These tours, hosted by New York jazz expert Gordon Polatnick, are the real deal for jazz buffs. Polatnick's private tours are tailor-made to the jazz interests of his clients. If you're into bebop, he'll show you Minton's Playhouse, the jazz club that was the supposed birthplace of bop. From there he'll take you to other active Harlem clubs that embody Minton's bebop spirit. If you're into the 1960s bohemian Village scene, he'll take you to clubs that represent that golden era of Village jazz clubs. The tour fee is $75 per hour, with a 4-hour minimum for most tours, plus cost of entrance fees, drinks, transportation, and so forth. He also offers three set tours: "Great Day in Harlem Jazz Tour" ($49, Sun), "Boulevard of Dreams Harlem Walking Tour" ($30, Fri and Sun), and "Harlem Juke Joint Crawl" ($99, Sun, limited to eight guests). For reservations, call ℅ **718/606-8442.**

combined with a traditional soul-food meal. A variety of options is available, including a tour of Harlem sights with gospel service or a soul-food dinner. The Harlem jazz tour includes a neighborhood tour, a stop at Apollo Theater, and a visit to a local jazz club. Bronx and Brooklyn tours are also an option for those who want a taste of the other outer boroughs. Prices start at $55, $39 for children 5–11, for a "Harlem Gospel" tour, and go up from there based on length and activities/meals. All tours leave from Harlem Spirituals' Midtown office, 690 Eighth Ave. (btw. 43rd and 44th sts.), and transportation is included.

Active visitors with an adventurous spirit can hook up with **Bike the Big Apple** (℅ **877/865-0078** inside the U.S., 347/878-9809 outside the U.S.; www.bikethebigapple.com). Bike the Big Apple offers guided half-day, full-day, and customized tours through a variety of city neighborhoods, including fascinating but little-explored upper Manhattan and Harlem; a "Secret Streets" tour that takes you over the legendary Brooklyn Bridge, through Chinatown and the East Village, to Ground Zero and around Wall Street. You don't have to be an Ironman candidate to participate; tours are designed for the average rider, with an emphasis on safety and fun; shorter rides are available, but the rides generally last around 5 to 7 hours. Tours are offered year-round; prices run from $80 and include all gear and a bike.

For a bit more whimsy on your tour, The **Levys' Unique New York!** (📞 **877/692-5869;** www.levysuniqueny.com) offers a lighter look at the city's history and landmarks. The tours are all custom planned, depending on the size and needs of the group; travel is by foot, subway, and private vehicle. A few of their most popular tours include the "Bohemians and Beat Poets of Greenwich Village: Sightseeing Literature Tours," and "Hey Ho! Let's Go! Punk Rock on the Bowery Pub Crawl and Walking Tour," which contrasts the culture of the 1850s with the punk rockers of the 1970s. The group is Brooklyn based, and they are extremely knowledgeable about their home borough; tours of Coney Island and another called "Edible Ethnic Brooklyn Eats" are just a few that feature Brooklyn. Tours are $25 per person, depending on group size and duration.

TALK OF THE TOWN: TV TAPINGS

The trick to getting tickets for TV tapings in this city is to be from out of town. Visitors have a much better chance than we New Yorkers; producers are gun-shy about filling their audiences with obnoxious locals and see everybody who's not from New York as being from the heartland—and therefore their target TV audience.

If you're set on getting tickets to a show, request them as early as possible—6 months ahead isn't too early, and earlier is better for the most popular shows. Most shows have "ticket request" areas on their websites, which will ask you the number of tickets you want, your preferred dates (be as flexible as you can), and your address *and* phone number. Tickets are always free. Even if you send in your request early, don't be surprised if tickets don't arrive at your house until shortly before the tape date.

If you come to town without any tickets, all is not lost. Because they know that every ticket holder won't make it, many studios give out a limited number of standby tickets on the day of taping. If you can just get up a little early and don't mind standing in line for a couple (or a few) hours, you have a good chance of getting one (note that the Letterman show no longer has standby lines; you have to call 📞 **212/247-6497** starting at 11am on the day of the taping you wish to attend). Now, the bad news: Only one standby ticket per person is allowed, so *everybody* who wants to get in has to get up at the crack of dawn and stand in line. And even if you get your hands on a standby ticket, it doesn't guarantee admission; they usually only start seating standbys after the regular ticket holders are in. Still, chances are good.

For additional information on getting tickets to tapings, call the **NYC & Company** at 📞 **212/484-1200.** And remember—you don't need a ticket to stand on Rockefeller Plaza in front of the *Today* show.

If you do attend a taping, be sure to bring a sweater, even in summer. As anybody who watches Letterman knows, it's *cold* in those studios. And bring ID, as proof of age may be required.

The Colbert Report   Jon Stewart's star reporter Steve Colbert, of *The Daily Show,* became so popular he was given his own show on Comedy Central. Now he is giving Stewart a run for his money in the ratings. For standby tickets, arrive

A taping of The Colbert Report is a hot ticket in NYC.

at the studio beginning at 4pm to sign up: 513 W. 54th St., between Tenth and Eleventh avenues. Check the website, **www.colbertnation. com/tickets**, for ticket information.

The Daily Show with Jon Stewart Comedy Central's irreverent, often hilarious mock newscast tapes Monday through Thursday at 5:45pm, at 733 11th Ave. *The Daily Show* no longer takes phone requests. For tickets, use the online ticket reservation system at **www.thedailyshow.com/tickets**. For more information, call ✆ **212/ 586-2477.**

Late Night with Jimmy Fallon Tapings are Monday through Friday at 5:30pm (plan on arriving by 4:15pm if you have tickets), and you must be 17 or older to attend. You can reserve up to four tickets in advance by calling ✆ **212/664-3056.** Standby tickets are distributed on the day of taping at 9am outside 30 Rockefeller Plaza, on the 49th Street side of the building (under the NBC Studios awning), on a first-come, first-served basis (come *very* early to get one).

The Late Show with David Letterman Here's the most in-demand TV ticket in town. Submit ticket requests online at **www.cbs.com/late_night/late_ show/tickets**; or stop by the Ed Sullivan Theater Monday to Friday from 9:30am to 12:30pm or Saturday and Sunday from 10am to 6pm to submit an in-person request. (Do not line up prior to 9am or you will not be eligible for tickets.) Tapings are Monday at 4:30 and 7pm, Tuesday and Wednesday at 5:30pm, and Thursday at 4:30pm. You must be 18 or older to attend. On tape days, there are no standby lines anymore; call ✆ **212/247-6497** at 11am; start dialing early, because the machine will kick in as soon as all standbys are gone. If you do get through, you may have to answer a question about the show to score tickets.

Live! with Regis and Kelly Tapings with Regis Philbin and Kelly Ripa are Monday through Friday at 9am at the ABC Studios at 7 Lincoln Sq. (Columbus Ave. and W. 67th St.) on the Upper West Side. You must be 10 or older to attend (children 17 and under must be accompanied by a parent). Send a postcard or regular-size envelope (four tickets max) up to a *full year* in advance to *Live With Regis and Kelly* Tickets, Ansonia Station, P.O. Box 230-777, New York, NY 10023-0777. Or, request tickets online at **http://www.dadt.com/live**. Standby tickets are sometimes available. Arrive at the studio as early as 7am and request a standby number; standby tickets are handed out on a first-come, first-served basis, so earlier is better.

Rachael Ray Show You can apply to be featured on the show (if you fit one of the topics they are doing a segment on, like "Do you have a crush on a reality TV star?" or "Kids not turning out the way you expected?") or request tickets on the website (**www.rachaelrayshow.com/show-info/audience-tickets**). Demand

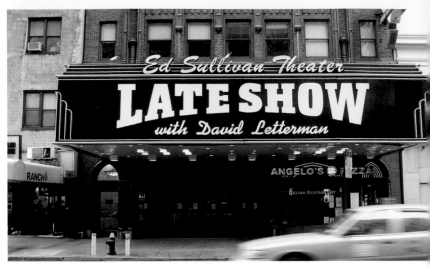

The Late Show with David Letterman tapes at the Ed Sullivan Theater.

for the tickets is high, and you may be in for a long wait. When it's in production, the show tapes twice a day on Tuesdays, Wednesdays, and Thursdays at Ray's studio at 222 East 44th St. (btw. 2nd and 3rd aves.). You must be over 16 years old to attend a taping, and bring a valid photo ID. There's a rather detailed dress code (no capris! no sequins!). You can also stop by on the day of taping to see if standby tickets are available.

Saturday Night Live *SNL* tapings are Saturday at 11:30pm (arrival time 10:45pm); there's also a full dress rehearsal at 8pm (arrival time 7:15pm). You must be 16 or older to attend. Here's the catch: E-mail requests (snltickets@ nbcuni.com) are taken only in August and the odds are always long. However, you can try for standby tickets on the day of the show, which are distributed at 7am outside 30 Rockefeller Plaza, on the 49th Street side of the building (under the NBC Studios awning), on a first-come, first-served basis; only one ticket per person will be issued. If you want to try your luck with advance tickets, call ✆ **212/664-3056** *as far in advance of your arrival in New York as possible* to determine the current ticket-request procedure.

The Today Show Anybody can be on TV with Matt, cuddly weatherman Al Roker, and Meredith Vieira. All you have to do is show up outside *Today's* glass-walled studio at Rockefeller Center, on the southwest corner of 49th Street and Rockefeller Plaza, with your HI, MOM! sign. The show airs live Monday through Friday from 7 to 11am, but come at the crack of dawn if your heart's set on being in front. Who knows? If it's a nice day, you may even get to chat with Ann, Matt, or Al in a segment. Come extra early to attend a Friday Summer Concert Series show.

The View ABC's hugely popular girl-power gabfest tapes live Monday through Thursday at 11am (ticket holders must arrive by 9:30am). Requests, which should be made 12 to 24 months in advance, can be submitted online (**http:// theview.abc.go.com/tickets**). Since exact-date requests are not usually accommodated, try standby: Arrive at the studio (320 W. 66th St) between 8 and 9am to pick up a number; earlier is better, as tickets are handed out on a first-come, first-served basis. You must be 16 or older to attend.

ESPECIALLY FOR KIDS

Some of New York's sights and attractions are designed specifically with kids in mind, and I've listed those below. But many I've discussed in the rest of this chapter are terrific for kids as well as adults; so I've included cross-references to the best of them.

Probably the best place of all to entertain the kids is in **Central Park ★★★**, which has kid-friendly diversions galore (see the section beginning on p. 282). For kid-friendly theatrical performances, see the "Kids Take the Stage: Family-Friendly Theater" box, on p. 392.

For general tips and additional resources, see "Family Travel" under "Planning Your Trip to New York City," p. 465.

Museums

In addition to the museums specifically for kids detailed below, consider the following, discussed elsewhere in this chapter: The **American Museum of Natural History ★★★** (p. 220), whose dinosaur displays are guaranteed to wow both you and the kids; the **New York City Fire Museum ★** (p. 261), in a real firehouse; the **Museum of the Moving Image ★** (p. 330), where you and the kids can learn how movies are actually made (and play vintage video games); the **Lower East Side Tenement Museum ★** (p. 255), whose weekend living-history program intrigues school-age kids; the **New York Transit Museum** (p. 324), where kids can explore vintage subway cars and other hands-on exhibits; the **South Street Seaport & Museum** (p. 268), which little ones will love for its theme-park-like atmosphere and old boats bobbing in the harbor; and the **Brooklyn Children's Museum,** 145 Brooklyn Ave. (✆ **718/735-4400;** www.brooklynkids.org), which in 2008 completed a decade-long $80-million renovation.

Children's Museum of the Arts ☺   Interactive workshop programs for children 10 months to 14 years old and their families are the attraction here. Kids dabble in puppet making and computer drawing or join in singalongs and live performances. Also look for rotating exhibitions of the museum's permanent collection featuring WPA work. Call or check the website for the current exhibition and activities schedule.

182 Lafayette St. (btw. Broome and Grand sts.). ✆ **212/274-0986.** www.cmany.org. Admission $10 for ages 1–65, pay-what-you-wish Thurs 4–6pm. Wed–Sun noon–5pm (Thurs to 6pm). Subway: 6 to Spring St.; R to Prince; N to Canal St.

Children's Museum of Manhattan ★ ☺   Here's a great place to take the kids when they're tired of being told not to touch. This museum is strictly hands-on, with interactive exhibits and activity centers that encourage self-discovery. "Adventures with Dora and Diego" takes children through different animal habitats as they help Diego on an animal rescue mission. "Discover Ancient Greece" introduces them to art, science, and literature. This isn't just a museum for the 5-and-up set—there are exhibits designed for babies and toddlers, too. The schedule also includes craft classes and storytellers, and a full slate of entertainment on weekends.

The Children's Museum of Manhattan is strictly hands-on.

212 W. 83rd St. (btw. Broadway and Amsterdam Ave.). ℂ **212/721-1234.** www.cmom.org. Admission $10 children and adults, $7 seniors, children 1 and under free, free for all on the first Friday of every month from 5–8pm. Tues–Sun 10am–5pm. Subway: 1 to 86th St.

New York Hall of Science ★ ☺ Children of all ages will love this huge hands-on museum in the borough of Queens, which bills itself as having the city's largest collection of hands-on science exhibits. This place is amazing for school-age kids. Exhibits let them float on air in an antigravity mirror, compose music by dancing in front of light beams, and explore the more-than-miniature world of microbes. There are even video machines that kids can use to retrieve astronomical images, including pictures taken by the *Galileo* in orbit around Jupiter. There's a Preschool Place for the really little ones. But probably best of all is the summertime outdoor Science Playground—ostensibly lessons in physics, but really just a great excuse to laugh, jump, and play on jungle gyms, slides, seesaws, spinners, and more.

The museum is in **Flushing Meadows–Corona Park,** where kids can enjoy even more fun beyond the Hall of Science. Not only are there more than 1,200 acres of park and playgrounds, but there's also a zoo, a carousel, an indoor ice-skating rink, an outdoor pool, and bike and boat rentals. The park is also home to the **Queens Museum of Art** (p. 332) as well as the U.S. Open Tennis Center.

47-01 111th St., in Flushing Meadows–Corona Park, Queens. ℂ **718/699-0005.** www.nyscience. org. Admission $11 adults; $8 seniors, students with college ID, and children 2–17; free for all Fri 2–5pm and Sun 10–11am except for July–Aug. Additional $4 for Science Playground. Rocket Park Mini Golf: $6 per person, $5 for children and seniors. Sept–March Tues–Thurs 9:30am–2pm, Fri 9:30am–5pm, Sat–Sun 10am–6pm; Apr–Aug Mon–Thurs 9:30am–2pm (till 5pm July–Aug); Fri 9:30am–5pm; Sat–Sun 10am–6pm. Subway: 7 to 111th St.

Sony Wonder Technology Lab ☺ This place is not as much of an infomercial as you'd expect. Both kids and adults love this four-level high-tech science-and-technology center, which explores communications and information technology. You can experiment with robotics, explore the human body through medical imaging, edit a music video, mix a song, design a video game, and save the day at an environmental command center. The lab also features the first high-definition interactive theater in the United States. Admission is absolutely free; this place is extremely popular, however, so it's wise to make reservations in advance. Reservations can be made up to 3 months in advance by calling ℂ **212/833-8100** Tuesday through Friday between 9am and 2pm. Otherwise, you may not get in, or you may get tickets that require you to return at a different time.

Sony Plaza, 550 Madison Ave. (at 56th St.). ℂ **212/833-8100.** www.sonywondertechlab.com. Free admission. Sun noon–5pm; Tues–Sat 10am–5pm; last entrance 30 min. before closing. Subway: E, M to Fifth Ave.; 4, 5, 6, N, R to 59th St.; F to 57th St.

Other Kid-Friendly Diversions

SHOPPING   Everybody loves to shop in New York—even kids. Don't forget to take them to Books of Wonder; that temple of sneakerdom, NIKETOWN; the NBA Store; Dylan's Candy Bar, for a real Willy Wonka experience; and Toys "R" Us in Times Square, with its very own indoor Ferris wheel. See chapter 7 for details.

SKY-HIGH VIEWS   Kids of all ages can't help but turn dizzy with delight at views from atop the **Empire State Building ★★★** (p. 232). The Empire State Building also has the **New York Skyride** (ℂ **888/759-7433;** www.skyride.com), which is a short motion-flight-simulation sightseeing tour of New York, in case the real one isn't enough for your kids. Skyride open daily 8am to 10pm; *when purchased online,* tickets are $19 for adults, $18 for seniors, $16 for kids; tickets cost more when purchased at the Empire State Building. Combination Empire State observation deck/New York Skyride tickets are available at a discount.

Kids love the high-tech exhibits at the Sony Wonder Technology Lab.

SPECIAL EVENTS Children's eyes grow wide at the yearlong march of parades (especially Macy's Thanksgiving Day Parade), circuses (Big Apple and Ring-ling Bros. and Barnum & Bailey), and holiday shows (the Rockettes' Christmas performances). See the "New York City Calendar of Events," in chapter 2, for details.

ZOOS & AQUARIUMS Bigger kids will love the legendary **Bronx Zoo,** while the **Central Park Zoo** ★, with its **Tisch Children's Zoo** (p. 287), is particularly suitable for younger kids. At the **New York Aquarium** at Coney Island (p. 323), kids can touch starfish and sea urchins and watch bottle-nosed dolphins and California sea lions stunt-swim in the outdoor aqua theater. **Brooklyn's Prospect Park** ★★ (p. 326) also boasts a wonderful little zoo.

HIGHLIGHTS OF THE OUTER BOROUGHS
In the Bronx

In addition to the options below, literary buffs might also want to visit the Edgar Allan Poe Cottage, the last home of the brilliant but troubled author of *The Raven, The Tell-Tale Heart,* and other masterworks. See the sidebar "In Search of Historic Homes," on p. 274.

Bronx Zoo ★★★ ☺ Founded in 1899, the Bronx Zoo is the largest metropolitan animal park in the United States, with more than 4,000 animals living on 265 acres, and one of the city's best attractions.

It's the eye of the tiger at The Bronx Zoo.

Bronx Highlights

Bronx Museum of the Arts **7**
Bronx Zoo Wildlife Conservation Park **4**
City Island **6**
New York Botanical Gardens **3**

Pelham Bay Park **5**
Wave Hill **1**
Woodlawn Cemetery **2**
Yankee Stadium **8**

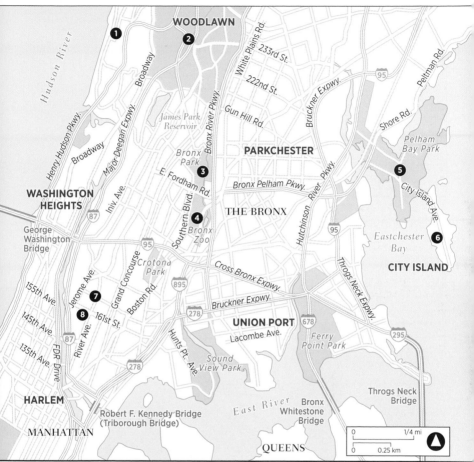

One of the most impressive exhibits is the **Wild Asia Complex.** This zoo-within-a-zoo comprises the Wild Asia Plaza education center; JungleWorld, an indoor re-creation of Asian forests, with birds, lizards, gibbons, and leopards; and the Wild Asia Monorail (May–Oct), which takes you on a narrated ride high above free-roaming Siberian tigers, Asian elephants, Indian rhinoceroses, and other nonnative New Yorkers (keep your eyes peeled—the animals aren't as interested in seeing you). The **Himalayan Highlands** is home to extremely rare snow leopards, as well as red pandas and white-naped cranes. The 6½-acre **Congo Gorilla Forest** is home to Western lowland gorillas, okapi, red river hogs, and other African rainforest animals.

The **Children's Zoo** (Apr–Oct; admission $3) allows young humans to learn about their wildlife counterparts. Kids can compare their leaps to those of

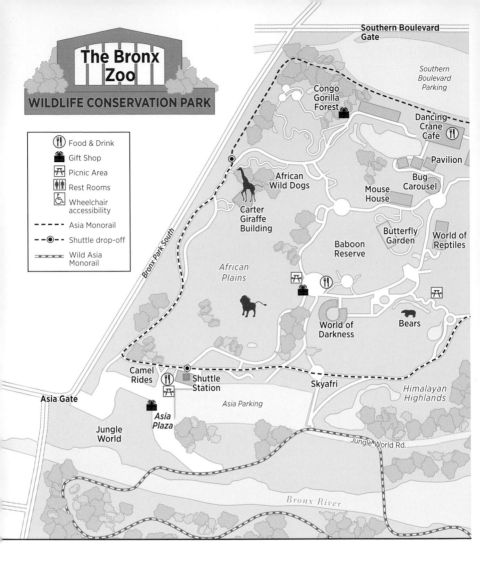

a bullfrog, slide into a turtle shell, climb into a heron's nest, see with the eyes of an owl, and hear with the ears of a fox. There's also a petting zoo. Camel rides are another part of the summertime picture, as is the Butterfly Garden (an extra $3 charge).

If the natural settings and breeding programs aren't enough to keep zoo residents entertained, they can always choose to ogle the two million annual visitors. But there are ways to beat the crowds. Try to visit on a weekday or on a nice winter's day. In summer, come early in the day, before the heat of the day sends the animals back into their enclosures. Expect to spend an entire day here—you'll need it.

Getting there: Liberty Lines' BxM11 express bus, which makes stops on Madison Avenue, will take you directly to the zoo; call ✆ **718/652-8400.** By

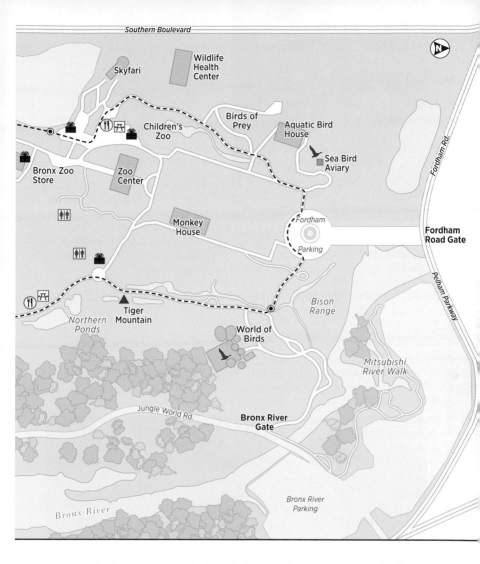

subway, take the no. 2 train to Pelham Parkway and then walk west to the Bronxdale entrance.

Fordham Rd. and Bronx River Pkwy., the Bronx. ✆ **718/367-1010.** www.bronxzoo.com. Admission $16 adults, $14 seniors, and $12 for children 3–12; pay-what-you-wish Wed year-round. There may be nominal additional charges for some exhibits. Nov–Mar daily 10am–4:30pm; Apr–Oct Mon–Fri 10am–5pm, Sat–Sun and holidays 10am–5:30pm. Transportation: See "Getting there," above.

New York Botanical Garden ★ A National Historic Landmark, the 250-acre New York Botanical Garden was founded in 1891 and today is one of America's foremost public gardens. The setting is spectacular—a natural terrain of rock outcroppings, a river with cascading waterfalls, hills, ponds, and wetlands.

Highlights of the Botanical Garden include the 27 specialty gardens, an exceptional orchid collection, and 40 acres of uncut forest, as close as New York gets to its virgin state before the arrival of Europeans. The **Enid A. Haupt Conservatory,** a stunning series of Victorian glass pavilions that recall London's former Crystal Palace, shelters a rich collection of tropical, subtropical, and desert plants, as well as seasonal flower shows. There's also the **Children's Adventure Garden.** Natural exhibits are augmented by year-round educational programs,

A lemur enjoys his lunch (and habitat) at the Bronx Zoo.

musical events, bird-watching excursions, lectures, special family programs, and many more activities. Best of all is the annual **Holiday Train Show** (late Nov to early Jan; call for exact dates), where railway trains and trolleys wind their way through more than 100 replicas of historic New York buildings and attractions—such as the Statue of Liberty, the Metropolitan Museum of Art, and the Garden's own Enid A. Haupt Conservatory—all made from plant parts and other natural materials. There are so many ways to see the garden—tram, golf cart, walking tours—that it's best to call or check the website for more information.

Getting there: Take Metro-North (© **212/532-4900;** www.mta.info/mnr) from Grand Central Terminal to the New York Botanical Garden station; the ride

It's blooming pretty at the New York Botanical Garden.

Wave Hill overlooks the Hudson River with a panoramic view.

takes about 20 minutes. By subway, take the D or 4 train to Bedford Park, then take bus Bx26 or walk southeast on Bedford Park Boulevard for 8 long blocks.

200th St. and Kazimiroff Blvd., the Bronx. ✆ **718/817-8700.** www.nybg.org. Admission $6 adults, $3 seniors and students, $1 children 2–12. Free to all Wed and 10am–noon Sat. Extra charges for Everett Children's Adventure Garden, Enid A. Haupt Conservatory, Rock and Native Plant Gardens, and narrated tram tour; All-Garden Pass $15 adults, $10 seniors and students, $4 children 2–12, free children 1 and under (prices change depending on season). Tues–Sun 10am–6pm. Transportation: See "Getting there," above.

Wave Hill ★ 🎁   Formerly a private estate with panoramic views of the Hudson River and the Palisades, Wave Hill has, at various times in its history, been home to a British U.N. ambassador, Mark Twain, and Theodore Roosevelt. Set in a stunningly bucolic neighborhood that doesn't look anything like you'd expect from the Bronx, its 28 gorgeous acres were bequeathed to the city of New York for use as a public garden that is now one of the most beautiful spots in the city. It's a wonderful place to commune with nature, both along wooded paths and in beautifully manicured herb and flower gardens, where all of the plants are clearly labeled by careful horticulturists. Benches are positioned throughout the property for quiet contemplation and spectacular views. It's a great spot for taking in the Hudson River vibe without having to rent a car and travel to Westchester to

---

A Trolley in the Bronx

Proving that the Bronx is not the bad-boy borough it has often been portrayed as in movies, the **Bronx Tourism Council** (✆ **718/590-3518;** www.llovethebronx. com) and the **Bronx Council on the Arts** (✆ **718/931-9500;** www.bronxarts.org) sponsor the Bronx Cultural Trolley. On the first Wednesday of every month, the quaint trolley-replica bus takes you on a free cultural tour of the lower Grand Concourse area of the south Bronx (✆ **718/931-9500,** ext. 33; www.bronx trolley.com).

🎁 THE BRONX YOU NEVER KNEW EXISTED

The Bronx is far more than just the home of a great zoo and baseball stadium. Here are a few under-the-radar highlights of that underappreciated borough.

The Point Community Development Corporation
940 Garrison Ave. (☎ **718/542-4139;** www.thepoint.org; Subway: 6 to Hunts Point Ave.): The Point Community Development Corporation, or just "the Point," is a community space to keep the young people of the neighborhood out of trouble. It has grown from its humble beginnings in the early 1990s into a cultural mecca. At the Point you can check out photographic exhibitions of works produced by talented young people under the tutelage of the International Center of Photography (ICP), or check out the a menu of movies, plays, musical performances, and other art-related activities staged at Live from the Edge Theater. At the Point you'll also find Angel Rodriguez, one of NYC's most important Puerto Ricans, with over 40 years' experience in performing salsa and mambo music, not to mention his legendary conga sessions, which you can catch at the Edge Theater.

Pelham Bay Park
Most tourists think the largest park in New York City is Central Park. Surprise! It's the Bronx's own Pelham Bay Park. In the northeast corner of the Bronx, Pelham Bay Park was created in 1888 and covers over 2,700 acres. It is also the playground for residents of nearby Co-op City, the biggest private-housing development on the East Coast. The park boasts an equestrian center where you can take lessons or go on guided horseback tours, lagoons where you can canoe, and trails along which you can bike or hike. Subway: 6 to Pelham Bay Park.

City Island (www.cityisland.com):
Take the no. 6 train to its last stop, Pelham Bay Park. Then transfer to City Bus Bx29 toward hidden-treasure City Island (pictured at left). During Colonial times, City Island was known as Minneford Island, which reflected the area's connection to its traditional owners, the Sinawoy Minneford tribe. Today City Island is connected to the mainland by a 600-foot-long bridge that takes you from parkland to fishing village. The island itself is a little over a mile long and a quarter of a mile wide and houses native Bronxites, whose heritage on the island can be traced back more than 150 years. On City Island, marinas dot the tiny coast. City Island also

visit the Rockefeller estate; in 2004, a 28-acre public garden and cultural center opened, making it even more attractive and accessible. Programs range from horticulture and environmental education to landscape history and forestry to dance performances and concerts.

Getting there: Take the no. 1 subway to 231st Street, then take the Bx7 or Bx10 bus to the 252nd Street stop; or take the A train to 207th Street and pick up the Bx7 to 252nd Street. From the 252nd Street stop, walk west across the parkway bridge and turn left; at 249th Street, turn right. Metro-North trains (☎ **212/532-4900;** www.mta.info/mnr) go from Grand Central to the Riverdale station; from there, it's a 5-block walk to Wave Hill.

675 W. 249th St. (at Independence Ave.), the Bronx. ☎ **718/549-3200.** www.wavehill.org. Admission $8 adults, $4 seniors and students, $2 children 6–12; free children 5 and under. Tues Nov–Apr and July–Aug, Sat 9am–noon year-round, and Tues 9am–noon May–June and Sept–Oct. Oct 15–Apr 14 Tues–Sun 9am–4:30pm; Apr 15–Oct 14 9am–5:30pm. Transportation: See "Getting there," above.

offers an abundance of top-quality sea-food restaurants.

The Bronx Museum of the Arts
1040 Grand Concourse, at 165th Street (© **718/681-6000;** www.bronxmuseum.org; subway: B, D to 167th St./Grand Concourse): The Bronx Museum of the Arts was founded in 1971 and specializes in contemporary art produced by talented New Yorkers of Latin, Asian, and African-American descent. The museum displays a number of works inspired by the Bronx itself, with over 700 pieces in the permanent collection. The artwork was made public in 1986, and exhibitions over the years have included "One Planet Under a Groove Hip-Hop, Contemporary Art" and "Urban Mythologies: The Bronx Represented Since the 1960s." For those travelers on a budget, admission to the museum won't set you back much at $5 for adults, $3 for students and seniors, and free for children. The museum is a 15-minute walk from Yankee Stadium and a good complement to a day watching the Yankees play.

Woodlawn Cemetery Webster Avenue and East 233rd Street (© **718/920-0500;** www.thewoodlawncemetery.org; subway: 4 to Woodlawn Station):

Woodlawn Cemetery is no ordinary cemetery. It was created in 1863 and is best known for its ornate and imaginative mausoleums and monuments. The grounds stretch over 400 acres and house the country's first community mausoleum, which opened in 1967. Woodlawn Cemetery is one of the city's most famous, and you'll find a number of notable people laid to rest here, including salsa superstar Celia Cruz, jazz geniuses Miles Davis (whose headstone is pictured above) and Duke Ellington, former mayor of New York City Fiorello La Guardia, Joseph Pulitzer, songwriter George M. Cohan, and theater impresario Oscar Hammerstein. Weekend guided tours are available.

In Brooklyn

For details on walking the **Brooklyn Bridge** ★★, see p. 228.

It's easy to link visits to the Brooklyn Botanic Garden, the Brooklyn Museum of Art, and Prospect Park, as they're all an easy walk from one another, just off **Grand Army Plaza.** Designed by Frederick Law Olmsted and Calvert Vaux as a suitably grand entrance to their Prospect Park, it boasts a Civil War memorial arch designed by John H. Duncan (1892–1901) and the main Brooklyn Public Library, an Art Deco masterpiece completed in 1941 (the garden and museum are on the other side of the library, down Eastern Pkwy.). The area is a half-hour subway ride from Midtown.

Brooklyn Bridge Park ★★ 📱 It only took 20 years of haggling, but this truly amazing park finally opened in March 2010—or at least a small part of its eventual 85 acres, which will stretch from just north of the Brooklyn Bridge down to Atlantic Avenue. It will take years for the entire park to be completed. Most of it

Brooklyn Botanic Garden offers an oasis of tranquility.

will be built on a series of massive piers, where ships were formerly unloaded. One of the piers (# 5) for example, will offer outdoor soccer and softball fields. Others will have volleyball courts and even pebble beaches. As *New York Times* architecture critic Nicolai Ouroussoff points out, Brooklyn Bridge Park "is an attempt to come to terms with the best and worst of our era: on the one hand, concern for the environment and an appreciation for the beauty of urban life and infrastructure; on the other, the relentless encroachment of private interests on the public realm." In recognition of that concern for the environment, the designer, Michael Van Valkenburgh, has envisioned series of small water pools, salt marshes and tidal coves, framed by piles of granite rocks, as the park extends to the south. This will be an ongoing event for years and years, but enough of it is completed to make it well worth a visit—especially in the summer. The views of Manhattan are gorgeous.

Main entrance is at Main and Plymouth sts. in Brooklyn. © **718/802-0603.** www.brooklynbridge park.org. Subway: A, C to High St.; 2, 3 to Clark St.; F to York St. (Consult website for directions after exiting subway.)

Brooklyn Botanic Garden ★

Down the street from the Brooklyn Museum of Art (see below) is the most popular botanic garden in the city. This 52-acre sanctuary is at its most spectacular in May, when the thousands of pink blossoms of cherry trees are abloom. Well worth seeing are the spectacular Cranford Rose Garden, one of the largest and finest in the country; the Shakespeare Garden, an English garden featuring plants mentioned in his writings; the Children's Garden; the Osborne Garden, a 3-acre formal garden; the Fragrance Garden, designed for the blind but appreciated by all noses; and the Japanese Hill-and-Pond Garden. The renowned C. V. Starr Bonsai Museum is home to the world's oldest and largest collection of bonsai, while the impressive

First Saturdays at the Brooklyn Museum are a popular free event.

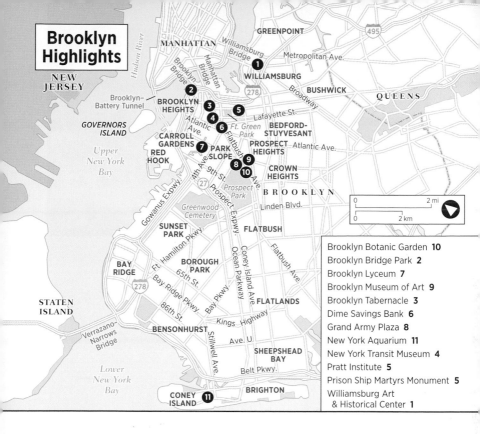

$2.5-million Steinhardt Conservatory holds the garden's extensive indoor plant collection.

900 Washington Ave. (at Eastern Pkwy.), Brooklyn. ℂ **718/623-7200.** www.bbg.org. Admission $8 adults, $4 seniors and students (free for seniors Fri), free for children 11 and under. Mar 15–Nov 6 Tues–Fri 8am–6pm, Sat–Sun 10am–6pm; Nov 8–Mar 11 Tues–Fri 8am–4:30pm, Sat–Sun 10am–4:30pm. Subway: Q to Prospect Park; 2, 3 to Eastern Pkwy./Brooklyn Museum.

Brooklyn Museum of Art ★★　One of the nation's premier art institutions, the Brooklyn Museum of Art rocketed into public consciousness in 1999 with the controversial "Sensation: Young British Artists from the Saatchi Collection," which drew international media attention and record crowds who came to see just what an artist—and a few conservative politicians—could make out of a little elephant dung.

Indeed, the museum is known for its consistently remarkable temporary exhibitions as well as its excellent permanent collection. The museum's grand Beaux Arts building, designed by McKim, Mead & White (1897), befits its outstanding holdings, most notably the Egyptian, Classical, and Ancient Middle Eastern collection of sculpture, wall reliefs, and mummies. The decorative-arts collection includes 28 American period rooms from 1675 to 1928 (the extravagant Moorish-style smoking room from John D. Rockefeller's 54th St. mansion is my favorite). Other highlights are the African and Asian arts galleries, dozens of works by Rodin, a good costumes and textiles collection, and a diverse collection

The Brooklyn Museum of Art contains many classic and modern works.

of both American and European painting and sculpture that includes works by Homer, O'Keeffe, Monet, Cézanne, and Degas.

2007 brought the opening of the Elizabeth A. Sackler Center for Feminist Art, which features permanent and rotating exhibitions of art made by women. One of the prizes of the collection is Judy Chicago's famous "The Dinner Party."

200 Eastern Pkwy. (at Washington Ave.), Brooklyn. ✆ **718/638-5000.** www.brooklynmuseum. org. Suggested admission $10 adults, $6 seniors and students, free for children 11 and under; free to all 1st Sat of the month 11am–11pm. Wed and Sat–Sun 11am–6pm, 1st Sat of the month 11am–11pm, Thurs–Fri 11am–10pm. Subway: 2, 3 to Eastern Pkwy./Brooklyn Museum.

Brooklyn Tabernacle ★　Under the direction of passionate orator Pastor Jim Cymbala and his choral-director wife, Carol, this nondenominational Christian revival church has grown into one of the largest—with a congregation of nearly 10,000 from all walks of city life—and most renowned inner-city churches in the nation. Folks come from all over the world to see the 285-voice, six-time Grammy Award–winning Brooklyn Tabernacle Choir, one of the nation's most celebrated gospel choirs.

The gloriously renovated 1918 building is the fourth-largest theatrical space in the five boroughs, and seats nearly 4,000 for each service. Still, come early for a prime seat, especially when the choir sings (at 9am and noon Sun services).

17 Smith St. (btw. Fulton and Livingston sts.), downtown Brooklyn. ✆ **718/290-2000.** www. brooklyntabernacle.org. Services Sun 9am, noon, and occasionally 3pm. Subway: A, C, F to Jay St./Borough Hall; 2, 3 to Hoyt St.; 4, 5 to Borough Hall; M, R to Lawrence St.

Coney Island ★★ 📷　Coney Island has been snatched from the jaws of death and has a whole new lease on life. After a complicated passage, which included its near-demise, a developer buying the land on which the park resides, then selling it to New York City, which, in turn, sold it to yet another developer, this fabled Brooklyn institution re-opened Memorial Day in 2010, as it has for so many decades. But don't expect an exact replica of the Coney Island of old. Some rides and attractions remain—the harrowing **Cyclone** roller coaster ride, for example and the **Wonder Wheel**—but there are 19 new rides that made their debuts in 2010. What used to be Astroland is now dubbed **Luna Park (www. lunaparknyc.com),** after Coney Island's famous precursor, a vast, glittering playland that opened in 1903 and closed in the 1940s. The new developer's representative promised the new rides would "flip you, launch you, drop you and splash you." The best amusement of all, however, is still the people-watching. Maybe because it is at the extreme edge of New York City, but Coney Island attracts more than its share of the odd, freaky, and funky. It's here where Nathan's Famous hot dogs holds its annual hot-dog-eating contest on July 4 at noon; where the entertaining **Mermaid Parade ★** spoofs the old bathing-beauty parades in the late spring; and where members of the Polar Bear Club show their masochistic gusto by taking a plunge into the icy ocean on January 1. The best time to visit is between Memorial Day and mid-September, when the rides and amusement park are open. Bring your bathing suit and test the waters.

If you are here in the summer, or even if you are not, I recommend a visit to Coney Island just to see it; and you can always visit the nearby **Coney Island Museum,** 1208 Surf Ave. (② **718/372-5159;** www.coneyisland.com). Open Saturdays and Sundays noon to 5pm year-round, here you will find relics from Coney Island's heyday as the premier amusement park in the world. Check out an original "steeplechase horse," vintage bumper cars, or fun-house distortion mirrors. And for a mere 99¢, even if all you want to do is use the clean bathroom, the museum is a bargain.

Brooklyn. Subway: D, F, N, Q to Coney Island–Stillwell Ave.

New York Aquarium ☺ Because of the long subway ride (about an hour from midtown Manhattan) and its proximity to Coney Island, it's best to combine the two attractions, preferably in the summer. This surprisingly good aquarium is home to hundreds of sea creatures. Taking center stage are California sea lions that perform daily at the Aquatheater. Also basking in the spotlight are gangly Pacific octopuses, sharks, and a brand-new sea-horse exhibit. Black-footed penguins, California sea otters, and a variety of seals live at the Sea Cliffs exhibit, a re-creation of a Pacific coastal habitat. But my absolute favorites are the beautiful white beluga whales, which exude buckets of aquatic charm. Children love the hands-on exhibits at Touch Pool. There's an indoor oceanview cafeteria and an outdoor snack bar, plus picnic tables.

Many consider Coney Island's Cyclone roller coaster one of the finest of its kind.

Coney Island's Boardwalk is still the home of a traditional sideshow.

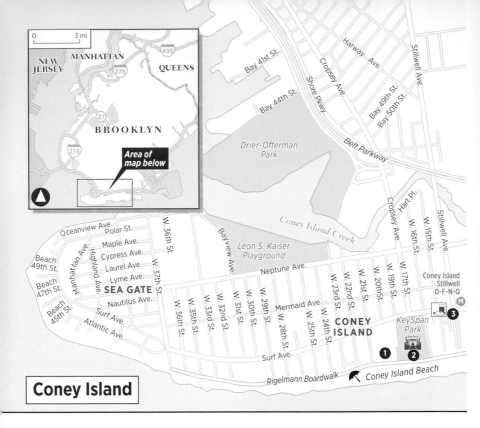

502 Surf Ave. (at W. 8th St.), Coney Island, Brooklyn. ℰ **718/265-FISH** (265-3474). www.nyaquarium.com. Admission $13 adults, $10 seniors, $9 children 3–12, Fri pay-what-you-wish 3pm-close. Nov 1–Apr 1 daily 10am–4:30pm; Sept 9–Oct 31 and Apr 2–May 27 Mon–Fri 10am–5pm, Sat–Sun and holidays 10am–5:30pm; May 28–Sept 8 Mon–Fri 10am–6pm, Sat–Sun and holidays 10am–7pm; Subway: F, Q to West 8th St.

New York Transit Museum ★ ☺
Housed in a real (decommissioned) subway station, this underground museum is a wonderful place to spend an hour or so. The museum is small but very well done, with good multimedia exhibits exploring the history of the subway from the first shovelful of dirt scooped up at groundbreaking (Mar 24, 1900) to the present. Kids and parents alike

Sea lions perform at the New York Aquarium's Aqua-theater each summer.

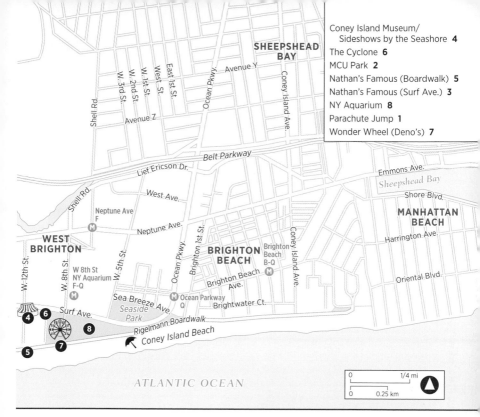

will enjoy the interactive elements and the vintage subway cars, old wooden turnstiles, and beautiful station mosaics of yesteryear. Recent exhibits include the photo show "Last Day of the Myrtle Avenue El" and "The Triborough Bridge: Robert Moses and the Automobile Age," which focused on what's now called the Robert F. Kennedy Bridge.

The smaller Gallery Annex & Store at Grand Central Station also houses rotating exhibitions and a terrific transit-themed gift shop. Boerum Place and Schermerhorn St., Brooklyn. ⏀ **718/694-1600.** http://mta.info/mta/museum. Admission $6 adults, $4 seniors and children 3–17, free for seniors Wed. Tues–Fri 10am–4pm; Sat–Sun noon–5pm. Subway: A, C to Hoyt St.; F to Jay St.; M, R to Court St.; 2, 3, 4, 5 to Borough Hall.

Take the subway to the past at the New York Transit Museum.

Gallery Annex: In Grand Central Terminal (on the main level, in the shuttle passage next to the Station Masters' office), 42nd St. and Lexington Ave. (℃ **212/878-0106.** Subway: 4, 5, 6, 7, S to 42nd St./Grand Central.

Prospect Park ★★   Designed by Frederick Law Olmsted and Calvert Vaux after their success with Central Park, this 562 acres of woodland, meadows, and ponds is considered by many to be their masterpiece and the *pièce de résistance* of Brooklyn.

Brooklyn's favorite spot of green is Prospect Park.

The best approach is from **Grand Army Plaza,** presided over by the monumental **Soldiers' and Sailors' Memorial Arch** (1892) honoring Union veterans. For the best view of the lush landscape, follow the path to Meadowport Arch, and proceed through to the Long Meadow, following the path that loops around it (it's about an hour's walk). Other park highlights include the 1857 Italianate mansion **Litchfield Villa** on Prospect Park West; the **Friends' Cemetery** Quaker burial ground (where Montgomery Clift is eternally prone—sorry, it's fenced off to browsers); the wonderful 1906 Beaux Arts **boathouse;** the 1912 **carousel,** with white wooden horses salvaged from a famous Coney Island merry-go-round (Apr–Oct; rides $2.00); and **Lefferts Homestead Children's Historic House Museum** (℃ **718/789-2822**), a 1783 **Dutch farmhouse,** with a museum of period furniture and exhibits geared toward kids (hours vary by season; see website for details). There's a map at the park entrance that you can use to get your bearings.

On the east side is the **Prospect Park Zoo** (℃ **718/399-7339**), a modern children's zoo where kids can walk among wallabies, explore a prairie-dog town, and more. Admission is $8 for adults, $6 for seniors, $5 for children 3 to 12. From April 1 through November 1, it's open daily from 10am to 4:30pm; October 31 through March 27, open Mon–Fri 10am–5pm and Sat–Sun and holidays 10am to 5:30pm.

At Grand Army Plaza, bounded by Prospect Park West, Parkside Ave., and Flatbush Ave., Brooklyn. (℃ **718/965-8951** (general info), or 718/965-8999 (events information). www.prospect park.org. Subway: 2, 3 to Grand Army Plaza (walk down Plaza St. West 3 blocks to Prospect Park West and the entrance) or Eastern Pkwy./Brooklyn Museum.

BROOKLYN HEIGHTS HISTORIC DISTRICT

Just across the Brooklyn Bridge is **Brooklyn Heights ★**, a peaceful neighborhood of tree-lined streets, more than 600 historic houses built before 1860, landmark churches, and restaurants. Even with its magnificent promenade providing sweeping views of lower Manhattan's ragged skyline, it feels more like its own village than part of the larger urban expanse.

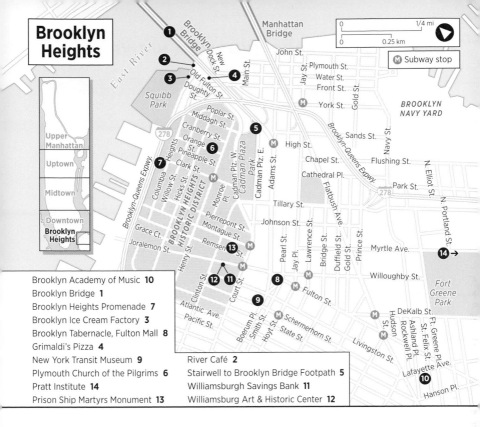

Brooklyn Heights

Upper Manhattan

Uptown

Midtown

Downtown

Brooklyn Heights

Brooklyn Academy of Music **10**
Brooklyn Bridge **1**
Brooklyn Heights Promenade **7**
Brooklyn Ice Cream Factory **3**
Brooklyn Tabernacle, Fulton Mall **8**
Grimaldi's Pizza **4**
New York Transit Museum **9**
Plymouth Church of the Pilgrims **6**
Pratt Institute **14**
Prison Ship Martyrs Monument **13**

River Café **2**
Stairwell to Brooklyn Bridge Footpath **5**
Williamsburgh Savings Bank **11**
Williamsburg Art & Historic Center **12**

This is where Walt Whitman lived and wrote *Leaves of Grass,* one of the great accomplishments in American literature. And in the 19th century, fiery abolitionist Henry Ward Beecher railed against slavery at Plymouth Church of the Pilgrims on Orange Street between Henry and Hicks streets (his sister wrote *Uncle Tom's Cabin*). If you walk down Willow Street between Clark and Pierrepont, you'll see three houses (nos. 108–112) in the Queen Anne style that was fashionable in the late 19th century, as well as an attractive trio of Federal-style houses (nos. 155–159) built before 1829. Also visit lively Montague Street, the main drag of Brooklyn Heights and full of cafes and shops. On Water Street, under the Brooklyn Bridge, is the **River Café** (© **718/522-5200;** www.river cafe.com), where a drink or dinner at twilight, as the lights of Manhattan begin to flicker on, will offer an unforgettable view.

GETTING THERE   Bounded by the East River, Fulton Street, Court Street, and Atlantic Avenue, the Brooklyn Heights Historic District is one of the most outstanding and easily accessible NYC sights beyond Manhattan. The neighborhood is reachable via a number of subway trains: the A, C, F to Jay St.; the 2, 3, 4, 5 to Clark Street or Borough Hall; or the R to Court Street.

It's easy to link a walk around Brooklyn Heights and along its promenade with a walk over the **Brooklyn Bridge ★★** (p. 228), a tour that makes for a lovely afternoon on a nice day. Take a no. 2 or 3 train to Clark Street (the first stop in Brooklyn). Turn right out of the station and walk

HOW TO SEE BROOKLYN LIKE A NATIVE

Here are five Brooklyn sights that, according to Norman Oder of the above-mentioned "New York Like a Native" tours, are often missed by guidebooks but much appreciated by Brooklyn natives.

1. **Downtown Brooklyn:** The 1907 Beaux Arts-style **Dime Savings Bank,** now operated by Chase, is a spectacular example of the financial cathedral. Check the Mercury dimes at the top of the interior Corinthian columns as well as the aphorisms about thrift carved into the marble benches. It's open 8:30am to 6pm Monday to Friday and 9am to 3pm on Saturday; no interior photos are allowed. Next door is the iconic restaurant Junior's, famous for its cheesecake (try the chocolate mousse variety). The bank is at 9 DeKalb Ave., just west of Flatbush Avenue.

2. **Williamsburg Art & Historical Center:** Located in the 1867-built Kings County Savings Bank at 135 Broadway, this is the largest gallery space in Williamsburg (② 718/486-7372; www.wahcenter.net). The shows here are funky and diverse. Not far from **Peter Luger Steakhouse** (p. 205), browsing the museum is a good way to work off one of Luger's porterhouses. Subway: L to Bedford Ave. or J, M, Z to Marcy Ave.

3. **Prison Ship Martyrs Monument:** In Fort Greene Park (www.fortgreene park.org), this oft-overlooked monument, designed by the legendary architectural firm of McKim, Meade & White, was dedicated by President Taft in 1908 and commemorates the sacrifices of more than 11,000 patriots during the Revolutionary War. It's open for outside views during daylight hours. Subway: B, Q, R to DeKalb Avenue or 2, 3, 4, 5 to Nevins Street.

4. **Pratt Institute,** 200 Willoughby Ave. (② 718/636-3600; www.pratt.edu): Before Brooklyn native Pete Hamill went on to a celebrated writing career, he studied art here. The campus has a terrific sculpture garden and a wide array of works, surrounded by buildings both modern and classic. Subway: G to Clinton/Washington.

5. **Brooklyn Lyceum,** 227 Fourth Ave. (② 718/857-4816; www.brooklyn lyceum.com): On the edge of the very residential neighborhood known as Park Slope, this quirky and cavernous performance space for music, theater, and more was once a public bathhouse (pictured below). Subway: R to Union St.

toward the water, where you'll see the start of the Brooklyn Promenade. Stroll along the promenade admiring both the stellar views of lower Manhattan to the left and the gorgeous brownstones to the right, or park yourself on a bench for a while to contemplate the scene.

The promenade ends at Columbia Heights and Orange Street. To head to the bridge from here, turn left and walk toward the Watchtower Building. Before heading downslope, turn right immediately after the playground onto Middagh Street. After 4 or 5 blocks, you'll reach a busy thoroughfare, Cadman Plaza West. Cross the street and follow the walkway through little Cadman Plaza Park; veer left at the fork in the walkway. At Cadman Plaza East, turn left (downslope) toward the underpass, where you'll find the stairwell up to the Brooklyn Bridge footpath on your left.

BROOKLYN TOURS

What better way to experience history-rich Brooklyn than **A Slice of Brooklyn Pizza Tour** ★ (© 917/678-9733; www.asliceofbrooklyn.com). And Brooklyn has no dearth of good pizza. Guided by affable and knowledgeable Brooklyn native and pizza aficionado Tony Muia, the bus tour begins in Manhattan and heads over the Manhattan Bridge for a look at DUMBO, the Brooklyn Bridge, and Fulton Ferry Landing, and then stops at **Grimaldi's** (p. 178) for Neapolitan pizza. From Grimaldi's, the bus keeps to the south of the borough, passing the Brooklyn waterfront, the neighborhood of Red Hook, and then into Bay Ridge and Bensonhurst, where Tony will show you film locations for movies such as *Saturday Night Fever, Goodfellas,* and *The French Connection.* The bus stops at L&B Spumoni Gardens in Bensonhurst for authentic Brooklyn Sicilian pizza, and then on to Coney Island where, if it is summer, you can ride the famous Cyclone roller coaster and attempt to keep all the pizza you have just eaten in your stomach. The 4½-hour tour is $75 ($65 children 11 and under), including pizza at both pizzerias and soft drinks.

There are New York natives and there are Brooklyn natives—please don't confuse the two. Norman Oder is the latter and proud of it. His **New York Like a Native tours** (© 718/393-7537; www.nylikeanative.com) cover the borough, the fourth-largest city in America, as extensively as anyone, from his "Brooklyn 101," which takes visitors to the heart of Brooklyn, Grand Army Plaza, Prospect Park, Park Slope, and Brooklyn Heights, to the more neighborhood-specific tours like that of the Polish-populated Greenpoint and the Orthodox and Hasidic Jewish Borough Park. Tours run about 2½ hours and cost around $15.

In Queens

For details on the **New York Hall of Science** ★ and **Flushing Meadows–Corona Park** (also home to the Queens Museum of Art; see below), see p. 310.

Louis Armstrong House Museum ★ 🎁 What is it about celebrities' homes that we find so fascinating? Is it that we get to see how they lived away from the glare of the cameras; how they functioned on a daily basis just like the rest of us? Armstrong was an international celebrity and could have lived anywhere, yet this unassuming, bi-level house in the working-class neighborhood of Corona, Queens, was the great Satchmo's home from 1943 until his death in 1971. It was bought and designed by his fourth wife, Lucille, who lived in it until her death in 1983. No one has lived in the house since, and in 2003 the house, a National Historic Landmark and a New York City landmark, opened its doors to the public as a museum. The 40-minute tour takes you through the small, impeccably preserved home and explains the significance of each room to both Louis and Lucille. My favorite is Armstrong's den, where he kept his reel-to-reel tape recordings, cataloging everything he taped—music, conversations, and compositions, some of which are displayed on his desk. The house also includes a small exhibit with some of his memorabilia, including two of his trumpets, and a gift shop, where many of his CDs are for sale along with other Satchmo-centric items. If you have any interest in jazz and in Armstrong, this is a must-see. 34–56 107th St., Corona, Queens. ✆ **718/478-8274.** www.louisarmstronghouse.org. $8 adults; $6 seniors, students, and children; children 3 and under free. Tues–Fri 10am–5pm; Sat–Sun noon–5pm; last tour at 4pm. Subway: 7 to 103rd St./Corona Plaza.

The home Louis Armstrong lived and worked in is now a museum.

Walk north on 103rd St., turn right on 37th Ave., turn left onto 107th St., and the house is a half-block north of 37th Ave.

Museum of the Moving Image ★ The museum reopened after a 3-year, $67 million renovation that doubled its size to a capacious 98,000 square feet. The

The Museum of the Moving Image offers glimpses of the history of film.

museum is built on the site of Astoria Studio, and this part of Queens was where many of the early American films were made. This is an amazing place that, as its describes itself, "incorporates all aspects of film, television and digital media from 19th century optical toys to the latest development in the Internet." For example, you have a wide array of early motion picture-making equipment including huge cameras that seem like they could power a battleship; cumbersome old editing machines that seem more like Franklin stoves; and giraffe-tall sound booms—all real, all used to make movies, many of which have become America's legacy. You have a great panoply of old television sets, too, some 95% cabinets with a tiny green cyclopean screen, others looking like they were props from bad science fiction films. You have original costumes, wigs (the one Bette Davis wore in Jezebel), and step-by-step examples of make-up, such as how the screen face of the Elephant Man was created. Hundreds of examples of games and dolls and other merchandise created for movie stars are also on display. Interactive features abound, even one that enables you to dub your voice over famous movie sequences. All this and more, plus a splendid 267-seat movie theater that can show 70mm and 3-D. The overall experience is to see how far we've come in so brief a span of time, and just how powerful is the human imagination.

35th Ave. at 37th St., Astoria, Queens. ✆ **718/777-6800.** www.movingimage.us. Admission $10; $7.50 seniors and college students with ID; $5 children 5–18; free members and children 5 and under. Tues–Thurs 10:30am–5pm; Fri 10:30am–8pm; Sat–Sun 10:30am–7pm; Fri 4pm–8pm free. Subway: R, M to Steinway St.; N to 36th Ave.

Isamu Noguchi Garden Museum ★ 🎁 No place in the city is more Zen than this marvelous indoor/outdoor garden museum showcasing the work of Japanese American sculptor Isamu Noguchi (1904–88). The museum showcases the beautifully curated collection of the artist's masterworks in stone, metal, wood, and clay; you'll even see theater sets, furniture, and models for gardens and playgrounds that Noguchi designed, as well as a gallery that highlights the artist's work in interior design.

9–01 33rd Rd. (at Vernon Blvd.), Long Island City, Queens. ✆ **718/204-7088.** www. noguchi.org. Admission $10 adults, $5 seniors and students, pay-what-you-wish first Fri each month from June–Sept 5:30–8pm. Wed–Fri 10am–5pm; Sat–Sun 11am–6pm. Subway: N to Broadway. Walk west (toward Manhattan) on Broadway until Broadway ends at Vernon Blvd.; turn left on Vernon and go 2 blocks.

The Isamu Noguchi museum has both indoor and outdoor exhibits.

P.S. 1 Contemporary Art Center
If you're interested in contemporary art that's too cutting-edge for most museums, don't miss this MoMA affiliate museum. Originally a public

The International Express

The **no. 7 train**—which originates in Manhattan at Times Square, makes three stops in that borough, and then snakes, mostly above ground, through the heart of ethnic Queens—is also popularly known as the International Express. Built by immigrants in the early 1900s, the no. 7 IRT (Interborough Rapid Transit) brought those same immigrants to homes on the outer fringes of New York City. That tradition has continued as immigrants from around the world have settled close by the no. 7's elevated tracks. Get off in Sunnyside and see Romanian grocery stores and restaurants; a few stops farther in Jackson Heights, you'll see Indians in saris and Sikhs in turbans; go all the way to Flushing and you'll think you are in Chinatown. You are—Flushing's Chinatown, as big or bigger than Manhattan's. In 1999, the Queens Council on the Arts nominated the International Express for designation as a National Millennium Trail, and that resulted in its selection as representative of the American immigrant experience by the White House Millennium Council, the United States Department of Transportation, and the Rails-to-Trails Conservancy. For more information and for events, visit the **Queens Council on the Arts** website, at **www.queenscouncilarts.org** (✆ **347/505-3010**).

school (hence the name), this is the world's largest institution exhibiting contemporary art from America and abroad. You can expect to see a kaleidoscopic array of works from artists ranging from Jack Smith to Julian Schnabel; the museum is particularly well known for large-scale exhibitions by artists such as James Turrell. In 2008, the museum featured a well-received and popular exhibit by Danish-Icelandic artist Olafur Ellisson, whose four man-made waterfalls in the New York harbor were simultaneously on display. If you've visited MoMa, you can present your ticket stub (within 30 days) for free admission.

22–25 Jackson Ave. (at 46th Ave.), Long Island City, Queens. ✆ **718/784-2084.** www.ps1.org. Suggested admission $10 adults, $5 seniors and students. Thurs–Mon noon–6pm. Subway: E, M to 23rd St./Ely Ave. (walk 2 blocks south on Jackson Ave. to 46th Ave.); 7 to 45th Rd./Court House Sq. (walk 1 block south on Jackson Ave.).

Queens Museum of Art   One way to see New York in the shortest time (albeit without the street life) is to visit the Panorama, created for the 1939 World's Fair, an enormous building-for-building architectural model of New York City complete with an airplane that takes off from LaGuardia Airport. The 9,335-square-foot Gotham City is the largest model of its kind in the world, with 895,000 individual structures built on a scale of 1 inch=100 feet. A red, white, and blue ribbon is draped mournfully over the Twin Towers, which still stand in this "Big Apple."

Also on permanent display is a collection of Tiffany glass manufactured at Tiffany Studios in Queens between 1893 and 1938. History buffs should take note of the museum's NYC Building, which housed the United Nation's General

You'll find interesting art, and a great view at the Socrates Sculpture Park.

Assembly from 1946 to 1952. Art exhibitions, tours, lectures, films, and performances are part of the program, making this a very strong museum on all fronts. Next to the Unisphere in Flushing Meadows–Corona Park, Queens. ☏ **718/592-9700.** www. queensmuseum.org. Suggested admission $5 adults, $2.50 seniors and students, free for children 4 and under. Wed–Sun noon–6pm (Fri until 8pm July 9–Aug). Subway: 7 to Willets Point; follow the yellow signs for the 10-min. walk through the park to the museum, which sits next to the Unisphere).

Socrates Sculpture Park ☺   This former riverside landfill is now the best exhibition space for large-scale outdoor sculpture in the city. No velvet ropes and motion sensors here—interaction with the artwork is encouraged. It's well worth a look, especially on a lovely day, and has a spectacular view of Roosevelt Island and the East Side of Manhattan. Check the website for the current exhibition schedule—or just let yourself be happily surprised. The park also offers outdoor movie screenings and free tai chi, Pilates, capoiera, and yoga classes in the summer. The Noguchi Museum is only about a block away, so you can swing by there as well.

32-01 Vernon, at Broadway, Long Island City, Queens. ☏ **718/956-1819.** www.socratessculpture park.org. Free admission. Daily 10am–sunset. Subway: N to Broadway; walk 8 blocks along Broadway toward the East River.

SPECTATOR SPORTS

For details on the New York City Marathon and the U.S. Open tennis championships, see the "New York City Calendar of Events," in chapter 3.

BASEBALL   With two baseball teams in town, you can catch a game almost any day, from Opening Day in April to the beginning of the playoffs in October.

YANKS & METS SETTLE INTO THEIR NEW(ISH) HOMES

Not just one, but two brand-new Major League Baseball stadiums opened in New York (New York) in 2009. The New York Yankees' spanking-new **Yankee Stadium** opened for business, and pleasure, on April 16, when the Bronx Bombers lost to the Cleveland Indians, 10–2 (ouch!). The Yankees recovered (and how!) to win their first World Series in a decade in 2009.

The new ballpark, which cost over $1 billion, is a stone's throw from the old. The reviews of the new stadium have generally been strong, with expected grumblings about the prices for seats and food. Ownership—that is, the Steinbrenners—has retained much of the style of the old stadium. The field dimensions are the same, for example (though home runs have been flying out in great number, a trend that seems to be continuing). But the seats are wider, there are more restrooms (1 for every 60 fans vs. 1 for every 89 in the old) and, overall, as the *New York Times* reports, "the new stadium does provide the baseball version of upward mobility."

And now you have the opportunity to buy sushi along with your classic Nathan's hot dog. The prices for seats? The new stadium was built when asking $900 for field level seats didn't seem like such a reach. By the time it opened, fans complained loudly (and successfully) about the high ticket prices, and some of them, at least, came down.

The Yankees had better luck with their new stadium than the Mets did in theirs. Across from where Shea Stadium used to stand, the Mets now occupy **Citi Field.** The old stadium, built in 1964, has been razed. The new stadium opened on April 13, 2009, when the Mets hosted the San Diego Padres. They lost, 6–5. That trend continued through much of the 2009 season, as the Mets failed to make the playoffs.

Inside Citi, there are 15,000 fewer seats than Shea, but, as with Yankee Stadium, the seats are wider, there is more legroom, and there are more restrooms. The start of the 2010 season saw the opening of the **Mets Hall of Fame & Museum** at Citi Field, which features artifacts, interactive exhibits, and memorabilia of great moments in the franchise's history, including the famous ball hit by Mookie Wilson that Bill Buckner booted in game 6 of the 1986 World Series.

While the field dimensions are not precisely the same as at Shea, they're close. Some fans have complained about the sightlines and that the new stadium doesn't honor the past Met stars and glory as prominently as it should, though the praise for the **Jackie Robinson Rotunda** has been universal.

For information on pricing and availability of tickets for the Metropolitans, call the **Mets Ticket Office** at ✆ **718/507-TIXX** (507-8499), or visit http://newyork.mets.mlb.com. Also keep in mind that you can buy game tickets (as well as logo wear and souvenirs, if you want to dress appropriately for the big game) at the **Mets Clubhouse Shop,** which has a midtown Manhattan location (p. 378).

New Yankee Stadium is across the street from the old one (Subway: C, D, 4 to 161st St./Yankee Stadium). **NY Waterway** (p. 299) offers baseball cruises to games; call ✆ **800/533-3779,** or visit **www.nywaterway.com**

The Mets' and Yankees; Staggered (and Staggering) Ticket Prices

For the 2011 season, ticket prices at new Yankee Stadium started at $15 for the bleachers (and as little as $5 for obstructed view seats), and you can purchase bleachers tickets in advance; other single-game ticket prices, when purchased in advance, range from $22 to $29 for grandstand seats, $48 to $80 for terrace seating, $57 to $150 for main level seats, and $95 to $325 for field-level seats. If purchased on the day of the game, add from $1 to $50 to the cost of the ticket.

At Citi Field, the Mets have a staggered pricing plan that charges different rates based on the visiting team and the time of the year, from the highest-priced "Marquee" games (the Yankees series), to the low-end "Value" games (early- and late-season contests). "Promenade Reserved" is the lowest-priced seating, ranging from $12 to $36; there are nearly 40 categories of seating, the most expensive being $440 for Delta Club Platinum for a Yankees' game.

for more info. For single-game tickets, contact **Yankee Stadium** (*©* **718/ 293-6000;** http://newyork.yankees.mlb.com) or go to the team's clubhouse shop in Manhattan (p. 378). Serious baseball fans check the schedule well in advance for Old Timers' Day, usually held in July, when pinstriped stars of years past return to the stadium to take a bow.

You can also buy Mets and Yankees tickets by contacting **Ticketmaster** (*©* **800/745-3000;** www.ticketmaster.com), visiting the stadium on the day of the game, or trying online resale sites such as **StubHub** (www. stubhub.com).

MINOR-LEAGUE BASEBALL ★ coexists with "the Show" in the boroughs, with the **Brooklyn Cyclones,** the New York Mets' minor-league farm team, and the **Staten Island Yankees,** the Yanks' minor leaguers. Boasting their very own

Citi Field draws the faithful to root for the Amazin' Mets.

The Brooklyn Cyclones play in MCU Park, where the Atlantic Ocean is just beyond the outfield wall.

waterfront stadium, the Cyclones have been a major factor in the revitalization of Coney Island; MCU Park sits right off the boardwalk (Subway: D, F, N, Q to Stillwell Ave./Coney Island). The SI Yanks also have their own playing field, the Richmond County Bank Ballpark (RCB Ballpark), just a 5-minute walk from the Staten Island Ferry terminal (Subway: N, R to Whitehall St.; 4, 5 to Bowling Green; 1 to South Ferry). What's more, with

New Yankee Stadium calls to mind the old one, and the club's storied history.

Amar'e Stoudemire's arrival in NYC was a boon to the Knicks.

bargain-basement ticket prices (which ran from $8–$16 for the Cyclones, $15–$17 for the Yanks in the 2011 season), this is a great way to experience baseball in the city for a fraction of the major-league hassle and cost. Both teams have a rabidly loyal fan base, so it's a good idea to buy your tickets for the June through September season in advance. For the Cyclones, call ✆ 718/449-8497 or visit **www.brooklyncyclones.com**; to reach the SI Yanks, call ✆ 718/720-9265 or go online to **www.siyanks.com**.

BASKETBALL There are two pro hoops teams that play in New York at **Madison Square Garden,** Seventh Avenue, between 31st and 33rd streets (✆ **212/465-6741,** or 800/745-3000 for tickets; www.thegarden.com or www.ticketmaster.com; Subway: A, C, E, 1, 2, 3 to 34th St.). The **New York Knicks** (✆ **877/NYK-DUNK** [695-3865] or 212/465-JUMP [465-5867]; www.nba.com/knicks) are the NBA team from NYC, and their tickets (when bought at the box office) range from $13 to $3,085. The WNBA's **New York Liberty** (✆ **212/564-9622;** www.wnba.com/liberty) have vacated MSG for the duration of renovations, which are being done in the summer and running through 2013. You can find them at Newark's Prudential Center until then.

FOOTBALL Both the New York Giants and the New York Jets play in the New Meadowlands Stadium, which opened in 2010. Located not in New York City—though (unsuccessful) efforts were made to build a stadium here—but in East Rutherford, New Jersey. *Note:* This stadium will host the Superbowl in 2014, the first cold-weather stadium ever to host this classic.

ICE HOCKEY NHL hockey is represented in Manhattan by the **New York Rangers,** who play at Madison Square Garden, Seventh Avenue between 31st and 33rd streets (✆ **212/465-6741;** http://rangers.nhl.com or www.thegarden.com; Subway: A, C, E, 1, 2, 3 to 34th St.). Rangers tickets are hard to get, so plan well ahead; call ✆ **800/745-3000,** or visit **www.ticketmaster.com** for online orders. Ticket prices range from about $42 to $290.

7

SHOPPING

t's true that in New York City you can buy just about anything. There are countless flagship stores, designer and discount retailers, and iconic department stores. But what's even more special about shopping in the Big Apple is the abundance of locally owned shops—many of which sell goods designed and made right here in the five boroughs.

So while big chain stores are included in this guide, many modest, unique New York shops are listed, too. This way savvy shoppers can get the best this city, and only this city, has to offer—while supporting local designers, artists, and retailers selling the coolest of the cool stuff.

This chapter will give you a head start on where to find some of the city's best shops, streets, and specialty boutiques. And because this is New York, the land of endless retail, you'll inevitably find other gems on your own. (For great strips to stroll for shopping and other local draws, check out "Best Streets to Walk Up or Down" on p. 10.)

THE TOP SHOPPING STREETS & NEIGHBORHOODS

Here's a rundown of New York's most interesting shopping scenes, with highlights of each to give you a feel for the neighborhood. If a location is not given, refer to the store's full listing by category in "Shopping A to Z," later this chapter.

Downtown
LOWER MANHATTAN & THE FINANCIAL DISTRICT

The mother of all discount department stores is **Century 21 ★**, across Church Street from the World Trade Center site. New inventory flows in literally all day, as do throngs of customers. Despite its often elbow-to-elbow aisles, the store is worth a visit—just aim to go on a weekday morning to take advantage of its bargains before the crowds appear. A little farther north by City Hall is local electronics megamart **J&R,** with reasonable prices on everything from cameras and computers to CDs and software. It's wise to buy electronics here rather than at the perpetually "going-out-of-business" joints in Midtown (with the exception of **B&H ★★** on 34th St.).

Head toward the East River via Fulton Street to visit the **South Street Seaport ★★** (© 212/732-8257; Subway: 2, 3, 4, 5, A, C, J, M to Fulton St.). Familiar names such as Gap, Abercrombie & Fitch, and Coach fill the cobblestone-paved, open-air mall. Cross South Street to visit **Pier 17,** one of the biggest indoor malls in Manhattan. But don't let the word "mall" discourage you. Though it's filled with largely nondescript shops and a forgettable food court, this retail-laden locale is worth the trip for the historic ambience and stunning harbor vistas. Be sure to hit the pier's top outdoor deck for a one-of-a-kind Brooklyn

FACING PAGE: **Even the dishes love New York at Fish's Eddy!**

Century 21 is an anchor of the downtown shopping scene.

Say hello (kitty) to a great souvenir at Pearl River Mart in Chinatown.

Bridge view. For store directories, visit **www.southstreetseaport.com** and **www. downtownny.com**.

Meanwhile, the Financial District/New York Stock Exchange zone has become quite the little high-end haven in recent years. On Wall Street, check out designer retailers like **Tiffany & Co. ★**, **True Religion Brand Jeans** (② 212/ 791-5930), **Thomas Pink** (② 212/514-7683), and **Tumi** (② 212/742-8020), as well as **Hermès** (② 212/759-7585) on Broad Street. And if you're sick of the subway, there's also a **BMW of Manhattan** salesroom at 67 Wall St.—apparently there for stockbrokers who get lucky.

If you need a magazine, and maybe a rest, head to **Borders** at 100 Broadway (② 212/964-1988; www.borders.com), where you can gaze out to Trinity Churchyard from the window of Dean & Deluca cafe inside.

CHINATOWN

Don't expect to find the bargain of a lifetime on Chinatown's crowded streets, but there's always great browsing. The fish and herbal markets along **Canal, Mott, Mulberry, and Elizabeth streets** are fun for their bustle and exotica—as well as for the handful of Italian joints still hanging on from the Little Italy days. Dispersed among them (especially along Canal), you'll find a mind-boggling collection of knockoff sunglasses, handbags, fragrances, shoes, and watches. It can be a fun browse, but quality is questionable, and usually so are the sellers—and remember to bargain *before* busting out your wallet! (Also, skip the bootleg CDs, videos, and software—these are stolen goods, and you will be disappointed with the product.) I'd steer clear of electronics altogether, but if you *must* buy, at least open the package before exchanging money to make sure you're not buying a brick in a name-brand box.

Perhaps the best matrix of Chinatown shops are the side streets tucked south of Canal, between Mott Street and the Bowery. The sidewalks are jammed, the stores are cramped, and vendors sell $1 eggrolls from carts—it's enough to make you question what country you're in. If it's Chinese housewares, spices, and delectables you're after, try wandering **Centre Street** and **Grand Street,** where you'll surely enjoy the photo opps if not the merchandise.

If you're out for cool and colorful mementos, duck into **Ting's Gift Shop,** 18 Doyer St. (✆ **212/962-1081**), one of the oldest operating businesses in Chinatown. Under a vintage pressed-tin ceiling, the shop sells good-quality Chinese toys, kits, and lanterns. Tea lovers should not miss **Ten Ren Tea & Genseng ★**, 75 Mott Street (✆ **212/349-2286**), where the lovely staff will help you select delectable teas and all the right brewing accessories.

No visit to Chinatown is complete without getting lost among the teapots, Buddha statues, kitchenware, and other wildly affordable items at **Pearl River Mart ★★** at 477 Broadway (✆ **212/431-4770**), where you should plan to spend at least a half-hour souvenir shopping (see "Gifts" in "Shopping A to Z," later in this chapter).

THE LOWER EAST SIDE

The bargains aren't what they used to be in the **Historic Orchard Street Shopping District,** which basically runs from Houston to Canal along Allen, Orchard, and Ludlow streets, spreading outward along both sides of Delancey Street. Prices on leather goods, shoes, luggage, linens, and fabrics on the bolt are still good; and the district is a nice place to discover a part of New York that's disappearing. Come during the week, since many stores are Jewish owned and close Friday afternoon and all day Saturday.

The artists and other trendsetters who have been turning this neighborhood into a bastion of hip have also added a cutting edge to its shopping scene in recent years. You'll find a growing—and increasingly upscale—crop of alterna-shops south of Houston and north of Grand Street, between Allen and Clinton streets to the east and west, specializing in up-to-the-minute fashions and edgy club clothes, plus funky retro furnishings, Japanese toys, and other offbeat items. Among them are **Reed Space,** 151 Orchard St. (✆ **212/253-0588**), a cool "lifestyle boutique" home to local and international designers, along with art, music, books, and magazines.

Before you head into the Orchard Street thicket, pick up a shopping guide at the **Lower East Side Visitor Center,** 54 Orchard St., between Hester and Grand streets (✆ **866/224-0206;** Subway: F to Delancey St.). Or you can preview the list and learn all things LES online at **www.lowereastsideny.com.**

SOHO

Over the past few decades SoHo has gone from undiscovered to uber-fashionable. It's true, **J. Crew** and **Old Navy** are two of many big names that supplanted many of the artists' lofts that used to fill SoHo's historic buildings. But the fact is,

---

〽 Sales Tax

At the time of this writing, the combined New York State and City sales tax totals 8.875%. But the city has made clothing and footwear under $110 exempt from sales tax, leaving only the state to charge 4.375% on those items. Plans to reinstate the state's clothing-and-footwear exemption are planned to return by April 2012 (depending of course on the gap in this year's state budget).

SoHo's Uniqlo offers fashions with a Japanese flair.

Funky St. Marks Place offers glam and grunge.

no neighborhood rivals the ambiance here. The elegant cast-iron architecture, the cobblestone streets, and the distinct artist vibe give SoHo a look and feel unlike any other neighborhood, which is why it's a landmarked district. And by the way, you can still buy original art direct from the artists lined up on Spring, Prince, and other high-traffic side streets (right outside designer storefronts).

SoHo's shopping grid runs from Broadway west to Sixth Avenue, and Houston Street south to Canal Street. **Broadway** is the most commercial strip, with big names like **Levi's, Hilfiger, Guess, Club Monaco, Bebe,** and **H&M,** the economical Swedish department store with cutting-edge fashions. **Bloomingdale's** has a downtown branch on Broadway, while nearby, **Prada**'s flagship store is worth visiting for its spacious, almost soothing design alone (by Dutch "starchitect" Rem Koolhaus). An atypical highlight is the two-story **Pearl River Mart ★★** Chinese emporium, which offers everything from silk cheongsam (traditional Chinese high-necked dresses) to teaware.

The 'hood also boasts some fabulous recent additions, like Spain's colorful **Desigual,** 594 Broadway (© **212/343-8206**), Japan's sleek **Uniqlo,** 546 Broadway (© **917/237-8800**), and London's brilliant **Topshop ★**, 478 Broadway (© **212/966-9555**), a women's megaclothier. But one longstanding hipster fave, **Yellow Rat Bastard,** 483 Broadway (© **212/925-4377**), is a counterpoint to the big chain stores as a haven for hip-hop/urban/skateboard-style punks.

There are plenty of avant-garde fashion shops (see "Clothing" in "Shopping A to Z," later in this chapter) in SoHo, and you'll find shoe stores galore and high-end housewares, as well as one-of-a-kind boutiques—like the **Hat Shop,** 120 Thompson St., between Prince and Spring streets (© **212/219-1445**), a full-service milliner for women that also features plenty of off-the-rack toppers.

If you're still hungry for the ultramodern and artistic, stop by the **Museum of Modern Art Design Store** ★, 81 Spring St. (© **646/613-1367**). The Midtown museum has a grand SoHo outpost, and it offers the original's same classic and contemporary artists' designs, ranging from books to furniture from the museum's collection. There also are several hot galleries along West Broadway and sprinkled throughout SoHo. So whether you're looking to expand your art collection or just see the work of the Next Big Thing, be sure to come to SoHo with plenty of time to wander. You can find a full list of shops and galleries (most are closed Monday) at **www.artseensoho.com**.

NOLITA

Not so long ago, **Elizabeth Street** was a quiet adjunct to Little Italy. Today it's one of the hottest shopping strips in the neighborhood known as Nolita (**No**rth of **Li**ttle **Ita**ly). Elizabeth and neighboring **Mott** and **Mulberry streets** are dotted with stylish shops between Lafayette Street and the Bowery, below Houston to Kenmare. It's an easy walk from the Broadway/Lafayette stop on the F or M line to the neighborhood, as it starts just east of Lafayette Street; you can also take the no. 6 train to Spring Street, or the N, R to Prince Street and walk east from there.

Nolita is the cousin of SoHo—making it cute and not cheap. Its curb-to-curb boutiques are largely the province of shopkeepers specializing in high-quality fashion-forward products. More and more, it's become a beacon of niche designs from around the world. **Calypso,** 280 Mott St. (© **212/965-0990;** www.calypso-celle.com), has evolved into a successful brand of boho-hippie-chic styles for women, children and babies, with stores in Nolita and SoHo. Nearby you'll find laid-back, military-inspired men's fashions at **Unis,** 226 Elizabeth St. (© **212/431-5533**), which are within reach of most wallets.

Nolita is also an accessories bonanza; stop in at **Sigerson Morrison,** 28 Prince St. (© **212/219-3893**), for chic, colorful women's shoes and handbags, or **Push,** 240 Mulberry St. (© **212/965-9699**), for eye-catching, funky jewelry. You'll find more standouts in the listings in "Shopping A to Z," later in this chapter, but just cruising the blocks will do the trick.

THE EAST VILLAGE

The East Village has long personified bohemian hip, though many New Yorkers would argue the area, with its shiny new condos, has been engulfed by gentrification. Nevertheless, it's a can't-miss neighborhood. The easiest subway access is the no. 6 train to Astor Place, which is just east of the prime hunting grounds.

Additional Sources for Serious Shoppers

If you're looking for specific items or sales, check the daily shopping listings at **www.newyork.citysearch.com, www.timeoutny.com**, and **www.nymag.com** before you leave home. Once you're here, consider picking up the hard-copy magazines: You can find details about the week's sales and newest shops in the "Seeking" and "Shopping" pages of *Time Out New York* or the "Sales & Bargains," "Best Bets," and "Wish List" sections of *New York* magazine.

If you don't already, you should know about **www.dailycandy.com**, a newsletter that often lists store openings and the day's hot tips on sale locations. Two more sites, **www.ny.racked.com** and **www.refinery29.com** are two more sites that list NYC store openings, great sample sales, and fashion trendspotting.

That said, if it's funky, sassy, and usually pretty cheap, it's probably for sale on **St. Marks Place,** which is the alternate name for 8th Street between Third Avenue and Avenue A. The strip between Third and Second avenues, however, is a permanent street market with countless T-shirt stands, tattoo parlors, and boho jewelry storefronts. Beyond endless sunglasses and hat stands, here used-record and rock-memorabilia collectors can have a field day (see "Music," in "Shopping A to Z," later this chapter). And don't forget to check out the bargains at **East Village Books,** 99 St. Mark's Pl. (✆ **212/477-8647**). If you're in search of the harder-edge East Village, head eastward toward the lettered streets that are "Alphabet City" (home turf of the musical *Rent*).

For chi-chi stuff, walk on **East 9th Street,** between Second Avenue and Avenue A, to find an increasingly smart collection of boutiques, clothing, and otherwise. Designers like **Jill Anderson,** 331 E. 9th St. (✆ **212/253-1747**), and **Huminska,** 315 E. 9th St. (✆ **212/677-3458**), stand out for their excellent quality and original fashions for women.

That same strip also draws shopping hawks circling for vintage duds, which are bountiful in the East Village. Highlights include: **Cobblestones,** 314 East 9th St. (✆ **212/673-5372**), specializing in '30s and '40s authentic garb; **Archangel Antiques,** 334 East 9th St. (✆ **212/260-9313**), with accessories, clothing and home décor; and **Argosy,** 428 East 9th St. (✆ **212/982-7918**), specializing in men's vintage clothing and boots.

LAFAYETTE STREET FROM SOHO TO NOHO

Lafayette Street has a retail character all its own, distinct from the rest of SoHo. It has grown into something of an Antiques Row, especially strong in furniture. Prices are high, but so is quality. The stretch to stroll is between 8th Street to the north and Spring Street to the south. Take the no. 6 train to Astor Place and work your way south, or get off at Spring Street and walk north, or take the F or M to Broadway–Lafayette and you'll be in the heart of the action. Highlights include **Gallery 440,** 440 Lafayette St. (✆ **212/979-5800**), for vintage 20th-century lighting and furniture pieces from American, French, and Italian designers. **Elan Antiques** and **Alan Moss Studios** also house great domestic and international collections.

Also stop by **Other Music** ★★ at 15 E. 4th St. (✆ **212/477-8150**) to browse their amazing selection of new and used CDs and vinyl records. Let the knowledgeable staff help you find the right new band or album to get you in the local NYC-music mood. (See the "Music" section later in this chapter for more.)

GREENWICH VILLAGE

The West Village is great for browsing and gift shopping. Specialty bookstores and record stores, antiques and craft shops,

You'll find all kinds of curiosities (and cards) in the Vi

Take a Shopping Tour

If you want some help in your shopping and feel a bit intimidated by all the options Manhattan has to offer, you might want to consider taking a shopping tour. **Shop Gotham** (☎ 212/209-3370; www.shopgotham.com) offers walking tours of SoHo and Nolita (Fri–Sat at 11am, Sun at noon) and the Garment Center "Insider" Tour (Wed and Fri at 10am). They can also customize private and group tours like the Sweet Sixteen Shopping Tour. Tours range from 2 to 4 hours and from $38 to $58.

---

and gourmet food markets dominate. On 8th Street—NYU territory between Broadway and Sixth Avenue—you can find trendy footwear and affordable fashions.

But the biggest shopping boom of late has happened on **Bleecker Street** west of Sixth Avenue. Between Carmine Street and Seventh Avenue, foodies will delight in the strip of tantalizing food shops, including **Amy's Bread, Wild Edibles,** and **Murray's Cheese ★**. In between are record stores, guitar shops, and a sprinkling of artsy boutiques. On **Christopher Street,** you'll find such wonders as **Aedes De Venutas ★** at 9 Christopher St. (☎ 212/206-8674; www.aedes.com), a lovely little outfit selling perfumes and scented candles that are hard to find in the States, and the **Porcelain Room,** 13 Christopher St. (☎ 212/367-8206; www.theporcelainroom.com), which is located below street level and offers amazing antique and contemporary porcelains from Europe and Asia.

Along Christopher Street you'll also find all manner of LGBT shops, like **Rainbow Greetings** at No. 98 (☎ 212/638-3310), for all your pride decor and much more.

Follow Christopher westward, where Bleecker becomes boutique alley, and one jewel box of a shop follows another. Among them: **Intermix, Olive & Bette, Ralph Lauren, Lulu Guinness, Marc Jacobs,** and the new **Michael Kors** emporium.

Great browsing also abounds among the shops **west of Seventh Avenue** and along **Hudson Street/Eighth Avenue.** One of them is the **House of Cards and Curiosities** at 23 Eighth Ave., between Jane and 12th streets (☎ 347/694-4215), which one could argue is more curiosities than cards. **The Ink Pad** (☎ 212/463-9876; www.theinkpadnyc.com), across the street, is "New York's only rubber stamp art shop," and is home to a remarkable array of cool and crafty stamps, along with classes to make clever art with them. The Village is full of adorable, locally owned storefronts like these.

CHELSEA/MEATPACKING DISTRICT

When 23rd Street was the epitome of New York fashion a century ago, the major department stores stretched along **Sixth Avenue** for about a mile from 14th Street up. These elegant stores stood in huge cast-iron buildings that eventually were abandoned. Fortunately, the past decade has seen those grand structures transform into to new superstores. **Filene's Basement, TJ Maxx,** and **Bed Bath & Beyond** are all at 620 Sixth Ave., with the **Container Store** across the street so you can figure out how to store all your purchases.

New to Chelsea in 2010 is **Limelight Marketplace,** 656 Sixth Ave. (☎ 212/359-5600)—both a former church and a former nightclub, now renovated as a three-story shopping mall. If the shopping doesn't impress you (and it probably won't), at least the architecture will.

Far west Chelsea, meanwhile, has been transformed into the **Chelsea Art District,** where more than 200 galleries have sprouted up in a once-moribund enclave of repair shops and warehouses. The district unofficially stretches between 14th to 29th streets and the West Side Highway and Seventh Avenue, but the high-density area lies between 20th and 26th streets, between Tenth and Eleventh avenues.

The Meatpacking District has also zoomed from quaint to hot (and some say over) in no time, with such big-name designers as **Stella McCartney,** 429 W. 14th St. (✆ **212/255-1556**); **Christian Louboutin,** 59 Horatio St. (✆ **212/255-1910**); and **Alexander McQueen,** 417 W. 14th St. (✆ **212/645-1797**) in residence.

Fashionistas flock to the Meatpacking District to top designer stores.

For those "metrosexual" fashion slaves, the strip of Eighth Avenue between about 17th and 20th Street also offers a series of cool, mostly menswear shops, such as **Universal Gear, EFOR,** and **Camouflage,** and there's **Barneys Coop** around the corner at 236 W. 18th St. (✆ **212/593-7800**).

If you're seeking unique souvenirs over fancy clothes, stop by **Chissholm Larsson Gallery,** 145 Eighth Avenue (✆ **212/741-1703**), which has sold original vintage posters for nearly four decades. You don't have to be a collector to marvel at the huge array of original movie, advertising, propaganda, and other posters.

UNION SQUARE/THE FLATIRON DISTRICT

The hottest shopping/eating/hangout zone in the city may be Union Square. The long-forlorn south side of the square is now a megashopping zone with **Whole Foods, Forever 21,** and **DSW (Designer Shoe Warehouse).** And while the city's first **Nordstrom Rack** replaced the music wonderland known as Virgin Megastore in 2010, you can still browse for a melodic memento at **Academy Records** up on 18th Street (or head down Broadway to **Other Music** in NoHo).

On the north side of the Square, **Barnes & Noble** fills a beautifully restored 1880 cast-iron building, but for a real New York experience go to the one-of-a-kind **Strand Bookstore ★**, at Broadway and 12th Street. Of course, the beating heart of Union Square is the 4-days-a-week **Greenmarket ★**, the biggest farmers' market in the city and the best place to see how Manhattanites shop for fresh local groceries. In November and December, the Square also partly turns into a pop-up mall with the **Holiday Market,** brimming with hand-crafted art, jewelry, gifts, clothes, and everything else.

On Broadway, just a few blocks north of Union Square, is the shopping emporium **ABC Carpet & Home,** where the loft-size floors hold brilliantly decadent displays of furniture, housewares, linens (thread counts off the charts), and tchotchkes of all sizes and shapes.

Upscale retailers who have rediscovered the architectural majesty of **lower Fifth Avenue** include **Banana Republic, Victoria's Secret,** and **Kenneth Cole.** You won't find many small-name shops along Fifth, so head down its side streets for something more unique.

And then, *certo,* there is **Eataly,** at the stately northwest corner of Broadway and Fifth Avenue (⏱ **212/229-2560**). Legendary chef, restaurateur and Italian-American Mario Batali and partners have splayed seemingly all of Italy's gastronomic delights across 50,000 square feet of prime Flatiron real estate (see "Edibles," p. 368).

Midtown

HERALD SQUARE & THE GARMENT DISTRICT

Herald Square—where 34th Street, Sixth Avenue, and Broadway converge—is dominated by **Macy's,** the self-proclaimed "biggest department store in the world." At Sixth Avenue and 33rd Street is the **Manhattan Mall** (⏱ **212/465-0500;** www.manhattanmallny.com), home to typical mall standards like **Aeropostale** and **Express.** And there's plenty of big shopping all around the mall, including an outlet of **Lush,** England's penultimate bath-supply store.

A long block over on Seventh Avenue, not much goes on in the grimy, heavily industrial Garment District. This is, however, where you'll often find sites for that quintessential New York event, the **sample sale** (the box titled "Additional Sources for Serious Shoppers," above, points you to upcoming sample sales around the city).

ABC Carpet & Home offers a plethora of unique furnishings.

Take home your favorite Italian specialty from Eataly.

TIMES SQUARE & THE THEATER DISTRICT

You won't find much in the heart of Times Square to entice the serious shopper. But among the most dazzling mega-stores is the **Toys "R" Us** flagship on Broadway and 44th Street, which even has its own full-scale indoor Ferris wheel.

West 47th Street between Fifth and Sixth avenues is the city's famous **Diamond District;** see "Jewelry & Accessories" in "Shopping A to Z," later in this chapter.

You'll also notice a wealth of **electronics stores** throughout the neighborhood, many perpetually trumpeting GOING OUT OF BUSINESS sales. These joints have been going out of business since the Stone Age—but one thing's certain, just like a real out-of-business store, you won't be able to return a lemon camera you bought there. Better to stick with buying souvenir trinkets and T-shirts at these joints. Electronics are more wisely purchased at B&H or J&R superstores for real bargains with set prices—and legitimate warranties. (See "Electronics" later in this chapter for more.)

Don't leave the neighborhood just yet. Stop by the **Drama Book Shop** ★ at 250 W. 40th St. to browse hard-to-find plays in print, and maybe meet a real-life starving actor. Then head up **Ninth Avenue** in Hell's Kitchen, between 42nd and 57th streets, home to a wealth of little shops and charming restaurants. One of the more interesting is **Scent Elate,** 313 W. 48th St., between Eighth and Ninth avenues (✆ **212/258-3043;** www.scentelate.com), which stocks candles, handmade soaps, essential oils, an array of products made by local artists, and the legendary Lampe Berger perfume lamps (one of the few places to find them in the city).

Rivaling the delightful fragrances at Scent Elate are the sweets at **Ruby et Violette,** 457 W. 50th St., between Ninth and Tenth avenues (✆ **212/582-6720;** www.rubyetviolette.com). Stop in and gorge on the 18 daily-rotating flavors (out of 120 total) of utterly divine cookie and ice cream flavors. If you've still got room for a meal, you're in luck: You're a stone's throw from **Restaurant Row,** 46th Street between Eighth and Ninth avenues, where you'll find interesting

T-Rex presides over the Times Square Toys "R" Us.

When Is It Open?

Open hours can vary significantly from store to store—even different branches of Gap can keep different schedules depending on location and management. Generally, stores open at 10 or 11am Monday through Saturday, and 7pm is the most common closing hour—with exceptions, of course. Both opening and closing hours tend to get later as you move downtown; stores in the East Village often don't open until 1 or 2pm, and they stay open until 8pm or later.

All of the big department stores are open 7 days a week. However, unlike department stores in suburban malls, most of these stores don't keep a regular 10am-to-9pm schedule. The department stores and shops along major strips, such as Fifth Avenue, usually stay open later 1 night a week (often Thurs), while smaller boutiques may close 1 day a week. Sunday hours are usually noon

to 5 or 6pm. In addition, some neighborhoods virtually shut down on a particular day—namely the Lower East Side on Saturday, the East Village on Monday, and most of the Financial District for the weekend. But at holiday time, anything goes: Macy's often stays open until midnight for the last few weeks before Christmas.

Your best bet is to **call ahead** or check a particular store website if your heart's set on visiting it.

And if you're in town in early September, you may be able to catch the city's annual **Fashion's Night Out** extravaganza. Launched in 2009, this one night of the year sees designers turn their shops into discos with late-night hours, open bars, and great bargains. Check out **www.fashionsnightout.com** for more, including a countdown clock. It's good enough to plan your trip around.

shopping interspersed among the multiethnic restaurants. (Find out more at **www.restaurantrownyc.com.**)

Wander over to 42nd Street to hit the big-name shops, like **Lids,** a chain that carries the official on-field baseball cap of every single major-league baseball team, and what seems like every variation, too.

FIFTH AVENUE & 57TH STREET

The heart of Manhattan retail spans Fifth Avenue from the upper 40s to 57th Street and across. **Tiffany & Co.,** which has long reigned supreme, sits a stone's throw from **NIKETOWN** and the huge **Louis Vuitton** flagship at the corner of 57th Street and Fifth Avenue. In addition, a good number of mainstream retailers, such as **Banana Republic,** have flagships along Fifth, shifting the breadth of higher-end shopping to Madison Avenue north of 59th Street. You will find a number of big-name, big-ticket designers radiating from the crossroads, including **Versace, Chanel, Dior,** and **Cartier.** You'll also find big-name jewelers here, as well as grand old department stores such as **Bergdorf Goodman, Henri Bendel,** and **Saks Fifth Avenue**—all Fifth Avenue mainstays that must at least be browsed, even if your budget won't allow for more than longing glances.

Uptown

MADISON AVENUE

Madison Avenue from 57th to 79th streets boasts the most expensive retail real estate in the world. Bring lots of plastic. This ultradeluxe strip—particularly in the high 60s—is home to *the* most luxurious designer boutiques, with **Barneys New**

York ★ as the anchor. For a sampling of local designers, see "Clothing" in "Shopping A to Z," later in this chapter.

Don't be intimidated by the glamour of this shopper's mile or any of the celebrities you're likely to cross paths with. The luxury boutiques of Madison Avenue will be happy you stopped by if only to peruse their treasures, and maybe even discover a bargain in the racks. There's also the joy of fine architecture among many of these upscale retailers, like the stunning **Ralph Lauren Store,** housed in a revamped mansion at 72nd Street.

If you're in the market for something different, two of the more diverse retailers are the Chinese luxury boutique **Shanghai Tang,** 600 Madison Ave. (✆ **212/888-0111;** www. shanghaitang.com), and French crystalier **Lalique** at 609 Madison Ave. (✆ **212/355-6550**), both with merchandise you won't find anywhere else in town.

Head for Maxilla & Mandible for all your skeletal needs.

UPPER WEST SIDE

The Upper West Side's best shopping street is **Columbus Avenue.** Small shops catering to the neighborhood's white-collar mix of yuppies and families line both sides of the avenue from 66th Street to about 86th Street. Highlights include **Maxilla & Mandible** ★ for its museum-quality natural-science-based gifts, and perhaps the world's best tagline: "The world's first and only osteological store." (See "Museum Stores" later in this chapter.)

The browsing continues along Amsterdam Avenue, but go one more block west to main-drag **Broadway** for some gourmet edibles at **Zabar's** and **Fairway** markets (see "Edibles," in "Shopping A to Z," later in this chapter). You can also score some comfy kicks at **Harry's Shoes** on Broadway at 83rd Street, or down Broadway at **Tip Top Shoes** on 72nd Street. (See "Shoes" for more.)

Mall with a View: The Shops at Columbus Circle

The Shops at Columbus Circle mall, in the Time Warner Center, features not only some of the biggest (and priciest) names in retail, but it also offers shopping with a view of Central Park. Situated just off the southwest corner of "the city's playground," the mall is 2 blocks long and four stories high. But for shoppers who set their sights on such retailers as **Williams-Sonoma, Sisley, Coach, Hugo Boss, Eileen Fisher, Thomas Pink, Borders, Bose,** and the massive 59,000-square-foot **Whole Foods Market,** does the picturesque view really matter? For more information and a complete list of stores, check the mall's website at **www.shopsatcolumbuscircle. com,** or call ✆ **212/823-6300.**

SHOPPING ONE-TWO-FIVE STREET

Few neighborhoods are now free of big chain stores, and now 125th Street, Harlem's central boulevard, is among them. The heart of this shopping thoroughfare is between St. Nicholas Avenue and Fifth Avenue, where you'll find **American Apparel, H&M, MAC Cosmetics,** the **Body Shop, Starbucks, Old Navy,** and **Modell's.** Fortunately smaller local retailers are peppered in between. Among them are elegant beauty and skincare shop **Carol's Daughter,** 24 W. 125th St. ((© **212/828-6757**), and clothier the **Brownstone Woman,** 24 E. 125th St. ((© **212/996-7980**).

Also sprinkled among the big names are stores that represent the unique Harlem character. Hip-hop boutiques are 1-2-5 mainstays, including two locations of **Jimmy Jazz,** 132 and 239 W. 125th St. ((© **212/663-2827**), and **Jersey Man Cap USA,** 112 W. 125th St. ((© **212/222-7942**), where you can get anything from a Kangol to Girbaud Femme. For a decade now, **Hue-Man Books,** 2319 Frederick Douglass Blvd., just south of 125th Street ((© **212/665-7400**), has been the neighborhood joint for books and readings—specializing in Harlem-based authors and local bestsellers, as well as "voices from the 'hood" categorized under "Street Fiction." And while 125th has no shortage of sidewalk vendors selling incense, African importer **Nicholas Variety,** 5 E. 125th St. ((© **212/289-3628**), may be an even better spot to pick up scented oils, bath salts, and other aroma therapy aids.

For a cultural diversion, stop in at the **Studio Museum in Harlem,** 144 W. 125th St., between Lenox Avenue and Adam Clayton Powell Jr. Boulevard ((© **212/864-4500**)—also home to a cool gift shop (for more, see chapter 6). Head east for the most eye-catching, uniquely Harlem T-shirts and hoodies at the modest **Harlem Underground Clothing Company,** 20 E. 125th St. ((© **212/987-9385**), which sports the coolest Barack Obama gear possibly in all of New York.

And with plenty more shopping to be found on side streets, you can also do a little online browsing to zero in on specific shops or merchandise at **www.harlemonestop.com,** which also does local walking and trolley tours.

Still further south, the **Shops at Columbus Circle** offers a world of upscale choices for shopping. (See the box "Mall with a View.")

The Outer Boroughs

Brooklyn is a shopping destination in its own right, and some of the best and most interesting things can be found in Park Slope, Williamsburg, Fort Greene, Cobble Hill/Carroll Gardens, DUMBO, and other neighborhoods. See the box "Take the L Train" (p. 361) for more on **Williamsburg** in particular.

In recent years, **Park Slope** became officially great shopping territory, lined with endless adorable and diverse, independently owned retailers selling unique wares. The main action is along **Fifth and Seventh avenues,** both starting from Flatbush Avenue all the way down to about 15th Street (see chapter 1 for "Best Streets to Walk Up or Down," p. 10). There's also the centrally located **Atlantic Terminal Mall,** should you need to visit Brooklyn's superbusy **Target** or another big chain store like **Gamestop, Daffy's,** or **Guitar Center.** Mostly I skip the mall and wander down **Atlantic Avenue** toward **Smith Street** and **Court Street** in Cobble Hill to browse the wealth of charming boutiques—and, as of

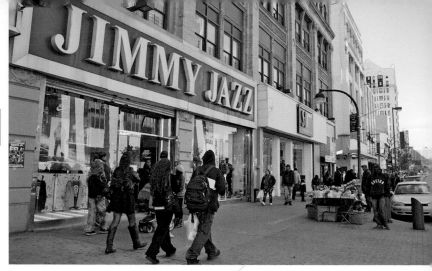

Hip-hop boutique Jimmy Jazz is on 125th Street (see box on p. 351).

late 2010, a new **Barney's Co-Op** at 194 Atlantic Ave. (☏ **718/637-2234**). Duck into the little side street called Boerum Place to check out what cool vintage plus-size garb is for sale at **Re/Dress** (☏ **212/522-7962**).

Closer to Manhattan you'll find the very scenic, cobblestoned **DUMBO** (that's **D**own **U**nder the **M**anhattan **B**ridge **O**verpass), with high-end stores in spacious shops, including local-fashion retailer **Loopy Mango** at two locations, and **Jacques Torres Chocolate** (see the sidebar "NYC Is Chocolate City," later in this chapter). Over in Fort Greene, the **Brooklyn Flea** ★★ weekend market (www.brooklynflea.com), should not be missed in either its Saturday warm-weather outdoor location on Lafayette Ave., or Sunday indoors at Skylight One Hanson, open year-round.

THE BIG DEPARTMENT STORES

ABC Carpet & Home ★   Shopping ABC has often been compared to taking a fantasy tour of your very rich and well-traveled ancestor's attic. This two-building emporium is legendary and deserves to be: It's the ultimate home-fashions-and-furnishings department store. On the west side of the street is the stunning 10-floor home emporium one blogger called a "wonderful mega boutique." The goods run the gamut from sustainable harvested Goodwood furniture to hand-painted Tuscan pottery to Tiffany-style lamps to chemical-free cotton bedding to much, much more. An entire floor of on-the-bolt upholstery fabrics rivals the best interior-design stores. These are high-end goods, but sales also bring substantial bargains. The parlor floor boasts an eclectic collection of beautiful gifts, antiques, and housewares, and some of the smaller items are quite affordable. Across the street is the multifloor carpet store, which boasts a stunning collection of area rugs. 881 and 888 Broadway (at 19th St.). ☏ **212/473-3000.** www.abchome. com. Subway: L, N, R, 4, 5, 6 to 14th St./Union Sq.

Barneys New York ★★   New York's self-made temple of chic still reigns supreme. While the store focuses on hot-off-the-runway women's wear, its men's wear runs the gamut from classic to cutting edge. Bring your platinum card, because nothing comes cheap here, although house brands are solidly made and aren't off-the-chart expensive. Both the downtown (in two locations), uptown, and Brooklyn **Barneys Co-Ops** have blossomed into real fashion hot spots, sisterly but separate from the chic Barneys New York Madison Avenue flagship. At Barneys Co-Op, more downtown-casual fashions for men and women—from designer names like Alexander Wang, John Varvatos, and Jil Sander—set the tone. Prices are more reasonable than on Madison Avenue but certainly not cheap.

Tip: Twice a year, Barneys hosts its famous **warehouse sale** in Chelsea. Prices change daily, but markdowns are 50% to 80% off the original retail prices on all clothing and gifts. So if you are planning a shopping trip to the city, check the website for sale dates—and arrive early. With diligence, you will score a designer item that makes the wait and the chaos worth it. 660 Madison Ave. (at 61st St.). ✆ **212/826-8900.** www.barneys.com. Subway: N, R to Fifth Ave. Barneys Co-Ops: 116 Wooster St. (btw. Prince and Spring sts.). ✆ **212/965-9964.** Subway: N, R to Prince St. 236 W. 18th St. (btw. Seventh and Eighth aves.). ✆ **212/593-7800.** 194 Atlantic Ave. (btw. Court and Clinton sts.). ✆ **718/637-2234.** Subway: 2, 3, 4, 5 to Borough Hall. 2151 Broadway (btw. 75th and 76th sts.). ✆ **646/335-0978.** Subway: 1 to 79th St. Barneys Warehouse: 256 W. 17th St. (btw. Seventh and Eighth aves.). ✆ **212/450-8500.** Subway: 1 to 18th St.

Bergdorf Goodman ★ Bergdorf's a store for the shopping sensualist. Housed in the former Vanderbilt Mansion, the store is spacious and sophisticated. Although the customer base is mainly "ladies who lunch" and businesswomen with gobs of money but no time for nonsense, fashionistas in the know appreciate Bergdorf's little secret: Sales can garner fantastic bargains, with designer-clothing prices slashed to the bone. Finely tuned designer salons represent both couture powerhouses and downtown darlings—from Chloe and Gaultier, to DKNY and Theory. The fifth floor is usually filled with fashions for younger women at more reasonable prices (including good end-of-season sales). The jewelry on the main floor and the unparalleled gift and tabletop floor are worth a browse alone. The store has two ladies' shoes departments, one tops for one-stop designer shopping in the $300-and-up range, and the less expensive fifth-floor salon. On the seventh floor is **BG Restaurant,** overlooking Central Park, where you can enjoy a full lunch menu (think $30 entrees), afternoon tea, and cocktails. Just across the street is the men's store, a similar palace of fine fashion. 754 Fifth Ave. (at 57th St.). ✆ **800/558-1355** or 212/753-7300. www.bergdorfgoodman.com. Subway: E, F to Fifth Ave.

Bloomingdale's ★ More accessible than Barneys and more affordable than Saks, Bloomingdale's has a certain New York pizzazz. Taking up an entire city block, Bloomie's stocks just about anything you could want, from clothing (both designer and everyday basics) and fragrances to housewares and furniture—not necessarily a good thing, because sometimes it feels too stuffed full of merchandise for comfort. It pays to make a reconnaissance trip to get the overview, then move in for the kill. The main entrance is on Third Avenue, but pop up to street level from the 59th Street subway station and you'll be right at the Lexington Avenue entrance. A smaller downtown branch opened on Broadway in SoHo, offering pricier and edgier items. 1000 Third Ave. (Lexington Ave. at 59th St.). ✆ **212/705-2000.** www.bloomingdales.com. Subway: 4, 5, 6 to 59th St. 504 Broadway (at Broome St.). ✆ **212/729-5900.** Subway: N, R to Prince St.

Century 21 ★ 🗲 There's a reason for this institution's charming tagline, "Fashion Worth Fighting For." Yes, it's worth a battle to get designer goods 40% to 70%

off what you would pay at a department store or fine boutique. Don't think that $250 Armani blazer is a bargain? Look again at the tag—the retail price is upward of $800. This is the place to find things like supercheap Calvin Klein tees, last season's Lucky jeans, this season's Dolce & Gabbana sunglasses, or a jazzy Missoni sweater. Kids' clothes, linens, luggage, and housewares are also part of the extensive stock (head to the basement for the latter). Just go on weekday mornings to avoid being elbowed. The expansive shoe outlet next door is less jammed, and it's hard to leave without a real score. **Note:** Rumor has it that a new "C21" will open on the Upper West Side in 2011. 22 Cortlandt St. (btw. Broadway and Church St.). 212/227-9092. www.c21stores.com. Subway: 2, 3, 4, 5, J, M to Fulton St.; A, C to Broadway/Nassau St.; E to Chambers St.; R, W to Cortlandt St.

Henri Bendel ★★ 🎁 This landmark Fifth Avenue store is fun to browse. It feels like you're shopping in the town house of a slightly offbeat, moneyed lady. It's a superstylish, high-ticket collection for ladies with flair, always open to funky accessories, gorgeous handbags, and the highest-quality makeup. The usual suspects are represented alongside lesser known but stellar brands—from Immupure and Perfekt to Mali and Laura Mercier. What's even more amazing is the caliber of customer service. These ladies (and a few gentlemen) will soothe your skin, share samples, and make you over with the perfect skincare suite for any occasion. 712 Fifth Ave. (btw. 55th and 56th sts.). 212/247-1100. www.henribendel.com. Subway: N, R to Fifth Ave. or the 4, 5, 6 to 59th. St.

Lord & Taylor You wouldn't head to Lord & Taylor for cutting-edge designers, but this New York institution has an understated, elegant manner all its own. It remains a classic in part by maintaining that sophisticated sensibility. Long known as an excellent source for women's dresses and coats, L&T stocks all the major labels for men and women, with an emphasis on American designers. Their house-brand clothes (khakis, blazers, turtlenecks, and summer sportswear) are well made and a bargain. Sales, especially around holidays, can be stellar. The store is big enough to have a good selection (especially for petites) but doesn't overwhelm. 424 Fifth Ave. (btw. 38th and 39th sts.). 212/391-3344. www.lordandtaylor.com. Subway: F, M to 42nd St.

Macy's ✋ A four-story sign on the side of the building trumpets MACY'S, THE WORLD'S LARGEST STORE—a hard fact to dispute, since the 10-story behemoth covers an entire city block, dwarfing even Bloomie's uptown. Macy's can be a hard place to shop: The layout impedes traffic flow, the service is forgettable, and the best part about its Herald Square flagship usually is leaving it. But they do sell *everything*. Many departments are organized into more manageable "ministores"—there's a Metropolitan Museum Gift Shop, a Swatch boutique, and cafes and makeup counters on different floors—but the store's one-of-a-kind flair is just a memory now (with the exception of the cool wooden escalators on the Seventh Ave. side of the building, which make you feel like you're stepping back in time). Still, sales run constantly, holiday or not (1-day sales are popular on Wed and Sat), so bargains are a sure thing. And because so many feel adrift in this retail sea, the store provides personal guides/shoppers at no charge. At Christmastime, come as late as you can manage, because the store is usually open until midnight in the final shopping days before the holiday. At Herald Sq., W. 34th St., and Broadway. 212/695-4400 or 212/494-7300. www.macys.com. Subway: B, D, F, N, Q, R, 1, 2, 3 to 34th St.

Saks Fifth Avenue ★ There are branches of Saks all over the country now, but this is it: Saks *Fifth Avenue*. No other store better typifies the Big Apple than

SALE SEASONS

These may be obvious to the serious shopper, but for those on the learning curve, here are New York's prime sale seasons:

Thanksgiving: "Black Friday," or the day after Thanksgiving, is the beginning of the holiday shopping season. Many stores inaugurate this high time with major sales. Stores are open wildly early and late, and entice shoppers with some amazing deals, usually involving buying multiple items.

Pre-Christmas: Retailers bent on making their sales quotas go to great lengths to draw in eager shoppers. Bargains abound, though they may not dazzle as much as prices on December 26. Which leads me to . . .

Post-Christmas: With the Christmas returns and overstocked storerooms come the markdowns.

Whites: Usually in January, this is a sale of linens . . . and these days, rarely white.

January Clearance: You'll find the European boutiques advertising clearance around the third week of January.

Valentine's Day: Anything red, chocolaty, or with a heart shape will be advertised "on sale."

Presidents' Day: This February long weekend brings great deals on winter inventory.

Memorial Day: Promotional sales sail in the last weekend in May.

Fourth of July: Blowouts on bathing suits and summer attire are summoned by the long weekend.

Midsummer Clearance: If there is anything summer related left on the racks after the Fourth of July, you'll find it through about mid-August.

Back-to-School: A dreaded term as a child now means terrific deals on shoes, sweaters, bags, and outerwear.

Columbus Day: Coats and winter gear go on sale on this long weekend, usually the second one in October.

Election Day: Columbus Day sale leftovers are usually on the supersale racks by this early November government holiday.

this legendary flagship store, which is well worth your time—and the smaller-than-most size makes it manageable. There's something for everyone here. Saks carries a wide range of clothing; departments err on the pricey designer side, but run the gamut to affordable house-brand basics. The men's department is the finest in the city, and in 2008 opened a 2,000-square-foot boutique devoted to Italian luxury brand Kiton. The cosmetics and fragrance departments on the main floor are justifiably noteworthy—they carry many hard-to-find and brand-new brands, including Laura Mercier, the Big Apple's own Kiehl's, and more—as are the extensive fine and costume jewelry counters. And the location, right across from Rockefeller Center, makes it a convenient stop for those on the sight-seeing circuit. 611 Fifth Ave. (btw. 49th and 50th sts.). ✆ **212/753-4000.** www.saksfifth avenue.com. Subway: B, D, F, Q to 47th–50th sts./Rockefeller Center; E, F to Fifth Ave.

SHOPPING A TO Z
Antiques & Collectibles

Antiques lovers and collectors will be dazzled by the bounty that New York has to offer, often with top-dollar pricetags to match.

Traditionalists will love the blocks off **Broadway near 10th** and **11th streets,** where the scene includes **Kentshire Galleries** (see below); and **East 59th, 60th,** and **61st streets** around Second Avenue, not far from the **Manhattan Art and Antiques Center,** at 1050 Second Ave. between 55th and 56th streets (☏ 212/355-4400; www.the-maac.com), where about two dozen high-end dealers line the street and spill over onto surrounding blocks. Fans of mid-century furniture and Americana with a twist should browse **Lafayette Street** in SoHo/NoHo.

The famous **Hell's Kitchen Flea Market** (☏ 212/243-5343; www.hells kitchenfleamarket.com) used to be a outdoor emporium on Sixth Avenue, but now the bargain bonanza is spread across three locations. The first is in Hell's Kitchen, also known as Clinton, on 39th Street, between Ninth and Tenth avenues, on Saturday and Sunday. Despite the quality vendors, the assemblage is hit or miss—some days you'll find treasures galore, and others it seems like there's nothing but junk. The truly dedicated arrive early on Saturday, but Sunday is consistently good. In addition, there's an indoor branch called the **Antiques Garage,** with antiques spread across two floors of an indoor garage in Chelsea, on West 25th Street, between Sixth and Seventh avenues. It's open Saturday and Sunday from 9am to 5pm. If you don't find what you (probably weren't even) looking for, try the **West 25th Street market,** on a lot between Broadway and Sixth Avenue, also open on weekend days.

In 2008, the **Brooklyn Flea ★★** (www.brooklynflea.com) popped up in Fort Greene, Brooklyn, garnering much fanfare for its enormous, varied selection of art, collectibles, jewelry, clothing, and housewares. The outdoor Brooklyn Flea is open on Saturdays from April to early December, filling the schoolyard of Bishop Loughlin High School with scores of amazing new and used goods—and usually live or DJ'ed music as well as local restaurants' booths—from April to December (rain or shine). Find it on Lafayette Avenue between Clermont and Vanderbilt avenues (Subway: A, C, G to Clinton/Washington). Meanwhile the Flea heads indoors on Sundays, to the Skylight at One Hanson Place (the former Williamsburg Savings Bank building) at Flatbush Ave. (Subway: 2, 3, 4, 5, B, D, N, Q, R to Atlantic-Pacific aves.). The Brooklyn Flea quickly became so cool that it's opened winter-holiday outlets in varying locales (including NoHo)—check the website for the latest.

Kentshire Galleries Still going strong after a half-century, this large and lovely gallery is the city's prime stop for 18th- and 19th-century English antiques, ranging from jewelry and tabletop items to formal furnishings. Furniture is displayed in richly appointed rooms that make for great browsing. 37 E. 12th St. (btw. University Place and Broadway). ☏ **212/673-6644.** Uptown galleries at 700 Madison Ave. (btw. 62nd and 63rd sts.). ☏ **212/421-1100.** www.kentshire.com. Subway: L, N, R, 4, 5, 6 to 14th St./Union Sq.

Lost City Arts Lost City features vintage modern furnishings and a quirky selection of accessories (station signs, 3-D photos, and the like), plus their own new midcentury-inspired furniture and accessories, including one inspired by the otherwise forbiddingly expensive custom designs of Machine Age genius

Warren MacArthur. A real treat. 18 Cooper Sq. (Third Ave. at 5th St.). 🕾 **212/375-0500.**
www.lostcityarts.com. Subway: N, R to 8th St.; 6 to Astor Place.

Mood Indigo   This dandy of a shop is the city's top dealer in glassware, dishware, and kitchen accessories from the 1930s through the 1950s. The charming
shopkeepers also specialize in Bakelite jewelry and 1939 World's Fair memorabilia and boast a whopping collection of 1950s novelty salt and pepper shakers
and just plain cool vintage barware. Everything is pristine, so expect to pay
accordingly. 40 W. 25th St., no. 112 and no. 222. (btw. Broadway and 6th Ave.). 🕾 **212/254-
1176.** www.moodindigonewyork.com. Subway: F, R to 23rd St.

New York Galleries Antiques   You'll feel like you're privy to designers' discounts at this fine arts and antiques assemblage in the heart of Chelsea. The
goods run the gamut from 18th-century chandeliers, to collectors' crystal and
brass, to a century's worth of radios, jewelry, and toys. It's also easy to make a
bargain, with a 20% discount for cash payments. Open daily. 111 W. 25th St. (btw.
Sixth and Seventh aves.). 🕾 **212/352-1819.** Subway: F to 23rd St.

Art

See the box titled "Art for Art's Sake: The Gallery Scene," on p. 262.

Beauty

In addition to the choices below, consider visiting one of the many locations of
the French beauty superstore **Sephora** (🕾 **212/980-6534;** www.sephora.
com). For high-quality skincare products based on natural formulas and ingredients (think sugar, milk, and soy)—as well as makeup not tested on animals—
check out **Fresh** at five locations around the city, including 57 Spring St.
(🕾 **212/925-0099;** www.fresh.com), where you can invest in a glorious facial.
You can also stop by **Henri Bendel** (p. 354) for a free makeover at their fab
beauty counters.

C. O. Bigelow   Who'd think that a 170-year-old apothecary would carry the
city's most eclectic, enjoyable, and international collection of healthy-skin and
personal-care products? The goodies range from their own line Bigelow creams,
salves, and haircare, to dozens of hard-to-find brands—hence the tagline, "If you
can't get it anywhere else, try Bigelow." As an added treat, enjoy the old-school
architecture of this shop, including leather ceilings and gas-powered lamps. 414
Sixth Ave. (btw. 8th and 9th sts.). 🕾 **212/533-2700.** www.bigelowchemists.com. Subway: A,
C, E, F, M to W. 4th St.

Kiehl's ★   Kiehl's is more than a store, it's a virtual cult. Models, stockbrokers,
foreign visitors—they all flock to this old-time apothecary (ca. 1851) for its simply packaged, wonderfully formulated products for women and men. Kiehl's now
has counters in several department stores (evidence of the brand's growth), but
stop into the original if you can and go home with a bag full of free samples. 109
Third Ave. (btw. 13th and 14th sts.). 🕾 **212/677-3171.** www.kiehls.com. Subway: L, N, R, 4, 5, 6
to 14th St./Union Sq.

Mario Badescu ★★   Here in the modest building where the founder once
lived and made his first product sample, a team of skin-care specialists will customize an assemblage of products that will absolutely pamper your epidermis. A
dozen "facialists" are on staff 7 days a week, and the smallish space also includes
an immaculate spa. But it's the unparalleled product line that's most worth the

visit. 320 E. 52nd St. (btw. First and Second aves.). **☎ 212/758-1065.** www.mariobadescu. com. Subway: 6 to 51st St.; E, M to Lexington–53rd St.

Ricky's ★ This chain of funky drugstores also features a wide range of beauty products. It's a haven for makeup mavens, with multicolored wigs, rainbow-colored lipstick, glitter galore, green nail polish, over 80 kinds of hairbrushes, and even edible undies. And in October, look out for their Halloween-costume pop-up shops all over Manhattan. Since there are more than two dozen Ricky's in NYC alone, check out their website for locations near you. Some of the biggest and most convenient are: 44 E. 8th St. (at Greene St.). **☎ 212/254-5247.** Subway: N, R to 8th St. Also at 466 Sixth Ave. (at 11th St.). **☎ 212/924-3401.** Subway: A, B, C, D, E, F to W. 4th St. 112 W. 72nd St. (btw. Columbus Ave. and Broadway). **☎ 212/769-3678.** Subway: 1, 2, 3 to 72nd St. 728 Ninth Ave. (btw. 49th and 50th sts.). **☎ 212/245-1265.** www.rickysnyc.com. Subway: C, E to 50th St.

Zitomer's This three-story drugstore is more a mini-department store than a pharmacy. You'll find everything from electronics to pet supplies. But the first floor is where you'll spend most of your time if you're looking for beauty products. They have their own very good line of cosmetics called Z New York. Big Apple lip gloss will make a great souvenir, and you won't find it in your local chain drugstore. 969 Madison Ave. (at 76th St.). **☎ 212/737-5560.** www.zitomer.com. Subway: 6 to 77th St. Z Chemists at 40 W. 57th St. (btw. 5th and 6th aves.). **☎ 212/956-6000.** Subway: E, F to 5th Ave.

Books

Bookstores are a good example of the big chains vs. the little guys. And since the biggies are easy enough to find, this section will point you to the independently owned and specialty bookstores that underscore just how literary New Yorkers really are. Not to mention how much local bookdealers will value your patronage.

In addition to the following, don't forget the giant **Scholastic Store** ☺ in SoHo for children's books and events. Then for more politically driven readers, there's **Revolution Books,** 146 W. 26th St. (**☎ 212/691-3345**), which specializes "progressive, radical and revolutionary intellectual life."

Argosy Books Antiquarian-book hounds should check out this stately, family owned store nearly 90 years young. With high ceilings, packed shelves, and a quietly intellectual air, it stocks an outstanding collection of rarities, including 18th- and 19th-century prints, maps, and autographs. They have something for every price range, like $1 books and $10 prints (great gift idea!) to a $150,000 early edition of Shakespeare. 116 E. 59th St. (btw. Park and Lexington aves.). **☎ 212/753-4455.** www.argosybooks.com. Subway: 4, 5, 6 to 59th St.

Bauman Rare Books Dealing strictly in highly prized volumes with topics ranging from philosophy and science to children's classics, Bauman is one of the foremost resources for serious collectors willing to spend big money (think hundreds of thousands of dollars) for pristine first editions, ranging from early Bibles and old-English classics, to *Huckleberry Finn* and *To Kill a Mockingbird* first editions (some signed by the authors). 535 Madison Ave. (btw. 54th and 55th sts.). **☎ 800/99-BAUMAN** (800/992-2862) or 212/751-0011. www.baumanrarebooks.com. Subway: 6 to 51st St.

Bluestockings ★ 🎁 The self-proclaimed "radical bookstore, fair-trade cafe, and activist center" in the Lower East Side packs a lot of literature and activity into its Allen Street storefront (a block south of Houston St.). In addition to books on queer and gender studies, capitalism, feminism, democracy, and liberation, they also carry "good ol' smutty fiction," as well as a variety of indie magazines, journals, and alternative menstrual products (probably the only bookstore in Manhattan so equipped). Bluestockings is one of the last bastions of alternative media in this city, so even if it's not your cup of tea, stop by for souvenirs for your liberal-minded family members back home. 172 Allen St. (btw. Stanton and Rivington sts.). ✆ **212/777-6028.** www.bluestockings.com. Subway: F to Second Ave.; J, M, Z to Essex/Delancey St.

Books of Wonder ☺ You don't have to be a kid to fall in love with this fun and charming bookstore, which served as the model for Meg Ryan's shop in *You've Got Mail.* (Meg even worked here for a spell to train for the role.) Kids will love BOW's story readings; call or check the website for the latest schedule for regular author readings. 18 W. 18th St. (btw. Fifth and Sixth aves.). ✆ **212/989-3270.** www.booksofwonder.com. Subway: L, N, R, 4, 5, 6 to 14th St./Union Sq.

Complete Traveller Whether your destination is Texas or Tibet, you'll find what you need in this prestigious travel bookstore. There are travel accessories as well, plus a rare collection of antiquarian travel books whose facts may be outdated but whose writers' perceptions continue to enlighten. 199 Madison Ave. (at 35th St.). ✆ **212/685-9007.** www.ctrarebooks.com. Subway: 6 to 33rd St.

Drama Book Shop ★ This performing-arts bookstore has an in-house performance space, where you can head for discussions, panels, staged readings, and book signings with members of the theater community. The knowledgeable staff can guide you through thousands of plays, from translations of Greek classics to the season's biggest hits, plus the shop also sells books, magazines, and newspapers on the craft and business of the performing arts. 250 W. 40th St. (btw. Eighth and Ninth aves.). ✆ **212/944-0595.** www.dramabookshop.com. Subway: A, C, E to 42nd St.

Forbidden Planet Here is the city's largest collection of sci-fi, comic, and graphic-illustration books, as well as some great sci-fi themed cool toys. The proudly geeky staff really knows what's what. 840 Broadway (at 13th St.). ✆ **212/473-1576.** www.fpnyc.com. Subway: L, N, R, 4, 5, 6 to 14th St./Union Sq.

Housing Works Bookstore Cafe ★★ 🎁 Here's a way to do something good for yourself and others at the same time: Buy your reading material at this spacious yet cozy new and used book shop, stocking thousands of books, records, and comics. It's part of Housing Works, a not-for-profit outfit that provides housing, services, and advocacy for homeless people living with HIV and AIDS. The collection is terrific and well organized, with lots of well-priced paperbacks, hardbacks, advance copies, and coffee-table books. There's also a cafe in back that serves beverages (alcoholic and non) and light bites. The bookstore often hosts readings by well-known writers as well as music, comedy, and trivia performances; call or check the website for the current listings. 126 Crosby St. (south of Houston St.). ✆ **212/334-3324.** www.shophousingworks.com Subway: B, D, F, m to Broadway/Lafayette St.; N, R to Prince St.

Hue-Man Bookstore One of the nation's largest black-owned bookstores—their tagline is "A SKU for every hue"—Harlem's Hue-Man stocks the area's largest selection of African-American literature and books. Lines snaked around the block back in 2004, when Bill Clinton staged a signing of his memoir. This is *the* place for readings by today's top African-American authors. 2319 Frederick Douglass Blvd. (btw. 124th and 125th sts. at Eighth Ave.). ✆ **212/665-7400.** www.huemanbookstore.com. Subway: A, B, C, D to 125th St.

Idlewild Books Taking its name from the former New York International Airport, which became JFK Airport in 1963, this friendly upstairs bookstore is a stone's throw from Union Square. Along with an amazing collection of travel guides, the shop also has a wealth of travel fiction and essays—along with lots of cool souvenirs, gifts, and globes, and language classes. 12 W. 19th St. (btw. Fifth and Sixth aves.). ℂ **212/414-8888.** www.idlewildbooks.com. Subway: L, N, Q, R, 4, 5, 6 to 14th St./Union Sq.

Kitchen Arts & Letters Foodies, take note: Here's the ultimate cook's and food-lover's bookstore. You'll be wowed by the depth of the selection, which includes rare, out-of-print, and foreign-language titles focusing on food and wine. The superseasoned staff will conduct free searches for hard-to-find titles—including editions dating back to the 1870s. So if cooking is your bag (or cauldron), you'll be browsing for hours. 1435 Lexington Ave. (btw. 93rd and 94th sts.). ℂ **212/876-5550.** www.kitchenartsandletters.com. Subway: 6 to 96th St.

Manhattan Judaica *The* Jewish bookstore of New York City, covering all manner of Judaica—everything from cookbooks and Kaballah, to funky menorahs and mezuzahs, and much much more. 62 W. 45th St. (btw. Fifth and Sixth aves.). ℂ **212/719-1918.** www.manhattanjudaica.com. Subway: B, D, F, M to 42nd St.

McNally Jackson Books ★ A welcome respite from the fashion circus that is SoHo, McNally Jackson offers an impressive array of titles, beautiful stationary, and a corner cafe for weary shoppers. Open daily until 10pm (9pm on Sundays), come here to get recommendations from the lovely staff or to check out near-daily events and readings—including book clubs and kids storytime every Saturday. 52 Prince St. (btw. Lafayette and Mulberry sts.). ℂ **212/274-1160.** www.mcnallyjackson.com. Subway: N, R to Prince St.; 6 to Spring St.

The Mysterious Bookshop No, the shop itself is not the mysterious part—but there is something curious about the inventory. Oh, right, it's that this place offers "the best in mystery, crime, suspense, espionage, and detective fiction." New and vintage inventories are stocked, and the store has specialized "clubs" for collectors, where members receive first edition and signed copies of books in their favorite sub-genres. 58 Warren St. (at W. Broadway). ℂ **212/587-1011.** www.mysteriousbookshop.com. Subway: 1, 2, 3, A, C, E to Chambers St.

Rizzoli This clubby Euro-centric bookstore is the classiest and most relaxing spot in town to browse for fine-art, fashion, and design books across its three floors, plus quality fiction, architecture volumes, gourmet cookbooks, and other upscale reading. There's a decent selection of foreign-language (mostly Italian, French and Spanish), music, and dance titles as well. 31 W. 57th St. (btw. Fifth and Sixth aves.). ℂ **212/759-2424.** www.rizzoliusa.com. Subway: N, R to Fifth Ave.

The Strand ★ 🖉 It's a New York legend, so don't miss the Strand and its staggering "8 miles of books," as well as its extensive downstairs inventory of review copies and bargain titles at up to 85% off list price (not to mention $1 books on outdoor racks). It's unquestionably the city's best book deal—there's almost nothing marked at list price—and the selection is phenomenal in all categories. Still, you'll work for it: The narrow aisles mean you're always getting bumped and the books are only roughly alphabetized. Nevertheless, it's a book lover's paradise in a great Union Square south location. There's also a rare-book department on the third floor. 828 Broadway (at 12th St.). ℂ **212/473-1452.** www.strandbooks.com. Subway: L, N, Q, R, 4, 5, 6 to 14th St./Union Sq.

TAKE THE L TRAIN

For New Yorkers, the L subway is the primary crosstown/cross-river link to the hipster enclave that is Williamsburg, Brooklyn. Years ago, the cool kids getting priced out their East Village apartments migrated via the L to what was then a much more affordable neighborhood, filled with a mix of dilapidated lofts, dive bars, and sidewalk junk sales. You'll still find all of that in Williamsburg, but now it's intermingled with indie fashion designers, pricey (but great) second-hand stores, and miscellaneous boutiques, clubs, and restaurants—almost all of which feel like tomorrow's Next Big Thing. Here are some shopping highlights, all reachable via the L train's first stop in Williamsburg: Bedford Avenue.

Beacon's Closet 88 N. 11th St., between Berry Street and Wythe Avenue (© **718/486-0816;** www.beaconscloset. com). This converted warehouse is not only Brooklyn's best vintage clothing, it also just may be New York City's as well. You can find men's and a huge selection of women's clothing here, along with hats, coats, jewelry, belt buckles, and novelties. A smaller Beacon's is also in Park Slope at 92 Fifth Ave. (© **718/230-1630**).

Brooklyn Industries 162 Bedford Ave., at North 8th Street (© **718/486-6464;** www.brooklynindustries.com). There are several outlets of this quality clothing and sturdy shoulder-bag brand in Brooklyn, and a few in Manhattan (in case you needed proof of its coolness). Here's the place for high-quality hoodies, jackets, T-shirts, dresses, and other wardrobe items sold in hip stores with sexy staffers. The label stands out for being authentically local owned, using unique fabric patterns, embroidered details, and quality silkscreening.

Earwax 218 Bedford Ave., at North 5th Street (© **718/486-3771**). This music outpost draws flocks of hipsters for its eclectic décor and selection. They also have an impressive collection of new and used CDs, and vinyl for the DJs among us.

Mini Mini Market 218 Bedford Ave., near North 6th Street (© **718/302-9337;** www.miniminimarket.com). The stock is geared for women, especially the inexpensive antique jewelry. The store also features beauty products, hats, bags, and throwback toys. Go around the corner to 160 N. 6th St. to check out their new **Shoe Market** shop (© **718/388-8495**).

Pema 225 Bedford Ave., near N. 5th St. (© **718/388-8814;** www.pemany.com). High style and cool casualwear fill this women's clothing, jewelry, hat, bag, and shoe store, which will add flair to every wardrobe.

Three Lives & Company For more than 30 years Three Lives has helped their customers answer the questions, "What to read next?" It's a real reader's bookstore—the Greenwich Village Historical Society called it a "pocket of civility." The staff knows every inch of the place, but you're welcome to peruse its nooks and corners on your own, too. 154 W. 10th St. (at Waverly Place). © **212/741-2069.** www.threelives.com. Subway: A, B, C, D, E, F, M to W. 4th St. or 1 to Christopher St.

Urban Center Books Housed in the 1882 Villard Houses (an architectural landmark designed by McKim, Mead & White's), the Municipal Art Society's bookstore Urban Center boasts a terrific selection of new books on architecture, urban planning, and landscape design. 457 Madison Ave. (at 51st St.). © **212/935-3595.** www.urbancenterbooks.org. Subway: 6 to 51st St.; E, M to 53rd St.

Clothing

RETAIL FASHIONS

The Top Designers

The legendary locale for the classic designer names has always been Fifth Avenue and 57th Street. There's been some exodus to Madison Avenue (see below), but with luxurious flagships like **Gianni Versace Boutique** at 647 Fifth Ave., between 51st and 52nd streets (✆ 212/317-0224; www.versace.com), the avenue still reigns supreme. Other deluxe designer tenants from Italy's haute couture world are **Prada** (see "For Men & Women," below) and **Salvatore Ferragamo,** no. 655, between 52nd and 53rd streets (✆ 212/759-3822; www.ferragamo.com). **Gucci** still shines at Fifth Avenue and 56th Street (✆ 212/826-2600; www.gucci.com) as well as their Madison Avenue location at 840 Madison Ave. (✆ 212/717-2619), while classic **Chanel** is at 15 E. 57th St., between Fifth and Madison avenues (✆ 212/355-5050; www.chanel.com), with the freshly hip tartans of **Burberry** just down the block at 9 E. 57th St. (✆ 212/407-7100; www.burberry.com).

To add to the panache of the glamorous strip, **Giorgio Armani** recently added an enormous, stunning new store at 645 Fifth Ave., at 51st Street (✆ 212/980-3037; www.giorgioarmani.com). The opening took place in 2009, filling all four floors of the ultramodern space with celebrities who came to ogle selections from each of the designer's collections.

The Upper East Side's Madison Avenue is the heartland of haute couture these days. The biggest names in modern designs line up along the platinum-coated boulevard; between 59th and 80th streets, you'll find **Calvin Klein, Valentino, Bottega Veneta, Dolce & Gabbana, Emanuel Ungaro, Givenchy, Hermès, Issey Miyake, Krizia, Max Mara, Prada** (see below), **Polo/Ralph Lauren** (see below), **Roberto Cavalli, Versace** (see above), and many more; the density is greatest in the high 60s.

Uptown is nice, but established avant-garde designers hold court in SoHo. Highlights include **Anna Sui,** 113 Greene St., just south of Prince Street (✆ 212/941-8406; www.annasui.com), who specializes in boho fashions with a glam edge. **Marc Jacobs,** 163 Mercer St., between Houston and Prince (✆ 212/343-1490; www.marcjacobs.com), excels at modern takes on classic cuts. Girlie designs are the specialty of **Cynthia Rowley,** 376 Bleecker St., at Perry Street (✆ 212/242-3803; www.cynthiarowley.com). SoHo has become so designer hot that plenty of established names have moved in, including **Louis Vuitton,** 116 Greene St., between Prince and Spring streets (✆ 212/274-9090; www.vuitton.com); always avant **Helmut Lang,** 142 Greene St., near Spring Street (✆ 212/563-0586 or 212/334-2487).

And there's a new power-shopping contender in Manhattan: **Bleecker Street** in the West Village, which already is being compared to Rodeo Drive and the Champs-Élysées for its sky-high rents and elite retailers. Stroll this street to check out the new **Michael Kors** and **Burberry** shops, as well as **Jack Spade, Ralph Lauren,** and **Juicy Couture.**

Talented up-and-comers have set up shop on and around **Bond Street** in NoHo; on **Elizabeth, Mott,** and **Mulberry streets** in Nolita; along **East 9th Street** in the East Village (see "For Men & Women," below); and on the **Lower East Side,** in the blocks south of Houston Street.

Fashion Flagships

Visits to New York flagship stores are an experience you won't find anywhere else, including at their smaller city storefronts and boutiques. These sites are display cases for the complete line of fashions, so come here to see everything you might only expect on the Internet. Check out **Ann Taylor** at 645 Madison Ave., at 60th Street (☎ **212/832-2010;** www.anntaylor.com); the Art Deco–styled **Banana Republic** flagship at Rockefeller Center, 626 Fifth Ave., at 50th Street (☎ **212/974-2350;** www.bananarepublic.com); and the reliably chic **DKNY,** 655 Madison Ave., at 60th Street (☎ **212/223-DKNY** [223-3569]; www.dkny. com). **J. Crew** has a big bi-level SoHo store at 99 Prince St., between Mercer and Greene streets (☎ **212/966-2739;** www.jcrew.com), as well as a large store on Rockefeller Plaza at 50th Street (☎ **212/765-4227**). **Old Navy's** mega-flagship, featuring its affordable basics and signature trendwear, is at 610 Sixth Ave., at 18th Street (☎ **212/645-0663;** www.oldnavy.com). And you can see the full line of bags, shoes, accessories, and more at the **kate spade** flagship at 454 Broome St. in SoHo (☎ **212/274-1991;** www.katespade.com).

One of the newest additions to affordable, superstylish fashion is the U.S. flagship of **Topshop,** a U.K. competitor of H&M, which opened in SoHo in 2009 at Broadway and Broome Street (☎ **212/966-9555;** www.topshopnyc. com). Two blocks up is the "global flagship" of sleek Japanese clothier **Uniqlo,** 546 Broadway (☎ **917/237-8800;** www.uniqlo.com).

For Men & Women

Atrium It may mostly be about the denim at this NoHo bastion of fashion, but you can stop by for accessories, shoes, even kid's wear. As long as you're browsing for trendy-but-quality clothing from tons of top designers—heavy on the jeans— Atrium is a great place to start dressing like a rock star. 644 Broadway. (at Bleecker St.). ☎ **212/473-3980.** www.atriumnyc.com Subway: 6 to Spring; R, W to Prince; F, M to Broadway/Lafayette St.

Brooks Brothers The perfect definition of all that is preppy lies behind this clubby storefront filled with pastels and clean cuts. The label is synonymous with quality, quiet taste, and classic tailoring. Some might argue it's dull, but no one can say it's not smart. 346 Madison Ave. (at 44th St.). ☎ **212/682-8800.** www.brooks brothers.com. Subway: S, 4, 5, 6, 7 to 42nd St./Grand Central. Also at 1934 Broadway (at 65th St.). ☎ **212/362-2374.** Subway: 1 to 66th St. and 1 Liberty Plaza. ☎ **212/267-2400.** Subway: 2, 3, 4, 5, A, C, J, M, Z to Broadway/Nassau St.

H&M 🎔 The Swedish superdiscounter Hennes & Mauritz is officially all over New York City. The loud, bustling stores are mostly multilevel lofts, but the departments are usually organized, if crowded. Both men's and women's clothing is ultrachic, and the prices are low, low, low—which is apparent in the quality, but who cares since it's only supposed to be worn one season. Teens especially love it for obvious reasons. The main Herald Square store carries all lines, including babies', children's, and maternity wear. (Check the website for more locations.) 1328 Broadway (at 34th St.). ☎ **646/473-1165.** www.hm.com. Subway: B, D, F, M, Q, R to 34th St./Herald Sq. Also at 640 Fifth Ave. (at 51st St.). ☎ **212/539-8391.** Subway: E, F to Fifth Ave. Smaller location at 558 Broadway (btw. Prince and Spring sts.). ☎ **212/343-2722.** Subway: N, R to Prince St.

Jeffrey New York ★ It used to be the only haute couture in the Meatpacking District, but Jeffrey New York still stands out for its impeccable merchandise. This outpost of the famed Atlanta megaboutique caters to the Barneys crowd, with prices to match on great clothes, accessories, and shoes galore. The collection is mostly geared to women, with a modest makeup counter to boot—but there's a stylin' men's department, too. 449 W. 14th St. (near Tenth Ave.). ℭ 212/206-1272. www.jeffreynewyork.com. Subway: A, C, E, L to 14th St.

Nordstrom Rack The first Nordstrom outpost to open in New York City did so in 2010, filling its racks with discounted clothes, shoes, bags, and jewelry from its regular stores. It serves as a competitor to local bargain faves like Century 21 and Filene's Basement, but so far has not been able to beat their markdowns on fashion-forward styles or designer labels. Still, the Rack is getting the hang of what NYC shoppers want, and with its prime location on the south side of Union Square should only get better with age. 60 E. 14 St. (btw. Broadway and Fourth Ave.) ℭ 212/220-2080. www.nordstrom.com. Subway: L, N, R, 4, 5, 6 to 14th St./Union Sq.

Paul Stuart Paul Stuart is a touch more hip and a touch more expensive than Brooks Brothers. It's is the classic New York haberdasher—gorgeous fabrics, flawless tailoring, and expensive price tags on everything from suits to weekend wear. And while Paul Stuart still focuses on men, this outpost's women's section was recently expanded with more fine suits and color palette. Madison Ave. at 45th St. ℭ 212/682-0320. www.paulstuart.com. Subway: 4, 5, 6, 7, S to 42nd St./Grand Central.

Polo/Ralph Lauren ★ Among all the high-ticket designers whose shops line Madison Avenue, Ralph Lauren deserves special mention for the stunning beauty of his flagship store, housed in a 1898 landmark mansion. One of New York's first important free-standing American designer homes, it has continued to wear as well as the classics Ralph churns out. Housewares and infants' clothing as well as women's and men's clothes are for sale in adjacent storefronts. The activewear and sporty country looks are at Polo Sport. On Madison Avenue Nos. 867 (men's), 888 (women's and home), 878 (boys and girls), 872 (infant and toddler) (all btw. 71st and 72nd sts.). ℭ 212/606-2100. www.ralphlauren.com. Subway: 6 to 77th St.

Prada Few designer labels are more body conscious, cachet laden, and downright chic than this sleek Italian line, which reaches beyond clothing to embrace shoes, accessories, and some of the sharpest handbags on the planet. 841 Madison Ave. (at 70th St.). ℭ 212/327-4200. Subway: 6 to 68th St. Also at 575 Broadway (at Prince St.). ℭ 212/334-8888. Subway: R, W to Prince St., 724 Fifth Ave. (btw. 56th and 57th sts.). ℭ 212/664-0010. Subway: N, R to 5th Ave. 45 E. 57th St. (at Park Ave.). ℭ 212/308-2332. Subway: 4,5,6 to 59th St./Lexington Ave.

Rag & Bone ★★ The designers behind Rag & Bone founded the label in 2002 with one goal: To make clothes that they and their friends would love to wear every day . . . even though they had no fashion experience. Today the high-quality, high-ticket brand, comprised of everything from tailored shirts and classic-cut jeans, to well-sewn leather and sophisticated runway pieces, is sold in high-end stores of all sizes around the world—but it's hard to beat its own, adorably cozy shop in the Village. (Check website for more locations.) 104 and 100 Christopher St. (btw. Bedford and Bleecker sts.). ℭ 212/727-2990. www.rag-bone.com. Subway: 1 to Christopher St.

Ted Baker London This hip Brit import, housed in a store that feels like an old-school country club, is one of Manhattan's most finely detailed designer. Specializing in cool variations on classics, this is the place to come for well-made, versatile classics. Shoes, hats, and coats will add to your sophisticated look—whether you're heading to a wedding, cocktail party, or big business meeting. 107 Grand St. (at Mercer St.). ℭ 212/343-8989. www.tedbaker.com. Subway: J, M, N, R, Z, 6 to Canal St.

Uniqlo 🎁 They call this place "the Japanese Gap," but it may be more comparable to H&M. Here you'll find hip apparel for men and women at very affordable prices. After a series of "pop-up" stores around the city with Uniqlo's clothes, in late 2006, Uniqlo opened a 36,000-square-foot, trilevel global flagship in SoHo. The towering rows of shelves are stocked with cashmere sweaters, brightly colored sweatpants, jeans, and painted T-shirts. With space-conscious displays, it's easy to browse here and, at these prices, hard to leave the store empty-handed. 546 Broadway (btw. Prince and Spring sts.). ⓒ **917/237-8811.** www.uniqlo.com. Subway: N, R to Prince St.

Zara   This Spanish retail brand rolls out affordable collections inspired by Calvin Klein, Chanel, and other big designers. Elegant suits, boho-chic dresses, and versatile, office-to-evening garments are the reason Zara now has stores around the globe, with five New York locations alone (check the website for additional sites). Midtown and downtown locations are at: 689 Fifth Ave. (at 54th St.). ⓒ **212/371-2555.** Subway: E, F to Fifth Ave. Also at 580 Broadway (btw. Prince and Spring sts.). ⓒ **212/343-1725.** www.zara.com. Subway: N, R to Prince St.

Just Women

Anthropologie   Funky, slightly exotic, and affordable wearables and accessories mix with fun gifts, furniture, and home-decorating items. Geared to funky-chic postcollegiate young women who've outgrown Urban Outfitters but still enjoy splashy, comfy clothes. 375 W. Broadway (btw. Spring and Broome sts.). ⓒ **212/343-7070.** www.anthropologie.com. Subway: C, E to Spring St. Also at 85 Fifth Ave. (at 16th St.). ⓒ **212/627-5885.** Subway: L, N, R, 4, 5, 6 to 14th St./Union Sq.

Eileen Fisher ★   Fisher's separates are a dream come true for stylish women looking for easy-to-wear classics that transcend the latest fads. She designs with a neutral palette and natural fibers that don't sacrifice comfort for style. The beautifully austere SoHo location is the prime showcase for the full collection, including both petite and women's. The closet-size East 9th Street location basically functions as a sample outlet store. (Check the website for more locations.) 395 W. Broadway (btw. Spring and Broome sts.). ⓒ **212/431-4567.** www.eileenfisher.com. Subway: C, E to Spring St. Also at 521 Madison Ave. (at 53rd St.). ⓒ **212/759-9888.** Subway: 6 to 51st St. 341 Columbus Ave. (near 76th St.). ⓒ **212/362-3000.** Subway: B, C to 81st St. 314 E. 9th St. (btw. First and Second aves.). ⓒ **212/529-5715.** Subway: 6 to Astor Place.

Flirt ★   Three artistic friends started this adorable Brooklyn shop to bring unique clothing, hats, and other miscellaneous treasures to women seeking more inspirational dress. They have succeeded, and now Flirt is the place to find unique wardrobe items you surely will be complimented on later. 93 Fifth Ave., Park Slope, Brooklyn (btw. Park and Prospect places). ⓒ **718/783-0364.** www.flirt-brooklyn.com. Subway: 2, 3 to Bergen St.

Huminska   If you're addicted to colorful, flirty dresses and shapely swirl skirts—and have a very liquid budget—make a beeline for this shop. The offerings change with the whims of the designer, but generally the look is retro chic, in sleek fabrics, with flair-filled patterns from polka dots and leopard prints, to florals and plaids (and the occasional simple, sleek solids). 315 E. 9th St. (btw. First and Second aves.). ⓒ **212/677-3458.** www.huminska.com. Subway: 6 to Astor Place.

Intermix   The place to dress and accessorize in style, with big brands spanning a range of prices—including frequent sales. The Flatiron location is the original, and remains the best of the New York branches. 125 Fifth Ave. (btw. 19th and 20th sts.). ⓒ **212/533-9720.** www.intermixonline.com. Subway: N, R to 23rd St. Also at 98 Prince

St. (at Mercer St.). ℂ **212/966-5303.** Subway: R to Prince St. 365 Bleecker St. ℂ **212/929-7180.** Subway: 1 to Christopher St. 1003 Madison Ave. (at 78th St.). ℂ **212/249-7858.** Subway: 6 to 77th St. 210 Columbus Ave. (btw. 69th and 70th sts.). ℂ **212/769-9116.** Subway: B, C to 72nd St.

Jill Anderson 🎁 A true New York local retailer, this narrow, peaceful shop and studio is lined on both sides with Jill's simple, clean-lined designs, which drape beautifully and accentuate a woman's form without clinging. They're wearable for all ages and many figure types. (Her small sizes are small enough to fit petites, and her XLs generally fit a full-figured 14.) Her clothes are feminine without being frilly, retro reminiscent but completely modern, understated, and utterly stylish. 331 E. 9th St. (btw. First and Second aves.). ℂ **212/253-1747.** www.jill anderson.com. Subway: 6 to Astor Place.

Searle ★ If you're looking for a winter coat or jacket, there aren't many better choices than Searle, whose shops are sprinkled around upper Manhattan. But the stores are not only known for their jackets—they also feature great clothes in beautiful colors and fabrics. 635 Madison Ave. (at 59th St.). ℂ **212/750-5153.** www.searle nyc.com. Subway: 4, 5, 6, N, R to 59th St. Also at 1051 Third Ave. (at 62nd St.). ℂ **212/838-5990.** Subway: 4, 5, 6, N, R to 59th. 1296 Third Ave. (at 74th St.). ℂ **212/717-5200.** Subway: 6 to 77th St. 1124 Madison Ave. (at 84th St.). ℂ **212/988-7318.** Subway: 4, 5, 6 to 86th St.

Vera Wang The powerhouse designer is still the big name in bridal fashions. Vera dresses many celebrities (particularly petite ones with great figures) for their weddings and award shows in her simple, elegant designs. Vera's bridal studio is open by appointment only, so brides-to-be should call ahead—otherwise stop by the flagship next door. There's also a Vera Wang salon on the third floor at **Bergdorf's** (p. 353). Ask about the annual warehouse sale, usually in September. 991 Madison Ave. (at 77th St.). ℂ **212/628-3400.** www.verawang.com. Subway: 6 to 77th St. Bridesmaids' store at 980 Madison Ave., 3rd floor (btw. 76th and 77th sts.). ℂ **212/628-9898.** Subway: 6 to 77th St.

Topshop ★ When this British women's retailer opened in SoHo in 2009, the line of hard-core shoppers wrapped around the block. Must be the versatile basics, fashion-forward frocks, and seductive designer collections that lure the ladies to this four-level U.S. flagship. Plus the great sales. And the amazing third-floor shoe lounge. Stop by the personal shopping department for an in-store consultation. 478 Broadway (at Broome St.). ℂ **212/966-9555.** www.topshopnyc.com. Subway: 6 to Spring St.

Just Men

Frank Stella This refined Brooks Brothers alternative sells casually elegant clothes for the well-dressed 21st-century man, including clean-lined blazers, quality knits, and beautifully cut trousers. 440 Columbus Ave. (at 81st St.). ℂ **212/877-5566.** www.frankstellanyc.com. Subway: B, C to 81st St. Also at 921 Seventh Ave. (at 58th St.). ℂ **212/957-1600.** Subway: A, B, C, D, 1 to 59th St./Columbus Circle.

John Varvatos ★ It was a hard to take for most New Yorkers when Varvatos took over the space long occupied by legendary punk-rock club CBGB back in 2006. But time has passed and it's hard to deny that this collection is a wealth of hot, well-made men's clothes—fittingly inspired by rock 'n roll. To that end, the shop hosts live local musicians the first Thursday of the month, exhibits signed guitars and memorabilia, and has preserved CBGB's original makeshift wallpaper of show posters and graffiti. You'll find his sexy suits and other gear at most high-end department stores and boutiques, but nothing compares to the Bowery shop.

315 Bowery (at Bleecker St.). ☎ **212/358-0315.** www.johnvarvatos.com. Subway: F to 2nd Ave. Also at 122 Spring St. (at Greene St.). ☎ **212/965-0700.** Subway: N, R to Prince St.; B, D, F to Broadway/Lafayette.

Paul Smith   This temple of new English fashion is a can't-miss. When it comes to menswear that's at once fashion forward and undisputedly classic, Paul Smith is the master—with tailored jackets, suits, pants, shoes, sportswear, and accessories that are luxury priced but worth every penny. 108 Fifth Ave. (at 16th St.). ☎ **212/627-9770.** www.paulsmith.co.uk. Subway: F to 14th St. Also at 142 Greene St. (btw. Houston and Prince sts.). ☎ **646/613-3060.** Subway: N, R to Prince St.; B, D, F to Broadway/Lafayette.

Saint Laurie Merchant Tailors 👔   Family-owned since 1913, this fine men's tailor stocks a huge selection of fabrics—from Scottish worsted wools to Italian silks—and offers you a selection of styles to choose from. A custom-made suit will set you back about $1,900 (less when sales are going on), but off-the-rack slacks, shirts, and vests are just as superb and more affordable. 22 W. 32nd St. (at Fifth Ave.). ☎ **212/643-1916.** www.saintlaurie.com. Subway: B, D, F, N, Q, R, M to 34th St.

Sean John   Fellas, take note: You don't have to head to P. Diddy's native Harlem to find his sexy urban streetwear. In 2004, he opened a flagship on Fifth Avenue and 41st Street featuring his signature hip-hop clothing line. Head to this elegant venue for all kinds of cool, quality gear, including fragrances, eyewear, and casualwear. Big and tall sizes and kids clothes are in the house, too—but only jackets for women. 475 Fifth Ave. (at 41st St.). ☎ **212/220-2633.** www.seanjohn.com. Subway: B, D, F, M, 4, 5, 6, 7 to 42nd St.

Just Kids

If you need the basics, you'll find branches of **Gap Kids, Baby Gap,** and the **Children's Place** all over town—in fact it's usually harder to avoid one than to find one. The department stores are also great sources, of course.

TriBeCa is home to an especially good stock of excellent children's stores, both affordable and elite. In addition to the ones listed below, wander around West Broadway, lower Hudson Street, and their side streets to explore tiny shops like **Babesta,** "for trendsetting tots," at 66 W. Broadway (☎ **212/608-4522**). Also duck into the East Village's **Dinosaur Hill** for one-of-a-kind clothing (see "Toys," p. 384).

Bu & the Duck 👔   This adorable shop sells its own unique vintage-inspired clothing and shoes that your kids can wear comfortably. Delightful sock puppets and other vintage-inspired toys and furniture are also in the mix in both locations. 106 Franklin St. (btw. Church St. and W. Broadway). ☎ **212/431-9226.** www.buandtheduck.com. Subway: 1 to Franklin St.

Shoofly   Top-quality clothing, footwear, and accessories for kids from newborns through teens. You'll find lots of distinctive outfits here, including imported lines. The shoe selection, in particular, isn't too pricey, and will make your kids rule the school. You'll also find one-of-a-kind toys and infant gifts at this downtown shop. 42 Hudson St. (btw. Duane and Thomas sts.). ☎ **212/406-3270.** www.shoofly nyc.com. Subway: 1, 2, 3 to Chambers St.

Space Kiddets 👔   This sleeper in the Flatiron District has been around for 3 decades now, and features children's clothing in refreshing styles—a cut way above chains like the Children's Place. But the prices are also a cut above; good thing sales are frequent. 26 E. 22nd St. (btw. Broadway and Park Ave.). ☎ **212/420-9878.** www.spacekiddets.com. Subway: N, R to 23rd St.

Vintage & Consignment Clothing

Vintage finds are tucked into many a corner of NYC, with a few strips even doubling as second-hand shopping clusters. Two great ones are East 9th Street in the East Village, and West 17th Street in Chelsea, where among their shops you can find broken-in boots, used fur coats, unique hats, and funky eyewear. Specifically for the latter, don't miss **Fabulous Fanny's,** 335 E. 9th St. (℃ **212/533-0637**), and **Eye Candy,** 329 Lafayette St. (℃ **212/343-4275**).

West 25th Street in Chelsea is another good vintage strip, home to "upscale resale" boutique the **Thrifty HoG,** 11 W. 25th St. (℃ **212/206-1174**), whose proceeds benefit homeless mothers and children.

Allan & Suzi 💼 Breeze past the colorful front windows to discover one of New York's best consignment shops. Allan and Suzi specialize in gently worn 20th-century designer wear, with a selection so good they even outfit celebrities, on camera and off. Their extensive vintage and contemporary couture collection—which ranges from conservative Chanel to over-the-top Halston, Mackie, and Versace—is well within reach of the average shopper's budget. 416 Amsterdam Ave. (at 80th St.). ℃ 212/724-7445. www.allanandsuzi.net. Subway: 1 to 79th St.

Michael's 🔖 This consignment boutique stocks top-drawer designer wear for women, including such names as Chanel, YSL, Prada, Gucci, Richard Tyler, and Escada, at a fraction of the original cost. The bridal salon is an unbeatable find for engaged gals looking for a top-quality dress at an off-the-rack price. 1041 Madison Ave., 2nd Floor (btw. 79th and 80th sts.). ℃ 212/737-7273. www.michaelsconsignment. com. Subway: 6 to 77th St.

Rags-a-GoGo ★ Finding specific second-hand items is the pride and joy of owner Joshua Suzanne, who has drawn together an affordable, very cool collection of denim, T-shirts, cowboy boots, and more. Here you'll find a nice alternative to the big-name stores around Union Square and the Village. You never know what you'll find on these very organized racks. 218 W. 14th St. (btw. Seventh and Eighth aves.). ℃ 646/486-4011. www.rags-a-gogo.com. Subway: A, C, E, 1, 2, 3 to 14th St.; L to Eighth Ave.

Re/Dress ★ 💼 New York's first and only plus-size vintage shop fills out a fabulous storefront in Cobble Hill, Brooklyn. Owner Deb Malkin believes that "plus-size women do too much aspirational shopping," so her shop offers a wealth of colorful accessories, frocks, and outerwear (all size 14+) for ladies who rue the teensy sizes churned out by the big designers. 109 Boerum Place, Brooklyn (btw. Dean and Pacific sts.). ℃ 718/522-7962. www.redressnyc.com. Subway: F, G to Bergen St.

Screaming Mimi's 🔖 Think you hate vintage shopping? Think again: Screaming Mimi's is as neat and well organized as any high-priced boutique, yet prices are totally reasonable, especially given the pricey vintage shops that have popped up around the city in recent years. Also a great place to find unique hats, ties, suspenders, sunglasses, bags, and more. 382 Lafayette St. (btw. E. 4th and Great Jones sts.). ℃ 212/677-6464. www.screamingmimis.com. Subway: 6 to Astor Place.

Edibles

In addition to these New York classics, you'll also find **Trader Joe's** bargain-priced groceries and wine shop just southeast of Union Square, at 142 E. 14th St. (℃ 212/529-4612). The **Essex Street Market** (℃ 212/388-0449; www. essexstreetmarket.com), on the Lower East Side at Delancey Street, rivals larger markets in town with its fresh, locally sourced produce, cheeses, and specialty goods.

Chelsea Market ★   Located in an old Nabisco factory, this big, dazzling food mall is the city's largest. Come for both raw and ready-to-eat foods, with an emphasis on local and gourmet lines. Choices include divinely inspired baked goods and cappuccino from **Amy's Bread;** yummy soups from **Hale and Hearty;** Manhattan's best brownie at **Fat Witch Bakery;** and much more, including the wonderful **Chelsea Wine Vault.** Stop by **Ronnybrook Dairy** for the best low-fat chocolate milk or yogurt smoothie you'll ever have. **Chelsea Market Baskets** is a great place to pick up gifts for home (they also ship). 75 Ninth Ave. (btw. 15th and 16th sts.). ℭ **212/243-6005.** www.chelseamarket.com. Subway: A, C, E to 14th St.; L to Eighth Ave.

Dean & DeLuca   This, the original location, is a bright, clean store that offers premier quality across the board: In addition to the excellent butcher, fish, cheeses, desserts, and beautiful fruits and veggies, you'll find a dried-fruit-and-nut bar, a huge coffee-bean selection, lots of imported waters and beers in the refrigerator case, and a limited but quality selection of kitchenware in back. Ready-to-eat foods like hot sandwiches and pizza can be ordered from the friendly professionals at the counter. 560 Broadway (at Prince St.). ℭ **212/226-6800.** www.dean-deluca.com. Subway: N, R to Prince St.

DiPalo's Dairy ★   Before there was Mario Batali or Anthony Bourdain, there was Lou DiPalo, a true New York food celebrity. But Lou won't be hosting any food shows—he's too busy behind the counter of his 1910 family-run store, putting together packages of the best and hardest-to-find Italian cheeses and cured meats around, for some of the city's most acclaimed restaurants and chefs. The tiny store is one of the last authentic Italian vestiges in the now sort-of tacky neighborhood of Little Italy. And do check out **Enoteca DiPalo** next door, where Lou's offspring founded an Italian wine "library." 200 Grand St. (at Mott St.). ℭ **212/226-1033.** www.dipaloselects.com. Subway: B, D to Grand St.

Eataly ★   An Italian revolution happened in 2010, when the cult of Batali finally took root in the heart of Manhattan at a temple to ethnic food called *Eataly*. Along with his partners, chef Mario founded this lofty gourmet emporium filled with bona-fide Italian imports and fresh local meats and produce—oh, and five different restaurants, a pasticceria, cheese and espresso counters, bakery, gelateria, butcher, and an adjoining wine store. No doubt this may be the city's most noteworthy gastronomic destination of late, with its authentic ingredients and delectable details (and throngs of customers). But this "place where food is more sacred than commerce," as Batali called it, doesn't make fine imported goods any more affordable. 200 Fifth Ave. (at Broadway). ℭ **212/229-2560.** www.eataly. com. Subway: N, R to 23rd St.

Fairway ✦   There is no better all-in-one, affordable grocery chain in New York. Here you'll find the best and most modestly priced vegetables in the city. Cheeses are top of the line; the fish counter is excellent; and the selection of hard-to-find health foods and organic produce is unrivaled. Fairway also carries gourmet items at a fraction of the usual costs. The Harlem store is huge and features a walk-in freezer, complete with down jackets provided for customers' use. (See their website for more locations.) 2127 Broadway (btw. 74th and 75th sts.). ℭ **212/595-1888.** www. fairwaymarket.com. Subway: 1, 2, 3 to 72nd St. Also at 2328 Twelfth Ave. (at 130th St.). ℭ **212/234-3883.** Subway: 1 to 125th St.

NYC IS chocolate city

The Big Apple has become a city consumed by a near-feverish craving for chocolate. Many sweets shops around the city now are turning out homemade chocolates in every variety that are so good, the stores, like four-star restaurants, are bona fide destinations.

One of New York's best and most famous chocolatiers is **Jacques Torres Chocolate** ★★. The variations of this luxury-chocolate brand are dazzling and include chocolate peanut brittle, chocolate-covered corn flakes, and champagne truffles. Take home a tin of the "wicked" hot chocolate, which features allspice, cinnamon, sweet ancho chile peppers, and hot chipotle peppers. The Torres chain has several locations, including one uptown at 285 Amsterdam Ave., at 73rd Street, and 350 Hudson St., at King Street, in the Hudson Square neighborhood (✆ **212/414-2462**). The 66 Water St. shop in DUMBO, Brooklyn lets you watch chocolate being made—just don't neglect his nearby **Ice Cream Store** at No. 62. (✆ **718/875-9772;** www.mrchocolate.com).

Just east of the Metropolitan Museum of Art is the Madison Avenue incarnation of the Paris import **La Maison du Chocolat** ★, 1018 Madison Ave., at 78th Street (✆ **212/744-7117;** www. lamaisonduchocolat.com). This boutique takes its chocolate very seriously. Here you will find possibly the best pure chocolate you've ever tasted. They abhor any bitterness in their chocolate and make it a point to claim that they use nothing stronger than 65% cocoa. It is serious chocolate. If you're downtown, stop by their new shop at 63 Wall St. (✆ **212/952-1123**), or duck into the midtown 30 Rockefeller Center store (✆ **212/265-9404**).

Lily O'Brien's Chocolate Cafe, across from Bryant Park at 36 W. 40th St. (✆ **212/575-0631;** www.lilyscafenyc. com), is the place to try superb 100% Belgian chocolate in many forms, served alongside some of the city's

Zabar's ★ More than any other of the city's gourmet food stores, Zabar's is a New York institution. This giant deli sells prepared foods, packaged goods from around the world, coffee beans, excellent fresh breads, and much more (no fresh veggies, though). This is also the top shop for lox in all of Manhattan. You'll also find an excellent—and well-priced—collection of housewares and restaurant-quality cookware on the second floor. Prepare yourself for serious crowds. The attached cafe serves delicious sandwiches and takeout, ideal for a Central Park picnic. 2245 Broadway (at 80th St.). ✆ **212/496-1234.** www.zabars.com. Subway: 1 to 79th St.

COFFEE & TEA

Ito En 🎁 You want green tea? You want black tea? Herbal tea? White tea? No problem. There are so many varieties of teas here you need a catalog to peruse the selections. Located in a Madison Avenue town house, Ito En is like an art gallery of teas predominantly from China, Japan, India, and other international locales. Products are neatly displayed in this serene store, home to bona fide tea experts. 822 Madison Ave. (at 69th St.). ✆ **212/988-7111.** www.itoen.com. Subway: 6 to 68th St.

McNulty's Tea & Coffee Company ★ McNulty's has been around since 1895, making it one of the oldest coffee purveyors in the country. And it still has best pastries—a great follow-up to winter ice skating in the park.

One of the oldest chocolate shops in the city is the 1923-established **Li-Lac Chocolates,** 40 Eighth Ave., at Jane Street (© **212/924-2280;** www.li-lac chocolates.com), home to new batches of handmade fudge daily. Nearby is Allison Nelson's sublime **Chocolate Bar,** 19 Eighth Ave., at West 12th Street (© **212/366-1541;** www.chocolate barnyc.com). For those who worship the cocoa gods, go for the superdark 72%—so dark and rich you might speak in tongues after a few bites.

Head to the Bowery for more diverse temptations, like the strawberry balsamic dark chocolate, vegan hazelnut chocolate, or the signature pretzel covered in sea-salted caramel at **Bespoke Chocolates,** 6 Extra Place, off 1st Street between Second Avenue and Bowery (© **212/260-7103;** www.bespoke chocolates.com).

More unconventional chocolate is found at **Kee's Chocolates,** 80 Thompson St., near Spring Street (© **212/334-3284;** www.kees chocolates.com), where owner Kee Ling Tong makes her own unique creations 7 days a week, like mango green tea and Thai chili.

Head east to **Bond Street Chocolate ★,** 63 East 4th St. (© **212/677-5103;** www.bondstchocolate.com), for chocolate in much more innovative forms—like miniature skulls and the "divine collection" of Virgin Mary, Jesus, and Ganesh chocolate statues. Lots of darks on the menu at Bond, as well as flavors ranging from tequila, elderflower, and absinthe truffle. Addicted locals are even calling her milk chocolate bar with caramelized almonds and sea salt the "crack bar."

If none of these sources are decadent enough for you, head to the Lower East Side's **Essex Street Market,** at Delancey Street, for some homemade truffles, caramels, or "pig candy"—that is, chocolate-covered bacon, if you can wrap your head around that—at **Roni Sue's Chocolates** (© **212/260-0421**).

that old-time feel, with overflowing sacks of coffees and rare teas cluttering the quaint West Village store—and they roast their own coffees right there. The Colombia Supremo is as perfect as it gets, but there are plenty of choices for decaffers and light-roast fans. 109 Christopher St. (btw. Bleecker and Hudson sts.). © **212/242-5351.** www.mcnultys.com. Subway: 1 to Christopher St.

SWEETS

Dylan's Candy Bar ★ Dylan (daughter of Ralph) Lauren is the owner of this bazaar for sugar addicts. Located across the street from Bloomingdale's, you'll find all the candy classics, such as Pixy Stix, Wack-o-Wax Wax Lips, collector Pez sets, and favorite childhood chewing gums like Black Jack and Gold Mine. The place always draws a crowd—but for those with sweet tooths it's a worthy wonderland. 1011 Third Ave. (at 60th St.). © **646/735-0078.** www.dylanscandybar.com. Subway: 4, 5, 6, N, R to 59th St.

Economy Candy Store ★★ While Dylan's is the new generation of candy store, Economy Candy, which has been selling sweets in its modest Lower East Side shop since 1937, is a scrumptious blast from the past. Here you'll turn up old-school treats like Bubble Gum Cigars, Bit O'Honey, Kosher rock candy,

A Taste of New York: Get an Edible Souvenir

Do you want to bring back a *real* New York souvenir—something that evokes the genuine flavor of New York more than an I ♥ NEW YORK T-shirt or an Empire State Building figurine? Possibly the best place to pick up food souvenirs is the Lower East Side. This neighborhood, home to so many immigrants over the years, is where a number of traditional New York foods originated. One could argue the real anchor of the LES is **Katz's Delicatessen** (p. 149) on Houston and Ludlow, where you can "send a salami to your boy in the army," or ship any number of their other delicacies around the world.

You don't need to know exactly what a bialy is to enjoy one, thank heavens. But since 1936 you can sample some of the best, hot baked local faves at **Kossar's Bialys,** 367 Grand St., between Norfolk and Essex streets (✆ 877/4BIALYS [424-2597]; www. kossarsbialys.com). A dozen goes for around $11 and are sold in many tasty flavors like sesame, poppy, and garlic, as are the fresh bagels.

East Houston Street features two New York food-souvenir choices worth bringing home. Start with knishes from the 1910-established **Yonah Schimmel Knishes** at 137 E. Houston St., between First and Second avenues (✆ 212/477-2858; www.knishery.com). The choices range from savory potato to spinach to mushroom; a box of 12 runs $45 plus shipping. And of course, you can just buy one or two to eat right there. At 179 E. Houston St., between Allen and Orchard streets, you'll find **Russ & Daughters** (✆ 212/475-4880; www. russanddaughters.com), which began as a push cart operation in 1908, and today is still family-run four generations later. They sell incomparable smoked fish and nova (similar to lox); try the tantalizing smoked-salmon medley package, which serves six and sells for about $89—and worth every penny.

Finally, there's **Ess-a-Pickle,** formerly known as Guss Pickles (✆ 917/701-4000). Once a Lower East Side staple, Ess-a-Pickle relocated to Borough Park, Brooklyn in mid-2010 (1470 39th St., to be exact). Owner Pat Fairhurst said high rents priced her out of Manhattan—but she'll still make phone orders for her flavorful half- or full-sour pickles and green tomatoes.

Atomic Fireballs, and Necco Wafers—alongside hand-dipped chocolate creations and penny candy. You'll also find a fine selection of dried fruits and nuts and gourmet chocolate here. This delectable time-capsule purveyor is family owned, one of a kind, and positively worth a visit. 108 Rivington St. (btw. Delancey and Norfolk sts.). ✆ **800/352-4544.** www.economycandy.com. Subway: F to Delancey St.

MarieBelle 👔 Stop by this cozy SoHo shop for the impeccably packaged chocolates, fine teas, coffees, and caramels—stay for the singularly delicious and pudding-thick hot chocolate in Aztec, dark, spicy, and coffee flavors. Stocked with a nice variety of goods, including creamy white chocolates and "mini ganache jewels," the edibles here are unrivaled and almost seem too pretty to eat. Almost. 484 Broome St. (btw. Wooster St. and W. Broadway). ✆ **212/925-6999.** www. mariebelle.com. Subway: A, C, E to Canal St.

Electronics

The Apple Store The largest Apple Store, at 18,000 square feet, opened in early 2006, and hasn't closed yet (it's open 24/7). Descend a glass staircase or elevator inside this edifice on Fifth Avenue and 59th Street, topped by a clear cube, to the store below, where there is a 46-seat theater and 14 Internet-connected computers fully loaded with games—an iPhone/iTouch/iPod/Mac-lover's paradise. It's almost impossible to walk by without popping in to see what the fuss is all about. If you're not into investing in all the Apple gadgets sold here, it's still fun to try out the floor samples. 767 Fifth Ave. (at 59th St.). © **212/336-1440.** www. apple.com. Subway N, R to Fifth Ave. Also at 103 Prince St. (at Greene St.). © **212/226-3126.** Subway: R to Prince St. Also at 401 W. 14th St. © **212/444-3400.** Subway: L to 8th Ave.

B&H Photo & Video ★   Looking for a new digital camera at a good price? You won't do any better than B&H, the largest camera store in the country. This electronics superstore has everything a pro or amateur shutterbug could want—and almost everything else that requires an outlet, from computers to projectors to mixing boards. If you are new to B&H, don't let it intimidate you. The staff is quite knowledgeable once your number's finally called, just have your questions ready. Also remember to check out the refurbished section for bargains. (**Note:** B&H is closed Sat.) 420 Ninth Ave. (at 34th St.). © **800/606-6969** or 212/444-6615. www.bhphotovideo.com. Subway: A, C, E to 34th St.

J&R Music & Computer World   This block-long Financial District emporium is a locally owned computer, electronics, music, small appliance, and office-equipment retailer. Prices are decent, but the downside of J&R is a gruff sales staff whose advice isn't always trustworthy. But don't feel pressured by their vibe—take your time and find what you need. 23 Park Row (at Ann St., opposite City Hall Park). © **800/806-1115** or 212/238-9000. www.jandr.com. Subway: 2, 3 to Park Place; 4, 5, 6 to Brooklyn Bridge/City Hall.

Gifts

For first-rate Fifth Avenue gifts, don't forget **Tiffany & Co.,** whose upper level boasts wonderful small gifts, all crafted in signature Tiffany silver or crystal and wrapped in the unmistakable turquoise box (see "Jewelry & Accessories," below).

For additional suggestions, see "Antiques & Collectibles," earlier in this chapter, and "Home Design & Housewares," below.

John Derian Company ★   It's hard to describe this wonderful store, in which owner and artist John Derian creates and stocks some of the most beautiful and unique goods in the city. His twin shops in the East Village are almost like affordable fine-art galleries, selling one-of-a-kind glass dishes, silver trays, small furniture, handmade paper goods, and assorted metal ware. If you're not in a buying mood, come here just for the comfort and class the stores evoke—though it will challenge you to leave empty-handed. 6 E. 2nd St. (btw. Bowery and Second Ave.). © **212/677-3917.** www.johnderian.com. Subway: F to 2nd Ave.

Pearl River ★★ ✦   This three-story Chinese emporium overflows with all things Asian, at almost shamefully affordable prices. Whether you're there just browsing or on the hunt for something as specific as silk pajamas or a themed mah-jongg set, you're covered. I never miss a chance to take my visiting parents here, because it's perhaps the single best place in New York for cheap souvenirs with personality—New York knickknacks among them. Plus, where else can you enjoy the sound of a bubbling two-story waterfall while you shop for hand-painted teapots and miniature Buddhas? 477 Broadway (at Grand St.). © **212/431-4770.** www. pearlriver.com. Subway: R, W to Prince; 6 to Spring.

Steuben Glass This is the flagship store for America's premier manufacturer of fine glass and crystal, said to be the world's purest. The store is gorgeous, and the pieces—which run the gamut from fruit bowls to sculptures—are spectacularly crafted and refract light beautifully. Prices start around $250 for a "hand cooler" (a small collectible, often animal shaped, that fits in your palm) and run into the five figures. Sports buffs will love the Major League Baseball collection of logo-etched crystals. The Corning Gallery, on the lower level, hosts rotating art exhibits. 667 Madison Ave. (at 61st St.). © **800/STEUBEN** (783-8236). www.steuben.com. Subway: N, R to Fifth Ave.

Handbags & Leather Goods

Anya Hindmarch This London-based designer makes beautiful bags of all kinds in innovative styles and patterns, as well as shoes and clothes inspired by classic styles. Always colorful, these are the day and evening bags that will get you noticed, all for reasonable prices. 115 Greene St. (at Prince St.). © **212/343-8147.** www.anyahindmarch.com. Subway: R to Prince St. Also at 29 E. 60th St. (at Madison Ave.). © **212/750-3974.** Subway: N, R to 5th Ave.

Jutta Neumann 🔖 In 2009, Neumann downsized from a small storefront to an even more modest studio. Now you'll (usually) find her at work cutting and stitching her own fine, clean-lined, bold-hued leather goods like bags, wallets, boots, and more. Her mules and strappy sandals are also sturdy and stylish. 355 E. 4th St. (btw. aves. C and D). © **212/982-7048.** www.juttaneumann-newyork.com. Subway: F to Second Ave.

Jack Spade Looking for a gift for the man who has everything? Then head to Jack Spade, which specializes all manner of "guy toys." The inventory changes all the time, but expect a great choice of smart wallets, key chains, and bags galore—from messenger style to briefcases to travel kits. This shop was launched by Kate Spade's husband, so you can expect a smart, upmarket collection. 56 Greene St. (btw. Spring and Broome sts.). © **212/625-1820.** www.jackspade.com. Subway: C, E to Spring St.; N, R to Prince St. Also at 400 Bleecker St. (at W. 11th St.). © **212/675-4085.** Subway: 1 to Christopher St.

kate spade Spade revolutionized the high-end handbag market with her practical yet chic rectangular handbags, which for a time kind of took over the planet. The classic styles and colors have expanded to include chic baby bags, luggage, sexy shoes, and comfy pajamas. You can also find signature bags at Saks, Barneys, Bergdorf Goodman, and Bloomingdale's. 454 Broome St. (at Mercer St.). © **212/274-1991.** www.katespade.com. Subway: R to Prince St. 135 Fifth Ave. (at 20th St). © **212/358-0420.** Subway: R to 23rd St. kate spade baby: 59 Thompson St. (btw. Spring and Broome sts.). © **212/965-8654.** Subway: C, E to Spring St.

Longchamp ★ This Parisian brand's leather bags and accessories (for men and women) are sold in high-end stores the world over, but the selection at its two New York boutiques can't be beat. Visit the SoHo shop for one of the most architecturally striking staircases ever built—a testament to the unique personality of this very expensive designer label. 132 Spring St. (btw. Wooster and Greene sts.). © **212/343-7444.** www.longchamp.com. Subway: C, E to Spring St. Also at 655 Madison Ave. (btw. 60th and 61st sts.). © **212/223-1500.** Subway: N, R, W to 5th Ave.

Manhattan Portage Come here for the hippest nylon and canvas carryalls in town. True to its name, Manhattan Portage manufactures its bags right in the city, and they're made from hard-wearing materials built for urban life. Styles are colorful and span all-purpose messenger bags, wallets, laptop covers, and backpacks (in both standard and one-shoulder styles). Manhattan Portage bags are sold mainly through other outlets, but you'll find the most complete selection at their token store. This brand is only rivaled by the similar sturdy bags of Brooklyn-based Yak Pak and Brooklyn Industries (see the box "Take the L Train" on p. 361). 258 Elizabeth St. (btw. Prince and Houston sts.). © 212/226-9655. www.manhattan portage.com. Subway: F to Broadway-Lafayette; 6 to Bleecker; N, R to Prince St.

Home Design & Housewares

Dealers line **Broadway** around the queen of home-furnishings department stores, **ABC Carpet & Home** (p. 352). The second floor of **Zabar's** (p. 370) is another excellent source for high-end kitchenware, while **Pearl River** (p. 373) is the go-to for affordable Asian dishware and teapots.

Broadway Panhandler   If you're looking for restaurant-quality cookware and kitchen tools, you've found your place. The best combination of selection, prices, and service in town, including novelty and New York–themed dishware and savvy supplies for the serious home chef. 65 E. 8th St. (btw. Broadway and University Place). © **866/266-5927.** www.broadwaypanhandler.com. Subway: N, R to 8th St.

Fishs Eddy ★★ *✦*   A happy kitchen store just north of Union Square, Fishs Eddy is a browsing mecca. Its in-house designs are equally wonderful, especially its series with the New York skyline and other landmarks. The inventory spans basic vintage and retro-inspired flatware, American industrial china, heavy crockery bowls, and classic restaurant-supply glassware, such as soda-fountain and pint glasses, that can be hard to find in regular stores. 889 Broadway (at 19th St.). © **877/347-4733.** www.fishseddy.com. Subway: L, N, R, Q, 4, 5, 6 to 14th St./Union Sq.

Frette   This Italian linen maker has taken the hotel world by storm with its silky cotton sheets and plush terry towels and robes. If you've slept on some and now you want your own, head to Frette's dedicated boutique or to ABC Carpet & Home (p. 352) for the best selections. 799 Madison Ave. (btw. 67th and 68th sts.). © **212/988-5221.** www.frette.it. Subway: 6 to 68th St.

Jonathan Adler   Anyone who reads home-decorating magazines will instantly recognize this hot potter's unique vases, lamps, and bowls. His style merges organic shapes, geometric patterns, natural hues, and mod ideas into a one-of-a-kind style that works in almost any décor—really. Great frames, lamps, and throw pillows, too. (Check website for more locations.) 47 Greene St. (at Broome St.). © **212/941-8950.** www.jonathanadler.com. Subway: N, R to Canal St. Also at 1097 Madison Ave. (btw. 83rd and 84th sts.). © **212/772-2410.** Subway: 6 to 86th St.

Leader Restaurant Equipment & Supplies *✦*   The Bowery is the place to find restaurant-supply-quality kitchenware, and Leader is the best dealer on the block. This big, bustling, friendly shop is a good source for Chinese and Japanese wares—chopsticks, rice and noodle bowls, sushi plates, sake cups, and the like. You'll see a lot of the same styles you'd find at the high-end home stores in SoHo or the Village but at a fraction of the prices (this is where they buy, too). 134 Bowery (btw. Broome and Grand sts.). © **800/666-6888** or 212/677-1982. Subway: 6 to Spring St.

Moss   If you have any interest in modern industrial design, don't miss this sleek, bright store. All kinds of everyday objects are reinvented by cutting-edge

European designers, from staplers to flatware to shelving units. The products were designed with 21st-century homes in mind, so they're surprisingly utilitarian and space efficient (not to mention pricey). 150 Greene St. (btw. Houston and Prince sts.). © **866/888-6677.** www.mossonline.com. Subway: N, R to Prince St.

Terence Conran Shop Sir Terence Conran rules the London design and restaurant world, and now he's looking to make inroads in America with this bold, sleek home shop. It's like an upscale—and, frankly, overpriced—version of IKEA, with lots of sleek contemporary lines, lightweight materials (chrome, blond woods, colorful plastic), and fun twists on standard household goods. Still, he's helped set the tone for contemporary design, plus the store is conveniently located inside ABC Carpet & Home. 888 Broadway, lower level. (at 18th St.). © **212/755-9079.** www.conran.com. Subway: L, N, R, Q, 4, 5, 6 to 14th St./Union Sq.

Jewelry & Accessories

Every big-name international jewelry merchant has a shop on Fifth Avenue in the 50s: glam Italian jeweler **Bulgari,** 730 Fifth Ave., at 57th Street (© **212/315-9000;** www.bulgari.com); royal jeweler **Asprey & Garrard,** no. 725 at 56th Street (© **212/688-1811**); ultraglamorous **Harry Winston,** no. 718, also at 56th Street (© **212/245-2000;** www.harrywinston.com); **Cartier,** housed in a stunningly restored mansion at 653 Fifth Ave., at 52nd Street (© **212/446-3400;** www.cartier.com); and, best of all, **Van Cleef & Arpels,** 744 Fifth Ave., at 57th Street (© **212/644-9500;** www.vancleef.com), which also has a boutique at Bergdorf's.

Some of the smaller boutique names are on Madison Avenue in the 60s. **Fred Leighton,** 773 Madison Ave., at 66th Street (© **212/288-1872;** www. fredleighton.com), specializes in magnificent estate jewelry.

Among the following shops, also consider stopping by the East Village's **New York Adorned,** 47 Second Ave. (© **212/473-0007;** www.nyadorned.com), one of the city's best tattoo parlors, which recently opened a jewelry outpost in Nolita at 269 Elizabeth St., sells an amazing collection of handmade, unique, local jewelry for all budgets.

Doyle & Doyle 🎁 The Doyle sisters' lovely antiques boutique offers further evidence of the transformation of the Lower East Side from old-world cheap to exceptionally chic. Doyle & Doyle specializes in fine antique and estate jewelry, from the Georgian period to contemporary items. Pieces are all carefully chosen and beautifully displayed. 189 Orchard St. (btw. Houston and Stanton sts.). © **212/677-9991.** www.doyledoyle.com. Subway: F to Second Ave.

Folli Follie 🦋 "Affordable, fashionable, luxury" is the motto of this Grecian boutique tucked among the uptown elites. The brand's understated jewelry designs appeal to younger fans, who come here for bargains on 18-karat investments peppered with colorful gemstones. Among the bracelets, rings, and necklaces you'll also find well-made handbags and watches. 575 Madison Ave. (near 57th St.). © **212/421-3155.** www.follifollie.com. Subway: N, R, to Lexington Ave.–59th St; 4, 5, 6 to 59th St.

Jill Platner ★★ 🎁 Platner's Aboriginal- and nature-inspired silver pieces are bold enough to look great on both men and women. Many are strung on brightly colored Tenara (a Gore-Tex-like thread) for a prehistoric-meets-21st-century feel. Prices are quite reasonable; it's easy to find a cool pair of earrings or a sexy ring for just a little more than $100. Plus all inventory is made locally in Platner's

West 47th Street between Fifth and Sixth avenues is the city's famous Diamond District. They say more than 90% of the diamonds sold in the United States come through this neighborhood first, so there are some great deals to be had if you're in the market for a nice rock or other fine jewelry. The street is lined with showrooms; and you'll be wheeling and dealing with the largely Hasidic dealers, who offer quite a juxtaposition to the crowds. For a complete introduction to the district, including smart buying tips, point your Web browser to **www.diamond district.org**. If you're in the market for wedding rings, there's only one place to go: Herman Rotenberg's **1,873 Unusual Wedding Rings**, 4 W. 47th St., booth 86 (© **800/877-3874** or 212/944-1713). For semiprecious stones, head 1 block over to the **New York Jewelry Mart**, 26 W. 46th St. (© **212/575-9701**). Virtually all of these dealers are open Monday through Friday only.

NYC studio. 113 Crosby St. (btw. Houston and Prince sts.). © **212/324-1298.** www.jill platner.com. Subway: N, R to Prince St.

Karen Karch Often featuring rough-hewn finishes and asymmetrical gems and stones, Karen Karch's eye-catching jewelry has attracted an A-list clientele to her Nolita shop. This is the place to find a finely weighted silver or gold piece that sing with personality—just be ready to splurge because fine craftsmanship doesn't come cheap. 240 Mulberry St. (btw. Prince and Spring sts.). © **212/965-9699.** www.karenkarch.com. Subway: 6 to Spring St.

Tiffany & Co. ★ The most famous jewelry store in New York—and maybe the world—deserves all the kudos. Its glamorous multilevel Fifth Avenue store offers a breathtaking selection of jewelry, signature watches, tableware and stemware, and a handful of surprisingly affordable gift items. The store is full of tourists, which perhaps is why a second one opened way downtown for wealthy Wall Street types. Believe it or not, it's not hard to find a lovely wearable piece in stunning silver for around $200. If you do indulge, anything you buy—even a $50 silver bookmark or key chain—comes wrapped in that unmistakable blue box with a perfect white ribbon. 727 Fifth Ave. (at 57th St.). © **212/755-8000.** www.tiffany. com. Subway: N, R to Fifth Ave. Also at 37 Wall St. (btw. William and Broad sts.). © **212/480-4587.** Subway: 2, 3 to Wall St.

Tourneau Time Machine The snazzy three-floor flagship on East 57th Street is, they say, the world's largest watch emporium, carrying more than 90 brands and 8,000 different styles. The mind-boggling selection runs the gamut from Von Dutch to Rolex, and Swiss Army knives, too. 12 E. 57th St. (btw. Fifth and Madison aves.). © **212/758-7300.** www.tourneau.com. Subway: N, R to Fifth Ave. Also at 500 Madison Ave. (at 52nd St.). © **212/758-6098.** Subway: 6 to 51st St. 200 W. 34th St. (at Seventh Ave.). © **212/563-6880.** Subway: 1, 2, 3 to 34th St. 10 Columbus Circle (the Shops at Columbus Circle). © **212/823-9425.** Subway: A, B, C, D, 1 to Columbus Circle.

Logo Stores

In addition to the following, the **NBA Store** (also home to the WNBA, let's not forget) was relocating from its Fifth Avenue megastore as of press time. The new address has not been announced; call © **212/515-6221** or check **www. nba.com/nycstore** for current details.

Adidas   Unlike NIKETOWN, this three-story NoHo flagship store has regular sales and an expansive collection of Adidas-branded sportswear and shoes. The still-cool old-school "Originals" collection will take you back to the Run-DMC days of "My Adidas"—think matching sweat suits and loose-laced sneaks. 610 Broadway. (at Houston St.). ☎ 212/529-0081. www.shopadidas.com. Originals store also at: 136 Wooster St. (at Houston St.). ☎ 212/673-0398. Subway: F, M, B, D to Broadway/ Lafayette.

Firestore ★ 🎒   What better way to spend your souvenir budget than by saluting New York's bravest and finest? Here's the place to purchase Fire- and Police-Department logo wear. The goods are top quality, and a portion of the profits support the families of firefighters lost in the September 11, 2001, terrorist attacks, as well as NYPD-related charities. The store, along with its next-door neighbor, formerly known as **New York 911,** is a one-stop shop for all things FDNY, NYPD, EMS, FBI, and NYC-coroner gear. The bounty includes shirts, caps, badge pins, patches, logo toys, and much more. The store is well stocked and fun to browse. 17 Greenwich Ave. (west of 8th St. and Sixth Ave.). ☎ 212/226-3142. www.nyfirestore.com. Subway: 1 to Christopher St.

Mets Clubhouse Shop   Stop in for logo goods galore—baseball caps, T-shirts, posters, jerseys, '69 Miracle Mets memorabilia, and much more Met-tastic merchandise. You can buy regular-season game tickets here, too. 11 W. 42nd St. (btw. Fifth and Sixth aves.). ☎ 212/768-9534. http://newyork.mets.mlb.com. Subway: B, D, F, M to 42nd St.

The MTV Store   This petite boutique sits streetside on Broadway, below the MTV studio in Times Square. It's predictable wares, with lots of colorful gear for your favorite teenager. Flyers advertising for audience members for MTV shows are sometimes on hand at the register—and if you don't want to attend a taping, just enjoy the occasional screaming groupies outside on the sidewalk. 1515 Broadway (at 44th St.). ☎ 212/846-5655. www.mtv.com. Subway: 1, 2, 3, 7, N, R, S to 42nd St./Times Sq.

NBC Experience   This neon-lit store sits directly across from the *Today* show studio and sells all manner of NBC-themed merchandise, from Matt and Al's favorite mugs to a *Biggest Loser* cookbook to *The Office* bobbleheads. And yes, there is a clearance department with merch from canceled shows. NBC Studio Tours also leave from here; call for details. 30 Rockefeller Plaza (at 49th St.). ☎ 212/664-3700. www.nbcuniversalstore.com. Subway: B, D, F, N, R, M, W to 47th–50th sts./Rockefeller Center.

NIKETOWN   More multimedia advertorial than sportswear store, NIKE-TOWN fills five floors with overly logo'ed athletic wear and slick merchandising displays. Customers are assailed by images of celebrity pitchmen and women, and Michael Jordan branding is still Nike's favorite. No sales or bargains here— "swoosh" fans will pay top dollar for the high-style athletic wear. 6 E. 57th St. (btw. Fifth and Madison aves.). ☎ 212/891-6453. www.niketown.com. Subway: N, R to Fifth Ave.

Yankees Clubhouse Shop   For all your Bronx Bombers needs—hats, jerseys, jackets, and so on. Tickets for regular-season home games are also for sale, and there's a limited selection of other New York team jerseys (well, maybe not the Mets). 245 W. 42nd St. (btw. Seventh and Eighth aves.). ☎ 212/768-9555. http://newyork. yankees.mlb.com. Subway: A, C, E to 42nd St./Port Authority. Also at 393 Fifth Ave. (btw. 36th and 37th sts.). ☎ 212/685-4693. Subway: 6 to 33rd St. 110 E. 59th St. (btw. Park and Lexington aves.). ☎ 212/758-7844. Subway: 4, 5, 6 to 59th St. 8 Fulton St. (in the South St. Seaport). ☎ 212/514-7182. Subway: 2, 3, 4, 5 to Fulton St.

Museum Stores

Maxilla & Mandible ★ 🎁 This shop is not affiliated with the American Museum of Natural History, but a visit here makes a good adjunct to your trip to the museum (which is around the corner). It may look like a bit freaky at first, but it's really a fascinating natural-history emporium. Inside you'll find unusual rocks and shells from around the world, luminescent butterflies in display boxes, even surprisingly affordable real fossils containing prehistoric fish and insects that come with details on their history and where they were excavated. There's also a good variety of natural-history-themed toys for the kids. 451 Columbus Ave. (btw. 81st and 82nd sts.). ✆ **212/724-6173.** www.maxillaandmandible.com. Subway: B, C to 81st St.

Metropolitan Museum of Art Store   Given the scope of the museum itself, it's no wonder that the gift shop is outstanding. Many treasures from the museum's collection have been reproduced as jewelry, china, and other *objets d'art*. The range of art books is dizzying, and upstairs is an equally comprehensive selection of posters and inventive children's toys. 1000 Fifth Ave. (at 82nd St.). ✆ **212/570-3894.** www.metmuseum.org/store. Subway: 4, 5, 6 to 86th St. Also at Rockefeller Center, 15 W. 49th St. ✆ **212/332-1360.** Subway: B, D, F, M to 47th–50th sts./Rockefeller Center. On the mezzanine level at Macy's, 34th St. and Sixth Ave. ✆ **212/268-7266.** Subway: B, D, F, N, Q, R to 34th St./Herald Sq.

SHOP THE museum STORES

New York is a memorable place, which means beyond the museum stores listed above, there several more worthy shops to check out. And most of them will allow you into their shops without having to pay the museum admission charge. For information about the museums listed here, see chapter 6.

Brooklyn Museum of Art   200 Eastern Pkwy., Brooklyn (✆ **718/638-5000;** www.brooklynmuseum.org). Where better to find a genuine "Brooklyn" coffee mug? For the kids back home, Spanish Bingo might be a fun challenge, while Global Feminism coffee mugs will enrich your feelings of sisterhood.

Cooper Hewitt National Design Museum   2 E. 91st St., at Fifth Avenue (✆ **212/849-8355;** www.cooperhewitt shop.org). Here you will find smart, artistic gifts, housewares, books, toys, and the coolest office accessories, all for (mostly) reasonable prices.

Lower East Side Tenement Museum   108 Orchard St., between Delancey and Grand streets (✆ **212/982-8420;** www.tenement.org). You've searched everywhere, but only here can you find those "Heroes of the Torah" glass set you've always wanted. There's also an impressive collection of Irish-, Italian-, and Jewish-themed books and other terrific and unique New York souvenirs here.

Morgan Library & Museum   225 Madison Ave., at 36th Street (✆ **212/590-0390;** www.morganlibrary.org). There are always new and interesting gifts at this charming museum gift shop, from bags to stationery to jewelry to—what else?—books.

Museum of Sex   233 Fifth Ave., at 27th Street (✆ **212/681-6337;** www.museumofsex.com). Finally, a museum store where you can buy faux-fur handcuffs! Among much more exotic things.

MoMA Design Store Across the street from the Museum of Modern Art is this one-of-a-kind shop, whose stock ranges from museum posters and clever toys for kids to fully licensed reproductions of many of the classics of modern design, including free-form Alvar Aalto vases, Frank Lloyd Wright chairs, and Eames recliners. If these high-design items are out of your reach, choose from plenty of more affordable outré home accessories. The SoHo store is equally fabulous. 44 W. 53rd St. (btw. Fifth and Sixth aves.). *C* **212/767-1050.** www.momastore. org. Subway: E, F to Fifth Ave.; B, D, F, Q to 47th–50th sts./Rockefeller Center. Also at 81 Spring St. (at Crosby St.). *C* **646/613-1367.** Subway: 6 to Spring St.

New York Transit Museum Store Lots of cool transportation-themed gifts here, like cufflinks made out of subway tokens—a true memento, since the MetroCard officially replaced tokens in 2003. There are also shower curtains showing the full subway map and even notebooks and things made from actual maps. Unfortunately, most items are overpriced, but then the perpetually cash-strapped New York City Transit system needs all the extra cash it can get. Grand Central Terminal (on the main level, in the shuttle passage next to the Station Masters' office), 42nd St. and Lexington Ave. *C* **212/878-0106.** www.transitmuseumstore.com. Subway: 4, 5, 6, 7, S to 42nd St./Grand Central. Also at Boerum Place (at Schermerhorn St.), Brooklyn. *C* **718/694-5100.** Subway: 4, 5 to Borough Hall.

Music

In addition to the following music specialists, consider a visit to **J&R Music & Computer World** (p. 373) across from City Hall to browse a nice-size CD and DVD inventory.

Academy Records & CDs This Flatiron District staple has a cool intellectual air that's more reminiscent of a good used-book store than your average used-record store. Academy is always filled with classical, opera, and jazz junkies perusing the extensive and well-priced collection of used CDs and vinyl. In addition to the extensive classical and jazz collection is a variety of other audiophile favorites, from rare '60s pop songsters to spoken word. Check out its pop/rock/jazz-LPs store in the East Village, and Annex in Williamsburg. 12 W. 18th St. (btw. Fifth and Sixth aves.). *C* **212/242-3000.** www.academy-records.com. Subway: L, N, R, 4, 5, 6 to 14th St./Union Sq. Also at 415 E. 12th St. (btw. First Ave. and Ave. A). *C* **212/780-9166.** Subway: L to First Ave. Also at 96 N. 6th St., Williamsburg, Brooklyn. (btw. Berry and Wythe sts.). *C* **718/218-8200.** Subway: L to Bedford Ave.

Bleecker Street Records *🖉* It's small, friendly and well located in the heart of Greenwich Village. It's also the place to score both new and used vinyl and CDs of any genre, sometimes as cheap as $1. T-shirts, posters, and an personable staff with great musical tastes make Bleecker a favorite with the locals. 239 Bleecker St. (btw. Carmine and Leroy sts.). *C* **212/255-7899.** www.bleeckerstreetrecordsnyc.com. Subway: A, B, C, D, E, F, M to W. 4th St.

Colony Music Center ★ This long-lived Theater District shop ("since 1948") is housed in the legendary Brill Building, among what was known as Tin Pan Alley back in the day. It's the perfect home for Colony, a nostalgia emporium filled with a pricey but excellent collection of vintage vinyl and new CDs—from "Oklahoma!" to "Glee." You'll find a great collection of Broadway scores and cast recordings; decades worth of recordings by pop-song stylists both legendary and obscure; the city's best collection of sheet music and karaoke discs (including some hard-to-find international stuff); and a great selection of original theater and movie posters. 1619 Broadway (at 49th St.). ℰ **212/265-2050.** www.colonymusic. com. Subway: N, R to 49th St.; 1 to 50th St.

Generation Records 🎁   This tidy little store sells mostly CDs and is an excellent source for "import" live recordings. Originally specializing in hard-core, punk, and heavy metal, the new collection upstairs still has a heavy edge but has since diversified appreciably. Downstairs is a well-organized and well-priced used-CD selection that runs the genre gamut. There's also a good selection of new and used LPs, and regular in-store performances. Despite the staff's tough look, they're actually real friendly. 210 Thompson St. (btw. Bleecker and 3rd sts.). ℰ **212/254-1100.** www.generationrecords.com. Subway: A, B, C, D, E, F, M to W. 4th St.

House of Oldies 🎁   The store claims to have more than a million vinyl records in stock—everything from R&B to doo-wop to surf music. But even if it's only a few hundred thousand, it's still the best place for both well-worn and collectible vinyl, mostly from the '50s, '60s, and '70s. 35 Carmine St. (at Bleecker St.). ℰ **212/243-0500.** www.houseofoldies.com. Subway: A, B, C, D, F, M to W. 4th St.

Jazz Record Center   This is *the* place to find rare and out-of-print jazz records. In addition to the extensive selection of CDs and vinyl (including 78s), videos, books, posters, magazines, photos, and other memorabilia are available. Prices start in the single digits for vinyl, $10 for CDs, and soar from there, befitting the rarity of the stock. These guys know all, so come here if you're trying to track down something obscure. (The shop does mail-order as well.) 236 W. 26th St., 8th Floor (btw. Seventh and Eighth aves.). ℰ **212/675-4480.** www.jazzrecordcenter.com. Subway: 1 to 28th St.

Other Music ★★   You won't find mega record labels at Other Music—the experts here focus exclusively on independent and small international labels, especially those on the cutting edge. The bizarro runs the gamut from underground Japanese spin doctors to obscure Irish folk; so needless to say, the world-music selection may blow your ear buds right off. But there's plenty of familiar bands too, in new and used form. This is the kind of place you come to find the music you didn't know you needed to know. Ask the lovely staff for some guidance, and for tips on the best upcoming live shows. 15 E. 4th St. (btw. Broadway and Lafayette St.). ℰ **212/477-8150.** www.othermusic.com. Subway: F, M to Broadway/Lafayette St.; 6 to Astor Place.

Paper & Stationery

JAM Paper and Envelope ★   This megastore of all things paper, envelopes, boxes, and wrappings is terrifically affordable (especially for bulk purchases), and wonderfully colorful. Head to the back for the coolest stationery ever, made from old maps. 135 Third Ave (btw. 14th and 15th sts.). ℰ **212/473-6666.** www.jampaper.com. Subway: L to 3rd Ave. Also at 466 Lexington Ave. (btw. 45th and 46th sts.). ℰ **212/684-6666.** Subway: B, D, F, M, 7 to 42nd St.-Bryant Park; 4, 5, 6 to Grand Central.

Kate's Paperie   Three cheers to Kate's for keeping the art of letter writing alive in our computer age. You could browse for hours among this cosmopolitan shop's handmade stationery and wraps, innovative invitations and thank-yous, imported notebooks, writing tools, and other creative paper products, including cool paper lampshades. Lovely art cards, too—perfect for writing the folks back home. 72 Spring St. (btw. Crosby and Lafayette sts.). ℰ **212/941-9816.** www.katespaperie.com. Subway: N, R to Prince St. Also at 8 W. 13th St. (btw. Fifth and Sixth aves.). ℰ **212/633-0570.**

Subway: F to 14th St. 140 W. 57th St. (btw. Sixth and Seventh aves.). ✆ **212/459-0700.** Subway: N, R to 57th St.

Shoes

Designer shoe shops start on **East 57th Street** and amble up **Madison Avenue,** becoming pricier as you move uptown. But down in **SoHo** you'll track down the more trendy styles. Cheaper copies of chic shoes are sold at the few remaining shops on **8th Street** between Broadway and Sixth Avenue in the Village, formerly known as "Shoe Row"; alternately, you can roam Broadway between Union Square and Canal Street for your kicks at places like **David Z** and **Shoe Mania.** Uptown, **Tip Top Shoes,** 155 72nd St. (✆ **212/787-4960**), is a true shoe bonanza.

Most department stores have two shoe sections—one for designer stuff and one for daily wearables. See "The Top Shopping Streets & Neighborhoods" and "The Big Department Stores," earlier in this chapter. For **Prada** and **Polo/Ralph Laren,** see "Clothing," and for **NIKETOWN** and **Adidas,** see "Logo Stores," both earlier in this section.

Camper Visit the Big Apple outposts for the full line of made-in-Spain Camper footwear for men and women. At both retail stores and in various other shops you'll be able to score some of these sturdy walking shoes and boots, made for people with an eye for style and craving for comfort. 125 Prince St. (at Wooster St.). ✆ **212/358-1842.** www.camper.com. Subway: N, R to Prince St.; C, E to Spring St. Also at 635 Madison Ave. (at 59th St.). ✆ **212/339-0078.** Subway: N, R to Fifth Ave.

Dr. Martens The 1990s are back, bigtime, with the comeback of this heavy-leather boot and shoe brand. The new New York storefront opened late in 2010 and instantly hit its stride among new and old generations of men and women who appreciate quality footwear at reasonable prices. 148 Spring St. (btw. W. Broadway and Wooster St.). ✆ **212/226-8500.** www.drmartens.com. Subway: B, D, F, M to Broadway/Lafayette St.; N, R to Prince St.; 6 to Spring St.

Harry's Shoes 🛠 This shoe store was an Upper West Side institution even before gentrification hit the neighborhood decades ago. It was one of the first NYC shoe stores to carry New Balance, and now their selection of brands ranges from Bruno Magli to retro Keds. Home to a huge selection of children's brands, Harry's is *the* place for kids' shoes—just beware of the annual August back-to-school frenzy. 2299 Broadway (at 83rd St.). ✆ **866/4-HARRYS** (442-7797). www.harrys-shoes.com. Subway: 1 to 86th St.

Jimmy Choo Its reputation precedes itself, so you know this is the place to buy your sexy stilettos. Besides the inventory, the shoe display alone is gorgeous at the sophisticated three-floor Fifth Avenue emporium. 645 Fifth Ave. (at E. 51st St.). ✆ **212/593-0800.** www.jimmychoo.com. Subway: E, F to Fifth Ave. Also at 716 Madison Ave. (at 63rd St.). ✆ **212/759-7078.** Subway: F, M to Lexington Ave.

Manolo Blahnik These wildly sexy women's shoes are iconic for their cut and sway, though many may think them notorious for the pain they'll cause with their aesthetic-over-comfort designs—perhaps a sign of too many male designers in the house? Ah, the agony of high fashion. For those ladies longing for healthy feet after the age of 50, there are a few more sensible pumps, too. Custom shoes in your own fabric are also available. 31 W. 54th St. (btw. Fifth and Sixth aves.). ✆ **212/582-3007.** www.manoloblahnik.com. Subway: E, F to Fifth Ave.

Sigerson Morrison 🎁 Women who love shoes and are willing to pay in the neighborhood of $200 to $300 for something really special should make a beeline for this UK company's NYC shops. These fashion-forward originals wow with their immaculate details, bright color palette, and sexy, strappy retro appeal. You'll also find some of their styles at Bergdorf Goodman and Saks if you don't want to go downtown. Bargain hunters should check out the great late-season sales in January and August. 28 Prince St. (btw. Mott and Elizabeth sts.). ✆ **212/219-3893.** www.sigersonmorrison.com. Subway: B, D, F, M to Broadway/Lafayette St.; N, R to Prince St.; 6 to Spring St. Also at 19 E. 71st St. (at Madison Ave.). ✆ **212/734-2100.** Subway: 6 to 68th St.

Ugg The original U.S. flagship of this Australian shoe and famed bootmaker was in SoHo, but now has sisters uptown. You'll find all the staples of the surfing-inspired brand, including its iconic sheepskin-and-suede boots, as well as sandals, slippers, and other comfort-minded kicks. 79 Mercer St. (at Spring St.). ✆ **212/226-0602.** www.uggaustralia.com. Subway R to Prince St. Also at 160 Columbus Ave. (at 67th St.). ✆ **212/671-1190.** Subway: 1 to 66th St. 600 Madison Ave. (at E. 58th St.) ✆ **212/845-9905.** Subway: N, R to 5th Ave.; 4,5,6 to 59th St./Lexington Ave.

Sporting Goods

In addition to the following sports shacks, consider a visit to the city's most intimate (some may say jampacked) family-owned sportswear and outdoor-equipment retailer, **Tent & Trails,** at 21 Park Place (✆ **212/227-1760**), just a stone's throw from City Hall.

Eastern Mountain Sports (EMS) ★ Yes, in New York you can find just about anything and everything for sale—but it is just plain hard to find a good pair of crampons for your next glacier climb. Head to this SoHo outlet (newly expanded in 2009) for all your camping, climbing, cycling, sportswear, and winter-sports-gear needs. 530 Broadway (at Spring St.). ✆ **212/966-8730.** www.ems.com. Subway: R to Prince St.

Modell's It's hard to argue with low prices, which is what you'll find at this New York sporting-goods chain. And even if you don't want some "pleather" Reeboks, you can still come here for an official, fitted wool Yankees cap. (Check the website for more locations.) 1293 Broadway (at 33rd St.). ✆ **212/244-4544.** www.modells.com. Subway: B, D, F, N, R, M to 34th St. Also at 300 W. 125th St. (at Frederick Douglass Blvd.). ✆ **212/280-9100.** Subway: A, B, C, D to 125th St. 51 E. 42nd St. (at Vanderbilt Ave.). ✆ **212/661-4242.** Subway: 4, 5, 6, 7, S to Grand Central. 55 Chambers St. (at Broadway). ✆ **212/732-8484.** Subway: E to Chambers St.

Paragon Sporting Goods The emphasis at this excellent all-purpose sporting-goods store is on equipment and athletic wear for virtually every sport, from tennis to biking to mountain climbing. End-of-the-season sales, especially on sneakers and outdoor clothing, bring serious discounts. Just try to overlook the unfriendly staff (since they're overlooking you). 867 Broadway (at 18th St.). ✆ **800/961-3030** or 212/255-8036. www.paragonsports.com. Subway: L, N, R, 4, 5, 6 to 14th St./Union Sq.

Patagonia Expensive it may be, but Patagonia deserves kudos for its commitment to producing efficient and eco-friendly sports and adventure wear—fleece pullovers made from recycled plastic soda bottles, shell jackets in ultralight weatherproof materials, and organic cotton T-shirts. It is a truly happy place to shop, especially during their February and August mega-sales. 101 Wooster St. (btw. Prince and Spring sts.). ☎ **212/343-1776.** www.patagonia.com. Subway: N, R to Prince St.; C, E to Spring St.

Toys

If your kids love to read, don't miss **Books of Wonder** (p. 359). For vintage toys, stop by one of New York's great flea markets (see "Antiques & Collectibles"). There's also the mammoth **Toys "R" Us** in Times Square, 1514 Broadway (☎ **800/869-7787**), which is so big and bustling you may forget you're in New York at all, and instead think you've landed in a toy-driven theme park complete with Ferris wheel.

American Girl Place   Your little princess may never forgive you if you don't take her to this 43,000-square-foot emporium for little girls, featuring a cafe, bookstore, and theater. If you come, don't forget to bring her favorite doll so it can get a makeover at the store's own doll salon. The store also hosts birthday parties, so if you want to plan one during your NYC visit, book well in advance. 609 Fifth Ave. (at 49th St.). ☎ **800/247-5223.** www.americangirl.com. Subway: B, D, F, M to 47th–50th sts./Rockefeller Center.

Dinosaur Hill ★★   Find handmade toys, kidswear, and a great book collection at this cute neighborhood shop that's delighted children and parents alike since 1983. Specialties include marionettes from around the world, hand puppets, quilts, and wooden toys, as well as knit and crocheted clothes. 306 E. 9th St. (btw. First and Second aves.). ☎ **212/473-5850.** www.dinosaurhill.com. Subway: 6 to Astor Pl.; N. R to 8th St.

FAO Schwarz   A true wonderland for kids—and some adults—this famous three-story toy store is a must-see if you're at all interested in stuffed animals, games, dolls, and character-themed collectibles. There's also a soda fountain where the kids can load up on sugar to fuel their romp through the magical rumpus. 767 Fifth Ave. (at 58th St.). ☎ **212/644-9400.** www.fao.com. Subway: N, R to Fifth Ave. or 4, 5, 6 to 59th St.

Kidding Around ★   This boutique is a longtime favorite among New Yorkers for its high-quality toys, many imported from Europe. The emphasis is on the old-fashioned—low-tech goodies such as puzzles, rocking horses, and tops. One wall is devoted exclusively to tub toys, windups, and other stocking stuffers. A great place for kids who haven't been sucked in by the mainstream. 60 W. 15th St. (btw. Fifth and Sixth aves.). ☎ **212/645-6337.** www.kiddingaroundnyc.com. Subway: F to 14th St.

Wine & Spirits

The decidedly less fancy **Trader Joe's Wine Shop** in Union Square, 142 E. 14th St. (☎ **212/529-4612**), may not have the high-end bottles you'll discover at the following retailers, but it is the best place for quality on a budget (though the place is invariably so crowded you might have to wait in line to get in!). Also, **Eataly Wine,** located next door to the main store on 23rd St., has perhaps the city's most extensive line of Italian vintages (see "Edibles," p. 368).

Acker Merrall & Condit Co.   In business since 1820—which makes Acker America's oldest wine shop—this attractive little store is the Upper West Side's best wine source. There are no bad bottles here, and some are quite rare. The careful selection is well displayed, with authoritative cards attached to each bin to help you choose. A supremely knowledgeable staff is on hand for additional assistance. 160 W. 72nd St. (btw. Broadway and Columbus Ave.). © **212/787-1700.** www. ackerwines.com. Subway: 1, 2, 3 to 72nd St.

Astor Wines & Spirits 🍷 This large store is a great source for excellent values on liquor and wine; their stock is deep and diverse. The staff is always willing to recommend the perfect vintage for any budget. Astor hosts excellent wine tastings two or three afternoons a week, often paired with edibles from local restaurants and gourmet shops; call or check the website for a current schedule and pricing. 399 Lafayette St. (at E. 4th St). © **212/674-7500.** www.astoruncorked.com. Subway: 6 to Astor Place.

Morrell & Company One of the leading wine retailers in America boasts a friendly, helpful staff and has a fine-wine division that hosts high-profile auctions. Adjacent is the **Morrell Wine Bar & Cafe** (© 212/262-7700; www. morrellwinebar.com), an ideal place to sample the goods. 1 Rockefeller Plaza (at 49th St.). © **212/688-9370.** www.morrellwine.com. Subway: B, D, F, M to 47th–50th sts./Rockefeller Center.

Sherry-Lehmann ★ Zagat's has called Sherry-Lehmann the "Rolls-Royce of wine shops," and *Wine Enthusiast* magazine named it "Retailer of the Year" in 2011. Their vast inventory is mind boggling and includes ritzy gift baskets that make luxurious presents. Service is excellent and free wine tastings are often offered. Though expensive, this is the place to come if you're looking for a special bottle. 505 Park Ave. (btw. 59th and 60th sts.). © **212/838-7500.** www.sherry-lehmann. com. Subway: N, R to Lexington Ave.; 4, 5, 6 to 59th St.

Union Square Wines and Spirits ★★ 🎒 This lovely wine store squeezes in more than 4,000 varieties of wines. Come for wine tastings throughout the week to get the latest tips from sommeliers from local restaurants. The store has a perfect location across from the Union Square Greenmarket (p. 296). If you're loaded up with fresh produce for a picnic, have the friendly clerks pair a wine with your food. 140 Fourth Ave. (at 13th St.). © **212/675-8100.** www.unionsquarewines. com. Subway: L, N, R, 4, 5, 6 to 14th St./Union Sq.

8

NEW YORK CITY AFTER DARK

N ew York's nightlife scene is like a self-propagating machine—the more you learn what's going on, the more you discover. There's so much to see and do in this city after the sun goes down; your biggest problem is probably going to be choosing.

Fortunately, there's no shortage of New York publications to help guide us, which is why you'll see many a subway rider reading one of the local periodicals to check out what's coming up. The latest, most comprehensive event, music, and nightlife listings are in **Time Out New York** (www.timeoutny.com), published every Thursday, listing the week's theater, dance, comedy, music, and other options. It also notes free and cheap events, has a full gay and lesbian section, and whole separate edition for kids. For a little more selectivity, grab **New York** magazine (new every Monday) for their latest listings in "Agenda," or check out the thorough venue and show reviews as well as invaluable reader comments at **www. nymag.com**.

The free weekly **Village Voice** (www.villagevoice.com), the city's legendary alternative weekly, hits newsstands early on Wednesdays, with even more listings online. The arts and entertainment coverage is extensive, and just about every live-music venue advertises its shows here.

As the hometown paper, the **New York Times** (www.nytimes.com), of course, is a staple and consistently offers thoughtful reviews and to-dos in its two-part Friday "Weekend" section. It's a great source of cabaret, classical, and theater information, with daily listings and forecasts. Another reliable source is the **New Yorker** (www.newyorker.com), in its weekly "Goings on About Town" section.

For the biggest plays and musicals, theatergoers head for Broadway. FACING PAGE: The Village Vanguard has been a hot spot for jazz fans for more than 75 years.

NEW ON THE arts/nightlife SCENE THIS SEASON

The iconic New York performing-arts complex **Lincoln Center** (p. 404) marked its 50th anniversary in 2009 with completion of most of its major renovation. But 2012 will bring to a close the last few projects—including the newly constructed **Elinor Bunin-Munroe Film Center** (opening summer 2011) and the Claire Tow Theater (opening in 2012). Other recent milestones include the rebuilt Columbus Avenue in front of the main plaza, a new restaurant now open outside the Vivian Beaumont Theater, and the reopening of **Alice Tully Hall,** which earned fanfare and critical acclaim for its pristine acoustics and innovative architecture.

Another NYC landmark venue also is transforming itself for the new millennium: Madison Square Garden in 2010 launched an $850 million renovation that will continue through 2014. Improved areas will open in phases over the coming years, from new seats to concourses with open views.

In Times Square, **Bowlmor** brought bowling to the Great White Way in 2010. Downtown, the **Slipper Room** by late 2011 will expand from a modest cabaret into a spacious "French opera-style setting" for its legendary burlesque and other performances.

Across the river in Queens, 2011 brought completion of the 3-year, $67 million **Museum of the Moving Image** (p. 330) renovation, doubling its size and expanding its screening and exhibit spaces as well as providing film lovers a spectacular place of worship.

But no matter what, to find the shows you most want to catch, do check listings and calendars as soon as you get to town, or even before you arrive.

As for bars and lounges, in addition to places listed in this chapter, there's also **Shecky's NYC Nightlife** (www.sheckysnightlife.com), a website that's supercurrent and searchable by some two dozen criteria, from dive to karaoke to swanky and neighborhood bars. Another good online bar source is **www.murph guide.com**. This website has all the latest happy-hour info by neighborhood and is especially big on Irish pubs—just be wary of being led to noisy sports bars.

To find the latest gay and lesbian goings-on, pick up free copies of **Next** (www.nextmagazine.com) and **GO** (www.gomag.com) magazines at **the Center** (www.gaycenter.org), **Bluestockings** (p. 358), or virtually any gay bar in town (see "The Gay & Lesbian Scene" at the end of this chapter for more).

For theater, the folks behind the TKTS Discount Booths (see "The ABCs of TDF," on p. 394) operate the **Theatre Development Fund** (© **212/912-9770;** www.tdf.org). You can subscribe to a daily newsletter that alerts you to what tickets will be discounted at its three booths. There's also a full list of Broadway shows at **www.ilovenytheater.com**, compliments of the Broadway League.

And beware, when it comes to New York nightlife, many cocktail lounges have decided to capitalize on the profit margins behind $20-plus drinks. Usually you're paying for the atmosphere more than the cocktail. So if that scene isn't worth blowing your budget, there are plenty of more affordable, friendlier places to try.

ALL THE CITY'S A STAGE: THE THEATER SCENE

Nobody does theater better than New York. No other city—not even London—has a big-ticket theater scene with so much breadth and depth, with so many diverse alternatives. Broadway, of course, gets the most ink and airplay. It's where you'll find the big stage productions, from crowd-pleasing warhorses like *The Lion King* to more recent hits like *Jersey Boys*. But today's scene is thriving beyond the bounds of Broadway—smaller, "alternative" theater fills spaces large and small. With bankable stars on stage, crowds lining up for hot tickets, and hits popular enough to generate major-label cast albums, Off-Broadway isn't just for culture vultures anymore. (And Off-Off Broadway is the cheapest theater in town, usually around only $20 a ticket.)

Helping to ensure the recent success of the New York theater scene has been the presence of movie and television stars such as Scarlett Johanson, Julianne Moore, Jude Law, Nathan Lane, Catherine Zeta-Jones, Denzel Washington, James Gandolfini, and Daniel Radcliffe (plus directors like Sam Mendes). But keep in mind that stars' runs are often limited, and tickets tend to sell out fast. If you hear that there's a celeb you'd like to see on the New York stage, be sure to jump on those ticket-buying plans. (Check to see how long a star is contracted for a role, and if he or she is playing all eight shows a week.)

Remember, since shows, venues, and calendars are ever-changing, check the publications listed at the start of this chapter and additional websites listed in "Online Sources for Theatergoers & Performing-Arts Fans," below, to settle on which shows you want to see and what's available.

The Basics

The terms **Broadway, Off-Broadway,** and **Off-Off Broadway** refer to theater size, pay scales, and other arcane details. Most of the Broadway theaters are in Times Square, around the "Great White Way" (so named for its millions of lights), but not directly on it. Instead, you'll find them dotting the side streets that intersect Broadway, mostly in the mid-40s between Sixth and Eighth avenues, but running north as far as 53rd Street. There's even a Broadway theater fully outside of Times Square: the Vivian Beaumont in Lincoln Center, at Broadway and 65th Street.

Off-Broadway, on the other hand, is less about location and more about the contract the production has with Actors Equity (the actors' union). These productions usually are staged on the eight-shows-a-week performance schedule for longer runs. The theaters are all over town, but there are mini–Theater Districts within Midtown and on the Upper West Side, as well as downtown. Off-Off Broadway shows tend to be more avant-garde, experimental, and/or nomadic, generally in theaters with less than 100 seats, with fewer performances overall—and many of them staging brilliant works by yet-undiscovered talents.

Broadway shows tend to keep pretty regular **schedules.** There are usually eight shows a week: Tuesday through Saturday evenings, plus matinees on Wednesday, Saturday, or Sunday. Evening shows are usually at 8pm, while matinees are usually at 2pm on Wednesday and Saturday, and 3pm on Sunday, but schedules can vary, especially Off and Off-Off Broadway.

In recent years, especially with stagings that are popular with a younger audience, shows sometimes offer more matinees, or earlier curtain times for evening performances, particularly shows early in the work week (a 7:30pm curtain on a Tues night is a relief!). **Broadway shows usually start right on time,** so if you arrive late, you may have to wait until after the first act to be ushered to your seat (and with more and more shows *sans* intermission, you could have to watch the whole thing on a monitor in the lobby—your own Broadway tragedy).

Ticket prices for Broadway shows vary dramatically. Expect to pay a *lot* for good seats; the high end for any given show is likely to be $100 or more (though some shows have charged "premium" prices for the very best seats, competing with the licensed ticket brokers). The cheapest end of the price range can be as low as $20 or as high as $50, depending on the theater configuration (or if they offer student, standing-room, or same-day rush tickets). Matinee tickets are cheaper than evening tickets, and midweek evenings are usually cheaper than weekend evening performances.

If all tickets are the same price or close to it, you can pretty much count on all of the seats being pretty good. But if you're buying tickets at the low end of a wide range, be wary of obstructed-view seats. Price is your barometer. These historic theaters (most Broadway theaters date from the early 20th century) are architecturally stunning both inside and out—the drawback may mean sitting behind a column that partially blocks the stage, seats way off to the side or upper rear mezzanine, and/or a lack of legroom. Tall folks should try for orchestra aisle seats; theater fanatics should splurge on reliably good seats.

Off-Broadway and Off-Off Broadway shows tend to be cheaper, with tickets as low as $10 or $15. However, seats for the most established plays and those with star power can command prices as high as $50 to $75.

Don't let price be a deterrent to enjoying the theater. There are ways to pay less if you're willing to make the effort and be flexible, especially closer to curtain time. Read on.

Top Ticket-Buying Tips
BEFORE YOU LEAVE HOME
Phone ahead or go online to buy tickets to the most popular shows as far in advance as you can—in the case of such shows as *The Lion King* (yes, even after all these years), it's never too early, and it will yield much better seats.

Buying tickets can be simple if the show you want to see isn't sold out. You need only call or surf to **Telecharge** (ⓒ **212/239-6200;** www.telecharge.com), which handles most Broadway and Off-Broadway shows and some concerts, or **Ticketmaster** (ⓒ **212/307-4100;** www.ticketmaster.com), which also handles Broadway and Off-Broadway shows and most concerts. You will pay a service fee per ticket, and sometimes a "restoration" fee for a show in an older theater.

Theatre Direct International (TDI) is a ticket broker that sells tickets for select Broadway and Off-Broadway shows, including some of the most popular crowd-pleasers, such as *Jersey Boys* and *Wicked!*, directly to individuals and travel agents. Check to see if they have seats to the shows you're interested in by calling ⓒ **800/BROADWAY** [276-2392] or 212/541-8457; you can also order tickets through TDI via their commercial website, **www.broadway.com.** (Disregard the discounted prices, unless you're buying for a group of 20 or more.) Because there's a minimum service charge of $15 per ticket, you'll definitely do better by trying Ticketmaster or Telecharge first; but because they act as a consolidator, TDI may have tickets left for a specific show even if the major outlets don't.

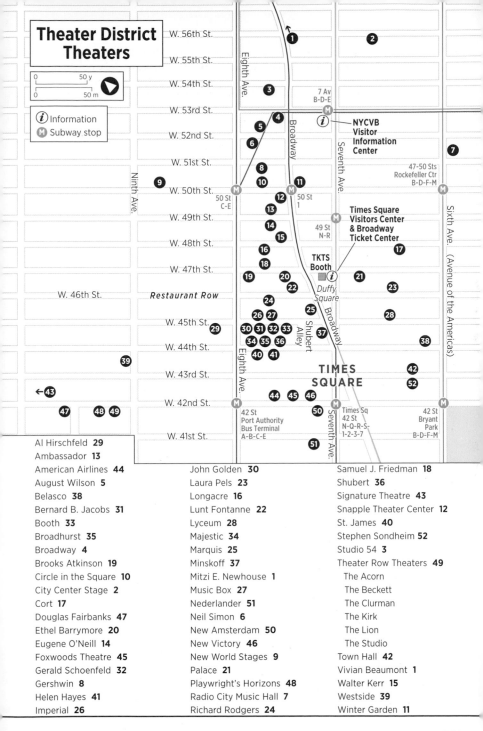

Theater District Theaters

0 — 50 y
0 — 50 m

ⓘ Information
Ⓜ Subway stop

W. 56th St.
W. 55th St.
W. 54th St.
W. 53rd St.
W. 52nd St.
W. 51st St.
W. 50th St.
W. 49th St.
W. 48th St.
W. 47th St.
W. 46th St.
W. 45th St.
W. 44th St.
W. 43rd St.
W. 42nd St.
W. 41st St.

Eighth Ave.
Ninth Ave.
Seventh Ave.
Broadway
Sixth Ave. (Avenue of the Americas)

7 Av B-D-E
NYCVB Visitor Information Center

47-50 Sts Rockefeller Ctr B-D-F-M

50 St C-E
50 St 1
49 St N-R

Times Square Visitors Center & Broadway Ticket Center

TKTS Booth

Duffy Square

Restaurant Row

Shubert Alley

TIMES SQUARE

42 St Port Authority Bus Terminal A-B-C-E

Times Sq 42 St N-Q-R-S-1-2-3-7

42 St Bryant Park B-D-F-M

Another reputable ticket broker is the international **Keith Prowse & Co.** (✆ **800/669-8687;** www.keithprowse.com). For a list of other licensed ticket brokers recommended by the New York Convention & Visitors Bureau (NYCVB), get a copy of the *Official NYC Guide*. (See "Visitor Information," in chapter 9, for details.)

If you don't want to pay a service charge, head to the theater **box office** directly; just be sure to go during their limited open hours. Broadway theaters don't sell tickets over the telephone—except for the always excellent **Roundabout Theatre Company** (✆ **212/719-1300;** www.roundabouttheatre.org), with its $6-per-ticket handling fee—but a good number of Off-Broadway theaters do.

Also, before you call a broker to snag tickets to a hot show, consider utilizing the **concierge** at the hotel where you'll be staying. If you've chosen a hotel with a well-connected concierge, he or she may be able to have tickets waiting for you when you check in—for a premium, of course. For more on this, see "When You Arrive," below.

For details on how to obtain advance-purchase theater tickets at a discount, see "Reduced-Price Ticket Deals," below.

KIDS TAKE THE STAGE: family-friendly THEATER

The family-friendly theater scene has been flourishing over the past years. There's so much going on that it's best to check *Time Out New York Kids, New York* magazine, or the Friday *New York Times* for current listings and special offers. Besides larger-than-life Broadway shows, the following offer some dependable kid-targeted entertainment options.

The **New Victory Theater,** 229 W. 42nd St., 10th Floor, between Seventh and Eighth avenues (✆ **646/223-3010;** www.newvictory.org), is a full-time family-oriented performing-arts center, and stages everything from jugglers to puppet masters to Shakespeare for kids.

Since 1958 the **Paper Bag Players** (✆ **212/353-2332;** www.paperbag players.org) have performed funny tales for children ages 4 to 9 in a set made from bags and boxes, at a few different theaters around the city. It's one of the top kid-oriented companies in the country, so look into upcoming, always affordable performances.

TADA! Youth Theater ★, 15 W. 28th St., between Fifth Avenue and Broadway, Third Floor (✆ **212/252-1619;** www. tadatheater.com), is a vivacious youth ensemble that performs musicals and plays with a multiethnic perspective for kids, including teens, and their families (pictured at right).

The **Swedish Cottage Marionette Theatre** (✆ **212/988-9093;** www. centralpark.org) puts on marionette shows for kids at its 19th-century Central Park theater throughout the year. Reservations are a must.

The "World Voices Program" of the **New Perspectives Theatre,** 456 W. 37th St., at Tenth Avenue (✆ **212/630-9945;** www.newperspectivestheatre.org), has different seasonal puppet shows based on famous figures and fables from different world cultures.

While David Mamet hardly seems like a playwright for the kiddies, the "Atlantic for Kids" series is making a go

ONLINE SOURCES FOR THEATERGOERS & PERFORMING-ARTS FANS

Some of your best, most comprehensive, and up-to-date information sources for what's going on about town are in cyberspace.

Three competing commercial sites—**Broadway.com** (www.broadway.com), **Playbill Online** (www.playbill.com), and **TheaterMania** (www.theatermania.com)—offer complete information on Broadway and Off-Broadway shows, and links to their ticket-selling agencies. Each has its own free **online club,** for which you register your e-mail address in exchange for savings on advance-purchase Broadway and Off-Broadway tickets. Discounts range from a few bucks up to 50% off regular ticket prices. Subscribing to e-mail newsletters also helps you keep track of changing offers—especially handy if you're a New York regular or have a longer stay. The Playbill Club was the first of the bunch, though Theater-Mania's *TM Insider* and Broadway.com's discount services are similar enough to compare and track down the best deals.

The **Broadway League** (✆ 888/BROADWAY [276-2392]; www.live broadway.com) is another now-playing resource, but only points you in the

of it at the **Atlantic Theater Company,** 336 W. 20th St., between Eighth and Ninth avenues (✆ **212/645-8015;** www. atlantictheater.org), which Mamet co-founded with Academy Award–nominated actor William H. Macy.

Another award-winning troupe that excels at youth theater is the **Vital Theatre Company,** 2162 Broadway, between 76th and 77th streets (✆ **212/579-0528;**

www.vitaltheatre.org). It's definitely worth seeing what's on, and maybe making time for your child to participate in a postshow workshop.

Look for Young People's Concerts and Kidzone Live!, in which kids get to interact with orchestra members prior to curtain time, at the **New York Philharmonic** (www.nyphil.org/education; p. 400). Also check to see what's on for the entire family at **Carnegie Hall** (www. carnegiehall.org; p. 404), which offers family concerts at prices as low as $6; plus the CarnegieKids program, which introduces kids ages 3 to 6 to basic musical concepts through a 45-minute music-and-storytelling performance. For kid-friendly classical music, see what's on at **Bargemusic** (p. 400), which presents occasional chamber-music concerts geared for kids. And don't forget Jazz for Young People, Wynton Marsalis's stellar family concert series and curriculum at **Jazz at Lincoln Center** (www.jalc.org/educ; p. 406).

THE abcs OF TDF

TDF is the **Theatre Development Fund.** They offer many programs for theater professionals, children, families, and for people with disabilities, but the most visible aspect of TDF, whether you're a New Yorker who loves to go to the theater or a visitor who wants to see as many shows as you can pack into a long weekend, is "the booths," the three TKTS locations in NYC.

Starting in 1973, in the heart of the Theater District at Father Duffy Square, the organization started selling half-price, same-day tickets for Broadway and Off-Broadway shows. In 1983, TKTS added a downtown branch, and 2008 saw the addition of a TKTS outlet in Brooklyn. Here's the deal:

1. The **Times Square Booth** sells day-of-performance tickets only (and has a "Play Express" line for non-musical shows).

2. The **South Street Seaport Booth** sells tickets to evening performances on the day of the performance, and matinee tickets the day before.

3. The **Downtown Brooklyn Booth** sells tickets to evening performances on the day of the performance, and matinee tickets the day before, as well tickets to Brooklyn performing arts events.

All locations sell tickets at 50%, 40%, 30%, and 20% off full-price (plus a $4 per-ticket service charge, which helps support other TDF services and programs). The booths accept credit cards, cash, traveler's checks, or TKTS Gift Certificates.

And you don't even have to trudge to Midtown, South Street Seaport, or Metro-Center to find out what's on the "board." When you subscribe to the **TKTS Today e-mail,** you'll get a daily message listing what's available at the downtown and Brooklyn booths on and Off-Broadway, the curtain time(s), and the daily operating hours.

Of the three booths, Times Square/ Father Duffy can have the longest wait, particularly during holidays and other high-visitor periods, so if you're comfortable navigating the subway, it's definitely worth the trip to get the tickets downtown or in Brooklyn.

Here are a few more tips and hints for making your TKTS booth experience go more efficiently:

1. Don't ask for a show that's not listed. You're probably not going to see tickets for *Wicked, Jersey Boys,* or *The Lion King.* (But if you do, grab 'em!)

2. Have more than one choice in mind when you get to the window. If *Mamma Mia* is gone when it's your turn, have an idea of another show you'd enjoy.

3. Half price can still be a lot. A $128 ticket is $64 (plus service charge) at 50%. That's not as much as a lot of other things in New York City (a courtside seat at the Knicks game, if you can get it, can run a grand or more), but keep in mind that if you want to see a big show with a big star, you'll pay (half) a big price.

—Kathleen Warnock

direction of special offers and discounts before sending you off to the box office, Telecharge or Ticketmaster. It's also the host of **www.ilovenytheater.com**, home to show details and their venues, and special-partner offers for nearby restaurants and hotels. Free Broadway shows, if you can believe it, await kids ages 6 to 18 (with purchase of a full-price adult ticket) at **www.kidsnightonbroadway.com**—though you have to fork over your address and stuff to join the League's Broadway Fan Club. With the promotions only for the first Tuesday and Wednesday shows of each month, you should also jump on this deal weeks or months in advance.

WHEN YOU ARRIVE

Once you arrive in the city, getting your hands on tickets can take some street smarts—and failing those, cold hard cash. Even if it seems unlikely that seats are available, always **call or visit the box office** and try for single seats, since they're often easiest to score.

You should also try the **Broadway Concierge & Ticket Center,** run by the League of American Theatres and Producers (the same people behind www.livebroadway.com, above) at the **Times Square Visitor's Center,** 1560 Broadway, between 46th and 47th streets (Mon–Fri 9am–7pm; Sat–Sun 8am–8pm; hours subject to seasonal changes; www.timessquarenyc.org). They may have tickets for otherwise sold-out shows, both for advance and same-day purchase, and charge only about $5 extra per ticket.

Even if saving money isn't an issue for you, check the boards at the **TKTS Booth** in Times Square (see the box "The ABCs of TDF," p. 394) for seats to same-day shows.

In addition, your **hotel concierge** may be able to arrange tickets for you. These are usually purchased through a broker and a premium will be attached, but they're usually good seats and you can count on them being legitimate. (A $20 tip to the concierge for this service is reasonable—maybe more if the tickets are for a hot show.) If you want to deal with a licensed broker directly, **Keith Prowse & Co.** has a local office that accommodates drop-ins at 234 W. 44th St., Ste. 1000, between Seventh and Eighth avenues (© **212/398-4175;** Mon–Sat 9am–8pm, Sun noon–7pm).

If you buy from one of the **scalpers** selling tickets in front of the theater doors, you're taking a risk. They may be perfectly legitimate—say, a couple from the 'burbs whose companions couldn't make it for the evening—but they could be swindlers passing off fakes for big money. It's probably not a risk worth taking.

One preferred **insiders' trick** is to make the rounds of Broadway theaters at about 6pm, when unclaimed house seats are made available to the public. These tickets—reserved for VIPs, friends of the cast, the press, or other hangers-on—offer great locations and are sold at face value.

Also, note that **Monday** is often a good day to cop big-name show tickets. Though most theaters are dark on that day, some of the most sought-after choices aren't. Locals are usually at home on the first night of the workweek, so odds favor the avid ticket hunter. But generally, your chances will always be better on weeknights, or for Wednesday matinees, rather than weekends. *Note:* If you're in town especially to see a big star in a show, check to see that said big star is playing all eight shows a week. While most big stars' contracts (think Catherine Zeta-Jones or Denzel Washington) require them to play every performance, if it's a vocally demanding role, they may hand the matinees off to their understudies.

REDUCED-PRICE TICKET DEALS

The cheapest tickets are found in advance. If you can be flexible, consider purchasing them before scheduling your trip to New York. You can also buy **reduced-price theater tickets** over the phone, in person, or at the box office, or by joining one or

MORE dramatic VENUES WORTH SEEKING OUT

When you want a spectacle, there's no place like Broadway, home to the top-dollar ticket. But this is New York, where you can see amazing stage productions and performers sometimes for less than the cost of a cinema ticket (that's around $14, as of early 2011). Off-Broadway, expect to pay $20 to $65 or so for tickets; Off-Off Broadway rarely charges more than $20—a price that rarely lets you down, even if the show does.

One favorite local tip is to volunteer-usher at **Atlantic, Signature,** and **Roundabout Theatres,** and a few others, where you can hand out playbills and in return, see the show for free. See each company's website for information about how far ahead you should sign up, and whether to do so by phone, e-mail, or in-person.

Where do you find the hidden gems? The *Village Voice* (which sponsors the annual Obies, or Off-Broadway Awards) is a good source. *Time Out New York* has excellent listings and capsule descriptions for major Off-Broadway productions, as well as a decent listing of Off-Off shows. For more offerings Off-Off Broadway, check the reviews on **Theatermania.com** (which also lets you purchase tickets and offers regular discounts) and **NYTheatre.com,** which probably has the most comprehensive listings and reviews of the Off-Off scene.

Three resident nonprofit theaters in New York—**Lincoln Center Theater** (p. 405), the **Roundabout,** and **Manhattan Theatre Club** (www.manhattan theatreclub.com)—present work in Broadway houses, as well as in smaller venues Off-Broadway. You'll pay

Broadway prices (or whatever discount you can get) for the best seats in the big houses, but you can also usually find special, lower prices for students or seniors or last-minute rush tickets. In their smaller spaces (MTC's Stage II; the Roundabout's Laura Pels Theatre; Lincoln Center's Mitzi Newhouse), you can find good seats for less than $50 to see excellent new plays and revivals by the likes of Terrence McNally and John Patrick Shanley. Following are a few other notable Off- and Off-Off Broadway venues, but these are just the tip of the iceberg; check out the sources listed above for many, many more options.

In addition to the following venues, also see what's on at downtown faves **HERE Arts Center** (www.here.org), **P.S. 122** (www.ps122.org), **Theater for the New City** (www.theaterforthenewcity. net), and the women-strong **La MaMa E.T.C.** (www.lamama.org), where you can see new, innovative, and experimental work by cutting-edge international artists—*très* New York. If you want to dig even deeper, try the **Brooklyn Lyceum** in Park Slope, with it's wild mix of events (www.brooklynlyceum.com). Uptown, check out Harlem's **National**

more of online theater clubs. The "membership" (which is mostly just giving up your e-mail) is free and can score you discounts of up to 50% on select Broadway and Off-Broadway shows. More details are above, under "Online Sources for Theatergoers & Performing-Arts Fans." In addition to those sites, **BroadwayBox.com** is a source for the all-important "discount codes" you can plug into ticket-selling sites, in some cases for significant discounts. (Discount codes frequently expire, get pulled or change, so don't rely on them until your purchase is complete.)

Black Theatre (www.nationalblack theatre.org), which stages African-centric plays, cabaret, and other performances.

- **Joseph Papp Public Theater ★★**, 425 Lafayette St. (☎ **212/539-8500;** www.publictheater.org), is the legacy of the late visionary theater producer Joseph Papp. Legendary among Off-Broadway theaters, the Public draws top talent with its ground-breaking stagings of new plays, classical dramas, and solo perfor-mances. The Public also hosts New York's best annual alfresco event, **Shakespeare in the Park,** each summer (see the box "Park It! Shakespeare, Music & Other Free Fun," on p. 408). If that's not enough, it's also home to **Joe's Pub** (p. 422).

- **Atlantic Theater Company,** 336 W. 20th St., between Eighth and Ninth avenues (☎ **212/645-8015;** www. atlantictheater.org), "produces great plays simply and truthfully, utilizing an artistic ensemble," according to its mission statement. With some regularity it presents plays by David Mamet and Sam Shephard, as well as the occasional musical.

- **Signature Theatre Company,** 555 W. 42nd St. (☎ **212/244-PLAY** [244-7529]; www.signaturetheater.org), presents season-long explorations of a playwright's work. A corporate grant guarantees $20 tickets for the start of each run, sometimes the full run. The Signature will be moving into a brand-new Frank Gehry–designed space for its 2011–12 season.

- **New York Theater Workshop,** 79 E. 4th St. (☎ **212/460-5475;** www. nytw.org), has been around since 1979, but it was *Rent* that put it on the map. Since the great success of the long-running musical, several other plays developed by NYTW have gone on to award-winning commercial runs. NYTW specializes in new work, rethought revivals, and collaborations. All Sunday evening performances are $20; there are discounts for students and opportunities to usher.

- **Emerging Artists Theatre** (**EAT;** ☎ 212/247-2429; www.eatheatre. org) has been producing new plays Off-Off Broadway for more than 15 years and always has something good to offer. In addition to its Off-Broadway offerings, it presents spring EATFests of new American short plays, and an annual spring (Apr or May) "Illuminating Artists" new works series, which includes *One Woman Standing* and *One Man Talking* (solo shows), and *Notes from a Page* (musicals); ticket prices are around $10.

Broadway shows—even blockbusters—sometimes have a limited number of cheaper tickets set aside for students and seniors; call the box office directly to inquire. Some popular shows have "lotteries" for cheaper tickets each day; others offer student, general "rush," or "standing room" tickets, which are available only on the day of the show. **Playbill.com** usually keeps a comprehensive list of the rush/student/lottery and other special rates.

The best deal in town on same-day tickets for both Broadway and Off-Broad-way shows is at the **Times Square Theatre Centre,** better known as the **TKTS** booth, run by the nonprofit Theatre Development Fund in the heart of the Theater District (see the box "The ABCs of TDF" below). Its longtime home at Duffy Square, 47th Street and Broadway, was completely rebuilt in 2009. Now above the ticket-selling windows, you can relax and take in the "crossroads of the world" on the illuminated red stadium seats. Windows are open from 3 to 8pm (opening at 2pm on Tues) for evening performances, 10am to 2pm for Wednesday and Saturday matinees, and from 11am to 8pm on Sunday for all performances. You can also head to the two other TKTS booths for shorter lines.

At the Times Square Booth, TKTS offers a dedicated line for non-musicals. Any show with a "P" next to the title on the board is also available at the "Play Express" window. Play Express lines are almost always shorter than the lines for musicals. But overall, depending on the season (especially around the winter holidays), there's often a huge queue at the Times Square location (see box on p. 394 for info on the other TKTS locations), so show up early for the best availability and be prepared to wait (the usual story for big NYC entertainment)—but frankly, the crowd is all part of the fun. If you don't care much what you see and you'd just like to go to a show, you can walk right up to the window later in the day and something's always available. The shows available change throughout the day, and who knows—you might score a ticket to a big hit just before curtain time.

Line up at "The Booth" for deeply discounted theater tickets.

OPERA, CLASSICAL MUSIC & DANCE

While Broadway is the Big Apple's greatest hit, many other performing arts also flourish in this culturally rich and entertainment-hungry town.

In addition to the listings below, see what's happening at **Carnegie Hall** and the **Brooklyn Academy of Music,** two of the most esteemed and enjoyable performing-arts venues in the city. The **92nd Street Y** also regularly hosts events that are worth considering, though they lean towards the academic with great speakers and panels.

Operatic and symphonic companies housed at **Lincoln Center** are below, but check the center's full calendar for its abundant offerings. See "Major Concert Halls & Landmark Venues," below for the full Lincoln Center breakdown.

Opera

New York has grown into one of the world's major opera centers. The season generally runs September through May, but there's usually something going on at any time of year.

Metropolitan Opera ★★★   The Metropolitan Opera ranks first in the world for its full productions of the classic repertory and a schedule packed with world-class grand sopranos and tenors. Millions are spent on fabulous stagings, and the venue itself is a wonder of acoustics. Whatever is on the schedule, the quality will be second to none. Of course, with that comes hefty ticket prices that range up to $300—but the Met's programmers know how to appeal to varied audiences simply through affordability. With that, it makes 200 $20 rush tickets available for Monday through Thursday shows, 2 hours before curtain (get in line early!); 50 of them are set aside for seniors 65 and older, and can be obtained by calling the main number (proof of age required). Student rush tickets can be had for $25 on weekdays, $35 on Fridays and Saturdays, always starting at 10am.

To guarantee that its audience understands the words, the Met has outfitted the back of each row of seats with screens for subtitles—translation help for those who want it, minimum intrusion for those who don't. James Levine continues his role as the brilliant and popular musical director. At the Metropolitan Opera House, Lincoln Center, Broadway and 64th St. (✆ **212/362-6000.** www.metoperafamily.org. Subway: 1 to 66th St.

New York City Opera ★★   The New York City Opera takes a delightful different approach to opera, staging stunning, big-budget productions. It aims to reach wider audiences than the Met with its hipper art direction and significantly lower prices ($12–$140), showing its commitment to adventurous premieres, new operas, the occasional avant-garde work, American musicals (*Porgy and Bess*), and novels (*Of Mice and Men*) presented as fresh, innovative operettas—and even obscure works by mainstream or lesser known composers. Its mix stretches from the "easy" works of Puccini, Verdi, and Gilbert and Sullivan to the more challenging oeuvres of the likes of Arnold Schönberg and Philip Glass. What's more, recent renovations at the renamed David H. Koch Theater (formerly the New York State Theater) promise a much more comfortable operatic experience. At the David H. Koch Theater, Lincoln Center, Broadway and 64th St.

Bargemusic: chamber music on the water.

ⓒ **212/870-5570** (information or box office), or 212/307-4100 for Ticketmaster. www.nyc opera.com. Subway: 1 to 66th St.

New York Gilbert and Sullivan Players If you're in the mood for light-hearted operetta, try this lively company, which specializes in Gilbert and Sullivan's 19th-century English comic works. Tickets are usually in the $60-to-$85 range. Performances take place all year on an ever-changing schedule, since the company also tours year-round. There's also the annual New Year's Eve gala at **Symphony Space** (p. 409). At City Center, 131 W. 55th St. (btw. Sixth and Seventh aves.). ⓒ **212/247-0430.** www.nygasp.org or www.citycenter.org. Subway: F, N, Q, or R to 57th St.; B, D, E to Seventh Ave.

Classical Music

Bargemusic ★ 🔲 Many thought Olga Bloom peculiar when she transformed a 40-year-old barge into a floating concert hall. More than 20 years later, Bargemusic is an internationally renowned recital room boasting more than 100 first-rate chamber-music performances a year. The unique setting draws esteemed international and local musicians to the stage, mostly playing classical and jazz. There are four shows per week—Thursday, Friday, and Saturday evenings at 7:30pm and Sunday afternoon at 3pm. The venue holds 130 guests, who listen to musicians perform on a small stage, behind which is a glass wall facing the stunning skyline of lower Manhattan. The barge may creak a bit and an occasional boat may speed by, but the music rivals what you'll find anywhere in the city. Tickets are just $35 ($15–$25 for students), or $40–$50 for performances by larger ensembles. Reserve seats in advance. At Fulton Ferry Landing (just south of the Brooklyn Bridge), Brooklyn. ⓒ **718/624-2083** or 718/624-4061. www.bargemusic.org. Subway: 2 or 3 to Clark St.; A to High St.; F to York St.

The Juilliard School 🎵 During its school year, the nation's premier music-education institution sponsors about 550 performances of the highest quality—at the lowest prices. With most concerts either free or as much as $20, Juilliard is one of New York's greatest cultural bargains. Though most would assume that the school presents only classical-music concerts, Juilliard also offers other music as well as drama, dance, opera, and interdisciplinary works. The best way to find out about the wide array of productions is to call, visit the school's website (click on "Complete Calendar of Events"), or consult the bulletin board in the building's lobby. Note that tickets are sometimes required even for free performances. Watch for master classes and discussions open to the public featuring celebrity guest teachers. 60 Lincoln Center Plaza (Broadway at 65th St.). ⓒ **212/799-5000,** or 212/721-0965 to charge tickets. www.juilliard.edu. Subway: 1 to 66th St.

New York Philharmonic ★ A magical New York experience, the Philharmonic is a staple of sophisticated local entertainment. The nation's oldest orchestra made news in 2009 when it hired one of the youngest musical directors in its history, New Yorker Alan Gilbert. The conductor selects classics and new compositions that draw an enthusiastic audience, now revived with his fresh energy. Philharmonic tickets range from $26 to $109, with rush tickets available to students (with ID at pickup) and seniors (63 and older) when the box office opens at 10am Monday through Saturday and at noon on Sunday. If you can afford it—and if the tickets are available—it's well worth it to pay for prime seats. The acoustics of the hall are such that, at the midrange price points, the second tier (especially the boxes) offers better sound than the more expensive rear orchestra

Alan Gilbert conducts the New York Philharmonic.

seats. But you're sure to enjoy the program from any vantage point in the majestic Avery Fisher Hall.

Along with guest composers and musicians (usually top violinists), Gilbert and his orchestra play free summer concerts in Central Park as well as in the city's outer boroughs—perhaps the single best picnic opportunity in New York. At Avery Fisher Hall, 10 Lincoln Center Plaza, Broadway at 65th St. ✆ **212/875-5656.** www. nyphil.org. Subway: 1 to 66th St.

Dance

In general, dance seasons run September through February and then March through June, but there's always something going on year-round. In addition to the major venues and troupes discussed below, some other names to keep in mind are the **Brooklyn Academy of Music,** the **92nd Street Y, Radio City Music Hall,** and **Town Hall** (see "Major Concert Halls & Landmark Venues," below). For particularly innovative works, see what's on at the **Dance Theater Workshop,** in the Bessie Schönberg Theater, 219 W. 19th St., between Seventh and Eighth avenues (✆ **212/691-6500** or 212/924-0077; www.dancetheater workshop.org), a first-rate launching pad since 1965.

In addition to regular appearances at City Center (below), the **American Ballet Theatre** (✆ **212/362-6000;** www.abt.org) takes up residence at Lincoln Center's Metropolitan Opera House for 8 weeks each spring/early summer. The same venue also hosts such visiting companies as the Kirov, Royal, and Paris Opéra ballets.

The weekly *Time Out New York,* available on newsstands around town, has a section dedicated to dance events around town that's an invaluable resource to fans.

City Center   Modern dance usually takes center stage in this domed, Moorish-revival performing-arts palace (and former temple). The companies of Paul Taylor and Alvin Ailey, as well as the American Ballet Theatre are regularly on the calendar. The dance companies always perform in the pitch-perfect Mainstage Theater, with ticket prices ranging from $10 to $150, or more. Also in the City Center building, plays are presented in Manhattan Theatre Club Stage I and the smaller Stage II, at affordable prices ranging up to $90. 131 W. 55th St. (btw. Sixth and Seventh aves.). *C* **212/247-0430** or 212/581-1212. www.citycenter.org. Subway: F, N, Q, or R to 57th St.; B, D, or E to Seventh Ave.

The Art Deco marquee of the Joyce Theater.

Joyce Theater Housed in an old Art Deco movie house, the Joyce has grown into one of the world's greatest modern-dance institutions. You can see everything from Native American ceremonial dance to Maria Benites Teatro Flamenco to the innovative works of Pilobolus to the Martha Graham Dance Company. In residence annually is co-founder Eliot Feld's ballet company, Ballet Tech, which WQXR radio's Francis Mason called "better than a whole month of namby-pamby classical ballets." The Joyce has a second space, **Joyce SoHo,** where you can see rising young dancers and experimental works in the intimacy of a 70-seat performance space. In either space, seats range from $20 to $60. 175 Eighth Ave. (at 19th St.). *C* **212/242-0800** for tickets, or 212/691-9740 for theater. www.joyce.org. Subway: A, C, or E to 14th St.; 1 to 18th St. Joyce SoHo at 155 Mercer St. (btw. Houston and Prince sts.). *C* **212/431-9233.** Subway: R to Prince St.; 6 to Bleecker B, D, F, or M to Broadway/Lafayette.

New York City Ballet Highly regarded for its unsurpassed technique, the New York City Ballet is arguably the world's best. The company renders with happy regularity the works of two of America's most important choreographers: George Balanchine, its founder, and Jerome Robbins. Under the direction of Ballet Master in Chief Peter Martins, the troupe continues to expand its repertoire and performs to a wide variety of classical and modern music. The cornerstone of the annual season is the Christmastime production of *The Nutcracker,* for which tickets usually become available in early October. Ticket prices run from $20 to $125, with student same-day rush tickets available for $12. At the David H. Koch Theater at 20 Lincoln Center Plaza, Broadway at 64th St. *C* **212/870-5570** or Center Charge 212/721-6500. www.nycballet.com. Subway: 1 to 66th St.

MAJOR CONCERT HALLS & LANDMARK VENUES

Apollo Theater ★ 📷 Built in 1914, this legendary Harlem theater launched or abetted the careers of countless musical icons—including Billie Holiday, Duke Ellington, Ella Fitzgerald, Sarah Vaughan, Count Basie, and Aretha Franklin. It also played a vital role in the development and worldwide popularization of black music in America. By the 1970s, the Apollo had fallen on hard times, but a 1986 restoration breathed new life into the NY landmark, and then in 2009, a major restoration of the Apollo was completed in time for its 75th anniversary. The results are spectacular—from the refurbished terra-cotta facade, to the new box offices, to the high-tech marquee that still shines with 1940s timeless style. The theater remains internationally renowned for hosting African-American performers of all musical genres, from hip-hop acts to Wynton Marsalis's Jazz for Young People events. Since 1934, Wednesday at the Apollo means "Amateur Night"; forget *American Idol*—this rowdy, fun-filled, often hilarious production draws young talents with high hopes of making it big. 253 W. 125th St. (btw. Adam Clayton Powell and Frederick Douglass blvds). ✆ **212/531-5300** or -5301. www.apollotheater.com. Subway: B or D to 125th St.

Brooklyn Academy of Music ★ 🏠 BAM is the city's most renowned contemporary-arts institution, presenting cutting-edge theater, opera, dance, and music. Offerings have included historically informed presentations of baroque opera by William Christie and Les Arts Florissants; pop opera from Lou Reed and Laurie Anderson; Marianne Faithfull singing the music of Kurt Weill; dance by Mark Morris and Mikhail Baryshnikov; the Philip Glass ensemble accompanying screenings of Lugosi's original *Dracula;* and many more works by artists from around the world—including a growing number of celebrity actors and directors—as well as visiting companies from all over the world.

Of particular note is the **Next Wave Festival,** running September through December, the country's foremost showcase for major new experimental works (see the "New York City Calendar of Events," in chapter 2). The **BAM Rose Cinemas** show first-run and classic films, and there's free live music every Friday and Saturday night upstairs at **BAMcafé,** which ranges from classical to reggae and jazz to bluegrass. BAM is also an easy subway ride from Manhattan, just a

The Apollo Theater is a landmark in Harlem.

block from several stations. 30 Lafayette Ave. (off Flatbush Ave.), Brooklyn. 𝄐 **718/636-4100.** www.bam.org. Subway: 2, 3, 4, 5, M, N, Q, or R to Pacific St./Atlantic Ave.

Carnegie Hall ★★   Perhaps the world's most famous performance space, Carnegie Hall offers everything from grand classics to popular author readings to the music of legendary sitarist Ravi Shankar. The **Isaac Stern Auditorium,** the 2,804-seat main hall, welcomes visiting orchestras from across the country and the world. Many of the world's premier soloists and ensembles give recitals, as do contemporary singers like Rufus Wainwright. The legendary hall is visually and acoustically brilliant, so don't miss an opportunity to experience it.

Within the hall, there's also the intimate 268-seat **Weill Recital Hall,** usually used to showcase chamber music and vocal and instrumental recitals. Carnegie Hall has also, after being occupied by a movie theater for 38 years, reclaimed the ornate underground 599-seat **Zankel Concert Hall.**

Carnegie ticket prices greatly vary, and are for sale by phone and at the box office, both open 8am to 8pm daily; same-day rush tickets for students and seniors are available, as are $10 partial-view tickets on a first-come, first-served basis. And to answer the famous question, "How do you get to Carnegie Hall?" Either by practice . . . or by subway. 881 Seventh Ave. (at 57th St.). 𝄐 **212/247-7800.** www.carnegiehall.org. Subway: N, Q, or R to 57th St.

Lincoln Center for the Performing Arts   New York is the world's premier performing-arts city, and Lincoln Center is its foremost institution. If you're planning an evening's entertainment, check the variety here, which can include opera, dance, symphonies, jazz, theater, film, and more—from classic to contemporary. Lincoln Center's many buildings serve as permanent homes to their own companies as well as major stops for esteemed international performance troupes.

Resident companies include the following: The **Chamber Music Society of Lincoln Center** (𝄐 **212/875-5788;** www.chambermusicsociety.org) performs at

How do you get to Carnegie Hall? (Take the N, Q, or R trains!)

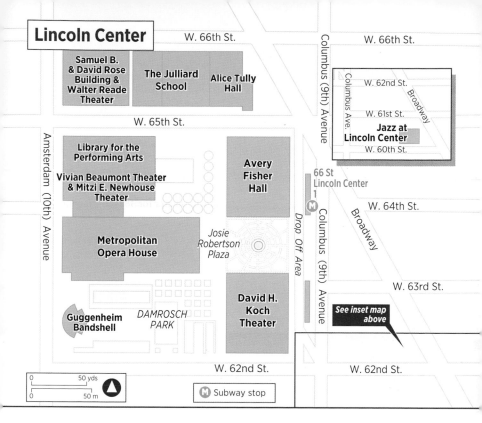

Lincoln Center

W. 66th St. — W. 66th St.

Samuel B. & David Rose Building & Walter Reade Theater | The Julliard School | Alice Tully Hall

Columbus (9th) Avenue

Jazz at Lincoln Center

W. 62nd St.
W. 61st St.
W. 60th St.

W. 65th St.

Library for the Performing Arts

Vivian Beaumont Theater & Mitzi E. Newhouse Theater

Avery Fisher Hall

66 St Lincoln Center
1

W. 64th St.

Amsterdam (10th) Avenue

Metropolitan Opera House

Josie Robertson Plaza

Drop Off Area

Columbus (9th) Avenue

Broadway

W. 63rd St.

Guggenheim Bandshell | DAMROSCH PARK | David H. Koch Theater

See inset map above

W. 62nd St. — W. 62nd St.

0 — 50 yds
0 — 50 m

Ⓜ Subway stop

Alice Tully Hall or the Daniel and Joanna S. Rose Studio, often in the company of high-caliber guests. The **Film Society of Lincoln Center** (℡ **212/875-5600** for automated schedule, or 212/875-5601 for box office; www.filmlinc.com) screens a daily schedule of movies at the Walter Reade Theater, and hosts notable film and video festivals, as well as the Reel to Real program for kids that pairs silent screen classics with live performance. **Lincoln Center Theater** (℡ **212/362-7600;** www.lct.org) consists of the Vivian Beaumont Theater, a modern, comfortable venue with great sightlines that has been home to much good Broadway drama, and the Mitzi E. Newhouse Theater, a well-respected Off-Broadway house that has also boasted numerous theatrical triumphs. Past seasons have included acclaimed productions of Tom Stoppard's *Arcadia, South Pacific* in revival, and the Tony Award–winning *Light in the Piazza*—and more are sure to come with the addition of the new Claire Tow Theatre on the Beaumont's roof (opening early 2012).

For details on the **Metropolitan Opera,** the **New York City Opera,** the **New York City Ballet, the Juilliard School,** the phenomenal **New York Philharmonic,** and the **American Ballet Theatre,** which takes up residence here every spring, see "Opera, Classical Music & Dance," earlier in this chapter.

Most of the companies' **major seasons** run from about September or October to April, May, or June. **Special series** such as Great Performers and the new American Songbook, showcasing classic American show tunes, help round out the calendar. Indoor and outdoor events are held in warmer months: Spring kicks

The Lincoln Center campus is vast—so much so it even applies to venues outside its borders, as is the case with **Jazz at Lincoln Center,** which resides a few blocks south in the Time Warner Center at Broadway and 60th Street (② 212/258-9800; www.jalc.org). Though technically the move was downtown (by a few blocks), it was definitely a move up. Its complex spans several floors of Time Warner's northern tower, featuring two amazing performance spaces, a jazz club, a mini jazz hall of fame, and a 7,000-square-foot atrium with views of Columbus Circle and Central Park.

The largest of the three venues is the **Rose Theater,** where you might see the incredible Jazz at Lincoln Center Orchestra with Wynton Marsalis. Acoustics are perfect and seating is spacious. The jewel of the Center is the **Allen Room** (pictured below), with its 4,500-square-foot glass backdrop behind the main stage offering glittering views of Central Park and the Manhattan night sky. Hard to believe that what was once played in smoky basements is now presented in venues as spectacular and opulent as these.

Also at Jazz at Lincoln Center is **Dizzy's Club Coca-Cola** (② 212/258-9595; p. 417), a stylish, intimate jazz club that's open every day and has a terrific Southern-inspired dinner menu.

off with the **Sing into Spring Festival** series at Dizzy's; July sees the **Midsummer Night's Swing,** with partner dancing, lessons, and music on the plaza; August's **Mostly Mozart** attracts such talents as Alicia de Larrocha and André Watts; **Lincoln Center Festival** celebrates the best of the performing arts; **Lincoln Center Out-of-Doors** is a series of free alfresco music and dance performances; there's also the **New York International Film Festival,** and more. Check the "New York City Calendar of Events" section, in chapter 2, or Lincoln Center's website to see what special events will be on while you're in town.

Tickets for performances at Avery Fisher and Alice Tully halls can be purchased through **CenterCharge** (② 212/721-6500) or online at **www.lincoln center.org** (click on "Event Calendar"). Tickets for all Lincoln Center Theater performances can be purchased thorough **Telecharge** (② 212/239-6200;

www.telecharge.com). Tickets for New York State Theater productions (New York City Opera and Ballet companies) are available through **Ticketmaster** (✆ **212/307-4100;** www.ticketmaster.com), while tickets for films showing at the Walter Reade Theater can be bought up to 7 days in advance by calling ✆ **212/496-3809.** For last-minute ticket-buying tips, consider "rush" tickets or a box-office pop-in, and see the "More Dramatic Venues Worth Seeking Out" box on p. 396.

Lincoln Center is also home to the **New York Public Library for the Performing Arts,** 40 Lincoln Center Plaza (✆ **212/870-1630;** www.nypl.org/research/lpa/lpa.html), with collections, services, and other resources available for true theater buffs.

Daily 1-hour **guided tours** of Lincoln Center tell the story of the great performing-arts complex, and even offer glimpses of rehearsals for $15 adults, $12 students and seniors, and $8 children. 70 Lincoln Center Plaza (at Broadway and 64th St.). ✆ **212/875-5350.** www.lincolncenter.org. Subway: 1 to 66th St.

Madison Square Garden   U2, Springsteen, the Rolling Stones, and other monsters of rock and pop regularly fill this 20,000-seat arena, which is also home to pro sports teams the Knicks, the Rangers, and the Liberty. A cavernous concrete hulk, it's better suited to sports than to concerts, or in-the-round events such as the Ice Capades, Ringling Bros. and Barnum & Bailey Circus, or the Westminster Dog Show. If you end up with seats in the back, bring binoculars.

The better sightlines are at the **Theater at Madison Square Garden** (www.theateratmsg.com) on the Seventh Avenue side of the block. This amphitheater-style auditorium with 5,605 seats that has also played host to some major pop stars, from Bob Dylan to Cher to Ozzy Osbourne. Watch for annual stagings of *Sesame Street Live, Cirque du Soleil,* and other family shows. Smaller events such as comedy shows, the NFL and NBA drafts, and family musicals also round out programming at the busy venue.

Through 2014, MSG is undergoing a phased, full-building renovation, which will close sections as work progresses—including full arena closures during the summers of 2012 and 2013. The latest plans and updates are posted at **www.msgtransformation.com**.

MSG's box office (which sells tickets *sans* surcharges) is located inside the concourse at Seventh Avenue and 32nd Street, or you can purchase tickets through **Ticketmaster** (✆ **212/307-7171;** www.ticketmaster.com). On Seventh Ave., from 31st to 33rd sts. ✆ **212/465-MSG1.** www.thegarden.com. Subway: A, C, E, 1, 2, or 3 to 34th St.

92nd Street Y ★★ ✦   This legendary non-profit community and cultural center offers a phenomenal line up of top-rated cultural happenings—there's classical, folk, jazz, and world music; cabaret; lyric theater; readings; comedy; workshops; and plenty more. Great classical performers—Robert Levin, Peter Serkin, Christian Tetzlaff, András Schiff, and Pinchas Zukerman—all perform regularly. The Tokyo String Quartet is in residence, and the full concert calendar often includes luminaries like Dave Brubeck; Jazz in July with Bill Charlap and guests; and Lyrics & Lyricists, the renowned American Songbook series. The lectures-and-readings calendar is unparalleled, with speakers that have included James Carville, Martha Stewart, Bill Gates, Jonathan Franzen, Margaret Atwood, Jon Stewart, Tony Blair, Erica Jong. . . the list goes on and on. There's a regular schedule of contemporary dance performances throughout the year and the annual 5-week Harkness Dance Festival in February and March. Best of all,

PARK IT! shakespeare, MUSIC & OTHER FRESH-AIR FUN

As the weather warms, New York culture goes outside to play.

Shakespeare in the Park, a New York institution since 1957, is as much a part of a New York summer as fireworks on the Fourth of July. The outdoor free event at the open-air Delacorte Theater in Central Park was the brainchild of the late Joseph Papp, former director of the Public Theater. Each summer usually features a revival of a Shakespeare play staged with a large company, including at least one or more film or TV stars—from Al Pacino (pictured at right in *Merchant of Venice*) to Liev Schreiber to Julia Stiles. The productions run from June to early September, and tickets are scarce.

The Delacorte Theater itself, next to Belvedere Castle near 79th Street and West Drive, is a dream—on a starry night, there's no better stage in town. Tickets are distributed at the theater free on a first-come, first-served basis (two per person) at 1pm on the day of the performance. The Delacorte might have 1,881 seats, but each is a hot commodity; whatever the show, people line up next to the theater 2 to 3 hours in advance (or early in the morning if a big

name is involved—a true New York cultural phenomenon). You can also sign up for the daily online ticket lottery. For more information, call the Public at ✆ **212/539-8500** or Delacorte at ✆ **212/535-4284,** or visit **www.public theater.org.**

Free concerts by the **New York Philharmonic** and the **Metropolitan Opera** are held beneath the stars on Central Park's Great Lawn and in parks throughout the five boroughs. For schedules, call the Philharmonic at

readings and lectures are usually priced between $20 and $40, dance is free up to $15, and concert tickets generally go for $25 to $70—a fraction of what you'd pay at comparable venue, and with discounts for those aged 35 and under.

Additionally, a full slate of entertainment—from comedy to film screenings to live music—is hosted by the well-curated **92YTribeca,** which also happens to have a great little cafe. 1395 Lexington Ave. (at 92nd St.). ✆ **212/415-5500.** www.92ndsty. org. Subway: 4, 5, or 6 to 86th St.; 6 to 96th St. 92YTribeca: 200 Hudson St. ✆ **212/601-1000.** www.92ytribeca.org. Subway: 1, A, C, or E to Canal St.

Radio City Music Hall ★ This stunning 6,200-seat Art Deco theater opened in 1932, and legendary Radio City continues to be a choice venue, where the theater alone adds a dash of panache to any performance. Star of the holiday season is the ***Radio City Christmas Spectacular,*** starring the legendary Rockettes. Touring chart toppers and old faves, from Neil Young to the Gipsy Kings, also perform here. Thanks to perfect acoustics and uninterrupted sightlines,

© **212/875-5656** or the Metropolitan Opera at © **212/362-6000**. The Philharmonic maintains a list of their upcoming gigs at **www.nyphil.org**; look under "Concerts & Tickets."

The most active outdoor music scene in Central Park, however, is **SummerStage,** at Rumsey Playfield, midpark around 72nd Street. SummerStage has featured everyone from Chaka Khan to Patti Smith; recent offerings have included concerts by the Jon Spencer Blues Explosion, the Flaming Lips, and Marianne Faithfull; cabaret nights; dance companies; and more. The season usually runs from mid-June through August. Big-name shows usually charge admission, but often tickets are free (donations always encouraged). Call the hotline at © **212/360-2777,** or visit **www.summerstage.org.**

Beyond Central Park, more free outdoor fun includes the **Bryant Park Summer Film Festival,** held in Bryant Park, just behind the main branch of the New York Public Library, at Sixth Avenue between 41st and 42nd streets. Every Monday night a classic film—think *Dr. Zhivago* or *Superman*—is shown on a large screen under the stars. The lawn typically opens by 5pm for blankets and picnicking; the movie starts at dusk (about 8 or 9pm). Rain dates are Tuesdays. For the schedule and more information, call © **212/512-5700.**

The biggest free summer arts festival is way downtown, where the **River to River Festival** inundates lower Manhattan from June to mid-September. Stages spring up at indoor and outdoor spots like the South Street Seaport, Battery Park, and the World Financial Center, showcasing live dance, readings, and a smattering of virtually every kind music you can think of. Free indie rock shows are an increasingly impressive presence at the Seaport in particular, so check out what's on at **www.riverto rivernyc.com.**

Calendars of free summer events come out earlier than you'd expect, around mid-spring, so you can plan ahead. There's also an overview of some of the city's outdoor events at the **Parks and Recreation Special Events Hot Line** at © **888/NY-PARKS** [697-2757] or 212/360-3456, or at **www.nycgovparks. org** under "Things to Do."

there's nary a bad seat in the house. The theater also hosts dance performances; family entertainment; and a number of annual awards shows, such as the Tony Awards, the Essence Awards, and MTV Video Music Awards. 1260 Sixth Ave. (at 50th St.). © **212/307-7171** for Ticketmaster. www.radiocity.com or www.ticketmaster.com. Subway: B, D, or F to 47th–50th sts./Rockefeller Center.

Symphony Space 🎁 An eclectic mix of culture can be found at this affordable Upper West Side institution. The variety of shows at the **Peter Jay Sharp Theater** includes music, with series by the World Music Institute as well as classical, rock, and blues; dance, with marathon tributes to such choreographers as George Balanchine and Zvi Gotheiner; literature, such as the selected shorts series introduced by writers like Jonathan Lethem, Edwidge Danticat, and Walter Mosley; and family, with performances by folk singer Tom Chapin and the Putuyamo Kids. Adjacent to the Sharp Theater is the **Leonard Nimoy Thalia.** The film-revival house that was known for its quirky sightlines was rescued by none other than Mr. Spock and has now been totally renovated. 2537 Broadway (at 95th St.). ℂ **212/864-1414.** www.symphonyspace.org. Subway: 1, 2, or 3 to 96th St.

Town Hall ★ This intimate landmark theater—a National Historic Site designed by McKim, Mead & White— is blessed with outstanding acoustics, making it an ideal place to enjoy many kinds of performances, including theater, dance, lectures, drama, comedy, film, and pop and world music. The calendar regularly includes such offerings as American tap and Brazilian tango exhibitions; doo-wop and global rhythms; live tapings of A *Prairie Home*

You might see a big name or an awards show at Radio City.

Companion with Garrison Keillor; lectures by luminaries such as Marianne Williamson and Frank Gehry; concerts by the likes of David Sanborn or They Might Be Giants; symphony, opera, and ballet companies from around the world; and much more. 123 W. 43rd St. (btw. Sixth and Seventh aves.). ℂ **212/840-2824,** or 212/307-4100 for Ticketmaster. www.the-townhall-nyc.org or www.ticketmaster.com. Subway: N, Q, R, S, 1, 2, 3, or 7 to 42nd St./Times Sq.; B, D, F, or M to 42nd St.

LIVE ROCK, JAZZ, BLUES & MORE

Here is a list of the top large and small music venues—but this is New York, so there are many others, and new ones cropping up all the time. For the latest, be sure to check the publications discussed in this chapter's introduction, as well as in the "Online Sources for Live-Music Fans" section, below.

Larger Venues

For coverage of **Madison Square Garden,** the **Theater at MSG,** and **Town Hall,** see "Major Concert Halls & Landmark Venues," above.

Beacon Theatre This lovely, midsize Upper West Side venue hosts mainly pop-music performances, usually for the over-30 crowd. Originally a 1928 Art Deco movie palace, its impressive lobby, stairway, and auditorium (seating about 2,700) were restored to their gorgeous glory back in 2009. Featured acts have ranged from street-smart pop diva Sheryl Crow to a Hall & Oates reunion to dazzling Rufus Wainwright. There's also an annual early-spring run of sellout Allman Brothers shows here. You'll also find all kinds of special guests and events on the mix-and-match calendar, for kids, comedy fans, and even devout Buddhists—the Dalai Lama and other monks have graced the Beacon. 2124 Broadway (at 74th St.). ℂ **212/465-6500.** www.beacontheatre.com. Subway: 1, 2, or 3 to 72nd St.

Roseland This still-very-active old warhorse of a venue—a 1919 ballroom— has hosted all kinds of music, performers, auctions, old-school dance parties, even trade shows. And with a general-admission capacity of 2,500, throngs of fans still get the house a-rockin'—to anyone from Paul Weller or Fiona Apple, to Busta

The noises of honking horns, car alarms, and sirens are not the only sounds you'll hear in your New York travels. Music is everywhere. In the warm weather, a guitarist or violinist will set up at a busy corner and play all day and night. In the winter, musicians head into subway stations, where, legally, they aren't allowed to play without permission—but not even the authorities want to stop free entertainment. Whether performers are great or groaners, they're all just trying to earn a buck. Some of the good ones, who audition for the opportunity, perform under a program sponsored by the Metropolitan Transportation Authority (MTA) called "Music Under New York." If selected, they can perform legally at designated subway stations, such as Times Square/42nd Street, 34th Street/Sixth Avenue, 14th Street/Union Square, and 59th Street/Columbus Circle. The variety of music is amazing and the quality is as good as you might see at some of New York's clubs. Traversing a busy subway station, you may hear a capella singing, gospel, blues, Cajun, classical piano, Andean, Brazilian drumming, barbershop quartets, or Dixieland jazz. If you're not in a hurry, the way most New Yorkers are, stop for a listen—just don't forget to tip! For more information, visit the MTA website (**www.mta.info/mta/aft/muny**).

Rhymes or Jeff Beck. There's plenty of room to either join the pit, or stand back get a drink and enjoy the show. Advance tickets can be purchased at the **Fillmore New York at Irving Plaza** box office (below) without the Ticketmaster service fee. Take a moment on your way through the lobby to check out the display cases memorializing Roseland's postwar heyday as the city's premier dance hall. 239 W. 52nd St. (btw. Broadway and Eighth Ave.). ℭ **212/777-6800,** or 212/307-7171 for Ticketmaster. www.roselandballroom.com. Subway: C, E, or 1 to 50th St.

Midsize & Multigenre Venues

Following are the main clubs where you can see virtually every kind of music passing through town, small or big. Also see what's on at the low-key **Joe's Pub** (p. 422), a sizeable cabaret that hosts intimate-feeling shows by popular performers; and **Webster Hall** (p. 441), where programming spans live music and dance parties nightly across its four floors.

B.B. King Blues Club & Grill   This overpriced, sometimes stuffy venue gets packed as one of the prime anchors of Times Square's "new" 42nd Street. Despite its name, B.B. King's seldom sticks to the blues; what you're likely to find instead is a bill full of pop, funk, and rock names, mainly from the past. George Clinton and the P. Funk All Stars are regulars here, as are a seemingly countless number of "tribute" bands, with an occasional cool dance party or only-in-NYC event like the New York Burlesque Festival. Tourist-targeted entry and bar prices make for an expensive night on the town, with sometimes convoluted seating policies or standing-room only (with near-impossible sightlines). At least the Sunday Gospel Bunch is soulful. 237 W. 42nd St. (btw. Seventh and Eighth aves.). ℭ **212/997-4144,** or 212/307-7171 for tickets. www.bbkingblues.com. Subway: A, C, E, Q, 1, 2, 3, or 7 to 42nd St.

The Bell House 🎵   Founded by the friends who run Union Hall (see below), the Bell House is one of the city's best new clubs (ca. 2008). Located in the gentrifying former industrial neighborhood called Gowanus—just across Fourth Avenue from Park Slope—this roomy club seems made for live music. A large front lounge with local beers leads to the giant performance space in back, outfitted with chandeliers, ambient lights, and a killer sound system. It's quickly proven to be one of the most diverse places to dance, see a local filmmaker's work, or catch great live music—from the Defibulators and A.C. Newman, to the French Kicks and Jewish rapper Matisyahu. 149 7th St. (btw. 2nd and 3rd aves., Brooklyn). ☎ **718/ 643-6510.** www.thebellhouseny.com. Subway: F or R to 9th St./Fourth Ave.; G or F to 9th St./Smith St.

The lovely Beacon Theatre has been restored to its original Art Deco style.

Bowery Ballroom ★ Run by the same people behind the **Mercury Lounge** (see below), the Bowery is bigger, accommodating a crowd of 500 or so. Plus the higher stage means way better sightlines. The sound couldn't be better, and Art Deco details give the place a sophistication that doesn't come easy to general-admission halls. The balcony has its own bar and seating alcoves. This place is a favorite with such alt-rockers as Vic Chesnutt, Travis, Steve Earle, the Delgados, and Toshi Reagon, as well as more established acts (Neil Finn, Patti Smith, Joan Jett and the Blackhearts), who thrive in an intimate setting. Save on the service charge by buying advance tickets at the Mercury's box office. 6 Delancey St. (at Bowery). ☎ **212/533-2111.** www.boweryballroom.com. Subway: F to Delancey St.; J, M, or Z to Bowery.

Highline Ballroom On the far West Side you'll find this venue situated below the namesake High Line, the abandoned elevated train structure that was recently rebuilt as an city park. The ballroom has a capacity of 700, and its diverse programming spans from rock to hip-hop, but tangos with eclectic and

---

📎 Ticket-Buying Tips

Tickets for events at all larger theaters as well as at Hammerstein Ballroom, Roseland, Irving Plaza, B.B. King's, and S.O.B.'s can be purchased through **Ticketmaster** (☎ 212/307-7171; www.ticket master.com).

Advance tickets for an increasing number of shows at smaller venues—including Bowery Ballroom and Mercury Lounge—can be purchased through **Ticketweb** (☎ 866/468-7619; www. ticketweb.com). Do note, however, that Ticketweb can sell out in advance of actual ticket availability. Just because Ticketweb doesn't have tickets left for

an event doesn't mean it's completely sold out, so be sure to check with the venue directly.

Even a sold-out show doesn't mean you're out of luck. There are usually a number of people hanging around at showtime trying to get rid of extra tickets for friends who didn't show, and they're usually happy to pass them off for face value. You'll encounter pushy professional scalpers too, who peddle forgeries for exorbitant prices and are best avoided. Be aware, of course, that all forms of resale on-site are illegal.

experimental musicians, too. A great sound system, wraparound balcony, and huge stage make this a rockin' venue for general-admission entry. 431 W. 16th St. (btw. Ninth and Tenth aves.). ℂ **212/414-5994.** www.highlineballroom. com. Subway: A, C, E, or L to 14th St.

Irving Plaza This high-profile mid-size music hall is the prime stop for national name rock bands that aren't quite big enough yet (or anymore) to sell out Hammerstein, Roseland, or the Beacon. Think Five for Fighting, the Eels, Morcheeba, Badly Drawn Boy, the Reverend Horton Heat, the New York Dolls, Cowboy Junkies, and Gang

Brooklyn's Bell House music club.

of Four. From time to time, big-name artists also perform—Bob Dylan, Prince, and Patti Smith have all played "secret" shows here. All in all, it's a good enough place to see a band, though when it's packed even the tall stage won't help your sightlines from the floor. Fortunately, there's an upstairs balcony with amazingly open views, but come early for a good spot along the rail. 17 Irving Place (1 block west of Third Ave. at 15th St.). ℂ **212/777-1224** or 212/777-6800. http://irvingplaza.com. Subway: L, N, Q, R, 4, 5, or 6 to 14th St./Union Sq.

Knitting Factory ★ The original Knitting Factory in TriBeCa closed in 2008, then quickly reopened in Brooklyn in 2009, drawing a steady crowd to its new home on a Williamsburg hangout strip. Maybe it's the great sound, or the cool industrial-style bar out front, or "the Knit's" solid reputation—either way, it's a great place to feel like you're catching a stellar band, like Ted Leo and the Pharmacists or Bitch and the Exciting Conclusion, in a local's-only New York stop. Don't be shy about making an impromptu visit, what with the good happy hour and bar DJs spinning virtually every night. Oh, and come for a laugh, too, on Sunday comedy night. 361 Metropolitan Ave., Williamsburg, Brooklyn (at Havemeyer St.). ℂ **347/529-6696.** http://bk.knittingfactory.com. Subway: L to Bedford Ave.; G to Metropolitan-Grand.

Music Hall of Williamsburg Brought to you by Bowery Presents, the concert promoters for the Bowery Ballroom, Mercury Lounge, and Terminal 5 (see below), this three-story Brooklyn venue (including up- and downstairs bars) holds 550 people and re-creates the style and substance of the Bowery Ballroom. Patti Smith was the debut concert in this impressive venue, which showcases old and new bands like Throwing Muses, OK Go, Cursive, and Gomez. 66 N. Sixth St., Williamsburg, Brooklyn (btw. Kent and Wythe aves.). ℂ **212/260-4700.** www.musichall ofwilliamsburg.com. Subway: L to Bedford Ave.

Terminal 5 The name of this huge club is a tribute to the famous JFK TWA terminal designed in 1962 by Eero Saarinen (it was demolished in 2008). But this relatively young, 40,000-square-foot boxy club has two upper-level balconies on three sides, open sightlines, and a state-of-the-art sound system that draws musicians like Tom Jones, Thievery Corporation, Ben Folds, and Broken Social Scene. 610 W. 56th St. (btw. Eleventh and Twelfth aves.). ℂ **212/260-4700.** www.terminal 5nyc.com. Subway: A, B, C, D, or 1 to 59th St./Columbus Circle.

Check these websites for the latest live-music schedules:

○ Ticketmaster: www.ticketmaster.com

○ Pollstar: www.pollstar.com

○ New York Citysearch: http://newyork.citysearch.com
  Additionally, *New York* (**www.nymag.com**), *Time Out New York* (**www.timeoutny.com**), and other hard-copy publications and their corresponding websites listed at the start of this chapter are full of the latest live-music listings.

(Mostly) Rock Clubs

Really, you can't throw, well, a rock downtown without hitting a rockin' club—though plenty of stellar (and more affordable) Brooklyn clubs are stealing their thunder. And remember, many of these places are half bars, in case you want to hang out without necessarily seeing a show.

Beyond the following venues, music fans on the hunt for diamonds in the rough should visit legendary folk-music joint the **Bitter End,** 147 Bleecker St., in the heart of the Village (✆ 212/673-7030; www.bitterend.com), and the quaint **Living Room,** at 154 Ludlow St. on the Lower East Side (✆ 212/533-7237; www.livingroomny.com). **(Le) Poisson Rouge** (p. 440) also hosts live music in addition to fun dance parties.

Arlene's Grocery ♪   This casual Lower East Side club is a friendly bar with good, smaller bands and musicians hitting the stage nightly. Shows aren't always free anymore, but the cover usually tops out at $10. Arlene's Grocery mainly serves as a showcase for hot bands looking for a deal or promoting their self-produced record. The crowd is an easygoing mix of club-hoppers, rock fans looking for a new fix, and industry scouts looking for new blood. The much-loved Rock and Roll Karaoke takes over on Monday nights at 10pm. 95 Stanton St. (btw. Ludlow and Orchard sts.). ✆ **212/995-1652.** www.arlenesgrocery.net. Subway: F to Second Ave.

The Knitting Factory moved to Brooklyn, but kept its cool.

All kinds of bands stop by the Music Hall of Williamsburg.

Mercury Lounge ★   The Merc is all that a live-music venue should be: unaffected, affordable, with a solid sound system. The rooms themselves are nothing special: a front bar and an intimate back-room performance space with a low stage and a few tables along the wall. The calendar is filled with a mix of accomplished local rockers and such national acts as Evan Dando, the Mekons, Cubic Zirconia, and the White Rabbits, along with occasional comedy shows. The crowd is grown up and easygoing. The only downside is that it's consistently packed. 217 E. Houston St. (at Essex St./Ave. A). ℭ **212/260-4700.** www.mercuryloungenyc.com. Subway: F to Second Ave.

Rodeo Bar 🏮   Here's New York's oldest and finest honky-tonk. Hike up your Wranglers and head those Fryes inside, where you'll find longhorns on the walls, peanut shells underfoot, first-class margaritas at the bar, and Tex-Mex on the menu. But this place is really about the music: urban-tinged country, foot-stompin' bluegrass, swinging rockabilly, Southern-flavored rock. Bigger names in country sometimes drop by—but regular acts like the Dixieland Swingers, cowpunk goddess Rosie Flores, and the good-time BBQ Bob and the Spareribs supply fine music, keeping the urban cowboys happy. It's happy hour until 7pm; the free music starts at either 9 or 10pm nightly and usually goes till at least 3am. 375 Third Ave. (at 27th St.). ℭ **212/683-6500.** www.rodeobar.com. Sub-way: 6 to 28th St.

Southpaw ★★   Always popular with the locals, Park Slope, Brooklyn's Southpaw has become a staple for all sorts of great music and events since it carved out a space in a former 99-cent store in 2002. The affordable spirit lives on though, at this club with an nice beer selection, large upstairs music space with elevated lounge seats, and intimate downstairs bar. All year round you can catch folk, hip-hop, rock, punk, and country music from around the world. Bands that have rocked this house include Cat Power, Mogwai, Ted Leo, Radio 4, and the singular Brooklyn band Clap Your Hands Say Yeah. 125 Fifth Ave. (btw. Sterling and St. Johns places, Brooklyn). ℭ **718/230-0236.** http://spsounds.com. Subway: R or M to Union St., or 2 or 3 to Bergen St.

Union Hall ★ 📷   Tucked away on Union Street in Park Slope is this classy, cozy-yet-huge multipurpose venue that feels like your grandpa's old boy's club.

Arrive early for a drink upstairs in a comfy leather chair by the fireplace, play a free game of bocce on the two indoor courts (yep—full size), or sit in the outdoor patio. Then head downstairs to hear mostly local bands in the well-wired basement, catch some comedy or burlesque, or join in on one of the fun monthly game nights. 702 Union St. (at Fifth Ave., Brooklyn). © **718/638-4400.** www.unionhallny.com. Subway: R or M to Union St.

Rodeo Bar: Midtown's own honky-tonk.

Jazz, Blues, Latin & World Music

Big-name jazz clubs can be really fun in New York, and likewise, expensive. Music charges and bar-tab/drink minimums can vary dramatically depending on who's playing; beware especially of a dinner requirement, even for a late show. Call ahead or ask the host so you know what you're getting into. Reservations are almost essential at top spots.

For those of you who like your jazz with an edge, see what's on at **City Winery.** Swingsters should consider **Swing 46** (p. 441). Weekends at **Carnegie Club** (p. 432) are ideal for Sinatra fans looking to relive the moment.

Despite its name, **B.B. King Blues Club & Grill** (p. 411) extends well beyond the blues genre to staging throwback acts of just about any ilk. You might also consider **Jazz at the Kitano,** in the mezzanine of the Kitano Hotel, 66 Park Ave., at 38th Street (© **800/548-2666** or 212/885-7119; www.kitano.com), for some first-rate jazz in a classy, comfortable setting. Likewise for **55 Bar,** 55 Christopher St., near Seventh Ave. (© **212/929-9883;** www.55bar.com), which bills itself as a "prohibition era dive bar with incredible jazz, funk and blues nightly in Greenwich Village." The **Kitchen,** 512 W. 19th St., between Tenth and Eleventh avenues (© **212/255-5793;** www.thekitchen.org), has a full slate of live music and performance art. In association with the 92nd Street Y, the **92YTribeca** (p. 408) offers a similarly eclectic mix, as does **Joe's Pub** (p. 422), which adds a cabaret spin.

There's also music at every first Friday of the month in the rotunda at the **Guggenheim Museum;** see chapter 6. And don't forget **Jazz at Lincoln Center,** the nation's premier forum for the traditional and developing jazz canon; see p. 406.

Some of the bars mentioned later in this chapter also have occasional live music. For an eclectic mix of jazz, Latin, and R&B, **Creole** (p. 437) in East Harlem offers a full schedule.

Bill's Place 🖰   Imagine hearing old-school, live jazz in your living room. That's the intimacy behind the Bill's Place experience. Bill is Bill Saxton, a jazz saxophonist extraordinaire and a Harlem legend. Saxton was a Friday night regular for many years at **St. Nick's Pub** (p. 418) and has played at clubs all over Harlem and downtown. In 2005 he opened his own club in the parlor level of a brownstone on West 133rd Street. In the 1920s, 133rd Street between Lenox and Seventh Avenue, with its speakeasies and jazz joints up and down the block, was the original "swing street," not just because a 17-year-old Billie Holliday was discovered singing in a club on 133rd Street. So it's appropriate that Saxton's place is on this historic block—jazz here is the real deal. There are no frills at Bill's Place: Come into the parlor, find a seat—there aren't many, so reservations are a must—and kick back with Saxton's quartet. Alcohol isn't served, but soft drinks are available and you can bring your own bottle. 148 W. 133rd St. (btw. Lenox and Seventh aves.). ℂ 212/281-0777. www.webbmmpr.com/billsplace.html. Reservations highly recommended. Admission $15. Subway: 3 to 135th St.

Birdland   This legendary club abandoned its distant uptown roost in 1996 for a more convenient spot in Midtown, where it has established itself once again as one of the city's premier high-end jazz spots. While the legend of Parker, Monk, Gillespie, and other bebop pioneers still holds sway, this isn't a crowded, smoky joint of yesteryear. The big room is comfy and classy, with great sound and great talent any night of the week (along with a Southern-cookin' dinner menu). Expect lots of accomplished big bands and jazz trios, plus occasional appearances by icons like Freddy Cole. The regular Sunday night show, starring Chico O'Farrell's Afro-Cuban Jazz Big Band, is always fun. 315 W. 44th St. (btw. Eighth and Ninth aves.). ℂ 212/581-3080. www.birdlandjazz.com. Subway: A, C, or E to 42nd St.

Blue Note   This Village classic once attracted some of the biggest names in jazz to its intimate setting: Dave Brubeck, Ray Charles, Manhattan Transfer, Dr. John, Chick Corea, David Sanborn, and others. But like a lot of NYC venues, the Blue Note now has slipped into a bit more routine programming and prices, with two shows nightly and up to $45 per ticket. The sound and sightlines are still good, but the charm is evaporating. 131 W. 3rd St. (at Sixth Ave.). ℂ **212/475-8592.** www.bluenote.net. Subway: A, B, C, D, E, or F to 4th St.

Dizzy's Club Coca-Cola ★   This luxurious jazz club is part of the Jazz at Lincoln Center complex in the Time Warner Center on Columbus Circle. You won't find a bad seat at this fifth-floor club, with a stage set in front of a large window with Central Park views. The club attracts an interesting mix of both up-and-coming and established artists. Every Monday the club starts with the student showcase Upstarts!, followed by 1-night-only shows from special guest musicians. Covers range from $20 to $35 and $10 for shows after 11pm, with $5 or $10 bar minimums; student discounts are available, and reservations aren't always necessary. Time Warner Center, 60th St. and Broadway. ℂ **212/258-9595.** www. jalc.org/dccc. Subway: A, B, C, D, or 1 to Columbus Circle.

Iridium   This well-respected, rather intimate jazz club is located just north of Times Square, and remains a legend in the New York music scene. Accomplished talent and big-name acts take the stage year-round, including Herbie Hancock, Jose Feliciano, Arturo Sandoval, Mose Allison, and saxophonist Houston Person. And even though the man himself isn't around to grace the stage anymore, the Iridium still puts on Les Paul tribute Mondays. Tapas and well-made cocktails should make it easy to reach your table minimum, in addition to tickets up to $50. 1650 Broadway (at 51st St.). ℂ **212/582-2121.** www.iridiumjazzclub.com. Subway: 1 to 50th St.

Jazz Standard ★★   Boasting a sophisticated retro-speak-easy vibe, the Jazz Standard is one of the city's largest jazz clubs, with well-spaced tables seating 150 and a reasonable $15 to $30 cover. The rule is straightforward, mainstream jazz

Live Rock, Jazz, Blues & More

by new and established musicians, including amazing artists and the occasional big name like Branford Marsalis. Three revolving tribute bands pay tribute to Charles Mingus tunes on weekly Mingus Mondays, and Sunday afternoons bring on the Jazz for Kids program. A limited menu from Danny Meyer's barbecue joint, **Blue Smoke** (p. 174), upstairs, is available. Jazz, blues, and barbecue—hard to go wrong with that. 116 E. 27th St. (btw. Park Ave. South and Lexington Ave.). ℂ 212/576-2232. www.jazzstandard.net. Subway: 6 to 28th St.

Lenox Lounge ★ 🍴 This frozen-in-time classic lounge is a symbol of Harlem's history and renaissance. The intimate, Art Deco–cool back room—complete with zebra stripes on the walls and built-in banquettes—hosts top-flight live jazz vocalists, trios, and quartets. Blues and R&B are the province of Thursday. The cover ranges up to $25, usually with a $16 bar minimum, and there's a local bar upfront that may make you feel like you've found a Prohibition-era speakeasy. With three shows per night, it's well worth the trip uptown for those who want a genuine Harlem jazz experience—consider a reservation while you're at it, and enjoy some authentic soul food. 288 Malcolm X Blvd. (Lenox Ave.; btw. 124th and 125th sts.). ℂ 212/427-0253. www.lenoxlounge.com. Subway: 2 or 3 to 125th St.

St. Nick's Pub 🎁 As unpretentious a club as you'll find, St. Nick's in Harlem's Sugar Hill district is the real deal, with live entertainment 7 nights a week and never a cover. On Saturdays it's West African music night, Mondays and special-guest Tuesdays bring trumpeter Melvin Vines to the stage, and Wednesdays mean Kumba Frank Lacy and his band Awareness. It's open daily from 1pm to 4am, with shows at 10pm nightly (and 7pm Sun). 773 St. Nicholas Ave. (at 149th St.). ℂ 212/283-9728. www.stnicksjazzpub.net. Subway: A, B, C, or D to 145th St.

Smoke ★ A relatively young star in the New York jazz scene, Smoke is a welcome throwback to the informal, intimate clubs of the past—the kind of place that on most nights you can just walk in and be amazed. And though it seats only 65, for no more than a $35 cover (not counting bar/table minimums), Smoke manages to attract such talents as the Steve Turre Quartet, Ron Carter, and Eddie Henderson. On Sundays, the club features Latin jazz; every Tuesday it's B3 grooves and soul jazz, and Wednesdays put the "Sideman in the Spotlight." There are three sets nightly, an affordable menu recently spruced up by a new executive chef sets apart this supper club, and makes for a very happy happy hour. 2751 Broadway (btw. 105th and 106th sts.). ℂ 212/864-6662. www.smokejazz.com. Subway: 1 to 103rd St.

S.O.B.'s If you like your music hot, hot, hot, visit S.O.B.'s, the city's top world-music venue, specializing in Brazilian, Caribbean, and Latin sounds. The packed house dances and sings along nightly to calypso, samba, mambo, African drums, *bhangra,* and other global grooves, sometimes preceded by free dance lessons. Bookings include top performers from around the globe. Astrud Gilberto, Mighty Sparrow, King Sunny Ade, Eddie Palmieri, Buckwheat Zydeco, Beausoleil, and Baaba Maal are only a few of the names who added their energy to this lively stage. The room's Tropicana Club style has island pizzazz that carries through to the Caribbean-influenced cooking and extensive (and pricey) tropical-drinks menu. Book ahead if you'd like dinner or a Bossa Nova brunch. Monday is dedicated to reggae, Friday is salsa, and Saturday is samba night. 204 Varick St. (at Houston St.). ℂ 212/243-4940. www.sobs.com. Subway: 1 to Houston St.

The Village Vanguard 📷 What CBGB was to punk rock, the Village Vanguard is to jazz. One look at the photos on the walls will show you who's been

AND FOR THE CINEMANIACS. . .

Just because it's New York City doesn't mean you have to commit solely to live entertainment. The Big Apple also is an unparalleled destination for cinephiles. Grab a *Time Out New York* or *Village Voice* for regular-release screenings at cool theaters like the **Angelika** or **Landmark Sunshine** and to find film festival listings. Or check out one of these legendary venues for something more memorable.

If you're a fan of the classics, you're in luck. **Film Forum** (✆ **212/727-8110;** www.filmforum.org) will delight the romantics among us who still love a good Hepburn-Tracy flick, or one from local-boy Martin Scorsese, in addition to first-run and foreign films. Classic, indie, and arthouse films screen daily at Brooklyn's **BAM Rose Cinemas** (also known as BAMcinématek; ✆ **718/636-4100;** www.bam.org), which usually themes its week- or month-long revivals by director or actor.

The 2011 renovation of the **Museum of the Moving Image** (✆ **718/784-0077;** www.movingimage.us) has made a trek to Astoria, Queens irresistible. The museum presents in-depth famous-film-maker talks and other one-of-a-kind events, in addition to new and historic film-related exhibits and special screenings (pictured at left). **IFC Center** (✆ **212/924-7771;** www.ifccenter.com) brings indies and classics to the Village's renovated Waverly theater. **Anthology Film Archives** (✆ **212/505-5181;** www.anthologyfilmarchives.org), **MoMA Film** (✆ **212/708-9400;** www.moma.org), and **92YTribeca** (✆ **212/601-1000;** www.92ytribeca.org) screens impressively obscure retrospectives and foreign films daily. **Film Society of Lincoln Center** (✆ **212/875-5600;** www.filmlinc.com), host of the autumnal New York City Film Festival and several others, presents diverse documentaries and themed film series that span silent, horror, musicals, animated, and more.

through since 1935, from Coltrane, Miles, and Monk to recent appearances by Bill Charlap and Roy Hargrove. Expect a mix of established names and high-quality local talent, including the Vanguard's own jazz orchestra on Monday nights. The sound is great, but sightlines aren't, so reserve or come early for a front table; tickets average around $25, with drink minimums. If you are looking for serious jazz, this is the place. 178 Seventh Ave. S. (just below 11th St.). ✆ **212/255-4037.** www.villagevanguard.com. Subway: 1, 2, or 3 to 14th St.

CABARET

An evening spent at a sophisticated cabaret just might be the quintessential New York night on the town. It isn't usually cheap: Covers can hit $100, depending on

AUTHOR! AUTHOR! WHERE TO hear SPOKEN WORD

Readings can be some of the most inexpensive and entertaining events in New York. Many readings are free; most others charge a small cover (unless it's for a big name).

Thorough weekly listings can be found in *Time Out New York*'s "Books" section. There's almost always a major author in town reading at one of the local **Barnes & Noble** stores (**www.bn.com**). You can also stop by **Housing Works Bookstore Café** (p. 359), **Bluestockings** (p. 358), and Brooklyn bar **Pete's Candy Store** (p. 438) for readings and discussions.

There are also two great traveling literary events: **The Moth** live storytelling performances (www.themoth.org) and the **Happy Ending Reading Series** (http://amandastern.com/happyending.html). Consult their websites for upcoming events.

So who are you likely to see at these diverse literary venues? Everyone from bestselling writers (Candace Bushnell, John Irving, Augusten Burroughs) to slam poets and spoken-word artists (Patricia Smith, Anne Elliott) to whoever's just scribbled a poem on the back of an envelope at an open-mic event.

In addition to the following top venues/series, check out the varied calendars of **Galapagos Art Space** in DUMBO, 16 Main St., at Water Street, Brooklyn (✆ **718/222-8500;** www.galapagosartspace.com), as well as the **Bitter End** (p. 414).

o **The Unterberg Poetry Center** at the 92nd Street Y, 92nd Street at Lexington Avenue (✆ **212/415-5740;** www.92y.org; Subway: 4, 5, or 6 to 96th St.). The 92nd Street Y has had all the heavy hitters in its lineup since 1939. In addition to talks and readings by the world's top poets, novelists, playwrights, and critics, the Y also offers Books & Bagels Sunday brunch series. Tickets are usually in the $20-to-$40 range. Some readings are in the 917-seat auditorium, which does on occasion sell out (for, say, a Nobel Prize winner or ex-president).

o **Nuyorican Poets Café ★,** 236 E. 3rd St., between avenues B and C (✆ **212/505-8183;** www.nuyorican.org; Subway: F to Second Ave.). For more than 30 years, the Nuyorican has presented poetry, drama, music, and film. The raucous, energetic **Poetry Slams** (the cafe fields a championship Slam Team) present poetry as a sport: Aspiring stars show up and throw down their work in front of mixed crowd and three teams of audience judges, who score them on the poetry and presentation. The Friday slams begin around 10pm (cover charge $10) and feature an invited slam poet. Slam Opens are held most Wednesdays ($7 cover). The storefront bar gets crowded quickly, so get there early on Slam nights.

o **Bowery Poetry Club,** 308 Bowery, at 1st Street, between Houston and Bleecker streets (✆ **212/614-0505;** www.bowerypoetry.com; Subway: F to Second Ave.). "Poetry Czar" (as anointed by the *Village Voice*) Bob Holman opened his "Home for Poetry" in a classic 1850 Bowery building. It's open all day for snacks, coffee, and that writerly essential, hanging out; a good happy hour precedes each evening's festivities. Poetry and fiction readings and slams, open mics, monologues, words with music, and all manner of other spoken word is presented from about 5:30pm each night, with covers ranging from free to

$10. National and rising stars on the poetry/spoken-word scene show up in this sizeable venue.

○ **KGB,** 85 E. 4th St., between Second and Third avenues ((𝄢 **212/505-3360;** www.kgbbar.com; Subway: F to Second Ave.; 6 to Astor Place). This second-floor bar (sadly not wheelchair accessible) in an old East Village brownstone was once a Ukrainian social club and is decorated with vintage Communist memorabilia (pictured below). There's never a cover, so it's affordable to refresh your drink often for the readings held almost every night of the week starting at around 7pm. It's a tiny bar, holding perhaps 40 to 50 comfortably, and double that for a hot reader (think Kaylie Jones, Eileen Myles, A. M. Homes), with theme nights curated by individual writers for poetry, science fiction, and other genres.

FESTIVALS & EVENTS

○ The *New Yorker* magazine (http://festival.newyorker.com) goes into the readings (and lecture and panel discussion) business with its *New Yorker* Festival every early October.

You'll pay around $30 for the privilege of seeing, say, Sherman Alexie or Malcolm Gladwell talk about their work at one of several venues, but the events usually sell out in a flash. There are also free events and book signings throughout the festival.

○ Every New Year's Day, the **Poetry Project at St. Mark's Church,** 131 E. 10th St. ((𝄢 **212/674-0910;** www.poetryproject.com; Subway: N or R to Union Sq.; 6 to Astor Place), presents a marathon poetry reading starting around 2pm, and running till . . . whenever. Poets and performers ranging from Patti Smith to Eric Bogosian, Maggie Estep, and many (many) more read to welcome in the new year and raise money for the Poetry Projects' year-round readings, workshops, and events. Tickets run about $20.

○ **Symphony Space,** 2537 Broadway, at 95th St. ((𝄢 **212/864-5400;** www.symphonyspace.org; p. 409), is the home of both **Selected Shorts** (Oct–Dec) and **Bloomsday on Broadway.** In Selected Shorts, modern and classic short stories are read by professional actors like Blair Brown, Cynthia Nixon, and Denis O'Hare, who read authors like Truman Capote, Jonathan Safran Foer, and Woody Allen. Tickets range from $20 to $30, with discounts for students and seniors. And each June 16 (the day Leopold Bloom took his stroll around Dublin in 1904 in James Joyce's *Ulysses*), an ensemble cast of actors and avid Joyceans does a marathon reading from the masterwork. Its tickets are usually sold out well in advance.

the showroom and the act, and require two-drink or dinner-check minimums. Always reserve ahead, and get the complete lowdown when you do.

Following are some classic venues, but if you like your cabarets on the fun 'n campy side, visit **Marie's Crisis Café** (☎ **212/3243-9323**) or the **Duplex** (p. 442) in Greenwich Village. Or if you're uptown (and into an older crowd) stop by 1924 speakeasy **Bill's Gay Nineties Restaurant and Piano Bar** at 57 E. 54th St. (☎ **212/355-0243;** www.billsnyc.com), which starts the piano sing-alongs around 8:30 nightly.

Ars Nova ★   You won't find traditional cabaret at this 99-seat Hell's Kitchen theater. But nothing is traditional about Ars Nova, and that's the point of the place. It's a venue for emerging artists from playwrights to cabaret acts, and the comedy you'll find here, such as Showgasm, is of the smart, sassy alternative variety. 511 W. 54th St. (at 10th Ave.). ☎ **212/481-9800.** www.arsnovanyc.com. Subway: B, D, or E to Seventh Ave./53rd St.

Cafe Carlyle   Cabaret doesn't get more elite than this—the place where the late, great singer/pianist Bobby Short held court for over 35 years. The club still attracts rarefied talents such as Betty Buckley and Barbara Cook. Expect a high tab—admission is up to $75 with a $30 per-person minimum; with dinner, two people could easily spend $300, but the ambiance is all there. Value-minded cabaret fans can save by reserving standing room (which usually results in a spot at the bar) for just $35. On most Mondays, Woody Allen joins the Eddy Davis New Orleans Jazz Band on clarinet to swing Dixie-style (at an overpriced $85 cover). At the Carlyle Hotel, 35 E. 76th St. (at Madison Ave.). ☎ **212/744-1600.** www.the carlyle.com. Closed July–Aug. Subway: 6 to 77th St.

Feinstein's at the Regency 🎁   Grammy-winning impresario Michael Feinstein calls this elegant cabaret-style supper club home. Cover charges push $100, but in return you get a memorable night of dining and song, and few other cabarets celebrate old-school cool so well. Recent high-wattage talent has included Keely Smith, Patti LuPone, and the man himself. Call ahead to reserve; you can also purchase tickets through Ticketweb. At the Regency Hotel, 540 Park Ave. (at 61st St.). ☎ **212/339-4095,** or 212/307-4100 for Ticketmaster. www.feinsteinsatthe regency.com or www.ticketweb.com. Subway: 4, 5, or 6 to 59th St.

Joe's Pub ★ 🎁   This charming, popular cabaret and supper club, named for the legendary theater icon Joseph Papp, is housed in the Public Theater building—and is everything a New York cabaret should be. The multilevel space serves up an American menu and an occasionally eclectic mix of talent you won't find on any other concert calendar. The sophisticated crowd comes for music and spoken word that ranges from operatic diva Diamanda Galas to solo shows from such Broadway stars as Daphne Rubin-Vega (*Les Miserables*), to first-class pop from husband-and-wife singer/songwriters Michael Penn and Aimee Mann, to modern rumba masters Los Munequitos de Matanzas. There's always jazz on the calendar, and don't be surprised if Broadway actors show up to show off on their off nights. 425 Lafayette St. (btw. Astor Place and 4th St.). ☎ **212/539-8778,** or 212/967-7555 for advance tickets. www.joespub.com. Subway: 6 to Astor Place.

Oak Room Supper Club   Opened in 1939 inside the legendary Algonquin Hotel, the Oak Room is one of the city's most intimate, elegant, and sophisticated spots for cabaret. Harry Connick, Jr., Peter Cincotti, and Diana Krall have played the Oak Room, and current regulars include singers KT Sullivan, Maude Maggart, Barbara Carroll, and Jack Jones, plus occasional smaller names on their way to greatness. Cover charges span $60 to $75. 59 W. 44th St. (btw. Fifth and Sixth aves.). ℭ **212/419-9331.** www.algonquinhotel.com. Closed July–Aug. Subway: B, D, F, or M to 42nd St.

STAND-UP COMEDY

Comedy cover charges are generally in the $8-to-$20 range, with a few exceptions. Most clubs also have a two-drink minimum. Be sure to ask about the night's cover when you make reservations, which are strongly recommended especially on weekends.

Beyond stand-up, you can also see sharp/silly improv at the low-key, affordable **People's Improv Theater,** 123 E. 24th St., near Lexington Avenue (ℭ **212/563-7488;** www.thepit-nyc.com). The Lower East Side's hidden gem the **Slipper Room,** 167 Orchard St., at Stanton Street (ℭ **212/253-7246;** www.slipperroom.com), is a great place to find original comedy through means other than (and in addition to) stand-up.

Carolines on Broadway   Caroline Hirsch presents today's biggest stand-up stars in her upscale, high-priced Theater District showroom—among them are Dave Chapelle, Andrew Dice Clay, Colin Quinn, Kathy Griffin, Gilbert Gottfried, Jimmie Walker ("Dyn-o-mite!"), Pauly Shore, or any number of *Saturday Night Live* alumni. 1626 Broadway (btw. 49th and 50th sts.). ℭ **212/757-4100.** www.carolines.com. Subway: N or R to 49th St.; 1 to 50th St.

Comedy Cellar 🎭   This intimate subterranean club is the venue of choice for stand-up fans in the know, thanks to the best, most consistently impressive lineups in the business. There are two shows a night, each with new and revolving comics like Darrell Hammond, Godfrey, Gregg Rogell, and Ben Bailey. 117 MacDougal St. (btw. Bleecker and W. 3rd sts.). ℭ **212/254-3480.** www.comedycellar.com. Subway: A, B, C, D, E, F, or M to W. 4th St. (use 3rd St. exit).

Dangerfield's   Dangerfield's is the nightclub version of the comedy club, with a mature crowd and a straight-outta-Vegas atmosphere. Claiming to be the "longest-running comedy club in the world," the comedians here are all veterans of the comedy-club and late-night talk-show circuit—"no amateurs or gimmicks," as its website says. 1118 First Ave. (btw. 61st and 62nd sts.). ℭ **212/593-1650.** www.dangerfieldscomedyclub.com. Subway: N or R to Lexington Ave.; 4, 5, or 6 to 59th St.

Gotham Comedy Club ★   Here's the city's trendiest and most sophisticated comedy club. The young talent—Tom Rhodes, Sue Costello, Mitch Fatel, the *Daily Show*'s Lewis Black—is red hot, and you never know what celebrity may take the mic. Comedy Central tapes *Live at Gotham* here with rotating hosts, Monday is the All Pro Show, while Tuesday is set aside for new talent. Gay and lesbian comics take the stage first Wednesdays at Homo Comicus. Call ahead for reservations. 208 W. 23rd St. (btw. Seventh and Eighth aves.). ℭ **212/367-9000.** www.gothamcomedyclub.com. Subway: F, N, or R to 23rd St.

Stand-Up New York   This modest Upper West Side stand-up comedy club hosts young and seasoned comics, plus an occasional pop-in from big-name comedians like Dennis Leary, Chris Rock, Robin Williams, and Mr. Upper West Side himself, Jerry Seinfeld. 236 W. 78th St. (at Broadway). ℭ **212/595-0850.** www.standupny.com. Subway: 1 to 79th St.

Upright Citizens Brigade Theatre ★ 🗲   You've seen their twisted, highly original sketch comedy on Comedy Central—now you can see the Upright Citizens Brigade, New York's premier alternative comedy troupe, live. The best of the

For all kinds of improv, visit the Upright Citizens Brigade.

nonstop hilarity is Sunday's *ASSSSCAT 3000*, the troupe's extra-popular long-form improv show, which often sells out in advance. The company has supplied and continues to invite back quite a few *Saturday Night Live* and other TV and film stars, including Amy Poehler, Tina Fey, and Seth Meyers. Reservations are a must, and tickets are a bargain at (mostly) $10 or less. 307 W. 26th St. (btw. Eighth and Ninth aves.). ✆ **212/366-9176.** www.ucbtheatre.com. Subway: 1 to 23rd St.

BARS & COCKTAIL LOUNGES
TriBeCa

Brandy Library Amber lit and sophisticated, this is your place to be schooled on the finer points of top-shelf liquors. So committed to fine brandy, scotch, and other adult beverages, even the walls are lined with bottles. Great place for a dimly lit date by the fireplace, just remember to dress "smart casual." 25 N. Moore St. (btw. Varick and Hudson sts.). ✆ **212/226-5545.** www.brandylibrary.com. Subway: 1 to Franklin St.

Bubble Lounge From the first cork that popped, this wine bar dedicated to the bubbly was an effervescent hit. More than 300 champagnes and sparkling wines are served in this glamorous living-room setting, more than 30 of them by the glass, to pair with caviar, foie gras, cheese, and sweets. There's live music and DJs most nights of the week. And they keep it classy—no jeans, sneakers, or baseball caps. 228 W. Broadway (btw. Franklin and White sts.). ✆ **212/431-3433.** www.bubblelounge.com. Subway: 1 to Franklin St.

Church Lounge The big, superstylish atrium-lobby bar and restaurant at the Tribeca Grand Hotel is a great place to enjoy a posh cocktail and rub elbows with the neighborhood's chic locals (including many a celebrity). Dress well and call ahead to see what's on tap that evening if you want to experience the height of the action—around 11pm. 2 Sixth Ave. (at White and Church sts.). ✆ **212/519-6600.** www.tribecagrand.com. Subway: 1 to Franklin St.; A, C, or E to Canal St.

Walker's 🎁 Walker's is an old holdout from prefabulous TriBeCa. It's got charm, a tin ceiling, a long wooden bar, oldies on the sound system, and cozy tables where you can dine on good, affordable meat-and-potatoes fare. No need

WHEN ALL THE CITY BECOMES A patio

In New York, nobody lets taxi exhaust or hordes of pedestrians stop them from sitting outside when it's nice out. Because after all, food and drink always taste better alfresco. Following are some standout places for cocktails out of doors, though many of this section's bar listings were included because they feature private patios.

The outdoors—what is it exactly? A balcony? Just an oversize steel step? Rowdy **Jeremy's Ale House,** 228 Front St. (© **212/964-3537;** www.jeremysalehouse.com), near the South Street Seaport, is a hidden, dirt-cheap spot with a view of the Brooklyn Bridge. Further south near Wall Street, you'll find Stone Street transformed into a virtual beer garden thanks to **Ulysses** at 95 Pearl St. (© **212/482-0400;** www.ulyssesfolkhouse.com), an Irish bar and restaurant that in warmer weather sets up long bench tables atop the cobblestones on its north side.

If you're going for trendy, some of the best outdoor drinking can be found at a few select hotels. To find where the eye candy mingles with spectacular views, take the elevator up to the top of the Hotel Gansevoort, 18 Ninth Ave., at 13th Street (© **212/206-6700**) to **Plunge,** where the you can gaze at the skyline by the rooftop pool, all the while sipping crazy-priced cocktails. A few blocks north at the Maritime Hotel, 363 W. 16th St., at Ninth Avenue, the scene on the roof at **Cabanas** (© **212/242-4300**), is like something out of Hollywood. In fact, you'll probably recognize a few

silver-screen denizens sunning themselves. Uptown near Lincoln Center, **the Rooftop** at the Empire Hotel, 44 W. 63rd St. (© **212/265-7400**), offers a glimmering view from its rooftop pool deck, open all summer—just call first to be sure it's not closed for a private event.

Riverside Park (see chapter 6) is a great overall destination, with two great spring/summer outdoor hangouts. There's the **79th Street Boat Basin Café,** 79th Street at the Hudson River (© **212/496-5542;** www.boatbasincafe.com), where starting every March you can sip a drink and watch the boats bob on the river as the sun sets. Also here is **Hurley's Hudson Beach Café,** Riverside Park and 103rd Street (© **917/370-3448**), where beach volleyball games and stunning sunsets are the entertainment, marred only by the constant automobile buzz of the nearby West Side Highway.

By the way, just because a bar has outdoor space doesn't mean it allows smoking in its enclosed space. Read the box "Smoke 'Em If Ya Got 'Em (in Designated Areas)" (p. 437) to find smoke-friendly establishments. Or just head to a more easygoing outer-borough bar.

to get fancy with your drink orders; stick with Guinness or one of the other fine draughts. 16 N. Moore St. (at Varick St.). © **212/941-0142.** Subway: 1 to Franklin St.

Chinatown & Nolita

Fontana's ★ Roomy and welcoming, Fontana's seems simultaneously appropriate for and out of place in upper Chinatown. But no matter—it's a great place to grab a cocktail in a old-school round booth and watch the hipsters flow by. And they will, after about 9 or 10pm, despite its good happy hour from opening (usually at 2pm, or whenever the bartender shows up) 'til 8pm. Also check out the live music downstairs, pool table in back, and punky jukebox. 105 Eldridge St. (btw. Baxter and Mulberry sts.). © **212/334-6740.** www.fontanasnyc.com. Subway: F to Delancey St.; J, M, or Z to Delancey/Essex sts.

Home Sweet Home This former factory on the eastern edge of Chinatown feels like a subterranean hideaway filled with taxidermied and found objects. Fortunately the drinks and DJs make it a draw for the hipster spillover from the Lower East Side who come to dance and flirt. Weekend cover charges are sometimes instituted depending on who's spinning. 131 Chrystie St. (btw. Broome and Delancey sts.). ℂ **212/226-5708.** www.homesweethomebar.com. Subway: B, D to Grand St.; J to Bowery.

Winnie's Karaoke bars are usually predictable, and often forgettable, but Winnie's is an exception. Maybe it's the überenthusiastic Asian singers battling on the mic, or maybe it's the Hawaiian Punch, a sickly sweet drink that, after a couple, will have you crooning in Cantonese. (At least it feels like Cantonese.) Even if you don't partake in the Chinatown embarrassment-fest, you will enjoy others as they throw themselves in the spotlight, fueled by liquid courage. 104 Bayard St. (btw. Baxter and Mulberry sts.). ℂ **212/732-2384.** Subway: J, M, N, Q, R, Z, or 6 to Canal St.

The Lower East Side

You won't be short of choices when it comes to LES bars, especially in the vicinity of Rivington and Allen. Among the following listings, there are many more lively mid- and low-end joints, including **Lolita** (ℂ **212/966-7223**), **Motor City** (ℂ **212/358-1595**), and **St. Jerome's** (ℂ **212/533-1810**).

Barramundi This fun, funky lounge has a friendly staff, daily 6 to 9pm happy hours, and a settled-in feel for a neighborhood overrun by hipster copycats. Come on a weeknight to snare a table in the little corner of heaven out back. A fireplace makes Barramundi almost as appealing on chilly nights. 67 Clinton St. (btw. Stanton and Rivington sts.). ℂ **212/529-6900.** www.barramundiny.com. Subway: F to Delancey St.

The Magician ★ As if with sleight of hand, the Magician somehow manages to be whatever you want it to be. A mellow early- or late-night happy-hour spot, a friendly hangout for groups, or a nonintrusive pickup scene. More than anything it's a conveniently located bar in the middle of all the LES hubbub. Disappear from it all with a good cocktail, and people-watch from the giant windows onto Rivington Street. 118 Rivington St. (at Essex St.). ℂ **212/673-7851.** Subway: F to Delancey St.

Mason Dixon Two words: mechanical bull. For $5 you can ride like an urban cowboy at this giant country-western honky-tonk that sells beer by the pitcher. It's also a sports bar with plenty of big-screen TVs—you can call it friendly fratboy paradise, but you can't say it's not country-fried heaven. 133 Essex St. (btw. Rivington and Stanton sts.). ℂ **212/260-4100.** www.masondixonnyc.com. Subway: F to Delancey St.

Sweet & Lowdown The spartan design of this downstairs wine bar says one thing: Focus on the wine and the fine company. New in 2009, this LES getaway showcases wines from around the country, with some especially good New York bottles at reasonable prices. A great place for good conversation, you can also cleanse your palate with tasty snacks. 123 Allen St. (btw. Delancey and Rivington sts.). ℂ **212/228-7746.** www.sweetandlowdown.com. Subway: F to Delancey St.; J, M, or Z to Delancey/Essex sts.

SoHo

Beyond the following recommendations, try one of western SoHo's new faves: **City Winery,** 155 Varick St. (ℂ **212/608-0555;** www.citywinery.com), makes its own bottles, and hosts a variety of music and special events almost nightly. And don't forget **Milady's** at 160 Prince St. (📞 **212/226-9340**)—perhaps SoHo's last remaining and most beloved dive.

Ear Inn 🎵 There are many debates about which is the oldest bar in New York, and with its 1870s origins and landmark status, Ear Inn is a serious contender for that crown. On the far west of superchic SoHo, this pub is an old-school relief. They pull an excellent Guinness and make a surprisingly good margarita. Live music and Saturday poetry readings often make this small bar feel even smaller. In warm weather, a few tables are set up outside. **Note:** Respect the no-cellphone policy or suffer the consequences. 326 Spring St. (btw. Greenwich and Washington sts.). 📞 **212/226-9060**. www. earinn.com. Subway: C or E to Spring St.; 1 to Houston St.

📎 Whiling Away the Happy Hours

Many of the city's best bars suddenly become more affordable from 4 to 8pm or thereabouts, when it's definitely a happy hour if you can snag one of those signature cocktails ($20 martinis, anyone?) at half price or two-for-one; or maybe there's some free bar food, or another value-saving offer. Happy hour is a great time to stop by those pricey places you've heard so much about. For rundowns on the city's joyful hours at many of the best watering holes, check online at www.sheckysnightlife.com or Murph's NYC Bar Guide at www.murph guide.com.

MercBar Notable for its long tenure in the fickle world of beautiful-people bars, the upscale MercBar has mellowed nicely. The decor bespeaks civilized rusticity with warm woods, a canoe over the bar, copper-top tables, and butter-leather banquettes—think SoHo goes to Yosemite. Look carefully to find it, because there's no sign. 151 Mercer St. (btw. Prince and Houston sts.). 📞 **212/966-2727**. www.mercbar.com. Subway: N or R to Prince St.

Pegu Club ★ Mixologist and co-owner Audrey Saunders, formerly of Bemelman's Bar in the Carlyle Hotel, makes magic with cocktails. In 2005 she opened this upstairs downtown gathering spot where the creative cocktails change seasonally. It helps that the staff uses fresh squeezed juices, homemade ginger beer, and the largest assortment of bitters in town. 77 W. Houston St., 2nd Floor (at W. Broadway). 📞 **212/473-PEGU** [473-7348]. www.peguclub.com. Subway: A, B, C, D, E, F, or M to W. 4th St.

Puck Fair 🍺 This homey pub looks as if it could have been lifted wholesale out of a stylish corner of London and plunked down on this side of the pond. It's genuine through and through, but a young crowd and a hip soundtrack make it feel fun and neighborhoody (unlike the more vintage **Fanelli's**, nearby). More than a dozen beers are on tap and there's a petite mezzanine for people-watching from above. 298 Lafayette St. (just south of Houston St.). 📞 **212/431-1200**. www.puckfair barnyc.com. Subway: F to Broadway/Lafayette St.

The East Village & NoHo

Don't forget to visit the East Village's **McSorley's Old Ale House** (p. 429, "Drinking with Ghosts"), **KGB Bar** (p. 420, "Author! Author! Where to Hear Spoken Word"), and the always dazzling **Holiday Cocktail Lounge** (p. 433, "The New York Dive Experience").

d.b.a. ★ d.b.a. has completely bucked the loungey trend that has taken over the city, instead remaining firmly and resolutely an unpretentious neighborhood

Meet a few comrades at KGB Bar in the East Village.

bar. It's a beer and scotch lover's paradise, with a massive drink menu on giant chalkboards. Owner Ray Deter specializes in British-style cask-conditioned ales (the kind that you pump by hand) and stocks a phenomenal collection of single-malt scotches. Out back is a huge terrace, creating one of the East Village's only beer garden–style spaces. 41 First Ave. (btw. 2nd and 3rd sts.). © **212/475-5097.** www.drinkgoodstuff. com. Subway: F to Second Ave. Also at 113 N. 7th St., Williamsburg, Brooklyn (btw. Berry and Wythe aves.). © **718/218-6006.** Subway: L to Bedford Ave.

Superdive I've never heard of another Manhattan bar that will wheel out a quarter-, half-, or full-size keg to your table. But if you like drinking beer in bulk, make a reservation and head to this Alphabet City joint. Or just stop by for cheap shots or a game of flip-cup. 200 Ave. A (at 13th St.). © **646/448-4854.** www. superdivebar.com. Subway: L to First Ave.

Temple Bar A staple in New York's low-lit lounge scene, Temple Bar is still a gorgeous Deco hangout, with a long L-shaped bar leading to a lovely seating area with velvet drapes, backlighting, and smooth background music. Though expensive, cocktails don't get any smoother than the classic martinis and manhattans served here. Look for the petroglyphlike lizards on the otherwise-unmarked facade. 332 Lafayette St. (just north of Houston St., on the west side of the street). © 212/925-4242. www.templebarnyc.com. Subway: 6 to Bleecker St.

Tom & Jerry's (288 Bar) ★ 🏠 A miraculously unpretentious, affordable neighborhood bar, untainted by SoHo scenesters. It's charm is set off by the vintage collection of *Tom & Jerry*–labeled punchbowl sets and the rotating collection of local artists' works. It's good for beer, good for mixed drinks, and there's almost always an open table or seats at the bar. There's no sign out front, but you'll spy the action through the big front window. 288 Elizabeth St. © **212/260-5045.** Subway: 6 to Bleecker St.

Zum Schneider You know New York has everything when you can find an authentic indoor/outdoor German beer garden in Alphabet City. With long tables and bench seating, it's a fun place for a group but gets crowded on weekends. There are more than a dozen varieties of German beer on tap here, and all are served in fitting steins and glasses. To complement those hearty beers, you can sample equally hearty German fare such as Bavarian blood sausage and homemade pretzels. 107 Ave. C (at 7th St.). © **212/598-1098.** www.zumschneider.com. Subway: F to Second Ave.; L to First Ave.

The Village & Meatpacking District

You could get lost barhopping in these very happening 'hoods. Beyond the following listings, also duck into **WXOU Radio Bar** at 558 Hudson St. (© **212/206-0381**)

DRINKING WITH GHOSTS

The ghosts are everywhere in New York. You might find them in the silent halls of some of the city's greatest structures. Or maybe wandering through narrow downtown streets. But the best place to find the ghosts is in a few of the city's more aged drinking establishments.

Three of the oldest bars in town are a good place to start when seeking out the ghosts. **Pete's Tavern,** 129 E. 18th St., at Irving Place (② **212/473-7676;** www.petestavern.com), claims to be the city's oldest continuing operating establishment. Warm up at Pete's on a cold winter night and after a few frothy pints, you might see writer O. Henry, a regular at Pete's over a century ago, sitting alone and unkempt in a booth, sipping his beer in between paragraphs of his famous 1906-written Christmas tale *Gift of the Magi.*

Across town in the West Village there's the **White Horse Tavern,** 567 Hudson St., at 11th Street (② **212/243-9260**). At this 1880s pub, through the maze of frat boys chugging domestics, you might see a desolate figure, head on table snoring, empty shot glasses in front of him. Could that be the ghost of Dylan Thomas, author of *A Child's Christmas in Wales* and White Horse regular who took his last sip at the legendary tavern in 1953? Or maybe it's just another tipsy yuppie.

McSorley's Old Ale House (pictured at right), 15 E. 7th St., between Second and Third avenues (② **212/474-9148**), is over 140 years old and—and while Pete's is the oldest tavern in New York, McSorley's claims to be the oldest "saloon." If there is indeed a difference, it probably doesn't matter to a ghost. Here, if you can avoid the busloads of fraternity Greeks (not from Greece) who come to pay respects to their shrine, and visit on, say, a quiet weekday afternoon, you might think you see a tall, well-dressed

man sitting at the bar taking notes, nursing an 8-ounce mug of ale. Could that be the ghost of *New Yorker* magazine writer Joseph Mitchell, author of *Joe Gould's Secret?* And are those notes for his 1943 book, *McSorley's Wonderful Saloon?* Well go up and ask him—before he disappears.

Meanwhile over in SoHo (or technically in the neighborhood newly labeled "Hudson Square"), you may hear creaks or cracks beyond the worn floorboards at the 19th-century **Ear Inn** (p. 427). It could be Mickey the sailor, a one-time regular rumored to goose female patrons, light the fireplace, and drain cellphone batteries.

for a nice happy-hour bev, or **Little Branch** at 20 Seventh Ave. S. (✆ **212/929-4360**) for a little live jazz with your cocktail.

In the Meatpacking District, you may like **675 Bar** at 675 Hudson St. (✆ **212/699-2410**) for a retro-cool alternative to the high-priced clubs—complete with comfy seating, video games, and foosball.

Bowlmor/Carnival   Bowlmor is the hipster version of a bowling alley: DJs spin, martinis flow, candy-colored balls knock down Day-Glo pins, and strikes and spares are auto-tallied into the wee hours. Upstairs you'll find an enormous Coney Island–inspired fun-house bar called Carnival, selling alcoholic snow cones and cotton-candy martinis. 110 University Place (btw. 12th and 13th sts.). ✆ 212/255-8188 (Bowlmor). www.bowlmor.com. Subway: 4, 5, 6, L, N, or R to 14th St./Union Sq.

Employees Only ★   Look for the glowing red PSYCHIC sign. Employees Only goes to great lengths to re-create a 1920s speak-easy, complete with tin ceiling and bartenders in period costume. But who needs gimmicks when the cocktails are this good? Drinks are made with the freshest ingredients and top-label liquors, some of them with homemade herb infusions. There's a full menu, but skip the entrees and order a few of the very good appetizers to accompany your drinks, like the ample Serbian charcuterie platter. 510 Hudson St. (btw. Christopher and W. 10th sts.). ✆ 212/242-3021. www.employeesonlynyc.com. Subway: 1 to Christopher St.

Hudson Bar & Books   One of three in New York, this elegant cigar bar has that old-tyme gentleman's-club appeal. Think cool jazz, a copper-topped marble bar, ambient lighting, cozy seating, and an extensive—and expensive—champagne, cocktails, cognacs, and malts menu. The crowd comprises more at-home locals than preening tourists. Open at noon daily, it's a great date place, and Monday nights ladies get free cigars. 636 Hudson St. (btw. Horatio and Jane sts.). ✆ 212/229-2642. www.barandbooks.net. Subway: A, C, or E to 14th St.; L to Eighth Ave.

Kettle of Fish   Take three steps down to enter this friendly neighborhood hangout, where Budweiser bottles are always cheap, and yet you can still get a perfect martini. Sports is usually on one of the three TVs, but thankfully isn't too loud and doesn't draw a fratty crowd. The back room is the place to play pinball, video games, or darts (as long as it's not league night). 59 Christopher St. (just east of

You can bowl, drink and play games of chance and skill at Bowlmor/Carnival.

LATE-NIGHT bites

What night of dancing and/or barhopping until the wee hours is complete without a plate of fries or cheesy omelet just before sunrise? Here's a sampling of some great late-night eats around Manhattan:

All-night diners are pretty common in Manhattan, but the centrally located **Hollywood Diner** at 574 Sixth Ave., at 16th Street (℃ **212/691-8465**), is a finer place to slide into a booth and grab a sobering burger deluxe.

On the higher end, and open until 4am nightly, **Blue Ribbon,** 97 Sullivan St., between Prince and Spring streets (℃ **212/274-0404**), is where the city's top chefs come to unwind after they close their own kitchens. Thanks to a top-notch oyster bar and excellent comfort food, this cozy bistro is always packed, so expect a wait.

You can also check out the West Village stalwart **Corner Bistro,** 331 W. 4th

St. (℃ **212/242-9502**), home to a nearly burgers-only menu 'til 4am. In Chinatown, many restaurants are open late or all night, but don't miss **Wo Hop** (p. 152), open 10am to 7am, for early-morning dumplings.

In the East Village, head to 24-hour **Veselka,** a bustling new-style diner offering eastern European comfort food at good prices, or **Katz's Delicatessen** (p. 149) for first-class Jewish deli eats available Friday and Saturday until 3am (11pm on weeknights).

The Theater District feast offers first-class pastrami and cheesecake until 4am at **Carnegie Deli** (p. 180), and until 2am at the **Stage Deli** (p. 180).

Seventh Ave.). ℃ **212/414-2278.** www.kettleoffishnyc.com. Subway: 1 to Christopher St.; A, B, C, D, E, F, or M to W. 4th St.

Chelsea

The simple alternative to fancy Chelsea bars is the happy-go-lucky **Bunga's Den** at 137 W. 14th St. (℃ **212/242-1040**), with daily happy hours, student discounts, and a beer pong table.

Black Door   Since 2002, this bar has built a solid reputation as a low-key hangout in otherwise trendy Chelsea. Backlit with mirrored walls and black wainscoting, the Black Door is a nice, atmospheric place to sip a cocktail, bottled beer, or any of a dozen good wines. There's plenty of seating, candles on every table, and a marked lack of attitude for a relatively pricey bar. 127 W. 26th St. (btw. Sixth and Seventh aves.). ℃ **212/645-0215.** Subway: 1 to 23rd St.

Bongo 🍸   This casual, comfortable retro-modern lounge is home to well-made, substantial cocktails. Don't miss the house drink, the Bongo 299, made with champagne and Lillet. Even better: Bongo boasts a full raw bar—a half-dozen varieties of oysters, cherrystones, and littlenecks, even lobster and caviar—and an excellent lobster roll. The crowd is hip but not too much so. Come early if you want to have space to sit and eat. 299 Tenth Ave. (btw. 27th and 28th sts.). ℃ **212/947-3654.** www.bongonyc.com. Subway: A, C, or E to 23rd St.

Dusk 🎁   This casual, fun lounge is a great place to hide out. There's a cool mirrored mosaic wall, cozy banquettes, a friendly bar serving affordable drinks, a pool table, and mostly U.K. tunes on the sound system. Expect an easygoing, youngish crowd that stays mellow well into the night. No sign, but look for the three blue lights attached to a dark storefront. Happy hour ends daily at 9pm; Mondays are karaoke night. 147 W. 24th St. (btw. Sixth and Seventh aves.). ℭ **212/924-4490.** www.dusklounge.com. Subway: F to 23rd St.

The Flatiron District, Union Square & Gramercy Park

Two of the city's oldest bars are in the Flatiron District, **Old Town Bar & Restaurant,** 45 E. 18th St. (ℭ **212/529-6713**), and **Pete's Tavern** (p. 429).

Flatiron Lounge ★   Sometimes you go into a swanky, stylish bar and it just feels right—a blend of classy, homey, hip, and straight-up Manhattan. That's the Flatiron. Go in ready for strong, old-fashioned drinks (it helps to overlook the double-digit prices), and you'll milk a chilled cocktail shaker full of joy and relaxation from this place. Inspired by the F. Scott Fitzgerald era, the Flatiron's underscored kitsch is amplified by concoctions added to the menu by expert guest mixologists. 37 W. 19th St. (btw. Fifth and Sixth aves.). ℭ **212/727-7741.** www.flatiron lounge.com. Subway: N, R or F, M to 23rd St.

Rye House   Come here for smoky, small-batch whiskeys and house-made punch served along a long granite bar. Rye House's dark wood suits the simple, rustic decor, and helps you focus on the important things, such as innovative cocktails like Creole daiquiri that combines New Orleans rum with chorizo-infused mescal. You can sober up a little with quality fare from the restaurant. 11 W. 17th St. (btw. Fifth and Sixth aves.). ℭ **212/255-7260.** www.ryehousenyc.com. Subway: F, M, 1, 2, 3 to 14th St.

Union Bar   Big with the after-work suits on weekdays, and the DJ-loving mobs on weekends, this longtime Union Square lounge serves up fancy cocktails, single-malt scotches and a large selection of beer, along with light fare to help soak it up. The bar is known to be a bit of a pick-up spot, so expect flirty dudes equally drawn to televised sports and date-free ladies. 200 Park Ave. S. (at 17th St.). ℭ **212/674-2105.** Subway: L, N, Q, R, 4, 5, 6 to Union Sq.

Times Square & Midtown West

Don't forget to go diving—this neighborhood is home to **Jimmy's Corner** and **Rudy's Bar & Grill** (see "The New York Dive Experience," above). There's also the new **Bowlmor Times Square** at 222 W. 44th St.—though you'll save more dough over at **Frames** or **Lucky Strike,** both just a few blocks west. Sports-themed honky-tonk **Johnny Utah's** is at 25 W. 51st St. (ℭ **212/265-8824**), if you're ready to saddle up a mechanical bull.

Carnegie Club 🎁   Like sister lounge the **Campbell Apartment** (see below), this swellegant lounge is another architecturally magnificent space, with soaring ceilings and an intimate mezzanine, plus a grand stone fireplace—a Gothic mood warmed up with plush, contemporary furnishings and a romantic vibe. *Weekends with Sinatra* stars the Stan Rubin Orchestra in a wonderfully evocative cabaret show devoted to Mr. New York (two shows nightly on Sat; cover $35, plus a two-drink minimum). There's also live swing on Friday. Reservations are recommended on live-music nights. And as one of the city's few cigar bars, be ready for some first- or second-hand smoking. 156 W. 56th St. (btw. Sixth and Seventh aves.). ℭ **212/957-9676.** www.hospitalityholdings.com. Subway: F or Q to 57th St.

THE NEW YORK DIVE EXPERIENCE

Not all of New York nightlife means bars and clubs with expensive cocktails, cover charges, and velvet ropes. There are places that you should be rewarded for braving—old, dark places where the top shelf is low and the characters colorful. Below are some dive bars that are just as New York as their trendy counterparts, but also check out the cheapo **Holiday Cocktail Lounge** at 75 St. Marks Place, near First Avenue (📞 **212/777-9637**)—complete with duct tape on the back booths. If a $9 pitcher and occasional bartender buyback suits you, try **the Patriot Saloon** near City Hall, at 110 Chambers St. (📞 **212/748-1162**).

Jimmy's Corner 140 W. 44th St., between Broadway and Sixth Avenue (📞 **212/221-9510**). Owned by a former boxing trainer, Jimmy's is a tough-guy joint that's been around for decades and survived the Disneyfication of Times Square. Pictures of boxers line the walls, and the jukebox plays lots of R&B and '70's disco. Beer is cheap and drinks aren't fancy. So maybe you should skip the area's theme bars and restaurants and go for an after-theater shot at Jimmy's instead.

Rudy's Bar & Grill 627 Ninth Ave., between 44th and 45th streets (📞 **212/974-9169**). This Hell's Kitchen bastion is no secret; the standing pig out front beckons the masses to suck down cheap beer, including the house brand, Rudy's Red, a weak brew served in pitchers or a huge plastic cup for 3 bucks. Arrive before 5 or 6pm, grab a seat at a duct-taped booth, and keep your eyes open for the bartender doling out free hot dogs. In the summer Rudy's opens its cement back garden for drinks 'n' smokes.

Subway Inn 143 E. 60th St., at Lexington Avenue (📞 **212/223-8929**). An all-time classic dive (pictured at right), the Subway has been around for over 60 years, and some of the regulars have been on their stools the entire time. The red

neon sign marks the spot where inside, no matter what time of day, it's midnight dark. The booths are wobbly and the dusty models of Godzilla and E.T. continue to decorate the shelves behind the bar. You might find workers from the neighborhood's upscale stores and office towers slumming at the Subway, but this joint remains the pinnacle of divedom.

Tap a Keg 2731 Broadway, between 103rd and 104th streets (📞 **212/749-1734**). This dog-friendly establishment owns the king of the dive-bar mottos: "Beer is much more than just a breakfast drink." Come here for the 7-hour happy hour; stay for the cheap pool table, dart board, video games, and three TVs.

Hudson Bar Hip and futuristic is Hudson Bar, in the Hudson Hotel, which glows from its underlit floor, while the low ceiling wears a Crayola-like fresco by Francesco Clemente. In between you'll find a tony, older-than-you'd-expect crowd and a one-of-a-kind cocktail menu. Enter at street level, on the Ninth Avenue side of the hotel's nondescript main entrance; dress well to avoid attitude, if that's

CHECKING INTO HOTEL BARS

A hotel bar should provide comfort and hospitality to the out-of-town visitor. And in New York, it's also likely to be a destination unto itself for locals, too. There are many fine ones whose throngs of moneyed patrons jockey for limited seats, like the **Lobby Bar** at the Bowery Hotel ((*C* **212/505-9100**) and **Bar Pleiades** at the Upper East Side's Surrey Hotel ((*C* **212/772-2600**), but here are the most noteworthy:

Ace Hotel Lobby Bar   in the Ace Hotel, 20 W. 29th St., at Broadway ((*C* **212/679-2222;** www.acehotel.com). The Ace is easily the hippest of its kind since it opened in 2009 in the former Hotel Breslin space. Get here before evening time if you want a shot at a seat; otherwise expect to sip your delightful $11 Breslin bloody mary while mingling amongst the well-dressed patrons in this gorgeous nouveau-classic setting. The sudsy, proprietary Breslin Aberdeen, a hand-pumped, cask-conditioned, Scotch-style ale, is not to be missed.

Bemelmans Bar   in the Carlyle Hotel, 35 E. 76th St., at Madison Avenue ((*C* **212/744-1600;** www.thecarlyle.com). A New York classic, here is everything you want in a hotel bar: white-coated service; lush seating with many dark romantic corners to sink into; a nice mix of locals and guests; and incredible cocktails, such as the Old Cuban, a mojito topped with champagne. The bar is named after children's book illustrator Ludwig Bemelmans, who created the *Madeline* books after he painted the whimsical mural here.

The Standard   in the Standard Hotel, 848 Washington St., at 13th Street ((*C* **212/645-4646;** www.standardhotels.com). Planted around the High Line elevated park, take your pick of the Top of the Standard, Le Bain, Living Room, or street-level Biergarten, and take in the views of the city and the beautiful people at this Meatpacking fashion hotspot. The place gets exclusive after about 9pm, so arrive on the early side to settle in and enjoy one of the zingy cocktails.

King Cole Bar   in the St. Regis, 2 E. 55th St., at Fifth Avenue ((*C* **212/753-4500;** www.kingcolebar.com). The birthplace of the bloody mary, this theatrical spot may just be New York's most historic hotel bar. The Maxfield Parrish mural (pictured below) alone is worth the price of a classic cocktail (ask the bartender to tell you about the "hidden" meaning of the painting). The one drawback is the bar's small size; after-work hours and holiday times, it's usually jammed.

Oak Room at the Algonquin in the Algonquin Hotel, 59 W. 44th St., between Fifth and Sixth avenues ((*C* **212/840-6800;** www.algonquinhotel.com). The splendid oak-paneled lobby of this venerable literati-favored hotel was made to linger over pre- or post-theater cocktails. You'll feel the spirit of Dorothy Parker and the Algonquin Round Table that pervades the room. Try the Matilda, a light, refreshing blend of orange juice, Absolut Mandarin, triple sec, and champagne, named after the Algonquin's legendary feline in residence.

possible. 356 W. 58th St. (btw. Eighth and Ninth aves.). 📞 **212/554-6000.** www.hudson hotel.com. Subway: A, B, C, D, or 1 to 59th St./Columbus Circle.

Mickey Mantle's   Opened in 1988, Mickey Mantle's is the sort of gimmicky sports bar that most grown-up cocktail seekers will want to avoid. But then, it's a good place for kids and baseball buffs, with plenty of Yankee memorabilia on the walls and sports on all the televisions—a great place to watch a game. Just stick with the basics: beer and burgers. 42 Central Park South (btw. Fifth and Sixth aves.). 📞 **212/688-7777.** www.mickeymantles.com. Subway: F to 57th St.

Morrell Wine Bar & Cafe   One of the leading wine purveyors in America, Morrell & Company, created the ideal place to sample the first-rate collection of vintages in comfort. Situated at the heart of Rockefeller Center, just across the alley from the plaza, the bi-level space is contemporary and attended by an extremely knowledgeable waitstaff. Make reservations if you're in for dinner. 1 Rockefeller Plaza (at 49th St.). 📞 **212/262-7700.** www.morrellwinebar.com. Subway: B, D, F, or V to 47th–50th sts./Rockefeller Center.

Russian Samovar ★   Of course it's a restaurant with Russian food—but the vodka is the main attraction of this Theater District legend. There are over 20 flavors of house-infused vodkas including dill, garlic, ginger, tarragon, and, host and impresario Roman Kaplan's favorite, cranberry-lemon. Despite their effects, it's difficult to resist sampling the diverse vodkas while listening to standards by the house pianist. You might want to soften the bite of the vodka with a few appetizers such as the Fish Platter, a selection of smoked fish and a little caviar. Just don't make this a pre-theater stop—you'll never make it to your show. 256 W. 52nd St. (btw. Eighth Ave. and Broadway). 📞 **212/757-0168.** www.russiansamovar.com. Subway: 1 to 50th St.

Midtown East

The Campbell Apartment ★   This unique, swank lounge is hidden away on the southwest mezzanine level inside Grand Central Terminal. It was created out of the former office of 1920s mogul John W. Campbell, who transformed the space into a pre-Renaissance palace worthy of a Medici. The high-ceilinged room has been restored to its full Florentine glory, and serves wines and champagnes by the glass, single-malt scotches, and haute appetizers to a well-heeled commuting crowd. Call ahead before heading over, as the space is sometimes closed for private parties. No sportswear allowed. In Grand Central Terminal, 15 Vanderbilt Ave. 📞 **212/953-0409.** www.hospitalityholdings.com. Subway: S, 4, 5, 6, or 7 to 42nd St./Grand Central.

The Ginger Man   The big bait at this upscale draught bar is the 66 gleaming tap handles lining the wood-and-brass bar, dispensing everything from Sierra Nevada to hard cider to cask-conditioned ales—and perfectly poured Guinness pints. The cavernous space has a clubby feel. It's the kind of place that balances the warmth of a dive bar with the posh spirit necessary for a thriving Midtown pub. 11 E. 36th St. (btw. Fifth and Madison aves.). 📞 **212/532-3740.** www.gingerman-ny. com. Subway: 6 to 33rd St.

Upper West Side

Dublin House   Like a welcoming beacon, the Dublin House's neon harp blinks invitingly. In 1921 this former orphanage was rebuilt as a no-frills Irish saloon. There's a long, narrow barroom up front and a bigger room in the back that's good for groups. Original wood veneer detail remains, adding to the pub's charm. The Guinness is cheap and drawn perfectly by the very able and sometimes crusty bartenders. Best enjoyed on weekday evening when the regulars rule, rather than on weekends and when the place is overrun with amateurs. 225 W. 79th St. (btw. Broadway and Amsterdam Ave.). ℂ **212/874-9528.** www.dublinhousenyc.com. Subway: 1 to 79th St.

Wine and Roses   This sophisticated wine bar serves dozens of monthly changing reds and whites by the glass and over 100 by the bottle, all sourced from boutique wineries. The impressive U-shaped granite bar makes for a great place to mingle with fellow winos—but with a seating capacity of only 35 the joint fills up fast, and they don't take reservations. 286 Columbus Ave. (btw. 73rd and 74th sts.). ℂ **212/579-9463.** www.wineandrosesbar.com. Subway: 1, 2, or 3 to 72nd St.

Upper East Side

The UES is littered with Irish pubs and sportsbars, but if you want to play 'em instead of just watching, drop by **Eastside Billiards & Bar** at 163 E. 86th St. (ℂ **212/831-7665**), with loads of games and happy hour 'til 7pm.

Auction House ★   Great drinks, red velvet couches, and a mahogany bar make this uptown lounge a welcome reprieve from the fratty hangouts that line Second Avenue. Dim lighting, candlelit fireplace, and chill jukebox enhance the joint's romantic vibe, though the tasty cocktails and 25 and older crowd help a lot, too. There's no sign so just look for an American flag in the front window. 300 E. 89th St. (at Second Ave.). ℂ **212/427-4458.** Subway: 4, 5, or 6 to 86th St.

Great Hall Balcony Bar 🔲   One of Manhattan's best cocktail bars is open only on Friday and Saturday—and only from 4 to 8:30pm. The Metropolitan Museum of Art transforms the lobby's mezzanine into a cocktail-and-classical-music lounge twice weekly, offering a marvelous only-in–New York experience. The music is usually provided by a piano and string quartet. You'll have to pay the $20 (suggested) museum admission, but the galleries are open until 9pm. Also check out the Roof Garden Martini Bar in warmer months. At the Metropolitan Museum of Art (Fifth Ave. at 82nd St.). ℂ **212/535-7710.** www.metmuseum.org. Subway: 4, 5, or 6 to 86th St.

Trinity Pub   One of the more pleasant of the seemingly endless neighborhood pubs, Trinity looks like a homey library but drinks like an Irish draught house. Women needn't be shy to come here alone—the matured frat boys who frequent the place know to keep their stares (and hands) to themselves. 299 E. 84th St. (at Second Ave.) ℂ **212/327-4450.** trinitypubnyc.com. Subway: 4, 5, or 6 to 86th St.

Harlem

It's hard to find a Harlem lounge that doesn't place a premium on good music, but **Shrine World Music Venue,** at 2271 Adam Clayton Powell Blvd. (ℂ **212/690-7807**), is a reliably cool place to hang with locals and hear live music and other multimedia art *sans* cover charge.

Bier International   Don't come here for cocktails—Harlem's proud beer garden centers on its 20 draught flavors (plus lots more international bottle brands) and hearty German food to match. It's giant glass front windows open in warmer weather to give an alfresco feel to its indoor picnic-table seating. 2099 Frederick Douglass Blvd. (btw. 113th and 114th sts.). ℂ **212/876-8838.** www.bierinternational.com. Subway: B, C to Cathedral Pkwy./110th St.

Creole   Tucked away in El Barrio (also known as east Harlem), Creole is a welcome addition to the uptown music scene. It's is an intimate bar/restaurant that features solid jazz, Latin, R&B, and, on Sunday, gospel. Sit at the bar or enjoy the music while chowing down on very good Southern/Cajun specialties—the gumbo might be the best in the city. Entertainment begins at 8:30pm, but you might want to venture in a little early for Creole's fun happy hour from 3 to 7pm. 2167 Third Ave. (at 118th St.). ✆ **212/876-8838.** www.creolenyc.com. Subway: 6 to 116th St.

67 Orange Street   Locale proprietor Karl Franz Williams opened this ambient Harlem outpost to evoke the first black-owned bar in the city—the 19th-century Almack's Dance Hall—which held this address in the 1840s. Sensational mixologist Kali Irwin whips up original cocktails with innovative ingredients, like artichoke, rhubarb, and pisco . . . all in drinks that go well with the raw bar. 2082 Frederick Douglass Blvd. (at 113th St.). ✆ **212/662-2030.** www.67orangestreet.com. Subway: B, C to Cathedral Pkwy./110th St.

Outer Boroughs

For the real New York experience you have to mingle with the locals—and a growing number of them are hanging out at cool bars in Brooklyn and Queens, where prices are reasonable, music is great, and tourists aren't jamming up the place.

It would take a whole separate book to list all of the amazing outer-borough haunts, but here's a small, subway-friendly sampling of the can't-miss variety.

Bohemian Beer Hall & Garden ★★ 🎁   At one time there were hundreds of outdoor German beer gardens in New York. They're almost all gone now, except for this Astoria survivor—with its football-field-size "garden" of tables and very happy honorary Bohemians. Try a pitcher of one of the Czech beers to drink under the stars on a balmy night from spring to autumn. If you're hungry, there are eastern European specialties such as pork schnitzel and Hungarian goulash to accompany your beer. The garden features live jazz every Thursday, and if you are a member of the Bohemian Benevolent Society of Astoria (because who isn't?), you get 10% off food. And even when the garden isn't open, you can still get a taste of Bohemia (and beer) indoors year-round. It's a supereasy walk from the elevated Queens subway. 29-19 24th Ave., Astoria, Queens (btw. 29th and 31st sts.). ℂ **718/274-4925.** www.bohemianhall.com. Subway: N to Astoria Blvd.

Floyd's You can't go wrong with this Brooklyn Heights favorite for bevs, indoor bocce, and beer cheese (yes, folks, it's house-made). Well-worn furniture is always a sign of a popular joint. Here the friendly bar staff is happy to pump out whatever you're drinking, and don't mind if you bring in takeout from one of the neighboring restaurants—a common occurrence outside of Manhattan. With a jukebox that covers everything from punk to honky-tonk, Floyd's is the kind of fun that only an outer-borough bar can be. 131 Atlantic Ave., Brooklyn Heights. (near Henry St.). ℂ **718/858-5810.** www.floydny.com. Subway: 2, 3, 4, or 5 to Borough Hall; A, C, or G to Hoyt/Schermerhorn; F or G to Bergen St.

Pete's Candy Store ★ This former candy store is Williamsburg's best place for live entertainment (readings? In a bar?) and games. The bar up front features the famous biweekly spelling bee held every other Monday, bingo on Tuesdays, a quiz-off on Wednesdays, and Scrabble on Saturdays. If games are not your thing, there is live music nightly featuring some of New York's most promising up-and-coming rock bands. 709 Lorimer St. (btw. Richardson and Frost sts.), Williamsburg, Brooklyn. ℂ **718/302-3770.** www.petescandystore.com. Subway: L to Lorimer St.

Spuyten Duyvil Hard-core beer aficionados should hop on the L train to Williamsburg to find the city's most interesting selection. But you need to know your stuff; otherwise, the vast offerings—from Peak Organic Espresso Amber on tap to Proef Flemish Primitive in bottle—will have your head spinning before you're done with your mini taste samples. Once you settle on some obscure microbrew, relax and enjoy the equally eclectic selection of songs from the jukebox. If you insist, wine is also served, along with cheese and meat platters. But, even better, cross Metropolitan Avenue and take out some of Spuyten Duyvil's sister establishment Fette Sau's (p. 206) barbecue to go with your beer. 359 Metropolitan Ave. (at Havemeyer St.). ℂ **718/963-4140.** www.spuytenduyvilnyc.com. Subway: L to Lorimer St.

DANCE CLUBS & PARTY SCENES

No New York trends fluctuate quite as much as the club scene. So remember: Finding and going to the latest hot spot is not worth agonizing over. Clubgoers spend their lives obsessing over "the Scene." But this is New York, and there are so many choices no one club is the empirical best.

By the way, "clubs" as actual, physical spaces don't mean much anymore. The hungry-for-nightlife crowd now often follow their favorite dance party, who keep trendsetting by switching nights and venues regularly.

The tracking game is best left to the perennial party crowds who know the guy at the door (who lets them in for free) and someone at the bar (who comps them drinks). So the best advice is to find a club you like and enjoy the crowd that enjoys it with you. And ladies, be prepared for that inescapable meat-market vibe.

Now then, here is rundown of popular dance clubs, most of which are accessible more than elite—since the elite clubs often lead to let-downs in many ways. Naturally, you can find more listings for the most current hot spots and touring parties in the **publications and online sources** listed at the start of this chapter—many will point you to the nightclub nexus of NYC, the Meatpacking District, where the cobblestone streets are littered with scenesters nightly.

Additional online sources that might score you reduced admissions or get on a guest list to select clubs include **www.clubplanet.com** and **www.sheckys nightlife.com**. Many clubs offer the guest-list sign-up service on their websites, too. No matter what, call ahead, because schedules change constantly and can do so at the last minute.

New York nightlife starts late, of course. With the exception of places that have scheduled performances, dancefloors stay almost empty until about 11pm. Don't depend on plastic—bring cash, and plan on most of it disappearing. Cover charges go up every year ($20 on average, and often mandatory $5+ coat check), and party producers usually increase the covers later in the evening to get more people in early.

Bar 13 ✦ This unpretentious, two-story club is a great place to dance the night away (with a bonus rooftop garden to cool off). It's stylish but unpretentious, with a steady roster of fun weekly parties. The nightly parties run the gamut from disco and '80s new wave, reggae, progressive house, and trance, to poetry slams and performance art. If there's a cover, it's usually $5 to $10. Happy hour offers two-for-one drinks from 5 to 9pm, with occasional open-bar specials (check the website). 35 E. 13th St. (btw. Broadway and University Place), 2nd Floor. ℂ **212/979-6677.** www.bar13.com. Subway: 4, 5, 6, L, N, Q, or R to 14th St./Union Sq.

Cielo At this longtime Meatpacking District fave, you'll find a great sound system pumping house and techno from some of the world's best DJs. There's a sunken dance floor with seating wrapped around it, a smoking patio out back, and lots of Wall Street types in untucked button-downs cruising for someone to dance with. Covers are usually $25. 18 Little W. 12th St. (btw. Ninth Ave. and Washington St.). ℂ **212/645-5700.** www.cieloclub.com. Subway: A, C, or E to 14th St.; L to Eighth Ave.

Greenhouse This bi-level party space used to be home to the old-school Club Shelter, but now dubs itself New York's first eco-friendly nightclub. It often hosts special parties on most Mondays through Wednesdays (most are open to the public), with house, electronica, and other fist-pumping DJ sets through the weekend when its alter-ego club (Area) Code takes over of the turntables. Expect to pay around $20 to enter. 150 Varick St., corner of Van Dam. ℂ **646/862-6117.** www. greenhouseusa.com. Subway: 1 to Houston St.; C or E to Spring.

(Le) Poisson Rouge Amid the local haunts of the NYU crowd is this afford-able versatile club. In addition to live rock, jazz, classical, and comedy shows, LPR is home to wild late-night parties like Friday's 11pm to 4am Freedom Party, which is heavy on the '80s, disco, and old-school hip-hop. It's on the affordable side with entry around $10, with original art for sale in its gallery spaces. 158 Bleecker St. (btw. Sullivan and Thompson sts.). (C) **212/505-FISH** (3474). www.lepoisson rouge.com. Subway: A, C, E, B, D, F to W. 4th St.

Pacha No, you are not on exotic Ibiza, but in Hell's Kitchen. Enter Pacha and wade through the club's four levels, marvel at the palm trees, and be awestruck by the bikini-clad go-go girls dancing in the red-lit showers. This is one of Man-hattan's busiest venues, often hosting multiple parties on most nights. Be ready to ogle and be ogled, and to leave broke. FYI, you can get on the entry list and pay your cover in advance online ($20–$35). 618 W. 46th St. (btw. Eleventh Ave. and the West Side Hwy.). (C) **212/209-7500.** www.pachanyc.com. Subway: A, C, E, or 7 to 42nd St.

Santos Party House ★ Things are always more easygoing downtown, like at this two-story bar and dance club in Chinatown. Huge, simple, and loud, Santos hosts live music and all kinds of DJs on two floors, regularly packing the house with its diversity (including all-ages nights). Check the calendar and take your pick from the bevy of music genres. Covers are around $10. 96 Lafayette St. (at Walker St.). (C) **212/714-4646.** www.santospartyhouse.com. Subway: J, M, N, Q, R, Z, or 6 to Canal St.

GETTING beyond THE VELVET ROPE

If you are somewhat masochistic, and are determined to get into that oh-so-trendy club you heard about back home, here are a few pointers that may help tip the scale in your favor:

○ **Dress well and fashionably.** Like it or not, the doorman is sizing you up to decide if you're hip enough to make the scene. If you want to get in, work it. Bribes can help too, whether it's a cool $50 or show/ballgame tickets.

○ **Call ahead.** A lot of places have Facebook pages and websites that make it easy to get your name on the list.

○ **Arrive early.** The bouncers just aren't as vigilant at 10pm when the place is half empty. Weeknights are also a better bet. Some may say that eager beavers are disdained for showing up too early, but it's the safer bet—plus you get to find a good spot inside and people-watch the night away.

○ **Be cool.** No matter how obnoxious the doorman may be (after all, it's their specialty), charm him. Giving attitude will always hinder your chances, but a nice smile and a little charisma won't. And remember to be on the down-low with your coaxing; it comes across more seasoned.

○ **Don't try to fast-talk your way in.** These guys have heard it all, so don't drop names or make up some story to get in the door. If you're not wanted, why bother? If it's like this outside, imagine inside. Take your business to a friendlier establishment, where you'll be happier in the long run.

Swing 46 🎁 And now for a little something different. Swing is a nightly affair at this Theater District jazz and supper club (supper not required). Music is live nightly except Monday, when a DJ takes over, and runs the gamut from big band to boogie-woogie to jump blues. Even first-timers can join in the fun, with free swing lessons usually offered Friday and Saturday at 9:30pm. No jeans or sneakers; music charges are $12, and $15 Friday and Saturday. 349 W. 46th St. (btw. Eighth and Ninth aves.). ✆ **212/262-9554.** www.swing46.com. Subway: C or E to 50th St.

Webster Hall ★ This New York institution may be the biggest club in the city, and its four wildly-decorated floors can make you feel like you were club-hopping even though you only paid one cover charge (usually around $30, cheaper if you buy online before the show). It's usually open Thursday through Sunday, when the music can span electro, new wave, disco, and indie—all in a single night. The place draws a great mix of club-goers, who flock for the high energy and eclectic atmosphere. 125 E. 11th St. (btw. Third and Fourth aves.). ✆ **212/353-1600.** www.webster hall.com. Subway: Subway: L, N, Q, R, 4, 5, 6 to Union Sq.

THE GAY & LESBIAN SCENE

To get a thorough, up-to-date take on what's happening in gay and lesbian nightlife, pick up copies of *Next* (www.nextmagazine.com), *GO Magazine* (www.gomag.com), or *Gay City News* (www.gaycitynews.com). They're available for free in bars and clubs all around town or at the **Lesbian and Gay Community Center,** at 208 W. 13th St., between Seventh and Eighth avenues (✆ **212/620-7310;** www.gaycenter.org). *Time Out New York* also has a solid gay and lesbian section. Also try **Metrosource NY** (www.metrosource.com), a bimonthly magazine with an extensive entertainment section.

Of course, in New York many bars, clubs, cabarets, and lounges are mixed with both gay and straight clientele (especially in 'hoods like the Village, Chelsea, and Hell's Kitchen). So in addition to the choices below, you'll find that several of the clubs listed above in "Dance Clubs & Party Scenes" cater to a gay crowd at least a few nights of the month.

New York is also home to dozens of gay bars (though only a small handful of dedicated lesbian bars), so always be friendly, because asking people in one bar can lead you to discover another new hotspot or otherwise dandy one we didn't have room for here.

Some LGBT parties (especially girl parties, like Tues night's long-running **Snapshot;** www.snapshotnyc.com) tour different clubs around town—the latest local sources will list them. That goes for country line dancing, too, where you can rely on the **Big Apple Ranch** (www.bigappleranch.com) to tip you off to where the gay cowboys and cowgirls are hitching up for the night.

There are also random gay events to be discovered around town all year round, like **Homo Comicus** stand-up at **Gotham Comedy Club** (p. 423).

Barracuda ★ Chelsea is central to gay life—and gay bars. In the heart of the 'hood is this relaxed bar that remains a favorite, repeatedly voted "Best Bar" by local gay mags. The hunky bartenders do not go unnoticed; they're complemented by the good music. Out front there's a sexy bar for cruising/sipping, and comfy couches in back. Look for regular cabaret shows, and be warned—the place gets crowded. 275 W. 22nd St. (btw. Seventh and Eighth aves.). ✆ **212/645-8613.** Subway: C, E, or 1 to 23rd St.

Boiler Room This down-to-earth East Village bar is a favorite gay dive. Despite the mixed guy-girl crowd, it's a serious cruising scene for well-sculpted beautiful boys and a perfectly fine hangout for those who'd rather play pool. Economical happy hours daily from 4 to 8pm. 86 E. 4th St. (btw. First and Second aves.). ☏ 212/254-7536. www.boilerroomnyc.com. Subway: F to Second Ave.

Brandy's Piano Bar Though mainly gay, this intimate, old-school Upper East Side piano bar attracts a mixed crowd for the friendly atmosphere and nightly entertainment. The talented waitstaff does most of the singing while waiting for their big break, but enthusiastic patrons regularly join in. 235 E. 84th St. (btw. Second and Third aves.). ☏ 212/744-4949. www.brandysnyc.com. Subway: 4, 5, or 6 to 86th St.

Cubby Hole ★ This longtime lesbian and gay hangout/watering hole is tiny, but its modest size only adds to the intimate appeal—even though "intimate" sometimes means way too packed. In some bars, being crowded can breed attitude—not so at the Cubby Hole, where the faces always seem to be smiling. Could it be the great jukebox, or free popcorn, or great daily drink specials . . . or maybe the crazy colorful décor? Best not to ask too many questions and just enjoy it. 281 W. 12th St. (at W. 4th St.). ☏ 212/243-9041. www.cubbyholebar.com. Subway: A, C, E, or L to 14th St.

The Duplex Here lies the heart of the gay cabaret and piano-bar scene. Expect a high camp factor and lots of good-natured fun that runs the gamut from mini-musicals to drag revues to stand-up comedy. Expect occasional small music charges or drink minimums. The summer's outdoor seating is lovely, and if the cabaret is not your thing head upstairs for plain old drinkin'. 61 Christopher St. (at Seventh Ave.). ☏ 212/255-5438. wwwtheduplex.com. Subway: 1 to Christopher St.; A, C, E, B, D, F to W. 4th St.

Downtown diva Hedda Lettuce presides over many festive events on the GLBT scene.

Gym Sportsbar   New York's gay sports bar has nine flatscreen televisions, a pool table, video games, and other jock paraphernalia. In fact, the Gym could pass for any fratty sports bar—a draw for some men all by itself. 167 Eighth Ave. (btw. 18th and 19th sts.). ✆ **212/337-2439.** www.gymsportsbar.com. Subway: A, C, E, or L to 14th St.

Henrietta Hudson   "Hank's" is well-known women's bar/lounge that attracts a good mix of uptown lipstick lesbians, clubgoers, and NYU gays, depending on the night. Dance parties, usually Thursday through Sunday, are primarily the domain "bridge-and-tunnel" suburban ladies who are fine paying $5 to $10 to jam onto the tiny dance floor. More local New York lesbians might head there too if not for the attitude that usually taints the vibe. Still, it's a place to go during calmer happy hours, or when Cubby Hole is too packed. 438–444 Hudson St. (at Morton St.). ✆ **212/924-3347.** www.henriettahudson.com. Subway: 1 to Houston St.

Julius 👬   Not only is this the oldest gay bar in New York, Julius is one of the city's all-time oldest barrooms, open since 1864. That age certainly lends it that authentic Village dive appeal. But no matter how weathered it is, men (and a few women) still flock here on weekends for its good burgers and reasonable prices, including half-price happy hour drinks. 159 W. 10th St. (btw. 21st and 22nd sts.). ✆ **212/243-1928.** juliusbarnyc.com. Subway: 1 to Christopher St.; A, C, E, B, D, F to W. 4th St.

Metropolitan ★   The giant patio out back is the main reason to come to this favorite Brooklyn semidive bar. Spacious it may be during the daily 3 to 8pm happy hour (when drinks are two for one), but the place usually gets crazy busy after 10pm—especially on Wednesday nights for the long-running women's party. 559 Lorimer St. (at Metropolitan Ave.). ✆ **718/599-4444.** Subway: L to Lorimer St.; G to Metropolitan-Grand.

Nowhere Bar   For a nice, roomy boys 'n girls space, this bar is usually notably quiet. It must be the somewhat unexpected location east of Union Square—because it can't be the cheap drinks, good beer selection, or friendly bartenders, most of whom will treat you more than right if you buy them a shot. There are also a great jukebox and pool table in back. 322 E. 14th St. (btw. First and Second aves.). ✆ **212/477-4744.** Subway: L to First Ave.

The Phoenix ★   Open daily until 4am, the Phoenix doubles as a neighborhood hang out (by evening) and crazy party (by late night). The bar is dark and friendly, has a punk-filled jukebox and cheap happy hours (from 4 to 8pm), and if the guys aren't doing anything for you there's both pool and a Ms. Pac-Man game for electronic diversions. 447 E. 13th St. (btw. First Ave. and Ave. A). ✆ **212/477-9979.** Subway: L to First Ave.

RF Lounge ★   The former lesbian landmark Rubyfruit's became RF Lounge in 2009, and is now outfitted with modern décor on its two floors, along with a young, beautiful bar staff. Daily happy hour (4–7pm) kicks off the nightly draw, with DJs and other party nights all through the week and weekend, including the Tea Dance every Sunday at 5pm. 531 Hudson St. (at Charles St.). ✆ **212/414-9500.** www.rflounge.com. Subway: A, C, E to 14th St.; L to Eighth Ave.

Splash/SBNY   Beautiful bartenders, sexy video screens, New York's best drag queens—Splash has it all. Theme nights are a big deal. The most fun is Musical Mondays, dedicated to Broadway and film musicals and video clips from 7pm to midnight. And with its wall-to-wall buff, hairless young bucks, this bar proudly

TIME TO HIT THE slope

Park Slope, Brooklyn, is commonly recognized as an ever-gentrifying family neighborhood—but don't be fooled, this is one of the gayest 'hoods in NYC. It just doesn't look that way since the population is generally so hip everyone blends together.

Many gay and lesbian bars in the Slope have come and gone, but there are plenty of queer parties that land at the Bell House, Southpaw, Bar 4, and other joints. And more importantly, there are two local anchors that draw both the guys and the gals, and they're essentially kitty-corner from one another.

Ginger's Bar, 363 Fifth Ave. (*(C)* **718/ 788-0924**), is the local lesbian pub where women gather for $5 pints, cheap pool, rowdy karaoke nights, and a nice back garden that's open year-round. It's happy hour 'til 8pm daily, and the place is consistently full of women from all five boroughs (and elsewhere) on weekends.

For the fellas, stop by **Excelsior,** 390 Fifth Ave. (*(C)* **718/832-1599**). There you'll find cute, down-to-earth Brooklyn guys, along with the expected bears and diva boys. The bartenders are the sweetest guys who ever served you a beer, and there's a back balcony and downstairs patio with seating under the stars.

wears the crown of "Best Gay Club" (GayCities.com, 2010) for its consistent Chelsea-boy appeal. 50 W. 17th St. (btw. Fifth and Sixth aves.). *(C)* **212/691-0073.** www. splashbar.com. Subway: F or M to 14th St.; 4, 5, 6, L, N, Q, or R to 14th St./Union Sq.

Stonewall Inn 📷   Here is the bar where it all started back in June 1969—the gay revolution that launched the global Gay Pride movement. Today, a mixed crowd—old and young, male and female, beautiful and fabulous—makes this an easy place to begin a tour of NYC queer history. Duck in to be part of the legend, then stay for one of the rotating theme nights or upstairs dance parties. And ladies, Stonewall is catering to lesbians much more than it ever has, including the Friday night Lesbo-a-Go-Go party at 10pm. 53 Christopher St. (east of Seventh Ave.). *(C)* **212/488-2705.** www.thestonewallinnnyc.com. Subway: 1 to Christopher St.; A, C, E, B, D, F to W. 4th St.

PLANNING YOUR TRIP TO NEW YORK CITY

9

A s with any trip, a little preparation is essential before you start your journey to New York City. This chapter provides a variety of planning tools, including information on how to get there and quick, on the ground resources.

GETTING THERE
By Plane

Three major airports serve New York City: **John F. Kennedy International Airport** (© 718/244-4444) in Queens, about 15 miles (1 hr. driving time) from midtown Manhattan; **LaGuardia Airport** (© 718/533-3400), also in Queens, about 8 miles (30 min.) from Midtown; and **Newark Liberty International Airport** (© 973/961-6000) in nearby New Jersey, about 16 miles (45 min.) from Midtown. Information about all three airports is available online at **www. panynj.gov/airports**. I prefer LaGuardia, because it's the closest airport to Manhattan. However, JFK has the best reputation for timeliness, such as it is, among New York–area airports; Newark has the worst. None will offer the best airport experience of your life. *Note:* As we all know, the experience of flying has gotten more and more complicated. Now we have body scans and patdowns. This, of course, is not limited to our fair city, but it's best to plan as best you can to deal with it all.

Almost every major domestic carrier serves at least one of the New York–area airports; most serve two or all three.

GETTING INTO TOWN FROM THE AIRPORT

Since there's no need to rent a car in New York, you're going to have to figure out how you want to get from the airport to your hotel and back.

For transportation information for all three airports (JFK, LaGuardia, and Newark), call **Air-Ride** (© 800/247-7433), which offers 24-hour recorded details on bus and shuttle companies and car services registered with the New York and New Jersey Port Authority. Similar information is available at **www. panynj.gov/airports**; click on the airport at which you'll be arriving.

The Port Authority runs staffed Ground Transportation Information counters on the baggage-claim level at each airport where you can get information and book various kinds of transport. Most transportation companies also have courtesy phones near the baggage-claim area.

Generally, travel time between the airports and Midtown by taxi or car is 45 to 60 minutes for JFK, 20 to 35 minutes for LaGuardia, and 35 to 50 minutes for Newark. Always allow extra time, especially during rush hour, peak holiday travel times, and if you're taking a bus.

PREVIOUS PAGE: **Times Square in your pocket...this chapter offers essential planning information for your trip.**

It's more convenient to fly into Newark than JFK if your destination is Manhattan, and fares to Newark are often cheaper than those to the other airports. Newark is particularly convenient if your hotel is in Midtown west or downtown. Taxi fare into Manhattan from Newark is roughly equivalent to the fare from JFK—both have **AirTrains** in place (see "AirTrains to Newark & JFK—the Very Good & the Not-So-Very Good," below), but the AirTrain to Newark from Manhattan is quicker.

SUBWAYS & PUBLIC BUSES   For the most part, your best bet is to stay away from the MTA when traveling to and from the airport. You might save a few dollars, but subways and buses that currently serve the airports involve multiple transfers, and you'll have to drag your luggage up and down staircases. On some subways, you'd be traveling through undesirable neighborhoods. Spare yourself the drama.

The only exception to this rule is the subway service to and from JFK (to a certain extent), which connects with the AirTrain (see the box "AirTrains to Newark & JFK—the Very Good & the Not-So-Very Good," below).

The subway *can* be more reliable than taking a car or taxi at the height of rush hour, but *a few words of warning:* This isn't the right option for you if you're bringing more than a single piece of luggage or if you have very young children in tow, since there's a good amount of walking and some stairs involved in the trip, and you'll have nowhere to put all those bags on the subway train. And *do not* use this method if you're traveling to or from the airport after dark or too early in the morning—it's not the safest or fastest way during those times. For additional subway information, see "Getting Around," below.

TAXIS   Despite significant rate hikes the past few years, taxis are still a quick and convenient way to travel to and from the airports. They're available at designated taxi stands outside the terminals, with uniformed dispatchers on hand during peak hours at JFK and LaGuardia, around the clock at Newark. Follow the GROUND TRANSPORTATION or TAXI signs. There may be a long line, but it generally moves quickly. Fares, whether fixed or metered, do not include bridge and tunnel tolls ($4–$6) or a tip for the cabbie (15%–20% is customary). They do include all passengers in the cab and luggage—never pay more than the metered or flat rate, except for tolls and a tip (8pm–6am a $.50 surcharge also applies on New York yellow cabs). Taxis have a limit of four passengers, so if there are more in your group, you'll have to take more than one cab. For more, see "By Taxi," p. 459.

- **From JFK:** A flat rate of $45 to Manhattan (plus tolls and tip and a 50¢ N.Y. state tax) is charged. The meter will not be turned on and the surcharge will not be added. The flat rate does not apply on trips from Manhattan to the airport.

- **From LaGuardia:** There's no set fare, but you can expect the meter to run about $24 to $28, plus tolls and tip.

o **From Newark:** The dispatcher for New Jersey taxis gives you a slip of paper with a flat rate ranging from $50 to $75 (toll and tip extra), depending on where you're going in Manhattan, so be precise about your destination. New York yellow cabs aren't permitted to pick up passengers at Newark. The yellow-cab fare from Manhattan to Newark is the meter amount plus $15 and tolls (about $69–$75, perhaps a few dollars more with tip). Jersey taxis aren't permitted to take passengers from Manhattan to Newark.

PRIVATE CAR & LIMOUSINE SERVICES Private car and limousine companies provide convenient 24-hour door-to-door airport transfers for roughly the same cost of a taxi. The advantage they offer is that you can arrange your pickup in advance and avoid the hassles of the taxi line. Call at least 24 hours in advance (even earlier on holidays), and a driver will meet you near baggage claim (or at your hotel for a return trip). You'll probably be asked to leave a credit card number to guarantee your ride. You'll likely be offered the choice of indoor or curbside pickup; indoor pickup is more expensive but makes it easier to hook up with your driver (who usually waits in baggage claim bearing a sign with your name on it). You can save a few dollars if you arrange for an outside pickup; call the dispatcher as soon as you clear baggage claim and then take your luggage out to the designated waiting area, where you'll wait for the driver to come around, which can take anywhere from 10 minutes to a half-hour. Besides the wait, the other disadvantage of this option is that curbside can be chaos during prime deplaning hours.

Vehicles range from sedans to vans to limousines and tend to be relatively clean and comfortable. Prices vary slightly by company and the size of car reserved, but expect a rate roughly equivalent to taxi fare if you request a basic sedan and have only one stop; toll and tip policies are the same. (**Note**: Car services are not subject to the flat-rate rule that taxis have for rides to and from JFK.) Ask when booking what the fare will be and if you can use your credit card to pay for the ride so there are no surprises at drop-off time. There may be waiting charges tacked on if the driver has to wait an excessive amount of time due to flight delays when picking you up, but the car companies will usually check on your flight to get an accurate landing time.

I've had the best luck with **Carmel** (✆ **866/666-6666;** www.carmel limo.com) and **Legends** (✆ **888/LEGENDS** [534-3637] or 718/788-1234; www.legendslimousine.com); **Allstate** (✆ **800/453-4099** or 212/333-3333; www.allstatelimo.com) and **Tel-Aviv** (✆ **800/222-9888;** www.telavivlimo.com) also have reasonable reputations. (Keep in mind, though, that these services are only as good as the individual drivers—and sometimes there's a lemon in the bunch. If you have a problem, report it immediately to the main office.)

For a bit more luxury and service, the best option I've found is **Luxor Limo** (✆ **866/998-4111;** www.luxorlimo.com), where the cars are spacious and the drivers as reliable as you will find, and with rates not much higher than the above-mentioned companies.

These car services are good for rush hour (no ticking meters in rush-hour traffic), but if you're arriving at a quieter time of day, taxis work fine.

PRIVATE BUSES & SHUTTLES Buses and shuttle services provide a comfortable and less expensive (but usually more time-consuming) option for airport transfers than do taxis and car services.

The world, it seems, is divided into two sorts of blogs. First, the blatantly commercial type in which advertising plays a *very* prominent role. It's very difficult to determine the objectivity of those blogs. Second is the ultra-personal blog—"Tom's New York From My Manhole" sort of blog in which the blogger often uses the blog as an excuse to rant about how his landlord hasn't fixed his bathroom sink despite 17 phone calls in 2 days. We want to spare you all that. (There is the obvious exception of Frommers.com section about New York City that is chock-full of useful and often real-time information about the Apple: **www.frommers.com/destinations/ newyorkcity**). But we do have a solid recommendation for you, and this is our own Brian Silverman's blog, **Fried Neck Bones . . . and Some Home Fries** (also known as "Adventures in Chow City"). Brian writes all the restaurant reviews for *Frommer's New York City.* But being adventurous and a lover of the city and hungry, he set himself the mission of finding great food at low prices in often out-of-the-way places. Décor is not always the prime attraction; the food is. So if you want to see what's good to eat in some of the lesser-known and lesser-traveled-to parts of our great city and have a terrific little romp, you couldn't have a better guide than Brian's blog: **http://friedneckbones.wordpress.com.**

SuperShuttle and **New York Airport Service** serve all three airports; **Olympia Trails/Coach USA** serves Newark. These services are my favorite options for getting to and from Newark during peak travel times because the drivers usually take lesser known streets that make the ride much quicker than if you go with a taxi or car, which will virtually always stick to the traffic-clogged main route.

The familiar blue vans of **SuperShuttle** (☎ 800/258-3826; www.supershuttle.com) serve all three area airports, providing door-to-door service to Manhattan and points on Long Island every 15 to 30 minutes around the clock. You don't need to reserve your airport-to-Manhattan ride; just go to the ground-transportation desk or use the courtesy phone in baggage claim and ask for SuperShuttle. Hotel pickups for your return trip require 24 to 48 hours' notice; you can make your reservations online. Fares run from about $13 to $28 per person, depending on the airport, with discounts available for additional residents in the same party.

New York Airport Service (☎ 718/560-3915; www.nyairport service.com) buses travel from JFK and LaGuardia to the Port Authority Bus Terminal (42nd St. and Eighth Ave.), Grand Central Terminal (Park Ave. btw. 41st and 42nd sts.), and Penn Station (Seventh Ave. btw. 31st and 32nd sts.). Look for the uniformed agent near the airport's ground transportation center. Buses depart the airport every 20 to 30 minutes (depending on your departure point and destination) between 6am and 11pm. One-way fare from JFK to Manhattan is $7, $20 round-trip; from LaGuardia it's $5 one-way and $25 round-trip.

Olympia Airport Express (☎ 877/863-9275; www.coachusa.com/ olympia/ss.newarkairport.asp) provides service every 15 minutes (every 30 minutes from 6:45 a.m. to 11:15 p.m.) from Newark Airport to Bryant Park (at 42nd St. and Fifth Ave.), the Port Authority Bus Terminal (on 42nd St.

AIRTRAINS TO NEWARK & JFK—THE VERY GOOD & THE NOT-SO-VERY GOOD

First the very good: **AirTrain Newark,** which connects Newark-Liberty International Airport with Manhattan via a speedy monorail/rail link.

Even though you have to make a connection, the system is fast, pleasant, affordable, and easy to use. Each arrivals terminal at Newark Airport has a station for the AirTrain, so just follow the signs once you collect your bags. All AirTrains head to **Newark International Airport Station,** where you transfer to a **NJ Transit** train. NJ Transit will deliver you to New York Penn Station at 33rd Street and Seventh Avenue, where you can get a cab or transfer to the subway or bus.

A trip from the Upper West Side to the Newark Alitalia terminal, for example, was quick and convenient, and cost me about $15 ($13 for the AirTrain link via Penn Station plus $2.50 for the subway to get to Penn Station). That's a savings of at least $54, compared to what it would have been if I took a cab, not to mention the time I saved. NJ Transit trains run at least six times an hour from 6am to 9pm and four times an hour from 9pm to midnight (there is no service from 2 to 5am), and depart from their own lobby/waiting area in Penn Station; you can check the schedules on monitors before you leave the airport terminal, and again at the train station. NJ Transit tickets can be purchased from vending machines at both the air terminal and the train station (no ticket is required to board the AirTrain). The one-way fare is $13 (children 11 and under ride free). On your return trip to the airport, the AirTrain is far more predictable, time-wise, than subjecting yourself to the whims of traffic.

Note that travelers heading to points beyond the city can also pick up Amtrak and other NJ Transit trains at Newark International Airport Station to their final destinations.

Now the not-so-very good: A few bumpy years after opening in 2003, at a cost of nearly $2 billion, AirTrain JFK is operating somewhat more efficiently. Though you can't beat the price—it's only $5 if you take a subway to the AirTrain, $13 if you take the Long Island Rail Road—you won't save much on time getting to the airport. From midtown Manhattan, the ride can take anywhere from 40 minutes to over an hour, depending on your connections. The connections can be confusing. Only a few subway lines connect with the AirTrain: the A, E, J, and Z; the E, J, Z to Jamaica Station and the Sutphin Blvd.–Archer Ave. Station; and the A to Howard Beach. The MTA is contemplating adding connections to the AirTrain in lower Manhattan sometime in the next decade, but there's not much else they can do now to speed up the trip.

A word of warning for both AirTrains: If you have mobility issues, mountains of luggage, or a bevy of small children, skip the AirTrain. You'll find it easier to rely on a taxi, car service, or shuttle service that can offer you door-to-door transfers.

For more information on AirTrain Newark and connection details, call ☎ **888/EWR-INFO** [397-4636], or go online to **www.panynj.gov**. For connections to trains, contact **NJ Transit** (☎ **973/275-5555;** www.njtransit.com) or **Amtrak** (☎ **800/USA-RAIL** [872-7245]; www.amtrak.com).

For more information on AirTrain JFK, go online to **www.panynj.gov**. For connection details, click on the links on the website or MTA's site, **www.mta.info/mta/airtrain.htm.**

btw. Eighth and Ninth aves.), and Grand Central Terminal (on 41st St. btw. Park and Lexington aves.). Call for the exact schedule for your return trip to the airport. The one-way fare runs $15, $25 round-trip; students $10 one-way, $20 round-trip; and seniors and passengers with disabilities $7.50 one-way, $15 round-trip.

By Bus

Busing to and from New York City from major East Coast cities has become the single most cost-effective way to get into town. Originally, these were cheap bus services created by Chinese-Americans as a means of getting between New York City and Boston, Philadelphia, and Washington, D.C., Budget travelers soon discovered the bus lines, and now a number of companies offer service between most of the major cities in the East (and as far west as Buffalo and Toronto) for a fraction of what you'd pay by train or plane. While the Chinatown buses remain the cheapest, we'd recommend that you check out the newer, larger services, which are both more comfortable and offer amenities like Wi-Fi, as well as a safer ride (Chinatown bus lines made the news in early 2011 after two fatal crashes).

From Philadelphia, the average ride might range from $10–$20; for the other two cities you'll pay $15 to $30, but there are times when specials reduce the fares to just $1. For information about the major lines (Megabus and Boltbus, as well as the Chinatown buses) as well as fare information and bookings, visit the well-designed agency site called **BusJunction** (**www.busjunction.com**).

You will probably wait for the bus to pick you up, or depart from a street corner, rather than a bus station, which some people might count as a bonus if you're not fond of bus stations.

For individual company websites, visit:

- **Megabus** (© 877/GO2-MEGA [462-6342]; www.megabus.com)
- **Boltbus** (© 877/BOLTBUS [265-8287]; www.boltbus.com)
- **Vamoose** (© 877/393-2828; www.vamoosebus.com)
- **DC2NY** (© 888/888-DCNY or 202/332-2691; www.dc2ny.com)

By Car

From the **New Jersey Turnpike** (I-95) and points west, there are three Hudson River crossings to the city's West Side: the **Holland Tunnel** (lower Manhattan), the **Lincoln Tunnel** (Midtown), and the **George Washington Bridge** (upper Manhattan). From **upstate New York,** take the **New York State Thruway** (I-87), which crosses the Hudson River on the Tappan Zee Bridge and becomes the **Major Deegan Expressway** (I-87) through the Bronx. For the East Side, continue to the **Robert F. Kennedy Bridge** (formerly called the Triborough Bridge) and then down the FDR Drive. For the West Side, take the **Cross Bronx Expressway** (I-95) to the **Henry Hudson Parkway,** or the **Taconic State Parkway** to the **Saw Mill River Parkway** to the Henry Hudson Parkway south. From **New England,** the **New England Thruway** (I-95) connects with the **Bruckner Expressway** (I-278), which leads to the Robert F. Kennedy Bridge and the FDR Drive on the East Side. For the West Side, take the Bruckner to the Cross Bronx Expressway (I-95) to the Henry Hudson Parkway south.

If you're traveling to a borough other than Manhattan, call **ETS Air Service** (© 718/221-5341) for shared door-to-door service. For Long Island service, call **Classic Transportation** (© 631/567-5100; www.classictrans.com) for car service. For service to Westchester County or Connecticut, contact **Connecticut Limousine** (© 800/472-5466 or 203/974-4700; www.ctlimo.com).

If you're traveling to points in New Jersey from Newark Airport, call **Olympic Airporter** (© 800/822-9797; www.olympicairporter.com) for Ocean, Monmouth, Middlesex, and Mercer counties, plus Bucks County, Pennsylvania; or **State Shuttle** (© 800/427-3207; www.stateshuttle.com) for destinations throughout New Jersey.

Additionally, **New York Airport Service** express buses (© 718/875-8200; www.nyairportservice.com) serve the entire New York metropolitan region from JFK, Newark, and LaGuardia, offering connections to the Long Island Rail Road; the Metro-North Railroad to Westchester County, upstate New York, and Connecticut; and New York's Port Authority terminal, where you head for New Jersey.

Note that you'll have to pay tolls along some of these roads and at most crossings. If your state has an **E-ZPass** program (**www.ezpass.com**), as most states in the Northeast do, your pass will allow you to go through the designated E-ZPass lanes.

Once you arrive in Manhattan, park your car in a garage (expect to pay $20–$45 per day) and leave it there. Don't use your car for traveling within the city. Public transportation, taxis, and walking will easily get you where you want to go without the headaches of parking, gridlock, and dodging crazy cabbies.

For information on car rentals and gasoline (petrol) in New York City, see "Getting Around by Car," later in this section.

By Train

Amtrak (© **800/USA-RAIL** [872-7245]; www.amtrak.com) runs frequent service to New York City's **Penn Station,** on Seventh Avenue between 31st and 33rd streets, where you can get a taxi, subway, or bus to your hotel. To get the best rates, book early (as much as 6 months in advance) and travel on weekends.

If you're traveling to New York from a city along Amtrak's Northeast Corridor—such as Boston, Philadelphia, Baltimore, or Washington, D.C.—Amtrak may be your best travel bet now that they've rolled out their high-speed Acela trains. The Acela Express trains cut travel time from D.C. down to 2½ hours, and travel time from Boston to a lightning-quick 3 hours.

GETTING AROUND

Frankly, Manhattan's transportation systems are a marvel. It's simply miraculous that so many people can gather on this little island and move around it. For the most part, you can get where you're going pretty quickly and easily using some combination of subways, buses, and cabs; this section will tell you how to do just that.

But between traffic gridlock and subway delays, sometimes you just can't get there from here—unless you walk. Walking can sometimes be the fastest way to navigate the island. During rush hours, you'll easily beat car traffic while on foot, as taxis and buses stop and groan at gridlocked corners (don't even *try* going crosstown in a cab or bus in Midtown at midday). You'll also see a lot more by walking than you will if you ride beneath the street in the subway or fly by in a cab. So pack your most comfortable shoes and hit the pavement—it's the best, cheapest, and most appealing way to experience the city.

By Subway

Run by the **Metropolitan Transit Authority,** also known as the MTA **(www. mta.info/nyct/subway),** the much-maligned subway system is actually the fastest way to travel around New York, especially during rush hours. Some 4.5 million people a day seem to agree, as it's their primary mode of transportation. The subway is quick, inexpensive, relatively safe, and efficient, as well as being a genuine New York experience.

The subway runs 24 hours a day, 7 days a week. The rush-hour crushes are roughly from 8 to 9:30am and from 5 to 6:30pm on weekdays; the rest of the time the trains are much more manageable. *Note:* In December 2009, in order to make up for a $400-million shortfall, the MTA passed a budget that mandates major cutbacks in service on both the subway and bus lines. Subways and buses are running with reduced frequency during weekends, late nights, and weekday afternoons. Some lines have been eliminated altogether (the W and V subway lines). These cuts, many of which took effect in late spring of 2010, have infuriated many New Yorkers, and various groups have been fighting them. Some cuts were restored after public outcry, but a number of bus and subway lines were affected.

PAYING YOUR WAY

A SingleRide subway fare is $2.50 (half price for seniors and those with disabilities), and children under 44 inches tall ride free (up to three per adult). *Note:*

Sidewalks of New York

What's the primary means New Yorkers use for getting around town? The subway? Buses? Taxis? Nope. **Walking.** They stride across wide, crowded pavements without any regard for traffic lights, weaving through crowds at high speeds, dodging taxis and buses whose drivers are forced to interrupt the normal flow of traffic to avoid flattening them. **Never take your walking cues from the locals.** Wait for walk signals and always use crosswalks—don't cross in the middle of the block. Do otherwise and you could quickly end up as a flattened statistic (or at least get a ticket for jaywalking).

Always pay attention to the traffic flow. Walk as though you're driving, staying to the right. Pay attention to what's happening in the street, even if you have the right of way. At intersections, keep an eye out for drivers who don't yield, turn without looking, or think a yellow traffic light means "Hurry up!" as you cross. Unfortunately, most bicyclists seem to think that the traffic laws don't apply to them; they'll often blithely fly through red lights and dash the wrong way on one-way streets, so be on your guard.

The prices listed in this section reflect the latest price increase by the MTA, which went into effect in December 2011. The fares are scheduled to go up again in 2013.

Tokens are no longer available. People pay with the **MetroCard,** a magnetically encoded card that debits the fare when swiped through the turnstile (or the fare box on any city bus). Once you're in the system, you can transfer freely to any subway line that you can reach without exiting your station. MetroCards also allow you **free transfers** between the bus and subway within a 2-hour period.

MetroCards can be purchased from staffed token booths, where you can only pay with cash; at the ATM-style vending machines now located in every subway station, which accept cash, credit cards, and debit cards; from a MetroCard merchant, such as most Rite Aid drugstores; Hudson News, at Penn Station and Grand Central Terminal; or at the MTA information desk at the **Times Square Information Center,** 1560 Broadway, between 46th and 47th streets. MetroCards come in a few different configurations:

Pay-Per-Ride MetroCards can be used for up to four people by swiping up to four times (bring the entire family). You can put any amount from $4.50 (two rides) to $80 on your card. Every time you put $8 or more on your Pay-Per-Ride MetroCard, it's automatically credited 15%—in other words, spend $20 and you get a free ride, plus a 50¢ balance. You can buy Pay-Per-Ride MetroCards at any subway station; most stations have automated MetroCard vending machines, which allow you to buy MetroCards using your major credit card or debit card. MetroCards are also available from many shops and newsstands around town in $10 and $20 values. You can refill your card at any time until the expiration date on the card, usually about a year from the date of purchase, at any subway station.

Unlimited-Ride MetroCards, which can't be used for more than one person at a time or more frequently than 18-minute intervals, are available in two values: the **7-Day MetroCard,** which allows you seven day's worth of unlimited subway and bus rides for $29; and the **30-Day MetroCard,** for $104. Unlimited-Ride MetroCards can be purchased at any subway station or from a MetroCard merchant. They go into effect the first time you use them—so if you buy a card on Monday and don't begin to use it until Wednesday, Wednesday is when the clock starts ticking on your MetroCard. Seven- and 30-day MetroCards run out at midnight on the last day. These MetroCards cannot be refilled.

Tips for using your MetroCard: The MetroCard swiping mechanisms at turnstiles are the source of much grousing among subway riders. If you swipe too fast or too slow, the turnstile will ask you to swipe again. If this happens, *do not move to a different turnstile,* or you may end up paying twice. If you've tried

Stand Clear of the Closing Stations

Since lower Manhattan will continue to resemble a giant construction zone for the next several years, be aware of **subway service reductions and station closures** south of Chambers Street. At the **World Trade Center,** the station for the No. 1 train is closed (probably until the site is rebuilt somewhere around 2014; see p. 246). The good news is that the **wheelchair-accessible South Ferry** station on the 1 line opened in 2009, while new elevators are up and running at the 2 and 3 line's **Chambers Street** station in TriBeCa.

subway stops FOR NEW YORK'S TOP ATTRACTIONS

MUSEUMS

American Museum of Natural History — **B, C** to 81st Street
The Cloisters — **A** to 190th Street
Ellis Island — **4, 5** to Bowling Green or N, R to Whitehall Street 1 to South Ferry

Guggenheim Museum — **4, 5, 6** to 86th Street
Intrepid Sea-Air-Space Museum — **A, C, E** to 42nd Street-Port Authority
Metropolitan Museum of Art — **4, 5, 6** to 86th Street
Museum of Modern Art — **E** to Fifth Avenue or B, D, F to 47th-50th streets-Rockefeller Center

HISTORIC BUILDINGS & ARCHITECTURE

Brooklyn Bridge — **4, 5, 6** to Brooklyn Bridge-City Hall
Chrysler Building — **4, 5, 6, 7, S** to Grand Central-42nd Street
Empire State Building — **B, D, F, N, R, Q** to 34th Street-Herald Square
Grand Central Terminal — **4, 5, 6, 7, S** to Grand Central-42nd Street
Rockefeller Center — **B, D, F** to 47th-50th streets-Rockefeller Center
Staten Island Ferry — **1** to South Ferry (first five cars)
United Nations — **4, 5, 6, 7, S** to Grand Central-42nd Street
Yankee Stadium — **4, B, D** to 161st River Avenue-Yankee Stadium

NEIGHBORHOODS

Chinatown — **6, J, M, Z, N, R, Q** to Canal Street
Greenwich Village — **A, C, E, B, D, F** to West 4th Street
Times Square — **1, 2, 3, 7, N, R, S** to 42nd Street-Times Square
Wall Street — **4, 5** to Wall Street or N, R to Rector Street

CHURCHES

Cathedral of St. John the Divine — **1** to Cathedral Parkway (110th St.)
St. Patrick's Cathedral — **B, D, F** to 47th-50th streets-Rockefeller Center or E to Fifth Avenue-53rd Street

repeatedly and really can't make your MetroCard work, tell the token booth clerk; chances are good, though, that you'll get the movement down after a couple of uses.

If you're not sure how much money you have left on your MetroCard, or what day it expires, use the station's MetroCard Reader, usually located near the station entrance or the token booth (on buses, the fare box will also provide you with this information).

To locate the nearest MetroCard merchant, or for any other MetroCard questions, call © **718/330-1234.** Or go online to **www.mta.info/metrocard**, which can give you a full rundown of MetroCard merchants in the tri-state area.

USING THE SYSTEM

As you can see from the full-color subway map of most of Manhattan on the inside back cover of this book, the subway system basically mimics the lay of the land aboveground, with most lines in Manhattan running north and south, like the avenues, and a few lines east and west, like the streets.

To go up and down the east side of Manhattan (and to the Bronx and Brooklyn), take the 4, 5, or 6 train.

To travel up and down the West Side (and also to the Bronx and Brooklyn), take the 1, 2, or 3 line; the A, C, E, or F line; or the B or D line.

The N, R, and Q lines first cut diagonally across town from east to west and then snake under Seventh Avenue before shooting out to Queens.

The crosstown S line, called the Shuttle, runs back and forth between Times Square and Grand Central Terminal. Farther downtown, across 14th Street, the L line works its own crosstown magic.

Lines have assigned colors on subway maps and trains—red for the 1, 2, 3 line; green for the 4, 5, 6 trains; and so on—but nobody ever refers to them by color. Always refer to them by number or letter when asking questions. Within Manhattan, the distinction between different numbered trains that share the same line is usually that some are express and others are local. **Express trains** often skip about three stops for each one that they make; express stops are indicated on subway maps with a white (rather than solid) circle. Local stops are usually about 9 blocks apart.

Directions are almost always indicated using "uptown" (northbound) and "downtown" (southbound), so be sure to know what direction you want to head in. The outsides of some subway entrances are marked UPTOWN ONLY or DOWNTOWN ONLY; read carefully, as it's easy to head in the wrong direction. Once you're on the platform, check the signs overhead to make sure that the train you're waiting for will be traveling in the right direction. If you do make a mistake, it's a good idea to wait for an express station, such as 14th Street or 42nd Street, so you can get off and change to the other direction without paying again.

The days of graffiti-covered cars are gone, but the stations—and an increasing number of trains—are not as clean as they could be. Trains are air-conditioned (move to the next car if yours isn't), though during the dog days of summer

---

📎 ## Subway Service Interruption Notes

The subway map featured on the inside back cover of this book was as accurate as possible at press time, but service is always subject to change, for reasons ranging from "a sick passenger" to regularly scheduled construction. Your best bet is to contact the **Metropolitan Transit Authority (MTA)** for the latest details; call ℂ **718/330-1234** or visit **www.mta.info,** where you'll find system updates that are thorough, timely, and clear. (You can also sign up online to receive service advisories by e-mail.) Also read any posters that are taped up on the platform or notices written on the token booth's whiteboard. Once in town, you can stop at the MTA desk at the **Times Square Information Center,** 1560 Broadway, between 46th and 47th streets (where Broadway meets Seventh Ave.) to pick up the latest subway map. (You can also ask for one at any token booth, but they might not always be stocked.)

the platforms can be sweltering. In theory, all subway cars have PA systems to allow you to hear the conductor's announcements, but they don't always work well. It's a good idea to move to a car with a working PA system in case sudden service changes are announced that you'll want to know about.

By Bus

Less expensive than taxis and more pleasant than subways (they provide a mobile sightseeing window on Manhattan), MTA buses are a good transportation option. Their big drawback: They can get stuck in traffic, sometimes making it quicker to walk. They also stop every couple of blocks, rather than the 8 or 9 blocks that local subways traverse between stops. So for long distances, the subway is your best bet; but for short distances or traveling crosstown, try the bus.

PAYING YOUR WAY

Like the subway fare, a SingleRide **bus fare** is $2.50, half price for seniors and riders with disabilities, and free for children under 44 inches (up to three per adult). The fare is payable with a **MetroCard** or **exact change.** Bus drivers don't make change, and fare boxes don't accept dollar bills or pennies. You can't purchase MetroCards on the bus, so you'll have to have them before you board; for details on where to get them, see "Paying Your Way," under "By Subway," above.

If you pay with a MetroCard, you can transfer to another bus or to the subway for free within 2 hours. If you pay cash, you must request a **free transfer** card that allows you to change to an intersecting bus route only within 2 hours of issue. Transfer cards cannot be used to enter the subway.

Mass Transit Fares in New York City

SUBWAYS, MTA BUS

Fare Type	Full**	Reduced*
Base Pay-Per-Ride MetroCard Fare	$2.25	$1.10
Minimum purchase for new MetroCard	$4.50	$4.50
Cash (Bus only)	$2.25	$1.10
Single-Ride Ticket	$2.50	N/A

UNLIMITED-RIDE METROCARD

7-day	$29.00	$14.50
30-day	$104.00	$52.00

* Reduced-fare customers who do not have a reduced-fare MetroCard pay $2.25 at a subway station booth for a round-trip.

** Reduced fare is not available during peak periods, 6–10am and 3–7pm weekdays.

USING THE SYSTEM

You can't flag a city bus down—you have to meet it at a bus stop. **Bus stops** are located every 2 or 3 blocks on the right-side corner of the street (facing the direction of traffic flow). They're marked by a curb painted yellow and a blue-and-white sign with a bus emblem and the route number or numbers, and usually an ad-bedecked Plexiglass bus shelter. Guide-a-Ride boxes at most stops display a route map and a hysterically optimistic schedule.

Almost every major avenue has its own **bus route.** They run either north or south: downtown on Fifth, uptown on Madison, downtown on Lexington, uptown on Third, and so on. There are **crosstown buses** at strategic locations all around town: 14th, 23rd, 34th, and 42nd (east- and westbound); 49th (westbound); 50th (eastbound); 57th (east- and westbound); 66th (eastbound across the West Side on 65th St., through the park, and then north on Madison, continuing east on 68th to York Ave.); 67th (westbound on the East Side to Fifth Ave., and then south on Fifth, continuing west on 66th St., through the park and across the west side to West End Ave.); and 79th, 86th, 96th, 116th, and 125th (east- and westbound). Some bus routes, however, are erratic: The M104, for example, turns at Eighth Avenue and 41st St. and goes up Broadway to West 129th St. Please note that the scheduled MTA cuts will affect some of the bus lines, especially at night.

Most routes operate 24 hours a day, but service is infrequent at night. Some say that New York buses have a herding instinct: They arrive only in groups. During rush hour, main routes have "limited" buses, identifiable by the red card in the front window; they stop only at major cross streets.

To make sure that the bus you're boarding goes where you're going, check the map on the sign that's at every bus stop, get your hands on a route map, or **just ask.** The drivers are helpful, as long as you don't hold up the line too long.

While traveling, look out the window not only to take in the sights but also to keep track of cross streets so you know when to get off. Signal for a stop by

---

📎 ## iPhone, BlackBerry apps

So much of the world now carries the Internet in the palm of his or her hand—literally. Whether you have an iPhone or a BlackBerry or some other type of ultra-modern phone/e-mail/Internet/God-knows-what-else device, there are apps associated with it that can make a visit to New York a little simpler. Frommer's has a free travel app called Travel Tools that includes a currency converter and a tip calculator. Find it here: **www.frommers.com/go/mobile.** (You can also purchase the entire New York City Guide via that link.) The iPhone has an app for finding the best subway route called, not unexpectedly, New York

Subway: **http://itunes.apple.com/app/new-york-subway/id301912130?mt=8.** You can download it for a mere \$.99. For \$9.99, you can purchase Zagat to Go, which has restaurant reviews not only for New York City but also from 44 of its other guides: **http://itunes.apple.com/us/app/zagat-to-go/id296428490?mt=8.** For BlackBerry apps, go here: **http://us.blackberry.com/apps-software/appworld.** Of course, it's good to know a 14-year-old, who probably knows everything about these and other apps and can upload or download them or whatever needs to be done for you in about 15 seconds.

For additional transit information, call the Metropolitan Transit Authority's **MTA/New York City Transit's Travel Information Center** at ℰ **718/330-1234.** Extensive automated information is available at this number 24 hours a day, and travel agents are on hand to answer your questions and provide directions daily from 6am to 10pm. Customers who don't speak English can call ℰ **718/330-4847.** For online information that's always up-to-the-minute, visit **www. mta.info.** *Note:* The MTA's website has been completely revamped, and it is surprisingly good. I would use it as often as possible in lieu of the telephone.

To request system maps, call the **Map Request Line** at ℰ **718/330-3322.**

Riders with disabilities should direct inquiries to ℰ **718/596-8585;** hearing-impaired riders can call ℰ **718/596-8273.** For MetroCard information, call ℰ **718/330-1234,** or go online to **www. mta.info/metrocard.**

You can get bus and subway maps and additional transit information at most information centers (see "Visitor Information" in "Fast Facts: New York City," p. 462). A particularly helpful MTA transit information desk is located at the **Times Square Information Center,** 1560 Broadway, between 46th and 47th streets, where you can also buy Metro-Cards. Maps are sometimes available in subway stations (ask at the token booth), but rarely on buses.

pressing the tape strip above and beside the windows and along the metal straps, about 2 blocks before you want to stop. Exit through the pneumatic back doors (not the front door) by pushing on the yellow tape strip; the doors open automatically. (Pushing on the handles is useless unless you're as buff as Hercules.)

Most city buses are equipped with wheelchair lifts, making buses the preferable mode of public transportation for travelers in chairs. Buses also "kneel," lowering down to the curb to make boarding easier.

By Taxi

If you don't want to deal with public transportation, finding an address that might be a few blocks from the subway station, or sharing your ride with 4.5 million other people, then take a taxi. The biggest advantages are, of course, that cabs can be hailed on any street (provided you find an empty one—often simple, yet at other times nearly impossible) and will take you right to your destination. I find they're best used at night when there's little traffic and when the subway may seem a little daunting. In Midtown at midday, you can usually walk to where you're going more quickly.

Official New York City taxis, licensed by the Taxi and Limousine Commission (TLC), are yellow, with the rates printed on the door and a light with a medallion number on the roof. You can hail a taxi on any street. *Never* accept a ride from any other car except an official city yellow cab (livery cars are not allowed to pick up fares on the street, despite what the driver tells you when he pulls over to see if he can pick up a fare).

The base fare on entering the cab is $2.50. The cost is 40¢ for every ⅕ mile or 40¢ per 60 seconds in stopped or slow-moving traffic (or for waiting time). There's no extra charge for each passenger or for luggage. However, you must pay bridge or tunnel tolls (sometimes the driver will front the toll and add it to your bill at the end; most times, however, you pay the driver before the toll). You'll pay

9

PLANNING YOUR TRIP TO NEW YORK CITY

Getting Around

a $1 surcharge between 4 and 8pm and a 50¢ surcharge after 8pm and before 6am. A 15% to 20% tip is customary.

Most taxis are now equipped with a device that allows you to pay by credit card, though some drivers will claim the machine is broken (there is a transaction fee for credit cards that cuts into their income) and ask you to pay in cash. You can choose to either add the tip to the credit card, or tip the driver in cash.

Many, if not most, taxi drivers may not have the best grasp of English. If their driving is scaring you, ask them to slow down, stop slamming on the brakes *quite* so hard, and taking off like a rocket when the light turns green. Wear your seat belt—taxis are required to provide them.

The TLC has posted a **Taxi Rider's Bill of Rights** sticker in every cab. Drivers are required by law to take you anywhere in the five boroughs, to Nassau or Westchester counties, or to Newark Airport. They are supposed to know how to get you to any address in Manhattan and all major points in the outer boroughs. They are also required to provide air-conditioning and turn off the radio on demand, and they cannot smoke while you're in the cab. They are required to be polite.

You are allowed to dictate the route that is taken. It's a good idea to look at a map before you get in a taxi. Taxi drivers have been known to jack up the fare on visitors who don't know better by taking a circuitous route between points A and B. Know enough about where you're going to know that something's wrong if you hop in a cab at Sixth Avenue and 57th Street to go to the Empire State Building (Fifth Ave. and 34th St.), say, and suddenly find yourself on Ninth Avenue.

On the other hand, listen to drivers who propose an alternate route. These guys spend 8 or 10 hours a day on these streets, and they know where the worst traffic is, or where Con Ed has dug up an intersection that should be avoided. A knowledgeable driver will know how to get you to your destination quickly and efficiently.

Another important tip: **Always make sure the meter is turned on at the start of the ride.** You'll see the red LED readout register the initial $2.50 and start calculating the fare as you go. I've witnessed unscrupulous drivers buzzing unsuspecting visitors around the city with the meter off, and then overcharging them at drop-off time.

Always ask for the receipt—it comes in handy if you need to make a complaint or have left something in a cab. In fact, it's a good idea to make a mental note of the driver's four-digit medallion number (usually posted on the divider btw. the front and back seats) just in case you need it later. You probably won't, but it's a good idea to play it safe.

Take a Free Ride

The Alliance for Downtown New York's **Downtown Connection** offers a free bus service that provides easy access to downtown destinations, including Battery Park City, the World Financial Center, and South Street Seaport. The buses, which run daily, every 10 minutes or so, from 10am to 7:30pm, make dozens of stops along a 5-mile route from Chambers Street on the west side to Beekman Street on the east side. For schedules and more information, call the Downtown Connection at ☎ **212/566-6700,** or visit **www.downtownny.com.**

A taxi driver is obligated to take you to your desired destination. If a taxi driver is on duty but refuses to take you to your desired destination (which happens on occasion when you want to go to an outer borough destination or very far uptown), get the driver's name and medallion number and file a complaint with the Taxi and Limousine Commission.

For all driver complaints, including the one above, and to report lost property, call © **311** or 212/NEW-YORK (639-9675; outside the metro area). For details on getting to and from the local airports by taxi, see "By Plane," under "Getting There," earlier in this chapter. For further taxi information—including a complete rundown of your rights as a taxi rider—point your Web browser to **www.ci.nyc.ny.us/taxi**.

By Car

Forget driving yourself around the city. It's not worth the headache. Traffic is horrendous, and you don't know the rules of the road (written or unwritten) or the arcane alternate-side-of-the-street parking regulations (in fact, precious few New Yorkers do). You don't want to find out the monstrous price of parking violations or live the Kafkaesque nightmare of liberating a vehicle from the tow pound. Not to mention the security risks.

If you do arrive in New York City by car, park it in a garage (expect to pay at least $25–$45 per day) and leave it there for the duration of your stay. (In our hotel chapter, we note if a hotel has a garage or offers discounted parking, and the rate). If you drive a rental car in, return it as soon as you arrive and rent another when you leave.

Just about all of the major car-rental companies have multiple Manhattan locations.

Traveling from the City to the Suburbs

The **PATH** (© **800/234-7284;** www.panynj.gov/path) system connects cities in New Jersey, including Hoboken and Newark, to Manhattan by subway-style trains. Stops in Manhattan are at the World Trade Center, Christopher and 9th streets, and along Sixth Avenue at 14th, 23rd, and 33rd streets. The fare is $1.75 one-way.

New Jersey Transit (© **973/275-5555;** www.njtransit.com) operates commuter trains from Penn Station, and buses from the Port Authority at Eighth Avenue and 42nd Street, to points throughout New Jersey.

The **Long Island Rail Road** (© **718/217-LIRR** [217-5477]; www.mta. info/lirr) runs from Penn Station, at Seventh Avenue between 31st and 33rd streets, to Queens (ocean beaches, Citi Field [the new home of the New York Mets], Belmont Park) and points beyond on Long Island, to even better beaches

WHERE TO CHECK YOUR E-MAIL IN THE CITY THAT NEVER SLEEPS

If your hotel doesn't offer free access to its business center or a terminal in the lobby to check your e-mail (and many do), where can you go to check it if you don't have a computer or smartphone with you?

All branches of the **New York Public Library** (**www.nypl.org**) feature computers that offer free access to the Internet, electronic databases, library catalogs, and Microsoft Office. Many branches also offer free Wi-Fi.

More free access is available at the **Times Square Visitors Center,** 1560 Broadway, between 46th and 47th streets (✆ **212/869-1890;** Mon–Fri 9am–8pm, and Sat–Sun 8am–8pm), which has computer terminals that you can use to send e-mails. You can even send an electronic postcard, with a photo of yourself, home to Mom.

CyberCafe (www.cyber-cafe.com)—in Times Square at 250 W. 49th St., between Broadway and Eighth Avenue (✆ **212/333-4109**)—can get expensive at $6.40 per half-hour, with a half-hour minimum (you're billed $3.20 for every subsequent 15 min.). But their connection is superfast, and they offer a full range of other cyber, copy, fax, and printing services.

and summer hot spots such as the Hamptons. You can also connect to the Fire Island ferry from the LIRR.

Metro-North Railroad (✆ **212/532-4900;** www.mta.info/mnr) departs from Grand Central Terminal, at 42nd Street and Lexington Avenue, for areas north of the city, including Westchester County, the Hudson Valley, and Connecticut.

BY BUS

Greyhound (✆ **800/231-2222** in the U.S.; ✆ **001/214/849-8100** outside the U.S. with toll-free access; www.greyhound.com) is the sole nationwide bus line. International visitors can obtain information about the **Greyhound North American Discovery Pass.** The pass, which offers unlimited travel and stopovers in the U.S. and Canada, can be obtained outside the United States from travel agents or through www.discoverypass.com.

[FastFACTS] NEW YORK CITY

Area Codes   There are four area codes in the city: two in Manhattan, the original **212** and **646;** and two in the outer boroughs, the original **718** and the newer **347.** Also common is the **917** area code, which is assigned to cellphones. All calls between these area codes are local calls, but you'll have to dial 1 + the area code + the seven digits for all calls, even ones made within your area code.

Business Hours   In general, **retail stores** are open Monday through Saturday from 10am to 6 or 7pm, Thursday from 10am to 8:30 or 9pm, and Sunday from noon to 5pm (see chapter 7). **Banks** tend to be open Monday through Friday from 9am to 5pm, with many open Saturday mornings, and some now even open on Sundays.

Customs **What You Can Bring into the U.S.**   Every visitor more than 21 years of age may bring in, free of duty, the following: (1) 1 liter of wine or hard liquor; (2) 200 cigarettes, 100 cigars (but not from Cuba), or 3 pounds of smoking tobacco; and (3) $100 worth of gifts. These exemptions are offered to travelers who spend at least 72 hours in the United States and who have not claimed them within the preceding 6 months. It is forbidden to bring into the country almost any meat products (including canned, fresh, and dried meat products such as bouillon, soup mixes, and so forth). Generally, condiments including vinegars, oils, spices, coffee, tea, and some cheeses and baked goods are permitted. Avoid rice products, as rice can often harbor insects. Bringing fruits and vegetables is not advised, though not prohibited. Customs will allow produce depending on where you got it and where you're going after you arrive in the U.S. International visitors may carry in or out up to $10,000 in U.S. or foreign currency with no formalities; larger sums must be declared to U.S. Customs on entering or leaving, which includes filing form CM 4790. For details regarding U.S. Customs and Border Protection, consult your nearest U.S. embassy or consulate, or **U.S. Customs (www.customs.gov).**

What You Can Take Home from the U.S.   If you're an international visitor, for information on what you're allowed to bring home, contact one of the following agencies:

U.S. Citizens: U.S. Customs & Border Protection (CBP), 1300 Pennsylvania Ave. NW, Washington, DC 20229 (✆ **877/227-5511;** www.cbp.gov).

Canadian Citizens: Canada Border Services Agency, Ottawa, Ontario, K1A 0L8 (✆ **800/461-9999** in Canada, or 204/983-3500; www.cbsa-asfc.gc.ca).

U.K. Citizens: HM Customs & Excise, Crownhill Court, Tailyour Road, Plymouth, PL6 5BZ (✆ **0845/010-9000;** www.hmce.gov.uk).

Australian Citizens: Australian Customs Service, Customs House, 5 Constitution Ave., Canberra City, ACT 2601 (✆ **1300/363-263;** from outside Australia, 612/6275-6666; www.customs.gov.au).

New Zealand Citizens: New Zealand Customs, the Customhouse, 17–21 Whitmore St., Box 2218, Wellington, 6140 (✆ **0800/428-786;** from outside New Zealand, 649/300-5399; www.customs.govt.nz).

Disabled Travelers   New York is more accessible to travelers with disabilities than ever before. The city's bus system is wheelchair-friendly, and most of the major sightseeing attractions are easily accessible. Even so, **always call first** to be sure that the places you want to go to are fully accessible.

Most hotels are ADA compliant, with suitable rooms for wheelchair-bound travelers as well as those with other disabilities. But before you book, **ask lots of questions based on your needs.** Many city hotels are in older buildings that have been modified to meet requirements; still, elevators and bathrooms can be on the small side, and other impediments may exist. If you have mobility issues, you'll probably do best to book one of the city's newer hotels, which tend to be more spacious and accommodating. At **www.access-able.com,** you'll find links to New York's best accessible accommodations (click on "World Destinations"). Some Broadway theaters and other performance venues provide total wheelchair accessibility; others provide partial accessibility. Many also offer lower-priced tickets for theatergoers with disabilities and their companions, though you'll need to check individual policies and reserve in advance.

Hospital Audiences, Inc. (☎ **212/575-7676;** www.hainyc.org) arranges attendance and provides details about accessibility at cultural institutions as well as cultural events adapted for people with disabilities. Services include "Describe!," which allows visually impaired theatergoers to enjoy theater events; and the invaluable **HAI Hot Line** (☎ **212/575-7676**), which offers accessibility information for hotels, restaurants, attractions, cultural venues, and much more.

Another terrific source for travelers with disabilities who are coming to New York City is **Big Apple Greeter** (☎ **212/669-8159;** www.bigapplegreeter.org). All of its employees are extremely well versed in accessibility issues. They can provide a resource list of city agencies that serve those with disabilities, and they sometimes have special discounts available to theater and music performances. Big Apple Greeter even offers one-to-one tours that pair volunteers with visitors with disabilities; they can even introduce you to the public transportation system if you like. Reserve at least 1 week ahead.

Doctors   If you get sick, consider asking your hotel concierge to recommend a local doctor—even his or her own. This will probably yield a better recommendation than any toll-free telephone number would.

There are also several walk-in medical centers, like **Beth Israel Medical Group,** 55 E. 34th St., between Park and Madison avenues (☎ **212/252-6000**), for nonemergency illnesses. The clinic is open Monday through Sunday from 8am to 8pm.

The **NYU Downtown Hospital** offers physician referrals at ☎ **212/312-5000.** You can also try the emergency room at a local hospital. Many hospitals also have walk-in clinics for emergency cases that are not life threatening; you may not get immediate attention, but you won't pay the high price of an emergency-room visit.

Pack **prescription medications** in their original containers in your carry-on luggage. Also bring along copies of your prescriptions in case you lose your pills or run out. Don't forget an extra pair of contact lenses or prescription glasses.

If you have dental problems on the road, a service known as **1-800-DENTIST** (☎ **800/336-8422**) will provide the name of a local dentist.

Also see "Hospitals," later in this section.

Drinking Laws   The legal age for purchase and consumption of alcoholic beverages is 21; proof of age can be requested at bars, nightclubs, and restaurants, especially if you're graced with youthful looks. However, this is New York City, which is a most tolerant place. Liquor and wine are sold only in licensed stores, which are open 6 days a week, with some choosing to close on Sunday, others on an early or midweek day. (You can usually find an open liquor store on Sun.) Liquor stores are closed on holidays and election days while the polls are open. Beer can be purchased in grocery stores and delis 24 hours a day, except Sunday before noon. Last call in bars is at 4am, though many close earlier. Do not carry open containers of alcohol in your car or any public area that isn't zoned for alcohol consumption. The police can fine you on the spot.

Driving Rules   See "Getting Around," earlier in this chapter.

Electricity   Like Canada, the United States uses 110 to 120 volts AC (60 cycles), compared to 220 to 240 volts AC (50 cycles) in most of Europe, Australia, and New Zealand. Downward converters that change 220–240 volts to 110–120 volts are difficult to find in the United States, so bring one with you.

Embassies & Consulates   All embassies are in the nation's capital, Washington, D.C. Some consulates are in major U.S. cities, and most nations have a mission to the United Nations in New York City. If your country isn't listed below, call for directory information in Washington, D.C. (📞 **202/555-1212**) or check **www.embassy.org/ embassies**.

The embassy of **Australia** is at 1601 Massachusetts Ave. NW, Washington, DC 20036 (📞 **202/797-3000;** www.usa.embassy.gov.au). Consulates are in New York, Honolulu, Houston, Los Angeles, and San Francisco.

The embassy of **Canada** is at 501 Pennsylvania Ave. NW, Washington, DC 20001 (📞 **202/682-1740;** www.canadainternational.gc.ca/washington). Other Canadian consulates are in Buffalo (New York), Detroit, Los Angeles, New York, and Seattle.

The embassy of **Ireland** is at 2234 Massachusetts Ave. NW, Washington, DC 20008 (📞 **202/462-3939;** www.embassyofireland.org). Irish consulates are in Boston, Chicago, New York, San Francisco, and other cities. See website for complete listing.

The embassy of **New Zealand** is at 37 Observatory Circle NW, Washington, DC 20008 (📞 **202/328-4800;** www.nzembassy.com). New Zealand consulates are in Los Angeles, Salt Lake City, San Francisco, and Seattle.

The embassy of the **United Kingdom** is at 3100 Massachusetts Ave. NW, Washington, DC 20008 (📞 **202/588-6500;** http://ukinusa.fco.gov.uk). Other British consulates are in Atlanta, Boston, Chicago, Cleveland, Houston, Los Angeles, New York, San Francisco, and Seattle.

Emergencies   For all emergencies—a fire, police, or health emergency—call **911.**

Family Travel   To locate accommodations, restaurants, and attractions that are particularly kid-friendly, look for the "Kids" icon throughout this guide. For more extensive recommendations, you might want to purchase a copy of *Frommer's New York City with Kids* by Alexis Lipsitz Flippin (Wiley), an entire guidebook dedicated to family visits to the Big Apple.

Good bets for the most timely information include the "Weekend" section of Friday's *New York Times,* which has a section dedicated to the week's best kid-friendly activities; the weekly *New York* magazine, which has a full calendar of children's events in its listings section; and *Time Out New York,* which also has a weekly kids section with a bit of an alternative bent. *Big Apple Parent* is usually available, for free, at children's stores and other locations in Manhattan.

The first place to look for babysitting is in your hotel (better yet, ask about babysitting when you reserve). Many hotels have babysitting services or will provide you with lists of reliable sitters. If this doesn't pan out, call the **Baby Sitters' Guild** (📞 **212/682-0227;** www.babysittersguild.com). The sitters are licensed, insured, and bonded, and can even take your child on outings.

Recommended family travel websites include **Family Travel Forum** (**www.familytravelforum.com**), a comprehensive site that offers customized trip planning; **Family Travel Network** (**www.familytravelnetwork.com**), an online magazine providing travel tips; and **TravelWithYourKids.com,** a comprehensive site written by parents for parents, that offers advice for long-distance and international travel with children.

For a list of more family-friendly travel resources, turn to the experts at Frommers.com.

Health   New York City has some of the best hospitals and doctors in the world. Hopefully, you won't need to avail yourself, but it's good to know, in case.

Hospitals   The following hospitals have 24-hour emergency rooms. Don't forget your insurance card.

Downtown: New York Downtown Hospital, 170 William St., between Beekman and Spruce streets ((✆) 212/312-5106 or 212/312-5000) and **Beth Israel Medical Center,** First Avenue and 16th Street ((✆) 212/420-2000).

Midtown: Bellevue Hospital Center, 462 First Ave., at 27th Street ((✆) 212/562-4141); **New York University Langone Medical Center,** 550 First Ave., at 33rd Street ((✆) 212/ 263-7300); and **St. Luke's/Roosevelt Hospital,** 425 W. 59th St., between Ninth and Tenth avenues ((✆) 212/523-4000).

Upper West Side: St. Luke's Hospital Center, 1111 Amsterdam Ave., at 114th Street ((✆) 212/523-4000); and **Columbia Presbyterian Medical Center,** 622 W. 168th St., between Broadway and Fort Washington Avenue ((✆) 212/305-2500).

Upper East Side: New York Presbyterian Hospital, 525 E. 68th St., at York Avenue ((✆) 212/746-5454); **Lenox Hill Hospital,** 100 E. 77th St., between Park and Lexington avenues ((✆) 212/434-3030); and **Mount Sinai Medical Center,** 1190 Fifth Avenue at 100th Street ((✆) 212/241-6500).

Insurance   For information on traveler's insurance, trip cancelation insurance, and medical insurance while traveling, please visit **www.frommers.com/planning**.

Internet & Wi-Fi   New York is rife with Wi-Fi (wireless fidelity) "hotspots" that offer free Wi-Fi access or charge a small fee for usage. A good directory of free hotspots in the city can be found at **www.openwifinyc.com**.

Your hotel may also provide Wi-Fi or broadband access in your room, sometimes for a hefty daily fee. It's always surprised us that the higher-end hotels are the ones who charge for Internet access, while the budget places are more likely to use free Internet as a selling point. (See "Where to Check Your Email in the City that Never Sleeps" on p. 462.)

You can access the Internet for free at **Starbucks (www.starbucks.com/coffeehouse/ wireless-internet**). So, have a cup of coffee and check your e-mail at your leisure. **FedEx Office (www.fedex.com/us/office/services/computer/index.html**) has free Wi-Fi at most locations, as well as computers you use for 30¢ per minute. There are dozens of locations around town.

Legal Aid   While driving, if you are pulled over for a minor infraction (such as speeding), never attempt to pay the fine directly to a police officer; this could be construed as attempted bribery, a much more serious crime. Pay fines by mail, or directly into the hands of the clerk of the court. If accused of a more serious offense, say and do nothing before consulting a lawyer. In the U.S., the burden is on the state to prove a person's guilt beyond a reasonable doubt, and everyone has the right to remain silent, whether he or she is suspected of a crime or actually arrested. Once arrested, a person can make one telephone call to a party of his or her choice. The international visitor should call his or her embassy or consulate.

LGBT Travelers   Gay and lesbian culture is as much a part of New York's basic identity as yellow cabs, high-rises, and Broadway theater. Indeed, in a city with one of the world's largest, loudest, and most powerful GLBT populations, homosexuality is squarely in the mainstream. So city hotels tend to be neutral on the issue, and gay couples shouldn't have a problem. Check out "The Gay & Lesbian Scene," in chapter 8 for nightlife suggestions.

All over Manhattan, but especially in such neighborhoods as the West Village (particularly Christopher St., famous the world over as the main drag of New York gay-male life)

PLANNING YOUR TRIP TO NEW YORK CITY

and Chelsea (especially Eighth Ave., from 16th to 23rd sts., and W. 17th to 19th sts., from Fifth to Eighth aves.), shops, services, and restaurants have a lesbian and gay flavor.

The **Lesbian, Gay, Bisexual & Transgender Community Center,** familiarly known as "the Center," is at 208 W. 13th St., between Seventh and Eighth avenues (📞 **212/620-7310;** www.gaycenter.org). The center is the meeting place for more than 300 lesbian, gay, and bisexual organizations. You can check the online events calendar, which lists hundreds of happenings—lectures, dances, concerts, readings, films—or call for the latest. The staff is also helpful in lending advice on gay friendly businesses in the area including hotels and guesthouses.

Other good sources for lesbian and gay events are the free bi-weekly newspaper *Gay City News* (**www.gaycitynews.com**) and the free magazines **Next** (**www.next magazine.com**) and **GONYC** (**www.gomag.com**), which is lesbian-oriented. You'll also find lots of information on their websites.

The weekly *Time Out New York* (**www.timeoutny.com**) boasts a terrific gay and lesbian section. *The Center* (see above) publishes a monthly guide listing many events (also listed on its website).

Mail   At press time, domestic postage rates were 28¢ for a postcard and 44¢ for a letter. For international mail, a first-class letter of up to 1 ounce costs 98¢ (75¢ to Canada and 79¢ to Mexico); a first-class postcard costs the same as a letter. For more information go to **www.usps.com**.

If you aren't sure what your address will be in the United States, mail can be sent to you, in your name, c/o General Delivery at the main post office of the city or region where you expect to be. (Call 📞 **800/275-8777** for information on the nearest post office.) The addressee must pick up mail in person and must produce proof of identity (driver's license, passport, and so on). Most post offices will hold mail for up to 1 month, and are open Monday to Friday from 8am to 6pm, and Saturday from 9am to 3pm.

Always include zip codes when mailing items in the U.S. If you don't know your zip code, visit www.usps.com/zip4.

Medical Requirements   Unless you're arriving from an area known to be suffering from an epidemic (particularly cholera or yellow fever), inoculations or vaccinations are not required for entry into the United States.

Money & Costs   Frommer's lists exact prices in the local currency. The currency conversions provided were correct at press time. However, rates fluctuate, so before departing consult a currency exchange website such as **www.oanda.com/currency/converter** to check up-to-the-minute rates.

New York City can be one of the most expensive destinations in the United States (and the world). You can pay more for lodging, dining, and transportation than almost anywhere else; however, in this book, we steer you to the best values for your money at every level.

For the last couple of years, with the dollar taking a beating on the international market, the city was flooded with overseas visitors taking advantage of the lopsided exchange

THE VALUE OF THE U.S. DOLLAR VS. OTHER POPULAR CURRENCIES

US$	A$	C$	€	NZ$	£
1.00	1.02	1.00	0.74	1.32	0.64

Cab from JFK airport to Manhattan (plus tolls)	45.00
Single full-fare subway or bus ride	2.50
7-Day Unlimited-Ride MetroCard for bus or subway	27.00
Double room at the Ritz-Carlton, Central Park view (very expensive)	1,045.00
Double room, Casablanca Hotel (moderate)	271.00
Double room, at the Hotel Newton (inexpensive)	144.00
Lunch for one at Becco (moderate)	18.00
Lunch for one at Nizza (inexpensive; lunch special)	8.75
Dinner for one, without wine, at The Post House (very expensive)	50.00
Dinner for one, without wine, at Marseille (moderate)	35.00
Massage (50 min.) at Elizabeth Arden Red Door Spas	120.00
Bicycle rental Central Park (1 hr.)	15.00
Ticket to a N.Y. Yankees game (Terrace)	85.00
Pint of beer (draft pilsner or lager)	7.00
Cup of coffee in a cafe or bar	2.50
Coca-Cola in a cafe or bar	3.00
Admission to Museum of Modern Art	20.00
Movie ticket	12.00
Ticket to a Broadway show (orchestra)	125.00

rate. Since most other currencies took a hit in the worldwide financial crisis of late 2008, the city's not such a bargain for international visitors at the moment, though as we discuss elsewhere, hoteliers and restaurants have lowered their prices in response to the downturn. In terms of how much to bring: not that much in cash. You never have to carry too much cash in New York, and while the city's pretty safe, it's best not to overstuff your wallet (although always make sure you have at least $20 in cash for small purchases).

ATMs   In most Manhattan neighborhoods, you can find a bank with **ATMs** (automated teller machines) every couple of blocks. Most delis, many restaurants and clubs, and other stores have an ATM on premises, so if you need cash quickly, you're probably never more than about 100 feet away from one. (Though keep an eye on the fees imposed for using the ATM; they will go on top of whatever fee your bank charges; and note that in some bars and clubs, where you can't leave once you've paid your admission, the withdrawal fee is hefty.)

Beware of hidden credit card fees while traveling. Check with your credit or debit card issuer to see what fees, if any, will be charged for overseas transactions. Recent reform legislation in the U.S., for example, has curbed some exploitative lending practices. But many banks have responded by increasing fees in other areas, including fees for customers who use credit and debit cards while out of the country—even if those charges

Avoid subways late at night, and splurge on a cab after about 10 or 11pm—it's money well spent to avoid a long wait on a deserted platform. Or take the bus.

Student Travel   There are student discounts at almost every museum in New York, for example, and so student travelers should bring their school IDs with them. In this case, "student" means high school or college—or any school, really.

Taxes   **Sales tax** is 8.875% on meals, most goods, and some services. **Hotel tax** is 5.875% plus a daily fee up to $2 depending on the cost of your room per night. **Parking garage tax** is 18.375%. The United States has no value-added tax (VAT) or other indirect tax at the national level. Every state, county, and city may levy its own local tax on all purchases, including hotel and restaurant checks and airline tickets. These taxes will not appear on price tags.

Telephones   Generally, hotel surcharges on long-distance and local calls are astronomical, so you're better off using your **cellphone** or a **public pay telephone.** Many convenience stores and drugstores sell **prepaid calling cards** in denominations up to $50; for international visitors these can be the least expensive way to call home. Many public pay phones at airports now accept American Express, MasterCard, and Visa credit cards. **Local calls** made from most payphones cost 50¢ (no pennies, please).

That said, there aren't as many payphones on the streets of New York City as there used to be because of the prevalence of cellphones, and the ones that are there are often out of order.

To make a **local call** in one of the five boroughs, **dial 1,** followed by the area code and the seven-digit number. Most long-distance and international calls can be dialed directly from any phone. **To make calls within the United States and to Canada,** dial 1. **For other international calls,** dial 011, followed by the country code, city code, and the number you are calling.

Calls to area codes **800, 888, 877,** and **866** are toll-free. However, calls to area code **900** (chat lines, bulletin boards, "dating" services, and so on) can be expensive—charges of 95¢ to $3 or more per minute. Some numbers have minimum charges that can run $15 or more.

For **reversed-charge or collect calls,** and for person-to-person calls, dial the number 0 then the area code and number; an operator will come on the line, and you should specify whether you are calling collect, person to person, or both. If your operator-assisted call is international, ask for the overseas operator.

For **directory assistance** ("Information"), dial 411 for local numbers and national numbers in the U.S. and Canada. For dedicated long-distance information, dial 1, then the appropriate area code plus 555-1212.

Mobile Phones   Just because your cellphone works at home doesn't mean it'll work everywhere in the U.S. (thanks to our nation's fragmented cellphone system). It's a good bet that your phone will work in New York City, but take a look at your wireless company's coverage map on its website before heading out.

If you need to stay in touch at a destination where you know your phone won't work, **rent** a phone that does from **National Geographic Talk Abroad Services** (© **800/287-5072;** cellularabroad.com) or a rental-car location, but beware that you'll pay $1 a minute or more for airtime.

You may even consider purchasing a cheap, pay-as-you-go phone in many locations (including convenience stores!) throughout the city.

If you're not from the U.S., you'll be appalled at the poor reach of the **GSM (Global System for Mobile Communications) wireless network,** which is used by much of the rest of the world. Your phone will probably work in most major U.S. cities; it definitely won't work in many rural areas. And you may or may not be able to send SMS (text messaging) home.

Many convenience groceries and packaging services sell **prepaid calling cards** in denominations up to $50. Many public pay phones at airports now accept American Express, MasterCard, and Visa. **Local calls** made from most pay phones cost 50¢. Most long-distance and international calls can be dialed directly from any phone. **To make calls within the United States and to Canada,** dial 1 followed by the area code and the seven-digit number. **For other international calls,** dial 011 followed by the country code, city code, and the number you are calling.

Calls to area codes **800, 888, 877,** and **866** are toll-free. However, calls to area code **900** (chat lines, bulletin boards, "dating" services, and so on) can be expensive—charges of 95¢ to $3 or more per minute. Some numbers have minimum charges that can run $15 or more.

For **reversed-charge or collect calls,** and for person-to-person calls, dial the number 0 then the area code and number; an operator will come on the line, and you should specify whether you are calling collect, person-to-person, or both. If your operator-assisted call is international, ask for the overseas operator.

For **directory assistance** ("Information"), dial **411** for local numbers and national numbers in the U.S. and Canada. For dedicated long-distance information, dial 1, then the appropriate area code plus **555-1212.**

Time   The continental United States is divided into **four time zones:** Eastern Standard Time (EST), Central Standard Time (CST), Mountain Standard Time (MST), and Pacific Standard Time (PST). Alaska and Hawaii have their own zones. For example, when it's 9am in Los Angeles (PST), it's 7am in Honolulu (HST),10am in Denver (MST), 11am in Chicago (CST), noon in New York City (EST), 5pm in London (GMT), and 2am the next day in Sydney.

Daylight saving time (summer time) is in effect from 1am on the second Sunday in March to 1am on the first Sunday in November, except in Arizona, Hawaii, the U.S. Virgin Islands, and Puerto Rico. Daylight saving time moves the clock 1 hour ahead of standard time.

For help with time translations, and more, download our convenient Travel Tools app for your mobile device. Go to www.frommers.com/go/mobile and click on the Travel Tools icon.

Tipping   In hotels, tip **bellhops** at least $1 per bag ($2–$3 if you have a lot of luggage) and tip the **chamber staff** $1 to $2 per day (more if you've left a big mess for him or her to clean up). Tip the **doorman** or **concierge** only if he or she has provided you with some specific service (for example, calling a cab for you or obtaining difficult-to-get theater tickets). Tip the **valet-parking attendant** $1 every time you get your car.

In restaurants, bars, and nightclubs, tip **service staff** and **bartenders** 15% to 20% of the check, tip **checkroom attendants** $1 per garment, and tip **valet-parking attendants** $1 per vehicle.

As for other service personnel, tip **cab drivers** 15% of the fare; tip **skycaps** at airports at least $1 per bag ($2–$3 if you have a lot of luggage); and tip **hairdressers** and **barbers** 15% to 20%.

For help with tip calculations, currency conversions, and more, download our convenient Travel Tools app for your mobile device. Go to **www.frommers.com/go/mobile** and click on the Travel Tools icon.

Toilets   You won't find many public toilets or restrooms on the streets in New York City, but they can be found in hotel lobbies, bars, restaurants, museums, department stores, and railway and bus stations. Large hotels and fast-food restaurants are often the best bet for clean facilities.

Public restrooms are available at the visitor centers in Midtown (1560 Broadway, btw. 46th and 47th sts.; and 810 Seventh Ave., btw. 52nd and 53rd sts.). You can find relief at the New York Public Library's main building on Fifth Avenue just south of 42nd Street. Grand Central Terminal, at 42nd Street between Park and Lexington avenues, also has clean restrooms. There are staffed bathrooms open from early in the morning until fairly late at night in the Times Square subway station (closer to Seventh Ave.). Your best bet on the street is Starbucks or another city java chain—you can't walk more than a few blocks without seeing one. The big chain bookstores are good for this, too. You can also head to hotel lobbies (especially the big Midtown ones) and department stores such as Macy's and Bloomingdale's. On the Lower East Side, stop into the Lower East Side BID Visitor Center, 54 Orchard St., between Hester and Grand streets (weekdays 9:30am–5:30pm, weekends 9:30am–4pm).

Visas   The U.S. State Department has a **Visa Waiver Program (VWP)** allowing citizens of the following countries to enter the United States without a visa for stays of up to 90 days: Andorra, Australia, Austria, Belgium, Brunei, Czech Republic, Denmark, Estonia, Finland, France, Germany, Greece, Hungary, Iceland, Ireland, Italy, Japan, Latvia, Liechtenstein, Lithuania, Luxembourg, Malta, Monaco, the Netherlands, New Zealand, Norway, Portugal, San Marino, Singapore, Slovakia, Slovenia, South Korea, Spain, Sweden, Switzerland, and the United Kingdom. (***Note:*** This list was accurate at press time; for the most up-to-date list of countries in the VWP, consult **http://travel.state. gov/visa**.)

Even though a visa isn't necessary, in an effort to help U.S. officials check travelers against terror watch lists before they arrive at U.S. borders, visitors from VWP countries must register online through the Electronic System for Travel Authorization (ESTA) before boarding a plane or a boat to the U.S. Travelers must complete an electronic application providing basic personal and travel eligibility information. The Department of Homeland Security recommends filling out the form at least three days before traveling. Authorizations will be valid for up to 2 years or until the traveler's passport expires, whichever comes first. Currently, there is a US$14 fee for the online application.

Existing ESTA registrations remain valid through their expiration dates. ***Note:*** Any passport issued on or after October 26, 2006, by a VWP country must be an **e-Passport** for VWP travelers to be eligible to enter the U.S. without a visa. Citizens of these nations also need to present a round-trip air or cruise ticket upon arrival. E-Passports contain computer chips capable of storing biometric information, such as the required digital photograph of the holder. If your passport doesn't have this feature, you can still travel without a visa if the valid passport was issued before October 26, 2005, and includes a machine-readable zone; or if the valid passport was issued between October 26, 2005, and October 25, 2006, and includes a digital photograph. For more information, go to **http://travel.state.gov/visa**. Canadian citizens may enter the United States without visas, but will need to show passports and proof of residence.

Citizens of all other countries must have (1) a valid passport that expires at least 6 months later than the scheduled end of their visit to the U.S.; and (2) a tourist visa.

For information about U.S. Visas go to **http://travel.state.gov** and click on "Visas." Or go to one of the following websites:

Australian citizens can obtain up-to-date visa information from the **U.S. Embassy Canberra,** Moonah Place, Yarralumla, ACT 2600 (✆ **02/6214-5600**) or by checking the U.S. Diplomatic Mission's website at **http://canberra.usembassy.gov/visas.html**.

British subjects can obtain up-to-date visa information by calling the **U.S. Embassy Visa Information Line** (✆ **09042-450-100** from within the U.K. at £1.20 per minute; or ✆ **866/382-3589** from within the U.S. at a flat rate of $16 and is payable by credit card only) or by visiting the "Visas to the U.S." section of the American Embassy London's website at **http://london.usembassy.gov/visas.html**.

Irish citizens can obtain up-to-date visa information through the **U.S. Embassy Dublin,** 42 Elgin Rd., Ballsbridge, Dublin 4 (✆ 1580-47-VISA [8472] from within the Republic of Ireland at €2.40 per minute; **http://dublin.usembassy.gov**).

Citizens of **New Zealand** can obtain up-to-date visa information by contacting the **U.S. Embassy New Zealand,** 29 Fitzherbert Terrace, Thorndon, Wellington (✆ **644/462-6000; http://newzealand.usembassy.gov**).

Visitor Information   **NYC & Company** runs the Official NYC Information Center at 810 Seventh Ave. (at 53rd St.), New York, NY 10019. You can call ✆ **800/692 8474** to request the *Official NYC Guide* detailing hotels, restaurants, theaters, attractions, events, and more. The guide (and a New York City map) is free and will arrive in 7 to 10 days. You can also download it online on the company's website, **www.nycgo.com**, where you will find a wealth of free information. To speak with a live travel counselor, call ✆ **212/484-1222,** which is staffed weekdays from 9am to 6pm EST, Saturday and Sunday from 9am to 5pm EST.

For visitors from the U.K., the NYC & Company office is located at Colechurch House, 1 London Bridge Walk, London, SE1 2SX (✆ 020/7367-0900). You can download or order the Official NYC & Company visitor guide online at **www.nycgo.com**. You can find a list of Frommer's travel apps at **www.frommers.com/go/mobile**.

Index

General

A

Abby Aldrich Rockefeller Sculpture Garden, 237
ABC Carpet & Home, 346–347, 352
Abode Apartment Rentals, 136
Abyssinian Baptist Church, 278
Academy Records & CDs, 380
Accommodations, 84–136. *See also* Accommodations Index; *specific boroughs and neighborhoods*
  alternative, 136
  best, 84–88
  budget chains, 134–135
  family-friendly, 115
  pet peeves, 120–121
  reservations services, 135
  tips on, 133–136
Ace Hotel Lobby Bar, 434
Acker Merrall & Condit Co., 384–385
Adidas, 378
African Burial Ground Memorial, 266
Airports, getting to and from, 446–452
Air-Ride, 446
Air tours, 301
AirTrains, 447, 450
Air travel, 446–451
Alexander and Bonin, 263
Alexander McQueen, 346
Allan & Suzi, 368
Allen Room, 406
Alliance for Downtown New York, 52
Alphabet City, 56
American Ballet Theatre, 401
American Folk Art Museum, 247
American Girl Place, 384
American Immigrant Wall of Honor, 231
American Jewish Historical Society, 248
American Museum of Natural History, 220–221, 228
American Sephardi Federation, 248
AMF Chelsea Piers Lanes, 298
Amtrak, 452
Anna Sui, 362
Ann Taylor, 363
The Ansonia, 271
Anthology Film Archives, 419
Anthropologie, 365
Antiques and collectibles, 43, 48, 356–357
Antiques Garage, 356

Anya Hindmarch, 374
Apartment rentals, 136
Apollo Theater, 402–403
The Apple Store, 372–373
Aquarium, New York (Brooklyn), 323–324
Archangel Antiques, 344
Architecture, 7–8, 27–32, 270–277
Area codes, 462
Argosy, 344
Argosy Books, 358
Arlene's Grocery, 414
Ars Nova, 422
Art Deco, 31
Art galleries, 262–263
Asia Society, 247–248
A Slice of Brooklyn Pizza Tour, 329
Astor Row Houses, 271
Astor Wines & Spirits, 385
Atlantic Theater Company, 392–393, 397
Atrium, 363
Auction House, 436

B

Bagels, 169, 194
BAM (Brooklyn Academy of Music), 403–404
BAM Next Wave Festival (Brooklyn), 47
BAM Rose Cinemas (Brooklyn), 403, 419
Banana Republic, 363
B&H Photo & Video, 339, 373
Banks, 463
Barbara Gladstone Gallery, 263
Barbecue restaurants, 174
Bargemusic, 400
Barneys Co-Op, 353
Barneys New York, 352–353
Bar Pleiades, 434
Barracuda, 441–442
Barramundi, 426
Bars and cocktail lounges, 424–438. *See also specific neighborhoods*
Bar 13, 439
Baseball, 333–337
Basketball, 337
Bateaux New York, 299
Battery Park, 290–292
Bauman Rare Books, 358
B.B. King Blues Club & Grill, 411, 416
Beacon's Closet (Brooklyn), 361
Beacon Theatre, 410
Beauty products, 357–358
Beaux Arts style, 29–30
Bed-and-breakfasts (B&Bs), 136
The Bell House, 411–412

Belmont Stakes, 44
Belvedere Castle, 283, 286
Bemelmans Bar, 434
Bergdorf Goodman, 353
Bespoke Chocolates, 371
Bier International, 436
Big Apple Circus, 47
Big Apple Jazz Tours, 305
Big Bang Theater, 220
Bike New York: The Five Boro Bike Tour, 44
Bike the Big Apple, 305–306
Biking, 44, 288
Bill's Gay Nineties Restaurant and Piano Bar, 422
Bill's Place, 416
Birdland, 417
Bird-watching, in Central Park, 288–289
The Bitter End, 414
BlackBerry apps, 458
Black Door, 431
Bleecker Street Records, 380
Blogs about New York City, 449
Bloomingdale's, 353
Blue Note, 417
Bluestockings, 358–359
Boathouse
  Loeb (Central Park), 283, 289
  Prospect Park (Brooklyn), 326
Boating, Central Park, 286
Bohemian Beer Hall & Garden (Queens), 437–438
Boiler Room, 442
Bond Street Chocolate, 371
Bongo, 431
Books, recommended, 32–34
Books of Wonder, 359
Bookstores, 358–361
Borders, 340
Bow Bridge (Central Park), 286
Bowery Ballroom, 412
Bowery Poetry Club, 420–421
Bowling, 298
Bowlmor/Carnival, 430
Brandy Library, 424
Brandy's Piano Bar, 442
Breakfast restaurants, 195
Broadway Concierge & Ticket Center, 395
Broadway League, 393
Broadway on Broadway, 46
Broadway Panhandler, 375
The Bronx, 67–68
  restaurants, 204–205
  sightseeing, 312–319
Bronx Cultural Trolley, 317
Bronx Museum of the Arts, 264, 319
Bronx Zoo Wildlife Conservation Park, 312–315

Joe's Pizza : Carmel Street : BM

Photo Credits